# HANDBOOK OF HEALTHCARE MANAGEMENT

# Handbook of Healthcare Management

*Edited by*

## Myron D. Fottler

*Professor Emeritus, College of Health and Public Affairs, University of Central Florida, USA*

## Donna Malvey

*Associate Professor, College of Health and Public Affairs, University of Central Florida, USA*

## Donna J. Slovensky

*Professor and Senior Associate Dean, Academic and Faculty Affairs, School of Health Professions, University of Alabama at Birmingham, USA*

Edward Elgar
PUBLISHING

Cheltenham, UK • Northampton, MA, USA

Published by
Edward Elgar Publishing Limited
The Lypiatts
15 Lansdown Road
Cheltenham
Glos GL50 2JA
UK

Edward Elgar Publishing, Inc.
William Pratt House
9 Dewey Court
Northampton
Massachusetts 01060
USA

Paperback edition 2017

A catalogue record for this book
is available from the British Library

Library of Congress Control Number: 2015938372

This book is available electronically in the **Elgar**online
Business subject collection
DOI 10.4337/9781783470167

ISBN 978 1 78347 014 3 (cased)
ISBN 978 1 78347 016 7 (eBook)
ISBN 978 1 78347 015 0 (paperback)

Typeset by Servis Filmsetting Ltd, Stockport, Cheshire
Printed and bound in Great Britain by TJ International Ltd, Padstow

# Contents

# Contributors

**Alicia Beardsley**, Graduate Program, Health Services Administration, College of Health and Public Affairs, University of Central Florida, USA.

**James W. Begun**, PhD, James A. Hamilton Professor of Healthcare Management, School of Public Health, University of Minnesota, USA.

**Nancy Borkowski**, DBA, CPA, FACHE, FHFMA, Professor, Department of Health Services Administration, School of Health Professions, University of Alabama at Birmingham, USA.

**Bryan K. Breland**, PhD, JD, MPH, MPA, Assistant Professor, School of Health Professions, University of Alabama at Birmingham, USA.

**Kurt Darr**, JD ScD FACHE, Professor, Department of Health Services Management and Leadership, School of Public Health and Health Services, George Washington University, USA.

**Clyde Deschamp**, PhD, Professor and Chair, School of Health Related Professions, University of Mississippi Medical Center, USA.

**Eric W. Ford**, PhD, Program Director, Master of Health Administration Program, Associate Department Chair, Johns Hopkins University, USA.

**Myron D. Fottler**, PhD, Professor, Department of Health Management and Informatics, College of Health and Public Affairs, University of Central Florida, USA.

**Leonard H. Friedman**, PhD, MPH, FACHE, Professor and Interim Chair, Department of Health Services Management and Leadership, Milken Institute School of Public Health, George Washington University, USA.

**John Gill**, PhD Candidate, College of Health and Public Affairs, University of Central Florida, USA.

**Peggy K. Howse**, MSH, MSE, Director of Business Services, University of Central Florida, USA.

**Timothy R. Huerta**, PhD, Associate Professor of Family Medicine, Ohio State University, USA.

**John C. Hyde**, PhD, FACHE, Professor, School of Health Related Professions, University of Mississippi Medical Center and School of Business, University of Mississippi, USA.

**Ross Kemp**, MSHA, Experienced Associate, PwC.

**Donna Malvey**, PhD, MHSA, Associate Professor, Department of Health Management and Informatics, College of Health and Public Affairs, University of Central Florida, USA.

**Ann Scheck McAlearney**, ScD, MS, Professor and Vice Chair for Research, Department of Family Medicine, College of Medicine, Professor, Health Services Management and Policy, College of Public Health, Ohio State University, USA.

**Nir Menachemi**, PhD, MPH, Professor and Chair, Department of Health Policy and Management, Richard M. Fairbanks School of Public Health, Indiana University, and Affiliated Scientist, Regenstrief Institute, Inc., USA.

**Carol Molinari**, PhD, MBA, MPH, Associate Professor, Health Systems Management, University of Baltimore, USA.

**Hannah Nguyen**, BBA, Graduate Program, Master of Science in Health Services Administration, College of Health and Public Affairs, University of Central Florida, USA.

**Stephen J. O'Connor**, PhD, FACHE, Editor, *Journal of Healthcare Management*, and Professor, Department of Health Services Administration, School of Health Professions, University of Alabama at Birmingham, USA.

**Pamela E. Paustian**, PhD, RHIA, Associate Professor, Department of Health Services Administration, School of Health Professions, University of Alabama at Birmingham, USA.

**Amanda Raffenaud**, MSHSA, PHD Candidate, Instructor, Department of Health Management and Informatics, College of Health and Public Affairs, University of Central Florida, USA.

**Saurabh Rahurkar**, DrPH, BDS, Department of Health Care Organization and Policy, School of Public Health, University of Alabama at Birmingham, USA.

**Sandra Ruff**, MNM/PA, Coordinator, Administrative Services, Department of Health Management and Informatics, College of Health and Public Affairs, University of Central Florida, USA.

**Carla J. Sampson**, MBA, FACHE, Instructor & Internship Director, Department of Health Management and Informatics, College of Health and Public Affairs, University of Central Florida, USA.

**Donna J. Slovensky**, PhD, RHIA, FAHIMA, Professor and Senior Associate Dean for Academic and Faculty Affairs, School of Health Professions, University of Alabama at Birmingham, USA.

**Dean G. Smith**, PhD, Professor of Health Management & Policy, School of Public Health, University of Michigan, USA.

**Patrice L. Spath**, MA, RHIT, Healthcare Quality Specialist, Brown-Spath & Associates, Oregon, USA; Adjunct Assistant Professor, School of Health Professions, University of Alabama at Birmingham, USA; and Adjunct Professor, School of Health Administration and Leadership, Pacific University, USA.

**Willi L. Tarver**, DrPH, MLIS, Post-Doctoral Fellow, Behavioral Oncology and Cancer Control Program, Indiana University School of Nursing, USA.

**Marcus Thygeson**, MD, MPH, Chief Health Officer, SVP, Healthcare Services, Blue Shield of California, USA.

**J.M. "Mickey" Trimm**, PhD, FHIMSS, Associate Professor and Director, Center for Healthcare Management & Leadership, School of Health Professions, University of Alabama at Birmingham, USA.

**Joseph G. Van Matre**, PhD, Professor, Collat School of Business, University of Alabama at Birmingham, USA.

**Charles F. Wainright**, III, Ph.D, MHA, FACHE, Director and Associate Professor, Jack C. Massey MBA Program in Healthcare Management, College of Business Administration, Belmont University, USA.

**James H. Willig**, MD, MSPH, Associate Professor, Department of Medicine, Division of Infectious Diseases, University of Alabama at Birmingham, USA.

**Tina Yeung**, MS, PhD Candidate in Public Affairs, Department of Health Management and Informatics, University of Central Florida, USA.

**Ting Zhang**, Assistant Professor, School of Public and International Affairs, College of Public Affairs, Associate Director, Jacob France Institute, Merrick School of Business, University of Baltimore, USA.

# 1. Managing complex healthcare organizations
## James W. Begun and Marcus Thygeson

## MANAGING COMPLEX HEALTHCARE ORGANIZATIONS

It is well established that healthcare organizations are among the most complex in society. It also is well established that effective management practice in any organization or setting is context-specific; that is, what works in one context may not work in another. Healthcare management theory built around the assumption that healthcare organizations are distinctively complex, therefore, is likely to be more useful in management practice.

We review several guidelines for managing complex healthcare organizations that emanate from the theoretical assumption that healthcare organizations are complex. Some guidelines derive from what is referred to as "complexity science" or "complexity theory"; most come from observers who "simply" appreciate, implicitly or explicitly, that healthcare organizations are complex. (There is much similarity between guidelines that derive from the two sources, as one might hope.) We then make recommendations for taking more seriously the complexity of healthcare management in the education and research arenas.

## WHAT IS COMPLEX ABOUT HEALTHCARE MANAGEMENT?

There are many ways to describe the complexity of healthcare management in the United States. A starting point for identifying complexity is the presence of multiple, diverse, interdependent agents. Interdependence among multiple, diverse agents produces novel outcomes, particularly when the agents and forces affecting the system are changing over time. Multiple, diverse, interdependent agents are present in healthcare organizations, most pointedly in the form of hundreds of specialized clinical healthcare professions and the administrators who attempt to help organize them into effective care delivery teams and units. The agents often diverge in their reporting and incentive structures. The specialized support and technical service workers add to the diversity of the delivery setting.

Putting a system of multiple, diverse, interdependent agents into motion, interacting to deliver healthcare, creates a vast level of complexity. In addition the agents themselves adapt and change over time, due to self-learning and development, or new requirements from regulatory, advisory, or legal sources, or other causes, and complexity is accelerated geometrically. Several authors have aptly summarized the resulting complexity of healthcare management in ways that help us comprehend and manage it.

The archetypal healthcare organization, the hospital, was labeled schizophrenic in its organizational structure by economist Jeffrey Harris (1977). Harris was referring to the formal administrative hierarchy versus the medical staff organization. The two personalities or sides of the hospital – administration and medical staff – are respectively characterized by formal hierarchy versus peer review, allegiance to the organization versus allegiance to the profession, and control versus autonomy. Complicating management decision-making is the fact that both sides of the hospital report separately to the governing board, and the medical staff often has more power than the administration, as the primary source of revenues and the arbiter of clinical quality.

A case can be made that nursing forms a powerful and semi-independent segment of the hospital as well. Nursing staffs have their own self-governance mechanisms and may be unionized, with significant power to force closure of the hospital during strikes. State laws may regulate the staffing requirements for different units in the hospital.

Members of the large number of other highly specialized clinical professions demand respect, a voice in decisions, and some degree of autonomy in setting quality standards. Most clinical professions, with pharmacy, physical therapy, and laboratory science being but three examples, have proud histories and strong socialization processes into the profession. The professionals typically are licensed and regulated by state boards rather than their employer organization. A consequence is that healthcare administrators generally shy away from interference in the clinical affairs of clinical health professionals (Mosser and Begun, 2013).

The concept of the professional bureaucracy nicely summarizes the challenge of managing in healthcare delivery (Mintzberg, 1983). Mintzberg's organizational archetype contains five parts: a strategic apex, middle management, support staff, technical staff, and an operating core. Managing an operating core comprised of clinical professionals and managing highly specialized support staff are quite different than managing workers in a production line and the relevant support staff

(Mintzberg's machine bureaucracy). The professional bureaucracy relies for coordination on standardization of skills, training, and socialization within each of the professions. Control over work is largely entrusted to those professions. For example, clinicians familiar with the latest technology make requests for new equipment and supplies, rather than such requests coming from administration. Best practices for clinical care are developed by groups of clinical professionals, rather than by administration. On many dimensions, administrators can effectively facilitate; they can rarely direct.

Glouberman and Mintzberg (2001) usefully convey the complexity of healthcare delivery by describing hospitals as consisting of four different worlds (or activities, ways of organizing, or mindsets): care (represented by the delivery team, particularly nurses); cure (represented by physicians and other medical professionals); control (represented by administrators); and community (represented by the governing board). All four are necessary but are "unnecessarily disconnected – by unreconciled values, incompatible structures, intransigent attitudes" (Glouberman and Mintzberg, 2001, p. 65). The "community" mindset of healthcare certainly adds to its complexity. The adage that "all healthcare is local" reflects the importance of meeting the needs of individuals and communities on their own terms and in geographic proximity. Governing boards are charged with representing such interests, particularly in not-for-profit healthcare organizations.

The above description refers to the hospital as a single, independent organization. Complexity is added when hospitals are linked to other hospitals and other types of delivery organizations, such as clinics and rehabilitation centers, in healthcare systems. The actions of one administrator then inevitably must take into account and feed back to other organizations within the system.

The above description of hospitals applies to varying degrees to other delivery organizations, such as nursing homes and clinics. The description also still largely applies in the face of growing physician employment by hospitals, which strengthens some powers of administrators to "direct" and "control" (Baker and Denis, 2011; Begun et al., 2011). But the fundamental need for administrators to facilitate autonomous practice by highly specialized professionals remains, as do the other sources of complexity in the structure and culture of healthcare organizations.

In addition to internal organizational complexity, a major source of complexity in healthcare management is the scope and diversity of what is typically called the "external environment." (The "external environment" is often difficult to classify as strictly "external," because linkages bring the external agents inside the boundaries of the organization.) A host of different agents are operating in the healthcare organization's external environment, including government organizations, suppliers of pharmaceuticals and medical technologies, professional and trade associations, research organizations, and educational organizations (Shi and Singh, 2014, p.3). Payers like Medicare and Medicaid and health insurance organizations are a key part of the environment of delivery organizations. One or more insurance organizations may be incorporated in a delivery organization's larger health system corporate structure, though most are external to the system. The existence of multiple payers, each with its own, usually different, way of doing business, means that hospitals deal with varying sets of payer-generated incentives and requirements. For instance, in many locations different insurance companies use different measures and incentive structures for promoting quality improvement. Also, with the recent increase in payer-mediated experimentation with care delivery structures like accountable care organizations, hospitals may be faced with varying and often conflicting financial incentives for how they deliver care.

Healthcare delivery organizations are a vital piece of the social and cultural fabric of societies, and thus are subject to social and cultural pressures from a variety of sources. Alexander and D'Aunno (2003) catalogue the diverse and often conflicting institutional and technical forces impinging on healthcare delivery organizations, ranging from the power of the professions, public regulators, voluntary and philanthropic supporters, and societal beliefs in healthcare as a right in the case of institutional forces to managed care, cost containment, and corporate ideology in the case of market or technical forces.

To convey complexity, many practitioners and scholars also find useful a further distinction of complex systems: they are characterized by causal ambiguity. One version of this distinction identifies two dimensions of decisions: consensus on the nature of the problem (the "what") and confidence in understanding cause and effect in solving the problem (the "how") (Stacey, 1996; Zimmerman et al., 1998). Snowden and Boone's (2007) framework, for example, distinguishes simple, complicated, complex, and chaotic contexts for decision-making. Simple contexts comprise repeated-pattern, clear cause-and-effect relationships that are evident to everyone, and fact-based or "rational" management. Complicated contexts are those where expert diagnosis is required. Cause-and-effect relationships are discoverable, but are not immediately apparent to everyone. It is a world of "known unknowns," and fact-based management is still possible. Complicated contexts call for analysis of several alternatives, some of which may be equally "good," and choice among them.

Many of the critical decisions in healthcare organizations can be

---

### BOX 1.1 COMPLEX FEATURES OF HEALTHCARE MANAGEMENT

- Multiple, diverse, interdependent agents.
- Dynamic system: agents change over time.
- Complex internal organizational structure:
  - two personalities: administrative and medical;
  - professional bureaucracy;
  - four mindsets: care, cure, control, community.
- Scope and diversity of "external environment":
  - conflicting institutional and technical forces.
- Low consensus on the nature of problems or understanding of cause and effect in solving problems.

---

characterized as occurring in a complex context. In complex contexts, flux and unpredictability are common; there are many competing ideas and no right answers, but instructive patterns do emerge. It is a world of "unknown unknowns." Complexities require that managers use dialectical inquiry, intuition, muddling-through, agenda building, and other "messier" decision-making means. Finally, chaotic contexts are largely "unknowable" and require many decisions and little time to think. Learning occurs largely by acting first, then learning from feedback.

### Summary of Complexity in Healthcare Management

Box 1.1 summarizes features of healthcare management that help convey its complexity. An extensive analysis by Welton (2004, p. 411) concludes: "Healthcare delivery organizations are complex systems that operate within the highly complex healthcare system." It is worth noting that this degree of complexity in both organizations and the overall system was not always the case. Scott (2003), for one, chronicles the growing dynamism and complexity in healthcare delivery. He characterizes healthcare delivery in the era from 1920 to 1960 as "the least changeable, most highly institutionalized sector" in US society, with healthcare delivery dominated by the power of physicians (Scott, 2003, p. 24). The sector has since moved to one in which the "systems involved are complex and varied, the forces at work manifold and intricately interrelated, the speed of change alarmingly swift" (Scott, 2003, p. 23). In summary, the work of healthcare managers today is rarely simple, straightforward, and predictable. How do managers work effectively in these circumstances?

## EFFECTIVELY MANAGING COMPLEX HEALTHCARE WORK

A number of authors offer guidelines for effectively managing in complex circumstances in general and in healthcare work specifically. Before discussing those guidelines, a brief note on the distinction between leadership and management is needed.

### Leadership or Management?

The two concepts, leadership and management, have much in common, because both refer to ways to get things done in organizations (and elsewhere). But for some purposes, such as describing work in simple or complicated settings versus work in complex settings, it is useful to separate the two (Kotter, 2013). To get things done, leadership works though mobilizing others by utilizing tools not necessarily possessed by managers (Begun and Malcolm, 2014, pp. 22–23). Managers largely rely on authority in order to mobilize others; leaders inspire others through discovering common purpose and passion. Authority "works" better in simple and complicated settings. An obvious problem with solely applying authority in healthcare organizations is that the power of authority held by managers is constrained by the power of professions held by those who deliver care. Clinical professions need to be "led" in addition to being "managed." In a complex organization setting, leadership tasks (for example, finding direction, building commitment, and overcoming challenges) are accomplished by emergent, relational dialogue among diverse individuals (Begun and White, 2008). Leadership becomes the responsibility of everyone in the organization (Heifetz et al., 2009).

Other distinctions between management and leadership include the notion that managers focus on efficiency (doing the most with the least), while leaders focus on effectiveness (goal attainment). This distinction relates to the shorter-term and operational focus of management compared to the longer-term and strategic focus of leadership. Management works better when there is agreement on goals and how to achieve them, which is more likely to be the case in the short term than the long term; leadership is needed when consensus on the "what" and knowledge about the "how" are relatively low, which again is more likely to be the case in the longer run.

Add to that the fact that change is ubiquitous in most healthcare delivery settings, and what worked in the past may not work in the future. This limits the effectiveness of a focus on efficiency, the bailiwick of managers. Healthcare delivery organizations are not only complex, but complex adaptive systems. This requires that managers "take off the blinders" and encourage change and innovation, relative to stability and control; more leadership, less management.

In summary, managers in complex organizations need the competencies of leaders. While we retain the terms "healthcare management" and "managing complex organizations" in this chapter, we see little difference in the terms "manage" and "lead" as they are applied to those individuals charged with managing or leading in complex healthcare organizations. We use the term "healthcare management" in the broadest sense, encompassing leadership activities.

## GUIDELINES FOR MANAGING (AND LEADING) IN COMPLEX ORGANIZATIONS

Scholars of complexity science draw conclusions about managing complex organizations largely from metaphor or extension of findings from complex system behavior in mathematics, biology, physics, and other physical and natural sciences. Choices regarding the exact content and wording of guidelines are fairly subjective; they depend on judgments by experts on what exactly is most important and relevant to management. An example of such conclusions comes from Snowden and Boone (2007), who offer five general guidelines for making decisions in complex contexts: (1) open up the discussion; (2) set simple rules; (3) stimulate attractors; (4) encourage dissent and diversity; and (5) manage initial conditions and monitor for emergence. Their guidelines 2, 3 and 5 flow directly from complexity science; the other two are consistent with a variety of theoretical traditions (as well as complexity science) and with experience. McDaniel and Driebe (2001, p. 24), positing that "Traditional views of health care managerial theory have been focused on organizational control," delineate six managerial strategies for managing complex systems: making sense, remembering (and forgetting) history, thinking about the future, dealing with surprise, taking action, and developing mindfulness. Again, their conclusions are interpretations of lessons drawn from the behavior of complex systems, particularly complex adaptive systems, as observed in the natural and physical sciences, tempered by their own view of experience with organizations. In a similar vein, Zimmerman et al. (1998) list such principles as: build a good-enough vision and provide minimum specifications; uncover and work with paradox and tension; and go for multiple actions at the fringes, letting direction arise.

Useful guidelines for managing complexity can derive from theoretical traditions other than complexity science, because many different theories and concepts in some way wrestle with complexity. For example, Drath (2001, 2004a, 2004b) focuses on three activities that are critical to successful action in complex organizations: shared sense-making, exploration, and connecting. All three concepts are familiar in the organizational literature, complexity science aside.

As theoretical guidelines (guidelines largely deduced from theory), such advice as the above may come across as too abstract and jargon-filled to many practitioners. Importantly, however, management practitioners induce from experience many of the same principles. White and Griffith (2010), for example, argue that the culture of healthcare organizations is the critical factor driving their performance. Excellent managers spend time promoting shared values, listening to their associates, and responding to their needs in ways that model the organization's values. The perspective is reflected in the common saying in healthcare that "Culture eats strategy for lunch." This perspective is quite consistent with complexity principles promoting the importance of underlying initial conditions in systems and the capacity of a few simple rules (reflected in an organization's culture) to guide complex behavior.

The popularity of the Studer Group philosophy (Studer, 2003, 2008) in healthcare organizations is another example of practice-driven guidelines that are consistent with a complexity viewpoint. Studer's philosophy emphasizes the important of human relationships – connections – in producing effective management and satisfied customers. His work devotes extensive attention to developing organizational culture to support patient or customer service. Again, organizational performance is built on the foundation of a strong culture that prioritizes a few key values.

Next we elaborate five guidelines that in our own view represent the wide breadth of knowledge about managing complex organizations, deriving from both theory and practice. Box 1.2 lists the guidelines. We emphasize guidelines that fit the management of complexity, rather than management guidelines that apply as well in simple and complicated

---

**BOX 1.2   FIVE GUIDELINES FOR MANAGING COMPLEX HEALTHCARE ORGANIZATIONS**

1. Encourage exploration.
2. Manage and reap the benefits of diversity.
3. Build connections.
4. Conduct shared sense-making.
5. Use simple rules.

settings. That is, these guidelines build on and around guidelines that apply in simple and complicated settings; they do not contradict or reject them.

First, encourage exploration. Exploration involves searching for new possibilities through experimentation, discovery, and innovation. It requires refining and extending existing products and services. Organizational scientist James March noted that organizations commonly tend to exploit known alternatives rather than explore unknown ones, resulting in stable and suboptimal equilibria in changing environments (March, 1991).

Managing in a complex environment means almost by definition that the organization is trying to find its way. There is insufficient clarity about what to do, and how to get it done. Learning about the world requires taking action and learning from those actions. This requires a level of comfort with decision-making under uncertainty. In such an environment, managers and leaders need to realize that they are in essence exploring a "solution space" or "fitness landscape," looking for adaptive next steps that move their organizations in the direction of higher performance. Like climbing an uncharted mountain, they are looking for the right path to the "fitness" summit for their organization. To get a better sense of what will work, managers and teams need to try out different approaches and methods, and see what works. Systematic "fail fast and learn" approaches to innovation, including user-centered design, rapid-cycle prototyping, and good-enough evaluation methods, enable modern organizations to maximize their chances of success when operating under conditions of complexity. Thus, a key principle of managing in a complex environment is to explore. Doing the same thing over again is likely to get you the same results; so try something new and see what happens.

Second, manage and reap the benefits of diversity. Complexity science teaches us that when properly used, diversity of thought and point of view helps teams and organizations explore their "solution space" with greater success and efficiency. Diversity does not just mean racial, ethnic, or gender diversity. It also applies to diversity in experience, knowledge, training, role, and perspective. Diverse groups of people working on a problem have a broader range of knowledge about the organization, its environment, and the challenges it faces than more homogeneous groups. Broader thinking engendered by diversity increases the probability that a good-enough solution will be found by the group. However, to harness the potential value of diversity, managers must enable two other capabilities. They must ensure that communication processes are such that all members of the group are able to speak up and be heard by the other members of the group. Diversity of knowledge and point of view serves little purpose if it remains silent or unheard. In addition, there must be a process of "curating" the work of the group, to ensure that quality standards are adhered to, and that dialogue, evaluation, and decision-making processes are high-quality. Diverse groups with good communication, respect, and trust that use best practices for collecting and evaluating evidence will be most successful at exploring their "fitness landscape" and identifying new approaches that improve performance.

Third, build connections. Connections among individuals, groups, teams, functional areas, departments, divisions, and agents outside the formal boundaries of the organizations are all necessary to provide the information flow necessary for organizational health. Network science provides insights here. The traditional organizational hierarchy, with its clear unidirectional reporting lines, generates highly clustered, centralized network structures that are characterized by slow information flow and decision-making. This is characteristic of bureaucracies, which do not generally perform well in response to complex challenges. Creation of "crosslinks" between agents in the organizational network, on the other hand, moves the organization in the direction of becoming a "small world network" characterized by rapid information flow and decision-making. Thus the organization is better positioned to leverage the "wisdom of the crowd" and to operate more effectively in complex environments.

More casual connections (what Granovetter, 1973, calls "weak ties") also add value and should be fostered. They are frequent sources for new ideas, information, and resources (for instance, a new team member with novel skills).

Building connections is not just about reporting relationships and acquaintances. Organizations get work done, and respond to complex challenges, by the work people do together. No individual, or set of individuals working by themselves, can enable organizational success. They must work together to explore the fitness landscape if the organization is to succeed. Such collaboration requires not just connections, but also relationships based on trust and shared goals. Thus, managers seeking success in a complex environment should not only build relationships, but also tend those relationships so that they are strong enough to sustain the adaptive work required to succeed.

One way to build relationships is to follow the fourth guideline, conduct shared sense-making. Sense-making refers to "the process through which people work to understand issues or events that are novel, ambiguous, confusing, or in some other way violate expectations" (Maitlis and Christianson, 2014, p. 57). Sense-making is related to mindfulness, because the ability to pick up cues enhances sense-making. It allows enacting a more ordered environment from which further cues can be drawn. Taking action and seeing what happens next can improve sense-making. Sense-making also can be a positive force for creativity and innovation, because it links employees to customers, patients, and the "external" world. The creation of novel understandings allows for new ways of doing business.

We emphasize the adjective "shared" in "shared sense-making." This is where the skills of listening and soliciting information are critical. Drath (2004b, p. 177) notes that complex challenges "cause confusion, ambiguity, conflict, and stress." Constructing responses to challenges and preferred futures is a collaborative task, because no one person has the knowledge or vision to see all its parts. Shared sense-making allows participants to understand the nature of problems and opportunities and to propose innovative solutions as a collective rather than as isolated individual "experts."

Finally, use simple rules. One of the fundamental teachings of complexity science is that all complex systems manifest emergent behavior that is the consequence of a small set of "rules" governing the behavior of the agents in the system (Plsek, 2001; Letiche, 2008). These rules are often described as "simple" because of the contrast between the simplicity of the rules and the complexity of the emergent behaviors. Examples of such rules in the organizational setting include incentives, culture, codes of conduct, and measurement systems. Typically, complex organizational systems have three types of simple rules: goal-setting rules, boundary-setting rules, and incentive rules. Goal-setting rules define the objectives of the organization, the pole star(s) with which the members of the organization align. Boundary-setting rules define the allowed behavioral norms to be followed in working to achieve the goals. Incentives define the rewards to the agents for making progress towards the goals while following allowable behaviors.

Organizations facing complex challenges often discover that the simple rules that previously enabled their success are no longer adaptive. Under these circumstances, stepping back, re-evaluating the organization's simple rules, and doing the adaptive work to modify them (in an exploratory fashion) may facilitate a shift to a more adaptive set of simple rules. Healthcare organizations implementing cultures of safety or collaborative care, for example, find that successful change requires revisions to the simple rules guiding the organizations.

## CHALLENGES FOR HEALTHCARE MANAGEMENT EDUCATION AND PRACTICE

We have recommended five guidelines for managing complex healthcare organizations: (1) encourage exploration; (2) manage and reap the benefits of diversity; (3) build connections; (4) conduct shared sensemaking; and (5) use simple rules. We offer two caveats about following these guidelines: do not follow them slavishly; and acquiring the ability to master them is not simple.

Like any strength or tool, over-reliance on these guidelines, and in particular the mistaken application of these methods to simple or complicated challenges, may yield bad results for the individual leader, as well as the organization. The utility of exploration versus exploitation, for example, depends very much on the organizational context. Likewise, there is a time for sense-making, and there is a time for giving orders. Managers need to leverage good judgment and a well-developed sense of situational awareness in deciding when to properly apply these complexity-informed guidelines.

That judgment, and the ability to apply these guidelines in behaviors, requires a level of maturity and psychological development that is rare in new managers and leaders. Developmentally, newer managers typically are focused on mastering their role and demonstrating their ability to achieve results. They are building the interpersonal skills that the guideline behaviors require, but are often "not there yet." Nevertheless, we think these skills can be learned.

How best can we develop managers who understand complex systems and use simple rules, shared sense-making, connections, diversity, and exploration to manage them? We identify two key approaches. First, give them experiences that enable them to learn. "Act your way to a new way of thinking" is a development adage that expresses this advice well. Second, support those experiences with feedback and coaching experiences that focus on and build insight into the skills required to successfully manage in a complex environment. Mentoring from more senior managers and leaders is also critical. It is a responsibility for more experienced leaders to bring their newer counterparts along on this developmental path as quickly as possible.

This combination of complexity experiences and coaching and mentoring can be extended to educational settings as well. New students are particularly driven to master technical skills that will help them attain and perform in entry-level jobs, and that is important, as is mastery of traditional management skills that work in simple and complicated systems. But at the same time, students can begin to experience and deal with complex challenges, through case studies and project work in "real-world" organizations, followed by mentored experiences in internships and residencies. Challenges involving longer-term issues (such as culture change) and interprofessional teams (requiring that students manage diversity) are particularly recommended.

In addition, complexity knowledge and related knowledge need to be a growing portion of the training and education curricula. Competency frameworks have become a common staple for guiding educational programs and development of employees in healthcare organizations. Accredited graduate education programs in healthcare administration are required to employ competency models as a basis for their curricula. Commonly used models include those developed by the National Center for Healthcare Leadership (NCHL) and the Health Leadership Alliance (HLA) (Calhoun et al., 2008; Healthcare Leadership Alliance, 2013; Stefl, 2008). As represented by those two educational program competency models, there is some appreciation for management of complexity, through competencies such as innovative thinking, information-seeking, collaboration, organizational awareness, interpersonal understanding, relationship-building, and self-development in the NCHL model and many of the competencies in the communication and relationship management domain and the organizational climate and culture cluster (in the leadership domain) in the HLA model. However, many of the more distinctive aspects of complexity, such as the concepts of simple rules and shared sense-making, are not directly represented. With growing recognition of healthcare as a complexity management field, more of the field's competencies for managers should reflect complexity content and practices.

Content areas related to complexity that may deserve more attention in curricula include innovation, change, and leadership, if those topics are approached with a complexity lens. For example, the change techniques of positive deviance, appreciative inquiry, and design thinking are consistent with complexity science (Bunker and Alban, 2006; Lockwood, 2009). The leadership approach known as adaptive leadership (Heifetz, 1994; Heifetz et al., 2009), among others, is quite consistent with complexity science (Begun and Thygeson, 2014; Thygeson et al., 2010). System dynamics is a systems thinking conceptual approach that provides a set of analytic tools including causal loop diagrams, system archetypes, and leverage point analysis, that can be used relatively intuitively for evaluating complex organizational problems and designing possible solutions (Begun and Thygeson, 2014; Meadows, 2008; Sterman, 2000).

## CHALLENGES FOR HEALTHCARE MANAGEMENT RESEARCH

Appreciation of complexity means changing the nature of questions investigated as well as the methods for doing so. Several scholars, including

McDaniel and Driebe (2001) and Zimmerman (2011), have suggested issues that help explore aspects of the complexity of healthcare management. Taking our five management guidelines as a guide, examples of research topics that would illuminate management of complexity include the following:

1.  Exploration. What is the relative balance of exploration and exploitation in the organization in different arenas? How and why has the balance changed over time? How does the exploration–exploitation balance in an organization affect performance?
2.  Diversity. What are the differential performance effects of diverse input into decisions of different types? How are diversity and efficiency of decision-making related?
3.  Connections. What key networks are underdeveloped in the organization? Overdeveloped? Where do new connections need to be made? How is team performance related to network structure and relationship function?
4.  Shared sense-making. What parties are involved in shared sense-making, about what issues? In what different ways are organizations making sense of current healthcare reform efforts? Is there an optimum amount of sense-making? How is attention to sense-making influenced by contextual factors like organizational size, pace of change, and organizational network structure?
5.  Simple rules. How are healthcare organizations distinguished by the simple rules they use? Under what circumstances are they altered (successfully or not)?

Studying complex processes requires appropriate research methods, as causality is more ambiguous, patterns are harder to discern, and variation is a prime source of knowledge rather than something to be eliminated (Begun et al., 2003; Byrne and Callaghan, 2013; McDaniel et al., 2009). Use of methods (and theories) that assume linear relationships and use of models with small numbers of variables can spawn misleading findings. In addition to system dynamics modeling and social network analysis, a third methodological tool that shows substantial recent promise and appears to be broadly applicable to studying or improving healthcare organizational performance is qualitative comparative analysis (Begun and Thygeson, 2014). Qualitative methods in general are well suited for complex organization research because rich and deep data are needed to truly understand variation. Tangled causal relations are difficult to discern quickly or with certainty. Qualitative comparative analysis (QCA) is a method based on set theory that is well suited to evaluating non-linear systems characterized by causal complexity, and its fuzzy set version is particularly useful for studying the association between combinations (configurations) of conditions and outcomes of interest where there may be multiple paths to the same outcome (equifinality), and causation may be asymmetric (the cause of A is different from the cause of not-A) (Ragin, 2008). Familiarity with the concepts of QCA, even if no formal QCA analysis is performed, can enable a healthcare manager to reframe a challenge using set-theoretic concepts, which are asymmetric and non-linear, rather than correlations, which are symmetric and linear. Several recent studies have illustrated the application of QCA to organizational management and health services research (Baltzer et al., 2011; Dy et al., 2005; Thygeson et al., 2012).

## CONCLUSIONS

As a result of their complexity, effective management in healthcare organizations requires different competencies than management in simple or complicated organizations. It requires more of what is typically called "leadership" than "management." We presented five guidelines for managing complex healthcare organizations: encourage exploration, manage and reap the benefits of diversity, build connections, conduct shared sense-making, and use simple rules. Effective managers of complexity are best developed through knowledge and through learning experiences supported with coaching and feedback. Greater appreciation of complexity in healthcare management education, practice, and research will expand the contribution of healthcare management to improvements in healthcare delivery and the health of patients and populations.

## REFERENCES

Alexander, J.A. and D'Aunno, T.A. (2003). Alternative perspectives on institutional and market relationships in the US health care sector. In S.S. Mick and M.E. Wyttenback (eds), *Advances in Health Care Organization Theory* (pp. 45–77). San Francisco, CA: Jossey-Bass.

Baker, G.R. and Denis, J. (2011). Medical leadership in health care systems: From professional authority to organizational leadership. *Public Money and Management*, 31: 355–362.

Baltzer, M., Westerlund, H., Backhans, M., and Melinder, K. (2011). Involvement and structure: A qualitative study of organizational change and sickness absence among women in the public sector in Sweden. *BMC Public Health*, 11: 318–335.

Begun, J.W. and Malcolm, J.K. (2014). *Leading Public Health: A Competency Framework*. New York: Springer Publishing.

Begun, J.W. and Thygeson, M. (2014). Complexity and health care: Tools for engagement. In S.S.F. Mick and P. Shay (eds), *Advances in Health Care Organization Theory* (2nd edn) (pp. 259–282). San Francisco, CA: Jossey-Bass.

Begun, J.W. and White, K.R. (2008). The challenge of change: Inspiring leadership. In C. Lindberg, S. Nash, and C. Lindberg (eds), *On the Edge: Nursing in the Age of Complexity* (pp. 239–262). Bordentown, NJ: PlexusPress.

Begun, J.W., White, K.R., and Mosser, G. (2011). Interprofessional care teams: The role of the healthcare administrator. *Journal of Interprofessional Care*, 25: 119–123.

Begun, J.W., Zimmerman, B., and Dooley, K.J. (2003). Health care organizations as complex adaptive systems. In S.S. Mick and M.E. Wyttenbach (eds), *Advances in Health Care Organization Theory* (pp. 253–288). San Francisco, CA: Jossey-Bass.

Bunker, B.B. and Alban, B.T. (2006). *The Handbook of Large Group Methods: Creating Systemic Change in Organizations and Communities*. San Francisco, CA: Jossey-Bass.

Byrne, D. and Callaghan, G. (2013). *Complexity Theory and the Social Sciences: The State of the Art*. New York: Routledge.

Calhoun, J.G., Dollett, L., Sinioris, M.E., Wainio, J.A., Butler, P.W., et al. (2008). Development of an interprofessional competency model for healthcare leadership. *Journal of Healthcare Management*, 53: 375–389.

Drath, W.H. (2001). *The Deep Blue Sea: Rethinking the Source of Leadership*. San Francisco, CA: Jossey-Bass.

Drath, W.H. (2004a). Leading together: Complex challenges require a new approach. In M. Wilcox and S. Rush (eds), *The CCL Guide to Leadership in Action* (pp. 171–180). San Francisco, CA: Jossey-Bass.

Drath, W.H. (2004b). The third way: A new source of leadership. In M. Wilcox and S. Rush (eds), *The CCL Guide to Leadership in Action* (pp. 153–163). San Francisco, CA: Jossey-Bass.

Dy, S.M., Garg, P., Nyberg, D., Dawson, P.B., Pronovost, P.J., Morlock, L., Rubin, H., and Wu, A.W. (2005). Critical pathway effectiveness: Assessing the impact of patient, hospital care, and pathway characteristics using qualitative comparative analysis. *Health Services Research*, 40: 499–516.

Glouberman, S. and Mintzberg, H. (2001). Managing the care of health and the cure of disease – Part I: Differentiation. *Health Care Management Review*, 26(1): 56–69.

Granovetter, M.S. (1973). The strength of weak ties. *American Journal of Sociology*, 78: 1360–1380.

Harris, J.E. (1977). The internal organization of hospitals: Some economic implications. *Bell Journal of Economics*, 8: 467–482.

Healthcare Leadership Alliance (2013). Introducing the HLA Competency Directory, Version 2.0. Retrieved from http://www.healthcareleadershipalliance.org/ (accessed 10 September 2014).

Heifetz, R.A. (1994). *Leadership without Easy Answers*. Cambridge, MA: Harvard University Press.

Heifetz, R.A., Grashow, A., and Linsky, M. (2009). *The Practice of Adaptive Leadership: Tools and Tactics for Changing your Organization and the World*. Boston, MA: Harvard Business Press.

Kotter, J.P. (2013). Management is "still" not leadership. HBR Blog Network, January 9. Retrieved from http://blogs.hbr.org/2013/01/management-is-still-not-leadership/ (accessed 10 September 2014).

Letiche, H. (2008). *Making Healthcare Care: Managing via Simple Guiding Principles*. Charlotte, NC: Information Age Publishing.

Lockwood, T. (2009). *Design Thinking: Integrating Innovation, Customer Experience and Brand Value*. New York: Allworth Press.

Maitlis, S. and Christianson, M. (2014). Sensemaking in organizations. *Academy of Management Annals*, 8(1): 57–125.

March, J.G. (1991). Exploration and exploitation in organizational learning. *Organization Science*, 2: 71–87.

McDaniel, R.R., Jr. and Driebe, D.J. (2001). Complexity science and health care management. *Advances in Health Care Management*, 2: 11–36.

McDaniel, R.R., Jr., Lanham, H.J., and Anderson, R.A. (2009). Implications of complex adaptive systems theory for the design of research on health care organizations. *Health Care Management Review*, 34: 191–199.

Meadows, D. (2008). *Thinking in Systems: A Primer*. White River Junction, VT: Chelsea Green Publishing.

Mintzberg, H. (1983). *Structure in Fives: Designing Effective Organizations*. Englewood Cliffs, NJ: Prentice-Hall.

Mosser, G.M. and Begun, J.W. (2013). *Understanding Teamwork in Health Care*. New York: McGraw-Hill.

Plsek, P. (2001). Appendix B: Redesigning health care with insights from the science of complex adaptive systems. In Institute of Medicine (ed.), *Crossing the Quality Chasm* (pp. 309–322). Washington, DC: National Academy Press.

Ragin, C. (2008). *Redesigning Social Inquiry: Fuzzy Sets and Beyond*. Chicago, IL: University of Chicago Press.

Scott, W.R. (2003). The old order changeth: The evolving world of health care organizations. In S.S. Mick and M.E. Wyttenback (eds), *Advances in Health Care Organization Theory* (pp. 23–43). San Francisco, CA: Jossey-Bass.

Shi, L. and Singh, D.A. (2014). *Delivering Health Care in America: A Systems Approach* (6th edn). Burlington, MA: Jones & Bartlett Learning.

Snowden, D.F. and Boone, M.E. (2007). A leader's framework for decision-making. *Harvard Business Review*, 85(11): 68–72.

Stacey, R.D. (1996). *Strategic Management and Organisational Dynamics* (2nd edn). London: Financial Times.

Stefl, M. (2008). Common competencies for all healthcare managers: The Healthcare Leadership Alliance model. *Journal of Healthcare Management*, 53: 360–373.

Sterman, J.D. (2000). *Business Dynamics: Systems Thinking and Modeling for a Complex World*. Boston, MA: Irwin McGraw-Hill.

Studer, Q. (2003). *Hardwiring Excellence*. Gulf Breeze, FL: Fire Starter Publishing.

Studer, Q. (2008). *Results that Last: Hardwiring Behaviors that Will Take Your Company to the Top*. Hoboken, NJ: Wiley.

Thygeson, M., Morrissey, L., and Ulstad, V. (2010). Adaptive leadership and the practice of medicine: A complexity-based approach to reframing the doctor–patient relationship. *Journal of Evaluation in Clinical Practice*, 16(5): 1009–1015.

Thygeson, M., Solberg, L.I., Asche, S.E., Fontaine, P., Pawlson, L.G., and Scholle, S.H. (2012). Using fuzzy set qualitative comparative analysis (fs/QCA) to explore the relationship between medical "homeness" and quality. *Health Services Research*, 47(1 Pt 1): 22–45.

Welton, W.E. (2004). Managing today's complex healthcare business enterprise: Reflections on distinctive requirements of healthcare management education. *Journal of Health Administration Education*, 21(4): 391–418.

White, K.R. and Griffith, J.R. (2010). *The Well-Managed Healthcare Organization* (7th edn). Chicago, IL: Health Administration Press.

Zimmerman, B. (2011). How complexity science is transforming healthcare. In P. Allen, S. Maguire, and B. McKelvey (eds), *The Sage Handbook of Complexity and Management* (pp. 617–635). Los Angeles, CA: Sage.

Zimmerman, B., Lindberg, C., and Plsek, P. (1998). *Edgeware: Insights from Complexity Science for Health Care Leaders*. Irving, TX: VHA.

# 2. Leadership resilience
## *Pamela E. Paustian*

## INTRODUCTION

Today's healthcare environment in the United States is impacted by many dynamic factors – new technologies, changes in the systems for delivery of healthcare, quality and patient safety concerns, evolving regulatory requirements, workforce shortages, workload requirements – all of which are changing far more rapidly than organizational performance structures can adapt. As a result, the gap between the rate at which change occurs and the ability of organizations to anticipate and plan for change is broadening. Evaluating the external environment and its impact on an organization's strategy and operations has long been seen as more difficult under conditions of uncertainty than during periods of predictability, thus many organizations experience less than satisfactory working conditions and leaders find themselves being more reactive to crisis situations than proactive in preventing them. Leaders faced with rapid change and uncertainty in their work environments often report such feelings as "being stretched too thin" or overstressed, experiencing internal conflict over difficult decisions, and being faced with adversity in their daily work routines. To remain effective in their leadership roles, individuals must develop resilience, the ability to regain previous (or improved) performance levels after experiencing a difficult or adverse situation, not only personally but also specifically regarding their leadership role.

Much of the research on resilience in the healthcare industry has been directed at the effects of stressors on employee health, job performance and job tenure, and coping mechanisms (Hodges et al., 2008; McCann et al., 2013; Zautra et al., 2008). Exploring the resilience of healthcare leaders specifically has not been pursued through robust research. Because the ways in which employees, healthcare practitioners, and leaders adapt to organizational change and the complexity of their work environments can impact individual resilience levels (Lambert et al., 2004; Lim et al., 2011; Luthans and Avolio, 2003; McCann et al., 2013; Sutcliffe and Vogus, 2003), the resulting effects on their job performance become of interest as well. Developing resilience helps build inner strength and shift individual attitudes toward working through periods of flux and turbulent times and experiencing work success through the ability to adapt personally as a member of a team.

Organizational leadership development programs may create a foundation of knowledge about the qualities needed to establish and maintain well-being in a challenging workplace. Individuals working in healthcare organizations, especially in positions of authority within an organization, can gain greater insight into their respective abilities to recover and bounce back from adverse occurrences in the increasingly complex organizational climate found in healthcare delivery systems. By understanding and developing leadership resilience skills, leaders can perform more effectively in unpredictable environments, manage their job demands, become more adaptive and avoid burnout.

Organizational survival in the healthcare industry requires that leaders accelerate their ability to change effectively in response to the demands imposed on healthcare organizations by regulators, payers, and patients. Developing and fostering resilient work environments and individuals within these healthcare organizations is seen as a way to reduce negative outcomes and increase positive outcomes. When considering how to provide psychosocial support, promote positive views and healthy activities, and create challenging and engaging intellectual stimulation, the question becomes how to prepare leaders in healthcare organizations to adapt effectively when faced with rapidly changing organizational complexity (McCann et al., 2013).

Research suggests that leaders who are armed with the necessary knowledge to demonstrate calmness and remain in control of their emotions, and who are able to inspire and motivate others, and make effective decisions when faced with adversity, will be better prepared to not only survive, but thrive, when confronted by crises (Jackson et al., 2007; Maddi and Khoshaba, 2003). Rapid change in healthcare today makes being able to adapt, manage, lead, and mentor in this environment a key component to overall success. These self-aware individuals are better equipped to become strong leaders who provide credible guidance with a sustained, long-term, positive impact on the success of their organizations (Boyatzis and McKee, 2005; Harland et al., 2005; Margolis and Stoltz, 2010; Patterson et al., 2009). Individuals who have built up emotional reserves are able to demonstrate resilience by returning from each adverse experience stronger, and are able to avoid resentful emotions and a negative mental attitude. They do not allow a negative environment to drain their resolve.

## DEFINING RESILIENCE

Grotberg (2003) concluded that resilience was based on a three-factor framework associated with external support, an individual's inner strength, and inner personal and problem-solving skills. Patterson et al. (2009) suggested that resilience incorporated nine different strengths: optimism, values, efficacy, support, well-being, courage, perseverance, responsibility, and adaptability. Furthermore, the authors suggested that the degree to which each of these strengths or factors is present in an individual may determine the extent of their overall resilience and the potential for success or failure with regard to a given venture in a complex and ever-changing environment.

Building upon these concepts, Patterson et al. (2009) postulated that objective assessment and articulation of their resilience might permit an individual to explore areas of self-development and increase any or all of the nine strengths. By understanding the limitations of personal resilience, an individual could fortify their reflexes, gaining advantage before the appearance of adversity occurs. Leaders need to develop a focus on self-care to prevent burnout and maintain a high level of psychological well-being (Barnett et al., 2007; McCann et al., 2013).

As Bennis and Thomas (2002) note, those in positions of leadership are often particularly interested in the potential to improve their resilience as a method of increasing their managerial skills. Research by Huey and Weisz (1997) suggests that resilient individuals become competent at recognizing employees with depleted levels of resilience based on a propensity to over-exaggerate reasons for a negative work outcome. Indeed, many leaders subscribe to the idea that their own success may, in fact, depend upon their ability to express a level of resilience that allows the larger group to recover from challenges and adversity (McFarland, 2009).

## UNDERSTANDING LEADERSHIP RESILIENCE

The study of resilience specifically among leaders is conceptualized as leadership resilience, and was characterized by Luc (2009) as "a condition and a consequence of the actualization and exercising of leadership in difficult and demanding situations" (Luc, 2009, p. 82). The intersection of leadership and resilience is graphically expressed through a Venn diagram, such as that shown in Figure 2.1, with the "X" representing those elements of resilience that are related to the leadership role and the importance of resilience to leaders.

An understanding of the boundaries of the "X" area is best achieved

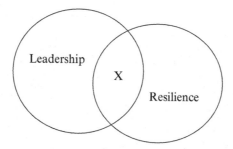

*Figure 2.1   Leadership resilience*

by summarizing key elements of resilience, leadership, and the integrated concept of leadership resilience. Each of these elements is developed by the bodies of work representing a synthesis of the seminal resilience and leadership literature, primarily in the fields of business, psychology, and education, but with strong application to healthcare leadership.

**Defining Leadership**

Understanding the importance of leadership resilience requires one to understand the more general concept of leadership and ideally endorse an articulated definition. As with many words, a single definition of "leadership" remains elusive and multiple definitions exist, some with similarities, some with unique elements (Bass and Bass, 2008).

A consensus definition for leadership remains elusive, even within the management and leadership community of scholars. Accordingly, Bennis and Nanus (1986) state: "leadership is like the Abominable Snowman, whose footprints are everywhere but who is nowhere to be seen" (Bennis and Nanus, 1986, p. 20). This sentiment was reminiscent of Stogdill's comment from the first edition of the *Handbook of Leadership*, wherein he stated that "there are almost as many definitions of leadership as there are persons who have attempted to define the concept" (Stogdill, 1974, p. 259). Now in its fourth edition, the *Handbook* continues to provide further evidence of the truth of this statement, currently identifying more than 1500 definitions of leadership (Bass, 2008).

Historically, the study of leadership was informed in part by Moore's definition of leadership as "the ability to impress the will of the leader on those led and induce obedience, respect, loyalty, and cooperation" (Moore, 1927, p. 124). When, almost 80 years later, Northouse stated, "leadership is a process whereby an individual influences a group of individuals to achieve a common goal" (Northouse, 2004, p. 3), it became evident that modern considerations of leadership now included broader concepts. Northouse's statement accurately reflects the attempt by recent researchers to "give more consideration to the dynamic aspects of leadership and to consider it an activity shared between the members of a team, group, or organization, much like communication" (Luc, 2009, p. ix).

Ciulla (1998) expanded the concept of leadership as a shared activity, stating: "leadership is not a person or a position but rather a complex moral relationship between people based on trust, obligation, commitment, emotion, and a shared vision of the common good" (Ciulla, 1998, p. xv). This foreshadowed the statement by Kouzes and Posner that leadership is the "art of mobilizing others to want to struggle for shared aspirations" (Kouzes and Posner, 2002, p. 30). Effective leadership, they asserted, can both engage workers and shape the culture and environment of the workplace, ultimately creating an environment where, as Stogdill observed, leadership goes beyond the individual and is about the totality of the workspace: people, processes, and relationships (Stogdill, 1974).

In his book *How the Mighty Fall*, Collins (2009) defines leadership as the leader's ability to motivate or influence others to the point of being a facilitator. While straightforward, this definition is also useful contextually in describing the need for a leader to quickly adapt while shepherding their charges through turbulent economic and competitive environments. By altering their leadership approach, a leader can provide the best direction, based on the problem encountered. This view is reflected in a number of leadership studies, including that of Hersey and Blanchard (1977), reinforcing the notion that there is no one best way to lead or influence others.

Recent work by Neck and Manz (2007) addresses the concept and emerging theory of self-leadership. Self-leadership in its simplest form is "the process of influencing oneself" (p. 5) meaning the behavioral and cognitive tactics people use for self-direction and self-motivation to achieve greater personal effectiveness in job or social performance. Self-leadership is divided into three strategies: "Self-imposed strategies," "Self-reward strategies," and "Self-punishment strategies" (Neck and Manz, 2007, pp. 20, 32, 34).

These diverse concepts of leadership form a spectrum of opinion that, while illustrating some unique traits, also contains common elements: specifically, the need of the leader to possess critical thinking skills. Regardless of which theory of leadership one embraces, critical thinking abilities are a key mechanism to an effective leadership process (Novelli and Taylor, 1993).

For the purposes of this chapter and for understanding leadership resilience, the definition grounding the idea of leadership is provided by

Bennis (1994), who stated that: "leadership revolves around vision, ideas, direction, and has more to do with inspiring people as to direction and goals than with day-to-day implementation. A leader must be able to leverage more than his own capabilities. He must be capable of inspiring other people to do things without actually sitting on top of them with a checklist" (Bennis, 1994, p. 139). This definition comes from Bennis's second edition work which focuses on the complexities and paradigm of leadership. The expansive text is composed of 28 leadership cases and experiences that allow the reader to absorb lessons from examples of successful leadership. Specifically, Bennis discusses the challenges associated with leadership, the role of leadership failure, the importance of knowing oneself, cultural awareness and the impact it has on leadership, the need to see beyond the here and now, the importance of operating on instinct, how to learn and improve from adverse experiences, and the crucial role of the follower. The type of leader described by Bennis embraces the challenges of change and is willing to work to overcome the barrier presented by change, which can often lead to the disruptions and challenges which require resilience.

## Leadership Theories

Given the wide span of definitions available, it is perhaps not surprising that multiple theories and models have emerged to help explain leadership. Among those theories, several stand as significant contributions to the field and they are summarized here to lend a focused perspective to the available body of knowledge.

"Trait theory" is rooted in the belief that distinct behavioral patterns, or traits, including extroversion, openness, neuroticism, agreeableness, and conscientiousness, are common among personality types and can be evaluated to predict future conduct. When applied to leadership, trait theory is often synonymous with "Great Man theory," the concept that highly influential individuals, so-called "Great Men," share common attributes that make them particularly well suited to utilize social power. Characteristics typically examined in these studies include position within society, level of education, gender, ethnicity, and the role of religion (Whittington, 1993).

Early subscribers to this theory included Wiggam (1931), who advanced the idea that intermarriage among the fittest individuals produces a biologically superior class, uniquely endowed with the character traits necessary to elevate them to positions of authority over their subordinates. "Thus, an adequate supply of superior leaders depends upon a proportionately high birth rate among the abler classes" (Stogdill, 1974).

More recent research has placed a greater emphasis on identifying the particular traits common to leaders, rather than linking Great Men through genetic lineage. Particular importance has been placed upon the qualities of integrity, self-confidence, dominance, sociability, persistence, extraversion, agreeableness, intelligence, and conscientiousness. The research of Judge et al. (2002) and Northouse (1997) indicates that a significant relationship exists between these traits and leadership (Gill, 2006).

Great Man theory also considers the environment in which the individual exists as essential to realization of one's ability. As Whittington (1993, pp. 184–185) notes, "social structures provide people with the potential for leadership," making it possible for the individual predisposed to leadership to translate that potential into actuality.

Intelligence, a commonly acknowledged characteristic of leaders, is thought to have multiple dimensions. One important aspect is intrapersonal intelligence (Gardner, 1983), or the capacity for self-awareness. Leaders who reflect on their own thoughts and feelings, and understand how their personal knowledge and values contribute to self-motivation, are empowered to better direct their own lives and careers. This self-awareness, developed over time as the leader learns from an inward focus, allows leaders to trust their instincts in challenging situations.

"Emergent leadership theory" suggests that an individual with the necessary characteristics and skills will naturally emerge as the leader of their group. This emergence will occur, it is suggested, regardless of any formal appointment or hierarchy, because the individual possesses the innate ability to lead. "Likely to be viewed as the most prototypical of the group" (Hogg, 2001, p. 204), the emergent leader is dependent upon the interaction with their followers and the ability to conform to the expectations of the group.

In considering the concept of emergent leaders, Greenleaf (1977) developed the theory of "servant leaders" to explain why certain individuals rise to positions of authority. Building upon classical references, the concept of servant leaders suggests that, endowed with aptitude, certain individuals will assume a mantle of responsibility to provide their followers with an enhanced sense of meaning and value. The leader will, in effect, serve the needs of their followers. Greenleaf (1977) further delineated the responsibility inherent in a natural leader along two tracks: strong leaders and strong servants. Leaders establish the direction and give orders to enforce their decisions. Servants view leadership as an opportunity to enrich their followers. While natural leaders express assertive and domineering qualities to attain a personal goal, natural servants are free of that drive, often instead seeking an altruistic aim and engendering an enhanced level of trust from others.

Leadership style theories center upon the actions of leaders rather than their individual traits. Proponents assert that by examining a leader's methods, procedures, and successes, one can measure the effectiveness and impact of that leader. In this case, what the leader produces is of greater importance than who they are, and how that person became a leader. While Statt (2000) cites Likert's leadership styles as being categorized into four classifications for use in organizations: "exploitative autocratic," "benevolent autocratic," "consultative," and "democratic" (p. 119), they can in practice be divided into two halves: "concern for task" (production orientation) and "concern for people" (employee orientation) (Katz et al., 1950; Katz, 1951). This suggests that when one balances their concern for the task at hand, with concern for the people who will be fulfilling that task, the leader is performing at an optimal level to achieve success.

The "psychodynamic theory" of leadership explores the role of the intrapsychic and interpersonal behaviors of leaders and followers in shaping a given organization. Departing from the view of people as a solely logical, rational, unified group dedicated to organized objectives, psychodynamic theory considers the individual, recognizing that obscure motivations often drive a leader and a follower. Dependent upon an understanding of both oneself and others, this concept requires each pair of leaders and members to be considered separately (Gill, 2006). The relationship between a leader and a follower, that leader's appreciation of the follower's motivations, and the effective exploitation of the follower's personality, contribute to the leader's ability to provide direction and guidance.

Contingency theories of leadership assert that each situation is unique and the most flexible leaders will enjoy the greatest successes. This approach recognizes no one style of leadership as "best," instead emphasizing the leader's ability to adapt their style to the current situation despite success with a particular style in a previous situation (Bass, 2008). Fiedler's (1967) "contingency model" expands upon the basic tenets of contingency theory, postulating that success in leadership results from the interaction of a given leader's style with the favorableness of the specific situation at hand. Fiedler's model is unique in suggesting that a leader's style and personality are relatively stable and not easily adapted to every situation. In cases where the leader and situation do not "match," Fiedler suggests that either the situation must be changed or a new leader possessing the desired style must be found. Fiedler's contingency theory is further developed through House's (1996) "path-goal theory" that recognizes how employee motivation affects the choice of leadership style chosen. By understanding employee motivation, the leader is able to clarify the path to success, inspiring the individual to achieve specific personal goals that stimulate satisfaction and ultimately fulfill the leader's own goals.

"Situational leadership theory" (Hersey and Blanchard, 1977), like other contingency theories, suggests that there is no single best style of leadership. This model asserts that effective leadership is dependent upon the specific situation and the relative maturity of those being led. A follower's level of maturity, or readiness, indicates their knowledge of a given task and ability to carry that task to completion. Accordingly, the effective leader must "adopt a directive or 'telling' style" (Gill, 2006, p. 48) to accommodate the subordinate's ability. Over time, the specific telling style utilized by the leader is expected to change as the employee continues to mature.

Reddin's (1987) "3-D theory of managerial effectiveness" builds upon the flexibility of situational and contingency theories, postulating four distinct styles of management with efficacy dependent on the situation. The major contribution of this work is Reddin's 3-D model of leadership, a relatively simple framework designed to indicate the best management style for a given scenario.

Although *The Transformational Leadership Report* (Transformational Leadership, 2007) credits J.V. Downton with introducing the term "transformational leadership" in a 1973 book, it is Burns's (1978) application of the term in the context of political leadership that is relevant to this chapter. Of particular interest is Burns's conceptualization of transformational leadership as a process rather than demonstrated behaviors, and his belief that such a process will change individuals as well as the organization. Bass (1985) extended Burns's work to focus on the effect this leadership approach has on the followers, in particular the trust and respect for the leader required to achieve a team goal focus.

Transformational theory suggests that empowerment is of primary importance to leaders looking to challenge themselves and their respective followers. By enabling "one of the four I's: individualized consideration, intellectual stimulation, inspirational motivation and idealized influence," the transformational leader charges their followers "to transcend their own self-interest for the greater good of the group" (Gill, 2006, p. 52). These newly empowered individuals are inspired to perform beyond expectations, to achieve goals that previously seemed out of reach. A visionary or charismatic leader may further inspire followers to excel through the manifestation of their personality (Weber, 1947).

**Qualities and Characteristics of Leaders**

Understanding the concept of leadership requires exploring descriptions of traits, behaviors, and classical models of leadership. What qualities, traits, and characteristics make a leader successful? Many have sought the answer to this question, but there is no one definitive list accepted by educators, researchers, or practitioners. Leaders have powerful effects on the organizations they lead. Because of this fact, many researchers have tried to define leadership traits while trying to define the relationship between the characteristics and the success of a leader.

Stogdill (1948) reviewed 124 trait studies in the seminal work 'Personal factors associated with leadership' derived from literature published from 1904 through 1948. These factors focused on main traits such as active participation, facilitation of others to achieve goals, intelligence, attention to the needs of others, task focus, initiative, problem resolution, self-confidence, accepting of responsibility, and the level of control desired. Additionally, Stogdill reviewed 52 leadership studies from 1945 to 1974 and identified an additional 26 general factors which appeared in at least three or more studies as the various qualities and abilities leaders needed to possess (Stogdill, 1974, pp. 92–97). These reviews conducted by Stogdill indicated that there is no specific set of traits that would indicate a strong leadership capability for any person in which the traits were observed. His findings indicate that it is possible to define a set of traits and characteristics for a good leader, but that those traits would change as the leadership situation changed.

Kouzes and Posner (2002, pp. 24–27) identified more than 225 different values, traits, and characteristics from surveys of more than 75 000 individuals. Northouse (2009) has developed a leadership trait questionnaire to aid leaders in identifying their personal strengths and weaknesses. These studies are merely examples; through these and many other studies some traits and characteristics of "successful" leaders have emerged and gained broad consensus. Many of the identified traits and characteristics, such as honesty, adaptability, vision, ability to inspire, courage, perseverance, and self-control, suggest that a leader must be able to accept and face reality the way it is, not how they wish it were (Welch, 2001). Through Stogdill's review of the many trait studies he identified that leaders are "characterized to an outstanding degree by persistence in the face of obstacles, [the] capacity to work with distant objects in view, [the] degree of strength of will or perseverance, and [the] tendency not to abandon tasks from mere changeability" (Stogdill, 1948, p. 50). This statement indicates that resilience was recognized as an important leadership skill in early management research.

## RESILIENCE

Individual leaders may encounter periods of adversity, change, difficulty, and stress during a career. How someone reacts to such events may well determine their success in a given job position or leadership role, or affect the individual's career progression beyond the current job.

A seminal work in the study of resilience was a longitudinal study conducted by Werner and Smith (2001). The study evaluated 500 children born in 1955 at predefined ages through age 40. The results of the Werner and Smith study identified several significant personal factors that allowed the children to overcome adversity. Personal factors included social responsibility, adaptability, tolerance, good communication skills, positive self-esteem, and an orientation to achievement (Werner and Smith, 2001, 2005). Although the Werner and Smith study began with children as subjects, the researchers followed these children into their adult years. The findings from this study provide a foundation of information about personal factors associated with resilience: social responsibility, adaptability, tolerance, good communication skills, positive self-esteem, and an orientation to achievement. The information provided by this research supports the idea of the relevance of resilience and personal strengths to personal and work success and demonstrates the success impact of positive capabilities and attributes rather than the failure impact of individual weaknesses (Werner and Smith, 2001, 2005).

Developing the capacity for resilience is vital for leaders to provide effective guidance to individuals about how to face and recover from or adapt to adversity or change (Luthans, 2002). Resilience has been acknowledged as one of the critical skills needed by leaders (Bennis and Thomas, 2002). Conner (1992, p. xv) defines resilience as "the ability to demonstrate both strength and flexibility in the face of frightening disorder . . . [and] the internal guidance system people use to reorient ourselves when blown off course by the winds of change". Stern (2003), in his report on the ten characteristics of mental toughness, identifies resilience as an ability to recover from setbacks due to the increased determination to succeed. He states that it is not the actual event being encountered that matters, but how an individual reacts and copes with the event.

George Vaillant in *Wisdom of the Ego* (1993) describes how the defenses in the mind work, and how these defenses evolve and change over time and change us as individuals. He refers to resilience as the "self-righting tendencies" of an individual to "bend without breaking and the capacity, once bent, to spring back" (1993, p. 248). In order to move forward past these "bending" events an individual must garner inner resources for coping with and even growing from these stressful and potentially damaging events. In essence, they must exhibit resilience. Variations of Vaillant's phrasing constitute the most common and consistent definition of resilience found across the literature: the ability to recover from or adapt to adversity (Coutu, 2003; Glantz and Johnson, 1999; Greene and Conrad, 2002; Neenan, 2009; Patterson et al., 2009; Siebert, 2008). Whether facing personal or professional adversity, how we "bounce back" determines success or failure (Coutu, 2003; Neenan, 2009). Coutu (2003) promotes the concept of resilience as "a reflex, a way of facing and understanding the world that is deeply etched into a person's mind and soul" (p. 17). An objective assessment and articulation of a leader's resilience level allows the individual in a leadership role to explore potential areas of self-development to strengthen that reflex to their benefit when adversity or challenge strikes. Coutu states that "resilient people share three traits: acceptance of reality; a deep belief that life is meaningful; and an uncanny ability to improvise" (Coutu, 2003, p. 2).

The ability to rebound from challenging situations is important for all persons from a social perspective, but is especially important for those individuals working in leadership positions. Research conducted by Patterson et al. (2009) suggests that resilience incorporates nine different strengths – optimism, values, efficacy, support, well-being, courage, perseverance, responsibility, and adaptability – that in varying levels determine the extent of one's overall resilience. They define a resilient leader as an individual who "demonstrates the ability to recover, learn from, and developmentally mature when confronted by chronic or crisis adversity" (p. 3) and who handles the pressures of adversity while maintaining the nine different strengths suggested by their research. Patterson and Kelleher (2005a, p. 10) claim, "It's not so much what you do. It's how you think about what you do that makes all of the difference. Your interpretation of the reality of the storm and your interpretation of your future after the storm strongly predict your ability to come through the storm in a better place." (See also Patterson and Kelleher 2005b.)

## LEADERSHIP RESILIENCE

Leadership resilience has become a focused strategic area of development for leaders, so that they will be prepared when challenge and adversity strike. Resilience in a leader is not an end in itself; it is seen more as a path to developing a capacity for accomplishment in the face of adverse conditions. Coutu, a psychology and business researcher, promotes the concept of resilience as "a reflex, a way of facing and understanding the world that is deeply etched into a person's mind and soul" (Coutu, 2003,

p. 17). An objective assessment and articulation of a leader's resilience level allows the individual in a leadership role to explore potential areas of self-development to strengthen that reflex to their benefit when adversity or challenge strikes.

Sutcliffe and Vogus (2003, p. 97) state that "resilience is the capacity to rebound from adversity strengthened and more resourceful." By increasing inner focus on well-being and professional development, potentially one can strengthen the human foundation in the nine strengths proposed by Patterson et al. (2009), and be prepared to face and rebound from adversity. In addition to increasing well-being, a leader may also need the ability to employ several styles of leadership to have a positive impact on an organization. Based on the studies of Around-Thomas (2004), "resilience may be the attribute most needed today by . . . leaders and organizations" (p. 1). In turbulent economic times the work environment is continually changing and a leader may have to rethink their leadership role in order to reshape and influence an emerging environment. Around-Thomas further states that resilient leaders should improve their ability to employ a variety of leadership styles. By moving "seamlessly between different styles from one situation to the next" the resilient leader is able to "promote organizational resilience" (2004, p. 4).

A key leadership strategy is a resilience focus. Hamel and Valikangas (2003) state that resilience is the "ultimate competitive advantage in the age of turbulence – when organizations are being challenged to change more profoundly, and more rapidly, than ever before" (p. 13). Thus, for a leader to invest in identifying their resilience strengths and weaknesses is to invest in the organization's strategy for success. When a leader identifies their leadership goals, develops an understanding of resilience, and identifies personal leadership resilience strengths and weaknesses, a positive association between leadership and resilience can occur if individuals focus their leadership development efforts toward increasing personal resilience levels. Whether facing personal or professional adversity, how we bounce back determines success or failure (Coutu, 2003).

Conner (1992) states that how well leaders absorb the implications of change dramatically affects the rate at which leaders successfully cope with the challenges they face. Based on the writings of Welch and Welch (2005), assessment of individuals for a leadership position should include evaluation of the characteristic of "heavy-duty" resilience. "It is so important that a leader must have it going into a job because if she [*sic*] doesn't, a crisis time is too late to learn it" (Welch and Welch, 2005, p. 90). Leadership resilience has become a focused strategic area of development for leaders, so they are prepared when challenge and adversity strike.

The leadership actualization model developed by Luc (2009) included seven main lines of strategies, with the fourth strategy being focused on building leadership resilience. Luc states that "the main lines for development of resilience stem from four key areas: personal, interpersonal, professional, and social" (Luc, 2009).

Patterson et al. (2009) identified three broad skill sets associated with leadership resilience. These authors state that "resilience thinking skills, capacity skills, and action skills" (p. 28) are all required of a resilient leader. Through a decade of research, Patterson et al. identified that resilience fluctuates infrequently; instead, capacity builds slowly over time.

The work of Reivich and Shatte (2002) has shown that resilience is more than an individual's capability of overcoming difficulty; it is also a skill that enables an individual to aid those around them to grow as well. This expectation of "developing others" is relevant to the leadership role, and the direct link with the resilience concept is important (Reivich and Shatte, 2002, p. 5). The research by Coutu supports this based on her statement that an "increasing body of empirical evidence shows that resilience – whether in children, survivors of concentration camps, or businesses back from the brink – can be learned" (Coutu, 2002, p. 48). With acknowledgement of the challenges and stresses faced in leadership, Reivich et al. (2002) conclude that resilience is a valuable skill to possess. They state that leaders need to develop a healthy "resilience quotient" to succeed in today's complex work environments (Reivich and Shatte, 2002, p. 33). When a leader identifies their leadership resilience strengths and weaknesses, a positive association between leadership and resilience can occur if individuals focus their leadership development efforts toward increasing personal resilience levels.

## TACTICS FOR DEVELOPING LEADERSHIP RESILIENCE

Today's healthcare organizations routinely experience rapid and complex changes that require leaders to be proactive, action-oriented, adaptable, flexible, and resilient. Leaders who repeatedly survive and even thrive during difficult times often are described as resilient. However, resilience is not an end in itself; it is best considered as a path to developing and renewing a capacity for accomplishment in the face of adverse conditions and complex work environments. This resilience capacity greatly benefits the leader's organization as well as the leader personally. Thus, for a leader to invest in identifying their resilience strengths and weaknesses is to invest in the organization's strategy for success. Resilience strength, therefore, has become an important area of personal development for leaders. Three areas where leaders should strive to enhance their individual resilience capacity in the context of their leadership roles are: proactive self-leadership, intrapersonal intelligence, and good personal health and well-being.

## Proactive Self-Leadership

Neck and Manz (2007) describe self-leadership as behavioral and cognitive tactics that an individual uses to direct and motivate their own behavior. Observed leader behaviors may, in fact, influence the resilience of their subordinates (Harland et al., 2005), thus contributing to organizational resilience. These tactics can be grouped into three areas: behavior, rewards, and constructive thinking. Self-leadership behaviors include prompt, decisive, appropriate, and principled action; accepting responsibility and accountability; and learning from role models and experiences. Through developing one's leadership behaviors a leader can positively impact their resilience level as well as those of their employees. Harland et al. (2005) suggest that employee resilience can be positively impacted by a leader's behavior and actions; therefore, it is critical that leaders be proactive in the development of skills to improve the capacity for resilience.

## Intrapersonal Intelligence

Gardner (1983) describes intrapersonal intelligence as an individual's ability to look inward, reflecting on how their thoughts and feelings direct their values and behaviors. Individuals are shaped by their past experiences. Leaders who systematically learn through an inward focus are empowered by their self-awareness to choose approaches and make decisions that are consistent with their values and supported by their skill sets. Self-consistency and values congruence are important, as their absence can produce extreme distress. Having an understanding of one's intrapersonal intelligence can empower a leader with the skills to transform an adverse event into a developmental challenge. A leader's focus should continuously anticipate and adjust to the challenges being faced so as to create an environment for employees where the challenges are faced with control and optimism, to gain new wisdom and experience from the successes and failures being experienced (Grotberg, 2003; Maddi and Khoshaba, 2003). Having the ability to effectively look inward and maintain an awareness of attitude, emotion, and self-regulation allows a leader to replace negative responses to situations with a response that moves not just the leader but the team forward beyond a perceived obstacle (Margolis and Stoltz, 2010).

**Personal Health and Well-Being**

Resilient individuals recognize the need to allocate time for managing their health. Conscious individuals pay attention to all facets of their well-being. Resilient leaders recognize the effect of personal health status on job performance. Resilient leaders know that physical and emotional health must be nurtured and managed. Therefore, they value healthy life-styles; reserve time to attend to their health needs and maintain a work–life balance; and take corrective action when symptoms of health decline emerge. Resilient leaders demonstrate high levels of self-care behaviors by maintaining a balance of mindful reflection, regular physical activities, and good nutrition. By practicing positive self-care and well-being, a leader has a greater tendency to view challenges and turmoil as less stressful. Their physical and mental capacity for resilience is improved by a clearer perspective and forward-looking attitude (Maddi and Khoshaba, 2003; Margolis and Stoltz, 2010). Resilient leaders must develop and maintain the ability to welcome adverse situations and transform these occurrences into opportunities.

## SUMMARY

Whether an individual leader must be visionary, or charismatic, or possess certain traits or abilities to be a "good" leader is arguable; however, effective leadership is considered essential to the success of any team. The concept of leadership is so integral to society that hundreds of interpretations have been posited and theories abound about how it is best practiced. As a result, while the importance of leadership is widely recognized, there remains no common definition of the concept upon which scholars are able to agree. No consensus has been reached among scholars or leaders in various professions about the definition of leadership or the specific traits and characteristics that successful leaders enjoy, although support has been found for many when examined in various contexts (Judge et al., 2002; Northouse, 1997; Gill, 2006).

Conversely, the trait of resilience, frequently deemed to be critical for success as a leader, is generally regarded by scholars as relatively definable. Albeit simplistic, resilience is described consistently as the ability to persevere in the presence of adversity (Coutu, 2003; Glantz and Johnson, 1999; Greene and Conrad, 2002; Neenan, 2009; Patterson et al. 2009, 2005; Siebert, 2008). Regardless of a leader's current level of attainment, resilience can be learned and developed.

The concept of leadership resilience brings the two singular concepts together into a blend informed by self-reflection and self-assessment. Leadership resilience is considered a valuable tool in improving the potential for the success of a team. It is the position of many of the researchers referenced in this chapter that if individuals identify their existing capacity, and work to develop to higher levels of leadership resilience by reinforcing those areas in which they are weak, they will ultimately strengthen their capabilities to contribute to the successful outcome of the team or organization. It is about continuously anticipating and adjusting to the challenges faced as leaders and using the skills that are developed during those situations to increase and maintain resilience levels. Elevated stress levels can impede performance on tasks that require attention to detail and strong decision-making abilities. Given the potential for the negative impact of adversity or stress on performance, and the individualistic ways in which people respond to adverse events, it is critical for leaders in healthcare organizations to develop leadership resilience skills to retain balance of meaning and work satisfaction. Resilient leaders will possess personal attributes such as an internal locus of control, professionalism, empathy, a positive self-image, optimism, and the ability to organize and lead complex operational responsibilities during unexpected adversity or rapid change (Friborg et al., 2003; LeBlanc, 2009; Maddi and Khoshaba, 2003; Margolis and Stoltz, 2010).

# REFERENCES

Around-Thomas, M. (2004). Resilient leadership for challenging times. *Physician Executive*, July/August: 18–21.
Barnett, J.E., Baker, E.K., Elman, N.S., and Schoener, G.R. (2007). In pursuit of wellness: The self-care imperative. *Professional Psychology: Research and Practice*, 38, 603–612.
Bass, B.M. (1985). *Leadership and Performance beyond Expectations*. New York: Free Press.
Bass, B.M. and Bass, R. (2008). *The Bass handbook of leadership: Theory, research, and managerial applications* (4th edn). New York: Free Press.
Bennis, W. (1994). *On Becoming a Leader* (2nd edn). Reading, MA: Addison-Wesley Publishing.
Bennis, W. and Nanus, B. (1986). *Leaders: Strategies for taking charge*. New York: Harper & Row.
Bennis, W. and Thomas, R.J. (2002). Crucibles of leadership. *Harvard Business Review*, 80, 39–45.
Boyatzis, R. and McKee, A. (2005). *Resonant Leadership*. Boston, MA: Harvard Business School Press.
Burns, J.M. (1978). *Leadership*. New York: Harper & Row.
Ciulla, J.B. (1998). *Ethics: The heart of leadership*. Westport, CT: Praeger Publishers.
Collins, J. (2009). *How the Mighty Fall: And why some companies never give in*. London: Random House Business.
Conner, D.R. (1992). *Managing at the Speed of Change*. New York: Villard Books.
Coutu, D.L. (2002). How resilience works. *Harvard Business Review*, 80 (5), 46–55.

Coutu, D. (2003). How resilience works. In *Harvard Business Review on building personal and organizational resilience* (pp 1–18). Boston, MA: Harvard Business School Press.

Fiedler, F.E. (1967). *A Theory of Leadership Effectiveness.* New York: McGraw-Hill.

Friborg, O., Hjemdal, O., Rosenvinge, J., and Martinussen, M. (2003). A new rating scale for adult resilience: what are the central protective resources behind healthy adjustment? *International Journal of Methods in Psychiatric Research,* 12 (2), 65–77.

Gardner, H. (1983). *Frames of Mind: The theory of multiple intelligences.* New York: Basic Books.

Gill, R. (2006). *Theory and Practice of Leadership.* London: Sage.

Glantz, M.D. and Johnson, J. (1999). *Resilience and Development: Positive life adaptations.* New York: Plenum.

Greene, R. and Conrad, N. (2002). Basic assumptions and terms. In R. Greene (ed.), *Resiliency: An integrated approach to practice, policy, and research* (pp. 1–27). Washington, DC: National Association of Social Workers Press.

Greenleaf, R.K. (1977). *Servant Leadership.* New York: Paulist Press.

Grotberg, E.H. (2003). *Resilience for Today: Gaining strength from adversity.* Westport, CT: London: Praeger.

Hamel, G. and Valikangas, L. (2003). The quest for resilience. *Harvard Business Review,* 81 (9), 52–63.

Harland, L., Harrison, W., Jones, J.R., and Reiter-Palmon, R. (2005). Leadership behaviors and subordinate resilience. *Journal of Leadership and Organizational Studies,* 11 (2), 2–14.

Hersey, P. and Blanchard, K.H. (1977). *Management of Organizational Behavior Utilizing Human Resources* (3rd edn). Upper Saddle River, NJ: Prentice Hall.

Hodges, H.F., Keeley, A.C., and Troyan, P.J. (2008). Professional resilience in Baccalaureate-prepared acute care nurses: First steps. *Nursing Education Perspectives,* 29 (2), 80–89.

Hogg, M.A. (2001). A social identity theory of leadership. *Personality and Social Psychology Review,* 5, 184–200.

House, Robert J. (1996). Path–goal theory of leadership: Lessons, legacy, and a reformulated theory. *Leadership Quarterly,* 7 (3), 323–352.

Huey, S.J., Jr. and Weisz, J.R. (1997). Ego control, ego resiliency, and the Five-Factor Model of personality as predictors of behavior problems in clinic-referred children. *Journal of Abnormal Psychology,* 106 (3), 404–415.

Jackson, D., Firtko, A., and Edenborough, M. (2007). Personal resilience as a strategy for surviving and thriving in the face of workplace adversity: A literature review. *Journal of Advanced Nursing,* 60 (1), 1–9.

Judge, T.A., Bono, J.E., Ilies, R., and Gerhardt, M.W. (2002). Personality and leadership: A qualitative and quantitative review, *Journal of Applied Psychology,* 87 (200), 765–780.

Katz, D. (1951). Introduction to the issue: Human relations research in large organizations. *Journal of Social Issues,* 7, 4–7.

Katz, D., Maccoby, N., and Morse, N.C. (1950). *Productivity, Supervision and Morale in an Office Situation.* Ann Arbor, MI: Institute for Social Research.

Kouzes, J.M. and Posner, B.Z. (2002). *The Leadership Challenge: How to get extraordinary things done in organizations* (3rd edn). San Francisco, CA: Jossey-Bass.

Lambert, V.A., Lambert, C.E., Itano, J., Inouye, J., Kim, S., Kuniviktikul, W., and Ito, M. (2004). Cross-cultural comparison of workplace stressors, ways of coping and demographic characteristics as predictors of physical and mental health among hospital nurses in Japan, Thailand, South Korea and the USA (Hawaii). *International Journal of Nursing Studies,* 41 (6), 671–684.

LeBlanc, V.R. (2009). The effects of acute stress on performance: Implications for health professions education. *Academic Medicine,* 84 (10 Suppl), S25–33.

Lim, J., Hepworth, J., and Bogossian, F. (2011). A qualitative analysis of stress, uplifts and coping in the personal and professional lives of Singaporean nurses. *Journal of Advanced Nursing,* 67 (5), 1022–1033.

Luc, E. (2009). *Unleashing your Leadership Potential: Seven strategies for success.* Lanham, MD: Rowman & Littlefield Education.

Luthans, F. (2002). Positive organizational behavior: Developing and managing psychological strengths for performance improvement. *Academy of Management Executives*, 16, 57–75.

Luthans, F. and Avolio, B.J. (2003). Authentic leadership: A positive developmental approach. In K.S. Cameron, J.E. Dutton, and R.E. Quinn (eds), *Positive Organizational Scholarship* (pp. 241–261). San Francisco, CA: Barrett-Koehler.

Maddi, S.R. and Khoshaba, D.M. (2003). Hardiness training for resiliency and leadership. In Paton, D., Violanti, J.M., and Smith, L.M. (eds), *Promoting Capabilities to Manage Posttraumatic Stress: Perspectives on resilience* (pp.43–58). Springfield, IL: Charles C. Thomas.

Margolis, J.D. and Stoltz, P.G. (2010). How to bounce back from adversity. *Harvard Business Review*, 88 (1), 86–92.

McCann, C.M., Beddoe, E., McCormick, K., Huggard, P., Kedge, S., Adamson, C., and Huggard, J. (2013). Resilience in the health professions: A review of recent literature. *International Journal of Wellbeing*, 3 (1), 60–81.

McFarland, K. (2009). *Bounce: The art of turning tough times into triumph*. New York: Crown Publishing Group.

Moore, B.V. (1927). The May Conference on leadership. *Personnel Journal*, 6, 124–128.

Neck, C.P. and Manz, C.C. (2007). *Mastering Self-Leadership: Empowering yourself for personal excellence*. Upper Saddle River: NJ. Pearson Prentice Hall.

Neenan, M. (2009). *Developing Resilience: A cognitive-behavioral approach*. New York: Routledge.

Northouse, P.G. (1997). *Leadership: Theory and practice*. Thousand Oaks, CA: Sage Publications, Inc.

Northouse, P.G. (2004). *Leadership: Theory and practice*. Thousand Oaks, CA: Sage Publications, Inc.

Northouse, P.G. (2009). *Leadership: Theory and practice* (5th edn). London: Sage Publications, Inc.

Novelli, L., Jr. and Taylor, S. (1993). The context for leadership in 21st-century organizations: A role for critical thinking. *American Behavioral Scientist*, 37, 139–147.

Patterson, J., Goens, G., and Reed, D. (2009). *Resilient Leadership for Turbulent Times: Guide to thriving in the face of adversity*. Lanham, MD: Rowman & Littlefield Education.

Patterson, J.L. and Kelleher, P. (2005a). Optimism in the face of the storm. *School Administrator*, 62 (2), 10–14.

Patterson, J. and Kelleher, P. (2005b). *Resilient School Leaders: Strategies for turning adversity into achievement*. Alexandria, VA: ASCD.

Reddin, W.J. (1987). *How to Make Management Style more Effective*. Maidenhead: McGraw Hill.

Reivich, K. and Shatte, A. (2002). *The Resilience Factor: Seven keys to finding your inner strength and overcoming life's hurdles*. New York: Broadway Books.

Siebert, A. (2008). *The Resiliency Advantage: Master change, thrive under pressure and bounce back from setbacks*. San Francisco, CA: Barrett-Koehler Publishers.

Statt, D.A. (2000). *Using Psychology in Management Training: The psychological foundations of management skills*. London: Routledge.

Stern, S. (2003). If you think you're hard enough. *Management Today*, March, 46–51.

Stogdill, R.M. (1948). Personal factors associated with leadership: A survey of the literature, *Journal of Psychology*, 25, 35–71.

Stogdill, R.M. (1974). *Handbook of Leadership: A survey of theory and research*. New York: Free Press.

Sutcliffe, K.M. and Vogus, T.J. (2003). Organizing for resilience. In K.S. Cameron, J.E. Dutton, and R.E. Quinn (eds), *Positive Organizational Scholarship: Foundations of a new discipline* (pp. 94–110). San Francisco, CA: Berrett-Koehler.

Transformational Leadership (2007). *The Transformational Leadership Report*. Available at http://www.transformationalleadership.net/products/TransformationalLeadershipReport.pdf.

Vaillant, G. (1993). *Wisdom of the Ego*. Cambridge, MA: Harvard University Press.

Weber, M. (1947). *The Theory of Social and Economic Organization*. New York: Oxford University Press.

Welch, J. (2001). *Jack: Straight from the gut*. New York: Warner Business Books.

Welch, J. and Welch, S. (2005). *Winning*. New York: HarperCollins Publishers.

Werner, E.E. and Smith, R.S. (2001). *Journeys from Childhood to Midlife: Risk, resilience and recovery*. Ithaca, NY: Cornell University Press.

Werner, E.E. and Smith, R.S. (2005). Resilience and recovery: Findings from the Kauai longitudinal study. *Research, Policy, and Practice in Children's Mental Health*, 19 (1), 11–14.

Whittington, R. (1993). *What is Strategy and Does It Matter?* London: Routledge.

Wiggam, A.E. (1931). The biology of leadership. In H.C. Metcalf (ed.), *Business Leadership* (pp. 13–32). New York: Pitman.

Zautra, A.J., Hall, J.S., and Murray, K.E. (2008). Resilience: a new integrative approach to health and mental health research. *Health Psychology Review*, 2 (1), 41–64.

# 3.  High-reliability organizations
## Patrice L. Spath

## INTRODUCTION

Since age 40 I have had an annual screening mammography, which is a radiological exam, intended to detect breast cancer. The facility where I get this exam is recognized by the American College of Radiology in the USA as having met the quality standards of its mammography accreditation program. Every year my experience is essentially the same: the test is scheduled, I arrive at the facility for the exam, which is efficiently performed, and a report of the negative results is mailed to me within a few days. A couple of years ago this scenario changed. After completing the routine exam I was contacted by the facility and told a suspicious spot had been found which required another exam, a breast ultrasound. Of course I was concerned and quickly scheduled the ultrasound. Upon arriving for the test, I was informed that an error had been made in the interpretation of my mammography results. When the written report was being created, a technician had entered the wrong results: a "key stroke" mistake they said. The exam findings should have been reported as negative. The ultrasound was cancelled and aside from a few days of significant apprehension about what might be my eventual diagnosis, and some inconvenience, thankfully no harm was done.

My mammography encounters illustrate the difference between quality and reliability. Most of the time the facility performed quite well, but quality "most of the time" is not reliable performance. In healthcare, reliability is defined as the "measurable ability of a health-related process, procedure, or service to perform its intended functions in the required time under commonly occurring conditions" (Weick et al., 1999, p.82). The innovation team at the Institute for Healthcare Improvement defines reliability as "failure-free operation over time" (Resar, 2006). An intended function of the mammography exam process is to produce an accurate report of the findings, which did not happen for me on one occasion. Thus the process was not reliable.

Unreliable healthcare processes can inconvenience consumers, as was the case with my mammography experience. Unreliable processes can also introduce unnecessary costs into the healthcare system. Some researchers estimate that as much as 40 percent of healthcare waste is coming from the overuse of medical resources (Physicians News Network, 2013). Unreliable processes can also adversely affect the financial bottom line of providers. Mistakes must be corrected and these rework costs can be substantial. For example, one group estimates that correcting errors in patient record databases can cost large hospitals more than $1 million per year (Smart Card Alliance Healthcare Council, 2009). Unreliable processes can also be life-threatening. Every year, people are harmed by mistakes as they transition from one healthcare setting to another (Bodenheimer, 2008). Surgeons occasionally operate on the wrong patient or the wrong body part (Joint Commission, 2014). It has been estimated that 210000 patients are harmed each year by medication errors that occur in US hospitals (James, 2013). Mark Chassin, President of the Joint Commission, notes that even amusement parks with their potentially dangerous fun rides do a better job of protecting the safety of consumers as compared to healthcare organizations (Clark, 2012).

Delivery of healthcare services involves numerous interrelated and complex processes, which could account for the high rate of errors. Yet industries outside of healthcare with similarly interrelated and complex processes have been able to achieve and maintain extraordinarily low levels of failure. There is less than a one in 1 million chance that a person will die in a catastrophic accident involving civilian aviation, nuclear power, and railroad transportation. In comparison, for every 10000 surgeries performed up to five people may be seriously injured or die due to a mistake (Amalberti et al., 2005). Chassin and Loeb (2013, p. 472) report knowing of "no hospitals that have achieved high reliability across all their activities."

Studies of very safe industries have yielded an understanding of what is needed to produce such high-quality and reliable performance. In this chapter readers are introduced to the high reliability principles and process improvement techniques that will help healthcare organizations narrow the gap between "most of the time" quality and high reliability.

## RELIABLE ORGANIZATIONS

The high-reliability organization (HRO) designation was first introduced into the safety lexicon in the 1980s by University of California Berkeley researchers, studying why some organizations have good safety records even though they operate in very trying conditions (Roberts, 1990; La Porte, 1996). The initial studies were done on air traffic control systems, nuclear power generation plants, and naval aircraft carriers.

The most commonly used definition of an HRO is a consistently reliable organization that operates in a complex environment where accidents might be expected to occur frequently, but which manages to avoid or seeks to minimize catastrophes. Chassin and Loeb (2011, p. 563) describe an HRO as one that shows "consistent performance at high levels of safety over long periods of time."

While HROs are often associated with good safety records, achieving reliable performance can impact all aspects of quality. As noted by Quint Studer, a high-profile healthcare management consultant, HROs "are organizations with systems in place that make them exceptionally consistent in accomplishing their goals" (Gamble, 2013, para. 5).

In the late 1990s it became clear that analysts had to consider ways to proactively improve safety management in complex systems, not just react after an accident occurred. For instance, how might senior leaders and managers encourage organizational safety to prevent accidents? Could it be deep-rooted into the system? To answer such questions, Weick et al. (1999) examined the various studies of HROs in the 1980s and early 1990s to identify commonalities among the better ones. These findings were synthesized by Weick and Sutcliffe (2001) and published in their seminal book on HROs, *Managing the Unexpected: Assuring High Performance in an Age of Complexity*. The researchers found that HROs place a heavy premium on maximizing learning opportunities, both within the organization and from other related organizations. This learning is used to identify and fix underlying systemic faults before they can cause an accident.

## COLLECTIVE MINDFULNESS

Weick and Sutcliffe (2007) found in HROs the characteristic of collective mindfulness: all individuals within the organization are aware of the dire consequences of even a small error, and are constantly alert to the potential for problems. Collective mindfulness is the idea that work teams can, by collaborating, develop a more comprehensive picture of what is happening than that of any one individual alone. In HROs the work culture stresses open communication among individuals at all levels of the organization. This culture allows for identification and response to signs of rapidly escalating failure conditions before the onset of a full-scale disaster.

Maintaining mindfulness is essential for high-quality, failure-free functioning. While every organization is fallible, effective HROs are "known by their capability to contain and recover from the errors they do make and by their capability to have foresight into errors they might make" (Weick et al., 1999, p. 51).

Researchers found five reliability principles (see Figure 3.1) that

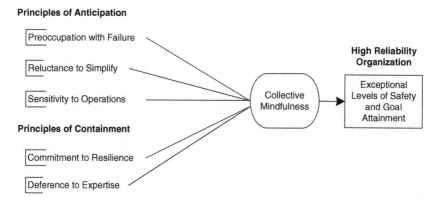

*Figure 3.1    Five principles that contribute to collective mindfulness in high-reliability organizations*

contribute to an organization's collective mindfulness (Weick and Sutcliffe, 2007). The first three principles – preoccupation with failure, reluctance to simplify, and sensitivity to operations – are considered to be principles of anticipation. These principles help the organization be mindful of what might go wrong so that preventive actions can be taken. The last two principles – commitment to resilience and deference to expertise – are considered to be principles of containment. These principles help the organization be mindful of what to do when it is evident that improvements are needed.

Although individual authors and studies sometimes debate the extent to which various principles apply, there is a reasonable level of consensus across the literature. The literature spans many fields, including energy, aviation, transport, military, fires, disasters, and healthcare. Chassin and Loeb (2013) argue that healthcare organizations can and should be HROs, with the goal of having zero defects in outcomes quality, and they assert that organizational leaders are the primary agents for advancing HRO principles.

**Preoccupation with Failure**

In an organization preoccupied with failure, people are vigilant in observing and tracking small failures and anomalies. Incident reporting systems are a cornerstone of this principle and all high-risk industries have them in place. Evidence shows that a safety-conscious environment where people are encouraged to speak up about mistakes and incidents without fear of retribution results in fewer mishaps and higher quality (Reason, 1990).

Such systems in healthcare are relatively new and underused (Shaw, 2012; Pham et al., 2013).

In an HRO even small failures are viewed as opportunities to better understand what went wrong so that more significant events can be prevented in the future. Examining these happenings allows people to see where processes are not working right or where expectations are not being met. A preoccupation with failure requires a trusting relationship between leadership and staff members. People who point out system flaws or express concerns about the status quo must trust that they will not be ostracized or otherwise punished for speaking up. Staff members must trust that leadership will examine reported defects and devote resources to address them if warranted.

### Reluctance to Simplify

HROs do not attempt to explain away the situation or make excuses when faced with problems. If a simple mistake occurs, all potential causes of the problem are investigated and all potential solutions considered. People do not apply simplistic fixes to complex system flaws. Satisficing, or selecting the first "good enough" solution, is not acceptable. Diverse opinions and experiences are embraced to arrive at the best solutions for avoiding or minimizing catastrophes. Many healthcare organizations use patient safety walk-arounds conducted by senior leaders to learn about the patient safety concerns of frontline staff, and gather their opinions on how risks can be reduced (Frush et al., 2006; Frankel et al., 2006).

Reluctance to simplify does not mean that HROs are averse to creating processes that are as simple as possible. Being reluctant to simplify means that HROs encourage workers to analyze a wide range of reasons why things go wrong, and not to presume failures are due to one simple cause that can be fixed by one simple solution. In healthcare organizations a reluctance to simplify also affects how patient care is provided. Treatment decision support systems do not channel patients' problems into overly simplistic solutions that fail to address each patient's uniqueness (Weaver, 2014).

### Sensitivity to Operations

People in HROs are very aware of the complexities of their work. Everyone – from senior leaders to staff members – individually and col-lectively understands the big picture of current operations, so anomalies and potential and actual mistakes can be quickly identified and addressed. Everyone, regardless of their job, values the importance of maintaining situational awareness. This means people constantly seek to understand what is happening right now and what is likely to happen next.

Effective communication among work team members is essential for maintaining situational awareness and resources are deployed to make sure this occurs. As noted by Hines et al., "a high reliability culture requires staff at every level to be comfortable sharing information and concerns with others – and to be commended when they do so" (Hines et al., 2008, p.9). Significant reductions in anesthesia-related adverse events over the past 30 years have been attributed, in part, to improved communication among physicians, nurses, technicians, and other medical professionals (Howard et al., 1992; Gaba et al., 2001).

**Commitment to Resilience**

A resilient organization is one that pays close attention to its ability to act regardless of what may happen. While most organizations try to anticipate impending problems, an HRO spends time improving the capacity of its systems and people to respond to any situation. Because there is a belief that all errors cannot be prevented, HROs allocate resources for activities such as simulation training and just-in-time learning to teach people how to quickly address and contain inevitable mistakes.

In an HRO, people are not caught by surprise when mistakes occur, and they know how to respond. Not only do people know how to react to mistakes, but the organization is actively concerned with developing people's skills and knowledge so that they can function effectively and safely in the work they do. Simulation-based training that exposes physicians and staff to new problems or unusual situations is an example of how healthcare organizations are building the capacity of people to respond to any situation (Louisiana State University Health Sciences Center, 2013; Shearm et al., 2013).

**Deference to Expertise**

Leaders in an HRO encourage people to seek input from those who are most knowledgeable, regardless of where they are in the organizational hierarchy. Adherence to rigid hierarchies is loosened, especially during high-risk situations or when the pace of operations is rapidly changing. The most experienced or senior person may not have the information needed to respond to a crisis, and relying solely on their input would be a mistake. Decision-making authority in HROs can be easily shifted to the individuals with the most expertise.

A de-emphasis on hierarchy is essential for organizations to prevent and respond to problems most effectively. There is an increasing realization in healthcare organizations that superior performance requires a team effort among and between professional and management support staff. As one respondent to a recent survey of high reliability in primary care put it, "While we recognize different levels of skill and responsibility . . . the lines become blurred as the entire office team becomes more involved in achieving clinical results" (Weaver, 2014, p. 5).

## SAFETY CULTURE

In addition to collective mindfulness, empirical research of HROs has identified another key characteristic: a positive and proactive safety culture. Organizational culture refers to what employees perceive to be the key beliefs, values, norms, and expectations that guide behavior and practice within an organization. Krause and Hidley (2009, p. 34) describe organizational culture as "the unstated and often unconscious assumptions about *how* things are done." Culture has the ability to enhance or impede performance. One aspect of organizational culture is the safety culture, as evidenced by Simon and Cistaro's (2009, p. 30) assertion that "safety excellence is a product not only of the right programs . . . but also of the right culture." Research in industries outside of healthcare has shown that a positive and proactive safety culture has a beneficial "impact upon an organization's quality, reliability, competitiveness and profitability" (Cooper, 2001, p. 1). The relationship between the safety culture in healthcare organizations and positive patient outcomes has yet to be clearly substantiated (Huang et al., 2007; Dicuccio, 2014).

The simplest definition of a safety culture is: making sure people are not harmed by how we do things around here (Collins, 2010). This culture provides an enabling environment for the five reliability principles that contribute to collective mindfulness. In a positive and proactive safety culture the organization's values and behaviors – modeled by its leaders and internalized by its members – make safety the overriding priority.

In HROs, the safety culture is supported by three fundamental leadership behaviors: commitment to excellence, commitment to integrity, and commitment to relationships (Collins, 2010). Leadership actions that demonstrate these commitments are summarized in Table 3.1.

Reason (1997) describes a positive and proactive safety culture as a "just culture" – one in which an atmosphere of trust in people is encouraged, but in which there are also clear lines drawn between acceptable and unacceptable behavior. Marx (2001) applied this concept to healthcare, indicating that an organization with a just culture expects people to

*Table 3.1*   *Actions that exemplify leadership commitment to a safety culture*

| Leadership behaviors | How leaders demonstrate this commitment |
| --- | --- |
| Commitment to excellence | • Publicize and model organizational values<br>• Communicate clear performance expectations<br>• Primary focus on performance results, not costs<br>• Provide training and resources necessary to achieve excellence<br>• Serve as a good problem-solver, mentor, and coach<br>• Promote organizational learning |
| Commitment to integrity | • Behave ethically (always do the right thing)<br>• Is transparent and honest in all communications<br>• Take stakeholders' views into consideration when making decisions<br>• Address issues quickly and properly<br>• Use mistakes as learning opportunities, not to blame<br>• Support appropriate accountability |
| Commitment to relationships | • Ask for and listen to suggestions<br>• Is respectful and welcoming<br>• Encourage diversity and personal development<br>• Do not undermanage or overcontrol<br>• Criticize little, compliment often<br>• Promote work–life balance |

*Source:*   Based on Collins (2010, p. 31).

perform according to certain standards. If they make a mistake while performing within those standards, the error is forgivable. A blatant violation of standards is subject to possible disciplinary action. In a positive and proactive patient safety culture it is wrong to hold employees accountable "without giving them the resources, information, leadership support, and encouragement they need for success" (Krause and Hidley, 2009, p. 132).

"Move beyond a culture of blame" is a commonly heard slogan in the patient safety movement. However, this is not a call to abandon systems of accountability. In HROs there is a constant vigilance to continually improving processes which includes building accountability into everyone's role. Excuses for missing training or not following accepted practices due to personal preferences are not acceptable. The right accountability system is just as important to an HRO as the right resources and the right leadership and organizational structure (Dekker, 2012; Shojania and Dixon-Woods, 2013).

Creating a culture of safety requires an integrated approach that focuses on having leaders and staff at all levels who are accountable for safety. The organization's senior leaders, beginning with the board and the chief executive officer (CEO), must be willing to sponsor the system changes necessary to create a culture of safety. This includes investments of people, time, and funding, and support of a non-punitive yet accountable environment.

## MEASURING RELIABILITY

Accepting that an HRO is able to achieve consistent, failure-free performance over long periods of time requires judging its consistency and performance level using some type of measurement process. Measuring the reliability of a system involves determining whether the system is performing all required functions without failure for a stated period of time. Before this measure can be calculated, several factors must be defined. First, the required functions must be specified. Next, a definition of failure is needed. For example, a failure may mean different things to a hospitalized patient and the hospital CEO. The environment in which the system is operating must be specified (for example, outpatient, home health, institutional care). Lastly, a period of time for measurement is identified.

Healthcare organizations use different methodologies to measure the reliability of performance. Sigma level, percentage, and an index based on an order of magnitude are three common reliability measurement methods.

## SIGMA LEVEL

In the Six Sigma quality methodology, process reliability is reported as a sigma level (Lighter, 2011). The higher the sigma level, the better the process is performing in terms of defect prevention (see Table 3.2).

The sigma level is based on the number of defects per million opportunities (DPMO). The DPMO calculation is based on three distinct pieces of information:

1. The number of units produced.
2. The number of defect opportunities per unit.
3. The number of defects.

The actual formula is shown in Box 3.1.

Recall my mammography experience described at the start of this

*Table 3.2    Sigma level and corresponding rate of defects*

| Sigma level | Defects per million |
|---|---|
| 1 | 697 672 |
| 1.5 | 501 350 |
| 2 | 308 770 |
| 2.5 | 158 687 |
| 3 | 66 811 |
| 3.5 | 22 750 |
| 4 | 6210 |
| 4.5 | 1350 |
| 5 | 233 |
| 5.5 | 31.7 |
| 6 | 3.4 |

*Source:*    Based on Kubiak (2009).

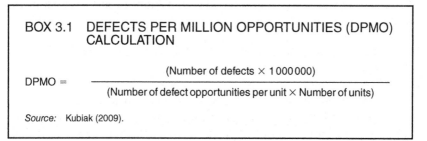

BOX 3.1    DEFECTS PER MILLION OPPORTUNITIES (DPMO)
CALCULATION

$$DPMO = \frac{(\text{Number of defects} \times 1\,000\,000)}{(\text{Number of defect opportunities per unit} \times \text{Number of units})}$$

*Source:*   Kubiak (2009).

chapter. Suppose the facility wants to calculate the DPMO for this process. The unit is a completed mammogram exam. The radiology department would need to decide how many opportunities there are for defects in this unit. To make this determination easy, let us presume there are five steps in the process and something could go wrong at each step. Since patient satisfaction is also important, dissatisfaction would also be a defect. Thus, there are a total of six defect opportunities per unit. Now data are gathered to determine the total number of defects the mammogram exam process is producing. A sample of completed exams is reviewed and the total defects in each exam are counted. Many exams will have no defects. Defects that might be found in a few include poor imaging techniques that cause the exam results to be unreadable, or findings are reported inaccurately (the defect I experienced).

Once data are gathered the DPMO can be calculated. Suppose 300 mammogram exams are reviewed and 90 defects are found. The calculation for the DPMO would be: $(1\,000\,000 \times 90) / (6 \times 300) = 50\,000$. This facility would reasonably be expected to have 50 000 defects for every 1 million mammogram exams it performs – a little better than a 3 sigma level of performance. Using Six Sigma methodologies to improve quality (for example, reduce waste, prevent failures, and improve cycle time) the facility could improve mammography performance to a higher sigma level.

## PERCENTAGE

Reliability can be reported as a percentage: the number of actions that achieve the intended results divided by the total number of actions taken (Kubiak, 2009). For example, suppose the average rate of urinary tract infections in a nursing home is 4.6 infections per 1000 resident days. This is a measure of the reliability of all actions taken to prevent residents from getting a urinary tract infection. Reliability of all these actions is calculated using the formula below:

Reliability calculation: $(1000 - 4.6)/1000 = 0.995$, or 99.5 percent reliability

A second method for measuring reliability using percentages is to determine the reliability of the individual actions or process steps. For example, suppose research has shown there are five interventions that help reduce the chance a hospitalized patient will develop a pressure ulcer (bed sore). The recommended actions are:

- Conduct thorough head-to-toe skin assessment of patient on admission and again at least once every shift.
- Evaluate patient's risk of pressure ulcers every day.
- Turn and reposition patients every two hours while in bed; every one hour while sitting in a chair.
- Use pillows or heel-lift devices to keep the patient's heels from touching the bed.
- Elevate the patient's bed-head less than 30 degrees, unless contraindicated for other medical reasons.

By measuring how reliably staff members are completing the recommended interventions, hospital leaders can pinpoint where improvements are needed. The reliability of each task is calculated by dividing the number of times the task is completed as expected by the total number of times the task should have been completed.

A third method for measuring reliability using percentages is to calculate system reliability. System reliability is calculated by multiplying the reliability ratings of the individual process steps. For example, suppose hospital leaders find that each of the five pressure ulcer prevention interventions are completed successfully 95 percent of the time. Using the formula below, the leaders discover that reliability of the entire ulcer prevention system in their hospital is only 77 percent:

Ulcer prevention system reliability calculation: $0.95 \times 0.95 \times 0.95 \times 0.95 \times 0.95 = 0.77$

Percentages can also be used to measure unreliability (the failure or defect rate). For instance, suppose of the 1000 skeleton X-rays taken of patient injuries in an emergency department, three were initially interpreted as negative when in fact the patient was later found to have a bone fracture. In three instances the expected outcome – an accurate initial X-ray reading – did not occur. The X-ray reliability rate would be 99.7 percent (997 divided by 1000). The failure or defect rate (reliability rate) for X-rays is 0.3 percent. This is calculated by subtracting the reliability rate (0.997) from 1.00 ($1.00 - 0.997 = 0.003$ or 0.3 percent).

## MAGNITUDE INDEX

A third way to express the defect rate of a process is by using an index number that expresses the magnitude of the rate. Rather than report the defect rate for X-ray interpretations as 0.3 percent or the reliability rate at 99.7, one could report the reliability level of accurate X-ray interpretations as being $10^{-3}$. Mathematicians that calculate reliability ratings often use a standardized form – an index of 10 – for reporting failure rates (Resar, 2006). Also referred to as a standard index form, it is a way of writing numbers that are too big or too small to be conveniently written in decimal form. For reliability calculations the math has already been done for you.

The standard index levels that relate to each level of process reliability are shown in Table 3.3. A process with 0.8–0.9 reliability and a 10–20 percent ($10^{-1}$) defect rate is considered unreliable. A process with 0.999999 reliability and a 0.0001 percent ($10^{-6}$) defect rate is considered extremely reliable. A process with less than 0.8 reliability and a more than 20 percent defect rate is considered chaotic and unpredictable.

When healthcare organizations report the reliability of various process

*Table 3.3    Range of process reliability levels*

| Defect or failure rate expressed as: | | |
| --- | --- | --- |
| Reliability | Percentage | An index of 10 |
| 0.8–0.9 | 10–20 | $10^{-1}$ (level 1): 1–2 failures out of 10 opportunities |
| 0.99 | 1 | $10^{-2}$ (level 2): up to 5 failures per 100 opportunities |
| 0.999 | 0.1 | $10^{-3}$ (level 3): up to 5 failures per 1000 opportunities |
| 0.9999 | 0.01 | $10^{-4}$ (level 4): up to 5 failures per 10000 opportunities |
| 0.99999 | 0.001 | $10^{-5}$ (level 5): up to 5 failures per 100000 opportunities |
| 0.999999 | 0.0001 | $10^{-6}$ (level 6): up to 5 failures per 1000000 opportunities |

*Source:*    Based on Spath (2013, p. 213).

outcomes they often use sigma levels or percentages. Staff and faculty at the Institute for Healthcare Improvement in Cambridge, MA and other authors refer to the index defect number when recommending actions to improve reliability (Resar, 2006). For this reason, it is important to understand the relationship between reliability and defect rates and the index of ten levels. More about this relationship will be covered in the next section.

## IMPROVING RELIABILITY

The principles of high reliability and a safe culture are necessary under-pinnings for creating and sustaining failure-free processes. Research in the healthcare setting has shown that an HRO can turn into an LRO (low-reliability organization) if there is not constant vigilance to maintain a supportive environment (Roberts et al., 2005). It is clear that achieving high-reliability status requires attention to both the organizational factors as well as what happens in the trenches. Thus, application of the sugges-tions in this section should be accompanied by an organizational strategy that advances HRO principles.

Improving reliability of activities within an organization starts with an assessment of the current state of reliability. Measurement data serves three purposes. It provides leaders with information needed to set priori-ties for improvement, it helps in determining the best course of action, and it serves as a baseline to judge the effectiveness of improvement actions.

---

## BOX 3.2   HIERARCHY OF IMPROVEMENT ACTIONS LISTED IN ORDER OF DECREASING EFFECTIVENESS

1. Fix environmental problems (e.g., reduce noise, eliminate clutter).
2. Implement forcing functions and constraints (e.g., computer data entry with feedback, access barriers).
3. Use automation and computerization (e.g., barcoded patient identification, electronic monitoring).
4. Use protocols, standards, and information (e.g., checklists, bed alarms).
5. Require independent verification and redundancy (e.g., double-checks, read-backs).
6. Implement rules and policies (e.g., staffing requirements, preventive maintenance).
7. Provide education and information (e.g., training, orientation).

*Source:* Thomadsen and Lin (2005).

---

## SETTING PRIORITIES

There are thousands of processes within an organization. Which of these should be targeted for improvement? Organizations committed to achieving high reliability would answer this question the same way as Lisa K. Jones, vice-president of clinical services at Owensboro (KY) Medical Health System (OMHC). Jones notes, "we have very intentionally incorporated high reliability into everything we do . . . it is the prevailing, defining attitude in our organization" (May, 2013, p. 18). Nevertheless, some improvement approaches are more effective than others. Box 3.2 provides a summary of common action categories ranked in order of effectiveness.

Many healthcare organizations focus improvement efforts on processes related to the quality goals set by outside organizations. For instance, OMHC targeted processes involved in preventing patient falls and hospital-acquired pressure ulcers, events deemed by the Joint Commission and Medicare as being important to avoid. Improvements in both processes at OMHC have resulted in a 75 percent reduction in patient falls and a rate of zero for hospital-acquired pressure ulcers (May, 2013). Like other organizations seeking high reliability, OMHC also works on preventing significant internal failures that are unrelated to goals of external groups. Mark Chassin, MD, President of the Joint Commission, observed: "As they strive for high reliability, organizations shift away from having outside bodies solely determine their quality agenda to developing an agenda that incorporates the organization's most important goals" (May, 2013, p. 22).

The radiology department at Cincinnati Children's Hospital Medical Center regularly measures several aspects of performance related to organization-wide and departmental quality goals. In the area of clinical services the department evaluates the reliability of processes related to patient safety, communications, patient access, peer review, and technical issues (Donnelly et al., 2010). Examples of clinical services measures include:

- Mean turnaround time (in hours) between completion of exam and approval.
- Imaging repeat rate.
- Intravenous (IV) contrast extravasation rate.
- Percent of preliminary report results changed in final report.
- Number of wrong procedure or patient events.
- Number of safety policy violations involving magnetic resonance imaging (MRI) exams.

Any process found to be unreliable and considered important to improve, for whatever reason, is a potential candidate for action. However, in any organization there are not sufficient resources to improve every process to Six Sigma reliability. This means priorities must be set. Dr. Roger Resar suggests healthcare organizations consider the following questions when selecting processes for improvement (Astion, 2008):

- Is the process potentially catastrophic for the patient immediately after it fails?
- If the process is potentially catastrophic, what is the likelihood of a catastrophic event if the process fails?
- What are the previous and current levels of performance for the process?
- Do users of the process have high expectations for reliability?

In reliability science there is a general rule of thumb used to set desired levels of process reliability. A reliability level of at least 99 percent ($10^{-2}$) should be the goal for non-catastrophic processes: processes that do not generally lead to patient death or severe injury within hours of a failure; for example, hand hygiene, medication reconciliation. A reliability level of at least 99.9 percent or better ($10^{-3}$ to $10^{-6}$) should be the goal for catastrophic processes: processes in which there is a high likelihood of patient death or severe injury immediately or within hours of a failure; for example, identification of correct surgery site, choosing and administering ABO compatible blood for a transfusion.

## ACTIONS TO IMPROVE RELIABILITY

How best to reduce process failures and improve reliability is a topic that has been debated and researched in the military and other high-risk industries for many decades. During the Second World War, efforts were made to improve the physical design of the aircraft cockpit and instrumentation to reduce pilot error (Wiener and Nagel, 1988). As technology advanced and mechanical failures within aircraft were significantly reduced, it became clear that human factors were a primary cause of airline accidents that continued to occur (Boeing, 1994). Similar investigations have been conducted in other high-risk industries, such as nuclear power. Although advanced technologies prevent many accidents, there is still a risk for human errors. For this reason, for several years the Nuclear Regulatory Commission has encouraged human reliability analyses in nuclear power plants (Bell and Swain, 1983). Many of the human factors developments in the military, aviation, nuclear power, and other settings are now being transferred to medicine.

## HUMAN FACTORS ENGINEERING

What has been learned about preventing mistakes in other industries can be applied to failure prevention in the delivery of healthcare services. This learning, known as human factors engineering (HFE), can help healthcare organizations design safer and more consistent, high-quality processes. HFE involves analyzing and applying information about human behavior, abilities, limitations, and other characteristics to the design of systems, tasks, jobs, and environments (Sanders and McCormick, 1993). Dr. Ken Catchpole, a human factors expert who has worked extensively in healthcare, suggests this definition of HFE as it relates to patient care services: "Enhancing clinical performance through an understanding of the effects of teamwork, tasks, equipment, workspace, culture, organization on human behavior and abilities, and application of that knowledge in clinical settings" (Clinical Human Factors Group, n.d., para. 4).

Decades of research in human factors have shown that interventions to reduce failures and improve reliability are most successful when they address both the needs of the system and the individuals who inhabit them. Optimal solutions to performance problems occur when system- and individual-level needs are addressed. Strong and effective systems make people more effective. Changes in procedures, rules, workflow, automation, the introduction of new technology and equipment, and other system changes help to make people effective. Something as simple as reducing unnecessary process steps can greatly reduce the chance of errors and improve process efficiency.

Strong and effective people make systems more effective. The organization must make certain that people working in the system have the competencies and skills required to do their job. Plus, work must be organized in a way that allows people to successfully apply their competencies and skills. Some of the ways in which organizations keep people from being successful include:

- Creating additional work for fewer people.
- Removing people from roles in which they were comfortable.
- Placing people in unfamiliar new roles as if they were interchangeable parts.

## SYSTEMS APPROACH

A systems approach is used in HFE. Humans are considered to be a critical system component. When analyzing how to improve the reliability of a system, analysis is focused on the people doing the work to determine what they are required to do to achieve system goals. The system is then analyzed to determine how it can be designed or modified to meet goals, considering the capabilities and limitations of the human component. For instance, if HFE were used to improve reliability of the mammography exam process at the facility where I get this test, the tasks required of those involved (receptionists, imaging technicians, clerical staff, radiologists, and others) and their common mistakes would be analyzed. Then the process steps and environment in which the people work would be modified to make it less likely that errors will occur.

Contemporary performance and safety improvement models incorporate aspects of HFE in the process improvement phase. For instance, Danbury (CT) Hospital conducted a Six Sigma project to reduce the billing time for nuclear cardiology charges which averaged 2.3 days with a high variation (standard deviation) of 4.22 days. Modifications were made to the electronic scheduling system and the process was streamlined by removing non-value added steps. These steps led to a reduction in average days to bill by 0.59 and a reduction in the typical variation (standard deviation) of 1.83 days. Much of this improvement came about as a result of making it easier for people to catch potential billing problems when a procedure is scheduled rather than spending time later researching and fixing problems (Nicholetti, 2009). The psychiatric unit at the Johns Hopkins Hospital used HFE to reduce the risk of inpatient suicides. The solutions included improving and standardizing the care team workflow for every shift, use of a feedback form for patient observers to document and review behavioral observations of their patient with the patient's nurse every shift, and changes in the hand-offs between shifts (Janofsky, 2009). All of these productivity, efficiency, and safety improvements are based on human reliability analysis and human factors research that began many decades ago.

## STRENGTH OF IMPROVEMENT ACTIONS

There are many ways of changing a process to improve its reliability. Research has shown, however, the various actions that might be taken differ in their power to effect changes. Some – such as real-time computer feedback to the nuclear cardiology procedure scheduler about variances – are very strong in preventing errors. Other actions – such as providing training to patient observers in the psychiatric unit – while necessary, often result in only small or transient improvements. Listed in Figure 3.2 are improvement actions derived from human factors research. These actions, based on human factors research, are considered to be effective way of decreasing errors to improve process reliability and safety. The actions are listed in order of decreasing effectiveness.

In a study of the effectiveness of actions taken to reduce events involving patients who wander away from the facility, the Veterans Administration found that strong actions such as environmental changes and constraints were 2.5 times more effective at preventing these events as compared to weaker actions such as new policies and staff training (DeRosier et al., 2007).

## STEPWISE APPROACH TO IMPROVED RELIABILITY

Based on the experience of HROs and human factors engineers, changing a chaotic, unpredictable process into a highly reliable process that achieves desired goals is best accomplished one step at a time. The first step is to simplify and standardize the process.

1. Fix environmental problems (e.g., reduce noise, eliminate clutter)
2. Implement forcing functions and constraints (e.g., computer data entry with feedback, access barriers)
3. Use automation and computerization (e.g., bar coded patient identification, electronic monitoring)
4. Use protocols, standards, and information (e.g., check-lists, bed alarms)
5. Require independent verification and redundancy (e.g., double-checks, read-backs)
6. Implement rules and policies (e.g., staffing requirements, preventive maintenance)
7. Provide education and information (e.g., training, orientation).

*Source:*   Thomadsen and Lin (2005).

*Figure 3.2   Hierarchy of improvement actions listed in order of decreasing effectiveness*

## Simplify

Simplifying the process involves looking at the tasks involved and how the process really works right now. There may be steps or decision points that are redundant or unnecessary. There may be process steps added in the past in an attempt to resolve problems that actually made the process more complex and created more problems. A study published in the *Archives of Surgery* found that current wrong-site surgery verification protocols often involve considerable complexity – multiple redundant checks – without clear added benefits (Kwaan et al., 2006). The study authors suggest that a simplification of protocols would improve adherence and efficiency.

### Involve Staff in Studying the Current Process and Identifying Ways to Simplify It

A quick tabletop analysis using sticky-notes may be sufficient for a simple process. A walk-through to observe the process can also be useful and especially important when there are environment or equipment issues. Process mapping should be used for complex processes. Whatever analysis techniques are used, answering the questions below for each step in the current process can aid in identifying where changes are needed.

- Can this step be done at the same time as other steps? Which steps must be completed before another can be started?
- What would happen if this step were eliminated? Would the process output be the same or would it be incomplete or have too many defects?
- Is the right person performing this step? Could another person more efficiently perform it?
- Was this step added as a work-around to prevent recurrence of a failure? Is it still necessary?
- Is this step a repeat of another step which could be eliminated?
- Does the step add value to the service produced by the process?

The above questions can help people gain insight into how the process can be simplified by doing away with wasteful steps, combining duplicative steps, or changing the flow of work. Eliminating unnecessary or redundant steps not only decreases the time it takes to complete the process, but it also reduces the chance for errors.

**Standardize**

Once the process is simplified, it must be standardized, meaning that everyone does it the same way. Procedures, instructions, checklists, and other related documents are created to support the streamlined process, and training is undertaken to be sure everyone knows how to follow the new standard process. Standardization of processes was ranked as the most effective action for reducing process failures by facility patient safety managers in the Veterans Health Administration (Bagian et al., 2011).

After completing standardization, data are gathered to confirm the process is being followed as expected, and it remains simplified (no unacceptable workarounds have evolved). For process simplification and standardization to be considered successful, an 80–90 percent ($10^{-1}$) level of reliability should be achieved and sustained.

Illustrated in Table 3.4 are the actions taken at one hospital to improve the reliability of hand hygiene by staff members. The hospital was not able to achieve a $10^{-1}$ level of reliability until steps were taken to simplify and standardize the process. In addition, the hospital had to rely on hard work and vigilance to sustain 80–90 percent compliance with hand hygiene practices.

After each process change is made, the impact of the intervention should be tested before implementing the next one. As shown in Table 3.4, the reliability level was calculated after each improvement action. What was

*Table 3.4  Steps taken to improve hand hygiene by hospital staff members*

| Process improvement actions | Reliability results |
| --- | --- |
| 1. Mandatory infection control training for all staff. | 40% compliance |
| 2. Weekly unit audits by infection control team, visual prompts ("clean your hands" posters, etc.), incentives, immediate feedback for non-compliance. | Up to 70% compliance |
| 3. Simplify the process using the World Health Organization "Five Key Moments for Hand Hygiene" and educate staff; gather data to better understand the causes of non-compliance so process can be changed to prevent these failures. | 60–70% compliance |
| 4. Standardize the process with "key moment" posters displayed in units and patient rooms, hand hygiene reminders included in daily unit briefings; ongoing daily audits by "cleanliness champions"; head of psychology trained champions in how to challenge staff non-compliance; continue to evaluate causes of staff non-compliance and make changes to prevent failures. | Sustained 80–90% compliance |

learned in evaluating failures was applied in design of the next improvement step. If attempts at standardizing the process had failed at achieving sustained 80–90 percent reliability, the hospital would have analyzed what was causing failures and tried other standardization strategies such as checklists and other visual reminders of the correct process.

If a higher level of reliability is desired, further process improvement actions are needed. These more sophisticated actions incorporate human factors and reliability science research. Resar refers to these more advanced process design principles as "model $10^{-2}$ change concepts" (Astion, 2008, p. 3). These design principles should not be applied until the process reliability has demonstrated a sustained level of 80–90 percent. Less than this level of reliability means that the process is chaotic and unstable, still relying on people's vigilance to achieve good results. It is a fundamental principle of statistics that cause-and-effect relationships cannot be effectively validated while the process is unstable. If $10^{-2}$ change concepts are applied to an unstable process, it is not possible to know with any certainty whether resulting improvements are a function of the change or merely due to random chance.

# ADVANCED PROCESS DESIGN PRINCIPLES

The more effective actions on the Thomadsen and Lin (2005) hierarchy of improvement actions, described earlier in this chapter, are considered to be advanced process design principles. A similar hierarchy, derived from human factors research, has been created by the Veterans Health Administration for use in patient safety improvement projects (Percarpio and Watts, 2013). Advanced process design principles in this list include:

- Making architectural or physical plant changes.
- Adding engineering controls or interlocks (forcing functions).
- Increasing staffing or decreasing workload for existing staff.
- Eliminating or reducing workplace distractions.
- Eliminating look-alike and sound-alike medications or treatments.
- Adding redundancies to the process, for example double checks.

The advanced process design principles listed below are suggested in the model for improving reliability promoted by the Institute for Healthcare Improvement (Nolan et al., 2004). These suggestions are similar to the more effective actions recommended by Thomadsen and Lin (2005, Figure 3.2) and the Veterans Health Administration:

- Decision aids and reminders are built into the system.
- Desired action is the default (based on scientific evidence).
- Habits and patterns are known and taken advantage of in the process design.
- Process risks are specified and actions for reducing risks are articulated.
- Scheduling is used to advantage.
- Redundant processes are utilized.
- Independent back-ups are in place.
- Measurement and feedback of information about compliance with specifications is performed.

Achieving 95 percent or better reliability requires an understanding of the cause of process failures and application of advanced process improvement design principles. Summarized in Box 3.3 are the actions taken in a rural healthcare system to improve the management of patients with diabetes.

Even with the best application of basic and advanced process designs, failures will still happen, because as noted by Luria et al., "To achieve

BOX 3.3   PROCESS DESIGNS TO IMPROVE COMPLETION
OF BODY MASS INDEX MEASUREMENT
REQUIREMENTS FOR PATIENTS WITH DIABETES

CareSouth, a rural healthcare system in the Pee Dee region of South Carolina, initiated a project aimed at improving the reliability of care provided to patients with diabetes. The improvement team identified five processes requiring high consistency of completion based on literature evidence of the relationship to patient outcomes:

- two $HbA_{1c}$ tests annually, at least 90 days apart;
- nutrition education;
- body mass index (BMI) performed and noted in chart at every visit;
- prescription of statins (if indicated);
- annual low-density lipoprotein testing.

The project started with a review of patient records to determine the current level of reliability for each process and the reasons for failures. Reviews of patient records continued as the project advanced to determine the success of the process changes. Below are the stepwise actions taken to improve one of these processes – BMI performed and noted in chart at every visit.

**Actions Taken to get to Reliability Level $10^{-1}$**

- Staff were educated about the need to obtain BMI at every visit of a diabetic patient;
- Chart reviews continued with performance feedback to staff.

**Actions Taken to get to Reliability Level $10^{-2}$ and Beyond**

- BMI included as a data element on the standardized core elements flow sheet which was placed on the front page of the patient record.
- Completion of the BMI during the visit was confirmed multiple times with redundant steps: by the nurse checking in the patient, by the physician, and by the patient's care manager.
- Job descriptions for all personnel were updated to include the task of ensuring BMI documentation at every visit.
- Patients helped to develop educational materials about BMI and other diabetes care requirements because the clinics initially received negative reactions from patients about how they were being counseled about BMI and other requirements.

The reliability of BMI completion improved from very low (< 20 percent) to a sustained level of 100 percent.

*Source:*   Based on Baker et al. (2009).

$10^{-3}$ performance or greater requires an understanding of which failures are occurring, how often they occur, and why they occur" (Luria et al., 2006, p. 8). For instance, one hospital made several process changes including alterations of its computerized order entry system to ensure physicians ordering opiate medications for patients also ordered a stool softener at the same time to prevent constipation. Despite the process changes, failures still occurred. By examining the failures the hospital discovered that some patients were designated NPO (*nil per os*, nothing by mouth) at the time the opiate was ordered, so they could not be given a stool softener at that time. Once the patients were allowed oral intake, the physicians did not remember to order a stool softener. The computerized system was altered again to prevent these types of failures (Luria et al., 2006).

Reaching very high levels of reliability, beyond 99.5 percent, often requires technology and advanced system design which can involve significant resource investments for the organization (Nolan et al., 2004).

## CONCLUSION

Although high reliability has been attained in other industries such as commercial air travel and nuclear power, it remains an elusive goal for most healthcare organizations. To be considered an HRO, the organization must have a consistently high level of performance with very few errors, and this performance must be sustained over long periods of time.

High reliability does not happen by accident. It must be valued and overtly planned and pursued by an organization. Two critical factors are required in the creation of HROs. First, senior leaders must create the right environment. A vital aspect of the environment in HROs is collective mindfulness. Collective mindfulness involves a heightened state of involvement, open communication, and attentiveness. People are sensitive to variations in their environment, aware of the potential for failures, and know how to respond to signs of rapidly escalating failure conditions. Five principles contribute to collective mindfulness: preoccupation with failure, reluctance to simplify, sensitivity to operations, commitment to resilience, and deference to expertise.

The organization's leaders also need to support a proactive, non-punitive safety culture. Information gleaned from reports of small mistakes and failures provides an important learning opportunity, one that will be missed if people are reluctant to report these events. People must be accountable for following accepted practices; however, they should not be blamed when the system sets them up for mistakes.

The second critical factor is creation of reliable work processes which result in tasks being performed as expected a high proportion of the time. Simplification and standardization should be the initial approach to improving process reliability. This means making it exactly repeatable, shift by shift. Then, and only then, should basic failure prevention strategies be incorporated into the process design. When these strategies have proven to be successful at maintaining reliability at 95 percent, and better reliability is desired, more sophisticated failure prevention and mitigation strategies are needed. This involves redesigning the system to prevent failures, making them more visible should they occur, and building capabilities for fixing failures or mitigating the failure effects. The inseparable combination of high reliability principles, safety culture, and more reliable processes is essential for HROs.

## REFERENCES

Amalberti, R., Auroy, Y., Berwick, D., and Barach, P. (2005). Five system barriers to achieving ultrasafe health care. *Annals of Internal Medicine*, 142(9): 756–764.

Astion, M. (2008). Getting realistic about reliability: An interview with Roger Resar. *Laboratory Errors and Patient Safety*, 3(4): 1–6.

Bagian, J., King, B., Mills, P., and McKnight, S. (2011). Improving RCA performance: The cornerstone award and power of positive reinforcement. *British Medical Journal Quality and Safety*, 20(11): 974–982.

Baker, N., Crowe, V. and Lewis, A. (2009). Making patient-centered care reliable. *Journal of Ambulatory Care Management*, 32(1): 8–15.

Bell, B. and Swain, A. (1983). A procedure for conducting human reliability analysis for nuclear power plants. Final report. Rep. NUREG/CR-2254. Washington, DC: Nuclear Regulatory Commission.

Bodenheimer, T. (2008). Coordinating care – A perilous journey through the health care system. *New England Journal of Medicine*, 358(10): 1064–1071.

Boeing (1994). *Statistical summary of commercial jet aircraft accidents. World-wide operations 1959–1993*. Seattle, WA: Boeing Corporation.

Chassin, M.R. and Loeb, J.M. (2011). The ongoing quality improvement journey: Next stop, high reliability. *Health Affairs*, 30(4): 559–568.

Chassin, M.R. and Loeb, J.M. (2013). High-reliability health care: Getting there from here. *Milbank Quarterly*, 91(3): 459–490.

Clark, C. (2012, December 20). Hospital care "3000 times less safe than air travel," says TJC chief. *HealthLeaders Media*. Retrieved from http://www.healthleadersmedia.com/print/QUA-287711/Hospital-Care-3000-Times-Less-Safe-Than-Air-Travel-Says-TJC-Chief (accessed 5 May 2014).

Clinical Human Factors Group (n.d.). Towards a working definition of human factors in healthcare. Retrieved from http://chfg.org/definition/towards-a-working-definition-of-human-factors-in-healthcare (accessed 5 May 2014).

Collins, D. (2010, February). HRO safety culture definition: An integrated approach. Presentation at a meeting hosted by the US Nuclear Regulatory Commission, Rockville, MD. Retrieved from: http://www.nrc.gov/about-nrc/safety-culture/sc-public-mtgs-presentations.html (accessed 5 May 2014).

Cooper, D. (2001). *Improving safety culture: A practical guide*. Hull: Applied Behavioural Sciences.

Dekker, S. (2012). *Just culture: Balancing safety and accountability* (2nd edn). Aldershot: Ashgate Publishing Company.

DeRosier, J.M., Taylor, L., Turner, L., and Bagian, J.P. (2007). Root cause analysis of wandering adverse events in the Veterans Health Administration. In A. Nelson and D.L. Algase (eds), *Evidence-based protocols for managing wandering behaviors* (pp. 161–180). New York: Springer Publishing Company.

Donnelly, L.F., Gessner, K.E., Dickerson, J.M., Koch, B.L., Towbin, A.J., Lehkamp, T.W., Moskovitz, J., Brody, A.S., Dumoulin, C.L., and Jones, B.V. (2010). Quality initiatives: department scorecard: a tool to help drive imaging care delivery performance. *Radiographics*, 30(7): 2029–2038.

Frankel, A., Grillo, S., and Pittman, M. (2006). The patient safety leadership walkrounds guide. Chicago, IL: Health Research and Educational Trust. Retrieved from http://www.hret.org/quality/projects/patient-safety-leadership-walkrounds.shtml (accessed 5 May 2014).

Frush, K.S., Alton, M., and Frush, D.P. (2006). Development and implementation of a hospital-based patient safety program. *Pediatric Radiology*, 36(4): 291–298.

Gaba, D, Howard, S., Fish, K., Smith, B., and Sowb, Y. (2001). Simulation-based training in anesthesia crisis resource management (ACRM): A decade of experience. *Simulation and Gaming*, 32(2): 175–193.

Gamble, M. (2013). 5 traits of high reliability organizations: How to hardwire each in your organization. *Becker's Hospital Review*, April 29. Retrieved from http://www.beckershospitalreview.com/hospital-management-administration/5-traits-of-high-reliability-organizations-how-to-hardwire-each-in-your-organization.html (accessed 4 April 2014).

Hines, S., Luna, K., Lofthus, J., and Marquardt, M. (2008, April). *Becoming a high reliability organization: Operational advice for hospital leaders.* (Prepared by the Lewin Group under Contract No. 290-04-0011.) AHRQ Publication No. 08-0022. Rockville, MD: Agency for Healthcare Research and Quality. Retrieved from http://www.ahrq.gov/hroadvice.pdf (accessed 15 May 2014).

Howard, S., Gaba, D., Fish, K., Yang, G., and Sarnquistm, F. (1992). Anesthesia crisis resource management training: Teaching anesthesiologists to handle critical incidents. *Aviation, Space, and Environmental Medicine*, 63(9): 763–770.

James, J.T. (2013). A new, evidence-based estimate of patient harms associated with hospital care. *Journal of Patient Safety*, 9(3): 122–128.

Janofsky, J.S. (2009). Reducing inpatient suicide risk: Using human factors analysis to improve observation practices. *Journal of the American Academy of Psychiatry and the Law*, 37(1): 15–24.

Joint Commission (2014). Sentinel event data event type by year, 1995–2013. Retrieved from http://www.jointcommission.org/assets/1/18/Event_Type_by_Year_1995-2Q2013.pdf.

Krause, T. and Hidley, J. (2009). *Taking the lead in patient safety: How healthcare leaders influence behavior and create culture.* Hoboken, NY: John Wiley & Sons.

Kubiak, T.M. (2009). Perusing process performance metrics: Selecting the right measures for managing processes. *Quality Progress*, 42(8): 52–55.

Kwaan, M., Studdert, D., Zinner, M., and Gawande, A. (2006). Incidence, patterns, and prevention of wrong-site surgery. *Archives of Surgery*, 141(4): 353–357.

La Porte, T.R. (1996). High reliability organizations: Unlikely, demanding and at risk. *Journal of Contingencies and Crisis Management*, 4(2): 60–71.

Lighter, D.E. (2011). *Advanced performance improvement in health care: Principles and methods.* Sudbury, MA: Jones & Bartlett.

Louisiana State University Health Sciences Center (2013). Simulation, team training improves performance, patient safety. *ScienceDaily*, November 1. Retrieved from www.sciencedaily.com/releases/2013/11/131101112408.htm (accessed 3 June 2014).

Luria, J., Muething, S., Schoettker, P., and Kotagal, U. (2006). Reliability science and patient safety. *Pediatric Clinics of North America*, 53(6): 1121–1133.

Marx, D. (2001). Patient safety and the "just culture": A primer for health care executives.

Retrieved from http://www.safer.healthcare.ucla.edu/safer/archive/ahrq/FinalPrimerDoc. pdf (accessed 2 May 2014).

May, E.L. (2013). The power of zero: Steps toward high reliability healthcare. *Healthcare Executive*, 28(2): 16–26.

Nicholetti, L.A. (2009). Using lean and six sigma to improve medical necessity workflow. *CT Scanner*, September (newsletter of the Connecticut Chapter of the Healthcare Financial Management Association). Retrieved from http://www.cthfma.org/site/files/473/ 18056/68537/420124/CT_Scanner_Sept_09.pdf (accessed 9 May 2014).

Nolan, T., Resar, R., Haraden, C., and Griffin, F.A. (2004). Improving the reliability of health care. IHI Innovation Series white paper. Boston, MA: Institute for Healthcare Improvement, available at www.IHI.org.

Percarpio, K.B. and Watts, B.V. (2013). A cross-sectional study on the relationship between utilization of root cause analysis and patient safety at 139 Department of Veterans Affairs Medical Centers. *Joint Commission Journal on Quality and Patient Safety*, 39(1): 32–37.

Pham, J. C., Girard, T., and Pronovost, P.J. (2013). What to do with healthcare incident reporting systems. *Journal of Public Health Research*, 2(e27), 154–159. Retrieved from http://www.jphres.org/index.php/jphres/article/view/jphr.2013.e27/109 (accessed 3 April 2014).

Physicians News Network (2013). Over-utilization driving up healthcare costs. March 4. Retrieved from http://www.physiciansnewsnetwork.com/news/article_6f436280-84e8-11e2-9161-0019bb30f31a.html (accessed 3 May 2014).

Reason, J. (1990). *Human error*. Cambridge: Cambridge University Press.

Reason, J. (1997). *Managing the risk of organizational accidents*. Aldershot: Ashgate Publishing.

Resar, R.K. (2006). Making noncatastrophic health care processes reliable: Learning to walk before running in creating high-reliability organizations. *Health Services Research*, 41(4 Pt 2): 1677–1689.

Roberts, K. (1990). Some characteristics of one type of high reliability organization. *Organization Science*, 1(2): 60–76.

Roberts, K., Madsen, P., Desai, V., and Van Stralen, D. (2005). A case of the birth and death of a high reliability healthcare organization. *Quality and Safety in Health Care*, 14(3): 216–220.

Sanders, M.S. and McCormick, E.J. (1993). *Human factors in engineering and design* (7th edn). New York: McGraw-Hill.

Shaw, G. (2012, August). Most adverse events at hospitals still go unreported. *Hospitalist*. Retrieved from http://www.the-hospitalist.org/details/article/2360341/Most_Adverse_ Events_at_Hospitals_Still_Go_Unreported.html (accessed 3 May 2014).

Shearm T., Greenberg, S., and Tokarczyk, A. (2013). Does training with human patient simulation translate to improved patient safety and outcome? *Current Opinion in Anesthesiology*, 26(2): 159–163.

Shojania, K.A. and Dixon-Woods, M. (2013). "Bad apples": Time to redefine as a type of systems problem? *British Medical Journal Quality and Safety*, 22(7): 528–531.

Simon, S.I. and Cistaro, P.A. (2009). Transforming safety culture: Grassroots-led/ management-supported change at a major utility. *Professional Safety*, 54(4): 28–35.

Smart Card Alliance Healthcare Council. (2009). A healthcare CFO's guide to smart card technology and applications. Retrieved from http://www.smartcardalliance.org/resources/ lib/Healthcare_CFO_Guide_to_Smart_Cards_FINAL_012809.pdf

Spath, P. (2013). *Introduction to healthcare quality management* (2nd edn). Chicago, IL: Health Administration Press.

Thomadsen, B. and Lin, S.W. (2005). Taxonomic guidance for remedial actions. In K. Henriksen, J.B. Battles, E.S. Marks, et al. (eds), *Advances in patient safety: From research to implementation. Volume 2: Concepts and methodology*. Rockville, MD: Agency for Healthcare Research and Quality. Retrieved from http://www.ncbi.nlm.nih.gov/books/ NBK20506/pdf/ch7.pdf.

Weaver, R.R. (2014). Seeking high reliability in primary care: Leadership, tools, and organization. *Health Care Management Review*, Epub ahead of print, DOI: 10.1097/ HMR.0000000000000022. Retrieved from http://journals.lww.com/hcmrjournal/Abstract/ publishahead/Seeking_high_reliability_in_primary_care_.99864.aspx.

Weick, K.E. and Sutcliffe, K.M. (2001). *Managing the unexpected: Assuring high performance in an age of complexity*. San Francisco, CA: Jossey-Bass.

Weick, K.E. and Sutcliffe, K.M. (2007). *Managing the unexpected: Assuring high performance in an age of complexity* (2nd edn). San Francisco, CA: Jossey-Bass.

Weick, K.E., Sutcliffe, K.M., and Obstfeld, D. (1999). Organizing for high reliability: Processes of collective mindfulness. *Research in Organizational Behavior*, 21: 81–123.

Weiner, E. and Nagel, D. (eds) (1988). *Human factors in aviation*. San Diego, CA: Academic Press.

# 4.  Organizational planning
## *J.M. "Mickey" Trimm and John Gill*

## THE CONCEPT OF PLANNING

Planning is one of the five basic managerial functions that organizational leaders must perform. Healthcare organizations must plan activities and acquire the resources necessary to achieve their goals for providing services and products. In addition to planning, managers must organize, staff, direct, and control resources within the organization (Figure 4.1). These last four managerial functions can only be undertaken once the organization plans what it wants to accomplish (Haimann and Hilgert, 1972). An organization's leaders must decide how many people will be required, what those people will do and how their activities will be monitored, how all of the organizational resources will be utilized, what the resources will be expected to accomplish, and whether those resources are effectively employed. The organization's plans allow for all of those activities to occur (Barnard, 1938).

Planning is often compared to the process of planning a trip. One's current location is known and there is a need to get to another location. Using a map, automobile or other form of transportation, fuel, time, and funds, an individual can develop a plan to get from the first point to the ending point. The plan may include multiple drivers or it may be just a short jaunt down the street. But thought must go into the best way to get there and what resources will be required. Business planning, likewise, should move the healthcare organization from its current situation in the

*Figure 4.1   The five functions of management*

healthcare environment to a future point where, through the expenditure of resources and effort, the organization has grown and developed and the community has benefitted from its services and products.

Organizations do planning at every level of management. Corporate leaders develop strategic plans that establish the overall direction for the entire organization. These plans should be based on an understanding of exactly what the organization is going to provide to the community and how it plans to provide that service or product. In order for an organization to achieve those strategic plans every segment of the organization – that is, every department and unit of the organization – develops plans that support the overall mission of the organization. Work units within each department must plan detailed activities, often on a daily basis, so that the departmental plans can be achieved, in turn allowing the strategic plans to be successful (Swayne et al., 2006). Consequently each individual in a department or subunit should follow a plan of activities that they will perform so that the departmental and corporate strategic plans are successful.

The thought process that considers how to employ resources in a way that assures the successful completion of a set of activities is the planning process. Good organizations employ their resources efficiently, therefore good organizations do good planning. They also find ways to use synergy to produce greater results. Good planning requires prior thought about resource utilization before the resources are put into action. Planning how resources will be used and the actions that will be undertaken with those resources requires that some future outcome has been envisioned. This future desired outcome or vision of what the organization should accomplish is what drives the organization to action.

Planning requires special effort and consideration when an organization is being formed and started. Many of the foundational requirements for organizations such as policies and procedures have not been developed and there is greater uncertainty about every aspect of the operation, such as human resource requirements and competition. Planning is critical when the organization encounters competition from other organizations. Dealing with competition is often equated to playing a chess game: the organization must anticipate the competitor's moves, often far beyond its current moves, and develop its planned responses accordingly.

Planning therefore takes place continuously as changes occur with the community needs, with changes in the resources available, and with changes from competitors. The plans must be executed throughout the organization to achieve its goals. And the planning must be done in advance of the organizing of the resources, the employing of staff, the executing of planned activities; and then planning must be adjusted based on community, organizational, and competitive changes (Hambrick and Fredrickson, 2001).

## THE DEFINITION OF PLANNING

Planning is the determination in advance of what should be done with organizational resources. Planning comes from the French word "*prévoyance*," which means to look ahead or have foresight (OED Online, 2014). The process of planning involves making decisions about what activities are going to be undertaken in the future. Planning can be complex with multiple activities or can be extremely simple, resulting in only very basic changes. In organizational terms planning is the process of deciding how to use resources to provide services and products to a community.

Planning involves the selection of specific activities and time frames from a set of multiple options. Often there are many ways to achieve a particular outcome and the planning process should select the most desirable course of action. But even before the organizational process activities have been selected and implemented, a decision on what are the desired services or products must be made by a planning process. Plans are focused on both the outcomes desired and the processes that must be put into place and carried out in order to achieve these outcomes.

Planning must be done on the execution of the other managerial activities, that is, organizing, staffing, directing, and controlling. The result of planning should be action. The success of planning lies in selecting the appropriate actions and then the successful execution of those activities. Good plans create positive outcomes when the appropriate goals and activities result in the proper impact for organizing, staffing, directing, and controlling the organization's resources (Haimann and Hilgert, 1972).

Planning is a key managerial function at every level of the organization. However, the amount of effort, time, and resources applied to the planning process will vary significantly depending on the level of management. Senior-level executives expend more time and effort planning then do lower-level managers and supervisors. The energy and effort put into planning is a direct function of the resources assigned to a manager. The more resources under the control of the manager, the more time will be required to plan the effective utilization of those resource (Swayne et al., 2006).

The time requirements and the lead time required to do proper planning are also functions of the level at which the plans are made. Senior executives with extensive resources must establish plans over long periods of time, sometimes as much as five to ten years in advance. Department supervisors and front-line managers plan on shorter time horizons. The span and magnitude of front-line supervisors' responsibilities and resources usually require time periods of a day to a year. The time and effort for the front-line supervisors to plan is typically far less than the time required for them to organize staff and direct the activities of the department.

## THE PURPOSE OF PLANNING

Every plan should support the goals and objectives of the organization. All planning therefore can only be effective if the organization has a clear understanding of what is to be accomplished by its existence. While this seems intuitive, many organizations evolve from activities undertaken by the participants but, due to a lack of understanding of an industry or its rules and regulations, may not clearly have a vision of what needs to be accomplished. For instance, a group of workers may decide to provide healthcare in the homes of neighbors, but without the understanding of how this can legally be undertaken and what is ultimately required, the group may not be able to sustain its activities. Random activities could result that do not accomplish the original intended care or might result in wasted resources and unsatisfactory clinical outcomes.

Planning is done to establish what work must be performed in under-taking the mission of the organization. The best planning starts at the upper echelons of the organization's leadership and is driven down by the management team. But the work at all levels must support an overarching and unified vision and mission. Effective leadership and management are achieved by assuring that all levels and units of the organization work together to accomplish the vision and mission.

The steps that are set forth to move the organization toward the vision are usually broken down into goals and objectives. While these terms are often used interchangeably and can be confusing, this chapter will define them in the following sense as a means of creating clarity for the assignment of work.

Goals are broad-based, complex, and longer-term accomplishments. They usually require multiple years to attain and require extensive resources. The complexity makes them difficult to measure in specific detail. An example of a healthcare goal might be "To expand the organization's market into adjoining counties."

Objectives are measurable, specific steps that can be achieved in a rela-tively short time period. They tend to be more concrete than goals, relative to identifying required resources and outcomes. Usually goals require multiple objectives to be completed in order to be successfully accomplished. An example of a healthcare objective might be "Establish three primary care centers in an adjacent county within one year."

Organizational planning requires the stakeholders of the organization, especially its leadership and management, to establish plans or actions that will result in the accomplishment of the goals and objectives necessary to achieve the vision of the organization in the future time frame (Zuckerman, 2012). The goals and objectives that the organization establish provide interim steps and incremental movement toward the corporate vision. Controlling the resources so that the goals are realized is the ultimate intention of planning and control must be applied at every level within an organization. The complexity of the organization will dictate the extent of the planning. More complex organizations will require more work to develop plans. Larger organizations with more services and products can expect to expend more time and effort on planning.

## TYPES OF PLANNING

For organizations the term "plan" can be found on many documents. There are many types of plans used in organizations and they all represent sets of activities that will accomplish some goal or objective for the organization. But all plans should be linked as components or segments of an overarching set of intended actions known as the "strategic plan." The organization's strategic plan provides a very broad set of goals or strategies that address the existing markets, identifying the services and products, and how the organization will generally compete to provide those. All other plans within an organization should be set up to support the strategic plan. The strategic plan should require a long time period to accomplish and should be far reaching in its desired outcomes. Hence the resources and effort to accomplish the strategic plan are enormous.

A quick survey of healthcare organizational literature will reveal multiple references to many types of plans. In Box 4.1 is a brief example of the types that might be found.

Many of these examples are specialized tactical plans. For instance, the marketing plan focuses on only the activities that will be used to market a service or product. Landscape planning is part of an operational plan that addresses space and facility operational plans. For this chapter the focus will be on examining the overall strategic plans, operational and tactical plans, contingency plans, and start-up planning since it has a unique purpose for organizations. These are the critical and the most important plans for achieving organizational success.

---

## BOX 4.1   TYPES OF PLANNING

- Architectural planning
- Business plan
- Capacity planning
- Comprehensive planning
- Contingency planning
- Economic planning
- Enterprise architecture planning
- Environmental planning
- Event planning and production
- Financial planning

- Land use planning
- Landscape planning
- Life planning
- Marketing plan
- Network resource planning
- Operational planning
- Site planning
- Spatial planning
- Strategic planning
- Succession planning
- Start-Up planning
- Tactical planning

*Source:*   Wikipedia (n.d.).

---

Operational plans and tactical plans are developed from breaking down the strategic plan into activities that must be addressed by various components of the organization. For instance, the cardiovascular division of a health system may adopt a plan to expand services to include new and upcoming technologies. This operational plan would involve an investment in new equipment, hiring and training new staff, more space, and a special marketing plan to promote the new technology. Such a plan will be costly, time-consuming, and will require a major focus of the clinical and administrative leadership of the organization. But it should also support a strategic plan for the organization that recognizes new technology in the cardiovascular area as part of a larger effort from the entire organization to compete in a particular market or community. The strategic plan may call for improved technology throughout the organization, not just in cardiovascular services.

Tactical plans, in turn, support the operational plans. A tactical plan involves specific departments or areas that will have to provide a component of the operational plan. As an example, the housekeeping department may have to develop a plan to regularly clean the newly constructed cardiovascular areas. These plans will be very specific, identifying responsible people, specific equipment required, and specific times required to accomplish the needed activities. These plans can be accomplished in very short time periods and are supported by budgeted funding and specific human resource plans. Multiple departments and units will need to develop tactical plans that support each operational plan (Moseley, 2009).

If the planned activities set up by the strategic plan, operational plans, and the tactical plans do not achieve the desired outcomes, an organization may create contingency plans that offer a different set of activities focused on achieving the organizational vision. The need for a contingency plan is driven by the extreme pace of change in today's healthcare environment and the ever-increasing presence of competition. Poor planning can result in the need for different plans but, most often, changing environmental factors drive the need for a contingency plan. Contingency plans allow for flexibility and force the organizational leaders to consider scenarios that expand their understanding and expectations of the market.

The start-up business plan is typically used to support the establishment of a business. The initial set of data that lays out the start-up activities and expectations for an organization is derived from the same information that a strategic plan uses. The purpose of this start-up plan is to secure the resources necessary to get the organization under way and assure its long-term success. This plan focuses on the resource acquisition aspects of a strategic plan. The typical audience for this plan is financial institutions and venture capitalists who may be requested to assist with funding the start up. The start-up business plan must convince the financiers that the organization is meeting a specific need in a way that can provide sustained operational success (Ford et al., 2007). The start-up business plan usually does not address the specific operational and tactical plans. Rather it shows that the general strategic plans are viable and that reasonable operational and tactical plans can be developed.

The need for more specific plans drives the tactical planning for areas such as facilities or training. The physical resources of a healthcare organization, hospital buildings and equipment, are often planned through a capital plan. Human resources and other costs may be planned through an operational budget that lays out the expected expenditure over the course of a year. The planned activities of individuals in the clinical and administrative areas of an organization may be established by a set of policies and procedures.

## STRATEGIC PLANNING

The concept of long-range or strategic planning has changed over the years. Turbulent environmental factors have forced a more dynamic approach to activities and the quickly changing needs of the healthcare customers. The purpose of strategic planning is to keep the organization moving and growing toward a long-term vision of a desired better situation for the organization and its stakeholders in the distant future. This is more difficult due to the high level of uncertainty that exists as business is projected farther out into the future.

In the mid-twentieth century, when hospitals became prominent components of communities in the United States, the scope and pace of the organizations did not require a lot of planning. Changes were minimal and the technology and clinical care processes were very stable. With the adoption of Medicare and Medicaid in the 1960s the environment started changing more quickly. Resource needs increased and the need to address longer-term plans developed. Long-range planning started out as an extension of budgeting, which only took into account the near future, typically only one year (Zuckerman, 2012).

Strategic planning evolved from that short planning time frame to address the more complex needs. More intense competition forced more dramatic and bold moves. Similar to a chess game, healthcare executives need to think farther out than their competitors.

Eventually executives realized that success required more than just planning. Implementation of the plans was just as critical and often more difficult to execute than the planning. Also, plans did not always go the way expected so control mechanisms had to be added. The result was the "strategic management model," a comprehensive cyclical approach to assessing the needs of the environment, evaluating the best way to serve those needs, assessing the competition, and assuring that the desired outcomes are achieved (Figure 4.2). Strategic management recognizes that

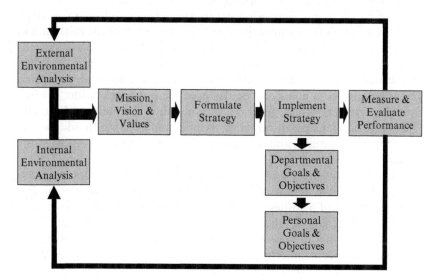

*Figure 4.2   The strategic management process*

strategic planning is just a component of the overall management of an organization, with the implementation of the plans and the correcting actions necessary for success.

Strategic management is the entire process of developing the strategy and then executing the actions necessary to achieve a desired outcome. Strategic management also includes the processes of reviewing and modifying or adjusting the strategies and implementation actions to correct for changes in the environmental situation or the competition.

The steps in the strategic management process are typically divided into the formulation phase and the implementation phase. During formulation the environmental factors affecting the organization are studied, the purpose or intent of the organization is developed and refined, and the strategies for competing and providing goods and services are selected. The implementation phase includes the dissemination of the strategies throughout the organization, and driving those plans down to all levels and locations within the organization where all the employees can work to implement component actions within departments and sections. The cumulative efforts, if properly selected, will propel the organization toward its goals and objectives (Swayne et al., 2006).

The process of developing strategy for the organization requires a thorough look at the environmental factors, both for the healthcare industry and for the general environment. Once the needs of the environment or community are determined, along with the understanding of the competition and the capabilities of the existing organization, the decision can be made as to what goods and services will be provided to meet the needs in the community. This determination of the mission and vision for what the future will hold if the organization is successful needs to be clearly articulated in mission, vision, and values statements. When the desired services and long-term outcomes are set, the strategy or plan for achieving these goals can be designed. The strategic effort is often articulated in very broad, general terms that allow flexibility and growth. The strategic plans detail how the organization is going to address the environmental issues, and overcome the competition to successfully sustain its services.

Once the strategic plans are formulated, the implementation phase begins. This is the action phase. Plans are translated into action. The implementation of a strategy drives action and change. The actions must be instituted throughout the organization, at all levels and in many ways. Regular follow-up and review is necessary to adjust for non-anticipated outcomes and for countermeasures instituted by the competition. When plans get off track, staff must do what is necessary to get the desired results back on track. This monitoring phase is followed by a return to the environmental analysis where regular updates to the analysis must be undertaken to stay ahead of the competition (Swayne et al., 2006).

The strategic management process works in all types of organizations, large for-profit corporations, small one-hospital corporations, rural hospitals, physician clinics, nursing homes, home health agencies, and even governmental healthcare agencies (Moseley, 2009).

# ENVIRONMENTAL ANALYSIS: MATCHING THE PLAN TO THE NEEDS

## External Environmental Assessments

Healthcare organizations exist to provide healthcare services and products that are needed by the community. These needs should drive the justification of the organization and be the basis for its existence. So this "external environment," which is made up of all the community factors beyond the bounds of the organization, provides the opportunities for service. It also presents the problems that must be overcome in order to provide those services, including the competitive elements in the environment. An analysis of all the factors will provide a clear understanding of the environmental opportunities and the threats that the organization will face while attempting to provide its services and products. An organization can use the identification of opportunities to plan for offering new services that are shown to be needed by the community. At the same time, the organization can develop plans to address threats to providing services. An example of such a threat or barrier might be a competitor's opposition to a Certificate of Need required by a US state governmental agency before a new facility could be built. To counter these challenges an organization might produce additional advertising or counteract legal challenges.

The external environment can be evaluated by examining different segments of the community. Opportunities and threats can be found in all of these. According to Fahey and Narayanan (1986) the five relevant segments that can be segregated and evaluated are:

1. Demographic elements.
2. Social elements.
3. Economic elements
4. Political elements.
5. Technological elements.

**Competition in the Healthcare Environment**

Organizations usually find that their ideas for providing services are not unique. Other organizations have similar desires to provide services and products for the community. Competition comes in various forms and for various reasons. But all organizations must face competition at some point in time. The intensity of the competition can vary. Sometimes the challenge is for the profits derived from the market. Other times the competitiveness may come from a desire to provide a better product or service. Competition often forces organizations to review their operations and activities more thoroughly, and better outcomes can be the result. Intense competition, however, can also result in destructive actions that hurt the entire market. Legal battles to protect exclusive territories protected by Certificates of Need can often result in millions of dollars expended. The patients ultimately pick up the bill for these battles (Porter, 1985).

Competition usually comes from the desire to perform better than the others in the healthcare market. Doing the same thing as others seldom works for the long run. What does work is performing activities that are different (and more desirable) than those of competitors. Performing the same activity in a different way or performing the activities at a lower cost can be attractive strategies. These two strategies are termed "differentiation" and "low-cost" strategies (Porter, 1980).

**Internal Environmental Assessments**

In order to compete in the community an organization must have the resources necessary to provide a healthcare service or product. The internal environmental assessment examines the various resources that make up the organization and assesses the strength or weakness of each. This will help develop a gap analysis of needed resources and existing resources. In the analysis several questions must be answered: "What are we doing right and what are we doing wrong?" "What can we do better?" "What can we do to better serve our customers and patients?" "How do our resources (financial, human, capital, real) compare to those of our competitors?" The organization should plan to take advantage of any strengths and find ways to "shore up" any resources that will be needed to provide its goods and services and compete with other organizations.

Resources can be tangible or intangible (Moseley, 2009). The resources of a healthcare organization can be segregated into several categories, as shown in Table 4.1:

*Table 4.1    Healthcare resources categories*

| Examples of Tangible Resources: | Examples of Intangible Resources: |
| --- | --- |
| • Human Resources<br>• Financial (Cash, Stocks, Bonds)<br>• Real Estate<br>• Buildings<br>• Equipment<br>• Information Technology<br>• Clinical Technology | • Creative Capabilities<br>• Knowledge<br>• Perceptual or Reputation<br>• Certificates of Need<br>• State Licensure |

1. Financial resources. A financial analysis follows standard accounting and financial review processes, incorporating income statement and balance sheet reviews, and ratio analysis. The financial strength of the organization will dictate the flexibility it has to develop strategies and move toward its goals.
2. Human resources. Human resources analysis involves an intense review of the capabilities and skills of the clinical and technical staff in the organization. Benchmarking against similar organizations can provide additional information about the cost factors related to the staffing. Comparisons of full-time equivalents (FTEs) per occupied bed and similar staffing measures may indicate opportunities for improving financial strength and improve efficiency.
3. Buildings and equipment. A thorough review of the buildings and equipment should offer a realistic evaluation of the appropriateness of these resources in providing the planned services and products. Often these resources need to be compared to those of competitor organizations. Organizational perceptions can often occur based on the visual impact of the buildings and the condition of the facilities.
4. Information technology. With its push for electronic medical records adoption, the American Recovery and Reinvestment Act is driving vast changes and upgrades in the information technology used in healthcare organizations in the US. Good information technology can be translated into more productive organizational processes and reduce costs. At the same time, the technology can improve quality and safety.
5. Clinical technology. Just as the overall information technology is quickly escalating in healthcare organizations, so the clinical technology is becoming more of a strategic factor. The implementation of mobile clinical capabilities may provide disruptive technologies that allow some organizations to offer better-quality and faster services that delight patients.

6.  Knowledge. As an intangible resource this element may be difficult to gauge. But a serious scanning of the healthcare environment should provide a benchmark to assess how well an organization is capable of learning and adapting new technologies, information, and skills.
7.  Creative capabilities. Translating knowledge into capabilities is critical for an organization to manage the tsunami of change flowing through the US healthcare industry today. Capabilities include medical and technical skills necessary to provide quality healthcare. But they also include the capabilities of operating a business in a turbulent environment.
8.  Perception. Success in a competitive environment often requires customers to feel they are getting value, whether there is concrete evidence for this or not. Perception comes from the visual and other sensory abilities. Reputation is a perception resource based on the opinions of patients, physicians, and others. The impressiveness of a new physical building and the cleanliness of the interior may suggest that the operation has a high level of quality, even if the clinical capabilities are not present. Federal surveys now provide opinion-based measures that allow organizational and physician comparisons. These perceptual metrics are becoming more important in evaluating what actions need to be planned to address the market.

**SWOT Analysis**

Using the first letter of each of the outcomes of the two assessments, a cumulative summary of the strengths, weaknesses, opportunities, and threats provides us with an organizational SWOT analysis. This summary of critical environmental factors will drive the plans that will allow the organization to accomplish its desired goals and objectives. Addressing the external needs and challenges while building the organizational abilities to meet these needs is the key to success (Coman and Romen, 2009).

# SUSTAINABLE COMPETITIVE ADVANTAGE

As the organization develops its strategic plans it should explore opportunities to develop customer-preferred competencies and resources that cannot be duplicated by the organization's competition. These attributes can be developed from natural resources, technology, clinical skills, or other resources that are difficult or impossible for the competition to acquire. The unique features differentiate its services and products from other organizations and cause demand over competitive services and products. When the competition cannot duplicate or find a suitable substitute for these, they are considered a competitive advantage. If that advantage can be maintained over time, it is considered a sustainable competitive advantage (Douglas and Ryman, 2003).

A good strategic plan will capitalize on any sustainable competitive advantages that an organization is able to develop. It will also protect those advantages with defensive strategies and plans.

## STRATEGIC INTENT: PINNING DOWN THE MISSION, VISION, AND VALUES OF THE ORGANIZATION

A good plan will always be based on the intent to provide for a need within the community or market. The clearer the purpose or intent of the organization, the more it is able to develop a viable plan to meet those needs. Often organizations develop a mission and vision statement that attempts to specify for customers, employees, and other stakeholders exactly what the organization is trying to accomplish.

The mission statement is an explanation of what the organization will actually do. It is therefore an action statement. A good mission statement will express its intent with active verbs that display energy and successful accomplishment of specific activities that will provide a service or product to meet a specific need. The statement should be short and broad. The best mission statements are only one or two sentences which succinctly express the plan of action (Swayne et al., 2006).

An example of a healthcare organizational mission statement is that of the University of Alabama at Birmingham Health Systems. Notice that it is broad but addresses key factors in the intent of the organization – innovative services, patient centeredness, research, and the education of health professionals: "To improve the health and well-being of society, particularly the citizens of Alabama, by providing innovative health services of exceptional value that are patient- and family-centered, a superior environment for the education of health professionals, and support for research that advances medical science" (UAB Medicine, n.d.).

Well-run organizations spend a great deal of time focusing on the "future state" of the organization. What will the organization look like and what will it do at some future point in time? How will it be different? What will be better about it? The plans for an organization should address these questions and offer a vision of that future state that is not only better, but inspiring to those who will move the organization to that vision.

This statement should establish the vision of what better situation the organization and the community will attain. Unfortunately many shirk this need and produce garble such as "We will be the organization of choice in our given market." This provides no understanding of what the organization will look like or what it will be doing that will cause everyone to flock to it for service. It is not clear and it is certainly not inspiring.

The vision should address not only the changes in the organization but also how those changes will affect those that the organization serves. More effective vision statements inspire stakeholders by offering a picture of a world made better by its work: "Our vision is a community free of unnecessary pain and suffering" offers a much better future than one where the organization has all the market share.

The vision is always a state of being. It is a statement of what the future will be. It should never contain active verbs. Active verbs connote action, and action connotes work that is being done to create the vision. This action that the organization undertakes is the mission of the entity. The mission is the work that must be done to achieve the vision.

Some organizations also produce values statements. These statements identify specific values that are important to the organization and steer decisions that might involve some ethical problems. Sometimes these statements are driven by previous indiscretions by the organization or its leaders. Sometimes the values are based on the religious beliefs or moral priorities of the leadership. Often the values will be incorporated into the mission statement rather than produced in another document (Moseley, 2009).

## FORMULATING THE STRATEGIES

Strategy formulation is simply deciding on a plan of action. Once the environmental assessments are complete and the mission and vision of the organization are as clear as possible, the leadership will have all the information it needs to decide what is necessary to compete in the community or market. The scope of the plans will be dictated by the environmental needs and the resources that the organization can marshal. The more resources that an organization is able to put toward a strategy, the greater the span of possible plans that it can administer. Organizations that are flush with cash (financial resources) will have an easier time expanding into new territory or building or buying another healthcare facility and adding services. Without significant finances, organizations must find other means of enhancing services that benefit the community.

Higher-skilled employees allow for more advanced technical procedures that may be difficult for competitive organizations to replicate. An attractive location, in a very affluent neighborhood, may offer advantages that cannot be overcome by an organization in a less desirable community.

Growth is a typical objective of organizational plans. Growing revenues, profits, and resources provide the opportunity for the organization to continue current services and to offer new and expanded services. Growth can occur in many ways. Expanding geographic territory is a primary means of growth. Adding services or increasing market share in an existing market are other means. Mergers and acquisitions are fast means of expanding if the financial resources allow. Internal growth is slower but takes less in the way of resources and can be an easy way to expand for non-profit organizations that do not have access to securities markets for support (Swayne et al., 2006).

Organizations can also grow by diversifying. If the market for current services and products is saturated, additional services and products may be warranted. A hospital might decide to enter the long-term care market. It might decide to open fitness and wellness centers. It could go into a non-related business such as real estate, although the farther an organization strays from its core competencies, the more risky the venture.

When an organization's environmental situation is not good – that is, financial resources are limited or their competitive stance in the market is weak – the organization may not be able to grow. Instead it may need to divest or liquidate some of its assets and redirect the plans to stabilize the situation. Retrenchment plans can allow the organization to buy time and get back to a more viable position in the market. An example of this is HealthSouth Corporation, which almost went bankrupt in 2004 but was able to jettison several business units and redirect its energies toward outpatient services, resulting in a strong expansive organization ten years later.

Organizations can also plan to maintain the status quo. Sustaining current operations is often an attractive plan when there has been a previous period of fast growth. The organization may decide to hold steady and solidify its current operational activities, catch its breath, or just observe the market before taking bold steps in the future (Swayne et al., 2006).

## IMPLEMENTING THE STRATEGIES

Great plans can be found on the shelves of many failed healthcare organizations. Having a plan that is innovative, bold and that addresses the needs of the community is not enough. The organization has to put those plans into action. Implementation of plans is often more difficult than developing the plan.

Implementation of plans falls short for many reasons. The organization may not have the ability to organize the work appropriately to complete the plans. It may not be able to find the resources necessary or it may have believed it had resources that were, in fact, non-existent. It may not have held the appropriate managers responsible for achieving specific actions. Often organizations get bogged down in the day-to-day activities and cannot pull away to focus on the important plans for the future.

The importance of implementation cannot be overstated. Effective leaders will be able to prioritize and help their managers focus on what is important and what can be accomplished. Unrealistic plans will be discarded and replaced with do-able plans that allow the organization to advance or grow.

Implementing organizational plans requires effort by everyone in the organization. While the plans are developed and adopted by the leadership, typically the senior executives and board of directors, the implementation has to be done by everyone at every level of the organization. This means that the plans must be communicated effectively and "sold" to the employees. They have to buy in to the plans and believe that the plans will provide success for the organization, and therefore success for themselves. The plans will make sense if they address the mission and vision of the organization and the employees understand how the plans will accomplish those goals (Swayne et al., 2006).

Strategic planning focuses on long-term, massive efforts with major commitments of resources, financial and human especially, to achieve extensive outcomes over long periods of time. In order to keep the organization on track and achieve these massive undertakings, the organization has to plan to move a little toward its objectives every day. This is accomplished by using its employees to undertake interim goals and objectives that have shorter time spans and that can be accomplished in shorter periods of time. Cumulatively these actions can result in the massive achievements. These interim steps are called operational plans and tactical plans.

# RATCHETING DOWN THE STRATEGY: OPERATIONAL AND TACTICAL PLANNING

Operational planning is the process of identifying the parts of the strategic plan that can be implemented in a measureable time frame. Typically organizations look at a one-year time frame for these operational plans. So the operational plan deals with activities of narrower dimensions, requiring less resources, and results are of lesser impact, focusing on what can be accomplished in the one-year time frame. The measurement of the outcomes allows organizations to plan and move forward in a way that encourages evaluation and adjustment at regular intervals but still allows it to focus on the long-term desired goals. The one-year time frame encourages an annual assessment and plan. This results in a one-year financial plan that is called a budget.

Working with the senior leadership the operational plans are developed by the mid-level managers who are responsible for specific departments and units of an organization. The operational plans will include the specific activities that support the strategies and long-term plans. They will identify resources needed, especially the staffing and financial needs, so that portions of the strategic plan can be achieved during a given operational period. Milestones and deadlines are set to keep the organization moving forward in a timely manner. The key elements of a good organizational plan are proper budgeting and good instructions for organizational staff on how to implement the needed activities.

## Budgeting

Deciding what can be accomplished in a year is the key factor that drives the detailed budgeting and operational activities within a healthcare organization. Each department and unit within the organization should have an annual operating plan and corresponding budget. Too often organizations focus more on the financial aspects of the budget, comparing increases from previous years and making accommodations to equalize resources for various department rather than using the overall goals and objectives to drive the financial needs to accomplish the necessary components of the operational plan (Walston, 2014).

## Policies and Procedures

Organizations use policies and procedures to help achieve goals and objectives. These rules, guidelines, and instructions provide boundaries for how specific activities are to be conducted. They standardize decision-making and ensure that the organization's processes for achieving specific out-comes are followed. While many policies and procedures address ethical and compliance issues, a key purpose is to standardize the planned activi-ties of individuals and groups so that the expected long-range strategies are successful.

Policies are the guidelines used by the organization to ensure con-sistency and compliance with its strategic plans. They can dictate how patients are treated and the specific activities related to clinical practices so that quality services occur consistently. By directing the tactical activities of the organization, broader goals can be realized.

Procedures are the methods or techniques that the organization wants to employ to accomplish specific outcomes and ensure that policies are fol-lowed. Standardizing the methods ensures that desired results are realized and that future outcomes occur as planned (Moseley, 2009).

## TACTICAL PLANNING

One-year budget plans are made for each component of the organization. The budgets drive the activities for each unit, department, or section of the organization. When this departmental planning is completed, the results are termed "tactical plans." The plans contain the basic action steps that each individual in a department must make to support operational objec-tives. Tactical plans involve actions such as purchasing a new piece of equipment or training a new staff member.

Tactical plans are the key to successfully accomplishing operational plans and strategic plans. Thousands of tactical activities must be under-taken in all the various units and departments in order for the broader goals to be realized. Since tactical plans affect smaller segments of the organization, usually one department, there are simpler activities and outcomes for each. Financial expenditures are much more modest at this level. Fewer employees are involved and responsibilities and action assign-ments can be focused on individuals or small groups where accountability is easier to maintain. Tactical plans are easier to achieve, measure, and evaluate.

Good tactical planning requires several elements to be successful. First, the activities must be broken down into action steps that can be clearly defined and easily accomplished. A specific individual should be assigned responsibility for the action step. The time frame for when the action step needs to be accomplished must be set, with specific start and completion times. The portion of the budget that is needed must be committed and available for the responsible person to use. Finally, a very clear outcome must be set that is tangible and demonstrable. The responsible person should be able to show clear evidence that the action step is completed. Often this outcome is termed the action's "feedback."

Tactical plans are developed by the department managers with support from the mid-level executives. The managers determine the action steps and assign them to staff within their departments based on the skills and knowledge needed for each step. The day-to-day responsibilities of the staff should be considered. Often adjustments in scheduled regular job functions are necessary, or the additional assignments can hinder the staff's ability to perform their regular activities and complete the added tasks.

Only one person can be responsible for each action step. If two or more are assigned responsibility there can be a tendency for finger-pointing or shifting blame when that action step is not completed satisfactorily. When a staff person understands that they will be held accountable, there is a greater likelihood of successful completion. There can be many support staff, both inside a department and in other parts of the organization, who can provide resources that can help the responsible person. These support staff should be consulted during the planning process to ensure that they understand the action step and the need for their assistance when the action step occurs.

The responsible person must understand what resources are available to accomplish an action step. The budgeted funding should be clearly spelled out and the time frame should be defined. Policies and procedures for addressing the action steps need to be in place, defining the rules for how to access the funds, how to engage other staff, and how to report progress.

The feedback that demonstrates the completion of the action step must be a tangible, concrete item. For instance, if an action step calls for a new piece of diagnostic equipment to be obtained, the bill of sale or bill of lading could be a viable feedback item. If a new employee is to be hired, the signed employment contract or a letter agreeing to a job proposal could be used as feedback. Certificates of occupation demonstrate that a building is complete. A signed contract shows that external resources are secured. The signed and approved minutes of a meeting can demonstrate that a board of trustees has agreed with a new plan or strategy.

Visual props such as an action plan chart can often help an organization to assure that all plans are developed properly and that no steps fall through the cracks. Table 4.2 is an example of an action plan that incorporates all the elements needed to assure that specific objectives are successfully completed. This action plan supports an operational plan to expand the surgical services within a hospital. Notice that the action steps could be further dissected to additional steps by the responsible party. But for

*Table 4.2  Example action plan – objective: strengthen depth and breadth of surgical service*

| Action Steps | Responsibility | | Schedule | | Resources | | Feedback |
| --- | --- | --- | --- | --- | --- | --- | --- |
| | Primary | Others | Start | Finish | Money | Time | |
| Hire Orthopedic Surgeon | CEO | Search Firm | February, 2007 | June, 2007 | $40 000 | 6 months | Signed Contract |
| Add 2 New OR Suites | Director of Engineering Services | Architects, Contractor | November, 2006 | July, 2007 | $1 450 000 | 8 months | Certificate of Occupancy |
| Plan and hire additional staff | Director of Nursing | Search Firm | November, 2006 | July, 2007 | $180 000/year | 3 months | Staff Oriented |
| Acquire new anesthesia and surgical equipment | Director of Material Mgt. | DON, Staff, Anesthesia MDs, Surgeons | November, 2006 | June, 2007 | $700 000 | 3 months | Purchases received and installed |
| Promote new services to primary care physicians and public | Director of Marketing | New Surgeon | June, 2007 | August, 2007 | $10 000 | 2 months | Presentations made, ads |
| Acquire outside financing for construction | CFO | Bond Counsel | November, 2006 | February, 2007 | $25 000 | 3 months | Loan or Bond Completed |
| Prepare plan for regular cleaning of new surgical areas | Director Enviro. Services | DON | November, 2006 | July, 2007 | $25 000/year | 3 months | Revised Cleaning Plan |

demonstration purposes, this table clearly shows how various segments of the facility will be responsible for the many steps necessary to complete the objectives and expand the operations.

## THE CONTROL SYSTEM: MEASURING AND EVALUATING OUTCOMES AND MAKING ADJUSTMENTS

Since planning takes place over long periods of time, environmental conditions, competition, and customer needs can all change. Assumptions about what will happen in the future do not turn out as expected. Adjustments and corrections to the plan will be necessary. This component of the planning process that measures and evaluates progress is considered the "strategic control system." Regular monitoring is required. In less turbulent times, the monitoring might have been done annually. Today ongoing, continuous monitoring is necessary due to the speed of changes in the US healthcare landscape (Moseley, 2009).

Essentially the control system asks the question: "Is the plan working?" Every organization needs to determine the relevant strategic dimensions that must be watched, and develop a plan for monitoring and modifying the plans based on this evaluation. Proper sources of good data must be determined. A system of collecting this data, analyzing it, and communicating it to the proper leadership must be developed. The challenge of identifying and organizing the process can be daunting.

One popular method for monitoring organizational progress toward goal attainment is the "balanced scorecard." Developed by Robert Kaplan and David Norton (1996) at Harvard, the model breaks the areas to monitor into four segments: financial, customer, internal business processes, and learning and innovation. Organizations identify specific metrics in each of these areas and track progress in each of these areas towards long-term plans. Other models work just as well. Organizations just have to find what works for them and consistently follow their progress.

## PERSONAL DEVELOPMENT PLANNING

Ultimately the success of the organization is dependent upon the success in having all the tactical plans completed. Motivating the staff to accomplish the action steps requires communication and constant oversight. Appropriate incentives and rewards should be employed as a budgeted component of the planning process. Usually the work on the action steps occurs during times when staff have regular day-to-day activities. The extra effort should be compensated.

More importantly, the employees should be able to understand how working toward the organizational strategic plans will also benefit themselves. Their personal goals should be aligned with those of the organization. While individuals have many varying goals, these can be fulfilled by their pay from the organization. But individuals also have needs for recognition, perceived worth, and other means for self-actualization. Good organizations will work with their employees to help them identify what they want to achieve in life and help them figure out how to attain those goals, especially through performing work in the organization.

For example, an individual may want to buy a home for their family. Obviously having a steady pay check is a means for obtaining that goal. But the organization could also encourage the employee by offering counseling on financial planning, corporate savings programs, insurance support, and other benefits that help with home ownership. Educational goals, smoking cessation, weight-loss programs, and other support services can be aligned with employee personal goals that breed loyalty and commitment. Better-educated, healthier, and motivated employees are more likely to produce successful work.

Some hospitals even help employees develop personal mission statements that set out individual goals and objectives. In addition to helping the employee achieve success, this type of effort builds an appreciation that the organization actually cares about its employees.

## CONTINGENCY PLANNING

Environmental conditions in today's economy can change quickly. A new political leader or a Supreme Court decision can quickly alter the healthcare landscape and require a change of direction for the healthcare organization. New competitors can appear overnight. Disruptive technology that completely changes the capabilities and costs of caring for a community makes planning a treacherous profession. And, of course, the patient demands and expectations are also changing due to national and local databases that allow comparisons of facilities and providers.

A contingency plan addresses the disruptive challenges of the healthcare environment, providing alternative courses of action when events assumed by the strategic plan do not happen as expected. Usually organizations consider contingencies for standard disaster-focused occurrences such as natural disasters, data breaches and losses, fires or other damaging incidents, and sabotage. But competitive changes can create severe challenges as well (Zuckerman, 2012). So having a "Plan B" is more than just a nicety. It is critical for well-run organizations. The contingency plan will provide flexibility and security. There are several advantages to developing a contingency plan for the organization.

First, the effort to develop a contingency plan forces the management to consider alternatives to the existing plan. Often the leadership is so entrenched in the details of the strategic plan that they fail to consider its weaknesses and vulnerabilities. Taking a different view will often turn up issues that could be overlooked otherwise. So the development of a contingency plan can help strengthen the originally developed plan.

When environmental factors blow up for the organization there can be a period of uncertainty and confusion that temporarily thwarts the efforts of that organization. Having a contingency plan and making sure the managers and key stakeholders know that a contingency plan exists can reduce anxiety and maintain order in times of uncertainty. Reducing the time to deal with disruptive changes can allow the organization to gain competitive advantage.

The key to an outstanding contingency plan is a comprehensive risk assessment for the organization. The environmental analysis of both internal and external factors should identify most of the risks that the organization faces. A potential new competitor checking out property in the community could pose a severe risk. So could the potential of losing a key physician. Or the possibility of a regulatory change in reimbursement methods could wipe out major income streams. Identifying and prioritizing potential threats can create a substantial list to consider (Redman, n.d.).

The intent of the contingency plan should be to maintain the strategic goals and objectives to the greatest extent possible. Playing "what if" games with the identified risk factors will provide some scenarios that help identify key resources and possible alternative courses of action that can assure survival and even greater prosperity.

The standard strategic planning model is used to work through the contingency plan development process with different environmental assumptions. How would the existing plan change if the organization's top-producing surgeon resigned? What would happen to revenues? How would that affect other parts of the organization? How many operating room employees would be needed for the reduced volumes? Financial and staffing are just a few of the considerations from such a scenario. Promotional plans may need to be changed. Budgets for recruiting may need to be adjusted. The organization's strategic plan may have to be totally revamped.

The same group of stakeholders that develop the original plan should be involved in the development of the contingency plans. Just as the strategic plan should be updated regularly, so should the contingency plan. At least annual reviews and updates are needed. Often outside consultants can help provide a frame of reference that may escape the internal leaders.

While most contingency plans address the disaster-related risks, these plans can also be developed for opportunity-related situations. Scenarios such as the decision of a competitor to exit the market or the acquisition of substantial resources from a former patient's estate can change the opportunities for advancing the organization and its ability to provide services and products to the community. Being flexible in such cases can be advantageous and organizations should plan for such situations.

Contingency plans differ from the plans developed in the strategic control component of the strategic management process. Strategic control monitors and modifies the existing plan with relatively minor adjustments over the course of the strategic effort. Contingency plans pose dramatic and often completely different strategies and are done prior to the realization that a change needs to be made. Contingency planning requires an investment of time, effort, and resources. But the long-term benefit gained from the flexibility can be invaluable.

## THE START-UP BUSINESS PLAN

The start-up business plan is a document that provides all the information one would need to justify why an organization should be created and what it plans to do to provide a product or service. These plans are typically prepared as an initial effort to obtain funding and support for a start-up business. In some cases a business plan may be developed to expand or substantially change an ongoing business. The elements of a good business plan will mirror the information found in other plans such as strategic plans, operational plans and tactical plans. But the start-up plan will address the unique situation where there is no historical evidence that the organization can be successful (Ford et al., 2007).

When individuals or groups decide to start a healthcare organization they need to sell the idea to other stakeholders who will provide resources such as capital, staff, and property. Investor banks and other businesses must be convinced that the new organization is worthy of support in order to commit.

When an organization has established its operations the business planning can be used to help focus the application of resources to the proper activities, allowing the organization to achieve its goals and maintain a viable operation.

There are several key elements which are found in most business plans. These include an executive summary explaining briefly what the organization expects to accomplish, milestones for specific operational activities, an explanation of the market forces that the organization will face, financial projections including sales, operational costs, other expenses, cash flow, and the existing and planned resources to be acquired, including staff (Barrow et al., 2012).

### The Executive Summary

The executive summary offers the developers an opportunity to make a good first impression. The summary will provide a quick overview of the mission of the organization, explaining why the organization should exist. It will contain extensive projections of the financial expectations, a projection of the market opportunities for the products or services to be offered, and the challenges to be faced by the organization, including existing and projected competition, regulatory requirements, and resource constraints.

### Target Market and Sales Plan

The next section of the plan introduces the products and services to be marketed. Any environmental problems that are to be solved by providing these products and services will be explained, along with how the environmental problems will be solved. The competitive landscape for the problem and how the business will gain a competitive edge over any existing competitors should be addressed here. Growth of the market will be projected and detailed plans for the marketing and sales of the products and services will be forecast.

### Milestones and Metrics

Specific activities and projected milestones for the development of the organization and its products and services are identified on a timeline. Specific outcomes along with due dates, the resources required to accomplish the outcomes, and the responsible parties for achieving the outcomes are shown on the timeline. Key metrics such as projected sales, staffing expectations, and other indications of growth are presented in this section of the plan.

## Management Team

A key factor in selling an organizational plan is the demonstration of management capability. Hence, an introduction of the management team that will guide the development of the organization and establish its services and products in the market is a critical part of the business plan. The management team biographies or résumés should be presented in a way that demonstrates that all of the necessary expertise required is onboard. If other human resource needs are identified, a plan for acquiring those resources should be included as part of this section.

## Financial Plan

The business plan must convincingly demonstrate a financial model that achieves the desired goals and objectives of the organization. A typical financial plan will include, but may not be limited to, the following information:

1.   a sales forecast;
2.   a personnel plan;
3.   other operating costs
4.   a profit and loss statement;
5.   a cash flow statement; and
6.   a balance sheet.

## Assumptions

Not all information necessary to evaluate an organizational plan will be available at the start of the organizational efforts. Some assumptions must be made regarding potential demand, expected competition, cost of operations, and cost of regulation. Depending on the market, other uncertainties will most likely exist. The uncertainty of the assumptions will play a critical factor in the acceptance of the business plan or its rejection by those who do are considering the investment of resources.

Properly presented, a well-prepared business plan will provide investors, customers, and other stakeholders with the information necessary to determine the viability of the proposed organization and the prospects of a successful operation. Once in operation many of the uncertainties will disappear as products and services are developed and the operations of the organization level out. Costs will become better known. Planning that occurs after the start-up is usually much more detailed, and evaluations of the viability, competition, environmental situation, and operational challenges will allow more detailed analysis and planning.

# RESEARCH JUSTIFICATION FOR STRATEGIC MANAGEMENT

The process of developing plans at all levels of an organization seems daunting. Much of the needed work is already known, and the process is extremely time-consuming. Why, then, should we really consider developing plans that are so detailed, specific, and costly? Research shows that there are actually many reasons that justify the effort and trouble:

1.  There is a good evidence that the effort will improve the organization's long-term financial performance. Recent research at hospitals across Texas by Amer Kaissi (2008) from Trinity University has demonstrated a strong correlation between organizations that have developed strategic plans and positive financial outcomes. Numerous other empirical studies over the years have shown similar outcomes. This could be because they develop better plans, or it could be that they simply understand their environment better as a result of the planning process. There is no doubt that the planning process yields positive results, no matter the causative factor.
2.  Related to the financial impact, the organizations that spend the effort to plan are able to more efficiently allocate resources. Using resources wisely creates better outcomes, but it also creates the internal impact of a more satisfied and stable workforce, less wasted energy, and a more attractive environment for customers and patients.
3.  Planning allows for an aggressive and proactive approach to the healthcare business. Often timing affects the success of plans. Early-adopter healthcare organizations can gain competitive advantage by establishing themselves as the dominant provider in their market with new and better services, technology, and access.
4.  Organizations that systematically plan are better aware of the external environment that they operate within. They know the forces that drive the market and the needs of the patients. They know what the competition has to offer and where they can fill the gaps in services. They understand the current environment. They have a better expectation of what the future holds and they understand the changes that must be employed to move the organization forward.
5.  Good planners are usually good communicators. Communications are critical to driving down all the strategic plans into operational and tactical planning elements. This overall understanding of the plans helps drive the success of the overall plans. Good metrics and good feedback on progress are communicated throughout the organization

both horizontally and vertically. Coordination of efforts results from the effective communications.

6.  Because employees are more involved in the planning and implementation process and understand their contribution and worth, they are more inspired and energized.

7.  Focusing on alternative plans for control and contingency efforts inspires innovation and creativeness in the plans. Change comes easier and often in ways that were unforeseen at the outset.

## BARRIERS AND PROBLEMS WITH PLANNING

Even the best of plans can create results that fall short of expectations. Assumptions sometimes are not realistic. Resources that should be available do not materialize. And, the competition can always come up with the unexpected. The typical problems involve short-falls with the implementation as much as bad planning. Many other issues can also create problems and barriers to success (Beer and Eisenstat, 2000):

1.  The organization's leadership may not be totally committed to the process of planning. Some leaders feel they know what needs to be done and that input from within the organization or from outside is not needed. Developing plans just to satisfy the board or for promotional value will usually create little commitment from the employees. A plan that is viewed as a dictate from the top leadership may be resented, especially if it does not consider the more realistic input of those who are performing the work.

2.  Lack of follow-through of the implementation phase of the plan is one of the most common problems with achieving success. Good plans must be executed to have an impact. When day-to-day activities and other distractions pull the energy and resources from the planned activities, the action plans do not come to fruition and goals are not realized.

3.  Some organizations get caught up in the analysis phase of the planning process. Analysis paralysis results. While good data is necessary and more data is usually better, an organization must make timely decisions or the plans will fail due to lack of time to implement or due to the changes in the environment that occur by the time the organization does move.

4.  The turbulence within the healthcare environment continues to grow. Changes are occurring much quicker. Data overload is becoming a problem. The attractiveness of big data is that it can provide better

information for decisions. But, the time needed for responding is getting shorter. Better data and information is good but it also can detract from the actions that are needed. Dissecting the additional information in a timely manner will be challenging.

5.  The Patient Protection and Affordable Care Act (ACA) is forcing changes in every aspect of US healthcare. Predicting the future as this politically charged legislation moves forward will be difficult. Judicial challenges could completely change its impact, and shifts in the political power in Washington could throw the entire industry into turmoil. Planning for how to provide services under the ACA will continue to be difficult until the political forces settle (Burns and Pauly, 2012).

6.  There has to be a good fit between the plans and the budgets. Plans that require more financial resources than the organization can muster are doomed to fail. Efficient use of funds is necessary, regardless of the scope of the plans.

7.  Some organizations set a plan and then stick to it regardless of the outcomes. Failing to monitor and adjust or to implement a contingency plan when disaster or critical environmental changes occur can cause less-than-optimum results or outright failure.

8.  Competition in healthcare is becoming more complicated. Organizations must compete nationally and globally now. Arrangements by national retail firms that direct patients from around the country to one provider creates a level of competitiveness far beyond the local challenges of the past. Medical tourism will force the competition even farther as the imbalance of wages in other parts of the world creates opportunities for US businesses to reduce their employee healthcare costs.

## SUMMARY AND CONCLUSIONS

Planning consumes much of a healthcare executive's time. And, it is one of the most important activities that healthcare leaders will undertake. Plans must be developed throughout the organization, and all must be coordinated. Plans direct all of the work throughout the organization, and the better the plans are developed and communicated, the better the organization performs.

While senior-level leadership tends to focus on the strategic planning process, the key to success for most organizations is the implementation and execution of thousands of action plans. The successful completion of all of these detailed activities forms the foundation that supports the overall goals and objectives. Budgets and policies and procedures must be established to guide the many individuals who will work towards and contribute to the implementation of the plans. Resources and competencies must be identified and secured to allow progress toward the identified "future state."

The challenge for healthcare leaders is to construct and implement plans while the US healthcare environment continues to increase in turbulence and change at astronomical speeds. The instability of the ACA does not help. Keeping plans current and responding to the disruptive technologies and to competition that is becoming global will create extreme barriers to success. Finding ways to speed the analysis of the environment and to quickly respond to environmental and competitive threats will tax even the best healthcare leaders.

# REFERENCES

Barnard, C. (1938), *The Functions of the Executive*. Cambridge, MA: Harvard University Press.

Barrow C., Barrow, P., and Brown, R. (2012), *The Business Plan Workbook*. London: Kogan Page.

Beer, M. and Eisenstat, R.A. (2000), The silent killers of strategy implementation and learning. *Sloan Management Review*, 41 (4), 29–40.

Burns, L.R. and Pauly, M.V. (2012), Accountable care organizations may have difficulty avoiding the failures of integrated delivery networks of the 1990s. *Health Affairs*, 31 (11), 2407–2416.

Coman, A. and Ronen, B. (2009), Focused SWOT: diagnosing critical strengths and weaknesses. *International Journal of Production Management*, 47 (20), 5677–5689.

Douglas, T.J. and Ryman, J.A. (2003), 'Understanding Competitive Advantage in the General Hospital Industry: Evaluating Strategic Competencies', *Strategic Management Journal*, 24 (4), 333–347.

Fahey, L. and Narayanan, V.K. (1986), *Macroenvironmental Analysis for Strategic Management*. St Paul, MN: West Publishing Company.

Ford, B., Bornstein, J., and Pruitt, P. (2007), *The Ernst & Young Business Plan Guide*, 3rd edn. Hoboken, NJ: John Wiley & Sons.

Haimann, T. and Hilgert, R.L. (1972), *Supervision: Concepts and Practices of Management*. Cincinnati, OH: South-Western Publishing.

Hambrick, D.C. and Fredrickson, J.W. (2001), Are you sure you have a strategy?. *Academy of Management Executive*, 15 (4), 48–59.

Kaissi, A.A. (2008), Strategic planning processes and hospital financial performance. *Journal of Healthcare Management*, 53 (3), 197–209.

Kaplan, R.S. and Norton, D.P. (1996), *The Balanced Scorecard: Translating Strategy into Action*. Boston, MA: Harvard Business School Press.

Moseley, G.B. (2009), *Managing Health Care Business Strategy*. Sudbury, MA: Jones & Bartlett Publishers.

OED Online (2014), Prevoyance. Oxford University Press, June, http://www.oed.com/view/Entry/151109?redirectedFrom=prevoyance (accessed August 2, 2014).

Porter, M.E. (1980), *Competitive Strategy: Techniques for Analyzing Industries and Competitors*. New York: Free Press.

Porter, M.E. (1985), *Competitive Advantage: Creating and Sustaining Superior Performance*. New York: Free Press.

Redman, B. (n.d.), Risk assessment and contingency planning. http://smallbusiness.chron. com/risk-assessment-contingency-planning-20948.html.

Swayne, L., Duncan, W.J., and Ginter, P.M. (2006), *Strategic Management of Health Care Organizations*, 5th edn. Malden, MA: Blackwell Publishing.

UAB Medicine (n.d.), Vision, culture, mission and values. http://www.uabmedicine.org/ about-us/about-us-vision-culture-mission-values (accessed August 3, 2014).

Walston, S. (2014), *Strategic Healthcare Management: Planning and Execution*. Chicago, IL: Health Administration Press.

Wikipedia (n.d.), Types of planning. http://en.wikipedia.org/wiki/Planning (accessed August 10, 2014).

Zuckerman, A.M. (2012), *Healthcare Strategic Planning*, 3rd edn. Chicago, IL: Health Administration Press.

# 5.  Customer service
## Myron D. Fottler and Tina Yeung

## INTRODUCTION

Management of customer service in healthcare requires addressing the service strategy, service staffing, and service systems. All are important contributors to the ultimate goal of meeting and exceeding the needs, wants, and expectations of internal and external customers. Key internal customers include physicians and staff. Key external customers include patients, families, third-party payers, and vendors.

Discussion of the service strategy involves looking at the current market reality and consumer expectations. The strategic planning process as it relates to service requires assessment of the external environment, developing appropriate action plans, forecasting the future, enhancing the healing environment, and creating a customer-focused culture. Staffing addresses the human resource activities which provide the professional and non-professional staff who develop, implement, improve, and monitor the service strategy. Such activities or functions include job analysis, recruitment, selection, leader and staff development, employee motivation, and patient co-production of services. Systems refer to the processes, standards, and other practices that support staff including information systems, various systems techniques, systems to reduce wait times, feedback systems, and service failure recovery systems.

Previously, healthcare organizations in the United States have focused on meeting the expectations of only two of their key stakeholders: medical staff and third-party payers (Blair and Fottler, 1990). More recently, the focus has been on customer satisfaction and meeting patient and clinical staffing needs. The passing of the Affordable Care Act (ACA) in 2010 has created incentives that emphasize the increase in customer satisfaction in the United States.

A survey commissioned by the National Coalition on Healthcare (2008) indicated low levels of consumer confidence in the quality, cost, and accessibility of healthcare services. Eight out of ten survey respondents believed something was seriously wrong with the healthcare system and six out of ten were pessimistic about its sustainability. Additionally, eight out of ten believed that healthcare is often compromised to help save money and quality services were not affordable for the average person.

**Customer Service Challenges**

We believe that we in healthcare organizations can learn from other service businesses that provide excellent customer services. These businesses have the following customer service characteristics (Ford and Bowen, 2008):

- The ultimate goal is to produce a memorable customer service experience.
- The customer co-produces or co-creates the value of the experience.
- Employee and customer attitudes and relationships are key to customer satisfaction.
- All tangible (visible to the customer) aspects of the service are managed.
- The customer determines how organizational effectiveness is measured.
- Culture is viewed as a mechanism for control and inspiration.
- Service errors are sought and fixed.

However, healthcare executives often find it difficult to provide superb customer service for three reasons: a shortage of primary care doctors, third-party reimbursement, and few rewards for good service or penalties for poor service. Firstly, primary care physicians are in short supply in the United States, because the US values its specialists more than its primary care physicians (Pho, 2008). Primary care demands too much work for too little pay. Insurance companies dictate the price for each service, and telephone and e-mail communications between doctors and patients are not reimbursed. The only way for primary care physicians to raise their income is to see more patients, which is antithetical to service excellence. Because of the shortage of primary care physicians, US patients have to wait longer for appointments than do patients in other countries (Arnst, 2007). This is one reason for the rapid rise of retail and other walk-in clinics (Fottler and Malvey, 2010).

Secondly, healthcare's unique reimbursement system acts as a barrier to great customer service. In contrast to other industries, the parties that pay for the product or service – such as a managed care company, Medicare, or Medicaid – are not the stakeholders who receive that product or service. These third-party payers impose rules, regulations, guidelines, clinical protocols, and incentives on providers that constrain the services and how they are provided to the patients and other customers. In other words, incentives for third-party payers are often antithetical to providing the excellent customer service found in other industries.

Thirdly, healthcare does not hand out monetary rewards for excellence nor penalties for mediocrity (Goodman, 2007). Service excellence, then, tends to be the result of the energy and enthusiasm of a few individuals who receive (and expect) no financial benefits for their efforts. Although the Affordable Care Act is beginning to make a change in these incentives, the process has a long way to go. The lack of innovation in healthcare customer service is tied to inflexible reimbursement systems which have not significantly modified incentives and disincentives.

Successful healthcare organizations are those managed by leadership teams who are committed to customer service and instill a service philosophy in their cultures (Studer, 2008). These leaders continually enhance their core competencies and set and sustain standards that enable their organizations to satisfy the needs of customers at all times in all service locations. They know that each interaction with a customer or potential customer represents a "moment of truth" that needs to be endowed with caring and courtesy. This chapter will address how the best healthcare organizations can and do manage all aspects of the service experience through strategy, staffing, and systems.

In healthcare, the primary goal is to achieve a positive clinical outcome. The rest of the patient experience, however, often receives much less attention, to the detriment of all concerned. Managing the total healthcare experience means ensuring that every component of care – the physical environment, organizational culture, clinician and staff behavior, interpersonal relations, communication system, administrative policies, clinical protocols, and standards of operation, to name but a few – is efficient, consistent, and responsive to the needs, wants, and expectations of all customers, especially patients.

**Customer Service Chain**

Figure 5.1 shows the processes by which higher and lower levels of customer service and loyalty are achieved as well as the organizational outcomes associated with both. The antecedent predictors (left box) include environmental incentives (that is, reimbursement rules) associated with both. Customers tend to develop their expectations based on both healthcare and non-healthcare service experiences. Their expectations (top center box) may be exceeded, met, or not met in terms of the clinical and service quality expected.

Healthcare organizations develop and implement strategies, staffing, and systems to address these expectations within the constraints of the reimbursement and other external constraints. Customer expectations regarding clinical and service quality and the organization's strategies, systems, and processes also influence one another.

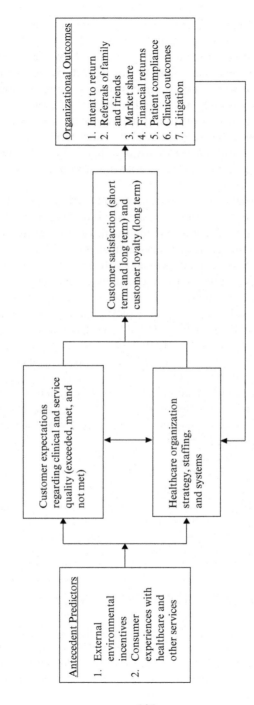

*Figure 5.1　The satisfaction–loyalty–outcomes chain*

101

Figure 5.1 also shows that customer expectations as well as the organization's strategies, staffing, and systems affect long-term customer satisfaction and long-term customer loyalty. Again, customer service expectations can be exceeded, met, or not met. If exceeded on a consistent basis, the result will be long-term customer satisfaction and customer loyalty. Previous research has found a strong empirical link between customer satisfaction and customer loyalty in the long term (Garman et al., 2004). If met, the result would be short-term customer satisfaction but not necessarily customer loyalty. If not met, the outcome will be short- and long-term customer dissatisfaction and no loyalty to the organization.

How can healthcare organizations create customer satisfaction that exceeds customer expectations? The answer is a combination of strategy, staffing, and systems which are aligned with each other and focused on providing high-quality customer service throughout the service experience for all customers. Specific management strategies for achieving such satisfaction and loyalty will be discussed throughout this chapter.

Once short-term and long-term customer service satisfaction and long-term customer loyalty have been achieved, a number of predictable organizational outcomes are likely (right box). These include: a customer's increased desire to return to the organization and refer others in the future; an increase in market share; improved financial returns; increased patient compliance with proposed regimens; improved clinical outcomes; and less legal litigation from both customers and regulatory agencies (Dube, 2003; Harkey and Vrakiu, 1992; Nelson et al., 1992; Pink and Murray, 2003). Conversely, low levels of satisfaction and loyalty are associated with negative outcomes for all variables.

More and more healthcare organizations now realize that patient loyalty and retention are major challenges (Bendapudi et al., 2006). A customer's intention to return and recommend are particularly associated with increased revenue, which positively impacts the organization's strategy, staffing, and systems (Evanschitsky and Wunderlich, 2006; Platonova et al., 2008). This process is continuous as more resources enhance the organization's environment, staffing, and delivery system.

## STRATEGY FOR CUSTOMER SERVICE

An organization's vision, mission, and values should precede development of a service strategy and should always include some focus on customer service. The vision articulates its aspirations or ideal state in the future. For a vision to gain strong support from stakeholders it must be clear, well communicated, and spell out the actual values of the organization. Examples are:

- World-class care in a community.
- Premier healthcare provider in the communities we serve.
- The best healthcare employer in our market.

The mission statement defines three organizational truths:

1. Why it exists (that is, to provide evidence-based and personalized health services to the local community).
2. What it does and how (that is, to provide quality, upscale, and cost-effective care to all service areas).
3. Who it serves (that is, to improve the health and wellness of our local community).

Where a vision represents an overarching goal, the mission identifies the purposes which underline these goals or how the organization will achieve its mission. A customer-focused mission states who the customers are, what they need, and how these needs will be met.

Results of one study of Canadian hospital mission statements found that the components most common among missions were purpose (76 percent), specific customers served (62 percent), one clear compelling goal (56 percent), values and beliefs (56 percent), products and services offered (52 percent), concern with satisfying customers (50 percent), and concern for employees (41 percent) (Barr, 1999). The survey also found that top management satisfaction with financial performance was significantly and positively correlated with a mission statement that contained statements concerning customers served, concern with satisfying customers, and products and services offered. Moreover, top management satisfaction with financial performance was highly correlated with management's satisfaction with how well the mission statement components were written: specific customers served, concern with satisfying customers, and concern for employees.

The service strategy is the detailed plan for meeting and exceeding the customers' expectations of a healthcare experience and is derived from the vision and missions statements. It should be based on informed judgment and should involve structured studies (environmental assessment) and consumer surveys. Led by the mission and vision, the service strategy guides the development of the service product, service setting, and service delivery system. The organization can craft the service product, its setting, and its delivery system based on the mission statement. For example, if the mission is to provide elective cosmetic surgery to an upscale, educated group in a specific geographic area, then the strategy should be to provide high-touch and high-tech services in an elegant environment.

The needs, opinions, preferences, and expectations of the targeted consumer group should be incorporated into the service strategy. Assessing the external and internal environment is not enough to gain insight into the key drivers of customer satisfaction. The organization must also ask its customers. Only customers can voice what they really think about the quality and value of a product or the role the organization's core competencies play in service delivery.

Service expert Len Berry (1999) suggests that an excellent service strategy commits the organization to four key factors: quality, value, service, and achievement. Press (2003) found that three key drivers were correlated with overall patient satisfaction based on data derived from 992 000 outpatients at 516 US outpatient facilities in 2001: "Staff sensitivity to your needs," "How well staff worked together to provide care," and "Response to concerns/complaints made during your visit." Each of these will be addressed in the chapter.

**Action Plans**

Action plans lay out the specific tactics of the service strategy; that is, how the organization will operate, what each department or employee group will be expected to do, and what time frame will be followed. Box 5.1 shows how a service strategy can be converted into action plans.

Action plans provide a road map and put the responsibility for achieving the service strategy into the hands of employees (managers and frontline staff alike). In this sense, everyone knows how their contribution helps the organization reach its mission, and everyone is held accountable for meeting and exceeding patient expectations. The most obvious and the biggest opportunity for delivering customer satisfaction is direct patient contact. Table 5.1 lists some behaviors to display during service delivery.

Previous research has found that when internal organizational factors (that is, mission, vision, values, and communication methods) are aligned with the strategic plan, employees feel higher levels of commitment and satisfaction (Ford et al., 2006). In turn, staff commitment and satisfaction lead to positive financial returns, competitive advantage, and customer satisfaction (Atkins et al., 1996; Fottler et al., 2006; Schneider et al., 1998). A study by Goldstein and Schweikhardt (2002) reveals that organizations that focus on the 19 dimensions of the Malcolm Baldrige National Quality Award provide high levels of customer service and satisfaction in the USA.

---

### BOX 5.1 CONVERTING SERVICE STRATEGY TO ACTION PLANS

**Service Strategy**

- Study similar organizations that excel in customer service and benchmark against them.
- Use a service audit to survey customers based on quality, value, service, and achievement. Develop a strategy to reduce the gaps between desired and actual customer service expectations.

**Action Plans**

- Use cross-functional teams to create tactical plans that focus all parts of the organization on customer service.
- Use cross-functional teams to integrate all of the tactical plans.
- Use various techniques, such as brainstorming, to create customer service initiatives in each tactical area.
- Carefully select one or two customer service priority areas for intense focus.
- Empower employees to meet customer expectations.
- Include customer outcome measures in assessment strategies.
- Ensure that key stakeholders support new strategic customer service initiatives through continued communication of benefits of change and risk of the status quo.
- Involve staff in identifying ways to implement strategy.
- Use social norms and opinion leaders to create support for strategic initiatives.
- Audit the alignment of customer service plans with mission, vision, values, strategies, staffing, and systems.

*Source:* Fottler et al. (2010, p.63).

---

*Table 5.1 Protocols and scripts for key drivers of patient satisfaction*

| Key Driver | Protocol (What you do) | Script (What you say) |
| --- | --- | --- |
| 1. Respect for privacy and dignity | Knock on patient's door and say patient's name | "Mrs.___? My name is ___. I am here to _____. Is this a good time?" |
| 2. Feel listened to | Ask if patient has any special needs or requests | "Is there anything else I can do for you?" |
| 3. Experience responsiveness to concerns and complaints | Ask if the previous concern (e.g., low room temperature) has been resolved | "Is the room temperature still uncomfortable? Can I get you another blanket?" |

*Source:* Scott (2001).

Sharp HealthCare is a recipient of the Baldrige Award and a proponent for aligning mission with all organizational components and activities.

**Alignment Audit**

An alignment audit should be conducted and structured as follows:

1. Define the goals of the mission in measurable terms (for example, scores on customer satisfaction surveys).
2. Identify key policies, procedures, practices, and communications that cue employee performance and behavior (for example, job descriptions).
3. Formulate questions that evaluate whether the mission is reflected in each key policy, procedure, practice, and communication.
4. Answer the questions honestly.
5. Develop a list of misaligned items for immediate or future corrections and improvements.
6. Compare the audit results (step 5) with the mission goals (step 1).

**Creating a Healing Environment**

One major component of the service strategy is the physical environment in which the customer experiences the services. Research has found that the physical environment of a healthcare organization can contribute to both positive- and negative-viewed outcomes (Ulrich et al., 2004). Examples include patient satisfaction and financial returns.

Nowadays, a patient's experience in the USA is very comprehensive, including comfort, convenience, safety, information, and even entertainment in the physical setting. (Fottler et al., 2010). Therefore, the environment in which healthcare is provided should not be forgotten. It is an integral component to customer service and vital to the healing process. It is not merely a background to the service experience; it is an important contributor to the patient's well-being, mood, attitude, and perception of value and quality. With this in mind, healthcare organizations need to pay close attention to the physical environment as an element of the patient's total healthcare experience.

The healing environment concept, defined as a place where the interaction between patient and staff produces positive health outcomes within the physician environment (Huisman et al., 2012), is based on evidence-based design (EBD). Ulrich (1984), who pioneered evidence-based design, conducted a study in which he exposed one group of recovering patients to a view of a brick wall, while another group of recovering patients were exposed to natural scenery. He found that the group who recovered with a view of natural scenery had shorter post-operative hospital stays, had fewer negative evaluative comments from nurses, took less moderately strong and strong medication, and had slightly lower scores for minor postsurgical complications. Since Ulrich's study, much attention has been focused on the design of healthcare facilities to promote a healing environment.

The redesign of a service setting needs to focus both on public spaces (that is, lobby, hallways, and waiting areas) and on private spaces (that is, patient and exam rooms) (Fottler et al., 2010). The Center for Health Design is a group of US healthcare and design professionals dedicated to advancing the idea that design could be used to improve patient outcomes in healthcare environments (Center for Health Design, n.d.). They recommend seven elements conducive to healing environments (Parrish Medical Center, n.d.). Table 5.2 expands on each of the seven elements.

The University of Minnesota Center for Spirituality and Healing (n.d.) states a simple guideline in the creation of a healing environment: look for ways to reduce stress in the environment. With this in mind, there are different ways in which to enhance a service setting. A family-friendly, home-like design, the use of animal therapy, the involvement of both patient and family in the healthcare process, and striving to meet the needs of employees are all strategies encompassed in the healing environment concept that impact the patient experience and their healthcare outcomes.

*Table 5.2   Elements conducive to a healing environment*

| Elements | Description |
| --- | --- |
| Nature | Large windows facing gardens and lush, green scenery |
| Color | Select color palettes that invokes a warm, home-like feeling |
| Health-building | Employ green initiatives and promote ecological sustainability by reducing wastes |
| Healthy lighting | Utilize and incorporate as much natural lighting as possible |
| Physical security | Clearly marked exit signs, have emergence plans in place |
| Wayfinding | Utilize signs that are clear and easy to understand |
| Cultural responsiveness | Provide training to clinicians and staff on respecting cultural differences. Employ bilingual employees. |

*Sources:*   Parrish Medical Center (n.d.) and Fottler et al. (2010).

For instance, in the nursing home world, striving to create a family-friendly, home-like design contributes to a patient's psychological well-being. The use and placement of home-like décor – using a desk instead of a nurse station, private bedrooms, indoor plants, pets, natural lighting – all contribute to a more family-friendly environment. However, family-friendly design is not limited to nursing homes. Other elements and trends adopted by new and renovated hospitals include the following:

- Positive distractions: indoor gardens, aquariums, display of artwork, large windows overlooking natural scenery.
- Natural light and control over lighting: allowing more natural light into public and private rooms and the ability to control lighting to create more ambient settings.
- Noise reduction: eliminating overhead paging and techniques to improve soundproofing by using carpet and sound-absorbing ceilings.
- Features to improve staff effectiveness: decentralized nursing stations to reduce time spent having to walk from the nursing station to a patient's room.
- Improved wayfinding: better signage through the use of color and images.
- Creating social spaces: social spaces that are inviting and comfortable, using small pieces of furniture and home-like décor (University of Minnesota Center for Spirituality and Healing, n.d.).

Adding pets to the environment is another way to enhance the mood and spirits of patients. As the saying goes "A dog is man's [or woman's] best friend." Is there a better way to recreate a home-like environment than having pets around? Pet therapy, which includes animal-assisted therapy and animal-assisted activities, has found its way into hospitals and nursing homes. Animal-assisted activities are more prevalent in nursing homes. Some nursing homes allow their residents' personal pets to visit, or utilize animal-assisted therapy groups (Veterinary Medicine and Biomedical Sciences, 2013).

The Mayo Clinic's Caring Canines program has over a dozen therapy dogs that make regular visits to various US hospital departments. Animal-assisted therapy can significantly reduce a patient's pain, anxiety, and depression and fatigue. Patient demographics and their use of animal-assisted therapy vary widely, ranging from small children to people suffering from chronic conditions and war veterans suffering from post-traumatic stress disorder. An example of the use of a therapy dog is with a five-year-old girl who was recovering from spinal surgery. The therapy dog helped the girl relearn how to walk. When the girl would take one

---

BOX 5.2   NEMOURS/ALFRED I. DUPONT HOSPITAL FOR
CHILDREN EXPANSION

Nemours/Alfred I. DuPont Hospital for Children in the USA is completing a massive expansion project that is slated to be completed in 2015. During the planning process, Nemours consulted with both parents and children to find out what they wished for most in a hospital. Inspired by the children and parents, Nemours is recreating its hospital to promote the physical, emotional, and spiritual healing of children. The expansion plans include private rooms with the following in every room: a view to the outside, refrigerators and closets, two TVs in every one – one for family and one for patient – and a shower. On every unit, there is a serenity room, a playroom, and a family room with a washer and dryer unit in each.

For their employees (that is care-givers), on every unit there is a conference room, and overnight sleeping accommodation for residents. Computers for patient documentation are available in every patient's room and care-givers have access to an award-winning electronic health record system. Other amenities as part of the expansion plan include: a five-story atrium with natural sunlight, a new dining area, serenity gardens, safety store, gelato shop, and a discovery zone for children. It is quite evident that Nemour's expansion plan strongly promotes a healing environment for the patient, family and employees (Nemours Children Health System, n.d.).

---

step forward, the dog would take one step backwards, causing her to step forward again (Mayo Clinic, n.d.).

In a healthcare setting, family plays a critical and important role in the healing process of a patient. As part of creating a healing environment, family members and patients need to be involved in their healthcare through building shared goals, sharing knowledge, and developing mutual respect among employees, patients and other informal caregivers (Fottler et al., 2010).

Lastly, in creating a healing environment it would be remiss if employees of the healthcare organizations were not considered as an integral part of the healing environment. Employees spend more time in the healthcare setting than anyone else. A well-designed, clean, well-lit, and safe work environment promotes employee satisfaction, which is highly correlated with patient satisfaction. More importantly, a healthcare setting that recognizes the needs and comfort of staff members will be reflected in their attitude and work ethic, which will be translated to their customer service when serving their patients. An example of this aproach is presented in Box 5.2.

**Environmental Strategies to Engender Customer Loyalty**

There are many trends and strategies through which to engender customer loyalty. One such way is to model a healthcare setting on that of a hotel. When people go on vacation, often the hotel that they stay at is selected based on the number and types of amenities offered at the hotel. Healthcare settings can emulate hotels and offer hotel-style amenities such as valet parking, spa services, free wireless internet, cable service, and a gym.

Climate change is real, although there are still some non-believers. Hospitals and other healthcare organizations alike are thinking of sustainability and green living when they construct new buildings or renovate existing structures. As for patients, sustainability is probably the last thing on their mind. However, more and more hospitals are adopting green initiatives and trying to reduce the exorbitant amount of waste that they generate. Hospitals do not operate in a closed system; they have a duty not only to the patient, but also to their ecological environment. As such, the creation of a healing environment not only needs to meet the needs of the patient, but it also has a responsibility in fostering ecological sustainability. Approximately 4 billion pounds (2 million tons) of waste are generated by hospitals in a single year. The majority of waste comes from unused medical supplies and equipment. Healthcare buildings come in second place as the most energy-intensive commercial sector buildings (Ananth and Kreisberg, 2011).

The Samueli Institute, an organization that fostered the Optimal Healing Environment (OHE), believes that healing has to occur within the larger landscape of the local environment and planetary health (Ananth and Kreisberg, 2011). Thus, ecological sustainability needs to be emphasized by all stakeholders, including the patient, clinicians, staff, and administrators. The Samueli Institute recommends a program in which to foster ecological sustainability that was developed by Health Care without Harm (HCWH) and the World Health Organization (WHO). There are seven elements to reducing a hospital's harmful footprint in our ecology:

1.  Energy efficiency: reduce energy consumption.
2.  Green building design: emphasis on reuse, reduce, recycle.
3.  Alternative energy generation: utilize renewable energy sources.
4.  Transportation: hybrid or electric vehicles.
5.  Food: support locally grown food.
6.  Waste: employ alternative methods to dispose of waste.
7.  Water: avoid bottled waste, and conserve.

# STAFFING FOR CUSTOMER SERVICE

The human resource department within a healthcare organization is tasked with an important responsibility: hiring competent, compassionate, experienced, and thoughtful employees to fill both clinical and administrative roles. Who is hired in the healthcare industry has a tremendous impact on a healthcare organization's ability to deliver patient-centered care. It begins with staff recruitment and selection based on both clinical and service competence, followed by staff training and, lastly, an emphasis on retention.

## Competency

Competency in healthcare is composed of four elements: knowledge, skills, behavior, and judgment (Howe, 2011). Competency applies to both administrative and clinical staff. Knowledge is required to perform one's job. Employees must learn skills to be successful in their position. Behavior defines one's ability to act according to the situations one has to deal with. And lastly, judgment is required when decisions need to be made with respect to patient care.

Cultural competence is defined as the ability to provide care to patients with diverse values, beliefs, and behaviors, including tailoring healthcare delivery to meet patients' social, cultural, and linguistic needs (Health Research and Educational Trust, 2013). As more and more emphasis is placed on patient-centered care in the US, a diverse staff composition is required to meet the needs of the diverse patient population served in the country. Furthermore, understanding diverse cultures helps to engage patients in their own healthcare.

Being a culturally competent healthcare organization benefits many stakeholders involved, including the patient, the community, clinicians, and the organization. Culturally competent organizations show a level of respect for their patients, thereby increasing trust. This also promotes the inclusion of all community members, while enhancing community involvement with their healthcare. Patients and family members also have a better sense of their health condition, which allows them to be more responsible in their healthcare (Health Research and Educational Trust, 2013).

Healthcare organizations that are culturally competent have been shown to reduce healthcare disparities, and also to reduce medical errors as patients and family members understand their healthcare. Moreover, culturally competent organizations have higher levels of efficiency, while being able to increase their market share and embrace a culture of strategies and ideas that are forward-thinking (Health Research and

Educational Trust, 2013). The Health Research and Educational Trust identifies three steps for an organization to become culturally competent:

1. Analyzing data and micro-targeting surveys to improve service for the local community.
2. Communicating survey findings to determine priorities.
3. Educating staff and aligning programming and resources to meet community needs (Health Research and Educational Trust, 2013).

It is important to analyze the demographics of a community to determine the composition of the local community population. Surveys can then be distributed to determine the needs of the community. Once the data is gathered and collected from the surveys, it is then necessary to analyze that data to determine the priorities for how the healthcare organization can best meet the needs of the community. Lastly, staff training and education on cultural competence is required to meet the cultural needs of the patients (Health Research and Educational Trust, 2013).

**Recruitment Process**

The recruitment process is critical to employing and hiring competent and diverse employees. A well-rounded staff depends on a healthcare organization's ability to adequately recruit and screen their candidates in order to best meet its needs. Organizations can choose to hire internal or external candidates. Hiring an internal candidate has its benefits and drawbacks. Internal candidates have an understanding of the organizational culture and are a known quantity within that organization. The internal candidate's strengths and weaknesses are well known. The drawback of hiring an internal candidate is the inability to inject new knowledge and experience from a previous position held.

External candidates can be a good fit for a healthcare organization that is looking for fresh ideas and new strategies. As much as a healthcare organization is looking for the perfect candidate to fill a vacancy, it is just as important for that healthcare organization to sell itself to the candidates. A highly qualified candidate will be sought after by multiple healthcare organizations. Therefore, it is important for an organization to market itself in a positive light to all candidates.

Some creative recruitment strategies for external candidates include a robust benefit package, university collaboration, a finder's fee, focus group and rehires. A successful recruitment effort is realized if there is a robust number of highly qualified and diverse applicants, a high retention rate of new hires, and a high percentage of those interviewed who are hired. Furthermore, increased customer satisfaction and a decrease in customer complaints is also demonstrative of successful recruitment.

**Selection and Screening Methods**

Once the recruitment of candidates is finished, the next step in the hiring process is to select and screen each candidate. Methods to utilize include the application form, an interview (phone or face-to-face), reference checks, and the use of social media. Every organization requires interested candidates to complete an application form for the position they are interested in. The application serves as a preliminary check on whether each candidate meets the minimum qualification of the position. Interviews will follow after the candidate meets the minimum requirements and then reference checks are completed if the candidate is the front-runner for the vacancy.

A newer method of selecting and screening applicants is through social media. LinkedIn is the world's largest professional network, with over 300 million members worldwide. LinkedIn is used by professionals to network and connect with others within their local community or worldwide. Most working professionals have a LinkedIn account. Scouring a candidate's social media profiles such as LinkedIn is a great way to ensure consistency and accuracy with what they have supplied on their application and resumé. Furthermore, LinkedIn offers a comprehensive window into a candidate's professional world that is extremely useful in the hiring process.

Should healthcare organizations choose to include social media as part of their hiring process, they do have to be careful with possible discrimination. Social media offers a wider lens through which to assess applicants than just looking at what is on paper, as the hiring personnel can assess the intangibles of an applicant. Therefore, a way to avoid possible discrimination is to utilize social media after you have interviewed a candidate (Bates, 2013).

Lastly, recent surveys have shown a disparate distribution of the types of users of social media such as LinkedIn. Reportedly, utilization by Latinos and blacks tends to be smaller as compared to the general US population. Therefore, it is important not to rely solely on social media, but to exercise all techniques in hiring to ensure a well-rounded and diverse group of employees to enhance patient-centered care at healthcare organizations (Bates, 2013).

## Leadership Development and Staff Training

Once the recruitment process is finished and the best candidate to fill the position has been selected, it is time to provide adequate training to enable staff members to do their jobs to the best of their abilities. Organizations need to emphasize leadership development and staff training. Even though leading is part of a chief executive officer's (CEO) daily responsibility, healthcare organizations still need to make leadership development a priority in their organization. In order to achieve excellence, organizations need to develop great leaders.

Staff training is another integral piece to ensuring excellent customer service to promote patient-centered care. Furthermore, if high-quality care is to be ensured, education and training are required to keep staff members knowledgeable. Effective training encompasses four elements: it is empowering, well-designed, interactive, and reoccurring. Staff members need to feel empowered to use the training they have acquired to make decisions in their workplace. If the training is not well designed, then it is useless. It will cause more harm than good, resulting in a drop in employee and organizational performance. Training is not always fun. So to engage staff members during their training, it must be made interactive. Make them a part of the training so that they are engaged, participating members. Lastly, training needs to be reoccurring. Organizational policies and continuous learning need to occur frequently, otherwise the knowledge gained will be lost.

## Emotional Intelligence

Many different operational strategies have been applied to the healthcare field from other industries such as Lean or Six Sigma. However, as emphasis is continually placed on patient-centered care, what role does emotional intelligence have in the healthcare field? Before trying to understand the role of emotional intelligence in the healthcare field, let us first define emotional intelligence. Emotional intelligence is defined as emotional and social abilities that enhance workplace performance. Emotional intelligence can be grouped into five core areas: self-awareness, self-regulation, self-motivation, social awareness, and social skills (Warren, 2013). Just as an intelligence quotient (IQ) score can be assessed, so can an emotional intelligence (emotional quotient, EQ) score. The areas of assessment to determine EQ include compassion, awareness, regulation, and social focus. EQ has shown to contribute positively to the physician–patient relationship, increased compassion, strengthened teamwork and communication, and increased overall physician and nurse satisfaction levels.

Of course, as with any skills, staff and clinicians need to be trained in EQ. The most successful patient-centered care training programs will combine service excellence principles with behavioral assessments that provide staff with useful insight into their own behavioral make-up, including healthcare-specific emotional intelligence (Warren, 2013).

**Retention**

Retention of highly qualified and reliable employees is a goal of all health-care organizations. Why would any healthcare organization want to go through the hiring process constantly? It is expensive and time-consuming to have to vet all of the candidates and then to have to provide training to the new hires. Strategies to retain employees include competitive compensation, autonomous jobs that can appeal to independent thinkers, being flexible, employing a highly effective supervisory team, and lastly, a ladder for career growth. Employees who are happy in their jobs will have a positive effect on their patients too. It is a win–win–win for the patients, the employee, and the organization.

**Motivation and Empowerment**

A highly motivated and empowered healthcare workforce is the difference between satisfied patients and dissatisfied patients. Therefore, in addition to a well-trained staff, employees need to be motivated and empowered in their workplace. Meeting the basic needs of employees, such as providing a robust benefit package, high salary, job security, and safe working environment, is important. However, truly successful organizations extend beyond meeting these basic requirements, such as making the workplace fun, fair, interesting, and important. Table 5.3 expands on each of these elements found within a truly employee-centered organization.

The Harvard Business Blog lists five criteria to motivate employees:

1. Employees need to understand the significance and relevance of their job responsibility as it pertains to the healthcare organization's mission.
2. Employees should be allowed the freedom to exercise their knowledge and expertise to make a difference in the organization.
3. Employers need to value empowerment and opportunities for growth.
4. Employees need to be given opportunities to collaborate and develop friendships with individuals from other disciplines or departments.
5. Employees require resources to provide support, and tools to be successful in their positions (Rimm, 2013).

*Table 5.3    Motivating mission-focused employees*

| Job is: | Because: |
| --- | --- |
| 1. Fun | A fun workplace makes employees happy. Happy employees are satisfied, which will translate to their work product and their customer service responsibilities. |
| 2. Fair | Equity is valued by employees. Employees want to know that their company values them and this can be shown through their compensation package, benefits, and professional development opportunities that are offered to those in similar positions within the organization as well as to those at external organizations. |
| 3. Interesting | Autonomy, empowerment, accountability are important. Additionally, the organization needs to promote a friendly and supportive work environment. |
| 4. Important | Positions need to be worthwhile; that is, valued by key stakeholders. |

*Source:*    Fottler et al. (2010).

Leadership and management teams are crucial in creating a happy, inviting, and interesting work environment. They need to intervene in employee conflict when necessary, and empower employees to encourage them to develop and grow themselves professionally See Box 5.3 for an example of a successful initiative.

## DELIVERY SYSTEMS FOR CUSTOMER SERVICE

Kumar et al. (2008) suggest that practitioners should focus on process management to positively impact upon service quality, rather than simply addressing service quality from a functional perspective. When problems arise, they need to review the service delivery system, which is a system of interconnected communication and structural processes which deliver value to the customers. Achieving patient satisfaction and avoiding problems in the healthcare experience can both be greatly affected by delivery system design (Prajogo, 2006). Every healthcare organization should invest time and energy in studying and planning the entire system to get it right. The total quality management (TQM) movement has taught organizational leaders two important lessons:

1. Everyone is responsible for delivering quality and monitoring the quality of the entire healthcare experience.

---

BOX 5.3   TEXAS HEALTH PRESBYTERIAN HOSPITAL
FLOWER MOUND NAMED #1 BEST PLACE
TO WORK IN HEALTHCARE BY MODERN
HEALTHCARE IN 2013

Texas Health Presbyterian Hospital Flower Mound, a mid-sized hospital that employs approximately 400 employees, was named the #1 Best Place to Work in Healthcare in the USA by Modern Healthcare in 2013. Areas which Modern Healthcare measures include leadership and planning, culture and communication, role satisfaction, working environment, relationship with supervisor, training and developing, pay and benefits, and overall satisfaction. All of these combined to determine the best mid-sized hospital to work for in 2013. This is a significant achievement for the hospital. The President of Texas Health Flower Mound, Spencer Turner, cited improved communication, competitive compensation, and employee recognition programs as contributing significantly to a working environment in which employees value and enjoy going to work every day. Furthermore, the hospital understands the needs of its physicians, nurses, and staff members and ensures that they have the resources and mindset to provide the absolute best medical care possible (Texas Health Presbyterian Hospital Flower Mound, 2013).

---

2.   When a service failure occurs, the system must first be checked for problems before blame is passed down to individual people; after all, even systems of high-performing service organizations fail from time to time.

In many cases system problems are blamed on employee deficiency even though the source of the problem may be the system itself. Although one person may end up being the cause of a service failure, the fault is frequently in the system and not in a person. Simply putting out one small fire (for example, "We are spending too much money on overtime") without thinking about the system can cause big problems elsewhere.

**Requisite System Components**

Any good delivery system must begin with careful planning, which is the first component. Years of experience in working with older people can give a new nursing home administrator a good head start in designing a comprehensive treatment, care, and recreation schedule. However, a careful analysis and detailing of every step in the entire service delivery process that provides comprehensive care and physical therapy for older people makes the difference between having it mostly right, and reaching the level of excellence that the very best service organizations deliver.

The second component is measuring for control. You cannot manage what you do not measure, and this is especially true of service delivery systems. Ideally, the measures should allow employees to monitor their own delivery effectiveness while simultaneously delivering the service. For example, if a nurse knows that the organizational standard for responding to a patient call is a maximum of three minutes, and a computerized device displays a running record of how many minutes it takes for the nurse to answer calls, she knows at all times where she stands in relation to the standard.

In addition to measuring employee performance, a good service delivery plan should include a way to measure how well the plan is being implemented at every step of the service delivery process, and how well the overall plan is succeeding. The measures should trigger an analysis of exceptions or variations from the plan and should quantify every critical part of the total healthcare experience. Patients usually know why they are satisfied or dissatisfied by the healthcare experience, whether the clinical outcome was successful or unsuccessful.

**Delivery System Design**

Service delivery system design is planning out the steps and processes in the entire system. At this stage, a detailed description of the steps involved is developed. Managers of benchmark service organizations start their planning by surveying their potential patients to determine the key drivers of the experience from the customer's perspective. Once those key drivers are identified, the delivery system can be designed to ensure that patients' expectations regarding those drivers are met or exceeded.

Four basic techniques – blueprinting, fishbone analysis, program evaluation and review technique/ critical path method (PERT/CPM), and simulation are commonly used to develop a detailed plan for delivering the healthcare experience. Managers can also use these techniques to focus on any aspect that patient feedback indicates is a problem area. These techniques are especially useful because they can readily incorporate the measurements necessary for control and analysis of problems that may appear in the system. Detailed discussion of these techniques, beyond the scope of this chapter, may be accessed elsewhere (Fottler et al., 2010).

Each technique has its own advantages, but all are premised on the idea that a detailed written plan leads to a better system for managing the people, organization, information, and production processes that deliver the total healthcare experience. If effort and care are devoted to the plan, failures should be minimized. If situations regularly get to the point where problem-solving and problem recovery techniques are necessary, some patients will inevitably become so dissatisfied that they will not choose to use the provider again, and the provider will lose market share.

**Communicating Systems**

Patient perspectives on customer service encompass many things. They evaluate customer service on their entire healthcare experience, including the healthcare environment, the competency and skill set of the clinicians and staff, the relationship with their physicians and nurses, and the communication between patient and their healthcare provider. With the advancement of healthcare technology and the emphasis on patient engagement, health information systems have become an invaluable tool with which to assist healthcare organizations in communicating with their patients.

The role of web-based technology has grown tremendously over the years. Healthcare organizations and healthcare providers use web-based tools to communicate frequently with their patients. Web-based technology is used by healthcare organizations and providers to advertise to patients, while patients utilize the internet for various purposes, including: to search for healthcare providers and hospitals; to access health-related information such as diseases, symptoms and types of treatments; and to shop for medical-related items.

Communication is essential in providing patient-centered care. Frequent communication has the ability to enhance the service environment, the service quality and the overall healthcare delivery system. The use of health information technology (HIT) only seeks to enhance communication. The value reaped from HIT includes: satisfaction amongst patients, doctors and staff members; improvement to treatments and clinical outcomes; the ability to gather and analyze data; prevention and patient education; and financial savings for the organization (HIMSS, 2014).

Patient portals are web-based and are a tool used by many hospitals, insurance companies and doctor's offices. They are a convenient and efficient way to communicate and share health information with patients. Patient portals supplement the management of a patient's healthcare. Some benefits of a patient portal include the ability to view test results and health documentation. Furthermore, patients can communicate with their physicians, knowing that it is a secure environment (Healthcase IT News, n.d.).

Other more advanced HIT tools used by hospitals include clinical decision support systems. These systems help to decrease adverse medical errors by using alerting systems to notify physicians of possible drug-to-drug interactions and other types of notifications. Furthermore, electronic submission of information reduces medical errors resulting from illegible handwriting (Handel et al., 2011).

### Service Failures

Service failures, like clinical errors, are inevitable. Many healthcare organizations do plan well for clinical problems, but they do not anticipate service problems with the same care. They incorrectly assume or hope that the service will be available as promised, the setting and delivery system will function as designed, and the staff will perform as they were trained – consistently, every time.

Despite the best-laid plans, service failure is a reality in all organizations. Complex organizations function as a system, with interdependent and tightly intertwined parts. One mistake in one part will affect the rest of the system, and the tighter the intertwining of these parts, the more susceptible the whole system is to disaster. The difference between an excellent and a poor service organization, however, is that the best one works hard not only to remedy failures, but also to prevent them from occurring at all. Service failures occur for two reasons: human error and system error.

Providers can fall short of a patient's expectations at any point in the healthcare experience. The product, setting, or delivery system may be inadequate or inappropriate, or the staff may perform or behave poorly.

### Evangelists and Avengers

According to Sherman and Sherman (1998), one "avenger" tells his unfortunate experience to at least 12 people. Each of those 12 then shares the story to five or more people. On average, an avenger has an audience of about 72 people. Furthermore, if eight avengers each spread the disappointing news to 12 others, each of whom in turn tells five of their associates, then 576 people hear the negative word of mouth that only eight patients actually experienced. A simpler calculation is this: each dissatisfied customer sends out, verbally or in writing, about 70 negative messages. "Evangelists" do not talk about their positive experience as widely as avengers do. Evangelists share their good stories to approximately six other people (Hart et al., 1990). In other words, if the number of highly satisfied customers equals the number of highly dissatisfied customers, the highly dissatisfied will send out more than 12 times the number of messages compared to the highly satisfied.

Unhappy patients react in one or a combination of three ways: never return, complain, and "bad-mouth" the organization. When a dissatisfied patient vows to never return, this is the worst customer reaction for an organization because it also means that the angry patient will tell others about the negative experience. In this situation, the organization loses not only the current business of this patient but also the future business of all the people the patient can influence. Service recovery should be especially focused on this group of unhappy customers.

The second option, to complain, is often encouraged by benchmark organizations. They view a complaint as an opportunity, not a challenge, because it gives the organization a chance to refine the system and make customers happy. Patients who complain, either verbally or in writing, allow employees and managers to fix the problem before the problem and the dissatisfaction are shared with others, resulting in widespread defections.

Complaining patients are less likely to defect to another provider and to bad-mouth the organization than those who do not express their dissatisfaction to the organization. Making sure no customer leaves unhappy is obviously advantageous to any organization. The best way to ensure this is to seek out and resolve patient complaints before they leave the hospital, clinic, or office.

If the negative experience is costly – financially and/or personally – the patient is more likely to spread the bad word. The greater the cost to the patient, the greater the motivation to tell. People who hear such negative stories will be discouraged from patronizing the same provider.

Angry customers (avengers) in the USA, who used to be limited to writing letters to corporate headquarters or the Better Business Bureau, putting up signs in their yard, or publicly referring to their car as a 'lemon' if it needed many repairs, now have a more powerful tool: the internet. For a minimal fee, anyone with internet access can create a website or a blog to tell the world about an offending company, and also invite others to share their stories of poor treatment. In this day of instant and global communication, a bad-mouther can spread the message to millions of people.

Word of mouth is important for several reasons. Friends, family, colleagues, and other associates tend to be more credible sources than impersonal testimonials (Lake, 2009). When a friend reports that a certain physician is cold and uncaring, you tend to weigh this information heavily in evaluating that physician. Personal accounts, either good or bad, from friends and family are also more vivid, more convincing, and more compelling than any paid commercial advertising.

Customer defection and negative word of mouth create an expensive problem for the organization. Over time, the loss of revenue from a patient who opts never to return, and from potential customers who listened to the unhappy patient's bad-mouthing, is tremendous. Because that dollar value is so high, hardly any effort to fix a service failure is too extreme. Results of previous research in healthcare and other industries indicated that the long-term cost of patient defection and negative word of mouth is usually much more than the expense of correcting a service failure immediately and appropriately (Fottler et al., 2010).

Berry (2009) argues that the organization should always apologize for service failures, but an apology alone is seldom sufficient. Three major strategies are available for dealing with service failures:

1. Proactive or preventive strategies for identifying problems before they happen; these strategies are built into the design of the service, employee training, and the delivery system.
2. Process strategies for monitoring the critical moments of the service delivery.
3. Outcome strategies for seeking out problems after the service experience has happened.

In their classic study, Hart et al. (1990) believe service recovery strategies should satisfy several criteria, as follows:

- Ensure that the problem is addressed in some positive way. Even if the situation is a total disaster, the recovery strategy should ensure that the patient's problem is addressed and, to the extent possible, fixed.
- Be communicated clearly to the employees charged with responding to patient dissatisfaction. Employees must know that the organization expects them to find and resolve patient problems as part of their job.
- Be easy for the patient to find and use, and be flexible enough to accommodate the different types of problems and the different expectations that patients have.
- Always recognize that because the patient defines the quality of the service experience, the patient also defines its problems and the adequacy of the recovery strategies.

The best recovery efforts are those that address the customer's problem. For example, suppose a patient tried to contact their physician by phone (as instructed) on a certain day and time, was put on hold, and ended up leaving a message asking the physician to return their call. If the return call was never made, a communications problem undoubtedly occurred, but the result for the patient is that the physician appears to be uncaring.

An appropriate recovery effort might be to provide the patient with the physician's personal cellphone number.

When severity is high and it is the organization's fault, the proper response is to go the extra mile in fixing the problem. The organization needs to bend over backward to apologize, communicate empathy and caring, and address the patient's problem, because it will take an outstanding recovery effort to overcome the patient's negative feeling. On the other hand, when the severity of failure is relatively mild and is not the fault of the organization, then it should be sufficient for organizational representatives to simply apologize and extend sympathy.

## MANAGERIAL IMPLICATIONS

Customer service excellence can be enhanced by the following strategies and tactics:

1. Start with the customer – both external patients and internal staff members – and determine the key drivers of their customer satisfaction.
2. Articulate a vision and strengthen the employees' ability to contribute more than the minimal requirements of any single job, which gives all staff a sense of value and worth in what they do.
3. Manage all three parts of the organization's service system – strategy, staffing, and systems – with the goal of exceeding customer expectations in order to build long-term satisfaction and loyalty.
4. Design a business strategy which focuses on achieving strategic goals related to customer service.
5. Build and continually reinforce a high-quality healing environment.
6. Build a strong customer service culture and sustain it with stories, deeds, and actions.
7. Organize, staff, train, and reward around the patient's needs, wants, and expectations.
8. Train all staff to think of the people in front of them as their guests.
9. Ensure that jobs are fun, fair, and interesting, to help employees provide superb experiences.
10. Keep in mind the strong relationship between highly satisfied employees and highly satisfied patients.
11. Incorporate customer satisfaction skills into employee training programs.
12. Never stop teaching; inspire everyone to keep learning.
13. Establish a standard of performance, measure it, and then manage it carefully.

14. Use information to improve strategy, staffing, and service elements identified by customers as deficient.
15. Link customer satisfaction scores to management and employee rewards and recognition.
16. Prevent every service problem you can; find every problem you cannot prevent; and fix every problem you find every time and, if possible, on the spot.

## REFERENCES

Ananth, S. and Kreisberg, J. (2011). Fostering ecological sustainability. *Explore*, 7(5): 332–333.
Arnst, C. (2007). The doctor will see you – in three months. *Business Week* (July 9/16): 100.
Atkins, P., Marshall, B.S., and Javalgi, R.G. (1996). Happy employees lead to loyal patients. *Journal of Healthcare Marketing*, 16(4): 14–23.
Barr, C.K. (1999). Mission statement content and hospital performance in the Canadian not for-profit health care sector. *Health Care Management Review*, 24(3): 18–29.
Bates, S. (2013). Use social media smartly when hiring. Society for Human Resource Management. Retrieved from http://www.shrm.org/hrdisciplines/technology/articles/pages/be-smart-when-using-social-media-for-hiring.aspx (accessed 16 May 2014).
Bendapudi, N., Berry, L., Frey, K., Parish, J., and Rayburn, W. (2006). Patients' perspectives on ideal physician behaviors. *Mayo Clinic Proceedings*, 81(3): 338–44.
Berry, L.L. (1999). *Discovering the soul of service*. New York: Free Press.
Berry, L.L. (2009). Competing with quality service in good times and bad. *Business Horizons*, 52(4): 309–317.
Blair, J. and Fottler, M. (1990). *Challenges in health care management: strategic perspectives for managing stakeholders*. San Francisco, CA: Jossey-Bass.
Center for Health Design (n.d.). About. Retrieved from https://www.healthdesign.org/chd/about (accessed 3 May 2014).
Dube, L. (2003). What's missing from patient-centered care? *Marketing Health Services*, 23(1): 30–38.
Evanschitzky, H. and Wunderlich, M. (2006). An examination of moderator effects in the fourstage loyalty model. *Journal of Service Research*, 8(4): 330–345.
Ford, R.C. and Bowen, D.P. (2008). A service-dominant logic for management education: It's time. *Academy of Management Learning and Education*, 7(2): 224–243.
Ford, R.C., Sivo, S.A., Fottler, M.D., Dickson, D., Bradley, K., and Johnson, L. (2006). Aligning internal organizational factors with a service excellence mission: An exploratory study in healthcare. *Health Care Management Review*, 31(4): 259–269.
Fottler, M.D., D. Dickson, R.C. Ford, K. Bradley, and L. Johnson (2006). Comparing hospital staff and patient perceptions of customer service: A pilot survey utilizing survey and focus group data. *Health Services Management Research*, 19(1): 52–66.
Fottler, M.D., Ford, R.C., and Heaton, C.P. (2010). *Achieving service excellence: Strategies for healthcare*. Chicago, IL: Health Administration Press.
Fottler, M. and Malvey, D. (2010). Human resources implications of low-cost disruptive innovation in healthcare: The case of retail clinics. *Advances in Healthcare Management*, 9: 137–162.
Garman, A.N., Garcia, J., and Hargreaves, M. (2004). Patient satisfaction as a predictor of return-to-provider behavior: Analysis and assessment of financial implications. *Quality Management in Healthcare*, 13(1): 75–80.
Goldstein, S.M. and Schweikhart, S.B. (2002). Empirical support for the Baldridge Award framework in US hospitals. *Health Care Management Review*, 27(1): 62–75.
Goodman, J.C. (2007). Perverse incentives in healthcare. *Wall Street Journal*, April 5: A13.

Handel, D.A., Wears, R.L., Nathanson, L.A., and Fines, J.W. (2011). Using information technology to improve the quality and safety of emergency care. *Academy of Emergency Medicine*, 18: 41–51.

Harkey, J. and Vraciu, R. (1992). Quality of health care and financial performance: Is there a link? *Health Care Management Review*, 17(4): 55–63.

Hart, C., Heskett, J., and Sasser, W. (1990). The profitable art of service recovery. *Harvard Business Review*, 68(4): 148–156.

Healthcare IT News (n.d.). Patient portals. Retrieved from http://www.healthcareitnews.com/directory/patient-portals (accessed 12 April 2014).

Health Research and Educational Trust (2013). *Becoming a culturally competent health care organization*. Chicago, IL: Health Research and Educational Trust.

HIMSS (2014). Value STEPS. Retrieved from http://www.himss.org/ResourceLibrary/ValueSuite.aspx#/steps- (accessed 4 May 2014).

Howe, L. (2011). What is competence in healthcare? HealthStream. Retrieved from http://blog.healthstream.com/blog/bid/77623/What-is-Competence-in-Healthcare-Part-I (accessed 23 May 2014).

Huisman, E., Morales, E., van Hoof, J., and Kort, H. (2012). Healing environment: A systematic review of the meaning of physical environmental factors on patient, family, carers (PFC) and staff outcomes. *Journal of Building and Environment*, 58: 70–80.

Kumar, V., Smart, P.A., Maddern, H., and Maull, R.S. (2008). Alternative perspectives on service quality and customer satisfaction: The role of BPM. *International Journal of Service Industry Management*, 19(2): 176–187.

Lake, L. (2009). Why word of mouth marketing? Retrieved from http://marketing.about.com/b/2009/08/24/why-word-of-mouth-marketing.htm. (accessed 13 May 2014).

Mayo Clinic (n.d.). Consumer Health. Retrieved from http://www.mayoclinic.org/healthy-living/consumer-health/in-depth/pet-therapy/art-20046342?pg=2 (accessed 7 May 2014).

Nelson, E.C., Rust, R.T., Zahorok, A., Rose, R.L., Batalden, P., and Siemanski, B.A. (1992). Do patient perceptions of quality relate to hospital financial performance? *Journal of Health Care Marketing*, 12(4): 6–13.

Nemours Children Health System (n.d.). Expansion: Building a healthier future for children. Retrieved from http://www.nemours.org/locations/nemoursdupont/expansion.html.

Parrish Medical Center (n.d). Healing environments. Retrieved from http://www.parrishmed.com/patients/healing-environment/default.aspx (accessed 12 April 2014).

Pho, Y. (2008). The value of volunteer labor and the factors influencing participation: Evidence for the United States from 2002–2005. *Review of Income and Wealth*, 54(2): 220–236.

Pink, G.H. and Murray, M.A. (2003). Hospital efficiency and patient satisfaction. *Health Services Management Research*, 16(1): 24–39.

Platonova, E.A., Kennedy, K.N., and Shewchuk, R.M. (2008). Understanding patient satisfaction, trust and loyalty to primary care physicians. *Medical Care Research and Review*, 65(6): 696–712.

Prajogo, D. (2006). The implementation of operations management techniques in service organizations. *International Journal of Operations and Production*, 26(12): 1374–1390.

Press, I. (2003). Patient satisfaction with the outpatient experience. *Healthcare Executive*, 18(3): 94–95.

Rimm, A. (2013). Tips for energizing your exhausted employees. Retrieved from http://blogs.hbr.org/2013/11/tips-for-energizing-your-exhausted-employees/ (accessed 23 May 2014).

Schneider, B., White, S., and Paul, M. (1998). Linking service climate and customer perceptions of service quality. *Journal of Applied Psychology*, 83(2): 150–163.

Scott, G. (2001). Accountability for service excellence. *Journal of Healthcare Management*, 46(3): 152–155.

Sherman, S.G. and Sherman, V.C. (1998). *Total Customer Satisfaction: A Comprehensive Approach For Health Care Providers*. San Francisco, CA: Jossey-Bass.

Studer, Q. (2008). *Results That Last*. Hoboken, NJ: John Wiley & Sons.

Texas Health Presbyterian Hospital Flower Mound (2013). Texas Health Presbyterian

Hospital Flower Mound named #1 Best Place to Work in Healthcare by Modern
Healthcare. Retrieved from http://www.texashealthflowermound.com/news/texas-health-
presbyterian-hospital-flowermound-named-1-place-work-healthcare-modern-healthcare/
(accessed 27 April 2014).

Ulrich, R.S., Zimring, J.A., Quan, X., and Choudhary, R. (2004). The role of the physical
environment in the hospital of the 21st century: A once-in-a-lifetime opportunity. Center
for Health Design. Retrieved from www.rwjf.org/files/publications/other/roleofthe physi-
calenvironment.pdf.

University of Minnesota Center for Spirituality and Healing (n.d.). What can i do to
create a healing environment?. Retrieved from http://www.takingcharge.csh.umn.edu/
explore-healing-practices/healing-environment/what-can-i-do-create-healing-environment
(accessed 4 May 2014).

Veterinary Medicine and Biomedical Sciences (2013). Pet therapy in nursing homes: Assisted
living may never be the same. http://vetmed.tamu.edu/news/pet-talk/pet-therapy-in-
nursing-homes-assisted-living-may-never-be-the-same#.U5Cj4bU_vL8 (accessed 3 May
2014).

Warren, B. (2013). Healthcare emotional intelligence: Its role in patient outcomes and
organizational success. *Becker's Hospital Review*. Retrieved from http://www.beckershos
pitalreview.com /hospital-management-administration/healthcare emotional-intelligence-
its-role-in-patient-outcomes-and-organizational-success.html (accessed 21 April 2014).

# 6. Human resources management
*Myron D. Fottler, Donna Malvey, John C. Hyde and Clyde Deschamp*

## INTRODUCTION

Like most other service industries, the healthcare industry is very labor-intensive. One reason for healthcare's reliance on an extensive workforce is that it is not possible to produce a "service" and then store it for later consumption. Human resources are all of the people who currently contribute to doing the work of the organization, as well as those who might contribute in the future and those who have contributed in the recent past.

The intensive use of labor and the variability in human resources in professional practice require that the attention of leaders in the industry be directed toward managing the performance of the persons involved in the delivery of these services. The effective management of people requires that healthcare executives understand the factors that influence individual and group performance of staff. Such factors include not only the traditional human resources management (HRM) activities (that is, recruitment and selection, training and development, appraisal, compensation, and employee relations) but also aligning these functions with strategy and other organizational aspects that impinge on human resources (HR) activities.

Strategic human resources management (SHRM) is the process of formulating HR strategies and implementation tactics which are aligned with and reinforce the organization's business strategy. It requires development of a comprehensive set of managerial activities and tasks related to developing and maintaining a qualified workforce. This workforce, in turn, should then contribute to organizational effectiveness, defined by the organization's strategic goals. SHRM occurs in a complex and dynamic milieu of forces within the organizational context. A significant trend that began within the last decade is for HR managers to adopt a strategic perspective of their job and to recognize critical linkages between organizational strategy and HR strategies.

Detailed discussions on how to manage each of the human resources functions are discussed elsewhere (Fried and Fottler, 2015). Rather, the present chapter will focus on the contemporary human resource challenges in healthcare:

- Role of HR in strategic management.
- Legal impacts on HR management.
- Managing with organized labor.
- Integration of clinical professionals.
- Work–family conflict.

Staffing the organization, designing jobs, building teams, developing employee skills, identifying approaches to improve performance and customer service, and rewarding employee success are as relevant to line managers as they are to HR managers. A successful healthcare executive needs to understand human behavior, work with employees effectively, and be knowledgeable about the numerous systems and practices available to put together a skilled and motivated workforce. The executive also has to be aware of economic, technological, social, and legal issues that facilitate or constrain efforts to attain strategic objectives.

# ROLE OF HR IN STRATEGIC MANAGEMENT

### Competitive Advantage

Healthcare organizations can gain a competitive advantage over competitors by effectively managing their human resources. This competitive advantage may include cost leadership (that is, being a low-cost provider) and product differentiation (that is, having higher levels of clinical and/or service quality). A 1994 study examined the HRM practices and productivity levels of 968 organizations across 35 industries in the United States (Huselid, 1994). The effectiveness of each organization's HRM practices was rated based on the presence of such benefits as incentive plans, employee grievance systems, formal performance appraisal systems, and employee participation in decision-making. The study found that organizations with high HRM effectiveness ratings clearly outperformed those with low HRM rankings. A similar study of 293 publicly held companies in the USA reported that productivity was highly correlated with effective HRM practices (Huselid et al., 1997).

Several more recent studies have also shown that effective management of human resources can increase profitability, annual sales per employee, productivity, market value, and growth and earnings per share (Messersmith and Guthrie, 2010). In these studies, a survey was used to study the sophistication of the organization's HR practices and responses created a score from 0 to 100, where high scores represented practices which were "state of the art." Performance was measured using accounting financial data. Results indicate that organizations with better HR practices experienced greater increases in financial performance relative to others (Becker et al., 2001). In addition, a survey of 200 chief financial officers (CFOs) revealed that 92 percent believed that managing employees effectively also improves customer satisfaction (Mayer et al., 2009). Customers also report that they are also more satisfied when the climate of the organization is more positive, employees generally get along well, and staff turnover is low (Nishii et al., 2008).

Table 6.1 summarizes HRM practices which appear to enhance the effectiveness and outcomes of organizations. These practices seem to be present in organizations that are effective in managing their human resources, and they recur repeatedly in studies of high-performing organizations. In addition, these themes are interrelated and mutually reinforcing; it is difficult to achieve positive results by implementing just one practice on its own.

While these HR practices generally have a positive impact on organizational performance, their relative effectiveness may also vary depending on the alignment (or lack thereof) of these practices with one another, and with the organization's mission, values, culture, strategies, goals and objectives (Ford et al., 2006). These HRM practices may vary in their impact on various types of healthcare organizations depending upon how well each one is aligned with and reinforces the others as well as how well it is aligned with various aspects with the overall business strategy.

No HR practice, even those identified in Table 6.1, are "good" in and of themselves. Rather, their impact is always dependent upon how well the process fits with the factors noted above. Fit, or alignment, leads to better performance, while lack of it creates inconsistencies (Ulrich et al., 2008). In general, however, organizational performance is enhanced when HR practices are aligned with business strategy, attuned to the external environment, and when they reinforce one another, enabling the organization to capitalize on its distinctive capabilities. Even though it is extremely difficult to prove a causal relationship between HR practices and organizational performance, it is reasonable for healthcare organizations to consider implementation of these practices associated with high-performing organizations.

The bad news about achieving competitive advantage through HRM is that it inevitably takes time to accomplish (Pfeffer, 1998). The good news is that, once achieved, this type of competitive advantage is likely to be more enduring and more difficult for competitors to duplicate. Measurement is a crucial component for implementing these HR practices. Failure to evaluate the impact of HR practices dooms these practices to second-class status, neglect, and potential breakdown. What gets

*Table 6.1   HRM effective practices for healthcare organizations*

| Essential HR function | Recommended practices |
| --- | --- |
| HR planning and job analysis | Encourage employee involvement so there is strong "buy-in" of HR practices and managerial initiatives. |
| | Encourage teamwork so employees are more willing to collaborate. |
| | Utilize self-managed teams and decentralization as basic elements of organization design in order to minimize management layers. |
| | Develop strategies to enhance employee work–life balance. |
| Staffing | Be proactive in identifying and attracting talent. |
| | In selecting new employees, use additional criteria beyond basic skills (i.e., attitudes, customer focus, and cultural fit). |
| | Provide opportunities for employee growth so employees are stretched to enhance all of their skills. |
| Training and organizational development | Invest in training and organizational programs to enhance employee skills related to organizational goals. |
| | Provide employees with future career opportunities by giving promotional priority to internal candidates. |
| | Include customer service in new employee onboarding and skill development. |
| Performance management and compensation | Recognize employees by providing monetary and non-monetary rewards. |
| | Offer high compensation contingent on organizational performance in order to reduce employee turnover and increase attraction to high-quality employees. |
| | Reduce status distinction and barriers such as dress, language, office arrangement, parking, and wage differentials. |
| | Base individual and team compensation on goal-oriented results. |
| Employee rights | Communicate effectively with employees to keep them informed concerning major issues and initiatives. |
| | Share financial, salary, and performance information to develop a high-trust organization. |
| | Provide employment security for employees who perform well so they are not laid off because of economic downturns or strategic errors by senior management. |

*Sources:*   Pfeffer (1995, 1998), Wright et al. (2005), Chuang and Liao (2010), Gomez-Mejia and Balkin (2011).

measured gets managed. Feedback from such measurement is essential in further development of or changes to practices, as well as in monitoring how each practice is achieving its intended purpose.

Why do the above practices have such a positive impact? The answer is that the strategic approach to human resource management has many benefits which improve various organizational outcomes, such as higher levels of employee competence, motivation, attitudes, commitment, retention, and satisfaction. In turn, these result in positive organizational outcomes such as improved financial performance, legal compliance, attainment of other strategic goals, and satisfaction of key stakeholders. Together, attainment of these organizational objectives enhance the organization's competitive advantage.

**The SHRM Model**

A strategic approach to human resources management is a process which includes the following (Fottler et al. 1990):

- Assessing the organization's environment and mission.
- Formulating the organization's business strategy.
- Identifying HR requirements based on the business strategy.
- Comparing the current HR inventory – in terms of numbers, characteristics, and practices – with future strategic requirements.
- Developing an HR strategy based on the differences between the current inventory and future requirements.
- Implementing the appropriate HR practices to reinforce the business strategy and to attain competitive advantage.

The implementation of an organization strategy through HR has become more and more dependent upon technology in recent years. Today in the USA, most Americans use mobile phones, which have thousands of applications that make their phones "smart." Healthcare organizations have quickly realized that HR applications can help them manage their employees more effectively by increasing operational efficiency and meeting expectations of different generations in the workforce. Mobile devices make it easier to deliver a variety of services, provide information to job applicants, offer training modules, manage interview skills, and coordinate work arrangements (Rafter, 2010).

When HR is viewed as a strategic partner, talking about the single best way to do anything makes no sense. Instead, the organization must adopt HR practices that are consistent with its strategic mission, goals, and objectives. In addition, all healthcare executives are HR managers.

Proper management of employees entails having effective supervisors and line managers throughout the organization. However, in order to develop and implement HR practices which are aligned with the organization's business strategy, HR needs a "seat at the table" when strategy is being developed (Fottler et al., 2006). Such is not always the case for healthcare organizations.

**The HR Scorecard**

The "HR scorecard" is one method to measure the contribution of HR. This tool is basically a modified version of the balanced scorecard (BSC), which is a measurement and control system that looks at a mix of quantitative and qualitative factors to evaluate organizational performance (Kaplan and Norton, 1996). The "balance" reflects the need for short-term and long-term objectives, financial and non-financial metrics, lagging and leading indicators, and internal and external performance perspectives. A book entitled *The Workforce Scorecard* (Huselid et al., 2005) extends research on the BSC to maximize workforce potential. The authors show that traditional financial performance measures are "lagging" performance indicators, which can be predicted by the way organizations manage their human resources. HR practices are the "leading" indicators, predicting subsequent financial performance.

The Mayo Clinic in the USA has developed its own HR balanced scorecard that allows the HR function to become more involved in the organization's strategic planning (Fottler et al., 2006). Based on the assumption "what gets measured gets managed," Mayo's HR balanced scorecard measures and monitors a large number of input and output HR indicators that are aligned with the organization's mission and strategic goals. This HR scorecard measures financial (that is, staff retention savings), customer (that is, employee retention, patient satisfaction), internal (that is, time to fill positions), and learning (that is, staff satisfaction, perceived training participation) areas.

**A Strategic Perspective on Human Resources**

US healthcare executives are now just beginning to demand that HR departments go beyond clerical functions (that is, payroll) and provide detailed forecasts of future HR needs, benefits, and costs over longer time periods (Becker and Huselid, 2006). They want to use new ways to acquire and utilize staff, measure their effectiveness, enter new markets, and manage crises.

Managers at all levels are becoming increasingly aware that critical sources of competitive advantage include appropriate systems for attracting, motivating, and managing the organization's human resources. Adopting a strategic view of human resources involves considering employees as human "assets" and developing appropriate policies and programs to increase the value of these assets to the organization and the marketplace. Effective organizations realize that their employees have value, much as the organization's physical and capital assets have value.

Viewing human resources from an investment perspective, rather than as variable costs of production, allows the organization to determine how best to invest in its people. This leads to a dilemma. An organization that does not invest in its employees may be less attractive to both current and prospective employees, which causes inefficiency and weakens the organization's competitive position. However, an organization that does invest in its people needs to ensure that these investments are not lost. Consequently, an organization needs to develop strategies to ensure that its employees stay on long enough so that it can realize an acceptable return on its investment in employee skills and knowledge.

Not all organizations realize that human assets can be strategically managed from an investment perspective. Management may or may not have an appreciation of the value of the organization's human assets relative to its other assets such as brand names, distribution channels, real estate, and facilities and equipment. Organizations may be characterized as human resources-oriented or not, based on their answers to the following questions:

- Does the organization see its people as central to its missions and strategy?
- Do the organization's mission statement and strategy objectives mention or espouse the value of human assets?
- Does the organization's management philosophy encourage the development of any strategy that prevents the depreciation of its human assets, or does the organization view its human assets as a cost to be minimized?

Often, an HR investment perspective is not adopted because it involves making a longer-term commitment to employees. Because employees can leave and most organizations are infused with short-term measures of performance, investments in human assets are often ignored. Organizations that are performing well may feel no need to change their HR strategies. Those that are not doing as well usually need a quick fix to turn things around, and therefore ignore longer-term investments in people. However, although investment in human resources does not yield immediate results, it yields positive outcomes that are likely to last longer and are more difficult to duplicate by competitors.

## LEGAL IMPACTS OF HUMAN RESOURCES MANAGEMENT

Issues of legal compliance and fairness pervade every area of HR in the USA. The legal framework consists of legislation, regulation, and court decisions. None of these are static and continual change in all three is the norm. Moreover, cultural change in society results in reinterpretation of many of these laws over time.

All three branches of US government have passed and expanded legal legislation and court decisions. However, federal statutes are the major foundation of the legal environment. State and local governments also enact and enforce laws which vary widely across the country: courts impact these laws by ruling in specific cases which often appealed up to the Supreme Court. Finally, Executive Orders are often issued by the President to guide government departments and manage their functions. Significant human resources legislation is summarized in Table 6.2.

As society's concerns change, so do the legal rights of employers and employees. Many years ago, US employers could discriminate against ethnicity and female employees. However, recent developments found these practices unethical. Federal government also issued regulations requiring government agencies and federal regulatory bodies to work at correcting the past results of discrimination. Such laws and regulations reflect societal values, are valued in courts of law, and balance the right of employers, employees, and other stakeholders. However, all such attempts are always imperfect.

Legal constraints on HR practices have become increasingly more complex due to new employment laws and recent court decisions which interpret existing laws. Such changes have made HR decisions more difficult and risky, thereby increasing the cost of poor decisions. The dynamism of the legal environment means healthcare executives must seek the advice of HR specialists and lawyers who add value to management decisions due to their expertise in employment law and regulations. However, executives should not feel as though they cannot make any decisions without legal counsel, and it would be a mistake to make legal considerations so important that they end up making poor business decisions.

*Table 6.2   Significant human resource legislation in the United States*

| Law | Year enacted | Description |
|---|---|---|
| Social Security Act | 1935 | Payroll tax to fund retirement benefits, disability, and unemployment insurance |
| Fair Labor Standards Act | 1938 | Established minimum wage and overtime pay |
| Equal Pay Act | 1963 | Prohibits unequal pay for the same job |
| Title VII of Civil Rights Act | 1964 | Prohibits employment decisions based on race, color, religion, sex, and national origin |
| Age Discrimination in Employment Act | 1967 | Prohibits employment decisions based on age when person is 40 or older |
| Pregnancy Discrimination Act | 1978 | Prohibits employers from discriminating against pregnant women |
| Drug-Free Workplace Act | 1988 | Covered employers must implement certain policies to restrict employee drug use |
| Americans with Disabilities Act (ADA) | 1990 | Prohibits discrimination based on disability |
| Family and Medical Leave Act | 1993 | Employers must provide unpaid leave for childbirth, adoption, illness |
| Patient Protection and Affordable Care Act | 2010 | Extends healthcare coverage to more people and makes it more affordable |

**Importance of the Legal Environment**

Compliance with the law is the right thing to do. In some cases, managers may disagree on specific applications of some of the laws, even though the goal of the laws is to mandate good management practices. However, violating the laws can result in financial liabilities: typical court awards to US victims of age, race, sex, or disability discrimination range from $50000 to $300000 and can actually be much larger.

Healthcare organizations may also face a public relations nightmare when discrimination charges are publicized. If managers make poor decisions on how to manage people, HR may not always be able to resolve the situation. If a manager discriminates on the basis of gender, age, or race, the HR may not be able to fix the problem before it has exploded. Moreover, a lack of transparency in hiring new employees may result in poor clinical or service quality when an applicant applies for a job and a previous employer refuses to provide a valid reference. This often occurs when a legal department warns managers about sharing any information about a former employee because of fear of a defamation lawsuit. The result is that bad employees are passed from healthcare organization to healthcare organization, doing damage to each one which ranges from murder to theft to customer dissatisfaction (Malvey et al., 2013).

Several challenges confront healthcare managers trying to comply with HR law. These include the legal dynamic landscape, complexity of regulations, conflicting strategies for fair employment, and unintended consequences. Not only do US courtroom and Supreme Court decisions change over time, but interpretations of regulations and legislations also change so there is room for different interpretations.

For example, in the USA sexual harassment regulations were adopted by the Equal Employment Opportunity Commission (EEOC) and accepted by the Supreme Court in 1986. Subsequently, employers, lawyers, and judges have been attempting to figure out what exactly they mean and require. Since opinions vary widely, different courts have made different decisions on what constitutes sexual harassment. Unless and until Congress clarifies sexual harassment laws or the Supreme Court makes more rulings, current managers will need to do everything possible to minimize both the perception and the reality of such harassment.

HR law in the USA is very complex and is accompanied by a set of regulations that is typically quite lengthy. The Americans with Disabilities Act (1990) is spelt out in a technical manual that indicates as many as 1000 different disabilities affecting Americans. It is very difficult for an expert in HR law, much less a non-lawyer, to understand all the implications of this law. However, in the vast majority of situations, healthcare managers should understand the basic intentions of HR laws without too much difficulty and obtain working knowledge they need to comply with these laws.

One of the major debates in HR law is how to obtain fair employment (a situation in which employment decisions are not affected by illegal discrimination). One strategy to reach this goal is for employment decisions to be made without regard to an individual's personal characteristics. A second strategy, affirmative action, aims to accomplish the goal by urging employers to hire individuals from groups which were discriminated against in the past. Obviously there is a conflict between these two strategies. While the battle for these competing strategies is being played out in society, the main legal doctrine has been made in the Supreme Court.

Based upon a series of Supreme Court decisions, the following conclusions seem warranted:

- Affirmative action strategy has been upheld and employers have been permitted to make employment decisions partly on a person's age, sex, race, and other characteristics.

- The employment decision cannot be made solely on the basis of these characteristics.
- Affirmative action is not permitted during lay-offs.

It is very common for a law, regulation, or employer policy to have numerous unanticipated consequences. The challenge for managers is anticipating the intended and unintended consequences of law. Affirmative action programs may be perceived, or actually do, only benefit women and minorities while lowering opportunities for men and non-minorities. The result is resentment and hostility at employer-initiated affirmative action programs (Amoroso et al., 2010). A number of Supreme Court cases have addressed this issue, with very close votes, including 5:4 decisions. The "bottom line" now seems to be that employers should emphasize the external recruitment and internal development of better-qualified minorities and female employees. Employment decisions should also be based on legitimate criteria so that only qualified applicants are hired or promoted (Liptak, 2009).

### Avoiding Legal Pitfalls

Employers can avoid many legal pitfalls associated with HR laws by engaging in sound management practices. Among the most important of these practices are training supervisors in the basics of HR law, establishing an employee complaint resolution system, documenting decisions, communicating honestly with employees, and asking job applicants for only information relevant to the particular job. As Chief Justice of the US Supreme Court, John Roberts, once said, "the way to end discrimination is to stop discriminating."

# MANAGING WITH ORGANIZED LABOR

### Overview

Managing with organized labor is challenging. Even though unionism in the USA has been declining nationally for decades, the relatively unorganized healthcare workforce has continued to grow and as such has become a serious target for unions (Malvey, 2010a). The labor relations process occurs when management (as the representative for the employer) and the union (as the exclusive bargaining representative for the employees) jointly determine and administer the rules of the workplace. A union is an organization formed by employees for the purpose of acting as a single unit when dealing with management about workplace issues, hence the term "organized labor."

Unions are not present in every organization because employees must authorize a union to represent them. Unions typically are viewed as threats by management because they interfere with management's ability to make and implement decisions. Once a union is present, management may no longer unilaterally make decisions about the terms and conditions of work. Instead, management must negotiate these decisions with the union. Similarly, employees may no longer communicate directly with management about work issues but instead must go through the union. Thus, the union functions as a middleman, which is relatively expensive to maintain for both parties. Employees pay union dues, and management incurs additional costs for such things as contract negotiations and any increases in salaries and benefits negotiated by the union (Freeman and Medoff, 1984).

Labor costs generally account for 70 percent to 80 percent of expenditures; consequently, controlling labor costs is critically important. A minor wage or benefit increase negotiated by the union will result in a significant increase in total operating costs for the organization. Subsequently, healthcare executives have a strong incentive to keep unions out of the organization (Scott and Seers, 1996). But doing so is challenging, and usually begins with management implementing a positive employee relationship program that incentivizes the employee to be an activist for the healthcare organization rather than for a union. However, given the trends of unionization in healthcare, managers are increasingly forced to work with unions (Malvey, 2010a).

The healthcare workforce comprises an estimated 16.4 million workers and represents one of the largest pools of unorganized workers in the United States and a prime target for union organizers. Only 7.2 percent of the healthcare workforce was affiliated with union membership in 2013 (Bureau of Labor Statistics, 2014). One-third of the projected job growth from 2012–2022 will occur in the healthcare field (Bureau of Labor Statistics, 2013).

In an attempt to protect workers' rights to unionize, the US Congress passed the National Labor Relations Act (NLRA) in 1935, which serves as the legal framework for the labor relations process. Although the NLRA has been amended over the years, it remains the only legislation that governs federal labor relations. The law contains significant provisions intended to protect workers' rights to form and join unions and to engage in collective bargaining. The law also defines unfair labor practices, which restrict both unions and employers from interfering with the labor relations process. The NLRA delegates to the National Labor Relations

Board (NLRB) the responsibility for overseeing implementation of the NLRA and for investigating and remedying unfair labor practices. NLRB rule-making occurs on a case-by-case basis.

Key participants in the labor relations process include: (1) management officials, who serve as surrogates for the owners or employers of the organization; (2) union officials, who are usually elected by members; (3) the government, which participates through executive, legislative, and judicial branches occurring at federal, state, and local levels; and (4) third-party neutrals such as arbitrators. The process also involves three phases that are equally essential: the recognition phase, the negotiation phase, and the administration phase (Malvey and Raffenaud, 2015).

**Recent Trends**

Because union membership and election activity have increased in US healthcare settings, managers must devote high-level attention to the application and maintenance of a positive labor relations program that integrates human resources functions, and especially includes social media networking sites and other Internet-based communications tools. Specifically, management must assure that there is a social media policy that will serve to guide both supervisors and employees with regard to what is permissible on social networking websites. Employees as well as managers must consider whether a post is protected and agreed upon, especially when the post could lead to disciplinary action or even termination (Brown and DeMarco, 2012).

The rise of claims of unfair labor practices and the increase in threats of strikes, walkouts, and other work stoppages suggest that the labor–management relationship is strained. Inconsistent and unfair application of disciplinary policies and procedures can create unnecessary grievance problems. At a minimum, the principle of just cause should guide the disciplinary process. When employees file grievances, they expect prompt attention to their requests. Delay in responding or ignoring complaints is a clear signal to employees that management does not care about their problems and thus cannot be trusted. Furthermore, management's credibility with employees will then deteriorate, creating an imbalance in the labor–management relationship that leads to employee perception that the union's position is the most honest (Malvey and Raffenaud, 2015).

Pressure from the shrinking economy and healthcare reform led to widespread lay-offs and reimbursement cuts. The growth of employed physicians could mean significantly more pressure on employers at the bargaining table, and rising costs to meet their demands. And the dissatisfaction expressed by nurses and their willingness to organize cannot be ignored. Management must prepare to deal with these challenges in the years ahead.

Nurses have become increasingly aggressive in having their voice heard through unionization, and the emergence of large and powerful nursing unions indicates that nurses will continue to be heard in the workplace. Nurses are among the most stressed workers, with 80 percent reporting that they are under more pressure this year than last and are experiencing physical ailments as a result. A recent *Nursing Times* survey reported:

- Nearly half (46 percent) said they work noticeably longer hours than this time last year.
- Seventy-three percent said they had suffered the side effects of work-related stress, such as physical or mental health problems, in the past year.
- More than a third (37 percent) have taken more sick leave in the past 12 months than they normally would.
- Seventy-four percent said they had felt under pressure from their organization to come to work when they were feeling ill this year (MacDonald, 2013).

With the advent of the Patient Protection and Affordable Care Act (ACA) and accountable care organizations (ACOs) and the trend towards hospitals employing physicians, physician unions could resurface as a major workforce challenge because physicians are increasingly becoming employees rather than self-employed. In 2012, approximately half of US physicians were already employed by large healthcare entities, and some industry experts predict that this number could reach 80 percent of all physicians. In addition, there is possibly a generational component to these numbers as younger physicians appear to be willing to give up income for a better quality of life, which means more regular working hours and less responsibility for patients after hours. Regardless, the trend toward employed physicians opens up possibilities for physicians at the bargaining table (Leffell, 2013).

**Managerial Implications**

Whether a healthcare organization is union or non-union, it should develop and utilize a policy on unionism. More importantly, this policy should be communicated to current as well as prospective employees. Above all else, management should strive to create and sustain a positive employee–management relationship. According to Malvey and Raffenaud

(2015), suggestions for doing so include, at minimum, the following five recommendations:

1. A positive employee–management relationship begins with the screening process. All prospective employees should be given information about the institution's position toward unions as well as its goals and strategies of fair and consistent dealings with unions. Employee handbooks and orientation represent other opportunities to communicate management's commitment to provide equitable treatment to all employees concerning wages, benefits, hours, and conditions of employment. Furthermore, management must also communicate that each employee is important and deserves respect, and that adequate funds and management time have been designated to maintain effective employee relations (Rutkowski and Rutkowski, 1984).
2. Management not only must have effective policies and procedures for selection of new employees but also must ensure proper fit of personnel with specific jobs. Job analyses, job descriptions, and job evaluations, as well as fair wage and salary programs, are essential in establishing a fundamental basis for fair representation.
3. Management must fulfill its roles and responsibilities to employees by providing necessary training, especially for first-line supervisors who are instrumental in determining how policies are implemented and in serving as liaisons between management and employees. If supervisors are not properly trained, grievances are less likely to be settled quickly and are more likely to escalate into substantive formal disputes. Training is especially critical in healthcare settings because of constant and rapid changes in technology and workplace safety issues.
4. Management's commitment to training must be consistent with fair and honest treatment of employees. Similarly, if management fails to establish objective performance policies and does not ensure that they are done routinely, the labor–management relationship is affected. Employees may perceive inequities and unfairness, and experience problems of declining morale and productivity, because rewards are not matched with performance.
5. Finally, to sustain a positive relationship, management should not make promises that cannot be fulfilled; at the same time, it should strive to do whatever is possible to improve employee relations. Monitoring employee attitudes through surveys is essential; otherwise, management is dependent on rumors. If there is a union, management must then rely solely on the union for communicating worker problems or change in attitudes.

**The Role of the Internet and Social Media**

With e-mails, websites, and blogs, unions have multiple communication channels that they can use to reach prospective members without alerting employers. Previously unions in the USA were restricted by specific rules about communicating with employees, especially visiting work premises to solicit workers during union recognition campaigns. Consequently, healthcare executives knew when unions would be at the worksite and what they were up to. Today, the Internet gives unions what is essentially free and unfettered access to employees, 24/7.

Unions now have the ability to grow e-relationships with employees and to nurture the growth of activists at facilities; all of which can occur under management's radar screen. This is a huge shift from the past when unions did most of their recruitment and nurturing in person. Today, healthcare executives have no idea how many and which of their employees are accessing union websites and resources. Furthermore, these websites offer a broader perspective of unionizing by giving employees information on what is going on at facilities across the United States, including sample contracts and bargaining issues, and methods for achieving successful outcomes (Malvey, 2010b).

The situation is not all one-sided, however. Employers also have the ability to disseminate information via the Internet. There are a variety of websites and blogs dedicated to sharing negative information about unions, such as the number of unfair labor practices filed against unions for coercive or intimidating behavior exhibited toward employees.

The Internet has also facilitated the ability of unions to engender support from the local community and in some instances actually create oppositional relationships with the healthcare facility and the community. The union strategy of turning the community against hospitals was explored in depth and reported on in 2006 (Haugh, 2006). This is a strategy in which the union launches a series of public efforts aimed at the hospital with the intent to discredit and embarrass the hospital in the community. The strategy is referred to as a "corporate campaign" by the industry. Its goal appears to be to exert sufficient pressure on the hospital to neutralize it so that does not interfere with union recruitment efforts of nurses and other employees.

Using the Internet, especially social media websites, unions have increasingly been able to tap into the emotional energy that underlies employee dissatisfaction. This can include employee feelings of powerlessness, or that they have no voice, or even worse, that management does not value them. Because of the Internet, unions have the capacity to nurture and grow employee activists. Management is thus challenged to make certain that their employees become activists for the organization, not the union. Doing so means working with HR to develop an action plan that goes beyond cheerleading. This is about getting employees involved in actively supporting the goals and plans of the organization and making room for them as participants in developing goals and plans and helping to implement them (Malvey, 2010b).

Management should avoid the temptation to rely almost exclusively on technology to relate and communicate with the workforce. Technology is only one resource. Managers should walk around the facility and observe and listen to what is occurring – first hand. E-mails and electronic communication do not tell the whole story. Healthcare executives often have "gut instincts" that derive from experience, education, and training. And they have common sense. If executives walk by a group of employees and the noise level drops, they pay attention. It is highly recommended that the HR department works with managers to develop a set of warning indicators and to monitor and report on them. Examples of such indicators might be staff turnover, especially to competing organizations, increases in reported grievances, and increases in employee-generated incidents such as staff fights or theft or damage to the organization's property (Malvey, 2010b).

# INTEGRATION OF CLINICAL PROFESSIONALS

## Two Parallel Systems

The healthcare organization utilizes a unique operating model composed of two parallel and semi-autonomous operating systems, one clinical and one business. These systems are mutually dependent; one cannot survive without the other. While there is a symbiotic relationship, the differences in philosophy and operation across these two systems offer ample opportunity for miscommunication, misunderstanding, and conflict to develop.

The clinical system is organized for the purpose of delivering healthcare. That system operates on an autocratic model, with a physician or physician surrogate serving in a "captain of the ship" role. The physician assesses each patient, provides a clinical diagnosis, and dictates the patient care plan. Nurses and other members of the healthcare team implement the care plan. Within this system, decisions are patient-centered and medically based. This tends to be a closed system whereby only medical personnel are involved in the decision-making process.

The operational side of the organization follows a more conventional business model. Within this system, decision-making follows a more traditional chain of command and standard financial indicators are utilized as benchmarks. Business leaders are responsible for overseeing the financial and operational performance of the healthcare system. While the dual system model is good for providing a basic understanding of the process, in reality there must be significant interaction and merging of resources between these two systems in order to maintain the health of the organization.

In order to maintain effective interaction across these two systems there must be established procedures for maintaining effective communication at all levels. That communication and interaction takes place at limited points of intersection and selected individuals are responsible for ensuring that communication is effective. These selected communicators must have some degree of credibility within both systems. The personnel who man these intersection points play a crucial role in the health of the organization.

**Potential Conflicts**

Given these two systems operating in tandem and the differences in mindset of those within the respective systems, there exist many opportunities for conflict. At the root of this potential conflict is an incomplete understanding of non-clinicians by clinicians, and of clinicians by non-clinicians. Clinicians often feel that non-clinicians do not fully understand the needs of healthcare because of their lack of clinical knowledge. Similarly, operational personnel view clinical personnel as being less than ideally qualified to make business related decisions due to their limited understanding of the overall business model and the macro operating environment.

Historically, operational employees were educated in traditional business programs and held degrees in business administration, accounting, and similar fields which did not offer much if any specialized knowledge related to healthcare. That situation has improved markedly over the past two decades as the number of healthcare administration (HCA) programs has grown and the MHA degree has emerged as the gold standard for preparation of healthcare administrators. This has afforded healthcare administrators better insight into the effective management of the clinical side of the healthcare system.

Healthcare professionals are required to complete long and demanding courses of study. Accreditation and board requirements strongly influence the composition of these programs. The clinical education demands are generally so high as to preclude the delivery of any significant amount of business content. However, once the clinical education program is complete, clinicians go to work in an environment which demands a high level of performance in both clinical and administrative systems. In short, clinical professionals spend prolonged periods of time preparing for a career in healthcare, but that preparation typically neglects the operational or administrative roles which are essential for success in such an environment.

However, just as healthcare administrators have gained insight into the clinical side of the operation, it has also become more common for physician leaders to further their formal education in healthcare administration or business administration in order to gain insight into the business side of the operation. This contralateral education has improved insight across the two systems and has led to more informed collaboration between healthcare professionals and business professionals.

Historically, the business component of the healthcare organization has been an intermediate level, sitting above medical operations but overseen by owners and investors who were typically physicians or physician groups. This created a sort of sandwich situation where physician practice was overseen by an administration but, in the same case, physicians oversaw the administration in their owner and investor roles.

**Recent Changes**

As US healthcare reform continues to evolve, a growing number of physicians and medical groups are being bought or absorbed into healthcare systems which are owned primarily by hospitals. This ongoing transition has prompted a move away from physician owner to physician employee. At present more than 50 percent of US physicians are healthcare system employees and that percentage is projected to grow. This represents a changing role for the physician in the healthcare workplace. While this change is certainly not free of controversy, many physicians have moved willingly into this new role, primarily due to the opportunity to eliminate non-clinical responsibilities and to gain access to enhanced support services.

On the business side of the organization, education, background, and experience are typically more diverse than on the clinical side. While upper-level managers will typically have a degree in healthcare administration or business administration, that is not an absolute, and it is not uncommon for clinical personnel to move to the business side of the organization as opportunities for advancement are presented. Hence, there may be more insight when looking from the business side to the clinical side than vice versa.

The extensive training required to become a physician instills a degree of self-confidence which is perhaps unequaled in other professions. While that self-confidence may be beneficial in the "captain of the ship" role which involves promptly diagnosing and managing complex medical conditions, it may have negative implications in environments requiring less autonomy and highly developed interpersonal skills. The "captain of the ship" role may not be as well received in non-clinical environments.

As healthcare systems have assumed more responsibility for clinical decision-making, evidence-based medicine (EBM) has assumed an increasingly important role. While the literature supports the fact that EBM results in improved quality of care and improved outcomes, it also takes away some of the physician's autonomy. That is a relatively common source of conflict between the individual physician and the healthcare system. Physicians may perceive a push toward EBM as being told how to practice medicine.

Affecting both sides of the organization are increasing regulatory demands for improved quality of care, combined with decreasing reimbursement. When all of these clinical and administrative stressors are combined we have all the ingredients for a high-stress environment. A statement from the American Health Lawyers Conflict Management Toolkit (Conard et al., n.d.) summarizes the potential for conflict well:

> The healthcare industry is subject to increasing strains due to demands for broader access to care, greater accountability to consumers, and improved quality of care, while facing more work for less pay, staffing shortages, stiffer regulatory enforcement, and decreased reimbursement. Little wonder that strains lead to stress that often leads to conflict.

Physicians and other clinicians with leadership roles in the clinical system often have responsibilities which carry over to the administrative side of the organization. When moving from one system to the other a rapid transition in behavior and management styles is often required. Making that transition can be difficult for clinical personnel who have no formal education outside the clinical realm. That sometimes leads to frustration and conflict with other healthcare providers and/or with administrators. Given the dual-track organizational structure, the all too common lack of insight across healthcare systems, and the stressful environment in which clinical professionals work, there is ample opportunity for conflict to develop both among clinical professionals and between clinical professionals and others within the healthcare setting.

The development of conflict within the healthcare environment is common enough that the Joint Commission requires healthcare organizations to have in place a plan for ameliorating and addressing conflict within the healthcare setting. Every organization should have in place a multistage plan for preventing and addressing conflict among healthcare professionals, and between healthcare professionals and non-clinical personnel and administrative personnel.

Programs which emphasize the need for a well-functioning system of communication, and which plan for some degree of miscommunication and misunderstanding, position themselves to identify and address developing conflict before it reaches a level where it may catalyze disruption in the interaction between these two systems. While clinical professionals and administrators will continue to have disagreements, the existence of a program which encourages ongoing communication across systems will eliminate a majority of potential conflicts before they develop.

**Managerial Implications**

At this point in time, the movement towards professional dominance of healthcare delivery in the USA seems virtually complete. With the fact that there are approximately 300 different healthcare occupations and professions, the HC organization has begun to reflect this complexity in both organizational structure, size and specialization. As such, the concept of managing clinical professionals must follow suit and keep up. Unfortunately, the HC organization has been slow and reluctant to impose any constraints that may appear to diminish the autonomy or expertise of the clinical professional. However, as Berenson et al. (2013) have pointed out:

> The United States is on the cusp of a new era, with greater demand for performance information, greater data availability, and a greater willingness to integrate performance information into public policy. This era has immense promise to deliver a learning healthcare system that encourages collaborative improvements in systems-based care, improves accountability, helps consumers make important choices, and improves quality at an acceptable cost.

The next steps require all healthcare providers, both facilities and clinical professionals, to embrace this challenge and strive to develop performance and quality measures that truly address the issues of quality of care, optimal outcomes, cost-effective and cost-beneficial care, and a patient-centered approach to the provision of healthcare.

The following action plan is offered as a beginning point for development of a healthcare performance measuring system:

1. Identify and evaluate the current system of performance measurement in terms of measures, evaluation processes, best practices, and patient outcomes.
2. Search for national quality and performance benchmarks, if necessary, to update and refocus the organization's performance system.

3. Elicit the input and expertise of various clinical professionals to validate and quantify the measures.
4. Implement the performance measurement system.
5. Establish a joint performance measurement committee comprises of various clinical professionals, administration, non-clinical professionals, and board members.
6. Establish a timeline for continuous quality improvement points.

While this action plan only offers major steps and must be tailored to each specific organization, it is incumbent upon management to lead this charge. As clearly presented in this chapter, the trend in healthcare is towards a system of care that may ultimately be rewarded on the quality of care delivered. This pay-for-performance mentality is "already in the works" and seems to be a foregone conclusion for the future of healthcare financing.

## WORK–FAMILY CONFLICT

For many employees, balancing their work and personal lives is a significant concern. The quality of their personal and family life is improved by flexibility of work, according to 68 percent of US HR professionals polled in 2010 (Miller, 2010). In particular, most employees do not feel they spend enough time with their families (McMillan, 2011). Work–life balance initiatives can enhance employee recruitment and retention by attracting and keeping staff who need or expect flexibility.

Employees today are less likely to define their personal success only in terms of financial gains. Many employees, especially younger ones, believe satisfaction in life is more likely to result from balancing their work challenges and rewards with those in their personal lives. Though most people still enjoy work and want to excel at it, they tend to be focused on finding interesting work and are more inclined to pursue multiple careers.

In fact, in a survey of more than 3000 workers, 86 percent said work fulfillment and work–life balance were their top priorities (Snell and Bohlander, 2013). Only 35 percent said being successful at work and moving up the ladder were their top priorities. People also appear to be seeking ways of living that are less complicated but more meaningful. These new lifestyles cannot help having an impact on the way employees must be motivated and managed. Consequently, HRM has become more complex than it was when employees were concerned primarily with economic survival.

Family-friendly companies have to balance the benefit they provide families versus their single employees. Most employees have no children under 18. Childless employees sometimes feel resentment against employees with children who are able to take advantage of these programs when they cannot (Carlson, 2004). Over the past decade the number of stay-at-home fathers in the USA has tripled which means mitigating work–family conflict has become a challenge for most families. Healthcare organizations must address this challenge if they wish to remain attractive to both men and women.

The issue is particularly relevant for nurses. Work and family responsibilities may be in conflict because the job of nursing is physically and psychologically demanding (Takeuchi and Yamazaki, 2010), and nursing has a high proportion of women, who tend to have greater family responsibilities than men. This tension between work and family can be seen in one study that described chronic work and family conflicts among 50 percent of nurses, and episodes of conflict among another 41 percent (Grzywacz et al., 2006). Furthermore, job and professional retention is problematic in the nursing profession (Auerbach et al., 2013), and early studies of work and family conflict indicate a connection between work and family conflict and intent to leave the job (Ganster and Schaubrock, 1991). For these reasons, awareness of factors that contribute to work and family conflict among nurses and how the conflict impacts nurses is necessary in order to reduce the impacts to the nurse practice environment and to retain nurses in the workplace (Leineweber et al., 2014).

Two general categories of antecedents or determinants of these work–family conflict/family–work conflict (WFC/FWC) phenomena are demographic or personal factors and work environment factors. Far more research has been done on the latter than the former among Registered Nurses (RNs). Among personal factors that predict either WFC or FWC or both are childcare responsibilities, lack of support at home, preschool children, number of children, and housework responsibilities (Fujimoto et al., 2008; Hoge, 2009; Takeuchi and Yamazaki, 2010).

Results of studies on work environmental factors suggest that lack of nurse involvement in decision-making, long work hours, being pressured to work overtime, staffing inadequacy, high workloads, and high job demands are all associated with higher work–family role conflict. Work schedule factors that contribute to higher levels of WFC include lack of flexible work hours, irregular working schedule, night or evening work, rotating shifts, and weekend work. Lack of management supportiveness is also associated with work–family conflict (Camerino et al., 2010; Cortese et al., 2010).

High perceptions of work–family conflict are associated with a number of significant impacts on the nursing workforce including low job satisfaction, and high levels of intention to leave the job or leave the profession of nursing (Cortese et al., 2010; Cortese et al., 2010). The presence of WFC fosters job dissatisfaction which leads to the intention to quit the job.

Antecedents that positively balance an RN's work–family conflict include flexibility in work hours, reduction of staff duties (if possible), supportive workplace polices regarding childcare, and supportive management as a whole (Fujimoto et al., 2008; Cortese et al., 2010). Predictability and control over working time also reduces work–family conflict (Simon et al., 2004; Taris et al., 2006). Competitive organizations are finding it advantageous to provide staff with more family-friendly options such as telecommuting, paid maternity leave, on-site daycare, extended leave, flexible work hours, elder care, part-time work, job-sharing, parental leave, adoption assistance, spousal involvement in career planning, and assistance with family problems.

## CONCLUSION

The HR challenges discussed in this chapter cover only the most obvious healthcare organizational challenges administrators face in managing their human resources in an efficient and effective manner. Changes in social, economic, and political environments as well as changes in HR management itself will continue to expand the number and potency of challenges HR professionals will need to address in the future.

## REFERENCES

Amoroso, M., Boyd, D.L., and Hoobler, J.M. (2010). "The Diversity Education Dilemma: Exposing Data Evidence Hierarchies without Reinforcing Them." *Journal of Management Education*, 34(6): 795–822.

Auerbach, D., Staiger, D., Muench, U., and Buerhaus, P. (2013). "The Nursing Workforce in an Era of Health Care Reform." *New England Journal of Medicine*, 368(16): 1470–1472.

Becker, B.E. and Huselid, M.A. (2006). "Strategic Human Resource Management: Where Do We Go From Here?" *Journal of Management*, 32(6): 898–925.

Becker, B.E., Huselid, M.A., and Ulrich, D. (2001). *The HR Scorecard: Linking People, Strategy, and Performance*. Boston, MA: Harvard Business School Press.

Berenson, R., Provonost, P., and Krumholz, H. (2013). "Achieving the Potential of Health Care Performance Measures: Timely Analysis of Immediate Health Policy Issues." *Urban Institute*, May. www.rwfj.org/content/dam/farm/Issue_briefs/2013/rwfj406195.

Brown, S.J. and DeLarco, M.E. (2012). "Health Care Institutions and Recent NLRB Activity: Preventative Action Is the Best Medicine." *Health Law Reporter*, July 12, Bloomberg BNA. Available at http://www.hoganlovells.cn/en-US/health-care-institutions-and-recent-nlrb-activitypreventative-action-is-the-best-medicine-07-12-2012/.

Bureau of Labor Statistics (2013). "Employment Projections: 2012–2022 Summary." Bureau of Labor Statistics Economic News Release, December 19. Available at www.bls.gov/pub/mir/2013.

Bureau of Labor Statistics (2014). "Union Members Summary." Available at http://www.bls.gov/news.release/union2.nr0.htm (accessed 24 April 2014).

Camerino, D., Sandri, M., Satori, S., Conway, P.M., Campanini, P., and Costa, G. (2010). "Shiftwork, Work–Family Conflict among Italian Nurses and Prevention Efficacy." *Chronobiology International*, 27(5): 1105–1123.

Carlson, L. (2004). "Flextime Elevated to National Issue." *Employee Benefit News*, September 15.

Chuang, C.H. and Liao, H. (2010). "Strategic Human Resource Management and the Service Concept." *Personnel Psychology*, 68: 409–446.

Conard, J.R., Franklin, J.F., Rothschild, I.S., and Vandecaveye, L.D. (n.d.). "Conflict Management Toolkit." American Health Lawyers Association. Available at https://www.healthlawyers.org/dr/SiteAssets/Lists/drsaccordion/EditForm/Conf%20mgmt%20toolkit.pdf.

Cortese, C.G., Colombo, L., and Ghislieri, C. (2010). "Determinants of Nurses' Job Satisfaction: The Role of Work–family Conflict, Job Demand, Emotional Charge and Social Support." *Journal of Nursing Management*, 18: 35–43.

Ford, R.C., Sivo, S.A., Fottler, M.D., Dickson, D., Bradley, K., and Johnson, L. (2006). "Aligning Internal Organizational Factors with a Service Excellence Mission: An Exploratory Investigation in Healthcare." *Health Care Management Review*, 31(4): 259–269.

Fottler, M.D., Erickson, E., and Rivers, P.A. (2006). "Bringing Human Resources to the Table: Utilization of an HR Balanced Score Card at Mayo Clinic." *Healthcare Management Review*, 31(1): 64–72.

Freeman, R.B. and Medoff, J.L. (1984). *What Do Unions Do?* New York: Basic Books.

Fried, B. and Fottler, M.D. (2015). *Human Resources in Healthcare: Managing for Success*, 4th edn. Chicago, IL: Health Administration Press.

Fujimoto, T., Kotana, S., and Suzuki, R. (2008). "Work–Family Conflict of Nurses in Japan." *Journal of Clinical Nursing*, 17: 3286–3295.

Ganster, D.C. and Schauroeck, J. (1991). "Work Stress and Employee Health." *Journal of Management*, 17(2): 235–271.

Gomex-Mejia, L. and Balkin, D. (2011). *Management: People, Performance, Change.* Upper Saddle River, NJ: Prentice Hall.

Grzywacz, J.G., Frone, M.J., Brewer, C.S., and Kovner, C.T. (2006). "Quantifying Work–Family Conflict among Registered Nurses." *Research in Nursing Health*, 29: 414–426.

Haugh, R. (2006). "The New Union Strategy. Turning the Community against You." *Hospitals and Health Networks/AHA*, 80(5): 32. Available at http://web.ebscohost.com (accessed February 11, 2010).

Hoge, T. (2009). "When Work Strain Transcends Psychological Boundaries: An Inquiry into the Relationship Between Time Pressure, Irritation, Work–Family Conflict and Psychosomatic Complaints." *Stress and Health*, 25: 41–51.

Huselid, M.A. (1994). "Documenting HR's Effect on Company Performance." *HR Magazine*, 39(1): 79–85.

Huselid, M.A., Becker, B.E., and Beatty, R.W. (2005). *The Workforce Scorecard.* Boston, MA: Harvard Business School Press.

Kaplan, R.S. and Norton, D.P. (1996). *The Balanced Scorecard.* Boston, MA: Harvard Business School Press.

Leffell, D.J. (2013). The Doctor's Office as Union Shop. *Wall Street Journal*, January 29. http://online.wsj.com/news/articles/SB10001424127887323375204578270401138739978 (accessed May 12, 2014).

Leineweber, C., Chungkham, H.S., Westerlund, H., Tishelman, C., and Lindquist, R. (2014). "Hospital Organizational Factors Influence Work–Family Conflict in Registered Nurses: Multilevel Modeling of a Nation-Wide Cross-Sectional Survey in Sweden." *International Journal of Nursing Studies*, 51(5): 744–751.

Liptak, A. 2009. "Supreme Court Finds Bias Against White Firefighters." *New York Times*, June 30: A1, A13.

MacDonald, I. (2013). "Survey: Nurses Overworked, Understaffed and Stressed." Fiercehealthcare.com, October 1. Available at http://www.fiercehealthcare.com/story/survey-nursesoverworked-understaffed-and-stressed/2013-10-01

Malvey, D. (2010a). "Unionization in Healthcare: Background and Trends." *Journal of Healthcare Management*, 55(3): 154–157.

Malvey, D. (2010b). "Unionization in Healthcare: Strategies." *Journal of Healthcare Management*, 55(4): 236–240.

Malvey, D., Fottler, M.D., and Sumner, J. (2013). "The Fear Factor in Healthcare: Employee Information Sharing." *Journal of Healthcare Management*, 58(3): 225–237.

Malvey, D. and Raffenaud A. (2015). "Managing with Organized Labor." In B. Fried and M.D. Fottler (eds), *Human Resources in Health Care: Managing for Success* (4th edn). Chicago, IL: Health Administration Press.

Mayer, D., Ehrhart, M.G., and Schneider, B. (2009). "Service Attribute Boundary Conditions of the Service Climate–Customer Satisfaction Link." *Academy of Management Journal*, 52: 1034–1047.

McMillan, H.S. (2011). "Constructs of Work/Life Interface." *Human Resource Development Review*, 10: 6–25.

Messersmith, J.G. and Guthrie, J.P. (2010). "High Performance Work Systems in Emergent Organizations: Implications for Firm Performance." *Human Resource Management*, 49(2): 241–264.

Miller, S. (2010). "Flexible Hours in the Ranks." *2010 HR Trend Book*. Alexandria, VA: Society for Human Resource Management, pp. 16–17.

Nishii, L.H., Lepak, D.P., and Schneider, B. (2008). "Employee Attributions of the Why of HR Practices: Their Effects on Employee Attitudes, Behaviors, and Customer Satisfaction." *Personnel Psychology*, 61: 503–545.

Pfeffer, J. (1995). "Producing Sustainable Competitive Advantages Through Effective Management of People." *Academy of Management Executive*, 10: 55–72.

Pfeffer, J. (1998). *The Human Equation: Building Profits by Putting People First*. Boston, MA: Harvard Business School Press.

Rafter, M. (2010). "Happy Days." *Workforce Management*, October: 21–26.

Rutkowski, A.D. and Rutkowski, B.L. (1984). *Labor Relations in Hospitals*. Rockville, MD: Aspen.

Scott, C. and Seers, A. (1996). "Determinants of Union Election Outcomes in the Non-Hospital Health Care Industry." *Journal of Labor Research*, 17(4): 701–15.

Simon, M., Kummerling, A., and Hasselhorn, H. (2004). "Work–Home Conflict in the European Nursing Profession." *International Journal of Occupational and Environmental Health*, 10(4): 384–391.

Snell, S. and Bohlander, G. (2013). *Managing Human Resources*. Mason, OH: South Western/Cengage Learning.

Takeuchi, T. and Yamazaki, Y. (2010). "Relationship Between Work–family Conflict and a Sense of Coherence Among Japanese Registered Nurses." *Japan Journal of Nursing Science*, 7: 158–168.

Taris, T., Beckers, D., Verhoven, L., Geurts, S., Kompier, M., and Van der Linden, D. (2006). "Recovery Opportunities, Work–Home Interference, and Well-Being Among Managers." *European Journal of Work and Organizational Psychology*, 15: 139–157.

Ulrich, D., Younger, J., and Brockband, W. (2008). "The Twenty-First Century HR Organizations." *Human Resource Management*, 47(4): 829–849.

Wright, P.M., Gardner, T.M., Moyniahan, L.M., and Allen, M.R. (2005). "The Relationship Between HR Practices and Firm Performance: Examining Cause and Order." *Personnel Psychology*, 68: 409–446.

# 7. Disaster preparedness and response
*Bryan K. Breland*

## DISASTER TERMINOLOGY

It should be noted at the onset of this exploration of the subject of disaster preparedness and response for healthcare organizations in the United States that, relative to many of the more mature areas in healthcare management research, it is a field in its infancy and is rapidly evolving in response to a broad spectrum of external stimuli, including newly discovered or created threats, resource and funding limitations and opportunities, political and societal pressures, regulatory and accreditation standards, among many others. The dynamic and evolving quality of our understanding of the topic is reflective of the chaotic nature of events and of our responses to those events, both of which are important aspects to study. Our shifting focus, in research and practice, on the various phases of the emergency management cycle can be observed in the preparedness lexicon, wherein we use the terms "disaster preparedness and response," "emergency management," "disaster management," "emergency preparedness," simply "preparedness" and a host of others to describe the continuum of activities undertaken to ensure the healthcare organization is capable of continuing operations during and directly after a catastrophic event that results in a rapid increase in demand for emergency services and medical care.

## DISASTER MANAGEMENT ACTIVITIES

In its early iteration, "disaster management" was used to describe the responsive mechanism of government to provide funding to stabilize local economies and rebuild infrastructure. The United States Congress authorized the first provision of federal monies in 1803 to a New Hampshire town devastated by fire. In the century following that first authorization, disaster relief was provided following more than 100 natural disasters including floods, hurricanes and earthquakes (FEMA, 2014). In the 1950s, disaster relief was first augmented by preparedness in the deployment of activities and measures developed by the US federal government as a means of preparing the public for nuclear attack. Considered a distinctly different approach, preparedness activities were labelled as "civil defense" and responsibility and authority remained fragmented across a number of federal, state and local agencies. It was in the aftermaths of numerous catastrophic events in the next two decades – hurricanes Carla, Camille, and Agnes and several powerful earthquakes – when authorities began to recognize the drawbacks and consequences of this fragmented approach. Two important federal policies followed. The first was passage of the 1974 Disaster Relief Act authorizing the presidential declarations of national disasters. The second, and arguably more pertinent to this chapter, was the creation of the Federal Emergency Management Agency (FEMA) in 1979, wherein US President Jimmy Carter consolidated a number of federal disaster-related agencies. States began to adapt their emergency management structures and resources to the FEMA model, consolidating preparedness and response efforts.

This consolidation evolved and expanded into the modern emergency management cycle construct, which now includes four distinct phases of activities intended to improve an organization's capacity to endure catastrophic events. Figure 7.1 is a visual representation of the cycle of emergency management activities that occur continuously through normal and disaster operations.

*Figure 7.1   Four-phase cycle of emergency management*

## Mitigation

Mitigation is the identification and redress of threats to individuals and organizations. The intent of activities in the mitigation phase of the emergency management cycle can be to eliminate or reduce the potential that a harmful event will occur, that is, to prevent the occurrence; or it may be intended to reduce the impact of an event that cannot be eliminated, that is, to protect lives and property in the event of the occurrence. Because the focus of the organization has influence on the perspectives and priorities of emergency management activities, some organizations consider a fifth, and perhaps sixth, phase: prevention and protection. I intend here that mitigation includes these important components.

## Preparedness

In the preparedness phase, the healthcare organization gathers supplies and equipment, trains personnel on processes and procedures to be used during disaster operations, and exercises and evaluates its capacity to react to crisis events, manage increased patient loads, and stabilize the event. Preparedness activities necessarily include the development and adoption of written plans, designating methods of communication, and considering how the organization operates within a larger structure established by the local, state, and federal governments.

## Response

During and immediately following a crisis event, implementation of emergency plans and management structures establish response priorities and operational objectives and direct available resources toward stabilizing the crisis and an eventual return to normal operations. These may include actions to protect the lives of staff and patients, triage and prioritization of medical services to accommodate increased patient loads, or assessing damage to the facility and arranging the transfer of patients to alternate locations.

## Recovery

Once the objectives of the response phase are met and the situation has stabilized, the organization must undertake the return to normal operations. The duration of the recovery phase is dependent on the extent to which the crisis event impacted the operations, personnel, and infrastructure of the organization. The transition from response to recovery may be difficult to identify, as objectives in the late stages of the response phase will include returning conditions to normal. As operations return to normal, lessons learned during the events should drive improvements in the next mitigation and preparedness phases.

While this four-phase emergency management cycle is useful in guiding the activities of a variety of types of agencies and organizations, it is important to consider the regulatory and societal obligations of various organizations during the response phase and the role of the organization in the broader context. Unlike many public and private sector organizations, a coordinated healthcare response during natural and man-made disasters is a necessary operational component in the context of the broader community. As such, the healthcare organization is responsible for much more than the safekeeping of existing patients and staff, but instead must plan, prepare, and respond in a manner consistent with community plans in order for emergency management at any level – local, state, or federal – to be successful in reducing the loss of life and stabilizing the local community following a widespread event. While it is difficult enough to continue normal operations during natural disasters – with potentially reduced staffing, damaged infrastructure, compromised communications, and a host of other disaster-related difficulties – some healthcare organizations will be asked, notwithstanding these challenges, to expand their operations to capacity.

## DISASTERS AND HEALTHCARE ORGANIZATIONS

Disasters, by definition, overwhelm an organization's capacity (FEMA, 1983, 1996; Quarantelli, 1985). In the context of healthcare, a disaster overwhelms the ability of a healthcare facility or system to meet the demand for medical services, creating a need for external resources and assistance (Zibulewsky, 2001). Disasters with widespread impact may overwhelm the collective healthcare and public health resources in an entire community.

An organization's capacity is determined by its level of resources, including staffing and infrastructure relative to demand (Hick et al., 2004). Infrastructure includes physical spaces, beds, support services such as laboratory and radiology, as well as clinical and non-clinical equipment and supplies (DHS, 2007). Following a disaster, demand at area hospitals swells rapidly as the injured arrive. The ability of the healthcare organization, operating under staffing conditions appropriate to routine demands, to expand staffing and infrastructure to accommodate the elevated demand is called "surge capacity."

# UNDERSTANDING THE MULTIDIMENSIONAL NATURE OF SURGE CAPACITY

This section will first examine the dimensions of surge capacity and capability and then shift to the importance of capacity in the public health and community context. The term "surge capacity" gained popularity at the turn of the century and considers the ability of the hospital to manage a sudden increase in demand; that is, the number of patients. Much of the research discussion prior to this involves overcrowding of emergency departments or variations that are experienced throughout the day or on certain days, with many researching solutions in distributing workforce to accommodate these variations. The transition in subject matter in the literature is noticeable as researchers began adopting terminology that would differentiate these phenomena, such as "routine surge" and "daily surge" in contrast with "disaster surge" capacity. Research on the topic of variation in demand for medical services and adaptive managerial approaches has provided a rather well-developed understanding of the workings of routine surges in demand on the emergency department and other services. However, the relative infrequency and complex nature of surges secondary to large-scale natural and man-made incidents hinders our efforts in properly defining and identifying the casual factors and consequences, and developing consistent measures of disaster surge capacity.

# SURGE CAPACITY DEFINITIONS

In the estimation of an organization's ability to managed increased patient load, normal patient volumes, daily or routine surge, and disaster surge must be simultaneously taken into account, because each acts upon the same pool of resources. To illustrate, a 500-bed facility with 70 percent occupancy does not have an inpatient surge capacity of 500 beds, but rather of 150 beds, assuming availability of staffing and necessary equipment and supplies. This concurrence of event phases is particularly important in the planning stages of the organization's approach to surge capacity. In 2012, the Institute of Medicine recognized three distinct modes of response that correspond to points along a continuum of surge capacity depending on the extent to which patient loads stress the organization and normal operating conditions (Hanfling et al., 2012). Figure 7.2 depicts the continuum of surge capacity, identifying the points along the continuum where some predetermined indicator (notice that the incident has occurred, scarcity of resources, patient volume, and so on) causes the organization to transition to the next operational mode.

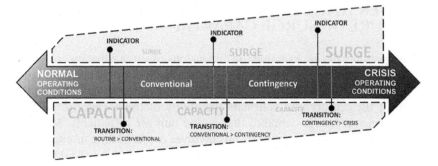

*Figure 7.2   Continuum of surge capacity*

**Conventional Capacity**

The organization operates within its conventional capacity in response to incidents that tax, but do not overwhelm, available resources when utilized in a manner consistent with routine practices and standard operating procedure. For example: a multiple or mass casualty incident that causes a sudden influx of patients, but is thought to be limited in scope and duration to a number of patients for which the hospital has adequate resource availability.

**Contingency Capacity**

To access its contingency capacity, the organization deviates slightly from routine practices and standard operating procedure in a way thought to be comparable with, or "functionally equivalent" to, routine practices; that is, the change in practice has a minimal impact on patient care. These spaces or practices may be used temporarily, as during a major mass casualty incident, or over an extended period during a disaster.

**Crisis Capacity**

During disaster operations healthcare providers attempt to provide sufficiency of care. Because the resources of the organization are overwhelmed, practices are adopted that deviate substantially from routine and are not consistent with usual standards of care. When demand following a disaster swells to the level that providing care at the usual standard is either impossible given the conditions and resources available, or would exhaust the ability to provide services to others, providers render care that is sufficient under the circumstances.

Some researchers differentiate surge capacity and "surge capability," a term describing the ability of the organization to provide specialized care and treatment to an expanded population of patients with particular needs (Hick et al., 2004). This distinction is important for two reasons. First, in communicating with other organizations involved in the response to a disaster, the differentiation between capacity and capability enables the hospital to indicate to authorities managing the incident response and other facilities that, while they have additional resources for generalized care, they are strained – by workforce, or infrastructure, or both – in the provision of care to special populations or conditions. This allows more efficient alignment of patients and resources (Hick et al., 2008). Second, it underscores the heterogeneous nature of disaster injuries and empha-sizes that even very large hospitals, or hospital systems, may be quickly overwhelmed when the population of injured is relatively different than the general population, as would be the case in disasters impacting a large number of pediatric patients or in incidents resulting in a specific injury type, like chemical or radiological burns. When this occurs, the hospital's ability to provide generalized care, or capacity, is not exhausted, but specific capabilities are compromised. Stated differently, capacity is a measure of one's command and control over resources, and capabil-ity is the measure of one's ability to direct those resources toward the attainment of an intended objective. It is noteworthy, however, that this differentiation of surge capacity and capability is not universally applied in the research literature, and many studies use the terms interchangeably with a presupposition that increased patient loads will almost certainly tax particular resources and specialties disproportionately. Table 7.1 con-tains definitions related to surge capacity that are often referred to in the literature.

## COMPONENTS OF SURGE CAPACITY

In the recent past, surge capacity was considered in much the same way as the organization's "routine" capacity; that is, the number of available beds. The Joint Commission on Accreditation of Healthcare Organizations in the US, now simply called the Joint Commission, in a 2003 effort to encourage emergency preparedness collaboration at the community level defined surge capacity in a broader context: "Surge capacity encompasses potential patient beds; available space in which patients may be triaged, managed, vaccinated, decontaminated, or simply located [structures]; available personnel of all types [staff]; necessary medications, supplies and equipment [stuff]; and even the legal capacity to deliver healthcare

*Table 7.1    Surge capacity definitions*

| Term | Definition |
| --- | --- |
| Surge capacity | Ability to manage a sudden, unexpected increase in patient volume (i.e., numbers of patients) that would otherwise severely challenge or exceed the current capacity of the healthcare system. |
| Surge capability | Ability of the healthcare system to manage patients who require specialized evaluation or interventions (e.g., contaminated, highly contagious, or burn patients). |
| Public health surge capacity | Ability of the public health system to increase capacity not only for patient care but also for epidemiologic investigation, risk communication, mass prophylaxis or vaccination, mass fatality management, mental health support, laboratory services, and other activities. |
| Facility-based surge capacity | Actions taken at the healthcare facility level that augment services within the response structure of the healthcare facility; may include responses that are external to the actual structure of the facility but are proximate to it (e.g., medical care provided in tenting in the hospital grounds). These responses are under the control of the facility's incident management system and primarily depend on the facility's emergency operations plans. |
| Community-based surge capacity | Actions taken at a community level to supplement healthcare facility responses. These may provide for triage and initial treatment, non-ambulatory care overflow, or isolation (e.g., off-site "hospital" facility). These responses are under the control of the jurisdictional response (e.g., public health, emergency management) and represent a public effort to support and augment the healthcare system. |

*Source:*    Hick et al. (2004, p. 254). Copyright 2004 by American College of Emergency Physicians. Reprinted with permission.

under situations which exceed authorized capacity" (Joint Commission on Accreditation of Healthcare Organizations, 2003).

Barbisch and Koenig soon after referenced the expansion as to include staff, stuff and structures, and later added a fourth component, systems, as necessary to manage and effectively utilize capacity (Barbisch and Koenig, 2006). The first three-component form became popular and appears throughout the literature, even recently. Though the addition of the fourth component was less popular, and some researchers continued to focus on staff, stuff, and structures in estimating surge capacity, it was nonetheless widely accepted that bed availability alone was insufficient to character-ize surge capacity, considering the multiple dimensions that comprise the ability to take on and manage rapidly increased patient loads. The list was not immutable, however, as demonstrated when, over time, some authors began to use "space" rather than the original "structures," reflecting a line of research suggesting expansion into any area, within or perhaps adjacent to, the facility: patient care on any "flat-space" available. Other modi-fications of the paradigm that can be found in the literature include the substitution of the word "supplies" for "stuff," when arguably, "stuff" is a better representation as it includes supplies as well as pharmaceuticals and equipment; references to the original term "structures," though the logic in support of that substitution was discussed above; and the omission of "systems," although there is a strong consensus that these are important aspects of the organization's surge capacity (Barbisch, 2005).

Recently, a trend in the literature is to include a component for vari-ability in the standard of care provided along the continuum of surge capacity discussed previously. Much of the operational research seems to conclude that during large-scale, high-volume operations following a catastrophic event it is more prudent to render what care you can provide under extreme circumstances than to withhold care in fear of falling short of customary standards. That viewpoint is shared by most practitioners and, recently, regulatory and accreditation agencies. With the addition of the "standards" component, I complete a list of the now "Five Ss of Surge Capability:"

- Staff: adequately trained healthcare providers and support personnel.
- Stuff: sufficient supplies and equipment for increased patient care.
- Space: physical facilities and infrastructure to support operational needs.
- Systems: policy, planning, and incident management systems that facilitate response time decision-making, clear lines of authority and communication.
- Standards: standard of care to be rendered as surge volume con-tinues to progress along a continuum and eventually overwhelms resources.

Tables 7.2, 7.3 and 7.4 summarize common activities of the organiza-tion while transitioning to the conventional, contingency and crisis opera-tions modes, respectively. It is important to note that these activities will vary between organizations according to organizational emergency plans, available resources, and function.

*Table 7.2   Conventional surge capacity and components*

| | |
|---|---|
| Conventional surge capacity | A measure of the organization's ability to provide patients medical services within the normal standard of care using all available organizational staff and resources in a manner consistent with routine practices. |
| Staff | All-hands approach.<br>Call in off-duty staff.<br>Suspend leave time.<br>Medical staff function within their traditional roles.<br>Non-medical duties are reassigned. |
| Stuff | Conservation of supplies; assessment and inventory of potentially scarce resources. |
| Space | Staffing of unattended beds; marshalling and use of unused and observation-use beds.<br>Initiate surge discharge.<br>Cancel routine appointments and elective surgeries. |
| Systems | Notification and warning.<br>Incident command: primarily hospital authority clinical decisions.<br>Operations: triage, medical services, support.<br>Logistics: facility resources.<br>Administrative: finance, human resources.<br>Communications: internal and external.<br>Public information. |
| Standards | Routine practices.<br>Standard operating procedures.<br>No deviation from established medical standard of care. |

### Surge Capacity: Staffing Levels

It is important to recognize that past practices estimating surge capacity based on bed counts did not necessarily discount the importance of staffing levels. To determine whether this occurred, one would need to clearly define "available beds." Estimation of licensed beds might include beds not currently in service and, therefore, not staffed. This may seem contrary to the intent of preparedness activities, but numerous studies indicate discrepancies between reported and actual available, staffed beds; either mistakenly, or through "occupancy-mitigating responses" (Fieldston et al., 2010; DeLia, 2006). One justification for such erroneous reporting is evident in the literature: one of the many variations by researchers in defining surge capacity – availability of resources. Many scholars subscribe sternly to the early position of the American College

*Table 7.3   Contingency surge capacity and components*

| | |
|---|---|
| Contingency surge capacity | A measure of the organization's ability to provide patients medical services comparable with or "functionally equivalent" to the usual standard of care by deviating slightly from routine practices of the organization. |
| Staff | Reassignment of medical duties to address need.<br>Expanded span of control for supervisors.<br>Interval assessments of inpatients changed to as needed. |
| Stuff | Conservation continues; wash and reuse of non- or minimally invasive disposable supplies. |
| Space | Utilize pre- and post-op beds; stepdown eligible Intensive Care Unit (ICU) patients; inpatient use of clinical areas routinely used for non-emergency, outpatient, and clinical appointments. |
| Systems | Notification and warning.<br>Incident command: expanded; primarily hospital authority and clinical decisions.<br>Operations: triage, medical services, support.<br>Logistics: facility resources.<br>Administrative: finance, human resources.<br>Coordination: primarily internal.<br>Communications: internal and external.<br>Public information. |
| Standards | Minor deviation from routine practices and standard operating procedures.<br>Functionally equivalent standard of care. |

of Emergency Physicians (ACEP); specifically, that surge capacity is the ability of the healthcare system "to manage a sudden or rapidly progressive influx of patients within the currently available resources" (ACEP, 2005). Others consider not only those resources available at a given time, but also those that may be readily mobilized in support of the incident. The proposition that the ability to manage surges in volume is constrained by current staffing levels is more rational in the context of an emergency department making routine operational decisions, than in the context of extraordinary surge following a catastrophic event. The ACEP has since revised that often-quoted policy statement and in its current form omits the phrase "within the currently available resources" (ACEP, 2011).

It is no more prudent, however, and no more methodically sound, to consider average or aggregate staffing levels a discrete measure of surge capacity. In the last decade, with the emerging consensus that surge capacity is multifaceted, one particular line of research suggests that healthcare workforce absenteeism is associated with a number of

*Table 7.4    Crisis surge capacity and components*

| | |
|---|---|
| Crisis surge capacity | A measure of the organization's ability to provide care that, while not consistent with usual standards of care, is sufficient under the extreme conditions of a disaster. |
| Staff | Assignment outside typical scope of practice; just-in-time teaching (JITT). Use of advanced or specialty practice limited to complex cases. |
| Stuff | Resource sharing of scarce resources; sterilize and reuse of more invasive disposable supplies. |
| | Rationing of critical items using benefit–demand analysis. |
| Space | Use of non-clinical space for clinical procedures; hallways, meeting and classrooms, any safe, available flat-space; transfer to alternative care site. |
| Systems | Notification and warning. |
| | Incident command: primarily hospital authority and clinical decisions. |
| | Operations: triage, medical services, support. |
| | Logistics: facility resources. |
| | Administrative: finance, human resources. |
| | Communications: internal and external. |
| | Public information. |
| Standards | Significant deviation from routine practices and standard operating procedures; crisis standards of care. |

variables (Kaji et al., 2006); among those appearing most often in recent studies are: (1) the nature and severity of the crisis event; (2) competing personal and family obligations; (3) the stability and leadership of the working environment; and (4) employee understanding of risks and whether those risks can be effectively mitigated (Connor, 2014). Whether reductions in the available healthcare workforce are based on ability or willingness to report to duty (Qureshi et al., 2005), these will undoubtedly have a detrimental effect on capacity. While a few scholars have included healthcare workforce absenteeism in surge capacity modeling, and several more have attempted to translate survey results into generalizable estimates of workforce depletion (Qureshi et al., 2005; Adams and Berry, 2012; Snipes et al., 2013), the measured balance of risk and duty to care is a profoundly personal one, and as such there is no universal threshold of risk after which we would expect absenteeism to rise (Iserson et al., 2008; Ehrenstein et al., 2006).

Widespread absenteeism, regardless of the underlying mechanisms, is a significant threat to capacity and requires attention during each phase of the emergency management cycle. There are three non-exclusive approaches to mitigating the effect of staffing shortfalls during crisis events, as follows.

### Prevent absenteeism to the extent possible

Lesperance and Miller (2009) propose that healthcare organizations can prevent absenteeism and promote resilience among the workforce by addressing identified needs and creating an organizational culture that values the provider's duty to their patients and colleagues. Needs to be addressed as part of the approach include leadership, communication, training, supplies and equipment sufficient to safeguard the employee, and assistance with practical needs (childcare, eldercare, transportation, lodging, and so on) and psychosocial needs (fear, stress, anxiety).

### Augment staffing with volunteers and reserve corps

Either through highly structured national systems of organizing volunteer healthcare personnel or the development of local resources, healthcare-trained volunteers allow an organization to offset reduced staffing levels or expand operations past routine capacity (Hoard and Tosatto, 2005; Frasca, 2010). There is some debate concerning the planned use of federal government resources to backfill or expand operations, anticipating that these workforces may be otherwise activated in support of a broader response, threat to the community, or in the interest of national defense (Sariego, 2006; Kearns et al., 2014).

### Temporary, conditional adaptation of roles and responsibilities

The organization develops a crisis staffing plan based on and providing guidance during each of the three responsive modes along the continuum of surge capacity: conventional, contingency, and crisis. While specific action to be undertaken during transition between one level and the next will be specific to the organization's unique characteristics, values, and objectives, the normative literature does provide some limited guidance (Hanfling et al., 2012): during the transition to "conventional capacity" (full utilization of assigned staff, often equated to a "busy day") documentation requirements are lessened and non-medical duties are reassigned; when transitioning to "contingency capacity," assignments and shifts are realigned to the incident need, supervision span of control changes to free up managerial resources, and routine patient assessments are discontinued in favor of assessment following an observed clinical change; once resources are overwhelmed and the organization is operating in a mode of "crisis capacity," staffing activities should include just-in-time training based on incident-specific mechanism of injury or illness (burns, trauma, respiratory infection, and so on). The focus of the training should be basic competencies and low-level intervention, which allows specialists to work on more complex cases (Hick et al., 2009).

**Surge Capacity: Equipment and Supplies**

Having gone the way of more traditional industrial and commercial consumers, hospitals often rely on a just-in-time inventory process to limit expenditures on storage, loss, and expiration (Schultz and Koenig, 2006; Jarrett, 2006). This substantially limits the organization from drawing on internal reserves during the first few hours or days of a crisis event. Hospitals have had varying degrees of success in reaching out to vendors and suppliers, and during widespread events there are constraints on equipment in use at other facilities, notwithstanding prior arrangements or agreements proposing shared resources as an alternative to costly stockpiling of assets. Ventilators, durable medical equipment, and pharmaceuticals are the dominant discussions in the management of scarce resources during a crisis.

There are a number of proposed strategies in the literature; two are particularly promising. Both were incorporated in the latest surge capacity planning toolkit published by the Institute of Medicine. The first is a focus on collaborative networks to facilitate the sharing of potentially scarce resources, augmented by interoperable computer-based tracking systems to identify the potential for depletion. There is support for using similar systems for US federal resources and government stockpiles of pharmaceuticals, and for a number of those resources implementation is under way at the agency level (CDC, 2014). The second is a further implementation of Hick's continuum of surge capacity. Over the first two response modes on the continuum – that is, conventional and contingency – providers begin to conserve supplies based on anticipated need, having relatively little impact on the standard of care. This includes the wash and reuse of minimally invasive equipment, such as immobilization boards and cervical collars that are designated as disposable items. During operations designed for crisis capacity, Hick et al. (2009) recommend sterilization and reuse of intravenous lines and other highly invasive equipment, as well as the rationing and distribution of medications to those who will achieve the greatest benefit with the lowest demand on resources.

**Surge Capacity: Medical Facility and Available Space**

I start with a statement that seemingly contradicts the previous discussion on bed count: an accurate count of available beds is an undeniable measure of surge capacity (Kelen et al., 2009; Satterhwaite and Atkinson,

2012). However, when bed count is the exclusively reported measure, it is insufficient to estimate surge capacity (Barbisch and Koenig, 2006). Bed availability, despite its occasional misuse as a single indicator of capacity, is nonetheless the most often cited issue with surge capacity in the research literature.

Following widespread criticism of the "available bed" measure of surge capacity, many organizations broadened their focus to the facility as a whole. In support of those efforts, numerous researchers considered cost-feasible approaches to building in reserve or flexible space, routinely used for non-medical purposes, but that could be readily converted to clinical or triage use during disaster operations (Walters et al., 2013). Because funding and space limitations make expansion impossible in some cases, the literature is strewn with a wide variety of alternatives to expansion (Hick et al., 2004); some proposing non-adjacent alternative care sites (Eastman et al., 2007), others proposing more creative use of existing space (Walters et al., 2013).

Applying the three-mode continuum approach to managing patient care space provides context and allows for considering more realistic, dynamic, and short-term alternatives to building, buying, or remodeling facility space. The healthcare organization transitions from routine to conventional response operations when there are indications that conservation of resources may be necessary to mitigate the effect of a surge in patient loads that will not overwhelm available hospital resources. Making space available in a systematic, clinically responsible way prolongs transition to higher response modes along the continuum – contingency or crisis – with the objective of providing care consistent with routine practices. Policies and operational decisions that achieve this objective include: calling in off-duty medical personnel to staff the organization's unstaffed beds; marshalling and reallocating unused beds and observation beds; activating surge discharge plans to move patients whose condition and acuity allow discharge to home or an alternative care facility; and cancellation of routine appointments and elective surgeries. Note that these cancellations will have little impact on availability of inpatient beds, but will create capacity in clinical and surgical rooms.

Estimates of the improvement in the number of patient beds are similar in studies where capacity is estimated by clinical evaluation of patient population at a given point for a period of time (Davis et al., 2005; Kelen et al., 2009), or by retrospective assessment of real-world large-scale events (Hick et al., 2004). The results of these studies in aggregate indicate that surge discharge can create a near-immediate capacity increase of 20 percent to 30 percent, and after 72 hours, 50 percent to 60 percent of pre-incident inpatients could be safely discharged. Hick et al. (2004), however, cautions that hospital characteristics and patient demographics play an important role in determining these estimates, and proposes that this should be estimated as a component of surge capacity planning.

When the organization reaches its capacity to provide care using conventional practices, the transition to contingency response mode begins with the clearing of patients from predetermined areas so that the space can be used for inpatient care; these areas typically include those routinely used for pre-induction, post-anesthesia, and surgical procedures. Intensive-care patients should be evaluated and, if stable enough, moved to stepdown units or floor beds. The goal in contingency mode is to provide space for functionally equivalent care: that which may deviate slightly from standard of routine procedures, but not so much as to reduce the standard of care provided to the patient.

If patient loads continue to surge to a point where contingency operations cannot accommodate needed services, patients may be provided inpatient care in areas of the facility that were never intended for patient care: any safe area with flat space, including hallways, meeting rooms, and common space. These areas were not included in estimations of surge capacity, and are utilized only when the planned capacity of the facility has been exhausted and the hospital is operating in a crisis response mode. The objective during crisis operations is to provide care that is sufficient under the extreme conditions of the event. With time, the incident stabilizes and the response mode moves in the direction of recovery, back toward conventional care and eventually normal operating conditions.

## SURGE CAPACITY: OPERATIONS MANAGEMENT AND SYSTEMS

A systems approach in the context of healthcare emergency management is a strategy that develops and progresses a standardized framework under which a number of relatively autonomous organizations are viewed as related components of a single system with the purpose of achieving a common objective (ICDRM, 2010).This framework consists of an identified management structure and processes that cross organizational boundaries, and a workforce familiar with the unified operational roles, pooled resources, and objectives.

Although there is broad consensus that an effective response is predicated on a systematic approach to the management of resources available for response operations, discussion on systems as a necessary consideration for surge capacity markedly decreased in the literature in the decade that followed Barbisch and Koenig's (2006) addition of systems to the surge capacity triad. Despite a number of initiatives to further develop incident management systems for healthcare, recent studies indicate that there is limited use and institutionalization of systems for command and management of resources during disasters outside of those designed for daily use (Jensen and Waugh, 2014). Research proposes two principal reasons for the aversion to the establishment of a separate and distinct management system for disaster-impacting healthcare operations: the first is that it is not needed, and the second is that it would not work.

First, there is widespread misconception that disaster operations differ from routine emergency operations only in the number of patients and perhaps the severity of injuries. Providers believe that routine operations can be scaled up to meet increased demand. This approach underestimates the qualitative differences in routine and disaster operations. In addition to psychosocial and behavioral effects on providers and patients, Quarantelli (1998) finds four qualitative differences between routine emergency and disaster operations at the organizational level. During disasters:

1.  Organizations must work collaboratively with others, often across several disciplines and organizational structures.
2.  Healthcare organizations lose some degree of autonomy as operational authority for coordinated response is vested in public officials.
3.  Standards of operation or performance are modified in an attempt to increase capacity or ensure personal safety.
4.  Boundaries between the public and private sector are crossed and individual and organizational rights may be pre-empted by public need.

The second obstacle to meaningful implementation of disaster management systems in healthcare exists in the concern that existing and proposed management structures are not practical for use in the healthcare environment. As is the case with disaster and emergency management terminology, there is some inconsistency in the usage of two terms "incident management" and "incident command." Most often, incident command systems are designated as those that facilitate the direction of response personnel. The term "incident management system" is used more broadly to include incident command system (ICS) and other systems intended to support response operations, including resource management, communications, and documentation and tracking of incident activities. An effective incident management system designates and describes essential functions, including command, control, communication, and coordination of incident resources (Hick et al., 2004), which consist of personnel, facilities, equipment, and supplies:

- Command. Through the delegation of authority of the individual, organization, or agency duly authorized to commit resources toward an identified objective, the incident commander determines and prioritizes response objectives and manages available resources in an effort to achieve them. The incident commander is charged with overall management of response activities.
- Control. Where "command" implies that an individual has the authority to commit resources and prioritize response objectives, "control" is the authority to make tactical decisions regarding how those objectives will be achieved. This includes directing personnel, facilities, and equipment, and available funding.
- Communication. The system must provide for the timely distribution of information pertinent to the response, including alerting and notification, situation status, and reporting of progress toward objectives. Communication includes the sharing of information with internal and external resources.
- Coordination. The incident management system must provide for the coordination of response activities of the organization with the broader community. This function is particularly important in response to widespread disasters that affect a number of public and private healthcare resources, as capacity and demand at one impacts the operational conditions at another.

These four components appeared in the literature in 2004, and since have been often interpreted to be essential to an incident command system, and a necessary element of an incident management system. Hanfling et al. (2012) include these in "the core functions and associated tasks of hospital facilities" in the Institute of Medicine's *Crisis Standards of Care: A Systems Framework for Catastrophic Disaster Response*. The core functions of an incident management system are shown in Table 7.5.

Several models for incident management have been described, some specific to healthcare (Barbera and Macintyre, 2002) and some standardized across emergency response disciplines, like the US National Incident Management System (NIMS). The Hospital Incident Command System (HICS) in the USA was developed in the late 1980s on the proposition that hospitals would benefit from incident command systems that had gained popularity in the fire services, and that those systems could be readily adapted to the specific needs of hospitals (CEMSA, 2006). In the decades that followed, HICS was revised to reflect changes in the evolution of healthcare from facility-based to systems-based. HICS is the most widely adopted system in hospitals accredited by the Joint Commission (Jensen and Waugh, 2014). In response to an event identified in the organization's emergency

*Table 7.5    Core functions of an incident management system*

| Function | Description |
| --- | --- |
| Monitoring and alerting | Monitoring established system used to alert the organization of impending threats |
| Notification and warning | The ability to notify responding personnel and relay information critical to operations and personal safety |
| Command | Clarity of roles and responsibilities under a delegation of authority from organization executives |
| Control | Authority to utilize the resources to achieve incident objectives and mitigate loss |
| Communications | Procedures and infrastructure that facilitates the sharing of information to and from internal and external units |
| Coordination | Planning and implementation of response actions that align and support activities of other responding agencies |
| Public information | The sharing of relevant, factual information regarding the status and operations of the organization |
| Operations | Providing triage, clinical care, and support operations in support of identified command objectives |
| Logistics | Providing or maintaining the facilities, equipment, staff, and supplies needed for operationalizing plans |
| Planning | Gathering information, tracking resources, and planning activities in support of the incident response |
| Administration | Providing guidance on legal, regulatory, and organizational directives in evolving conditions |

operations plan, the HICS management structure is initiated by establishing an incident commander, who is delegated the authority to direct operations in response to the incident by the chief executive officer. As the incident evolves and the potential to overwhelm the commander's ability to manage the various aspects of the response increases, the incident commander builds out a standardized hierarchical structure and delegates the authority to established functional sections of the incident management team. Disaster response activities are carried out in functional components called sections, which may be further subdivided into units designated to perform specific tasks in support of the operation. Figure 7.3 illustrates the basic structure of the HICS when all sections are activated. Units would be added to each section as warranted by the changing complexity of the response.

Although ICS is deeply institutionalized in emergency response

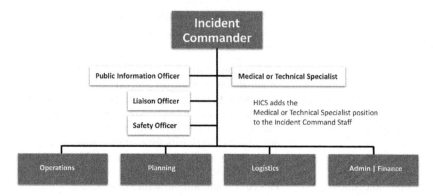

*Figure 7.3    HICS basic organizational structure*

organizations and enjoys near universal adoption in the United States, Wenger et al. (1990) enumerate a number of weaknesses of ICS including weak interagency coordination, and propose that these weaknesses may be attributable to the system's origin and evolution in the fire service, where the authority of the fire department to conduct fire ground operations is evident; there is a strong sense of community; and participants are well trained in the concepts and principles of ICS. Others suggest that the deficiencies identified in the literature are not innate weaknesses in ICS but are the results of flawed or fragmented implementation, where adoption of the incident management system was spurious, institutionalization of ICS has not occurred, or participants lack sufficient knowledge to operationalize system principles (Buck et al., 2006).

Despite these proposed shortcomings of ICS for the healthcare organization, an overwhelming majority of hospitals have adopted HICS as an incident command system. Adoption of the NIMS framework and annually reported measures of implementation are a condition of receiving preparedness funding. Additionally, recent changes in standards for Joint Commission accreditation require organizational adoption of an incident management system that is consistent and capable of integrating into the larger community response. Adoption, however, is not necessarily indicative of meaningful implementation and use (Jensen and Waugh, 2014).

## SURGE CAPACITY: STANDARDS OF CARE

Until researchers began to consider the effects of Hurricane Katrina in 2005 on the ability of the US healthcare system to provide medical care in the face of overwhelming demand, there was little overt discussion in the literature regarding the appropriate standard of care in disaster situations. Until the same time, most hospital emergency operations plans assumed no change in the standard of care to be delivered, and further assumed that the healthcare system was capable of expanding or consolidating resources, facilities, and staffing to support the delivery of care of the usual standard. In 2005, the Agency for Healthcare Research and Quality (AHRQ) in the United States proposed that under certain catastrophic conditions, that assumption is flawed, and that in events involving thousands of victims, maintaining a functioning healthcare system would require hospitals and practitioners to consider implementing "altered" standards of care. Acknowledging that there was no widely accepted definition for "altered," they generalized the term to mean "providing care and allocating scarce equipment, supplies, and personnel in a way that saves the largest number of lives in contrast to the traditional focus on saving individuals" (ARHQ, 2005). What follows in the literature is commentary, debate, and conjecture that together offer insight into the complexities of considering altered standards of care, as well as the diversity of opinion in the medical and emergency response communities as to the appropriateness of doing so.

One must initially consider the usual standard of care and the perspective from which it should be evaluated under routine operations. While it is important to differentiate medical and legal standards of care, the two are decidedly associated, as development and adoption of the medical standard influences over time the practice and approach of providers against which the legal standard will be evaluated.

The medical standard of care is a consensus of the profession; evaluation of the clinical decisions of a provider considering professional norms, statutory and regulatory requirements, and institutional objectives (Hanfling et al., 2012). Often the medical standard of care is reflected in the clinical practice guidelines developed by various associations of medical professionals that summarize the current state of research and knowledge on specific conditions. The medical standard of care is useful in evaluating patient progress and outcomes, and the professional judgment and conduct of providers.

The legal standard of care is useful only in the context of determining whether particular conduct by a provider constitutes medical negligence. The legal standard of care is an extension of the legal principle of "duty of care" in negligent tort law. When allegedly negligent conduct results in loss or injury to another, the court considers whether the conduct was that a "reasonably prudent person" would take under similar circumstances. In medical negligence cases, the legal standard of care considers whether the care rendered was consistent with other community providers under similar circumstances.

Even during normal conditions, clinical practices often vary slightly between geographic regions, as they are influenced by dissimilarities in local culture, state and county regulations, jurisdictional issues, resource availability, and a number of other internal and external factors. For this reason, the court often considers the "community standard," as providers in the same region experience the same influences and, as such, should practice in a relatively consistent manner.

Much of the debate concerning altered standards of care in disaster is centered on condoning alternative medical standards and practices in the healthcare community where providers may be liable for their conduct when the legal standard is later used to evaluate that conduct. Further, many propose that since the legal standard of care considers the level of care rendered by providers under similar circumstances, which necessarily includes conditions of overwhelming demand and scarce resources, altered standards of care are unnecessary and may even have a detrimental effect on quality of care provided (Schultz and Annas, 2012).

Similar events may have dramatically different consequences and impacts on the different organizations depending on the size, location, and resources of the facility (Hick et al., 2009). Because the implementation of crisis standards of care will be predicated upon a number of complex variables, including the baseline and disaster response resources, demands, capacity of healthcare organizations, duration, and so on, research currently provides little guidance on just how the standards should be altered, focusing more on the considerations and processes of planning for crisis standards of care (CSC). In developing surge capacity plans that include processes and indicators for initiation of altered or "crisis" standards of care, healthcare organizations must provide for:

- a strong ethical grounding that enables a process deemed equitable based on its transparency, consistency, proportionality, and accountability;
- integrated and ongoing community and provider engagement, education, and communication;
- the necessary legal authority and legal environment in which CSC can be ethically and optimally implemented;
- clear indicators, triggers, and lines of responsibility; and
- evidence-based clinical processes and operations (Gostin et al., 2009, p. 20).

Along the continuum of surge capacity, usual standards of care are maintained in the conventional and contingent phases by making temporary changes in operational processes and procedures intended to utilize any unused capacity. In the conventional phase, the marshaling and decidedly more conservative use of resources takes advantage of any excess organizational capacity. In the contingent phase, patient care practices that deviate from the routine practices of the organization but maintain either the usual standard of care or their "functional equivalent" are adopted. Converting clinical procedure areas to inpatient use, for instance, does not fall short of the standard of care, but would not be considered the "routine" practice of the hospital. When operating at its full potential, using all conventional and contingency capacity combined, further increases in demand for patient care will overwhelm resources. During and immediately following a disaster, demand outpaces resources in such a way that providers attempting to deliver care consistent with the usual standards of care will result in the demands of other patients going unaddressed. While under normal circumstances the best interests of the individual patient are paramount, there is widespread acceptance in the practice community that disasters shift the focus from the individual patient to the population of patients.

## BEYOND PATIENT DEMAND

Undoubtedly, increased demand for patient care is the primary focus of the healthcare organization's response during disaster operations, where injuries or illnesses are a direct result of the disaster. It is important, however, to recognize that the response to the disaster also requires resources and generates additional demand. Incident management can be made more efficient by differentiating event-generated and response-generated demand. Event-generated demands are those unique to the crisis. While planning activities in the preparedness phase will make assumptions regarding incident demands based on the nature of the events and the organization's vulnerabilities, actual demands cannot be determined prior to the event occurrence. Response-generated demands, in contrast, are consequences of response operations rather than of the incident. As Quarantelli (1998) put it: "there are problems created by the disaster itself, and there are problems generated by the organized effort to respond to the disaster."

The principles of incident management systematically identify incident demands either in the preparedness phase or in the response phase, depending on whether the demands are generated by the crisis events or by the response itself. Severe storms may generate a disaster surge in traumatic injuries in a localized region and result in damage to the closest hospital, all on relatively short notice. A hurricane provides a longer time frame in which to prepare for response operations, but consequences are far more widespread and may result in the loss of multiple hospitals and public health functions. Responsive actions and the nature of medical services needed will differ significantly between earthquakes and floods, or chemical accidents and disease epidemics. While some level of preparation and planning is necessary for individual hazards for which the organization identifies a potential, it is simply not possible to predetermine the demands generated by the unknown or to develop scripted responses.

Emergency managers in the healthcare setting must consider both event-generated and consequential response-generated demands in the preparedness phase through planning, and equipping and training response personnel appropriately. Because the organization designs the response structure, planning assumptions for response-generated demands are often more accurate and, therefore, more readily addressed at crisis occurrence.

## THEORY AND PRACTICE: MEASURES OF PREPAREDNESS

Evaluating healthcare preparedness is challenging for a number of reasons and the result is a lack of consensus in evaluation measures and methods (Nelson et al., 2007). Some are related to the collection and analysis of disaster-related data. Since disasters are rare, the occasions to evaluate systems and outcomes at or near capacity are limited (Alexander, 1993). In cases where measures are available, the chaotic nature of disasters makes it difficult to attribute positive or negative change in outcomes to preparedness efforts. It is, for example, impossible to compare the impact upon two communities during the same disaster, and to attribute loss of life or property to the level of preparedness; it is meaningless, also, to compare the losses of a community during one disaster to the losses of the same community in a subsequent disaster.

Other reasons are more academic. Some propose that because disaster outcomes cannot be isolated, preparedness research should focus on process evaluation or intermediate measures. Compared to evaluating objectives or structural measures, process evaluation is inherently more difficult and requires more complex methodology; structural measures are more easily addressed with policy or administrative change, whereas process measures are likely to require substantial effort and monitoring over a longer period of time (Krumholz et al., 2006). Mays et al. (2009) propose that one solution lies in establishing multidimensional measures of healthcare delivery, including preparedness, using theoretically sound intermediate outcomes expected to be associated with improved performance. As a result of the difficulties with data collection, interpretation, and a theoretical approach, even extraordinary findings presented using seemingly reasonable methodologies are cast in a negative light and progress toward a consensus measure is hindered.

Healthcare organizations predominantly evaluate preparedness and their underlying capacity of response to disaster scenario exercises. These may be conducted as relatively informal consideration and discussion of organizational responses to a hypothesized event, sometimes called a "tabletop exercise," or may be much more resource-intensive and designed to place the workforce in simulated conditions to test one or more functional components of the response plan and system. While training exercise design has improved in the last decade, and training and evaluation in public health agencies and organizations have gained acceptance, these methodologies still primarily test outcomes and capacity on a scale that permits ongoing operations and does not exhaust resources (Arch et al., 2008). This premise is difficult to reconcile with a broader understanding of disaster operations: that is, by definition, an overwhelming of resources. It is simply not either economically feasible or ethically prudent for organizations to test disaster preparedness to the point of failure.

Criticisms of exercises and self-assessment measures of preparedness should not be thought to indicate a lack of value in increasing readiness for a disaster event. The broad consensus is that these activities are meaningful to comprehensive emergency management, often identifying deficiencies that serve as the basis for future planning, mitigation, and preparedness activities. Rather, caution should be used in the interpretation of exercise outcomes as measures that are predictive of organizational capacity or performance during crisis events.

Further, the debate in usefulness of preparedness indictors extends beyond how to measure response potential. A lack of consensus on which activities undertaken by healthcare organizations, called "target capabilities," should be considered as indicators of preparedness was demonstrated by McCarthy et al. (2009). Thirty-five target capabilities were identified in the five agencies and organizations considered most influential in US healthcare emergency management. Only seven of the 35 activities were identified jointly by three or more of the organizations. That study concluded that the current focus on the development of tools for the evaluation of healthcare emergency management should be shifted to the development of a common and widely accepted framework for healthcare preparedness (McCarthy et al., 2009).

# THEORY AND PRACTICE: HEALTHCARE COALITIONS

It is widely acknowledged in healthcare emergency management that collaboration is an essential component of preparedness, with the caveat that these alliances often create challenges of their own: from conflicts over resource utilization, to priorities, to organizational culture (Kadushin et al., 2005). The underlying assumption in an organization's decision to participate in preparedness coalitions – like all preparedness activities – is that doing so definitively improves the organization's ability to respond effectively and efficiently to these large-scale events (Lindell et al., 2001). In addition, it is reasonable that participation in healthcare coalitions, because of increased training and access to additional resources, may actually improve the member organizations' routine operations (Hoge et al., 2005).

If these assumptions were incorrect, the member organizations would have no incentive to remain in the coalition. Individuals and organizations only join and remain in alliances when the benefits of being in the alliance outweigh the costs (Pretsby et al., 1990). It is necessary, therefore, to evaluate the ability of these coalitions to improve the capacity of individual organizational members to respond to disasters. Yet, relatively few published studies attempt this seemingly critical evaluation, and fewer still do so with more than nominal scientific rigor (Granner and Sharpe, 2004).

While healthcare coalitions for the purpose of emergency and disaster preparedness are a relatively recent endeavor, coalitions and partnerships have long been a mechanism used in public health to address a broad range of chronic conditions and social concerns (Cheadle et al., 1997; Butterfoss and Francisco, 2004). Partnerships and coalitions with clearly defined public health objectives more effectively utilize institutional and interorganizational resources, avoid duplication, and broaden the foundation of the initiative's knowledge and workforce (Reich, 2000). Healthcare coalitions are useful in mobilizing community and shared resources and providing coordination of public health activities (Berkowitz and Wolff, 2000; Wolff, 2001).

Reviewing the guidance documents published by numerous agencies and branches of the US federal government, and adopted in large part by the practice community, leaves one with the impression that healthcare coalitions have a measureable positive effect on capacity. But, despite a long history and anecdotal success of collaborative efforts to promote public health, healthcare coalitions suffer from the same shortcomings in theoretical consensus as do preparedness measures. There is no demonstrated consensus as to what constitutes effectiveness in coalition-building

(Zakocs and Edwards, 2006; Zakocs and Guckenburg, 2007); little agreement upon which measures the collaborative process should be judged; and no widely accepted methodological techniques to analyze either processes or outcomes (Granner and Sharpe, 2004).

Recent focus and the availability of grant funding have improved the US healthcare system's disaster readiness, but parts of the system remain fractured and dysfunctional, insufficiently prepared to effectively manage large-scale catastrophic events requiring the immediate treatment of large numbers of patients (Courtney et al., 2009). This is in large part because emergency preparedness is considered by most a function of government, and US healthcare is overwhelmingly in the private sector. As a result, comprehensive, integrated disaster preparedness is slow in coming.

Shortly after the markedly deficient public health response to the terrorist attacks on the World Trade Center in New York City and the anthrax attacks that began one week later, the National Hospital Preparedness Program (HPP) was established within the United States Department of Health and Human Services. Since that time, the focus of the program has expanded from bioterrorism response and readiness to hospital preparedness more generally. Management of the program was placed with the Assistant Secretary for Preparedness and Response (ASPR) as part of the 2006 Pandemic and All-Hazards Preparedness Act. The program funding increased from the initial appropriation of $125 million in 2002 to nearly $500 million in 2003, and has averaged just under $450 million per year since (HHS, 2013).

The HPP has been credited with a number of meaningful improvements to the US hospital system, many of those specific to the system's capacity for emergency response and disaster readiness. In 2009, an evaluation of the program by the Center for Biosecurity at the University of Pittsburgh Medical Center (UPMC) noted the major advancements in individual hospital preparedness measures and recognized the emergence of healthcare coalitions specific to emergency and disaster preparedness, but cautioned that such efforts were still in the early stages, and insufficient to effectively respond to widespread catastrophic events (Toner et al., 2009).

In the 2009 HPP program report, the Assistant Secretary for Preparedness and Response stated that among the priorities in moving forward "will be the increased emphasis on broader, community-wide, healthcare preparedness approaches, including building and strengthening healthcare coalitions . . . and . . . development and use of additional preparedness metrics" (ASPR, 2011a, Foreword). In support of these priorities, grant funding would "move from preparedness at the facility level to healthcare preparedness at the community level, through further development and operation of Healthcare Coalitions nationally" (ASPR,

2011b, p. 106). This economically incentivizes organizations to participate in emergency preparedness coalitions. While this important shift in strategy moves public health preparedness efforts toward meaningful collaboration and an increased capacity to respond to patient surge, existing measures are inadequate for scientifically rigorous evaluation of the effectiveness of collaborative relationships.

In 2013, of more than 6300 US hospitals, just over 85 percent received funding from the HPP and, thus, expressly agreed to participate in healthcare coalitions. Evaluation of measures proposed in the absence of a definitive theoretical framework for preparedness and preparedness coalitions potentially misaligns incentives for performance and demonstrated improvement, and is, therefore, detrimental to the coalition-building process, the cost-effectiveness of such efforts, and progress toward substantive improvements in preparedness at the facility and community level.

## THEORY AND PRACTICE: POLICY, MANAGEMENT, AND RESEARCH IMPLICATIONS

For a number of reasons, there is considerable opportunity for meaningful research in healthcare disaster preparedness and response: numerous operational and functional components; the varying nature and scope of disaster events; a growing continuum of healthcare facilities and services; and medical, legal, and ethical questions, to name a few. It is rational, then, that there should be as diverse a perspective on research priorities. On the contrary, healthcare and public health disaster researchers and practitioners chiefly agree on the relative importance of furthering understanding of several key elements in disaster preparedness. Since 2008, a number of national organizations focused on hospital and public healthcare systems have indicated the following issues as critical to the advance of healthcare emergency management and disaster preparedness (Altevogt et al., 2008; Lazar et al., 2009; McCarthy et al., 2009; Nelson et al., 2008).

### Evaluating Preparedness Measures

Research in the area of emergency management and preparedness should focus on the development and validation of conceptual frameworks for disaster preparedness that are relevant to and widely accessed by the healthcare sector. Lack of consensus as to the validity and reliability of existing or newly developed evaluations and instruments undermines progress in identifying and building strength in those measures associated with improved capacity and performance.

Setting aside the difficulties in collecting and analyzing data during a disaster, and issues of validity in even well-designed exercises and drills, the absence of consensus on essential components of healthcare management hinders progress on the development of useful evaluation tools and discourages commitment of resources to improve the current circumstances. The ultimate objective in this line of research must be clear and consistent criteria for evaluating healthcare disaster management programs and metrics for monitoring and reporting progress and cost-efficiency.

**Collaboration and Integration in a Systems Approach**

Healthcare organizations joining healthcare coalitions as a means of improving disaster preparedness and response perceive an increased capacity as well as improved organizational emergency management. As access to HPP and Public Health Preparedness Cooperative (PHEP) funding is conditioned upon participation, implementation is occurring in the absence of a sound theoretical framework for preparedness coalition-building. Research should build on existing coalition theory with the objective of developing and validating a healthcare preparedness coalition framework to guide the creation, maintenance, and periodic evaluation of collaborative efforts.

These efforts, as well as those of integrating healthcare organizations into the broader community response, must be supported with additional research in the implementation of systems specific to emergency and incident management. Existing systems are not well implemented and are often underutilized during crisis situations, creating operational disconnects between traditional emergency response functions – like police, fire, and emergency management – and healthcare, which plays a vital role in disaster operations. Investigators must identify the barriers to implementation of existing frameworks or propose alternative, but compatible, healthcare-specific management systems.

**Legal Issues on the Horizon**

Operations under implemented crisis standards of care are predicated on plans developed by the institution in collaboration with state and local governments and community partners that call for a formal declaration of the transition to a crisis response mode. The declaration of a disaster, a health power conferred by a state government upon public officials, is one of a number of unconventional powers that are rarely used, scarcely understood by the general public, and are likely to cause confusion if not discussed in detail with those in the organization who will ultimately be charged with conducting disaster operations. Many US state laws limit the liability of healthcare providers during declared emergencies and disaster, allow for changes in the scope of practice, authorize temporarily granting of privileges to providers licensed out-of-state, and temporarily suspend laws and regulations that under normal conditions guide clinical practice or hospital procedures.

Hospitals and providers must understand their legal rights and liabilities before the occurrence of an event that may result in a deviation from normal operations. Legal issues arising from disasters that result in increased demand and subsequent strain on resources may include medical negligence and malpractice claims, claims based on the application of triage protocols, liability in the organization's failing to adequately plan for emergencies, and violations of statutory and regulatory provisions regarding access, discriminatory conduct, and patients' rights.

Because there is no direct mechanism of healthcare to adjust the legal standard of care, implemented changes to the medical standard of care during disasters will predictably result in a number of legal actions on the basis of medical malpractice. This is an area that healthcare providers and hospital administrators should monitor, to ensure that adopted and future policies and practices are consistent with court decisions and do not create unanticipated liability.

## REFERENCES

Adams, L.M. and D. Berry (2012), "Who will show up? Estimating ability and willingness of essential hospital personnel to report to work in response to a disaster," *Online Journal of Issues in Nursing*, 17 (2), available at http://www.ncbi.nlm.nih.gov/pubmed/22686116.

Agency for Healthcare Research and Quality (AHRQ) (2005), "Altered standards of care in mass casualty events: Bioterrorism and other public health emergencies," Rockville, MD: AHRQ.

Alexander, David (1993), *Natural Disasters*, New York: Chapman & Hall.

Altevogt, Bruce M., Andrew M. Pope, Martha N. Hill, and K.I. Shine (2008), "Research priorities in emergency preparedness and response for public health systems. A letter report," Washington, DC: Institute of Medicine Committee on Research Priorities in Emergency Preparedness and Response for Public Health Systems.

American College of Emergency Physicians (ACEP) (2005), "Health care system surge capacity recognition, preparedness, and response," *Annals of Emergency Medicine*, 45 (2): 239.

American College of Emergency Physicians (ACEP) (2011), "Healthcare system surge capacity recognition, preparedness, and response," available at http://www.acep.org/Clinical-Practice-Management/Health-Care-System-Surge-Capacity (accessed 15 May 2014).

Arch, F.Z.D., R. Berry, M.P. Pietrzak, and A. Paratore (2008), "Integrating disaster preparedness and surge capacity in emergency facility planning," *Journal of Ambulatory Care Management*, 31 (4): 377–385.

Assistant Secretary for Preparedness and Response (ASPR) (2011a), "From hospitals to healthcare coalitions: Transforming health preparedness and response in our communities," US Department of Health and Human Services, available at http://www. phe.gov/Preparedness/planning/hpp/Documents/hpp-healthcare-coalitions.pdf (accessed 12 March 2014).

Assistant Secretary for Preparedness and Response (ASPR) (2011b), "FY11 Hospital Preparedness Program (HPP) guidance," US Department of Health and Human Services, available at http://www.phe.gov/Preparedness/planning/hpp/Documents/fy2011-hpp-funding-guidance.pdf (accessed 12 March 2014).

Barbera, Joseph A. and Anthony G. Macintyre (2002), "Medical and Health Incident Management (MaHIM) System: A comprehensive functional system description for mass casualty medical and health incident management: Final report, December 2002," Washington, DC: Institute for Crisis, Disaster, and Risk Management, George Washington University.

Barbisch, D.F. and K.L. Koenig (2006), "Understanding surge capacity: essential elements," *Academic Emergency Medicine*, 13 (11): 1098–1102.

Berkowitz, William and Tom Wolff (eds) (2000), *The Spirit of the Coalition*, Washington, DC: American Public Health Association.

Buck, D.A., J.E. Trainor, and B.E. Aguirre (2006), "A critical evaluation of the incident command system and NIMS," *Journal of Homeland Security and Emergency Management*, 3 (3). DOI: 10.2202/1547-7355.1252.

Butterfoss, F.D. and Francisco, V.T. (2004), "Evaluating community partnerships and coalitions with practitioners in mind," *Health Promotion Practice*, 5 (2): 108–114.

California Emergency Medical Services Authority (CEMSA) (2006), *The Hospital Incident Command System Guidebook*, available at http://www.emsa.CA.gov (accessed 27 March 2014).

Center for Disease Control and Prevention (CDC) (2014), "Countermeasure tracking systems," available at http://www.cdc.gov/phin/tools/imats/index.html?s_cid=fb1291 (accessed 5 April 2014).

Cheadle, A., W. Beery, E. Wagner, S. Fawcett, L. Green, D. Moss, A. Plough, A. Wandersman, and I. Woods (1997), "Conference report: community-based health promotion – state of the art and recommendations for the future," *American Journal of Preventive Medicine*, 13 (4): 240–243.

Connor, S.B. (2014), "When and why health care personnel respond to a disaster: the state of the science," *Prehospital and Disaster Medicine*, 29 (3): 1–5.

Courtney, B., E. Toner, R. Waldhorn, C. Franco, K. Rambhia, A. Norwood, T.V. Inglesby, and T. O'Toole (2009), "Healthcare coalitions: The new foundation for national health-care preparedness and response for catastrophic health emergencies," *Biosecurity and Bioterrorism: Biodefense Strategy, Practice, and Science*, 7 (2): 153–163.

Davis, D.P., J.C. Poste, T. Hicks, D. Polk, T.E. Rymer, and I. Jacoby (2005), "Hospital bed surge capacity in the event of a mass-casualty incident," *Prehospital and Disaster Medicine*, 20: 169–176.

DeLia, D. (2006), "Annual bed statistics give a misleading picture of hospital surge capacity," *Annals of Emergency Medicine*, 48 (4): 384–388.

Eastman, A.L., K.J. Rinnert, I.R. Nemeth, R.L. Fowler, and J.P. Minei (2007), "Alternate site surge capacity in times of public health disaster maintains trauma center and emergency department integrity: Hurricane Katrina," *Journal of Trauma and Acute Care Surgery*, 63 (2): 253–257.

Ehrenstein, B.P., F. Hanses and B. Salzberger (2006), "Influenza pandemic and professional duty: family or patients first? A survey of hospital employees," *BMC Public Health*, 6 (1): 311. DOI:10.1186/1471-2458-6-311.

Federal Emergency Management Agency (FEMA) (1983), *Capability Assessment and Standards for State and Local Government (Interim Guidance)*, Washington, DC: FEMA.

Federal Emergency Management Agency (FEMA) (1996), *Guide For All-Hazard Emergency Operations Planning*, Washington, DC: FEMA.

Federal Emergency Management Agency (FEMA) (2014), "About the agency," available at http://www.fema.gov/about-agency (accessed 27 March 2014).

Fieldston, E.S., M. Hall, M.R. Sills, A.D. Slonim, A.L. Myers, C. Cannon, S. Pati, and S.S. Shah (2010), "Children's hospitals do not acutely respond to high occupancy," *Pediatrics*, 125 (5): 974–981.

Frasca, D.R. (2010), "The Medical Reserve Corps as part of the federal medical and public health response in disaster settings," *Biosecurity and Bioterrorism: Biodefense Strategy, Practice, and Science*, 8 (3): 265–271.

Gostin, Lawrence O., Dan Hanfling, Sarah L. Hanson, Clare Stroud, and Bruce M. Altevogt (eds) (2009), *Guidance for Establishing Crisis Standards of Care for Use in Disaster Situations: A Letter Report*, Washington, DC: National Academies Press.

Granner, M.L. and P.A. Sharpe (2004), "Evaluating community coalition characteristics and functioning: a summary of measurement tools," *Health Education Research*, 19 (5): 514–532.

Hanfling, Dan, Bruce M. Altevogt, Kristin Viswanathan, and Lawrence O. Gostin (eds) (2012), *Crisis Standards of Care: A Systems Framework for Catastrophic Disaster Response*, Washington, DC: National Academies Press.

Hick, J.L., J.A. Barbera, and G.D. Kelen (2009), "Refining surge capacity: conventional, contingency, and crisis capacity," *Disaster Medicine and Public Health Preparedness*, 3 (S1): S59–S67.

Hick, J.L., D. Hanfling, J.L. Burstein, C. DeAtley, D. Barbisch, G.M. Bogdan, and S. Cantrill (2004), "Health care facility and community strategies for patient care surge capacity," *Annals of Emergency Medicine*, 44 (3): 253–261.

Hick, J.L., K.L. Koenig, D. Barbisch, and T.A. Bey (2008), "Surge capacity concepts for health care facilities: the CO-S-TR model for initial incident assessment," *Disaster Medicine and Public Health Preparedness*, 2 (S1): S51–S57.

Hoard, M.L. and R.J. Tosatto (2005), "Medical Reserve Corps: strengthening public health and improving preparedness," *Disaster Management and Response*, 3 (2): 48–52.

Hoge, M.A., J.A. Morris, A.S. Daniels, L.Y. Huey, G.W. Stuart, N. Adams, M. Paris Jr, et al. (2005), "Report of recommendations: The Annapolis Coalition conference on behavioral health work force competencies," *Administration and Policy in Mental Health and Mental Health Services Research*, 32 (5–6): 651–663.

Institute for Crisis, Disaster and Risk Management at George Washington University (ICDRM) (2010), *Emergency Management Principles and Practices for Healthcare Systems*, 2nd edn, available at http://www.gwu.edu/~icdrm (accessed 2 April 2014).

Iserson, K.V., C.E. Heine, G.L. Larkin, J.C. Moskop, J. Baruch, and A.L. Aswegan (2008), "Fight or flight: the ethics of emergency physician disaster response," *Annals of Emergency Medicine*, 51 (4): 345–353.

Jarrett, P.G. (2006), "An analysis of international health care logistics: the benefits and implications of implementing just-in-time systems in the health care industry," *Leadership in Health Services*, 19 (1): 1–10.

Jensen, J. and W.L. Waugh (2014), "The United States' experience with the Incident Command System: What we think we know and what we need to know more about," *Journal of Contingencies and Crisis Management*, 22 (1): 5–17.

Joint Commission on Accreditation of Healthcare Organizations (2003), "Health care at the crossroads: strategies for creating and sustaining community-wide emergency preparedness systems," Joint Commission on Accreditation of Healthcare Organizations.

Kadushin, C., M. Lindholm, D. Ryan, A. Brodsky, and L. Saxe (2005), "Why it is so difficult to form effective community coalitions," *City and Community*, 4 (3): 255–275.

Kaji, A., K. Koenig, and T. Bey (2006), "Surge capacity for healthcare systems: A conceptual framework," *Academic Emergency Medicine*, 13 (11): 1157–1159.

Kearns, R.D., B.A. Cairns, and C.B. Cairns (2014), "Surge capacity and capability: A review of the history and where the science is today regarding surge capacity during a mass casualty disaster," *Frontiers in Public Health*, 2, available at http://www.ncbi.nlm.nih.gov/pmc/articles/PMC4001022/.

Kelen, G.D., M.L. McCarthy, C.K. Kraus, R. Ding, E.B. Hsu, G. Li, J.B. Shahan, J.J. Scheulen, and G.B. Green. (2009), "Creation of surge capacity by early discharge of hospitalized patients at low risk for untoward events," *Disaster Medicine and Public Health Preparedness*, 3 (S1): S10–S16.

Krumholz, H.M., R.G. Brindis, J.E. Brush, D.J. Cohen, A.J. Epstein, K. Furie, G. Howard, et al. (2006), "Standards for statistical models used for public reporting of health outcomes," 113 (3): 456–462.

Lazar, E.J., N.V. Cagliuso, and K.M. Gebbie (2009), "Are we ready and how do we know? The urgent need for performance metrics in hospital emergency management," *Disaster Medicine and Public Health Preparedness*, 3 (1): 57–60.

Lesperance, A.M. and J.S. Miller (2009), "Preventing absenteeism and promoting resilience among health care workers in biological emergencies," available at http://www.pnl.gov/main/publications/external/technical_reports/PNNL-18405.pdf (accessed 30 March 2014).

Lindell, Michael K., Kathleen J. Tierney, and Ronald W. Perry (2001), *Facing the Unexpected: Disaster Preparedness and Response in the United States*, Washington, DC: Joseph Henry Press.

Mays, G.P., S.A. Smith, R.C. Ingram, L.J. Racster, C.D. Lamberth, and E.S. Lovely (2009), "Public health delivery systems: Evidence, uncertainty, and emerging research needs," *American Journal of Preventive Medicine*, 36 (3): 256–265.

McCarthy, M.L., P. Brewster, E.B. Hsu, A.G. Macintyre, and G.D. Kelen (2009), "Consensus and tools needed to measure health care emergency management capabilities," *Disaster Medicine and Public Health Preparedness*, 3 (S1): S45–S51.

Nelson, C.D., E.B. Beckjord, D.J. Dausey, E. Chan, D. Lotstein, and N. Lurie (2008), "How can we strengthen the evidence base in public health preparedness?" *Disaster Medicine and Public Health Preparedness*, 2 (4): 247–250.

Nelson, C., N. Lurie, and J. Wasserman (2007), "Assessing public health emergency preparedness: concepts, tools, and challenges," *Annual Review of Public Health*, 28: 1–18.

Pretsby, J., A. Wandersman, P. Florin, R. Rich, and D. Chavis (1990), "Benefits, costs, incentive management and participation in voluntary organizations: A means to understanding and promoting empowerment," *American Journal of Community Psychology*, 18: 117–149.

Quarantelli, E.L. (1985), "What is disaster? The need for clarification in definition and conceptualization in research," available at http://udspace.udel.edu/handle/19716/1119 (accessed 23 March 2014).

Quarantelli, E.L. (1998), "Major criteria for judging disaster planning and managing their applicability in developing countries," available at http://dspace.udel.edu/bitstream/handle/19716/286/PP268.pdf?sequence=1 (accessed 19 March 2104).

Qureshi, K., R. Gershon, M.F. Sherman, T. Straub, E. Gebbie, M. McCollum, M.J. Erwin, and S.S. Morse (2005), "Health care workers ability and willingness to report to duty during catastrophic disasters," *Journal of Urban Health*, 82 (3): 378–388.

Reich, M.R. (2000), "Public–private partnerships for public health," *Nature Medicine*, 6 (6): 617–620.

Sariego, J. (2006), "A military model for civilian disaster management," *Disaster Management and Response*, 4: 114–117.

Satterthwaite, P.S. and C.J. Atkinson (2012), "Using 'reverse triage' to create hospital surge capacity: Royal Darwin Hospital's response to the Ashmore Reef disaster," *Emergency Medicine Journal*, 29 (2): 160–162.

Schultz, C.H. and G.J. Annas (2012), "Altering the standard of care in disasters – unnecessary and dangerous," *Annals of Emergency Medicine*, 59 (3): 191–195.

Schultz, C.H. and K.L. Koenig (2006), "State of research in high-consequence hospital surge capacity," *Academic Emergency Medicine*, 13 (11): 1153–1156.

Snipes, C., C. Miramonti, C. Chisholm, and R. Chisholm (2013), "Reporting for duty during mass casualty events: a survey of factors influencing emergency medicine physicians," *Journal of Graduate Medical Education*, 5 (3): 417–426.

Toner, E., R. Waldhorn, C. Franco, B. Courtney, K. Rambhia, A. Norwood, T.V. Inglesby, and T. O'Toole (2009), "Hospitals rising to the challenge: The first five years of the US Hospital Preparedness Program and priorities going forward," Center for Biosecurity of UPMC for the US Department of Health and Human Services.

US Department of Health and Human Services (HHS) (2013), "HHS Fact Sheet: FY10 Hospital Preparedness Program (HPP)," available at http://www.phe.gov/preparedness/planning/hpp/pages/fy10hpp.aspx (accessed 2 March 2014).

US Department of Homeland Security (DHS) (2007), "Target Capabilities List: A companion to the National Preparedness Guidelines," available at http://www.fema.gov/pdf/government/training/tcl.pdf (accessed 12 March 2014).

Walters, E.L., T.L. Thomas, S.W. Corbett, K.L. Williams, T. Williams, and W.A. Wittlake (2013), "A convertible use rapidly expandable model for disaster response," *International Journal of Disaster Resilience in the Built Environment*, 4 (2): 199–214.

Wenger, D., E.L. Quarantelli, and R.R. Dynes (1990), "Is the Incident Command System a plan for all seasons and emergency situations?" *Hazard Monthly*, 10 (12): 8–9.

Wolff, T. (2001), "Community coalition building – contemporary practice and research: introduction," *American Journal of Community Psychology*, 29 (2): 165–172.

Zakocs, R.C. and E.M. Edwards (2006), "What explains community coalition effectiveness? A review of the literature," *American Journal of Preventive Medicine*, 30 (4): 351.

Zakocs, R.C. and S. Guckenburg (2007), "What coalition factors foster community capacity? Lessons learned from the Fighting Back Initiative," *Health Education and Behavior*, 34 (2): 354–375.

Zibulewsky, J. (2001), "Defining disaster: The emergency department perspective," *Proceedings* (Baylor University Medical Center), 14 (2): 144.

# 8. Organizational excellence

## Leonard H. Friedman

## INTRODUCTION

In 1964, the case of *Jacobellis v. Ohio* came before the United States Supreme Court (Chicago-Kent College of Law). The court was asked to judge on the purported obscenity of Louis Malle's motion picture, *The Lovers*. By a 6:3 majority, the court ruled that the movie was not obscene. What was most memorable was the language of Associate Justice Potter Stewart who wrote that while he could not precisely define obscenity, "I know it when I see it."

What does a 1964 Supreme Court decision on obscenity possibly have to do with excellence in healthcare delivery? While the intent here is not to equate a racy movie by 1964 standards with organizational excellence in healthcare, a similar challenge exists. In both cases, we do not have a uniform definition that is acceptable across the country and is not dependent on the community standards in place at one moment in time. Beyond defining organizational excellence (OE) is the larger question of whether this is a priority for healthcare leaders. In their annual survey of the top issues confronting hospital chief executive officers (CEOs), the American College of Healthcare Executives lists financial challenges, healthcare reform implementation, government mandates, patient quality and safety, care for the uninsured, patient satisfaction, hospital–physician relations, population health management, technology, personnel shortages, and creating an accountable care organization as their top ten concerns for 2013 (American College of Healthcare Executives, 2014). Examining the list, a case can be made that there are elements of OE that have the attention of the CEOs who responded to the survey. That said, there appears to be little or no obvious interest in creating and sustaining consistently high-performing organizations.

Given this premise, the intent of this chapter is to accomplish two goals. The first is to critically examine the forces and policies that have worked to restrain consistent OE in the USA. The second goal is to provide a seven-factor model that can serve as the framework for students and practitioners of healthcare management who wish to create and support organizations that aspire to become truly excellent in healthcare delivery.

## A SHORT HISTORICAL PERSPECTIVE

In 1994, William Kissick wrote about the presence of an "iron triangle" in healthcare, requiring trade-offs between cost, quality, and access as we think about the critical forces acting on healthcare delivery (Kissick, 1994). In the 20 years that have followed the publication of his book, little has changed. Healthcare organizations (HCOs) continue to face (at a micro system level) a balancing act requiring them to provide ever increasing levels of access to service, at high quality, combined with decreasing reimbursement. In order for healthcare leaders to achieve optimal levels of cost, quality, and access they are compelled to make difficult choices at the level of their individual organization and community. Let us consider the historical perspectives associated with each of the three vertices of Kissick's iron triangle.

First is cost. The cost of healthcare in the United States must be considered simultaneously with that of reimbursement. As readers of this book know, US healthcare costs have risen dramatically since 1960 in terms of total dollars, fraction of gross domestic product (GDP) and per capita spending, so that in 2012 almost $2.8 trillion was spent on healthcare, which represented 17.2 percent of GDP and $8915 per capita – the highest levels anywhere in the world (CMS, 2014a; Squires, 2012). The rate of spending represents the oft-discussed cost curve that the Affordable Care Act was intended to address. Along with ever-increasing costs of care has come a fundamental shift in the way that healthcare (primarily for hospital inpatient and physician services) services are paid from a retrospective, fee-for-service methodology to a prospective payment system embracing models including health maintenance organizations (HMOs), preferred provider organizations (PPOs), bundled payments, and capitation, among others.

Under a fee-for-service model, costs naturally rose since the incentive for providers was to do more tests and procedures knowing that they would be paid at a level commensurate with their effort. As prospective payment became the norm, the economic incentive for providers shifted so that they were rewarded for doing just enough for the patient and nothing more. A natural outgrowth of prospective payment is the imposition of value-based purchasing (CMS, 2014b), wherein reimbursement is directly tied to incentive payments to hospitals based on their achieving certain quality measures. Furthermore, a study recently published in the *Dartmouth Atlas of Health Care* found, "Among the 306 hospital referral regions in the United States, price-adjusted Medicare reimbursements varied twofold in 2010, from about $6900 per enrollee in the lowest spending region to more than $13000 in the highest spending region" (Dartmouth Institute, 2014).

The second element is quality. As noted in the cost discussion, Centers for Medicare and Medicaid Services (CMS) is attempting to drive improvement in hospital quality by creating specific financial incentives. This begs the question of why we have to provide hospitals (and ultimately physicians) incentives for providing the kind of high-quality care that we should expect to be the norm. While we expect healthcare to be of the highest possible clinical quality and patients be treated in a respectful, honest, and compassionate manner by all members of the healthcare team, this has not always been the case. In its groundbreaking publication *To Err is Human* the Institute of Medicine (2000) reported that in 1997 somewhere between 44 000 and 98 000 persons died in US hospitals due to an adverse event; a medical error. A more recent study found that upwards of 400 000 persons die in US hospitals each year due to some adverse event and that as many as 4 million persons annually are injured but do not die due to an adverse event (James J. T., 2013).

Beyond the number of persons who are killed or injured in US hospitals is the concern associated with patients' experience with healthcare delivery as another measure of quality. In 2006, the CMS launched the Hospital Consumer Assessment of Healthcare Providers and Systems (HCAHPS) program. The HCAHPS surveys recently discharged hospital inpatients on 32 questions about their level of satisfaction with the hospital experience (CMS, 2014b). Thirty percent of the total incentive provided to hospitals under value-based purchasing is linked to the HCAHPS scores. At issue for hospitals and physicians is the pressure they are under to make sure they do their part so that "top box" scores on the HCAHPS survey are obtained. For many physicians whose focus is on clinical quality, the issue is that the HCAHPS questions focus on the experience that patients have with all members of the care team and with their perceptions of the way in which they were treated during their stay in the hospital – factors which are out of the control of the individual physician.

The third aspect of the "iron triangle" is access. Access to healthcare in the United States has been a long-standing problem, given that up until the passage of the Affordable Care Act in 2010, access to private healthcare was dependent entirely on having employer-sponsored health insurance, eligibility for Medicare and/or Medicaid, availability of Veterans Administration health benefits, or sufficient personal funds. Up until the passage of the Affordable Care Act in 2010 and implementation of federal and state health insurance exchanges in 2013, there were an estimated 50 million citizens of the US without some form of health insurance (Galewitz, 2010). Among the 33 most economically developed nations on earth, the United States is the one nation that does not mandate universal healthcare for all its citizens (Fisher, 2012). Universal health insurance was initially supported by President Theodore Roosevelt, given his belief that no country could be strong whose people were sick and poor (Starr, 1982), yet it took a century of effort to design and pass the Patient Protection and Affordable Care Act. Even with the passage of the Affordable Care Act, tens of millions of US citizens will remain without the benefit of health insurance.

It is clear that the historical forces of cost, quality, and access remain at the forefront of challenges facing healthcare organizations today. Too often, healthcare leaders default to trying to optimize two of these three forces, with the net effect being that the larger system is suboptimized. As a way of illustrating this point, Shortell and Kaluzny crafted a visual depiction of a network of health service organizations that explicitly puts the patient in the center of the network (Shortell, 2014; Kaluzny, 1997). Frequently, healthcare organizations minimize the centrality of the patient in favor of financial performance, technology acquisition, or enhancing market share. While recent CMS initiatives are a step in the right direction to enhance the patient experience, there needs to be a renewed focus on creating and sustaining healthcare delivery organizations that uniformly deliver high-quality care to the greatest number of people at a price that is consistent across the country. Prior to laying out a roadmap for achieving organizational excellence in healthcare, I will take a moment to review what others have said on this topic.

## PRIOR WORK ON OE

There is comparatively little that has been written about the precise theme of organizational excellence in healthcare. However, service quality and service excellence (these terms are used interchangeably here) appear repeatedly in the academic and practitioner literature. Frei posits that the success or failure of a service business depends on how well the organization manages four elements: the service offering, funding mechanism to provide that service, employee management system, and customer management system (Frei, 2008). Warden and Griffith explicitly linked achieving the goals of the larger organization to excellence in management practice that is focused on the academic preparation of talented management candidates and the expansion of continuing education for managers (Warden and Griffith, 2001).

Service quality is a theme that appears repeatedly in the literature and is not a new concept. According to Kennedy et al., patient-centered care has been a part of the experience at the Mayo Clinic in the US for over 100 years (Kennedy et al., 2011). From their perspective, service quality requires sustained performance from physicians and allied health staff. Lasserre makes the point that "Patients' perception of *good* or *great* service is paramount to an organization's success" (Lasserre, 2010). Creating a culture of service is one of the core goals of highly effective healthcare leaders.

One of the most vocal advocates of OE in healthcare is Quint Studer. His 2003 book, *Hardwiring Excellence*, provides a widely adopted template for creating and sustaining excellence in hospitals and other healthcare organizations (Studer, 2003). Studer recommends that healthcare leaders deploy a core set of principles in a consistent manner throughout the organization, and that ultimately leaders be held accountable for the implementation of all the principles. The tools, techniques, and advice provided by StuderGroup coaches have been implemented by healthcare organizations in the United States, Canada, Australia, and New Zealand with the goal of improving clinical, operational, and financial outcomes (StuderGroup, 2014).

Finally, the Institute for Healthcare Improvement (IHI) developed a concept known at the Triple Aim that it envisions as a framework for health system improvement. The three parts of the Triple Aim include improving the experience of care, improving population health, and reducing the per capita cost of healthcare (IHI, 2014). According to IHI:

> Organizations and communities that attain the Triple Aim will have healthier populations, in part because of new designs that better identify problems and solutions further upstream and outside of acute health care. Patients can expect less complex and much more coordinated care and the burden of illness will decrease. Importantly, stabilizing or reducing the per capita cost of care for populations will give businesses the opportunity to be more competitive, lessen the pressure on publicly funded health care budgets, and provide communities with more flexibility to invest in activities, such as schools and the lived environment, that increase the vitality and economic wellbeing of their inhabitants. (IHI, 2014)

There is no lack of evidence supporting the interest and effort in providing healthcare services that are of high clinical quality, safe for the patient, and delivered in a way such that patients feel as though they are being cared for as real people and not just a sack of symptoms. Virtually every professional meeting in healthcare management and healthcare delivery will have multiple educational sessions centered on the themes of service quality, and improving the patient experience along with enhancing financial performance, reacting to changes brought about by the Affordable Care Act and best practices in information technology (IT), among others. Multiple organizations including (but not limited to) the Institute for Healthcare Improvement, American Health Quality Organization, Joint

Commission and the Agency for Healthcare Research and Quality all exist to make US healthcare delivery better.

Despite all of the time, effort, energy, and enthusiasm around improving healthcare, the US system continues to fall short of its aspirations. For the remainder of this chapter, a model of organizational excellence is proposed that has the potential to create a uniform level of improvement across multiple healthcare delivery organizations. It is important to keep in mind that none of the proposed elements to this model are possible without the strong and visible commitment of senior administration in the organization, including physician leadership. This model presumes the presence of a macro and micro organizational culture that permits and promotes continuous learning, clear and unambiguous communication, transparency in shared decision-making, real-time use of mission-critical data, and adherence to a mission that puts the patient at the center of the healthcare enterprise.

## A MODEL FOR HEALTHCARE ORGANIZATIONAL EXCELLENCE

This model for healthcare organizational excellence (OE) is a synthesis of prior literature and personal interactions with healthcare leaders over the past 20 years, coupled with an analysis of the strong and weak signals currently moving through the healthcare environment. A visual depiction of the model is found in Figure 8.1 and contains the following elements that contribute to achieving a sustained level of organizational excellence:

- Patients first.
- Clinical quality.
- Service.
- Alignment with organizational mission, vision, and values (MVV).
- Financial performance.
- Meeting healthcare needs of the community.
- Creation of a continuous learning environment.

### Patients First

"Patients first" represents a perspective that puts the patient at the center of the activities of the healthcare organization. This level of centrality encompasses two primary activities: patient safety and the patient experience. As noted earlier in this chapter, an unacceptably high number of

*Figure 8.1   Model for healthcare organizational excellence*

persons are killed or injured as a result of unintentional medical errors. We know that virtually no one sets out to intentionally harm a patient, yet hundreds of thousands of adverse clinical events occur each year across virtually all US healthcare organizations. While much has been written and discussed about the enormity of this problem, progress to improve patient safety is incremental at best. For too many healthcare organizations, the typical way of dealing with an unintended medical error is to "blame and shame" or "blame and train."

In both variations, the goal is to identify the individual bad actor, blame them for their actions, and force them to take responsibility by providing some sort of punishment (including possible termination) or have them take additional training to make sure they do not make the same mistake again. This type of linear approach to problem solving is something that Chris Argyris would refer to as single-loop learning (Smith, 2013). As Argyris would note, single-loop learning as a method of dealing with medical errors fails to recognize that healthcare delivery exists within a complex system in which simply trying to fix one part of the system (the person who made the mistake) ignores the effects brought about by the larger system.

A different way of thinking about the conditions that allows patients to be harmed is referred to as the "Swiss cheese model" (CMS, 2012), first mentioned by James Reason: errors occur when the holes in the Swiss cheese line up. As noted by the Agency for Healthcare Research and Quality (AHRQ):

> another of Reason's key insights, one that sadly remains underemphasized today, is that human error is inevitable, especially in systems as complex as health care. Simply striving for perfection – or punishing individuals who make mistakes – will not appreciably improve safety, as expecting flawless perfor- mance from human beings working in complex, high-stress environments is unrealistic. The systems approach holds that efforts to catch human errors before they occur or block them from causing harm will ultimately be more fruitful than ones that seek to somehow create flawless providers. (CMS, 2012)

While controversial, one robust model of ensuring patient safety involves adopting the principles and practices associated with commercial aviation. Whether that includes the enhanced use of checklists (Gawande, 2011), crew resource management (SaferHealthcare, 2014), sterile cock- pits (Oregon Patient Safety Commission, 2014), or the implementation of a safety culture (Air Safety Support International, 2006), there is no questioning that the annual fatal accident rate in commercial aviation is approaching zero (Boeing Aircraft Company, 2013). Might it be worth the time and effort to discover the best practices of commercial aviation and diffuse them into healthcare organizations?

**Clinical Quality**

For the purposes of this discussion, I will use the definition of medical quality put forth by the American College of Medical Quality (ACMQ), which reads as follows: "the degree to which health care systems, services and supplies for individuals and populations increase the likelihood for positive health outcomes and are consistent with current professional knowledge" (ACMQ, 1996). This definition suggests that healthcare organizations must provide the tools and staff necessary to achieve the sorts of "positive health outcomes" that are called for by the ACMQ. However, the latest tools and best-trained staff are a necessary but not sufficient condition. Clinicians must consistently employ the best science available in order to obtain the best possible clinical outcomes.

While the best science possible is the ideal, all too often clinicians depend on other heuristics including personal experience, recommendations from peers, conversations with vendors of medical devices or (in many cases) simple guesswork. A study in 1985 postulated that only 15 percent of medical practice was based on solid clinical trials (Eddy, 2005). Even if the figure is actually twice as high, the idea that 70 percent of clinical practice is based on anything other than good science is cause for much concern. It is said that medicine is often equal parts art and science. Given the rise of death and disability from chronic disease, and the availability of a wide range of diagnostic and treatment methods, there needs to be a concerted effort to make science a larger part of providing uniformly outstanding clinical care.

One of the best approaches available is the consistent use of "evidence-based medicine." The term was first coined in 1995 (Sackett and Rosenberg, 1995). According to Sackett and Rosenberg, five steps are required in order to practice evidence-based care: convert the information needed about diagnosis, prognosis, therapy, decision analysis, and cost into answerable questions; track down the best evidence with which to answer the questions; critically appraise that evidence performance for both validity and usefulness; apply the results of the appraisal to clinical practice; and evaluate performance.

In order to accumulate the basic data that can be transformed into information and then used as a guide for evidence based practice, a robust electronic health record is essential. In the wake of the Health Information Technology for Economic and Clinical Health Act (HITECH Act) in 2009, Health and Human Services, Office of National Coordinator (HHS/ONC) healthcare organizations have been moving to implement electronic health records in the hospital and physician practice settings. While progress in this area has been slow and inconsistent, there are examples of organizations that have meaningfully used health information technology to help clinicians make better decisions and to better manage the health of their respective populations. US organizations including Kaiser-Permanente, Banner Health, Mayo Clinic Health System, and Cedars-Sinai Medical Center (HIMSS, 2014) have achieved the top rating from the Health Information Management System Society (HIMSS) in IT maturity and use of electronic health records. While only 2 percent of US hospitals have achieved what HIMSS refers to as Stage 7 (Booker, 2014), the potential exists for the other 98 percent of hospitals to realize the full potential of IT to help assure clinical quality.

**Service**

All US healthcare organizations share a number of common attributes. Regardless of size or location, all are physical entities that contain similar types of equipment, are organized in a ways that are consistent with the guidelines of the Joint Commission, and exist to meet the needs of their respective communities. However, one important component is missing: the people who work in the HCO and provide the vital services, whether they include direct patient care, clinical support, ancillary services, or the administrative backbone. All staff members have a crucial role to play if organizational excellence is to be maintained.

Think for a moment about the nature of the work that clinical staff are expected to perform on a daily basis. Every person admitted into a hospital, whether through the regular admitting process or through the Emergency Department (ED), is in the organization because something is wrong and needs to be corrected. From the perspective of the patient, an inpatient or outpatient stay in a hospital is generally one filled with uncertainty, worry, and fear as the most common emotions. Patients are putting themselves completely in the hands of strangers, trusting them to do the right things and not harm them when they are in their care. This is truly an awesome level of responsibility and one would hope that the staff of truly excellent healthcare organizations would uniformly treat all patients and their families with compassion, dignity, and kindness.

Unfortunately, too often healthcare organizations fall short of their aspirations. They are so busy with their jobs that they fail to see the person who is lost amid the confusing signs in the buildings. They assume that everyone understands the language that they use and the vocabulary that makes up healthcare delivery regardless of the recipient's level of health literacy. They are so focused on the financial health and well-being of the organization that they sometimes forget that were it not for their patients, they would have no business at all. At their core, they are a service industry, and as with any service-oriented business, customers judge them by their perception of the type of service that they receive. While many patients have the information technology available to help them ask good questions about clinical care and treatment options, the most important variable for patients is the interaction with staff at all levels. Generally speaking, HCOs do well on the clinical side when dealing with patients (ignoring for a moment the all too frequent medical errors that occur). Unfortunately, in too many instances, they do a less than exemplary job of creating a uniformly high-quality healthcare experience.

Think for a moment about organizations that are well known for outstanding customer service. Nordstrom has a long reputation of providing amazing customer service. In a recently conducted Zogby Analytics poll, organizations including Amazon, Marriot, Hilton, UPS and FedEx were ranked as the top five firms providing outstanding customer service in the USA (MSN Money, 2013). Granted that healthcare is much more complex than selling shoes, providing an online shopping experience, offering hotel rooms, or delivering packages – the fundamentals remain the same. High-performing service firms do everything possible to make sure that customers have a uniformly outstanding experience with every employee in the organization. In the final analysis, this means creating and supporting a culture of service excellence.

In order to achieve a culture of service excellence, many health-care organizations are turning to the principles that make Disneyland, Disneyworld, EuroDisney, and the entire Disney enterprise an exemplar of creating a world-class experience that exceeds the expectations of each and every guest. Whether off-site at the Disney Institute in Orlando, Florida or at the organization itself, the objective of the training is to create a culture of service excellence (Walt Disney Company, 2013). Another example of the installation of Disney values into healthcare organizations can be found in the book, *If Disney Ran Your Hospital* (Lee, 2004) in which Lee provides a number of examples of how service excellence can drive organizational excellence.

All of this begs the question of why outstanding service is so difficult to obtain reliably in healthcare organizations. While people often cite issues like workforce shortages, lagging reimbursement, constantly changing technology, poor IT infrastructure, aging buildings, unreasonable regulatory demands, and a host of other things, service excellence has never been a high priority for HCOs. There is a glimmer of hope with the imposition of the Hospital Consumer Assessment of Healthcare Providers and Systems (HCAHPS) in which a portion of hospital reimbursement is tied to patients' perceptions of hospital care (CMS, 2013b). While HCAHPS has been met with objections by many clinicians, US hospitals are beginning to focus on helping to drive up HCAHPS scores. While there is a financial benefit to obtaining high patient perception scores, outstanding service should be an end in itself. A culture that supports and encourages service excellence will help to attract the very best employees, and assures patients that the care they receive will be uniformly exceptional – the very least that should be done for all who look to HCOs in time of personal need.

### Alignment with Mission, Vision, and Values

Virtually every organization has crafted a set of statements expressing their mission, vision, and values. Simply stated, the mission describes what the organization is and what it does; the vision states what the organization seeks to become; and the values are those core principles that guide the organization in its day-to-day operations. Examples of well-written mission, vision, and values statements from a number of different healthcare organizations are as follows.

Mission:

> The North Shore-LIJ Health System strives to improve the health of the communities it serves and is committed to providing the highest quality clinical care; educating the current and future generations of health care professionals; searching for new advances in medicine through the conduct of bio-medical research; promoting health education; and caring for the entire community regardless of the ability to pay. (North Shore LIJ, 2014)

Vision:

> Sharp HealthCare's vision is to be the best health system in the universe. Sharp will attain this position by transforming the health care experience through a culture of caring, quality, service, innovation and excellence. Sharp will be recognized by employees, physicians, patients, volunteers and the community as the best place to work, the best place to practice medicine and the best place to receive care. Sharp is known as an excellent community citizen embodying an organization of people working together to do the right thing every day to improve the health and well-being of those we serve. (Sharp Healthcare, 2014)

Values:

> Cleveland Clinic was established by visionary leaders who believed in simple, guiding principles. Six fundamental values form the foundation of the Cleveland Clinic's culture:
>
> Quality. We maintain the highest standards and achieve them by continually measuring and improving our outcomes.
>
> Innovation. We welcome change, encourage invention and continually seek better, more efficient ways to achieve our goals.
>
> Teamwork. We collaborate and share knowledge to benefit patients and fellow caregivers for the advancement of our mission.
>
> Service. We strive to exceed our patients' and/or fellow caregivers' expectations for comfort and convenience.
>
> Integrity. We adhere to high moral principles and professional standards by a commitment to honesty, confidentiality, trust, respect and transparency.
>
> Compassion. We demonstrate our commitment to world-class care by providing a caring and supportive environment for our patients, patients' families and fellow caregivers. (Cleveland Clinic, 2014)

You could look up almost any healthcare organization of your choice and find equally well-written and compelling mission, vision, and values statements. You could also legitimately ask what relevance these three statements have to organizational excellence. After all, the mission, vision, and values by themselves do not deliver health services of any sort; they are simply words on paper or an electronic imprint somewhere on an organization's web page. In an ideal world where organizational excellence is routinely sought, the mission, vision, and values become a set of guiding principles that keep everyone pointed in the same direction. The difference for truly excellent healthcare organizations, and those who fall short, is the extent to which the organization's leaders are held accountable for moving in the direction of the vision and upholding the values in a measurable and consistent manner.

In his book *Straight A Leadership*, Studer emphasizes the need for alignment, action, and accountability among healthcare leaders if they are going to achieve consistently outstanding organizational performance (Studer, 2009). It is necessary but not sufficient to have a well-written and engaging mission, vision, and values statement. All three of these must work together in such a way that leaders throughout the organization are accountable for fulfilling their parts. For example, assume that one of the values is to deliver high-quality care to the poor and vulnerable. Many faith-based healthcare organizations have a similar type of value. The question for the excellent healthcare organization is the extent to which this value is fulfilled, and then how senior leaders are held accountable for achieving this value. How is the value of high-quality care to the poor and vulnerable translated into measurable objectives?

What are the metrics that will be used consistently throughout the organization to determine whether the poor and vulnerable are being served, and if so, to what level? Simply abiding by the requirement of the Emergency Medical Treatment and Active Labor Act (EMTALA) is clearly not sufficient to live up to this stated value. Rather than doing the minimum to meet the legal requirements, measurable alternatives could include opening up and staffing a number of school-based primary care clinics in low-income areas, partnering with community health centers which already have a footprint in the community, and funding health promotion and disease prevention initiatives targeted at reducing the burden of common chronic conditions in the community. Regardless of the method or approach chosen, adherence to mission, vision, and values and holding leaders accountable for their successful completion is a critical part of every healthcare organization seeking to achieve excellence.

**Financial Performance**

Full risk capitation, bundled payments, global budgeting, and incentive payments are not vocabulary words out of some accountant's textbook. Rather, these represent but a few of the many ways that healthcare organizations are being – or are soon to be – paid for providing services to patients. Back in the "good old days" of healthcare reimbursement (from the perspective of the provider) hospitals and physicians were paid using one of several variants of fee-for-service, retrospective payment. Using what was referred to as usual, customary, and reasonable (UCR) charges, providers would set the rates for various services and then submit the bill either directly to the patient or to the third-party payer, typically a commercial insurance company. The incentive for providers was to do more tests, procedures, office visits, and admissions, since the more things that were done the more the providers would be paid.

In the years following the imposition of diagnosis related groups (DRGs) for inpatient Medicare services in 1982, more and more of the financial risk for care has been shifted away from the payers and towards the providers. Hospitals had an incentive to keep as many beds filled for as long as possible in order to generate maximum revenue. Typically, patients would be admitted at least a day before a surgery or other procedure and then allowed to stay until the admitting physician felt that they were well enough to be discharged. Today, patients are generally admitted the day that their procedure is scheduled to take place and then are discharged as soon as possible without exposing them to undue medical harm.

The issue for organizational excellence is that healthcare is fundamentally a human resource-intensive business. Salaries, wages, and associated fringe benefits are typically the single largest line item in the budget of any healthcare organization. In addition to salaries and associated costs are expenses linked to technology (both clinical and information technology), supplies and equipment, mortgage, food service, pharmaceuticals, utilities, licensure, and many more. Costs for all of the items listed have continued to rise, and at the same time the current reimbursement rules have sought to drive down payment in an effort to bend the cost curve downwards. A wise person once said that "Learning to do more with less and do it better is not a sustainable strategy."

The question for OE is how to balance the need to pay the bills for day-to-day operations, purchase new and replacement equipment and technology, put money away in a reserve fund for unplanned contingencies, and fund a host of other requirements in an environment that is driving down reimbursement. Unfortunately, there are no simple and easy answers. Citing another wise person, "Healthcare leaders must accept the fact that reimbursements will never get any higher than they are today." If we accept as legitimate the previous quote, there are a number of approaches that we can take and still maintain OE:

- Attend to mission-critical activities. Too often healthcare organizations continue to provide services simply because they have always done so, as historical precedent. Every service that the OE hospital or health system offers must line up with the stated mission of the organization. If the service is being used sparingly or if the outcomes of that service are below expectations, it might be time to discontinue that service and make those resources available for other, high-value items.

- Transparency of budgeting. Even when done well, budgeting and financial management can be a confusing and complex activity. In too many healthcare organizations, staff are told limited information about the budget and are left uncertain about the actual state of revenue and expense. Why is this information treated like a state secret? Truly excellent HCOs will share news, both good and bad, about the status of their department and organization budgets. In this way, when decisions need to be made about budget reductions or realignment, everyone has a clear understanding of what is happening and why.
- Look for lower-cost substitutes. It should come as no surprise that healthcare organizations continue to look for lower-cost substitutes for costly resources. As is the case with generic drugs, if the effect is the same for both the generic and name-brand product, why would you not choose the generic?

    In recent years, we have seen substitutions in the healthcare workforce where nurse practitioners are used instead of family practitioners or general internists, nurse midwifes substitute for obstetricians during uncomplicated deliveries of new babies, and pharmacy technicians are asked to perform many of the tasks previously performed by pharmacists. Another example is limiting the number of choices available to clinicians for a particular procedure, particularly among orthopedic surgeons. Rather than allow each surgeon to use their own vendor to supply joint replacement parts, the cost-conscious but still excellent hospital might employ clinical evidence (rather than personal preference) to select a single vendor.
- Everyone has "skin in the game." Earlier in this chapter, the idea of transparency was mentioned as a crucial element for all truly excellent HCOs. All staff members need to be told the truth. Not just the outcomes, but the reasons for those outcomes. The "why" needs to stand side by side with the "what" and "how." In the domain of financial performance, each and every staff member needs to understand their role in generating revenue and holding down expenses.

    It is easy to point out to the physician that their volume of patients seen is below that of their peers, or that their readmission rates are higher than the norm. Excellent HCOs will be able to make the case to the housekeeping staff for their role in keeping infection rates (and their associated costs) down by being meticulous in cleaning patient rooms. Excellent HCOs will be able to demonstrate to the parking attendants their role in creating an exceptional experience for patients and visitors, thereby giving people a reason to want to return to the HCO rather than take their business elsewhere. Regardless of where the staff member works in the organization, their consistently outstanding work helps to sustain the financial performance of the HCO.

## Meet Community Needs

One of the commonly used terms in healthcare management in recent years is that of "population health management" (Advisory Board Committee, 2014). According to the Advisory Board Committee:

> Environmental forces are combining to cause major changes to our industry. The Baby Boomers have started enrolling in Medicare. Information and data are increasingly available – and portable. Chronic disease incidence is reaching epidemic proportions. And health reform has set a new timeline for change. Together, these forces are pushing providers past the point of incremental change toward a new business model centered on delivery of comprehensive care and management of total cost risk. Organizations on the transition path to population health management must prioritize three foundational elements: 1) Information powered clinical decision making, 2) Primary care led clinical workforce and 3) Patient engagement and clinical integration.

As the focus of healthcare has shifted from acute care episodic illness to chronic disease management, the locus of care has also begun to shift. It is incumbent on HCOs that aspire to OE to work diligently to meet the healthcare needs of their respective communities. One of the outcomes of the Affordable Care Act is to make primary care available to a segment of the US population for whom these services were previously not easily accessed. If primary care works as designed, the members of a community are encouraged to see a primary care provider routinely with the goal of promoting good health and preventing disease. The objective is to help manage important chronic diseases including (but not limited to) diabetes, asthma, heart disease, and arthritis outside of the hospital, resulting in improved health with a lower financial burden on the individual and nation at large.

If we believe that population health management is more than the latest flavor of the month and will be with us for the long term, HCOs embracing OE must adjust their business models to anticipate the health needs of their respective communities. It is not enough to simply be available 24/7/365 to provide high-quality care as needed. The hospital and health system of tomorrow must effectively partner with other organizations embedded within the community to jointly manage the health of the population. Among the most important of those organizations are community health centers (CHCs). As a result of the Affordable Care Act, community health centers received an additional $300 million to expand and enhance critical primary care services to vulnerable populations who have typically previously not been able to access private healthcare (Wakefield, 2014). Rather than independently investing in stand-alone clinics, a better strategy might be to work collaboratively with one or more of the 1300 CHCs already in operation.

Another strategy that several HCOs have embarked upon to focus on community based care is via an Accountable Care Organization (ACO) model. According to CMS:

> Accountable Care Organizations (ACOs) are groups of doctors, hospitals, and other health care providers, who come together voluntarily to give coordinated high quality care to their Medicare patients. The goal of coordinated care is to ensure that patients, especially the chronically ill, get the right care at the right time, while avoiding unnecessary duplication of services and preventing medical errors. When an ACO succeeds both in both delivering high-quality care and spending health care dollars more wisely, it will share in the savings it achieves for the Medicare program. (CMS, 2013a)

As of 2014, over 500 ACOs are being funded through the public or the private sector, or both, and typically combine hospitals, physician practices, and insurance companies in a collaborative venture (Shortell, 2014). Evidence is still being collected about the effectiveness of ACOs in delivering high-quality care to Medicare patients in a cost-effective manner, but there appears to be general enthusiasm about this approach to meet the healthcare needs of Medicare recipients.

Regardless of the strategy, approach, or tactics chosen, organizational excellence demands that HCOs pay close attention to meeting the healthcare needs of their respective communities. That said, it may not be enough just to provide healthcare. Using a public health perspective, good health is a function of the total environment in which people live. Good health cannot be separated from the economic well-being of a community, availability of wholesome food at reasonable prices, the quality of air and water, community safety, and a host of other issues. This is not to say that excellent HCOs are responsible for addressing all of the issues mentioned. However, there are opportunities for HCOs to take a leadership role and begin to make a real difference in creating healthier communities.

**Continuous Learning**

The final attribute of excellent HCOs is the presence of continuous learning. While learning is typically considered to be confined to the individual person who takes a class, participates in a continuing education program, or goes so far as to obtain an advanced academic degree, OE demands much more. Before examining the phenomenon of organization-wide continuous learning, it is worth pointing out that a foundational part to every excellent HCO is the availability of a formal process of training and development for all staff members. Studer points out that HCOs with a culture of high performance (OE) are going to assure that individuals get the skill development needed to be successful (Studer, 2013). Too often, when HCOs find themselves in a difficult financial position, the budget for staff development and training is the first thing to be eliminated.

Beyond the need to have a robust staff training and development program in place is the requirement for a culture that encourages and permits continuous informal learning and innovation throughout the organization. Driving this need for learning and innovation is a level of continuous change in healthcare that is unlike anything seen prior to now (Studer, 2013). There is little or no time to develop elegant plans, analyze data generated by carefully designed longitudinal studies employing sophisticated statistical methods, or just sit around and wait until the organization emerges from the whitewater of unpredictable change. The fact is that change is constant and highly effective HCOs must take this as a given and act accordingly.

Part of the dilemma lies in the fact that healthcare organizations have been designed using the principles first put forth by Max Weber (1947) in which he describes the multiple components of an ideal bureaucracy. The structure and operation of most large HCOs contain the requisite division of a formal hierarchy, management by rules, employment based on technical expertise, and departmentalization. This type of organization structure is particularly well suited for an environment that is stable and predictable. Back in the day when a stable revenue stream was assured (as was the case in pre-prospective payment days) and both physicians and hospitals were relatively buffered from external environmental pressure, this type of bureaucratic structure was appropriate. Today, the level and intensity of change brought about by technology, consumer demands, workforce shortages, reduced reimbursement, and legal and regulatory demands have made the large, rigid organizational form incompatible with the current environment. Strict policies and procedures, rules and regulations, rigid organizational silos and formal reporting relationships severely limit the ability of the HCO to adapt to change.

Given the requirements set forth by Joint Commission and various US state agencies there are relatively few degrees of freedom that HCOs can use to restructure themselves in order to become more nimble and adaptable to change. This is where organizational learning comes in. Peter Senge, in his book *The Fifth Discipline* (Senge, 1990), highlights five practices that are essential for any learning organization: personal mastery, mental models, shared vision, team learning, and systems thinking. According to Senge, "Learning organizations [are] organizations where people continually expand their capacity to create the results they truly desire, where new and expansive patterns of thinking are nurtured, where collective aspiration is set free, and where people are continually learning to see the whole together" (Senge, 1990).

What would be the benefits to an HCO that seeks to transform itself into a learning organization? First and foremost, staff would learn to envision their organization as a system made up of multiple subsystems. Rather than try to optimize their small part of the larger system, they would understand that a change to one part of the organization impacts other parts in ways large and small with sometimes unintended consequences. Another important benefit is the co-creation of a unified vision for the HCO. Departments would be given the freedom of doing things in creative and innovative ways so long as they contributed to the overall mission and were in alignment with the values of the organization. Staff would be permitted to create with one another an HCO that is responsive to the needs of patients, staff, and the community at large. A final benefit is that when confronted with an environmental jolt such as might be encountered in an unexpected emergency or disaster (think about the events on September 11, 2001, a possible bioterror event, or pandemic spread of infectious disease), the HCO has the resiliency to effectively respond even when there is no contingency plan or policy and procedure manual covering this scenario (Friedman and Marghella, 2004).

Organizational excellence requires a high level of formal and informal learning in order to build the ability to effectively deal with continuous change. HCOs have frequently been described as high reliability organizations (HROs), given the potential for catastrophic errors when mistakes are made (Lewin Group, 2008). One of the key attributes to HROs is the need for ongoing training and preparation of leaders to deal with potential system failures. This type of training and continuous learning needs to be provided to everyone in the organization regardless of job title or span of responsibility. To do less puts the HCO in a position where it is diminished in its ability to effectively deal with environmental change.

## CONCLUDING THOUGHTS

This chapter can be distilled down into a single thought: organizational excellence is about crafting an intentional future. The seven-phase model described here is a structured way of thinking about the values a truly excellent HCO should possess in an environment that is driven by the forces described in the "iron triangle." It is important to emphasize the belief that truly excellent healthcare organizations must transcend exclusively clinical quality, which is a necessary but not sufficient condition. Clinical care that is safe, effective, and timely is taken by most patients as a given, although the unacceptably large number of medical errors suggests that there is a long way to go in order to assure the promise of safety (James, 2013). The attribute that makes HCOs truly excellent is a commitment to creating and sustaining an exceptional healthcare experience for patients, their families, and staff members of the organization. What makes this hard to accomplish is that all of us have a different perception of what that experience should be like. Much like the introduction to this chapter, most of us can describe only in general terms what an outstanding healthcare experience is like, but we know it when we experience it.

Organizational excellence and a uniformly outstanding healthcare experience require a commitment from senior leaders and the governing board that this is of the highest priority. There needs to be a public and consistent message from leaders that they are going to hold themselves accountable for putting into practice the methods and tactics associated with moving towards uniform organizational excellence. Bringing in external coaches will certainly help in the process, particularly when progress is slow and people in the organization begin to get discouraged. Creating clear goals, providing ongoing feedback, and encouraging both the head and the heart must be built in right from the start. Keep in mind that an outstanding healthcare experience exists as a perception within those who interact with the system. Allowing senior leaders or clinicians to define the boundaries of a healthcare experience without taking into account the voice of the end user is at best shortsighted, and at worst the ultimate of hubris.

The reader will note that the elements of the OE model do not provide a prescriptive list of tasks and activities. Every healthcare organization has its unique challenges and operates in an environment that is in many respects different even from similar HCOs in the same community. It is left to those for whom OE is a priority to determine how to best fit the parts of this model into their particular setting. The voyage will be long and sometimes hard, but with vision, energy, and determination they can create the sort of uniformly excellent healthcare delivery organizations that all of us want and deserve.

# REFERENCES

ACMQ. (1996, March 27). *Policy 1 – Definition of Medical Quality*. Retrieved July 25, 2014, from http://www.acmq.org/policies/policies1and2.pdf

Air Safety Support International. (2006, January 2). *Safety Culture*. Retrieved June 17, 2014, from Air Safety Support International: http://www.airsafety.aero/safety_development/sms/safety_culture/

American College of Healthcare Executives. (2014). Top Issues Confronting Hospitals: 2013. *Healthcare Executive*, 88.

Boeing Aircraft Company. (2013, August 1). *Statistical Summary of Commercial Jet Airplane Accidents: Worldwide Operations 1959–2012*. Retrieved June 17, 2014, from Boeing Aircraft Compant: http://www.boeing.com/news/techissues/pdf/statsum.pdf

Booker, E. (2014). *HIMSS Rates Hospital's IT Maturity*. Retrieved July 29, 2014, from Information Week Health Care: http://www.informationweek.com/healthcare/analytics/himss-rates-hospitals-it-maturity/d/d-id/1112939

Centers for Medicare and Medicaid Services. (2013, March 22). *Accountable Care Organization (ACO)*. Retrieved August 9, 2014, from CMS.gov: http://www.cms.gov/Medicare/Medicare-Fee-for-Service-Payment/ACO/

Centers for Medicare and Medicaid Services. (2014, January 7). *National Health Expenditure Data*. Retrieved May 14, 2014, from CMS.gov: http://www.cms.gov/Research-Statistics-Data-and-Systems/Statistics-Trends-and-Reports/NationalHealthExpendData/NationalHealthAccountsHistorical.html

Chicago-Kent College of Law. (n.d.). *Oyez*. Retrieved May 12, 2014, from Jacobellis v. Ohio: http://www.oyez.org/cases/1960-1969/1962/1962_11_2

Cleveland Clinic. (2014). *Mission, Vision and Values*. Retrieved August 1, 2014, from Cleveland Clinic: http://my.clevelandclinic.org/about-cleveland-clinic/overview/who-we-are/mission-vision-values.aspx

CMS. (2012, October 1). *AHRQ PSNet*. Retrieved June 13, 2014, from AHRQ Agency for Healthcare Research and Quality: http://psnet.ahrq.gov/primer.aspx?primerID=21

CMS. (2013, April 10). *HCAHPS: Patients' Perspectives of Care Survey*. Retrieved July 31, 2014, from CMS.gov: http://www.cms.gov/Medicare/Quality-Initiatives-Patient-Assessment-Instruments/HospitalQualityInits/HospitalHCAHPS.html

CMS. (2014, February 24). *Home*. Retrieved May 30, 2014, from CAHPS Hospital Survey: http://www.hcahpsonline.org/

CMS. (2014, May 8). *Hospital Value Based Purchasing*. Retrieved May 29, 2014, from CMS.gov: http://www.cms.gov/Medicare/Quality-Initiatives-Patient-Assessment-Instruments/hospital-value-based-purchasing/index.html?redirect=/hospital-value-based-purchasing/

Dartmouth Institute. (2014, January 10). *Total Medicare Reimbursements Per Enrollee, By Adjustment Type*. Retrieved June 3, 2014, from The Dartmouth Atlas of Health Care: http://www.dartmouthatlas.org/data/topic/topic.aspx?cat=21

Eddy, D. (2005). Evidence-Based Medicine: A Unified Approach. *Health*, 9–17.

Fisher, M. (2012, June 28). *Here's a Map of the Countries That Provide Universal Health Care (America's Still Not on It)*. Retrieved June 3, 2014, from The Atlantic: http://www.theatlantic.com/international/archive/2012/06/heres-a-map-of-the-countries-that-provide-universal-health-care-americas-still-not-on-it/259153/

Frei. (2008). The Four Things a Service Business Must Get Right. *Harvard Business Review*, 70–80.

Friedman, L., & Marghella, P. (2004). Environmental Jolt of Bioterrorism. In J. Blair, M. Fottler, & A. Zapanta, *Advances in Health Care Management* (pp. 141–162). London: Emerald Publishing Group.

Galewitz, P. (2010, September 16). *Uninsured Rate Soars, 50+ Million Americans Without Coverage*. Retrieved June 2, 2014, from KHN: Kaiser Health News: http://www.kaiserhealthnews.org/stories/2010/september/16/census-uninsured-rate-soars.aspx

Gawande, A. (2011). *The Checklist Manifesto*. New York: Metropolitan Books.

HHS/ONC. (n.d.). *Hitech Programs & Advisory Committees*. Retrieved July 29, 2014,

from      HealthIT.gov:      http://www.healthit.gov/policy-researchers-implementers/
health-it-adoption-programs
HIMSS. (2014). *Stage 7 Hospitals*. Retrieved July 29, 2014, from HIMSS Analytics: http://
www.himssanalytics.org/emram/stage7Hospitals.aspx
IHI. (2014). *The IHI Triple Aim*. Retrieved July 28, 2014, from IHI Triple Aim Initiative:
http://www.ihi.org/Engage/Initiatives/TripleAim/Pages/default.aspx
James, J. T. (2013). A New, Evidence-based Estimate of Patient Harms Associated with
Hospital Care. *Journal of Patient Safety*, 122–128.
Kaluzny, S., Shortell, S., Faluzny, A., & Monte, S. (1997). Organization Theory and Health
Services Management. In S. M. Shortell & A. D. Kaluzny, *Essentials of Health Care
Management* (pp. 10–11). Albany: Delmar Publishers.
Kennedy, D. M., Caselli, R. J., & Berry, L. L. (2011). A Roadmap for Improving Healthcare
Service Quality. *Journal of Healthcare Management*, 385–400.
Kissick, W. (1994). *Medicine's Dilemmas: Infinite Needs versus Finite Resources*. New Haven:
Yale University Press.
Lasserre, C. (2010). Fostering a Culture of Service Excellence. *Medical Practice Management*,
166–169.
Lee, F. (2004). *If Disney Ran Your Hospital*. Bozeman: Second River Healthcare.
Lewin Group. (2008). *Becoming a High Reliability Organization: Operational Advice for
Hospital Leaders*. Rockville: Agency for Healthcare Research and Quality.
Medicine, I. o. (2000). *To Err is Human*. Washington: National Academy Press.
MSN Money. (2013, July 17). *How We Did Our Survey*. Retrieved July 31, 2014, from
MSN Money: http://money.msn.com/investing/latest.aspx?post=29b455a7-8d44-4435-
9011-959655111596
North Shore LIJ. (2014). *Mission Statement*. Retrieved August 1, 2014, from North Shore
LIJ: http://www.northshorelij.com/hospitals/about-us/about-us-mission-statement
Oregon Patient Safety Commission. (2014, January 2). *A "Sterile Cockpit" for Healthcare*.
Retrieved June 17, 2014, from Oregon Patient Safety Commission: http://oregonpatient-
safety.org/healthcare-professionals/articles/sterile-cockpit-for-healthcare/527
Sackett, D., & Rosenberg, W. (1995). The Need for Evidence-Based Medicine. *Journal of the
Royal Society of Medicine*, 620–624.
SaferHealthcare. (2014, January 2). *Crew Resource Management in Healthcare*. Retrieved
June 17, 2014, from SaferHealthcare: http://www.saferhealthcare.com/crew-resource-
management/crew-resource-management-healthcare/
Senge, P. (1990). *The Fifth Discipline: The Art and Practice of the Learning Organization*.
New York: Doubleday.
Sharp Healthcare. (2014). *Mission, Vision and Values*. Retrieved August 1, 2014, from Sharp
Healthcare: http://www.sharp.com/choose-sharp/mission-vision-values.cfm
Shortell, S. (2014, March 26). *The State of Accountable Care Organizations*. Retrieved
August 9, 2014, from AHRQ Health Care Innovations Exchange: http://www.innovations.
ahrq.gov/content.aspx?id=3919
Smith, M. (2013, October 1). *Chris Argyris: theories of action, double-loop learning and organiza-
tional learning*. Retrieved June 13, 2014, from The Encyclopedia of Informal Education: http://
infed.org/mobi/chris-argyris-theories-of-action-double-loop-learning-and-organizational-
learning/
Squires, D. A. (2012, May 1). *Issues in International Health Policy*. Retrieved May 14, 2014,
from The Commonwealth Fund: http://www.commonwealthfund.org/~/media/Files/
Publications/Issue%20Brief/2012/May/1595_Squires_explaining_high_hlt_care_spending
_intl_brief.pdf
Starr, P. (1982). The Social Transformation of American Medicine. In P. Starr, *The Social
Transformation of American Medicine* (p. 243). New York: Basic Books.
Studer, Q. (2003). *Hardwiring Excellence*. Gulf Breeze: Fire Starter Publishing.
Studer, Q. (2009). *Straight A Leadership*. Gulf Breeze: Fire Starter Publishing.
Studer, Q. (2013). Leader Development. In Q. Studer, *A Culture of High Performance*
(pp. 151–174). Gulf Breeze: Fire Starter Publishing.

Studer, Q. (2013). The Times are Changing ... But the Values Remain the Same. In Q. Studer, *A Culture of High Performance* (pp. 1–19). Gulf Breeze: Fire Starter Publishing.

StuderGroup. (2014). *About StuderGroup*. Retrieved June 10, 2014, from StuderGroup: https://www.studergroup.com/

The Advisory Board Company. (2014). *Three Key Elements for Successful Population Health Management*. Retrieved August 9, 2014, from About Us: http://www.advisory.com/research/health-care-advisory-board/studies/2013/three-elements-for-successful-population-health-management

Wakefield, M. (2014, June 3). *Affordable Care Act Funds to Expand Services at the Nation's Community Health Centers*. Retrieved August 9, 2014, from HHS.gov/HealthCare: http://www.hhs.gov/healthcare/facts/blog/2014/06/expand-services-at-community-health-centers.html

Walt Disney Company. (2013). *Disney's Approach to Building A Culture of Healthcare Excellence*. Retrieved July 31, 2014, from Florida Unlimited Incentives, Inc.: http://www.floridaunlimitedincentives.com/disneyinstitute/pc/Disney-s-Approach-to-Building-A-Culture-of-Healthcare-Excellence-c18.htm

Warden, G. L., & Griffith, J. R. (2001). Ensuring Management Excellence in the Healthcare System. *Journal of Healthcare Management*, 228–237.

Weber, M. (1947). *The Theory of Social and Economic Organization*. New York: Free Press.

# 9. Communication

*Charles F. Wainright and Amanda Raffenaud*

---

> ## BOX 9.1 BRIEF VIGNETTE: WHY IS IT SO HARD TO GET THINGS DONE?
>
> Diane was recently hired as an experienced operating room (OR) circulating nurse to work in the outpatient surgery center in Nashville, Tennessee, in the USA. Diane had about three years of experience as a Bachelor of Science in Nursing (BSN) nurse who had worked in both cardiac intensive care units (ICUs) and in special procedures departments within other hospital units. She was very accomplished in her skills and knowledge around the OR, but had not had any experience with this new position within the ambulatory surgery setting of this clinic.
>
> Initially, upon employment, Diane was given a very general orientation of the facility and the procedures performed for about two or three days. After the initial orientation, Diane was rotated in various OR suites with various teams and procedures. During her rotations, she would ask other experienced nursing personnel what initial tasks needed to be performed to prep the OR for each procedure. Unfortunately, each surgery team would prep the rooms in different ways and in different steps, even though the surgical procedures were approximately the same. When Diane asked other nursing personnel why they were doing it differently from other teams, they would look perturbed and just say, "That is the way we do it" and would provide no other explanation. Diane was getting extremely frustrated since once she learned the preparation for the OR one way, another team would come in and say, "No, we want it done this way." Additionally, a team member would say, "Have you called the cleaning crew to clean the OR for the next case?" However, Diane never knew this had to be done, nor was she informed that she was the one who should perform this task.
>
> When Diane had her initial first month's evaluation meeting with her supervisor, she was told she was doing her job well, but needed to stop asking other team members so often why tasks were done a certain way. Diane explained that this was how she was able to learn the different procedures or methods used during the outpatient surgeries so that she could understand and retain the essential sequencing of steps to follow for the various surgical teams. The supervisor seemed a little annoyed, but appeared to understand. She indicated to Diane to just try harder to learn the system and unique nuances of the teams in other ways. Diane continued to learn by observing, but not asking very many questions. While she did improve her skills and techniques, she became more frustrated with the position and the lack of communication with all the team members.
>
> Why was Diane so frustrated with her work and her position at the ambulatory surgery center? Why did the other team members complain about Diane asking questions?

Why would the supervisor ask Diane to stop asking questions? How could communication be improved in this situation?

If you have ever experienced a similar situation in your work setting or had a difficult experience with other staff members, then you might begin to realize the major communication difficulties and the frustration for both Diane and the other team members.

# INTRODUCTION

In the opening passage, what appears to be the main difficulty surrounding this brief healthcare vignette? What might Diane, the other team members, and the supervisor have done to improve the communication among all parties and help to relieve the frustration created from the interactions among all the individuals involved? Why should we be concerned as to whether the communication activities among individuals in a healthcare setting actually work well? The answer is very straightforward: communication is critical to the smooth operations and flow of work processes with all organizations. However, this is especially true within healthcare facilities and organizations. Without appropriate, timely and accurate exchange of information among all parties within the healthcare setting, the consequences can be disastrous. Patients may get the wrong medication and/or treatments, or staff may create situations that damage the confidence of patients, families, and staff in each other. Serious mistakes may arise, resulting in injury and or death to any or all individuals working or being served in these facilities. If this is a critical aspect of patient care experience, then all healthcare personnel must understand what good communication is and how to effectively communicate with each other, patients, family members, and all other necessary parties. Communication is a deliberate process where information is exchanged between two or more individuals and usually has a specific reason or purpose for this information exchange activity (Shannon and Weaver, 1949).

# BASIC COMMUNICATION MODEL AND THE RELATIONSHIP TO HEALTHCARE PROFESSIONALS

The basic communication model is a very simple process, but it can have a variety of difficulties and problems if not facilitated properly. Communications can and often times appear to be one way, in that one individual conveys some specific information directly to another.

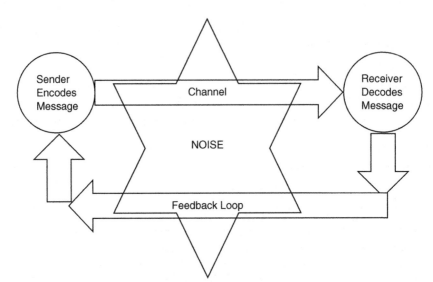

*Source:*   Adapted from Berlo, D.K. (1960), *The Process of Communication*, New York: Holt, Rinehart, and Winston, 24.

*Figure 9.1    Basic communication model*

However, while one-way communications can be effective, two-way communications allows for optimal feedback between all parties which allows for any additional information to be passed to the various individuals to ensure a completed communications session.

Even though the model seems very easy to comprehend, there are many complications that can arise with the communications process itself. The sender may not fully articulate the intended message to the receiver. The receiver may not understand the context of the message. The feedback may not be adequate to fulfill the needs of all parties to complete the communication process. This may be especially true when it comes to healthcare. Healthcare professionals may use specific references to medical terminology or specialty areas that are not familiar to the other individuals, and particularly to patients and family members. A healthcare clinician may be referring to a specific symptom as part of a patient's condition. However, the patient or family member really does not understand the clinical terms or phrases used by the clinician, but may be too embarrassed to ask for clarification. Also, the information being conveyed may not be easily translated to the frame of reference of the other individuals within the communication process. For example, a healthcare professional may discuss a specific US federal payment policy (for example, Medicare or Medicaid) with a colleague who may be thinking of an organizational policy, which is internally created and driven. This could create major confusion about which policy is being discussed. Mistakes can also occur when healthcare professionals are discussing multiple patients in various scenarios and the other clinicians may not know which case is being discussed. These are just a few examples of errors created during the communication between healthcare professionals as well as patients and family members. A discussion concerning these communication difficulties naturally gravitates to a discussion of the various barriers or interferences encountered during the communication process.

## COMMUNICATION BARRIERS: INTERPERSONAL, ORGANIZATIONAL, ENVIRONMENTAL

When entering into the communication process, it is important to recognize the barriers and interfering factors that may be encountered when attempting to communicate effectively. Communication barriers may be identified in various forms, but it is helpful to categorize these into three specific categories (Watson and Smeltzer, 1984).

- interpersonal (or individual);
- organizational;
- environmental.

The interpersonal (or individual) category would include language barriers, personality differences, gender differences, professionalism difficulties, cultural barriers, use of acronyms or slang phrases, and attitude or demeanor complications. Examples of this category of barriers can include female versus male commonalities, agreeable versus disagreeable personalities, lack of cultural awareness and traditions, and use of unfamiliar terms or phrases which can be misinterpreted or applied across different professions with different results. Professionalism difficulties can be seen when one individual believes that their profession is above another's profession in knowledge or capability, which can create barriers to effective communication. For example, a specialty physician may believe (in general) that their education is far superior to that of a pharmacist or healthcare manager and may convey this within the discussion, which can place a wedge or divide between the individuals attempting to discuss a specific issue on pharmaceutical usage. This can also be further complicated if the pharmacist has had specific education on the qualitative effectiveness of the pharmaceuticals and/or the healthcare manager is also trained and experienced in the effectiveness studies analyzing various pharmaceutical agents and outcome studies.

Most interpersonal barriers are considered very personal in nature to each specific individual and therefore can invoke high emotional responses in both parties during the communication process. These situations can often escalate into an emotionally charged shooting match, which further diminishes the effectiveness of the communication interaction. As messages are communicated, the receiver can also filter in their own feelings, emotions, status, and experiences through the process. It may even be difficult for the receiver to separate the actual message from their feelings about the messenger (Dunn, 2007). Therefore, it is paramount to be aware of these potential "hot buttons" during the communication process and to ensure that the information is conveyed in a professional and calm manner to avoid additional complications in the process. Realizing that these potential barriers or issues may be a problem can go a long way in helping all parties to understand these pitfalls, and to assist them in keeping the communications feedback at an acceptable and fruitful level for all concerned parties.

The organizational barrier category is composed of factors that may be attributed to the organization that affect the overall communications process. Organizational barriers can include, but are not limited to, segmentation of the departments or workforce within the organization, positions or ranks that further divide the employees, organizational policies and procedures that require specific steps and individuals to contact in sequence, limited technology or communication mechanisms used by the organization, regulations or rules that prohibit use of communication devices or other mechanisms for security purposes, and organizational culture or history which may inhibit the ability to make new communication structures or avenues, forcing individuals to follow previous (and sometimes outdated) procedures within the organization (Argyris, 1993).

Many of these organizational barriers are further exacerbated by the organizational missions and the established medical, clinical, and administrative cultures that have developed over time within the healthcare industry. For instance, the healthcare profession has generally divided up patient issues and treatment along body systems, procedural versus diagnostic, or some other type of division that often confines or restricts the ability of various providers in different divisions to discuss clinical or administrative issues among all parties. There are numerous examples of surgeons not relating to internists, interventional radiologists not communicating with cardiologists, healthcare managers failing to appropriately connect with clinicians, and other similar examples of weak communication processes. Additionally, many lower-level employees may feel intimidated or restricted to discussing matters with higher executives or clinical directors. This is especially true if a lower-level employee has had a past encounter where they felt diminished or berated for bring up an issue or topic. Many medical errors are often overlooked when a junior employee observes a mistake or error, but believes that speaking up will result in an adverse action levied at them. This further complicates the communication process as well as potentially providing harmful or inappropriate treatment. Healthcare mangers should take a proactive approach to guard against status and position barriers by fostering an organizational culture that values all employees and positions.

The third category of barriers is considered environmental in nature. The environmental barrier category may include noise, interference (electronic, or physical or structural), technological capability, weather conditions, geographic distance, and other man-made or natural phenomena, which inhibit the effective transmission of information. While most environmental barriers are similar in healthcare organizations as they are in other industries, the fact that life-and-death issues and/or information may be exchanged can highlight the importance of the awareness of these barriers. Medical software systems may not be compatible with each other, which can inhibit effective communication between parties and the electronic systems. Additionally, the necessity for patient privacy and the sensitive nature of various patient or clinical information make it necessary to artificially create structural or physical barriers to eliminate unauthorized transmission of critical information to individuals who do not have an official need for the information. Additionally, shielding for fire and safety and radiation protection can also limit the use or effectiveness of electronic devices. Noise and other interference generated by medical equipment and devices can further degrade the communication process. Finally, due to the necessity to provide services that may span large geographic distances, these distances and geographically remote areas may also create barriers to critical communication activities.

A final feature of environmental barriers is that of change. The healthcare industry is wrought with change; from political change to organizational change, there is only one thing constant in the field: change. Resistance to change is a common response by employees who feel insecure through change. As processes, regulations, and/or policies change, employees may reject new ideas that are communicated, or listen only selectively to new strategies being presented. Healthcare managers must strive to be effective in their communication strategies by utilizing the above tips, especially during times of change.

In order to avoid or mitigate these communication barriers, effective communication techniques and redundancies should be used to maximize the effectiveness of all communication endeavors. Some of the critical factors affecting the level of effectiveness of the communication process include:

- Understanding the purpose of the communications activity.
- Understanding the credibility of the sender, receiver, and all other parties.
- Understanding the importance or priority of the message.
- Understanding the urgency and timeliness of the message.
- Understanding the effects of the interpersonal, organizational, and environmental barriers on the communication process.
- Understanding the transmitting and listening skills of both the sender and the receiver, including persuasion and non-verbal communication skills.
- Understanding the major influencing factors related to gender and cultural differences.
- Understanding the best channels or medium to be used to maximize the communication process.

Taking these communication effectiveness factors into account can significantly improve the overall process and the level of understanding and exchange of information by all parties. Just being aware of these potential barriers and the effectiveness factors may assist in avoiding some pitfalls in the communications process. For example, if a senior healthcare professional realizes that a junior professional may feel too intimidated to make a comment or provide valuable feedback in a specific situation, it is incumbent on the senior professional to make the junior professional know it is OK, and even encourage them to provide feedback and put them at ease in the situation. Additionally, if the healthcare individuals are aware of significant interference, distractions, and/or other barriers, it may be necessary to communicate the message in multiple, different channels and to ask for specific feedback to ensure the exchange of information was completed and appropriate. Providing information to the receivers on urgency, importance, purpose, and other critical components can further assist the effectiveness of the information exchange. A major communication effectiveness factor is the use of appropriate channels to communicate the message to other parties. The channel or channels selected can be almost as important as the message itself in ensuring proper transmission and exchange of information.

In addition to the above tips for overcoming communication barriers, Dunn (2007) reveals that careful planning, feedback, listening, credibility, and sensitivity should be applied when communicating. Below are important keys to combatting communication barriers:

- Carefully plan and prepare what needs to be communicated.
- Strive to be reliable and credible in your communication.
- Offer feedback when sending and receiving messages to clarify intent.
- Pay attention and fully listen to the message sender.
- Clarify the message by asking, "Is this what you mean?"
- Repeat or rephrase messages using different channels (verbal versus written) as needed to reinforce the message.

## COMMUNICATION CHANNELS

Communication channels can occur in various forms. The commonly used communication channels – verbal, nonverbal, and written communications – have both advantages and disadvantages with use. The following subsections will discuss each channel in detail.

### Verbal Communication Channels

Verbal communication uses spoken language to convey a message. This use of words can be a very effective means of delivering information to patients or colleagues. Verbal communication can take place both formally and informally. For example, as a nursing supervisor briefs nurses on a new policy during monthly staff meetings, verbal communication might take place formally in a conference room. Or, as a physician discusses treatment options with a colleague, verbal communication might take place informally in a hospital hallway.

Verbal communication usually occurs face-to-face, synchronously in real time, where the message sender can visually see the message receiver. This face-to-face method might be in person or even online through Skype or another electronic meeting platform. Verbal communication can also occur without being face to face, but still take place synchronously. Telephone communication would be one such example.

The benefits of using verbal communication channels are vast. Verbal communication is usually more efficient than written forms because communicating orally is quicker and saves time. Additionally, verbal communication allows for two-way messages to be shared back and forth vis-à-vis the sender and receiver, including a necessary feedback loop as depicted above. This feedback loop allows for clarification to be pursued should the message receiver find the message difficult to understand. Thus, verbal communication is an efficient and clear method of delivery information.

The disadvantages of using verbal communication channels include misinterpreted semantics and the lack of formal message documentation. Semantics considers multiple meanings of words or phrases, and the context in which they are used (Dunn, 2007). A simple, verbal communication message can be construed differently by receivers, which can result in miscommunication. Another disadvantage with the use of verbal communication is the lack of a paper trail that results. A medication change order that is verbally instructed to the nurse illustrates this point. If the verbal order was incorrect, or interpreted incorrectly, there is no formal documentation to verify what was actually ordered. In healthcare especially, it is crucial to maintain a proper documentation trail, even if in an electronic format, to ensure mistakes are minimized.

**Non-Verbal Communication Channels**

Non-verbal communication includes various forms of body language that often carry meaning during communication. Facial expressions, head nods, body posture, and voice tone are just a few examples of non-verbal communication cues. Without using words, this form of communication can still communicate a message – either positive or negative. Eye-rolling, crossed arms, rigid posture, and lack of eye contact can portray disagreement or annoyance between the message sender and the message receiver. On the other hand, a smile, a slight head nod, and direct eye contact can signal engagement and understanding between the message sender and the message receiver.

In healthcare, it is important to remember that non-verbal communication is a powerful tool in communication. It is important to not only consider what is said, but how it is said (D'Agostino and Bylund, 2014). When practitioners communicate with patients who may struggle with language barriers, positive non-verbal cues can be a calming force. When superiors communicate with their subordinates, eye contact, positive tones, and friendly facial expressions can signal a positive demeanor. Non-verbal cues carry significant meaning that can either add or detract from the message being delivered.

**Written Communication Channels**

Written communication is vital in the healthcare field as a means to properly document patient information and organizational policies and procedures. Written communication can range from short and quick memos or e-mail messages to long and cumbersome policy manuals. As with verbal communication, written communication also has some advantages and disadvantages with use.

Written communication allows for the message sender to carefully think through what needs to be said and how it should be said. This includes utilizing correct terminology, rereading for clarity, and revising or editing the message before the receiver receives the message. This ensures appropriate transfer of the message contents. Further, utilizing written communication enables a paper trail to exist, which is often important when practitioners and healthcare managers must formally document processes.

Written communication, however, lacks the advantage of a synchronous feedback loop. Unlike the verbal communication channel, written communication feedback does not usually occur in real time. For instance, if the Radiological and Imaging Department head e-mails the department's technicians to communicate important equipment information, a feedback loop will not occur until the e-mail is received, read, and responded to, which can take time, and significantly impact the necessary follow-up that is needed. Another disadvantage of written communication, especially in the form of memos or e-mail messages, is the lack of face-to-face interaction. Tones are difficult to decipher through the mere written word without having the ability to hear the message and view the associated non-verbal cues.

Much of the written communication that occurs in healthcare organization is through electronic formats. There has been a strong push towards electronic medical records, replacing paper record formats. Additionally, old paper-based processes are now being replaced with electronic processes; such as, computerized physician order entry (CPOE) systems which allow for prescription requests and renewals to be sent electronically to pharmacies, rather than utilizing paper-based prescriptions. Additional forms of electronic-based written communication such as blogs and social media will be discussed in later sections of this chapter.

**Multiple Communication Channels**

Healthcare professionals should aim to utilize multiple channels when communicating with patients, colleagues, and other stakeholders. Relying on only one communication channel to convey important messages may potentially result in a less clear understanding of the information being presented. For example, as patients are discharged from the hospital, discharge instructions are communicated not only verbally, but also through written forms (that is, printouts of at-home instructions and follow-up guidelines). As another example, hospital executives typically convey important policy changes in multiple formats: verbal methods from supervisors to employees as well as e-mail reminders and updates. Utilizing multiple communication channels helps to ensure the message is not only heard and understood, but also remembered, allowing for appropriate follow-up actions to take place as needed.

## ORGANIZATIONAL COMMUNICATIONS MODELS AND ACTIVITIES

Formal and informal models of communication exist in the healthcare industry. Although these structures are distinct, both are important in sharing messages from one group to another (Dunn, 2007).

Formal communication models are usually dictated by organizational hierarchies. These models consist of downward communication, upward communication, horizontal communication, and diagonal communication. Downward communication flows from superiors to subordinates, in which someone from a higher point in the hierarchy communicates with lower levels of the hierarchy. For example, as the Director of Nursing sends e-mails, memos, or letters to shift nurses, downward communication is occurring. Upward communication can take place as subordinates communicate with their supervisors or supervisors communicate with their next-level supervisors. The flow of communication is upward and involves keeping superiors informed. This might encompass job complaints, patient complaints, or environment complaints. Or, a department director might want to pay a compliment to a technician by telling the next-level supervisor about the technician's skills and work ethic. Horizontal communication occurs across departments or peer managers or co-workers. For example, a hospital patient who is undergoing multiple procedures would require the surgical nurses to communicate with the unit nurses through horizontal communication. Diagonal communication consists of messages flowing from different parts of the organizational fields. As human resource managers discuss benefit packages with hospital staff, diagonal communication occurs. Further, diagonal communication occurs as the food service department discusses patient dietary needs with a unit nurse (Dunn, 2007).

An informal communication model (*aka* "the grapevine") occurs through various levels: downward, upward, horizontal, and diagonal flows. The grapevine entails general socializing between employees and usually lacks structure. This might include face-to-face or e-mail communication. The information shared via informal models may or may not be correct, and is typically dependent upon the employee's current working situation and the personal feelings and/or experiences of the employee. Although the grapevine can be a healthy form of socialization and communication between employees, managers must guard against the grapevine turning destructive. Effective formal communication channels will aid in creating effective informal commination channels (Dunn, 2007).

Within the healthcare environment, it is critical for the healthcare organization and its executive team to be fully aware of and to monitor both formal and informal communication activities throughout the organization. Failure to adequately monitor these activities and to correct inappropriate use of both formal and informal channels of communication can give the healthcare employees an impression of avoidance or a non-caring attitude towards inappropriate communications. Proper monitoring, dissemination, training, education, and creation of a professional culture towards all communication activities can prevent employees from harmful communication exchanges that will degrade both the morale and the smooth operations of the organization.

## COMMUNICATING WITH HEALTHCARE PROFESSIONALS AND PATIENTS

Communication barriers can often create larger-scale communication issues in the healthcare industry. This section will discuss health communication as it relates to the provider–patient relationship, the employer–employee relationship, and other complexities that arise between healthcare professionals and stakeholders.

### Provider–Patient Communication

Effective provider–patient communication refers to "the exchange of information between doctor and patient in which the meaning is mutually understood" (Ge et al., 2009). The provider–patient relationship centers on effective communication and considers patient attributes (health status, education, age, and so on), provider attributes (specialty, work demands, and so on) and their relationship attributes (trust, rapport) (Thompson et al., 2003). Patients typically have a desire to discuss their healthcare needs, to be listened to, and to understand their conditions and subsequent provider recommendations. Providers have a desire to communicate important health information, to be understood, and to work with compliant patients. Mutual understanding, confidentiality, trust, and patient-centered communication should drive the relationship between patients and providers (Matusitz and Spear, 2014).

The relationship between patients and providers can serve as a powerful indicator of healthcare quality and often determines patients' health behaviors and outcomes (Matusitz and Spear, 2014). The health communication literature consistently confirms that both the quality of medical practice and quality treatment outcomes center on positive interaction and communication between the patient and practitioner (Matusitz and Spear, 2014). Practitioners and healthcare managers alike should take note of these linkages and aim for healthy communication patterns with their patients, as doing so will influence health outcomes.

Some fundamental communication tips, according to Maturisz and Spear (2014), that medical professionals should employ when discussing healthcare-related information with their patients are as follows:

- Communicate health information directly and explicitly.
- When possible, avoid scripted communication and practice everyday discourse.
- Avoid overtalking or interrupting when the patient is speaking.
- Practice active listening when the patient is speaking.
- Pay attention to a patient's non-verbal cues and also practice sending positive non-verbal cues.

**Employer–Employee Communication**

Effective employee–employer communication will allow for organizational policies, procedures, and goals to be carried out. When effective communication is present, both short-term and long-term plans can be achieved and department activities coordinated and controlled; in essence, the organization's mission can be fulfilled (Dunn, 2007). In fact, much of an organization's success will depend on effective communication between supervisors and their employees. As discussed previously, communication between employers and employees can flow upward or downward. As employers communicate messages to their employees (downward flow), clarity should be a top priority. Further, employers should encourage an open dialogue with their employees, allowing for the feedback loop to be practiced. During times of increased organizational change such as legislative or healthcare policy changes, employers should commit to an increase in communicative efforts, utilizing multiple channels of both verbal and written formats.

When employees communicate with their employer (upward flow), employers should demonstrate respect for the messenger, regardless of the message being presented. Allowing employees to voice their work-related opinions, without fear of repercussions, will foster open communication habits. When necessary, healthcare managers should hold open forums or discussion sessions, allowing employees to voice their opinions and offer suggestions on workplace issues.

**Turf Wars**

Employed within the healthcare field are individuals with varying levels of education and scope of influence. At times, "turf wars" can occur between parties who have conflicting interests about workplace issues or industry conditions. Common turf wars might occur between a nurse and a physician, a physician and another physician, or a physician and hospital administration. These disagreements can be small-scale, between two employees of the same practice or hospital, or they can be large-scale, between multiple parties in large hospital systems or industry-wide participants. Nursing strikes, for example, illustrate a large-scale turf war between nurses and employers, typically revolving around workplace conditions.

Depending on the degree and intensity of the turf war, disagreements may be resolved by utilizing the effective communication practices described above. Managers should be equipped to handle conflict between employees, and aim to minimize such conflict. At the larger scale, it might be necessary to include a mediator or other neutral third party to serve as an intercessor between the involved parties. Minimizing turf wars requires the involved parties to utilize effective communication across multiple channels.

**Gender Complexities**

It is well documented within scientific literature than men and women are different. It is no surprise that men and women may also communicate differently. D'Agostino and Bylund (2014) note that female physicians usually engage in increased patient-centered communication behaviors compared to their male counterparts. Further, females usually spend more time with their patients, demonstrate increased empathetic communication, encourage more partnership-building with patients, and are less directive (D'Agostino and Bylund, 2014). Gender communication differences may also be evident outside of the practice environment. For instance, men may more easily break down the interpersonal communication barriers between each other, whereas women may have a more difficult time doing so. Regardless of gender, healthcare professionals should strive to communicate effectively with both patients and colleagues. Further, it is in the best interest of practitioners and managers to be aware of gender differences that may impact communication, and work to resolve these differences, for the good of the patient and the organization at large.

**Culture Complexities**

Knowledge, beliefs, experiences, and customs collectively make up one's unique culture (Matusitz and Spear, 2014). Patients, providers, healthcare managers, and other stakeholders possess individual cultural views that shape how they interact with others, especially in the healthcare field. Cultural differences can often present as barriers. Matusitz and Spear (2014) further contend that race, culture, gender, socio-economic status, spiritual beliefs, education level, and spoken language can all function as chasms in the communication process, especially if these traits are vastly different between the message sender and message receiver. In situations where cultural uniqueness exists – with either the message sender or message receiver – "cultural tailoring" should occur. Cultural tailoring is the "development of interventions, strategies, messages, and materials to cater to unique culture attributes" (Pasick et al., 1996). Understanding their patients' "world" – their needs, beliefs, and perceptions – will allow providers to value diversity while effectively communicating with their patients.

# COMMUNICATION AND TECHNOLOGY

The increased use of technology in the healthcare field has impacted communication among stakeholders. Although the benefits of using technology as a communication aid are vast, there are some important protocols to keep in mind. The following section will discuss the professional use of various online communication methods within the healthcare industry. Up to this point, the chapter has focused mostly on internal communication (that is, communication between providers and patients, or employers and employees). The section will shift the discussion to external communication and how healthcare organizations can reach outside stakeholders and community members by utilizing online communicative methods.

Healthcare organizations are remaining culturally relevant by communicating across various technological platforms. Websites, blogs, and social media such as Twitter, Facebook, LinkedIn and YouTube are many of the commonly utilized methods for online communication. These methods have distinct advantages when aiming to reach a particular audience.

**Websites**

It is rare to find a healthcare facility or practice in the USA that does not have an accompanying website. Creating an online presence allows healthcare organizations to appeal to patients and other community members while conveying information in a quick and efficient manner. Many healthcare facilities utilize their websites to provide basic healthcare information, contact information, secure payment platforms, and even patient registration tools.

**Blogs**

Blogs are content management tools that can range from a short exchange of information (Twitter and "microblogging") to a long exchange of information (personal or organizational blogs). Most healthcare organizations have blogs on their organization's website that provide helpful health tips and/or organizational updates. In addition, most healthcare organizations have Twitter handles, or accounts, and "tweet" brief information to those who follow the account.

**Social Media**

Social media such as Facebook, Twitter (discussed above), LinkedIn, and YouTube are commonly utilized by healthcare organizations to convey information to patients, employees, and the community at large. Facebook is a social networking site that individuals and organizations can join to gain an online presence and share pertinent information. LinkedIn is a business-oriented social networking site, and serves as a professional networking platform. Media-sharing social media platforms such as YouTube allow for organizations to share informational videos. For example, a hospital or group practice may feature a video series on "Getting Healthy" and post its videos to YouTube.

All social media sites aim to have followers or subscribers. These followers are interested in following the organization and receiving information that is sent out into the community. In essence, followers act as the organization's audience. It is important for healthcare organizations to understand their online audience and aim to communicate effectively in a way that benefits both patients and providers.

**Top 5 Hospitals and their Social Media Communication**

US News and World Report ranked the top five hospitals in the US in 2013–2014. These hospitals were judged on various criteria including reputation, patient survival, patient safety, and other care-related indicators (Leonard, 2013). To illustrate the point that social medial platforms prove to be an effective and necessary communication method, Table 9.1

*Table 9.1  Top five ranking US hospitals and their social media communication*

| Hospital | Website | Twitter | Facebook | LinkedIn | YouTube |
|---|---|---|---|---|---|
| 1. Johns Hopkins Hospital, Baltimore | http://www.hopkinsmedicine.org | @HopkinsMedicine 239000 followers | Johns Hopkins Medicine 158483 likes | https://www.linkedin.com/company/johns-hopkins-hospital?trk=company_name 6346 employees on LinkedIn | https://www.youtube.com/user/JohnsHopkinsMedicine 9341 subscribers |
| 2. Massachusetts General Hospital, Boston | http://www.massgeneral.org | @MassGeneralNews 16300 followers | Massachusetts General Hospital 7723 likes | https://www.linkedin.com/company/massachusetts-general-hospital?trk=company_name 10630 employees on LinkedIn | https://www.youtube.com/user/MassGeneralHospital 718 subscribers |
| 3. Mayo Clinic, Rochester, MN | http://www.mayoclinic.org | @MayoClinic 794000 followers | Mayo Clinic 520000 likes | https://www.linkedin.com/company/mayo-clinic?trk=company_name 19420 employees on LinkedIn | https://www.youtube.com/user/mayoclinic 19073 subscribers |
| 4. Cleveland Clinic | http://my.clevelandclinic.org/default.aspx | @ClevelandClinic 253000 followers | Cleveland Clinic 1 million likes | https://www.linkedin.com/company/cleveland-clinic?trk=company_name 18563 employees on LinkedIn | https://www.youtube.com/user/ClevelandClinic 8933 subscribers |
| 5. UCLA Medical Center Los Angeles | http://www.uclahealth.org | @UCLAHealth 13900 followers | UCLA Medical Center 827 likes | https://www.linkedin.com/company/ucla-health-system 5562 employees on LinkedIn | https://www.youtube.com/user/UCLAHealth 5028 subscribers |

*Note:* This table was created from a compilation of sources, including websites and social media sites, publicly available, for the above named hospitals. Information reflects data as of June 2014.

displays the top five hospitals and each of their social media statistics. As depicted in the table, all five hospitals capitalize on these social media methods to reach broad audiences. The number of followers, likes, and subscribers indicates the online audience each hospital has; the larger the audience, the more important the social media communication.

Benefits aside, there are some important professional components to keep in mind when communicating through social media or online tools. As organizations utilize websites, blogs, and social media sites, there should be protocols in place to check for message and content accuracy. Blogs, posts, updates, and tweets should contain accurate information that remains credible and professional. Organizations should provide proper training to those who are responsible for updating the institution's online platforms to ensure that proper protocols are followed. Most organizations have strict policies that govern both personal and organizational use of social media sites. The following are common rules regarding the use of social media, and pertain to both the employee's personal social media sites as well as the organization's public social media sites:

- Avoid posting individually identifiable patient information that will violate patient privacy and confidentiality.
- Uphold local, state, and federal regulations regarding copyright laws and intellectual property rights.
- Refrain from posting, uploading, or e-mailing information that is unlawful, disruptive, threatening, abusive, harassing, profane, defamatory, obscene, libelous, hateful, or an invasion of privacy.
- Discipline and/or job termination may occur for inappropriate use of social media sites.

Concerns about privacy often surface when individuals and organizations utilize social media. Organizations, typically transparent entities, must be careful to share only appropriate information and not information that should remain confidential such as specific patient information, diagnoses, or sensitive information about employees and the organization at large. In addition, strict access codes and passwords should be applied to organizational accounts in order to prohibit a breach of access by non-approved employees.

## COMMUNICATING DURING CRISIS SITUATIONS

Effectively communicating during a crisis situation is a priority for all organizations, but can be especially daunting for healthcare organizations. The actual crisis situation itself can be especially stressful and chaotic even without addressing the communication requirements. This emotionally charged period of time requires the best and most accurate communication exchanges possible given the crisis and potentially harmful situation. A crisis situation can be either a natural or a man-made disaster, which adversely affects the organization, or individuals within the organization. For healthcare organizations (and especially patient treatment facilities) it can affect the organization on multiple levels. A weather-related disaster such as a fire, flood, tornado, or other sizable event can directly affect and impact the facility. Other industries and organizations would also have similar affected areas, as would a healthcare organization. However, in the case of a patient treatment facility, the organization is seen as a safe haven or a place to be treated from the dangerous encounter. Therefore, the healthcare organization must not only take care of its own personnel and facility issues, but it must also extend its help and assistance to outside individuals who will expect to be treated or just be given shelter from the crisis event. This creates a situation where it is critical for the organization to have excellent communication procedures and standards for both the internal staff but also the incoming patients to the facility.

Healthcare organizations must deliberately prepare for effective communications activities during crisis events by creating various templates and examples of the types of messages that will be necessary during these events. Organizational instructions, warnings, preparation memos, media announcements, and other messages must be prepared in advance and then modified as the situation dictates in order to be able to rapidly transmit information to the needed parties. Attempting to create these announcements or messages from a totally blank page will cause unnecessary and significant delay in getting the right information to the right personnel. This type of communication is already difficult during a crisis period without adding the burden of creating these announcements without any specific examples to use. Therefore, it is absolutely essential that key personnel develop and practice with prepared communication messages, which will add realism to the practice sessions as well as provide enhanced training on how to modify these announcements. An example might be that a tornado, flood or other weather event is about to hit the community in the next hour or so. Hospitals, clinics, and other healthcare organizations can have these predefined announcements within a standard operating procedure manual as a part of a crisis management plan. These templates and examples can be quickly modified and sent out to all the required personnel along with specific instructions on how to react to the upcoming crisis. Providing practice drills and exercises prior to the real crisis event will further prepare all individuals and allow any necessary modifications to be made within the communications plan.

Additionally, during a crisis situation, the healthcare organization must have a mechanism to help with media requests and crowd control situations. The media will want to know the status of the emergency situation along with what the healthcare organization is doing to be prepared for the event. It is paramount that the healthcare organization has created a strong communication dialogue with the local media and has designated public affairs or press representatives within the healthcare organization who have worked with the local media in the past and have a good rapport with these agencies. This will help both sides to know who to contact, having pre-established connections with each other prior to the actual event. Along with the media relations activities, the healthcare organization must also prepare for crowd control during the crisis situation. During an emergency event, many individuals will quickly move to places that are considered safe-haven locations such as hospitals, clinics, and other healthcare facilities. Communicating effectively with the public using both local media sources as well as direct communication channels can help to reduce congestion and crowding of critical patient treatment areas. For example, during Hurricanes Katrina and Sandy, many citizens moved in large masses to the local emergency rooms and other medical facilities. This has the potential for clogging up the emergency access and treatment areas where both patients needing treatment and care-givers are not able to access the necessary areas of the healthcare facilities. Having specific communications activities such as barriers, signage, traffic control personnel, and other prepared instructive devices will assist in better patient and care-giver flow within the system. Early communication with local police, fire, rescue, public health, Federal Emergency Management Agency (FEMA), and other agencies, along with the media, is critical in order to ensure the proper flow and operations in the healthcare system (Eisenman et al., 2007).

Past research on crisis activities has provided useful information concerning communication techniques prior to a disaster. Some of these tips include:

- Plan activation and alert system. This activity includes circumstances for plan activation, activation stages (alert, standby, call-out, and stand down), procedures for notification, internal chain of command, alternate notification systems, staff rationing, prioritizing of closing patient areas due to staff shortages.
- Hospital disaster command control center readiness. This activity examines requirements for alternate disaster control locations to be

designated, and the establishment of appropriate operating procedures for the command center.

- Security, traffic flow and control considerations. This activity examines the ability to lock down and control entrance and exit points within a healthcare facility, as well as pedestrian and vehicular traffic flow. It also recognizes security issues regarding emergency service vehicle access, staff access, supply vendor access, police support, visitor control, vehicle parking, and removal of contaminated vehicles.
- Communications systems. Under this activity, the communications capabilities including telephone, fax, cellular service, e-mail, paging, and radio are addressed. Additionally, communication networks with local law enforcement, fire, health department, emergency medical services (EMS), and Emergency Management Agency should be assessed for vulnerabilities.
- Media relations. This activity examines the roles and responsibilities of the public information officer including media control, information requests by media representatives, designating an area for media representatives, designated areas for press briefings, and plans associated with internal staff communication with the media.
- Backup communication, power requirements, and supplies. These activities examine all forms of backup communications, power and supply systems, including alternative communications such as walkie-talkie systems, messenger/runner and schematic area layout maps in hard copy which should be in place. Auxiliary power systems, gas or diesel generators, battery packs, and calibration of specialized medical equipment must be thoroughly addressed. Rationing of food, water, medical supplies, clothing, and laundry support must also considered. Staff morale and welfare including rotations and sleep periods must be appropriately addressed.

All of these activities and examples are areas to consider before a crisis situation occurs. Addressing these and other similar activities associated with disaster planning can go a long way to ensuring that the healthcare facility is prepared for the challenges that may occur during a natural or man-made disaster within the community (Higgins et al., 2004).

## STRATEGIC INITIATIVES IN HEALTHCARE COMMUNICATIONS

When understanding and analyzing communication structures and processes, a fundamentally important aspect which should be addressed is the strategic initiatives associated with the communication within organizations. The main idea surrounding this topic is that in order for organizations to be successful, they should have a strong strategic focus. As part of the strategic focus, organizations should use specific and deliberate communication initiatives in order to support and attain their strategic goals and objectives. Finding ways to make the organization's communication activities strategic in nature is not always an easy task. Organizations must find the optimal and most effective ways to communicate all aspects of their strategic initiatives, and ensure that the flow of communications is constantly readjusted to ensure maximum information exchange. These initiatives can come in the form of strategic focus groups with employees and outside constituents to gain valuable information and sharing of best practices. They can also take the form of expert intelligence-gathering networks to allow organizations to be on the cutting edge of new innovations and opportunities available within the marketplace. Using current employees, board members, and other close constituents along with information sources that provide updated trends within the industry can improve the organization's strategic advantage within its respective industry. Having specific communication structures to help gather useful intelligence on trend data for the industry is essential for organizations to remain financially viable. In healthcare organizations, this can take the form of possible mergers, acquisitions, or other market consolidations where corporate executives, healthcare financial managers, or other entities are privy to select information on these situations and this information is considered very strategic in nature. It can also be a situation where a physician group is attempting to build an imaging center or outpatient surgery center that will rival the current hospital system's operations and undercut its financial viability. Having this information available through various intelligence-gathering channels would significantly help the healthcare system's strategic operations and planning guidance to gain the competitive advantage.

These strategic communication systems would also assist the healthcare organization in ensuring that the strategic vision and goals are communicated to all constituents and that the organization's interests are properly aligned with individual employee interests in the institution. Sometimes this can take the form of both formal and informal channels, to include focus groups, brainstorming sessions, supervisor counseling sessions, and other interactive meetings with the facility personnel. It may be necessary to hold training sessions on communication techniques, on listening, feedback, and both verbal and non-verbal methods of effective communications. Many healthcare personnel are very good at listening, but in many instances they are so focused on their work that they use a form of selective hearing and may tune out valuable communication activities during the workday. It is vital that healthcare supervisors and staff be especially vigilant to ensure that multiple communication processes and channels are used, to ensure that all-important messages are transmitted and correctly received in a timely and effective manner. Attempting to be strategic and think strategically in all communication activities can help an organization to link its strategic initiatives to all efforts of communicating and transmitting information concerning its strategic planning objectives.

Lastly, in attempting to create a culture that embraces a communications system that is strategic in focus, it is important to ensure that all employee groups are fully trained and brought into the entire process very early during the formulation of the organization's strategic initiatives. This essentially means that all employees have buy-in to the process, and have been able to voice both their reservations as well as their allegiance to the strategic process. Not providing both the necessary training and education, but also the time needed to engage the various employee groups in this process, can have disastrous consequences. Not allowing the employees to have time to fully understand and support the strategic communication process can create animosity within and isolation of various employee groups. These groups can actually feel so disenfranchised that they may engage in deliberate sabotage of the creative and innovative strategic initiatives of the organization. Therefore, it is crucial that employee groups are included in all strategic conversations and processes, using multifaceted channels to ensure a comprehensive approach to the strategic communications endeavor.

## MANAGERIAL TIPS FOR THE HEALTHCARE PROFESSIONALS

This chapter discussed important elements associated with effective communication within the US healthcare industry. Important takeaways for stakeholders, whether managers, practitioners, or aspiring professionals, are the following:

- Utilize multiple communication channels (that is, verbal, non-verbal and written forms) when conveying important messages. This will ensure proper understanding and delivery of the message.
- Non-verbal cues can add or detract from a message's content. Use non-verbal communication wisely.
- Work to overcome communication barriers. These often fall into

one of these categories: language barriers, status and position barriers, and general resistance to change.

- Understand that culture can play a part in communication, in both sending and receiving messages.
- The provider–patient relationship is built on effective communication and often influences health outcomes.
- Employers should create open forums of communication for their employees and allow for positive upward flow of communication.
- Engage in communication via social media platforms, but do so appropriately by upholding the law and honoring patient privacy and confidentiality with all updates and posts.
- Avoid posting individually identifiable patient information that will violate patient privacy and confidentiality.
- Uphold local, state, and federal regulations regarding copyright laws and intellectual property rights.
- Refrain from posting, uploading, or e-mailing information that is unlawful, disruptive, threatening, abusive, harassing, profane, defamatory, obscene, libelous, hateful, or an invasion of privacy.

## CONCLUDING THOUGHTS

As the authors close this chapter on communicating with healthcare professionals, it is important to redirect our thoughts back to the opening vignette with Diane and her supervisor. What are some of the lessons that can be learned within this scenario and the entire outpatient surgery center? Certainly all parties must realize that effective communication takes work from all individuals. Multiple channels should be used, as well as non-verbal cues to pick up on subtle differences in both the sender's and the receiver's communication abilities and concerns. All individuals must have a firm understanding of the various barriers, which can inhibit effective transfer of information. Employee forums are helpful mechanisms to all employees to provide valuable feedback to their employers in more acceptable pathways to excellent communication mechanisms. Both Diane and her supervisor need to be more open to the various approaches by which individuals may both send and receive knowledge. Both need to realize the subtle yet important cues each is attempting to communicate to the other. Increased open and honest feedback, along with using a variety of channels to better communicate with and understand both parties' needs and desires, can certainly help to reduce the frustration levels of both individuals, and assist movement towards a higher level of communication success.

# REFERENCES

Argyris, C. (ed.) (1993), *Knowledge for Action: A Guide to Overcoming Barriers to Organizational Change*, San Francisco, CA: Jossey-Bass.

D'Agostino, T. and C. Bylund (2014), "Nonverbal accommodation in health care communication," *Health Communications*, 29: 563–573.

Dunn, R. (ed.) (2007), *Haimann's Healthcare Management*, Chicago, IL: Health Administration Press.

Eisenman, D., K. Cordasco, S. Asch, J. Golden, and D. Glik (2007), "Disaster planning and risk communication with vulnerable communities: lessons from Hurricane Katrina," *American Journal of Public Health*, 97: S109–S115.

Ge, G., N. Burke, C.P. Smokin, and R. Pascik (2009), "Considering the culture in physician-patient communication during colorectal cancer screening," *Qualitative Health Research*, 19(6): 778–789.

Higgins, W., C. Wainright, N. Lu, and R. Carrico (2004), "Assessing hospital preparedness using an instrument based on the mass casualty disaster plan checklist: results of a statewide survey," *American Journal of Infection Control*, 32(6): 327–332.

Leonard, K. (2013), "US news and world report: best hospitals 2013–2014," available at http://health.usnews.com/health-news/best-hospitals/articles/2013/07/16/best-hospitals-2013-14-overview-and-honor-roll?int=a01008 (accessed June 2014).

Matusitz, J. and J. Spear (2014), "Effective doctor–patient communication: an updated examination," *Social Work in Public Health*, 29: 252–266.

Pasick, R. J., C.N. D'Onofrio, and R. Otero-Sabogal (1996), "Similarities and differences across cultures: questions to inform a third generation for health promotion research," *Health Education Quarterly*, 23: 142–161.

Shannon, C. and W. Weaver (1949), *The Mathematical Theory of Communication*, Chicago, IL: University of Illinois Press.

Thompson, T., A. Dorsey, K. Miller, and R. Parrott (eds) (2003), *Handbook of Health Communication*, Mahwah, NJ: Lawrence Erlbaum Associates.

Watson, K.W. and L.R. Smeltzer (1984), "Barriers to listening: comparison between students and practitioners," *Communication Research Reports*, 1(1): 82–87.

# 10. Healthcare marketing and social media
## *Donna Malvey, Alicia Beardsley,*
## *Peggy K. Howse and Sandra Ruff*

## INTRODUCTION AND OVERVIEW

Marketing is a science and as such is a complex discipline replete with theories and constructions. The American Marketing Association (2013) defines marketing as follows: "Marketing is the activity, set of institutions, and processes for creating, communicating, delivering, and exchanging offerings that have value for customers, clients, partners, and society at large." This is an acceptable definition for marketing, although it would be helpful to include some reference to monitoring and evaluation. Doing so would assure that what is being done, as well where the money is being spent, is achieving the intended goals.

Healthcare marketing is now recognized as a functional discipline to be used in the management of a healthcare organization. Marketing in healthcare is viewed primarily as a process that involves planning and execution of the four marketing mix variables: product, price, place, and promotion. While not always effectively practiced, the perspective that marketing is more than advertising has gained increasing recognition over the years. Although healthcare is undergoing significant structural change, the basic elements of marketing will be at the core of any healthcare organization's successful position in the marketplace (Thomas, 2010).

However, defining healthcare marketing remains unfinished business. The definitions for healthcare marketing, including the marketing concepts and core functions, often vary according to authors, consultants, and reputed experts who have attempted to adapt them to healthcare, albeit with some modification and limitation. There are those who would modify components of the marketing mix or replace them with variables more in line with the healthcare environment. Is the healthcare context so unique as to exempt it from the rigors of scientific principles on which marketing science is based? Not likely, but all four of the marketing mix variables (the "4 Ps"), are somewhat problematic when applied to healthcare because of the idiosyncratic characteristics of the industry (Thomas, 2010). Clearly, the lack of consensus about what is healthcare marketing makes it difficult when it comes to practical application.

*Table 10.1   Why marketing is different in healthcare*

| Variable | Description |
| --- | --- |
| Demand | Health services demand is highly unpredictable |
| End-user | May not be the target of the marketing campaign because the end-user (i.e., patient) typically doesn't directly purchase or pay for services. |
| Nature of the product | Extremely complex and often cannot be easily categorized or described. Also variability due to patient complexity, especially the impact of multiple chronic diseases. |
| Nature of the consumer | Not all consumers are considered desirable. For example, uninsured and underinsured patients represent financial losses to providers and as such would not be targets of marketing campaigns or strategies. |
| Outcomes | Complexity and difficulty in measuring outcomes in terms of provision of health services. |
| Comparison of service delivery across HCOs | Difficult to quantify differences between HCOs and services they delivery. |
| Goods vs. services | Marketing services more challenging to market. |
| Government Intervention | Impact of changes in regulations, reimbursement, and especially impact of ACA on assessing patient satisfaction with their experience with respect to service delivery. |

*Source:*   Based on Thomas (2010).

Table 10.1 discusses why marketing in healthcare is believed to be different. The application of marketing principles in the healthcare environment reflects the unique features of an industry in which the end-user is often not obvious. Who a health system attracts to its facilities and equipment may be two different populations. Too often in the past, healthcare organizations have defined their market by simply identifying who walked into the facility or who used the emergency room. In addition, the demand for health services is unpredictable and is often buffered by insurance. Furthermore, changes in reimbursement insurance programs in the United States such as Medicare and Medicaid can impact availability and demand for services.

In addition, the concept of the market, which is critically important in other industries, simply does not exist in healthcare. Furthermore, health professionals are unused to thinking in terms of products and services lines (Thomas, 2010). But context alone should not be an excuse for disregarding scientific principles and core functions. Marketing in health-care is a process that involves planning and execution of the four mar-keting mix variables: product, price, place, and promotion. Healthcare marketing should be viewed as different or unique only in the manner in which the process and variables are applied.

Marketing is clearly important in healthcare because it affects the bottom line, just as it does in other industries. Too often marketing is over-looked because its impact on the bottom line does not appear on balance sheets. That is about to change in the USA, especially for hospitals because of the Affordable Care Act (ACA) and the move to pay-for-value. Effective October 2012, the Centers for Medicare and Medicaid Services both rewards and penalizes hospitals based on patient satisfaction scores. The US government surveys patients – through the Hospital Consumer Assessment of Healthcare Providers and Systems (HCAHPS) survey – asking them a variety of questions ranging from how clean their room was to how well their pain was controlled. The patient experience will make up 30 percent of the total bonus payments; that is, Pay for Performance (P4P) for hospitals under the ACA. For the first time, reimbursement will be linked to outcomes. Thus, patient experience matters where it counts, literally: the bottom line. As such, marketing is expected to become an essential component of patient experience, especially through the use of social media.

In the past consumers did not have the expertise or access to informa-tion required to evaluate the service provided by US health professionals. In fact, as Table 10.2 illustrates, marketing's evolution in healthcare shows the impact of limited access to information and transparency for consum-ers. Because of the American Medical Association's (AMA) early ban on physician advertising, consumers were unable to gain information about their doctors. Prior to 1975, the AMA had a prohibition against advertis-ing within its codes of ethics. In 1975, the US Supreme Court ruled that the professional associations were subject to federal antitrust laws and that withholding information might be deemed as restraint of trade. The AMA eventually revised its code of ethics to be less stringent regarding advertis-ing. Today it is commonplace to see US healthcare organizations (HCOs) and physicians advertise.

In addition, marketing's ability to create demand and increase competi-tiveness was not beneficial to HCOs due to the inelastic demand for health services and insurance that essentially shielded the industry from compe-tition. As Table 10.2 also shows, the growth of competition, changes in reimbursement, and the passage of landmark health reform legislation in the form of the ACA resulted in an environment where marketing matters. Of course, the rise of consumerism that began in the United States in 1970s

*Table 10.2    Evolution of healthcare marketing in the United States*

| Decade | Description of Environment | Outcomes |
| --- | --- | --- |
| 1950s | None. HCOs shielded from competition by inelastic demand and insurance. Physician advertising was banned by AMA in 1947. | Healthcare marketing is not yet evident. While other industries became engaged in competitive behaviors post WWII, healthcare did not. And the AMA ban on physician advertising (1947) precluded such. |
| 1960s–1970s | Physician referrals mattered to hospitals because of the introduction of Medicaid and Medicare reimbursement. For profit hospitals entering healthcare. Volume became the key because of changes in reimbursement. 1975, the Federal Trade Commission called AMA ban on physician advertising restraint of trade. | Marketing efforts in terms of promotional activities aimed at select group – physicians – and patients were not recognized as an important constituency. |
| 1980s–1990s | Emergence of DRGs for inpatient care. Emphasis of payment associated with resource usage leads to substantive changes, including a move toward ambulatory care. AMA backs off advertising ban for physicians. | Healthcare environment grows competitive and by 1990s physicians and hospitals begin to openly compete to attract patients. |
| 2000–Present | Rising healthcare costs and increases in the number of uninsured lead to healthcare reform emerging as legislative agenda priority. Passage of ACA in 2009. Increase in regulations for hospitals and physicians alike. | Marketing becomes increasingly important because ACA elevates patient satisfaction as a component of reward/penalty system associated with reimbursement. |

also has greatly influenced the healthcare industry. Consequently, patients became customers over 40 years ago, and their needs and wants evolved to become important determinants of marketing plans and strategies, just as they would be for any business enterprise.

Evaluation of health services is becoming possible as consumers can go online and access reviews of physicians, hospitals and other healthcare organizations. In turn, organizations can discover what the healthcare experience means to a patient through a variety of mechanisms, including the Press Ganey experience assessment. This transparency has created new opportunities for both consumers and HCOs (Keller, 2014).

## THE MARKETING PROCESS

Marketing is not simply advertising, even though many believe this. Advertising is appropriate for "pull" functions: that is, creating consumer demand for a particular product. But marketing also needs to focus on "push" functions, the distribution methods. Marketing is a process that involves planning and execution of the four marketing mix variables: product, price, place, and promotion. A successful marketing strategy requires combining the four marketing mix variables (the "4 Ps") in such a way that the blend of elements will result in a successful exchange or transaction between two or more parties. Moreover, the service or product offered in the exchange has to be of value to the consumer and fill a need; in other words, provide a benefit (Thomas, 2010).

Specifically, there must be two or more parties with unsatisfied needs. One party might be the consumer trying to fulfill certain needs; the other, a company seeking to exchange service or product for economic gain. There must be either desire or ability of one party to meet the needs of another. Parties must have something to exchange. For example, a physician has the clinical skills that will meet an individual patient's need to have a torn meniscus repaired. A consumer might have the health insurance or financial resources to exchange with the physician for the receipt of these medical services. Finally, there must be a mechanism for communication among parties. That is, in order to facilitate an exchange between two parties each party must learn of the other's existence. It is this last aspect of healthcare that has formally evolved in recent years (Thomas, 2010).

# HEALTHCARE MARKETING VARIABLES ("4 PS")

### Product

To respond to customers, an organization must develop a product. In healthcare, products and services differ in terms of tangibility. Services are intangible in that they cannot be felt, touched, or heard before they are encountered. Cardiac surgery, for example, is intangible. Prior to undergoing such a procedure, the patient cannot see the surgery or examine it, as can be done with the purchase of a computer or automobile. A major challenge in the marketing of intangible services is to show the expected tangible benefits. For the most part, consumer interactions with the individuals who deliver the services are often the basis by which consumers evaluate the actual service itself.

### Price

In other industries this marketing mix variable is all about determining the price that customers are willing to pay. However, in US healthcare, price is often determined by the insurer, including the government. For example, the Medicare Program will establish a pricing list for procedures so that the customer or patient is not involved. Insurance also removes price from immediate consideration. In addition, prices can vary depending on insurance status so that self-pay patients who pay out-of-pocket might pay a very different price from a patient who has health insurance and whose carrier has negotiated a discounted rate. However, self-pay patients can also negotiate pricing with HCOs and physicians, especially if they have the ability to pay cash for services.

### Place

This variable includes identifying what place is most convenient for customers to purchase the product or access the service. With the advent of the Internet and the emergence of telemedicine and other virtual health services, consumers are increasingly accessing a variety of health services via their mobile phones or computers. This is a relatively new development for HCOs and expands their potential to gain new customers. At the same time, it also has the potential to increase competitiveness as consumers can choose to obtain services at HCOs outside their immediate community.

**Promotion**

The fourth marketing variable is promotion: promoting the product or service to customers to let them know of its availability. In the past, promotion was closely associated with advertising, and advertising was perceived as marketing. But promotion is just one variable of the marketing mix. Promotion represents a way of informing the marketplace that the HCO has developed a response to meet customer needs and wants. Promotion itself involves a range of activities, including publicity, advertising, and selling. With the emergence of social media and Internet resources such as websites, promotion has grown beyond mailing or handing out flyers or placing an advertisement in local newspapers or using radio and television spots. For example, most HCOs and some physicians have their own Facebook pages and use Twitter to alert customers about events such as the opening of new clinics or adding new specialty practices.

# BRANDING

When promoting any product, an organization must decide how well it will be branded. A brand is any name, term, colors, or symbols that distinguish one seller's product from another. We are all familiar with the graphic symbol for Apple Computer products, but healthcare has been slow to engage in branding. Branding is expected to become important and prevalent in healthcare, especially as a strategy, because of growth due in large part to the ACA. Moreover, branding and co-branding are perceived to be effective marketing techniques with the potential for expanded and enhanced promotional opportunities associated with social media. Thus branding in the digital age may expedite healthcare's engagement with social platforms, too.

Multiproduct branding strategy involves an organization placing one brand on all the products in its line. For example, a hospital puts its name on the outpatient surgery center, its walk-in emergency centers, and its sports medicine rehabilitation program. The rationale for this approach is the use of brand equity so that knowing the brand name, consumers have confidence that the new product should work as well as others in the line. Using a well-known name is expected to lead to expedited promotion in any new product introduction.

However, there are also risks for a multiproduct strategy, and these risks can be significant. Because the organization uses one name for all items of the line, each new product puts the brand equity at risk.

HCOs that follow this strategy must ensure that the new product meets the quality standards for which the HCO is known. Otherwise a failure in one item may negatively affect other similarly branded products.

Multibrand strategy is when the organization places a different name on each item. The downside to this type of strategy is that each brand must establish consumer recognition on its own. Consequently, promotional costs tend to be higher in the introductory period, but there is no risk to organization's brand if the product is not well received by consumers. An HCO that enjoys high visibility and brand equity may engage in a multibrand strategy when entering new product markets or offering new services.

Co-branding is when the organization markets its name alongside another brand name. Co-branding is a relatively new branding strategy in healthcare. This strategy has mostly occurred outside of healthcare. The advantage of this approach is a synergistic effect of two positive well-known brand names. For example, the prestigious Johns Hopkins University as well as Cleveland Clinic enjoy affiliations with CVS Minute Clinics in which they share their prestige and reputation for high-quality healthcare.

The real test of an organization's brand is in its performance. If consumers have a positive experience, they become sources of new business for additional products and services. Information therefore becomes critical to assessing brand performance. The HCO must develop a data collections system, methods of analysis and reporting that can continuously monitor and evaluate the success of its brand. In addition, the brand must be assessed in terms of the organization's business strategy and updated as required (Thomas, 2010).

Marketing as a corporate function in healthcare has occurred at different times for different types of organizations. For example, for-profit businesses have tended to be more aggressive in terms of having more formalized and mature levels of marketing activities compared with non-profits, which have tended to be slower to adopt and adapt marketing as a corporate function. In addition, very few of the marketing techniques from other industries can be utilized in healthcare because most HCOs confront multiple markets and customers. Finally, it is incredibly difficult, if not impossible, to generalize about HCOs' marketing activities because of the diversity of scope of marketing challenges. Academic medical centers, nursing homes, local community hospitals, rehabilitation and assisted living facilities all face different marketing challenges (Thomas, 2010).

# MARKETING RESEARCH

Marketing research is essential because it contributes to the strategy and decision-making processes in an organization. The ACA is shifting the focus toward population health outcomes, including consumer satisfaction, which will require healthcare executives to become more aware of who their customers are and what they want. Over the years, healthcare has become more market-driven. Executives can no longer afford to ignore changing characteristics of the market, nor can they afford to ignore technological innovations such as social media: Twitter and Facebook. In today's increasingly mobile environment, marketing departments have to be constantly searching for new opportunities as well as evaluating existing services and products. Marketing research efforts directed towards new and existing products and services, and distribution channels, will assist in decision-making.

Marketing research can be conceptualized as a multi-stage process. The number of stages will vary from problem to problem. The process begins with identification of the problem or issue and ends with the strategic decision. The stages in healthcare marketing research process are similar to those in other industries, although healthcare has some unique considerations such as the Health Insurance Portability and Accountability Act (HIPAA) that require some modifications. Healthcare organizations use both internal and external data. Healthcare organizations routinely produce a large volume of internal data as a byproduct of their normal operations, including information on patient characteristics, utilization patterns, referral streams, financial trends, staffing patterns and levels, and other types of information that impact and have implications for marketing (Thomas, 2010).

Current data are most valuable as a baseline against which past data can be compared and from which future figures can be projected. Because marketing is future-oriented, effective marketing depends on insight into possible future conditions affecting the environment and the organization. Because actual future data do not exist, future conditions relevant to the community or the healthcare organization must be projected. There are a variety of methods for projecting futures, including scenario analysis. Scenario analysis creates a variety of possible futures based on changing conditions. Because the healthcare environment is characterized by rapid and continuing change, scenario analysis might be useful.

Social media, smartphones, and Google tracking devices offer unprecedented opportunities for market researchers to acquire data at both the individual and the aggregate level. But with these opportunities come challenges. Security and privacy are two prominent challenges. Websites and apps can be perceived by consumers as intrusive and also as promoting identity theft. Consequently, healthcare marketing research has to carefully evaluate emerging opportunities for capturing data.

The federal government has led the way to make data available through the Internet and mobile applications. Agencies such as the Census Bureau, Centers for Disease Control (CDC), National Center for Health Statistics (NCHS) and Centers for Medicare and Medicaid Services (CMS) have expended significant effort posting their data files on the web. In addition, the open government initiatives called for by US President Obama are looking to federal agencies, departments, and units to make information available in easily accessible formats on websites and associated mobile applications (Malvey and Slovensky, 2014).

Perhaps the most formidable marketing challenge in healthcare may be the integration of social media. Using social media to facilitate the marketing exchange is both exciting and daunting for healthcare executives. Social media can create intimate and personal exchange relationships with HCOs, including physicians and nurses who interact online with patients; but social media can also lead to marketing disasters in which failures of market research produce misleading databases and security breaches.

## SOCIAL MEDIA

Healthcare has seen the emergence of social platforms that seek to reshape the way consumers share information about their health, physicians, and treatments. Yet even though there has been a rapid proliferation of mobile health apps that allow consumers to monitor many aspects of their health, including their exercise routines and eating habits, information technology has not yet revolutionized healthcare in the same way as it has radically upended shopping (Bradley, 2013). The recent release of Apple's new wearable smartwatch, called the Apple Watch, may just be the game-changer for this transformation. The watch's ability to monitor the wearer's health and fitness is at the forefront of Apple's sales pitch for the new product. Some speculate that the watch will be especially useful for doctors treating patients with chronic illnesses such as diabetes. The UK's National Health Service (NHS) has already qualified the technology as useful within the NHS (Boseley and Hern, 2014).

Social media is fundamentally changing the way organizations and providers need to connect with their patients. Social media is revolutionizing what it means to communicate. By way of illustration, consider that more than 250 million people are reporting as active Facebook users; over 346 million people read blogs, and 184 million people are bloggers themselves; Twitter has more than 14 million registered users; and YouTube claims more than 100 million viewers per month (Zarella, 2010). Social media is moving people away from a reliance on advertising in making purchasing decisions, towards relying more on the information they find online. For healthcare, this becomes increasingly relevant as the public has been gaining access to quality and cost ratings.

With the shift towards transparent healthcare, reduced healthcare costs, and the evolution of the informed consumer, connecting with the patient is becoming more important than ever. In 2013, it was reported that 31 percent of physicians and 26 percent of all US hospitals had adopted a social media presence. Forty-one percent of people said social media would affect their choice of a specific doctor, hospital, or medical facility (Honigman,2013). We have entered an era where society is in constant need of connection to people, places, and information, and the expectations are high. Although it is commonly known that not everyone likes change, social media has reputedly had a positive impact on healthcare in terms of showing increased patient and provider satisfaction, patient compliance, and improved clinical outcomes (Schaffer, 2013).

Social media can also have profound benefits for marketing. Unlike the traditional marketing plan, social media is significantly more cost-effective; reaches larger numbers of people and larger numbers of the target population; and allows for more creativity, frequency, and permanence of the message. And although traditional marketing offers several marketing outlets (TV, print, radio, billboards) these options tend to be more expensive than social media channels and not as vast.

## SOCIAL MEDIA CHANNELS

Social media has an extensive list of channels, ranging from social networking and professional networking, to videos and blogging. The variety of social media channels available and the number of active users may seem overwhelming and raise concerns in organizations joining social media for the first time. Therefore, it is recommended to break down social media into channels, and then to explore each one. This process makes it easier to identify which channel would work best for each marketing strategy and goal. In order to identify the channel, or channels, that would work best for an organization there needs to be an understanding of the purpose of each channel, whether the demographic of users aligns with the target market, and most importantly, an individual with the ability to implement and maintain the presence being created needs to be appointed (Mayo Clinic, 2012).

Depending on what the organization or practice's objective is, one specific channel may be able to fully meet the needs of a given marketing plan. However, larger organizations such as hospitals, long-term care facilities, and practices with multiple locations may need to adopt multiple social media channels to accomplish their full goal and the objective of their plan. The following social media channels have the greatest following and relativity:

- Facebook. In the United States, more than 80 percent of time spent on social media is on Facebook, which is where almost 11 percent of all online time is spent. However, Facebook is a difficult platform to maneuver as it has strict filters, and given the large scale of this channel along with its limited search tools, getting noticed and reaching your target audience may prove challenging. Facebook is best used for private practices to identify hours of operation, insurances accepted, and any news updates they wish to share with their patients (Schaffer, 2013).
- Twitter. Listed as the fastest-growing of social media channels, Twitter is where breaking news is often heard first and it offers real-time updates, making information-sharing quick and viral. Twitter serves as a practical and efficient social media channel for both large and small organizations, allowing the organization or practice to share blog posts, news articles, breaking news, or just simply to communicate with its target market on a regular, real-time basis (Schaffer, 2013).
- LinkedIn. Known as the professional networking site, this social channel is beneficial to organizations, especially their recruitment efforts. This holds true for individuals as well who are seeking to promote their expertise and availability to appropriate organizations. It is possible for an organization to identify potential job candidates by screening this site.
- YouTube. With over 1 billion users, YouTube has become a great resource in sending messages to target audiences. This channel allows opportunities for organizations and practices to promote their services, business, and information. The most promising use of this channel is to develop a mini-series of healthcare information, treatments, innovations, and tutorials. YouTube can help with post-care patients who may need to reference information or instructions on their aftercare, which in turn may help to reduce readmissions. It can also announce new services such as telehospice care, and for minimal expenditure share this information with wide audiences, who can also retrieve and view the information again and again.

- Blogging. Building a blog allows the organization to personalize its communication with its target audience by engaging them in current trends and topics discussions, acting as an informational resource, and addressing specific conversations occurring on social media. However, blogs have to be maintained, and hospitals and other HCOs must update information for them to be relevant.

Social media may also be viewed as a form of digital word-of-mouth marketing. In some respects, social media potentially represents the most effective marketing tool, inasmuch as the conversations that are being shared are about experiences, products, and services of consumers (Zarrella, 2010). Social media affords some control of word-of-mouth marketing online by allowing organizations and providers to see what is being talked about and address customer service problems more quickly and directly. HCOs that offer a venue for patients to share their positive experiences and personal stories can send a powerful message to consumers who are determining where to obtain their healthcare services (Backman et al., 2011).

Hospitals may find social media helpful in marketing, educational, and fundraising campaigns. Social media is also useful in hospital recruitment. Eighty-one percent of respondents in a patient preference survey indicated that hospitals will use social media like Twitter and Facebook to advertise campaigns towards organ donors and educational outreach (Bennett, 2011). Finding an avenue for connecting to the greatest quantity of individuals or companies is absolutely necessary under certain circumstances.

When engaging in social media, the focus of the healthcare organization should be on the patients and their well-being. Although social media is used in promotion, it should not be the primary focus for self-promotion. Finding what patients need is important. With so many healthcare websites and information hubs, social media should focus on offering wellness, general health, and community-specific information as an alternative approach (Boyer, 2011). Finding public interest will create a stage that invites interaction between the organization and the patient.

In healthcare, it is hard to predict disasters or emergencies. In times of communication necessity, social media can be valuable. In North Dakota, Innovios Health is a healthcare system that had planned to launch a social media initiative in the future. However, the flood of 2009 proved to be a starting point for the launch. During the flood, communications were reduced and Innovios found it effective to use its plan to relay important information to people in the community. This effort served as an emergency management initiative. Innovios Health learned many lessons from the flood outreach that can be used for future needs.

In addition to emergency management, Innovios is still using the social media method for recruitment, marketing, employee relations, and marketing of the organization's brand and service lines to patients (Squazzo, 2010).

Social media appears to have expanded the marketing role in healthcare because it enables executives to manage the patient as an asset across the integrated network, so that the patient uses the right care at the right time and in the right place. Traditional marketing, which involves the exchange of products or services with customers, has been disrupted by the Internet and the emergence of social media and also mHealth. How can managers best integrate social media with marketing initiatives? How can managers identify the limitations of social media for health services marketing, especially its impact on branding and co-branding partnerships?

Social, mobile, analytics, and cloud technologies are the underpinnings of new healthcare business models in which HCOs will be paid based on value rather than volume. These technologies will fundamentally alter how health organizations interact with patients and one another to deliver care and manage health while keeping costs down (PWC Health Research Institute, 2013). Facebook's chief executive officer (CEO) Mark Zuckerberg believes that individuals want to live their lives on Facebook, and do everything from paying bills to exchanging healthcare information on this platform. What he does not yet understand is that healthcare is special. It turns out that people may be less than comfortable with total transparency in their lives and posting everything on Facebook. When it comes to their personal healthcare data ... not so fast. People want their healthcare data to be secure and they want privacy assured when exchanging that data.

A patient's personal care should not be discussed in open social media outlets. Forums should serve patients by offering general information. Healthcare organizations must assess the risks of giving advice and breaching confidentiality. However, in certain situations, there are emergency concessions. If the only way to communicate lifesaving information to a patient is via a public social media channel, then a clinician should not worry about violating privacy, and provide care (Harlow, 2012). Considering privacy, healthcare organizations that use social media should set policies that provide guidelines towards organizational protection as well as patient protection. Having policies that protect physicians, clinicians, and staff offers the ability to engage effectively with others without having to review each post for violations. Most importantly, all users in an organization must be properly trained on how to engage and respond to social media feedback.

# PROACTIVE APPROACH TOWARD MANAGING SOCIAL MEDIA

Healthcare organizations should continually monitor open communications through social media. If comments are inappropriate or violate patients' privacy, the organization may face legal action. A survey conducted on the US state medical boards revealed that 92 percent of respondents reported at least one online violation of professionalism that led to a major action, including license revocation (Kling, 2013). Furthermore, these occurrences were in widespread demographics.

Inaccurate and misleading information can easily spread through social media, so hospitals and organizations need to be proactive in their polices and the approach on how to manage the protocol of public relations (Bird, 2013). Therefore, monitoring of social media outlets is necessary for organizations to oversee. This can be challenging if a strategy has not been established on how to address these risks. There is no way an organization can determine every discussion by people who join an organization's social networks, therefore organizations need to accept this fact and learn lessons from the experience (Anderson, 2011).

When managing risk, it is important to prepare your organization for potential risks and create policies that are straightforward and apply to all. Educating all members of an organization is important. Sharing responsibility with others in the organization concerning social behavior can encourage employees to feel a part of the online social community and the organization. When Methodist Hospital System in Houston, Texas, decided to jump on the social media bandwagon, the organization was concerned about the number of employees who could access the media outlets. The organization considered strategies such as banning use of social media on the organization's computers. However, Methodist decided on an educational plan that would remind employees about the privacy rules, their affiliation with the health system, and the standards of participating on social media sites managed by the hospital. The plan was effective, yet there were a few cases of privacy infringement (Angelle and Rose, 2011).

Twitter has come to the forefront in terms of communication. More people appear to be comfortable with and using Twitter. After all, you do not have to have much to say with Twitter: it is limited to about 140 characters. But what Twitter carries with that is a propensity for mobbing: mobs of followers commenting on as well as demanding that certain things occur. It does not take much to get a Twitter mob going, either. And this mobbing feature can work positively or negatively. For example, if a patient has something complimentary to say about a hospital stay using Twitter, the hospital can gain expanded positive publicity about the facility. However, if the Twitter comment is negative, the hospital may not be able to stop the barrage of bad publicity. There is no way to stop detractors from going online and making suggestions about problems at a facility.

We live in a world where mistakes can be recorded and uploaded for the world to see. Social media makes it harder to hide the truth, but it also alters our perceptions of the truth. Damage can be done by people who loudly shout misleading information or produce memorable tweets. If an organization uses social media, they must be prepared to deal with mishaps. Clearly there must be proactive policies and strategies for preventing and mitigating social media mishaps. More importantly, these policies must be monitored, updated, and evaluated continuously. What works today may be ineffective tomorrow.

The rules have not yet been written for the digital world. Most executives are adapting as best they can, as they go along. Some do better than others. But doing nothing in response to a social media mishap is almost always the wrong answer. Even though you can develop proactive strategies or policies for social media, you cannot predict the emergence of "rogue tweeters" or advertisers that post inappropriate ads on clinical websites. But you can predict that there will be problems if companies are unprepared. Clearly, knowing when to shut down a site, keep one open, or create additional sites to respond to complaints is an essential part of a social media program.

## EMERGING CHALLENGES FOR HEALTHCARE EXECUTIVES

Social media brings with it new challenges for healthcare executives. Embedded with the technology are new management responsibilities, including developing a proactive social media program. To do so involves the following activities:

1. Identifying the role of social media and m-health in marketing and understanding their advantages as well as limitations.
2. Identifying and assessing the impact of social media's marketing implications for health professionals.
3. Examining possible applications of social media for different products and services.
4. Recognizing implications of marketing online and potential legal concerns.

5.  Communicating to employees how a robust brand and marketing strategy rooted in the beliefs and values of the organization are more important than ever.
6.  Analyzing the impact of social media in bringing a new healthcare product to market.
7.  Discerning how social media will impact existing products and overall branding strategies.

Healthcare organizations (HCOs) have little time, expertise, or resources to devote to monitoring their social media programs. Social media is pretty much a 24/7, two-way street. Consequently, to be successful HCOs must constantly monitor postings as well as major social networks and digital channels to be aware of what is buzzing online. Executives must be fully engaged to the extent that they can take action quickly to change any perceptions that arise from a social media mishap.

## SOCIAL MARKETING

Not all marketing has a business orientation. Social marketing is the utilization of marketing to promote, design, and implement programs that are engaged to encourage socially beneficial behavioral changes. Examples of this type of marketing include: smoking cessation, increasing exercise, and reducing fat consumption and other preventable behaviors that affect health. Globally, social marketing has been used to create awareness of safe drinking water practices and to promote and encourage immunizations. This type of marketing has been shown to be successful; due to being relatively new there is a lack of understanding, causing it not to be as widely utilized as it should be (Wood, 2012).

Not to be confused with social media, this type of marketing utilizes the same basic principles as they relate to the "4 Ps". In social marketing the "4 Ps" are defined as they relate to social marketing. Product becomes the benefit as it is related to the desired behavior or service that it intends to change or influence. Price is the actual sacrifice that will take place for the possible reward or benefit; cost can be measured in time, or psychological distress (breaking a habit). Place would be where the consumer would make the behavior change or be provided with the support to alter the behavior, or it could be a class or event. Promotion is more directed and can include policy changes, activities that support the initiative, or public service announcements to further convince and reinforce the need for change (Kotler et al., 2002).

According to Grier and Bryant (2005) the concept of social marketing has not reached its full potential due to several factors, including:

1. Lack of formal education and training in the area.
2. Insufficient interfaces with funding organizations to create synergy between program grants and successful implementation of social marketing initiatives.
3. Insufficient research and evaluation of implemented projects to judge the effectiveness of social marketing tactics and evidence of cost–benefit ratio analysis.
4. Few community-based prevention initiatives to encourage social change related to the health of individuals as well as the community.
5. Failure of organizations to be more inclusive and include the consumer in the marketing process and research, and to listen to what they need to become healthier individuals.

However, what further complicates adoption is the confusion between social media and social marketing, and the inference that they are one and the same (Wood, 2012).

## CONCLUSIONS AND MANAGERIAL IMPLICATIONS

The Affordable Care Act (ACA) has created a situation in which marketing has become extremely important in the US, whether we are talking about marketing of the health insurance exchanges, or reimbursing providers based in part on customer satisfaction. Thus it is incumbent on every healthcare manager to answer the question, "What is marketing and how can I utilize marketing effectively?" Marketing is based on scientific principles and involves creating and sustaining relationships among suppliers and consumers. The core elements are product, price, place, and promotion. None of these aspects of marketing have changed; what has changed is technology and the ability to exchange information, communicate, and establish virtual relationships. This chapter has examined healthcare marketing through the lens of change.

One of the most successful companies in the world is Starbucks, which competes primarily on image and does not advertise. Starbucks is all about the experience, and has essentially grown by word of mouth, or what some now refer to as consumer advocacy. Consumers stand in long lines at Starbucks to purchase expensive beverages and food products, as well as CDs and other items that reflect co-branded arrangements with celebrities and organizations that want to share the popularity of Starbucks. And

Starbucks customers socially embrace products and the company on any number of social media websites, while Starbucks invites its customers to test new products and supply feedback on its social platforms.

Could the Starbucks marketing model work for healthcare organizations? Highly unlikely, and this is because marketing is not necessarily something that is easily replicable or transferrable across organizations and even industries. Context has a role in marketing. However, healthcare organizations could examine the Starbucks model to determine whether any of its marketing components might be applicable. For example, social media might lend itself to consumer advocacy for either a hospital or a physician group practice. And co-branding arrangements with large retailers such as CVS and Walgreens include partnering with prestigious hospital-led healthcare systems. CVS, for example, has a marquee partnership with the Cleveland Clinic in Cleveland and Jacksonville, Florida. Meanwhile, Walgreens has relationships with Johns Hopkins in Baltimore and Ochsner (Japsen, 2014).

# REFERENCES

American Marketing Association (2013). About AMA. Available at https://www.ama.org/AboutAMA/Pages/Definition-of-Marketing.aspx (accessed 7 September 2014).

Anderson, Dianne (2011). The Foray into Social Media: A Clinician, and Skeptic, Sold. *Frontiers of Health Services Management* 28 (2): 23–27.

Angelle, Denny and Rose, Clare (2011). Conversations with the Community: The Methodist Hospital System's Experience with Social Media. *Frontiers of Health Services Management* 28 (2): 15–21.

Backman, C., Dolack, S., Dunyak, D., Lutz, L., Tegen, A., and Warner, D. (2011). Social Media + Healthcare. *Journal of AHIMA* 82 (3): 20–25.

Bennett, E. (2011). Social Media and Hospitals: From Trendy to Essential. In American Hospital Association and Society for Healthcare Strategy and Market Development (eds), *Futurescan: Healthcare Trends and Implications 2011–2016*. Chicago, IL: Health Administration Press, pp.47–48.

Bird, Julie (2013). Social Media can Destroy or Boost Hospital Reputations. Fierce Healthcare. http:www.fiercehealthcare.com/node/80266/print (accessed 9 July 2013).

Boseley, S. and Hern, A. (2014). Apple Watch has Designs on Health Industry – but Is It Good for Doctors? 10 September. Available at http://www.theguardian.com/technology/2014/sep/10/apple-watch-health-app-iphone-smartwatch (accessed 22 September 2014).

Boyer, C. (2011). Social Media for Healthcare Makes Sense. *Frontiers of Health Services Management* 28 (2): 35–40.

Bradley, R. (2013). Social Media Comes to Healthcare. *Fortune* 167 (6): 52, 54.

Grier, S. and Bryant, C.A. (2005). Social Marketing in Public Health. *Annual Review Public Health* 26: 319–339.

Harlow, David (2012). Health Care Social Media – How to Engage Online Without Getting into Trouble (Part II). Healthblowg.typad.com http://healthblawg.typepad.com/healthblawg/2012/01/health-care-social-media-how-to-engage (accessed 11 January 2012).

Honigman, B. (2013). 24 Outstanding Statistics on How Social Media has Impacted Health Care. Available at http://getreferralmd.com/2013/09/healthcare-social-media-statistics/

Japsen, B. (2014). CVS, Walgreen Seek Long-Term Profits through Hospital Partnerships. 23 May. Available at http://www.fool.com/investing/general/2014/05/23/cvs-walgreen-seek-long-term-profits-through-hospit.aspx (accessed 30 August 2014).

Keller, P.A. (2014). What Marketing Can Do for Hospitals. 15 September. Available at http://www.forbes.com/sites/onmarketing/2014/09/15/what-marketing-can-do-for-hospitals/ (accessed 16 September 2014).

Kling, Jim (2013). New Social Media Guidelines Issued for Physicians. Medscape.com (accessed 15 April 2013).

Kotler, P., Roberto N., and Lee, N. (2002). *Social Marketing: Improving the Quality of Life.* Thousand Oaks, CA: Sage.

Malvey, Donna and Slovensky, Donna J. (2014). *mHealth: Transforming Healthcare.* New York, Heidelberg, Dordrecht and London: Springer.

Mayo Clinic (2012). *Bringing the Social Media Revolution to Health Care.* Rochester, MN: Mayo Clinic.

PWC Health Research Institute (2013). Top Health Industry Issues of 2014. December. Available at http://www.pwc.com/us/en/health-industries/top-health-industry-issues/index.jhtml (accessed 23 January 2014).

Schaffer, N. (2013). *Maximize Your Social: One-Stop Guide to Building a Social Media Strategy for Marketing and Business Success.* Hoboken, NJ: John Wiley & Sons.

Squazzo, J.D. (2010). Best Practices for Applying Social Media in Healthcare. *Healthcare Executive* 25 (3): 34–39.

Thomas, Richard K. (2010). *Marketing Health Services*, 2nd edn. Chicago, IL: Health Administration Press.

Wood, M. (2012). Marketing Social Marketing. *Journal of Social Marketing* 2 (2): 94–102.

Zarrella, D. (2010). *The Social Media Marketing Book*. Beijing: O'Reilly.

# 11. Employee motivation

*Stephen J. O'Connor, Nancy Borkowski and Ross Kemp*

## INTRODUCTION

Today's healthcare managers in the USA are faced with numerous issues and challenges regarding how best to motivate organizational employees to alter their behaviors to meet the needs of a changing industry. Not too long ago, a manager's major difficulty was balancing the motivational needs of generational differences in the workplace. Now the difficulties are more numerous and complex, due to various changes such as increasing physician employment, the use of multidisciplinary teams to deliver coordinated care to individuals and populations of patients, and the transformation of the industry to deliver patient-centered care with value-based outcomes. Moreover, managers need to understand the professional culture of physicians to minimize conflicts as they adjust into the employed workforce as well as develop an appreciation for the physicians' motivational needs. Although the use of teams to accomplish organizational goals has been well established over the years, the use of cross-discipline teams composed of both clinicians and non-clinical administrators to deliver efficient and effective care is a relatively new concept in many healthcare organizations. Managers need to establish the right balance of incentives, feedback, and so on for teams to develop the needed cohesiveness to support the "right" delivery of care. Finally, the constant change being experienced throughout the industry has caused numerous challenges for managers to obtain the required behaviors from employees, who are facing higher levels of ambiguity, in order to effectively achieve the organization's goals.

The purpose of this chapter is to provide healthcare managers with the knowledge necessary to successfully motivate the industry's changing workforce for obtaining high value-based care. To accomplish our goal, we first provide an overview of the various content and process theories of motivation. Next, we discuss the "new" employees in healthcare organizations, motivating teams, and issues related to generational differences in the workplace. We follow with a discussion of contemporary views of motivation as the US healthcare industry moves forward with the challenges of healthcare reform. In the final section, we present our thoughts for future research to further assist managers with motiving tomorrow's workforce.

## CONTENT THEORIES OF MOTIVATION

The content theories of motivation provide managers with a way to understand how employees identify and satisfy a need. In other words, content theories assist us with understanding what motivates goal-directed behavior in people.

### Maslow's Hierarchy of Needs

Abraham Maslow (1954) presented the theory that humans are motivated by a hierarchy of needs. This hierarchy has five levels comprised of both physiological and psychological needs (see Figure 11.1). Maslow believed that motivational needs were the same for all people and that there was a strict path progressing up the hierarchy (that is, lower-level needs must be satisfied first). Individuals do not attempt to fulfill multiple levels of

*Figure 11.1   Maslow's hierarchy of needs*

the hierarchy simultaneously, but are motivated to first fulfill the lowest unsatisfied need before moving to the next need level. Individuals go through a process of satisfaction progression where once they have satisfied the need of one level to an acceptable state, they will then progress to satisfy the needs of the next level. If an individual experiences a situation that causes a lower level need to become unmet, such as a job loss, they will be driven to re-satisfy the lower-level need again before continuing to a higher level.

Maslow theorized that basic physiological needs, such as food, water, and shelter, are the first needs that must be satisfied. From an employment viewpoint, this can be understood as individuals' need to earn, at a minimum, adequate wages to meet their basic needs for food, housing, clothing, and other necessities of life.

After the basic physiological needs are satisfied, individuals require an environment that provides them with a sense of safety and security. In the workplace, this can be described as an environment free of violence and/ or harassment, as well as job security. For example, in the United States starting in 2009, the Joint Commission requires accredited hospitals to have a comprehensive, zero-tolerance policy for dealing with disruptive and intimidating behaviors displayed by either physicians or staff in the workplace. This policy was initiated because the Joint Commission recognized that these types of behaviors negatively affect staff morale, which can indirectly and directly impact the delivery of quality care to patients.

Job security can be viewed not only as a formal written contract but also as a psychological contract, the unwritten agreement between an employee and the organization. According to Lester et al. (2002, p. 40): "the psychological contract is an individual's perceptions about what they expect the employer to provide (e.g., competitive wages, advancement opportunities, job security) in return for what they give the firm (e.g., a fair day's work, loyalty)." After satisfying safety and security concerns, individuals are motivated to the higher psychological levels of Maslow's hierarchy of needs. The third level involves the individual's need to belong. In the workplace this translates into positive interactions with co-workers and managers.

As individuals satisfy their lower-level needs and progress to the next-highest level of the hierarchy, the motivators move from extrinsic to intrinsic. The fourth level deals with the individual's need for self-esteem, which differs from person to person. Some individuals can be satisfied through recognition (promotion, appreciation), while others seek out a sense of accomplishment (confidence, autonomy). Managers need to create a positive work environment in which opportunities exist for

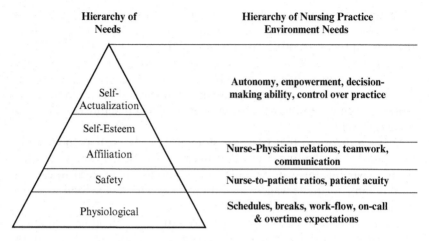

*Source:*    Adapted from Paris and Terhaar (2010).

*Figure 11.2    Using Maslow's hierarchy of needs to attain a healthier practice environment for nurses*

employees to participate in challenging, meaningful work and their abilities are recognized through advancement (Borkowski, 2011). When an individual has satisfied this need to an acceptable state, they reach towards the highest level, which is referred to as self-actualization. Maslow viewed self-actualization as the point where a person reaches their full potential. The US Army might have summed up self-actualization the best with their now-retired slogan, "Be All You Can Be." At this level, the individual desires to "become everything he is capable of becoming" (Maslow, 1943, p. 382).

Paris and Terhaar (2011) used Maslow's hierarchy of needs to show how managers can create a positive practice environment for nurses (Figure 11.2). Although they combined the self-esteem and self-actualization levels, their framework reflects the necessary motivators to increase nurses' job satisfaction and reduce their levels of stress that are contributable to their job context (that is, external factors), such as unpredictable workflow and schedules, poor physician–nurse relations, and perceived low-quality care.

Because Maslow's hierarchy of needs only allows for individuals to be motivated to satisfy one level of need at a time, it has received criticism from the research community. To address this concern, other motivational theories were developed which will be discussed in the following sections.

**ERG Theory**

In 1972, as a response to criticism of Maslow's restricted hierarchical needs, Clayton Alderfer introduced his existence, relatedness, growth (ERG) theory. Alderfer believed that individuals have three sets of needs that they simultaneously strive to satisfy: existence, relatedness, and growth. Existence relates to the need to satisfy basic physiological necessities: food, water, shelter, and so on. Relatedness refers to the individual's need to develop substantial connections, associations and involvement with others. Growth is defined by the person's need to be continually useful by making productive contributions. This need includes the individual's need for personal development with opportunities for personal growth. Although the ERG needs are organized in a hierarchical structure similar to Maslow's, the difference is that each need can be and is pursued simultaneously by the individual. For example, someone who is currently unemployed may seek out friendships through their social network, and professional growth opportunities through volunteering, while still seeking a new position to ensure future sustainability of their existence needs. This example also highlights the frustration-regression principle of the ERG theory. When a barrier prevents (that is, frustrates) an individual from obtaining a lower-level need (for example, a job), a person can seek satisfaction of a higher-level need before the lower-level need is satisfied. This frustration–regression principle also works in the opposite direction. When an obstruction averts an individual from obtaining a higher-level need (for example, they are passed over for a promotion), a person will regress for a period of time to a lower-level need such as relatedness to satisfy their unmet growth need until the person is able to pursue their growth need again. The frustration–regression cycle is continuous and exists throughout one's life.

The ERG theory's frustration–regression principle was applied by Labarda (2011) to explain the motivation of physicians in the Philippines to shift their careers and work as nurses abroad. Labarda found that the physicians' unmet growth needs (that is, career advancement and growth, advanced training for developing new skills, and feelings of personal accomplishment) had created an impetus to fulfill their lower-level existence needs (that is, salary or compensation, and job security). Since the doctors felt they were unable to alter their current career situations in the Philippines (frustration), they refocused their behaviors on satisfying other needs in the context of their families (regression) (Labarda, 2011).

**McClelland's Three-Needs**

In 1961, David McClelland theorized that individuals have three needs that have been acquired over time through life experiences: achievement, power, and affiliation. Although some may exhibit a strong bias towards one of the three needs, the majority's behavior is influenced by all three to some degree. The three needs are described as follows (McClelland, 1985):

1. The need for achievement (n-Ach). Those who have a strong need for achievement tend to be task-oriented, avoid teamwork, and are typically viewed as the "doers" of the organization. They are drawn to assignments that are challenging but have attainable goals. They require feedback to gauge how well they are fulfilling their task responsibilities.
2. The need for power (n-Pow). Individuals with a strong desire to influence others are those with a high need for power. There are two different variants that a need for power can manifest (Borkowski, 2011). Some individuals have a need for personalized power where they are focused on their own personal power. These individuals may use materialistic goods to showcase their power such as expensive cars or watches, or may be highly focused on professional titles. Individuals with a need for socialized power display attributes that are typically viewed as strong leadership traits. They want to make positive contributions to the organization, which drives their need for power.
3. The need for affiliation (n-Aff). When the need for affiliation is dominant, individuals are drawn towards harmonious interpersonal relationships. They will avoid confrontation and are naturally agreeable. Social acceptance for these individuals is very important and they enjoy working in groups and teams.

While each person possesses all three needs, there tends to be one that is stronger than the other two (and this can change from time to time). As such, managers need to not only create the ways and means for employees to fulfill their needs, but to be cognizant of what needs will motivate particular employees. In this way, a manager can set tasks, build teams, and develop leadership roles in accordance with employees' needs.

McClelland's theory of acquired needs has important implications for the motivation of employees. Managers' understanding of their employees' dominant needs will enable them to be better able to motivate them. For example, employees who have a high need for achievement will respond to challenging goals, those with a high need for power will seek out opportunities to influence others, and those with high affiliation needs will be motivated to obtain approval and acceptance of and from their peers and supervisors. Organizations need to have mechanisms in place to motivate employees, such as providing challenging assignments coupled with meaningful rewards (n-Ach), offering opportunities for advancement and increased responsibility (n-Pow), as well as creating positive team environments (n-Aff).

**Herzberg's Two-Factor Theory**

Fredrick Herzberg (1966) theorized that there are two sets of factors that influence an employee's motivation. One set of factors impacts the employee's degree of job satisfaction (motivators) while the other set affects the level of dissatisfaction experienced by the employee (hygiene factors). Herzberg's research identified several factors that serve as motivators (satisfiers) for an employee. The satisfiers are achievement, recognition, work itself, responsibility, and advancement. If these intrinsic factors are largely unfulfilled in an employee's job content they will have less job satisfaction. When certain job context factors (hygiene factors) are unmet in the work environment – such as good policies, supervision, salary, interpersonal relations, and working conditions – an employee will experience varying levels of job dissatisfaction. Managers need to be aware that job satisfaction is not the opposite of job dissatisfaction, or vice versa. The opposite of job satisfaction is no job satisfaction, and the opposite of job dissatisfaction is no job dissatisfaction. In other words, satisfiers provide the job content for employees to be motivated, whereas hygiene factors support and maintain the structure of the employee's job (Borkowski, 2011).

Research has shown over the past decade that nurses' dissatisfaction with their working environments is a predictor of their intent to leave their profession (Borkowski et al., 2007). For example, Aiken et al. (2002) reported that 40 percent of nurses in the USA were dissatisfied with their jobs and almost one in four nurses intended to leave within a year. The reasons cited as dissatisfiers were lack of: (1) autonomy; (2) control over one's work; (4) collegiality with physicians; and (4) organizational support. Therefore, Herzberg's two-factor theory provides managers with a strategy for providing a motivating environment for employees, by ensuring that an adequate level of hygiene factors is in place to meet employees' expectations and avoid job dissatisfaction, while providing the right elements for employees' personal growth and professional fulfillment. In addition, managers should focus on creating jobs in which employees perceive that their work is significant. According to Herzberg, the idea that the work that one does is significant will motivate employees and lead to satisfaction with the work itself (Borkowski, 2011).

Prior research has demonstrated that a relationship exists between job satisfaction and job characteristics. Hackman and Oldham (1980, pp. 78–80) listed five core motivational job characteristics:

1. Skill variety. The degree to which a job requires a variety of different activities in carrying out the work, involving the use of a number of different skills and talents of the person.
2. Task identity. The degree to which a job requires completion of a "whole" and identifiable piece of work; that is, doing a job from beginning to end with a visible outcome.
3. Task significance. The degree to which the job has a substantial impact on the lives of other people, whether those people are in the immediate organization or in the world at large.
4. Autonomy. The degree to which the job provides substantial freedom, independence, and discretion to the individual in scheduling the work and in determining the procedures to be used in carrying it out.
5. Feedback. The degree to which the work activities required by the job provide the individual with direct and clear information about the effectiveness of their performance.

Hackman and Oldham (1980) related that the combination of skill variety, task identity, and task significance leads to an employee perceiving job "meaningfulness." In addition, if employees possess: (1) the necessary knowledge and skills to perform their job well; (2) strong growth needs; and (3) satisfaction with the work context, they will exhibit high personal satisfaction, as well as high work motivation and performance.

## PROCESS THEORIES OF MOTIVATION

The process theories of motivation address the observed behavior of an employee as they satisfy a need. Unlike the content theories, the process theories of motivation attempt to explain from a cognitive perspective why individuals do what they do: what initiates the behavior, where is it directed, and how is it sustained.

### Expectancy Theory

Expectancy theory was introduced by Victor Vroom (1964) to describe how employees are motivated not only by personal needs but also by the ability to make a meaningful impact regarding their work. According to Vroom, the degree of motivation exhibited by an employee will

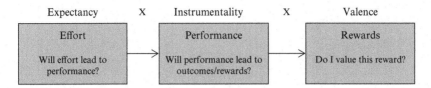

| Expectancy | X | Instrumentality | X | Valence |
|---|---|---|---|---|
| **Effort** <br><br> Will effort lead to performance? | | **Performance** <br><br> Will performance lead to outcomes/rewards? | | **Rewards** <br><br> Do I value this reward? |

*Figure 11.3    Vroom's expectancy theory*

be determined by three factors: valence, instrumentality, and expectancy (Figure 11.3). Valence is the employee's preference for an action's outcome. "An outcome has a positive valence when the person prefers attaining it to not attaining it, a valence of zero when the person is indifferent to attaining it or not attaining it, and a negative valence when the person prefers not attaining it to attaining it" (Borkowski, 2011, pp. 129–130). Instrumentality is the employee's belief that an outcome will occur given their performance related to the task. Expectancy is the employee's perception of the impact of their effort on a designated task.

Using expectancy theory, Smith et al. (2011) explored what motivated dentists to work in the Scottish prison system. Through in-depth interviews of ten dentists, the researchers found that although the clinicians possessed the necessary skills to improve their prisoner-patients' oral health, their efforts were often delayed by the need to fit into the prison system's operations processes and procedures (expectancy). Despite these operational difficulties, the dentists experienced the professional rewards associated with improving their patients' oral health (instrumentality). The dentists reported feelings of personal worth and a sense of professional commitment related to their care of the prisoners (valence). As Smith et al. (2011) pointed out, the dentists were motivated by their belief that their efforts would improve the prisoner-patients' clinical outcomes, which was rewarded by the satisfaction they experienced when they overcame the environmental obstacles and provided oral health care for their prisoner-patients.

Expectancy theory allows managers the ability to quantify the preferred outcomes of their employees in order to increase motivation. If any of the three factors – expectancy, instrumentality, or valence – equal zero then motivation for an employee to fulfill a task will be low. Therefore, managers need to provide the right environment to encourage high levels of performance by employees. This can be accomplished by illustrating to the employee the relationship between their efforts and the expectations for them to perform the task well, and how achieving (or exceeding) these task expectations will result in the employee obtaining the desired rewards.

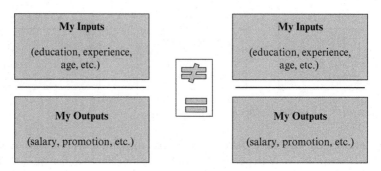

*Figure 11.4    Adam's equity theory*

**Equity Theory**

As Vroom (1964) was developing the expectancy theory, Adams (1963) introduced the equity theory. Equity theory proposes that an employee evaluates their inputs (efforts) and related outcomes (rewards/outputs) in comparison to another's inputs and outcomes whom the employee perceives to be similar to them. Perception of inputs/efforts will vary from individual to individual. The employee's inputs include education level, hours worked, age, years of work in an organization and so forth. Outputs/rewards may include compensation, fringe benefits, recognition, advancement, or a combination. If the employee perceives their ratio of efforts to rewards is favorable in comparison to another worker's inputs/outputs then an employee will be motivated to complete the required tasks. However, if the perceived comparison is unfavorable, the employee will be less motivated.

For example, one nurse is paid $35 per hour and works in an extremely busy and stressful inpatient unit due to staff shortages. Her colleague is paid the same wage but is assigned to work in a low-volume, low-stress ambulatory care unit. Assuming that both nurses have the same education, years of experience, time employed by the hospital, and are the same age, the first nurse has to exert more effort (input) than her peer but both receive the same outcome (that is, compensation). This causes an unfavorable or "inequity" condition for the nurse working in the busier inpatient unit. When an inequity is perceived by an individual, Adam (1963) relates that it creates tension within the person, which motivates them to relieve it. There are six methods that an individual may consider to relieve their inequitable tension:

1.  Reduce productivity by taking longer break times and/or using sick days for personal activities.

2. Secure a pay raise or a promotion.
3. Cognitively distort their inputs or outputs (that is, describe how much harder they are working).
4. Relocate to another department or resign from the organization.
5. Distort the inputs or outputs of the comparison other (that is, describe the other person's job as routine and unchallenging).
6. Seek out another person within the department or organization who is more like them as the comparison other.

To avoid creating a negative, demotivating environment, managers need to be cognizant of how employees perceive inequities in the treatment or favoritism of others in the workplace.

**Satisfaction–Performance Theory**

In 1968, Lyman Porter and Edward Lawler constructed their satisfaction–performance motivation model by including the elements missing from Vroom's expectancy theory and incorporating the components of Adam's equity theory. A criticism of the expectancy theory was that it failed to account for the relationship between employee performance and job satisfaction. Porter and Lawler's satisfaction–performance model theorizes that if an employee: (1) desires the outcome's reward; (2) perceives that their efforts will lead to those rewards; (3) believes that they possess the required abilities; and (4) understands their role, then higher performance will result (Borkowski, 2011). In addition, if both the intrinsic and extrinsic rewards related to higher performance are perceived as equitable, then the employee will experience job satisfaction. Managers need to be aware that for employees to willingly exert the efforts necessary for high performance and obtaining job satisfaction, rewards must be related to the employee's performance. Rewards such as annual pay raises that are issued across the board by an organization are counterproductive for increasing employee motivation and satisfaction.

**Goal-Setting Theory**

The research studies of Gary Latham and Edwin Locke revealed that individuals given specific and challenging tasks outperformed those who were given vague goals (Latham and Locke, 1979). Based on their experiments, Latham and Locke (1979) developed a model that outlines the steps necessary to motivate employees towards obtaining measurable, challenging, and achievable goals. As noted, goals should be specific and measurable, and avoid vague language. Vague goals such as "Always do your best" have been shown to be less effective than goals that are defined, such as "Sustain unit hand washing at 95 percent for two weeks." In addition, to obtain employee "buy-in," allow employees to develop their own work-related goals avoiding management-imposed objectives. Finally, managers need to communicate the rewards associated with the employee reaching their goals. These rewards can be either external such as a financial bonus, or internal such as the feeling of accomplishment. In either case, rewards need to be valued by the employee for them to be a motivating factor. In addition, managers should ensure that employees have the proper amount of resources in order to achieve the goals. If there are insufficient resources then employees will become frustrated and unmotivated.

**Reinforcement Theory**

In 1953, B.F. Skinner published his book titled *Science and Human Behavior* in which he theorized that human behavior is learned and adapted through positive, negative, and punishment reinforcements. Positive reinforcement occurs when an employee receives a desirable outcome associated with their actions. A nurse manager organizing a pizza party to recognize the unit's efforts achieving high patient satisfaction scores is an example of positive reinforcement. In contrast, a manager docking the pay of a nurse for routinely being tardy is an example of punishment reinforcement. The manager imposes a punishment in order to extinguish or curtail the behavior. Negative reinforcement occurs when a "specific behavior is no longer positively reinforced with valued consequences" (O'Connor, 1998, p. 458). If a nurse has been on time for work for a year, and never receives any positive reinforcement, that nurse encounters negative reinforcement which diminishes the value of being on time.

Reinforcement tends to occur in patterned intervals called reinforcement schedules. There are four main types of reinforcement schedules: fixed intervals, variable intervals, fixed ratios, and variable ratios.

1.  Fixed intervals. Set and consistent periods of time in which reinforcement is given. For example, at the end of each year, hospital employees receive a "thank-you" bonus.
2.  Variable intervals. Set but inconsistent periods of time in which reinforcement is given. For example, the hospital chief executive officer (CEO) attends departmental meetings periodically throughout the year.
3.  Fixed ratios. Reinforcement is given after a set number of occurrences of a behavior. For example, after a third disciplinary infraction an employee is suspended.

4. Variable ratios. Reinforcement is given when a variable number of behaviors have occurred. For example, the nurse manager recognizes employees' efforts sometimes on a monthly or quarterly basis depending on how busy the inpatient unit has been due to changing patient census.

We have concluded our discussion of the various content and process theories of motivations. In the following section, we will discuss three challenges that today's healthcare manager must deal with on a daily basis. First, we will discuss the "new" employee in healthcare: the physician. We follow with a discussion on the challenges presented with the use of cross-displine teams. The third issue focuses on the motivation of the multigenerational workforce.

## MOTIVATING THE "NEW" HEALTHCARE WORKFORCE

### Employed Physicians

Although physicians in the USA have long been employed in private practice, group practices or other physician-owned healthcare organizations, there has been an rapid upswing in physician employment by hospitals and other administratively-led organizations. According to a recent American Medical Association (2013) report, approximately 20 percent of all physicians in the USA are now employed by hospitals. In 2010, hospitals employed approximately 211 500 physicians, a 34 percent increase since 2000. This trend is expected to increase. Jackson Healthcare's recent staffing survey reported that between 2012 and 2013, hospital-employed physicians increased from 20 percent to 26 percent (Jackson Healthcare, 2013). Sadly, when asked what they disliked most about employment, 30 percent of surveyed employed physicians cited "being bossed around by management" (Medscape, 2014). As O'Connor and Lanning (1992) pointed out, physicians believe that administrators' roles should be limited to managing the non-medical health delivery operations that are needed to support the clinicians' work of practicing medicine. As such, physicians are viewed by administrators as difficult to manage, but in reality there is an inadequate knowledge base about managing highly trained professionals in any organization (Stamps and Cruz, 1994). Going forward, as health organizations attempt to achieve clinical integration of services and manage population health, physicians are and will continue to be critical to the success of these initiatives. As such, managers need to develop a deeper understanding of the professional culture of physicians to minimize the negative impacts as they become acclimatized to employed status.

Recently the question was asked, "Are physicians really different from any other professionals?" (Dye and Sokolov, 2013). The answer is yes, which is mainly attributable to their extensive educational process which forms their socialization into the medical profession.

As Borkowski (2000) pointed out, management of physicians is particularly complex because of their cosmopolitan versus local characteristics. Gouldner (1957, 1958) applied the terms "cosmopolitan" and "local" to describe latent social identities in a formal organization, so that management could understand the conflicts of employees' views of commitment to the organization and their profession. Cosmopolitans are described as those individuals who have low organizational loyalty and high commitment to their specialized role skills and professional growth (for example, physicians). Locals' social orientation reflects the opposite: strong feelings of loyalty to their employing organization, with less professional identity (for example, managers). Adding to the complexity of this relationship is the physician's identity with their role within the organization. This can be best explained using social identity theory (Tajfel and Turner, 1979). Whereas Gouldner's latent social identities relate to commitment, social identity theory describes how members of one group discriminate in favor of their "in-group" and against members in the perceived "out-group." For instance, practicing physicians viewed doctors who worked full-time in management roles as "outsiders" and "betrayers" to the medical profession (Hoff, 1999). As a result of perceived professional and organizational identifications, tension can and does occur between the two groups, of physicians and administrators.

Although more research is needed in the area of professional and organizational identifications, some researchers have found that physicians can cope with the conflicts arising from their multiple social identities and positively identify with their organizations. For example, Dukerich et al. (2002) found that physicians who identified strongly with their health systems were more likely to engage in cooperative behaviors. Likewise, Hekman et al. (2009b) found that physicians who more strongly identified with the organization and less with their profession were more receptive to administrator social influence. The opposite was found for the employed physicians who more strongly identified with the profession.

Because more US physicians are becoming organizational employees, understanding how to engage and motivate them is vital for today's healthcare manager in order to achieve organizational goals. As such, managers need to create an environment in which physicians perceive the organization as supporting and not in conflict with their professional identification (Hekman et al., 2009a). This can be accomplished, in part, by clearly communicating and demonstrating the shared values and culture between the profession and organization. For example, when processes are designed to support patient-centered care, and shared financial rewards are determined on value-based outcomes instead of levels of productivity, it has been found that work autonomy is maintained, and social relatedness to the profession is encouraged (Janus, 2011, 2014).

A word of caution regarding the use of financial reward systems such as pay-for-performance (P4P) programs as a motivator for behavioral change. Although P4P has been widely used to improve employee job performance in various organizational settings, including those within the healthcare industry, the results have been mixed (Cameron and Pierce, 1994; Jenkins et al., 1998; Rosenthal and Frank, 2006). In a recent study that focused on a P4P program implemented in a physician organization, Young et al. (2012) found that while physicians are generally responsive to financial incentives and will adjust their performance accordingly, the degree of performance change was dependent on the physician's attitude toward the incentive arrangement relative to their professional values and work autonomy. As Young et al. (2012) point out, physicians had a stronger response to the program if they were less concerned about the incentive program being a threat to their autonomy. They also had a stronger response if they believed that the program's goals were aligned with their own professional goals. As such, managers need to be cautious when implementing financial reward systems to ensure that they are consistent with physicians' professional values and autonomy needs.

**Multi-Disciplinary Teams**

Cohen and Bailey (1997, p. 234) define a team as: "a collection of individuals who are interdependent in their tasks, who share responsibility for outcomes, who see themselves and who are seen by others as an intact social entity embedded in one or more larger social systems, and who manage their relationships across organizational boundaries." Using this definition, Taplin et al. (2013, p. 280) describe four of the most common types of teams within healthcare:

1. Work teams accomplish tasks on an ongoing basis in a specific organizational setting (for example, a primary care team, surgical team, emergency department team).
2. Parallel teams address shared challenges, such as responding to a cardiac arrest or aiding the transition of patients from hospital care to

ambulatory care, and typically draw participants from several work teams.

3.  Project teams focus on a one-time deliverable and have limited terms (for example, an electronic health record implementation team).
4.  Management teams oversee all the others.

Although teams are commonplace throughout organizational settings, the required attention for building effective healthcare professional teams has not been adequately addressed within the industry. As noted by Frankel et al. (2006, p. 1700), "Currently, we can assure our patients that their care is always provided by a team of experts, but we cannot assure our patients that their care is always provided by expert teams." In a study exploring nurses' perceptions of multidisciplinary teamwork in a acute care setting, Atwal and Caldwell (2006) identified three barriers that hindered teamwork: (1) differing perceptions of teamwork; (2) different levels of skills acquisitions to function as a team member; and (3) the dominance of medical power that influenced interaction in teams. They found that the groups lacked specific goals, an evaluation process to measure outcomes, accountability of decision-making, and equal status and/or power of members. In the aviation industry, "pilots are regularly evaluated for both their technical skill and their ability to promote effective teamwork" (Frankel et al., 2006, p. 1694), which leads us to question why this practice is not duplicated in the healthcare industry with physicians and nurses.

Lemieux-Charles and McGuire (2006) reported that high-performing teams are usually associated with positive communication patterns and minimum conflict due to high levels of collaboration, coordination, cooperation, and participation (Pinto and Pinto, 1990; Poulton and West, 1999; Shortell et al., 2004; Temkin-Greener et al., 2004; Vinokur-Kaplan, 1995), but "taken as a whole, published studies do not provide clear direction on how to create or maintain high-functioning teams" (Lemieux-Charles and McGuire, 2006, p. 295). So the question remains: "How can managers motivate healthcare professionals to become high-performing teams?" This can be accomplished by creating an environment that supports team success.

Similar to Hackman and Olden's job design, for teams to work effectively, responsibility and authority must be clearly delineated and communicated. Furthermore, to reach a high-functioning level, teams must have cohesiveness. Cohesiveness is defined as "the total field of forces causing members to remain in the group" (Festinger et al., 1950, p. 164). This is not an easy task for cross-disciplinary health teams given the various members' (for example, physicians, nurses, pharmacists, therapists, administrators) social identities and levels of professional versus organizational commitment. It is not to say that intragroup and intergroup relations cannot be positive from the beginning of the team's formation; however, more times than not, the members experience communication and coordination difficulties due to lack of knowledge-sharing and the inability to cross professional boundaries (Bartunek, 2010; Nembhard and Edmondson, 2006). By understanding the stages of team development, one can appreciate the level of relationship-building that is needed to achieve cohesiveness among the group members. Tuckman (1965) identified four stages of group development that explain how members move from being joined together to a cohesive team. The final or fifth stage, referred to as "adjourning," represents the dissolution of the group due to task completion:

1.  Forming. During the forming stage, members try to determine what the appropriate behaviors and core values of the group are. They focus on exchanging functional information, task definition, and boundary development. They begin to establish tasks and determine how they might meet objectives. During this initial stage, members must gain an understanding about the reason or purpose for joining, and find a social niche in the group.
2.  Storming. The second stage of group development, storming, is characterized by high levels of emotion, because members are trying to find their group identity and exert their individuality. At this stage, members are claiming their social power within the group and a hierarchy is established as people question authority, react to what is supposed to be accomplished, and jockey for power within the group. Intermember criticism, scapegoating, and judgments may accompany this struggle for control.
3.  Norming. Within the third stage, the development of cohesion and structure occurs when the group's standards, key values, and roles are accepted. The gradual development of cohesion occurs after the conflict in the storming stage. In this third stage, the rules for behavior are explicitly and implicitly defined. There is a greater degree of order and a strong sense of group membership.
4.  Performing. In the fourth stage, members have found their role(s) within the group and their energy is focused on the task and the problems confronting them. The members pull together and display sensitivity to each other (Borkowski, 2011, p. 332).

There are many challenges faced by cross-disciplinary teams, such as diversity (for example, personality, backgrounds, experiences, values, culture, organizational responsibilities), time allocations, reward systems, and reporting relationships (Weber, 2002), in addition to social identities and organizational commitment previously discussed. These challenges cannot be overcome and cohesiveness achieved without the establishment of mutual trust among the team members. Trust increases connectedness among members and assists the development of group cohesion. However, the team climate of trust is not likely to emerge without specific interventions by managers.

Druskat and Wolff (2001) state that developing a team's emotional intelligence (EI) supports the behaviors for building trust, group identity, and group efficacy through established norms. The outcome is a more effective team that achieves better decisions, more creative solutions, and higher productivity (Druskat and Wolff, 2001). The researchers explain that team EI is more complex than individual EI due to the fact that teams interact at more levels. First, the team must be attentive to the emotions of its members and be able to regulate them if group norms are broken. Second, the team develops a self-awareness by seeking feedback from both inside and outside the organization. Third, the team regulates group emotions by providing stress relievers. Finally, the team ensures that it is aware of the needs and concerns of people outside the group and develops relationships with these individuals and groups. The key factor for building team EI is developing the group's norms, which include: (1) interpersonal understanding and perspective-taking; (2) team self-evaluation by internally assessing its effectiveness as well as seeking feedback from others outside the group; and (3) organizational understanding of the concerns and needs of others, and ensuring the team's actions are aligned with the firm's culture (Druskat and Wolff, 2001).

## GENERATIONAL DIFFERENCES IN THE WORKPLACE

The US workforce is largely comprised of three generations: Baby Boomers (born between 1945 and 1964), Generation X (born between 1965 and 1979), and Millennials/Generation Y (born in 1980 or later). Although much has been written about their differences, there still remains a gap in our understanding of each generational cohort's values and beliefs (Becton et al., 2014). Some scholars have found generational differences in organizational commitment (D'Amato and Herzfeldt, 2008), work values (Cennamo and Gardner, 2008), and leadership behaviors (Sessa et al., 2007), while others have found few variances (Wong et al., 2008; Trzesniewski and Donnellan, 2010). As such, generational differences may best be explained by "age, life stage, or career stage effects" (Becton et al., 2014, p. 176). For example, members of a certain generation (usually defined within a 20-year span) have shared similar life experiences which framed who they are: their characteristics, values, and beliefs. For example, the Baby Boomers grew up during a prosperous economy, society was optimistic, and the world was achieving great feats, such as landing on the moon. They also experienced other events in their living rooms, watching them unfold on TV: civil rights movements, leaders' assassinations, and the Vietnam War. The Baby Boomers were part of traditional households where commitment to the family and employer were valued and rewarded. They have been characterized as high achievers (promotions, titles, and other workplace recognition), resourceful, and hard workers (Meriac et al., 2010). In comparison, Generation X have grown up in an era of constant change: family units (for example, two-income households, divorce), economic conditions (recessions, inflation, unemployment), and technology. This generation has experienced corporate scandals, lay-offs, and technology advances that allow instant gratification. Becton et al. (2014) note that Generation X are viewed as being individualistic, with low organizational commitment, outcomes-focused, having a preference for mentoring and feedback for learning, and maintaining a work and personal life balance. They, like Generation Y, have low organizational commitment and are more interested in performing meaningful work, which they use to measure their success (Becton et al., 2014). In addition, Generation X place a higher value on their leisure time than the other two generational cohorts (Twenge, 2010).

Although generational cohort stereotyping is commonplace, managers need to understand that individuals have different motivational needs. For example, the popular press has reported stories of younger physicians moving away from private practice, the traditional career path of prior generations of physicians. This change may be attributable to the new physician generation's desire to balance their professional and personal needs as well as today's economics of practicing medicine (Harris, 2011). Overall, physicians are becoming more institutionalized. The American Medical Association (2013) reported that although 60 percent of physicians worked in physician-owned practices, 81 percent of them were over the age of 40 (Baby Boomers and Generation X). In addition, almost 36 percent of physicians treating Medicare beneficiaries practice in groups of 50 physicians or more, up from approximately 31 percent in 2009 (Welch et al., 2012). With estimates that 64 percent of newly hired physicians in the USA will be employed by hospitals in 2014 as compared to 11 percent in 2004, managers will need to address each age and career stage group's motivational needs. This is true for other clinicians as well.

Much has been published on nursing job satisfaction and intent to leave the profession (Borkowski et al., 2007; Coomber and Barriball, 2007), and how job dissatisfaction impacts patient satisfaction and quality of care (Aiken et al., 2012; McHugh et al., 2011). For example, McHugh et al. (2011) reported that patient satisfaction is lower in organizations where nurses report feeling burnt-out and dissatisfied with their work conditions than in other institutions. The researchers found that nurses' levels of burnout and job dissatisfaction were related to the perceived quality of their work environment, which included managerial support and responsiveness for correcting care issues, and physician–nurse relations. These issues were also significantly associated with nurses' satisfaction with employee benefits, including salary. These job dissatisfaction issues all relate to the extrinsic motivational components of a person's job, which is controllable by managers.

Clipper (2012) points out that individuals within each generational cohort have varying attributes relating to the importance of the meaningfulness of the work they do, the need to balance work–life commitments, aspirations for career advancement, and levels of organizational commitment, and that a manager's motivational strategies should be directly related to these differences (Table 11.1).

Clipper (2012, pp. 116–117) notes that there are five primary intrinsic motivators that are common to all generations: (1) healthy interpersonal

*Table 11.1   Meeting the needs of different generations*

| Generation | What they want | Motivation strategies |
|---|---|---|
| Boomers | • Recognition for experience and excellence<br>• Positive work environment<br>• Good pay and benefits<br>• Continuing education | • Give public recognition<br>• Find opportunities to share expertise<br>• Promote "gradual retirement" |
| Xers | • Career advancement<br>• Autonomy and independence<br>• Work–life balance | • Provide opportunities for skill development and leadership<br>• Involve in decision-making<br>• Avoid micromanaging |
| Millennials | • Meaningful work<br>• Stimulation, engagement, involvement<br>• Skill development<br>• Impatient for promotion: "move up or out" | • Encourage teamwork<br>• Offer a supportive work environment<br>• Begin leadership development early<br>• Provide feedback<br>• Develop skill base |

*Source:*   Adapted from Clipper B. (2012).

relationships; (2) meaningful work; (3) a sense of competence or self-efficacy; (4) autonomy or choice; and (5) achievement of progress and accomplishments. However, managers need to appreciate the differences associated with the generational cohorts and that these differences are aligned with each individual's age, and life and career stages, so that the proper motivational strategies can be used to develop and maintain an enjoyable work environment including positive interpersonal relationships (Apostolidis and Polifroni, 2006). The outcomes will be increased employee engagement (that is, organizational commitment) and higher levels of job satisfaction, which will lead to improved patient care.

## CONTEMPORARY VIEWS OF MOTIVATION

Most of the major content theories of motivation, such as Maslow's (1943) needs hierarchy, Alderfer's (1972) ERG theory, and McClelland's (1961) three needs theory have focused predominantly on human needs. The major process theories of motivation, such as Vroom's (1964) expectancy theory, Locke's (1968) goal-setting theory, and Adams's (1963) equity theory have emphasized human thought processes and elements including beliefs, perceptions, and goals. Both content and process theories of motivation are viewed as incomplete, as they do not incorporate human emotion within their explanatory frameworks, an element that has the capacity to influence human thought and action. Recent theoretical (Seo et al., 2004) and empirical work (Seo et al., 2010) has incorporated the emotional element as an important feature of work motivation and builds upon our traditional process and expectancy motivational theories by suggesting how emotional experiences can contribute to work motivation. Core affect is viewed as a key concept underlying motivational processes and outcomes, and has been described as feelings, mood (Morris, 1989), or affect (Watson and Tellegen, 1985). Seo et al. (2004) hypothesized that direct and indirect paths are likely to influence three major behaviors associated with work motivation: direction, intensity, and persistence. Direction reflects what actions a person chooses to engage in. Intensity refers to the amount of effort expended by an individual, and persistence refers to the length of a behavioral activity (Seo et al., 2004).

Figure 11.5 (Feldman Barrett and Russell, 1998, p. 970) shows the structure of core affect including the dimensions of pleasantness and activation. The pleasant–unpleasant dimension (x-axis) shows affective experience ranging from a positive very pleasant (happy and content) to a negative very unpleasant (upset and sad). The activation–deactivation dimension (y-axis) represents a vitality or behavioral readiness ranging from a

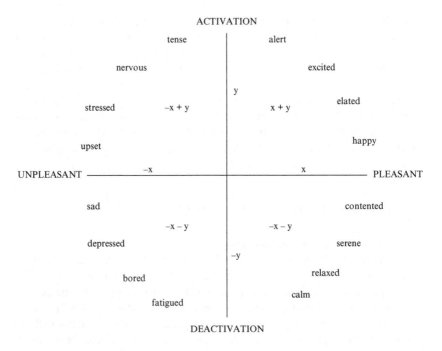

ACTIVATION

tense

alert

nervous

excited

y

stressed          −x + y

x + y          elated

upset

happy

UNPLEASANT ————— −x ——————————— x ————— PLEASANT

sad

contented

−x − y          −x − y

depressed

serene

−y

bored

relaxed

calm

fatigued

DEACTIVATION

*Note:*   The letters x and y represent semantic components: x = pleasantness; y = activation.

*Source:*   Feldman Barrett and Russell (1998, p. 970).

*Figure 11.5   A sematic structure of affect*

highly activated aroused state (tense and alert) to a very deactivated state (fatigued and calm). An individual at any moment in time will be in a state of core affect that is represented by a point location within Figure 11.5. This core affective state may be located closer to the center of Figure 11.5 (indicating a more neutral state) or towards the periphery (indicating more moderate or extreme states) (Russell, 2003; Russell and Feldman Barrett, 1999).

Seo et al. (2004) hypothesized that an individual's level of core affect could influence the motivational behavioral outcomes of: (1) generative–defensive orientation (active engagement to realize positive results); (2) effort (time and exertion dedicated to choosing and completing a task); and (3) persistence (continuing a chosen activity over time). They proposed that core affect could affect these behavioral outcomes directly or indirectly through three intermediary subjective cognitive judgments:

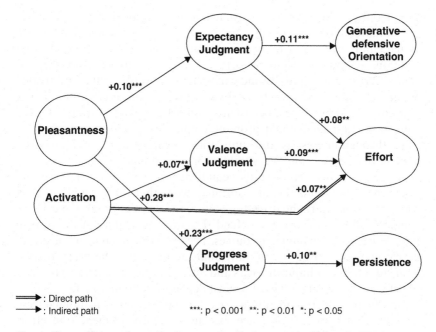

*Note:*   The coefficients shown above are standardized gamma coefficients in HLM regression models.

*Source:*   Seo et al. (2010).

*Figure 11.6   Direct and indirect effects of core affect on task behavior*

(1) expectancy (the probability that a certain action will result in anticipated outcomes); (2) valence (the desirability, positive or negative, of anticipated outcomes); and (3) progress (judgment of progress toward goal attainment).

Seo et al. (2010) tested the above hypotheses empirically using an ingenious research design and sample of investment club participants. The results of the study are summarized in Figure 11.6. Although not all of the hypotheses were supported, their results indicate that core affect (pleasantness–activation) is statistically significantly related (directly or indirectly) to the motivational behavioral outcomes of generative–defensive orientation, effort, and persistence. The results also show that pleasantness is significantly positively related to expectancy and progress judgments and activation is significantly positively related to valence judgment and to effort.

This research study has enhanced understanding of expectancy theory as not only a cognitive process, but one that is augmented by a wider emotional context. Practically, the results show the importance of individual emotion to work motivation. Conventional wisdom suggests that emotions are antithetical to performance in the workplace. However, Seo et al.'s (2010) research results indicate otherwise, as pleasant and activated emotional states lead to improved generative action orientation, greater task effort, and promote a persistence and determination towards a given work task. Managers could promote employees' pleasant and activated states through interesting and stimulating job assignments and the development of a positive and pleasurable workplace climate.

We next turn to research studies conducted by Nohria et al. (2008), who discovered four fundamental emotional needs that drive people in their endeavors. These are the drive to acquire, the drive to bond, the drive to comprehend, and the drive to defend. The drive to acquire relates to people's desire to obtain limited resources. The drive to bond is concerned with developing relationships with individuals and groups. The drive to comprehend fulfills our inquisitiveness and our desire to understand. The drive to defend is the desire to guard against dangers and to uphold fairness.

Nohria et al. (2008) operationalized the individual motivation concept through four typical workplace measures: (1) engagement (the effort and initiative an employee brings to the job); (2) satisfaction (employee perception of the degree to which an organization fulfills its explicit and implied agreements and meets workplace expectations); (3) commitment (degree to which employees exhibit organizational citizenship behavior); and (4) intention to quit (a good proxy measure for employee turnover). Behavioral intentions, such as intention to quit, have been shown to be closely linked to actual behavior (for example, job turnover) (Fishbein and Ajzen, 1975). Nohria et al. (2008) note that these four emotional drives cannot be substituted for each other, nor can they be hierarchically ordered. All four drives must be attended to simultaneously in order to fully motivate employees.

Nohria et al. (2008) note that each of the four basic emotional drives is best satisfied by a distinctive organizational approach, what the authors refer to as "levers." These levers and their associated emotional drives are: (1) the organization's reward system (drive to acquire); (2) the organization's culture (drive to bond); (3) job design (drive to comprehend); and (4) performance management and resource allocation processes (drive to defend). From their empirical research, the authors show that an organization's reward system is associated with the drive to acquire. When this system is functioning well, it is able to distinguish good performers from poor performers, offer the best work opportunities to the best employees, and clearly link rewards to performance. The organization's culture addresses the drive to bond when the culture is able to stimulate collaboration, friendliness, and teamwork. When managers truly care about workers and when workers care about each other, a climate of fitting in and teamwork will take root. Job design fulfills the drive to comprehend by addressing the extent to which jobs offer purposeful, engaging, satisfying, and challenging work. Performance management and resource allocation processes address the emotional drive to defend. Impartial, honest, and clear performance management and resource allocation processes fulfill this need.

Nohria et al. (2008) compared firms in their study in terms of worker motivation, with the baseline average firm at the 50th percentile for motivation. Enhancing any single emotional drive improved its motivational standing to the 56th percentile. However, when organizations focused on improving all four emotional drives simultaneously, worker motivation increased to the 88th percentile of all organizations.

The authors note that in addition to an organization's efforts in fulfilling the four basic emotional drives, the efforts of an employee's direct supervisor are equally important. Employees know that their immediate supervisor has control and discretion over how organizational efforts and processes are applied. Specifically, Nohria et al. (2008, p. 84) noted that as:

> employees look to different elements of their organization to satisfy different drives, they expect their managers to do their best to address all four within the constraints that the institution imposes. Our surveys showed that if employees detected that a manager was substantially worse than her peers in fulfilling even just one drive, they rated that manager poorly.

In sum, employees tend to harbor fairly accurate ideas as what their direct supervisors should be able to accomplish in satisfying their basic emotional needs, and in turn, increasing their level of motivation.

## FUTURE RESEARCH

The motivation of employees will continue to challenge managers into the future as the industry develops new methods of healthcare services delivery and reimbursements schemes for rewarding value-based, patient-centered organizations. These changes will directly impact tomorrow's workforce. Competencies needed by this workforce will include not only mastery of the technical aspects of their jobs, but also self-management. Managers will need to create environments in which employees are motivated to be fully engaged with high levels of satisfaction. "Organizations will need workers who are willing to take active responsibility for handling more and more of the uncertainties involved in the accomplishment of their work" (Thomas, 2009a, p. 19).

Thomas (2009a) states that employees are engaged when they accept responsibility for their performance through self-management. He describes the behavior associated with employees who are engaged and committed to their purpose. First, they use their intelligence to make choices about how best to accomplish their purpose. Second, they verify that they are performing their responsibilities well and that what they are doing is in fact accomplishing their purpose. By self-managing, employees can correct their behavior, if necessary, for goal attainment. The manager can shift focus to providing information and advice to employees as they gain experience and skills to self-manage. Through self-management, employees become fully engaged.

Thomas (2009a) describes the four intrinsic rewards that need to be in place to drive employee engagement: meaningfulness (what you are doing is worthwhile), choice (you determine how the activities should be performed), competence (performing the activities well), and progress (making significant advancement towards accomplishing your purpose). Recent studies regarding work engagement have found that employees who score high on the four intrinsic rewards experience high levels of positive emotions about their work, are rated as more effective by their managers, report higher satisfaction with their professional development and job, greater commitment to the organization, and fewer stress symptoms (Sparrowe, 1994; Thomas, 2009b; Thomas and Tymon, 1994). These preminlinary results are promising but more empirical research is needed for generalization.

As noted earlier in the chapter, more research is needed in the area of professional and organizational identification. As an increasing number of physicians in the USA are employed by hospitals and health systems, more knowledge is needed about how managers can motivate this group of employees to be engaged with and committed to the organization while balancing their need to protect their professional identification.

Another area where a gap remains is related to multigenerational cohorts. Although much has been written about the various generations' characteristics and work behaviors, only a few published reports have involved empirical studies. We need to add to our knowledge and better understand the values and beliefs for each generational cohort. To assist managers' understanding that each generation has different motivational needs, there needs to be less stereotyping and reliance on the popular press.

# CONCLUSION

This chapter is a resource for healthcare managers to better understand how to effectively motivate today's workforce. We provided an overview of the various content and process motivation theories. These theories create the foundation for managers to develop the right environment for employees to be motivated to obtain organizational goals. We discussed three challenges facing managers. The first challenge is the physician as the "new" employee in healthcare organizations. The second issue is how best to assist cross-disciplinary teams to build trust and cohesiveness so they can be more effective with less conflict. The third area relates to understanding the motivational needs of the industry's multigenerational workforce. The contemporary views of motivation provide managers with a new perspective in the field of motivation. An overview of needed future research was provided so we may continue to assist managers in motivating tomorrow's workforce as the industry continues to evolve.

# REFERENCES

Adams, J.S. (1963), "Toward an understanding of equity," *Journal of Abnormal and Social Psychology*, 67: 422–436.

Aiken, L.H., S.P. Clarke, D.M. Sloane, J. Sochalski, and J.H. Silber (2002), "Hospital nurse staffing and patient mortality, nurse burnout, and job dissatisfaction," *Journal of the American Medical Association*, 288 (16): 1987–1993.

Aiken, L.H., W. Sermeus, K. Van den Heede, D.M. Sloane, R. Busse, M. McKee, L. Bruyneel, A.M. Rafferty, P. Griffiths, T. Moreno-Casbas, C. Tishelman, A. Scott, T. Brzostek, J. Kinnunen, R. Schwendimann, M. Heinen, D. Zikos, I.S. Sjetne, H.L. Smith, and A. Kutney-Lee, (2012), "Patient safety, satisfaction, and quality of hospital care: cross sectional surveys of nurses and patients in 12 countries in Europe and the United States," *British Medical Journal*, 344 (7851): e1717.

Alderfer, Clayton P. (1972), *Existence, Relatedness, and Growth: Human Needs in Organizational Settings*. New York: Free Press.

American Medical Association (AMA) (2013), "Policy research perspectives: new data on physician practice arrangements: private practice remains strong despite shifts toward hospital employment," Chicago, IL: American Medical Association.

Apostolidis, B.M. and E.C. Polifroni (2006), "Nurse work satisfaction and generational differences," *Journal of Nursing Administration*, 36 (11): 506–509.

Atwal, A. and K. Caldwell (2006), "Nurses' perceptions of multidisciplinary team work in acute health-care," *International Journal of Nursing Practice*, 12 (6): 359–365.

Bartunek, J.M. (2010), "Intergroup relationships and quality improvement in healthcare," *BMJ Quality and Safety*, 20 (Suppl 1), i62–i66.

Becton, J.B., H.J. Walker, and A. Jones-Farmer (2014), "Generational differences in workplace behavior," *Journal of Applied Social Psychology*, 44 (3): 175–189.

Borkowski, Nancy M. (2000), "An examination of physician participation and levels of acceptance in the implementation of clinical practice guidelines," Unpublished doctoral dissertation, Nova Southeastern University, Fort Lauderdale, FL.

Borkowski, Nancy (2011), *Organizational Behavior in Health Care* (2nd edn). Sudbury, MA: Jones & Bartlett Publishers.

Borkowski, N., R. Amann, S. Song, and C Weiss (2007), "Nurses' intent to leave their profession: gender, ethnicity and educational level related issues," *Health Care Management Review*, 32 (2): 160–167.

Cameron, J. and W.D. Pierce (1994), "Reinforcement, reward, and intrinsic motivation: A meta-analysis," *Review of Educational Research*, 64 (3): 363–423.

Cennamo, L. and D. Gardner (2008), "Generational differences in work values, outcomes and person–organization values fit," *Journal of Managerial Psychology*, 23 (8): 891–906.

Clipper, Bonnie (2012), *The Nurse Manager's Guide to an Intergenerational Workforce*. Indianapolis, IN: Sigma Theta Tau International.

Cohen, S.G. and D.E. Bailey (1997), "What makes teams work: group effectiveness research from the shop floor to the executive suite," *Journal of Management*, 23 (3): 239–290.

Coomber, B. and K.L. Barriball (2007), "Impact of job satisfaction components on intent to leave and turnover for hospital-based nurses: A review of the research literature," *International Journal of Nursing Studies*, 44 (2): 297–314.

D'Amato, A. and R. Herzfeldt (2008), "Learning orientation, organizational commitment, and talent retention across generations: a study European managers," *Journal of Managerial Psychology*, 23 (8): 929–953.

Druskat, V.U. and S.B. Wolff (2001), "Building the emotional intelligence of groups," *Harvard Business Review*, 79 (3): 80–90.

Dukerich, J., B.R. Golden, and S.M. Shortell (2002), "Beauty is in the eye of the beholder: The impact of organizational identification, identity, and image on the cooperative behaviors of physicians," *Administrative Science Quarterly*, 47: 507–533.

Dye, Carson F. and J.J. Sokolov (2013), *Developing Physician Leaders for Successful Clinical Integration*. Chicago, IL: Health Administration Press.

Feldman Barrett, L. and J.A. Russell (1998), "Independence and bipolarity in the structure of core affect," *Journal of Personality and Social Psychology*, 74 (4): 967–984.

Festinger, Leon, S. Schachter, and K.W. Back (1950), *Social Pressure in Informal Groups*. New York: Harper & Row.

Fishbein, Martin and I. Ajzen (1975), *Belief, Attitude, Intention, and Behavior: An Introduction to Theory and Research*, Reading, MA: Addison-Wesley.

Frankel, A.S., M.W. Leonard, and C.R. Denham (2006), "Fair and just culture, team behavior, and leadership engagement: The tools to achieve high reliability," *Health Services Research*, 41 (4:II): 1690–1709.

Gouldner, A.W. (1957), "Cosmopolitans and locals: Toward an analysis of latent social roles I," *Administrative Science Quarterly*, 2 (3): 281–306.

Gouldner, A.W. (1958), "Cosmopolitans and locals: Toward an analysis of latent social roles II," *Administrative Science Quarterly*, 2 (4): 444–480.

Hackman, J. Richard and G.R. Oldham (1980), *Work Redesign*. Reading, MA: Addison-Wesley.

Harris, G. (2011), "More physicians say no to endless workdays," *New York Times*, 2 April, A1.

Hekman, D.R., G.A. Bigley, H.K. Steensma, and J.F. Hereford (2009a), "Combined effects of organizational and professional identification on the reciprocity dynamic for professional employees," *Academy of Management Journal*, 52 (3): 506–526.

Hekman, D.R., H.K. Steensman, G.A. Bigley, and J.F. Hereford (2009b), "Effects of organizational and professional identification on the relationship between administrators' social influence and professional employees' adoption of new work behavior," *Journal of Applied Psychology*, 94 (5): 1325–1335.

Herzberg, Fredrick (1966), *Work and the Nature of Man*. New York: World Publishing.

Hoff, T.J. (1999), "The social organization of physician-managers in a changing HMO," *Work and Occupations*, 26 (3): 324–351.

Jackson Healthcare (2013), "Filling the void: 2013 Physician Outlook and Practice Trends," http://www.jacksonhealthcare.com/media/191888/2013physiciantrends-void_ebk0513.pdf (accessed 14 July 2014).

Janus, K. (2011), "Pay-for-performance does not always pay – risks and side effects of incentives in healthcare," *Eurohealth*, 17 (4): 31–35.

Janus, K. (2014), "The effect of professional culture on intrinsic motivation among physicians in an academic medical center," *Journal of Healthcare Management*, 59 (4): 287–303.

Jenkins, G.D., A. Mitra, N. Gupta, and J.D. Shaw (1998), "Are financial incentives related to performance? A meta-analytic review of empirical research," *Journal of Applied Psychology*, 83 (5): 777–787.

Labarda, M.P. (2011), "Career shift phenomenon among doctors in Tacloban City, Philippines: lessons for retention of health workers in developing countries," *Asia Pacific Family Medicine*, 10 (13), http://www.apfmj.com/content/10/1/13 (accessed 28 July 2014).

Latham, Gary P. and E.A. Locke (1979), "Goal setting – a motivational technique that works," *Organizational Dynamics*, 8 (2): 68–80.

Lemieux-Charles, L. and W.L. McGuire (2006), "What do we know about health care team effectiveness? A review of the literature," *Medical Care Research and Review*, 63 (3): 263–300.

Lester, S.W., W.H. Turnley, J.M. Bloodgood, and M.C. Bolino (2002), "Not seeing eye to eye: differences in supervisor and subordinate perceptions of and attributions for psychological contract breach," *Journal of Organizational Behavior*, 23 (1): 39–56.

Locke, Edward A. (1968), "Toward a theory of task motivation and incentives," *Organizational Behavior and Human Performance*, 3 (2): 157–189.

Maslow, A. (1943), "A theory of human motivation," *Psychological Review*, 50 (4): 370–396.

Maslow, Abraham (1954), *Motivation and Personality*. New York: Harper Row.

McClelland, David C. (1961), *The Achieving Society*. New York: Free Press.

McClelland, David C. (1985), *Human Motivation*. Glenwood, IL: Scott-Foresman.

McHugh, M.D., A. Kutney-Lee, J.P. Cimiotti, D. Sloane, and L. Aiken (2011), "Nurses' widespread job dissatisfaction, burnout, and frustration with health benefits signal problems for patient care," *Health Affairs*, 30 (2): 202–210.

Medscape (2014), "Medscape Employed Physician Report," available at: http://www.medscape.com/features/slideshow/public/employed-doctors#8.

Meriac, J.P., D.J. Woehr, and C. Banister (2010), "Generational differences in work ethics: an examination of measurement equivalent across three cohorts," *Journal of Business Psychology*, 25 (2): 315–324.

Morris, William N. (1989), *Mood: The Frame of Mind*. New York: Springer-Verlag.

Nembhard, I.M. and A.C. Edmondson (2006), "Making it safe: The effects of leader inclusiveness and professional status on psychological safety and improvement efforts in health care teams," *Journal of Organizational Behavior*, 27 (7): 941–966.

Nohria, N., B. Groysberg, and L.E. Lee (2008), "Employee motivation: A powerful new model," *Harvard Business Review*, July–August: 78–84.

O'Connor, Stephen J. (1998), "Motivating effective performance," in W. Jack Duncan, Peter M. Ginter and Linda E. Swayne (eds), *Handbook of Health Care Management*. Malden, MA: Blackwell Publishers, pp. 431–470.

O'Connor, S.J. and J.A. Lanning (1992), "The end of autonomy? Reflections on the postprofessional physician," *Healthcare Management Review*, 17 (1): 63–72.

Paris, L.G. and M. Terhaar (2011), "Using Maslow's pyramid and the national database of nursing quality indicators to attain a healthier work environment," *OJIN: The Online Journal of Issues in Nursing*, 16 (1), available at http://www.nursingworld.org/MainMenuCategories/ANAMarketplace/ANAPeriodicals/OJIN/TableofContents/Vol-16-2011/No1-Jan-2011/Articles-Previous-Topics/Maslow-and-NDNQI-to-Assess-and-Improve-Work-Environment.html.

Pinto, M.B. and J.K. Pinto (1990), "Project team communication and cross-functional cooperation in new program development," *Journal of Product Innovation Management*, 7 (3): 200–212.

Porter, Lyman W. and E.E. Lawler (1968), *Managerial Attitudes and Performance*. Homewood, IL: Irwin-Dorsey Press.

Poulton, B.C. and M.A. West (1999), "The determinants of effectiveness in primary health care teams," *Journal of Interprofessional Care*, 13 (1): 7–18.

Rosenthal, M.B. and R.G. Frank (2006), "What is the empirical basis for paying for quality in healthcare?" *Medical Care Research and Review*, 63 (2): 135–157.

Russell, J.A. (2003), "Core affect and the psychological construction of emotion," *Psychological Review*, 110 (1): 145–172.

Russell, J.A. and L. Feldman Barrett (1999), "Core affect, prototypical emotional episodes, and other things called emotions: Dissecting the elephant," *Journal of Personality and Social Psychology*, 76 (5): 805–819.

Seo, M-G., Bartunek, J.M., and L. Feldman Barrett (2010), "The role of affective experience in work motivation: Test of a conceptual model," *Journal of Organizational Behavior*, 31 (7): 951–968.

Seo, M-G., L. Feldman Barrett, and J.M. Bartunek (2004), "The role of affective experience in work motivation," *Academy of Management Review*, 29 (3): 423–439.

Sessa, V.I., R.I. Kabacoff, J. Deal, and H. Brown (2007), "Generational differences in leader values and leadership behaviors," *Psychologist-Manager Journal*, 10 (1): 47–74.

Shortell, S., J.A. Marsteller, M. Lin, M.L. Pearson, S.Y. Wu, P. Mendel, S. Cretin, and M. Rosen (2004), "The role of perceived team effectiveness in improving chronic illness care," *Medical Care*, 42 (11): 1040–1048.

Skinner, Burrhus F. (1953), *Science and Human Behavior*. New York: Simon & Schuster.

Smith, P.A., M. Themessl-Huber, T. Akbar, D. Richards, and R. Freeman (2011), "What motivates dentists to work in prisons? A qualitative exploration," *British Dental Journal*, 211 (4): 176–177.

Sparrowe, R.T. (1994), "Empowerment in the hospitality industry: An exploration of antecedents and outcomes," *Hospitality Research Journal*, 17 (3): 51–73.

Stamps, Paula L. and T.B. Cruz (1994), *Issues in Physician Satisfaction: New Perspectives*. Chicago, IL: Health Administration Press.

Tajfel, Henri and Turner, J.C. (1979), "An integrative theory of intergroup conflict," in William G. Austin and Stephen Worchel (eds), *The Social Psychology of Intergroup Relations*. Monterey, CA: Brooks-Cole Publishing, pp. 33–48.

Taplin, S.H., M.K. Foster, and S.M. Shortell (2013), "Organizational leadership for building effective health care teams," *Annuals of Family Medicine*, 11 (3): 279–281.

Temkin-Greener, H., D. Gross, S.J. Kunitz, and D. Mukamel (2004), "Measuring interdisciplinary team performance in a long-term care setting," *Medical Care*, 42 (5): 472–481.

Thomas, Kenneth W. (2009a), *Intrinsic Motivation at Work* (2nd edn). San Francisco, CA: Berrett-Koehler Publishers.

Thomas, Kenneth W. (2009b), "Technical brief for the work engagement profile: Content, reliability and validity," available at http://www.psychometrics.com/docs/wep_tech_brief.pdf.

Thomas, K.W. and W.G. Tymon, Jr. (1994), "Does empowerment always work: understanding the role of intrinsic motivation and personal interpretation," *Journal of Management Systems*, 6: 1–13.

Trzesnieski, K.H. and M.B. Donnellan (2010), "Rethinking 'generation me' a study of cohort effects from 1976–2006," *Perspectives on Psychological Science*, 5 (1): 58–75.

Tuckman, B.W. (1965), "Developmental sequence in small groups," *Psychological Bulletin*, 63 (6): 384–399.

Twenge, J.M. (2010), "A review of the empirical evidence on generational differences in work attitudes," *Journal of Business Psychology*, 25 (2): 201–210.

Vinokur-Kaplan, D. (1995), "Treatment teams that work (and those that don't): an application of Hackman's group effectiveness model to interdisciplinary teams in psychiatric hospitals," *Journal of Applied Behavioral Science*, 31 (3): 303–327.

Vroom, Victor (1964), *Work and Motivation*. New York: John Wiley.

Watson, D. and A. Tellegen (1985), "Toward a consensual structure of mood," *Psychological Bulletin*, 98 (2): 219–235.

Weber, S.S. (2002), "Leadership and trust facilitating cross-functional team success," *Journal of Management Development*, 21 (3–4): 201–214.

Welch, W.P., A.E. Cuellar, S.C. Stearns, and A.B. Bindman (2012), "Proportion of physicians in large group practices continued to grow in 2009–11," *Health Affairs*, 32 (9): 1659–1666.

Wong, M., E. Gardiner, W. Lang, and L. Coulon (2008), "Generational differences in personality and motivation: Do they exist and what are the implications for the workplace?" *Journal of Managerial Psychology*, 23 (8): 878–890.

Young, G.J., H. Beckman, and E. Baker (2012), "Financial incentives, professional values and performance: A study of pay-for-performance in a professional organization," *Journal of Organizational Behavior*, 33: 964–983.

# 12. Organization change and transformation
## Nancy Borkowski

> It is not the strongest of the species that survives, nor the most intelligent that survives. It is the one that is most adaptable to change. (Charles Darwin)

## INTRODUCTION

No one would argue with the statement that there is a high degree of uncertainty about the future of the healthcare industry in the United States as reform initiatives roll out across all segments to increase access, improve quality, and slow the rate of spending. For health services organizations this means a paradigm shift as to how they will need to operate for future success. As a result, organizations are considering and engaging in redesign to include more alignment and inclusion across health systems (Fischer et al., 2009). For example, the new accountable care organizations (ACOs) are expected to "integrate and coordinate the various component parts of healthcare, such as primary care, specialty services, hospitals, home healthcare; and to ensure that all parts function well together to deliver efficient, high quality, and cost-effective patient-centered care" (Borkowski and Deppman, 2014, p. 195). To accomplish these goals requires individuals that appreciate the complexity of leading organizations through change, considering that for every successful corporate transformation there is at least one equally prominent failure (Ghoshal and Bartlett, 2000). Managing change is a complex, dynamic, and challenging process. Therefore, understanding change at both the organizational and individual levels is critical for success.

The purpose of this chapter is to provide healthcare managers with the knowledge necessary to successfully implement planned change within their organizations. The chapter is organized as follows. First, I discuss why health service organizations need to change. The most significant factor is environmental pressures. The next section provides an overview of types of change. The two main types discussed are incremental/transactional change and radical/transformational change. I then describe three theories of planned change: Lewin's change model, Burke–Litwin's model of organizational performance and change, and positive change. Within each of these models, I discuss the activities necessary to initiate and implement successful organizational change. The following sections address overcoming barriers to change and readiness for change. In the final section, I provide some thoughts for future research that would further assist managers with successfully implementing planned change.

## WHY ORGANIZATIONS CHANGE

There are a variety of pressures on managers to change their organizations. They come from many directions, such as the external environment, new visions for the future, or the need for internal improvements. For example, as the implementation of health reform rolls out across the USA's $2.8 trillion industry, new norms and opportunities are pressuring organizations to change. Healthcare organizations must adjust to empowered consumers, rapid innovation, and increasing competition from non-traditional players (PWC, 2013). The PricewaterhouseCoopers (PWC) Health Research Institute (PWC, 2013) offers insight into other environmental pressures:

> Changing traditional health care roles: Due to fiscal pressures, massive regulatory changes, and industry-wide shift to consumerism, health care organizations are reinventing themselves. For example, insurers are acquiring provider groups. Providers are entering the insurance business. Retailers are expanding their health offerings.
> Technologies enabling innovation: Social, mobile, analytics, and cloud technologies are causing the formation of new business models in which health organizations will be paid based on value rather than volume. These technologies will fundamentally alter how health organizations interact with patients and one another to deliver care and manage health while decreasing or maintaining costs.
> Price transparency: Cost-conscious employers will make price transparency a priority when negotiating with insurers for their employees' health coverage and large businesses will enter into exclusive contracts with high-value providers. Others will then need to improve quality and lower prices/costs to competitively compete in the marketplace. The health insurance exchanges (private and public) will require insurers to provide clear and easily understandable pricing and coverage information for payees.
> Long-term care: As life expectancy continues to increase, more Americans will require a complicated array of costly long-term care services. A shift toward managed long-term care will be a challenge for insurers and providers.

In addition to external forces, there are various pressures internal to the organization that may cause the need for change. Examples would be pressure for growth or the need for integration and collaboration in a new era (Palmer et al., 2009). As Goldman and Dubow (2007) point out, growth is an ongoing process, and successful growth requires organizations to be receptive to new ideas and the changes that will occur. For example, hospitals will need to change their frame of reference from being the hub for all services to being a member of a healthcare team that provides care to a defined population of patients. Their future growth will not be in the traditional inpatient setting due to increasing outpatient service utilization, new foci on preventive health and wellness strategies, and advancements in genetic counseling services. As such, more integration and collaborative efforts have emerged due to US healthcare's changing landscape of declining reimbursements, new payment models, increased transparency of quality, value, and patients' experiences, and the transition to population health management. For example, two sizable (and competing) US health systems, Ascension and CHE Trinity Health, formed a clinically integrated network of providers that covers the entire state of Michigan, encompassing 27 hospitals and hundreds of other care sites (Stempniak, 2014). Some hospitals are participating in ACO pilot projects or collaborating with other organizations to better understand how to change from a volume-based to a value-based delivery and payment environment. As an example, Baptist Health South Florida partnered with the state of Florida's largest health insurer (Florida Blue) and Advanced Medical Specialties, an oncology practice with 38 physicians and 17 offices in South Florida, to form an accountable care organization focused specifically on cancer treatment (Kutscher, 2012). Successful change whether due to growth, organizational redesign, or other factors requires energy and leadership, and the organization needs to be prepared with both (Goldman and Dubow, 2007).

## TYPES OF CHANGE

There are two basic types of change: incremental change (first-order) and radical change (second-order), representing opposite ends of the spectrum. Incremental or continuous change is described as small-scale adjustments to the status quo (Tushman and Romanelli, 1985). These types of changes are designed to support organizational continuity and order (Palmer et al., 2009), whereas radical change is considered transformational and therefore alters the organization at its core (Bate, 1995). It entails transforming the nature of the organization (Newman, 2000). Radical change is seen as large-scale and disruptive. For example, a study by Meyer et al. (1990, 1993) showed how changes in US hospitals during the 1960s were evolutionary and related to a stable environment (that is, incremental change). During the 1970s and 1980s, the environment changed with

BOX 12.1   TYPES OF CHANGE

The nature and size of the change impacts how much change management you need. Changes that are incremental in nature typically require less change management, because you are asking your employees to make a smaller leap from what they know and are comfortable with. Radical changes, on the other hand, require more change management. The future state is more unknown than in incremental change, and the comfort of the status quo is left farther behind when we ultimately make the change.

Think about a particular change – introducing Six Sigma – in the two scenarios below:

- Scenario 1: you are introducing Six Sigma into a manufacturing environment with a rich and long history of quality improvement efforts that focus on quality and systems already in place for measuring the amount of defective outputs. The quantity of outputs is right in line with what is required by Six Sigma analysis.
- Scenario 2: you are introducing Six Sigma into a hospital, where the notion of "quality" has taken on a very different definition and there are no tracking systems for measuring medical errors. The quantity of transactions processed is either extremely large (hospital) or very small (physician group practice) so the notion of medical errors per million does not make sense.

For the medical device manufacturing firm, Six Sigma is an incremental change to how it interprets and measures quality. For the hospital, Six Sigma is a radical change requiring new approaches to thinking about quality and measuring outputs. These two scenarios require significantly different amounts of change management. Communication plans will be different. The level of support and personal coaching required by managers and supervisors will be different. The amount of training required will be different. And how resistance occurs, where it comes from and how it should be managed will be different.

*Source:*   Prosci, Inc. (www.prosci.com, 2014). Adapted from copyrighted material and modified for use with permission.

high concerns about health costs, which led to revolutionary strategic and structural changes in US health service organizations (that is, radical change), similar to today (Meyer et al., 1990). For healthcare managers there is value in understanding the distinction between incremental change and radical change. This understanding assists in knowing the appropriate management practices to apply to the different types of change with the intent of making processes shorter, less expensive, and less uncertain (see Box 12.1).

## THEORIES OF CHANGING

Organizations may experience both unplanned and planned change. An unplanned change occurs without the involvement of a change agent and is considered unexpected and unintentional. For example, the sudden death of a key senior executive would constitute unplanned change. Although difficult to respond to effectively, when an unplanned change occurs the manager's objective would be to act as quickly as possible to minimize the adverse effects and maximize potential benefits, if any.

Planned change is an intentional and systematic effort by managers to move an organization to a new state. In this section, three theories of changing[1] will be described. Within each of these frameworks, the activities necessary to initiate and implement successful organizational change are summarized.

### Lewin's Change Model

Lewin's change model (1947, 1951) is one of the earliest frameworks that addressed the steps necessary for planned changed. Lewin states that before change can occur, managers need to identify the driving forces pushing the change initiative and the opposing forces that serve to resist the change. He describes this as a force field analysis with the current behavior set at equilibrium. For change to occur, this equilibrium state must be disrupted either by adding or strengthening forces positively affecting the change, or in the opposite direction, subtracting or weakening the resisting forces. Ultimately, the present behavior is changed and a new equilibrium state is achieved (see Figure 12.1). This change process is achieved by first unfreezing the current situation, followed by changing behavior to a new level, then refreezing this behavior so it becomes the new permanent equilibrium (see Box 12.2 and Figure 12.2). Unfreezing behavior is often the most difficult step due to individuals' and organizations' lack of readiness for change which leads to resistance to change. As Hanson et al. (2011, p. 274) point out, "while the industry is experiencing pressures for desired transformation, it is also constrained by numerous interests and forces that seek to maintain the status quo." The issues of resistance to change and readiness for change will be discussed later in the chapter.

Because Lewin's three-step model is "relatively broad, considerable effort has gone into elaborating it" (Cummings and Worley, 2009, p. 24). For example, Lippitt et al. (1958), as cited in Mitchell (2013), extended Lewin's model into seven phases: (1) development of a need for change; (2) establishment of a change relationship; (3) working toward change; (4)

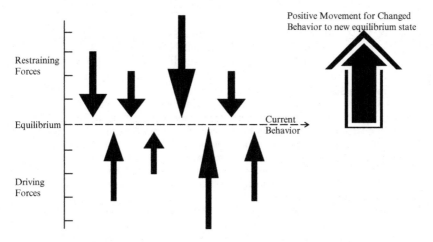

*Figure 12.1   Lewin's force field analysis*

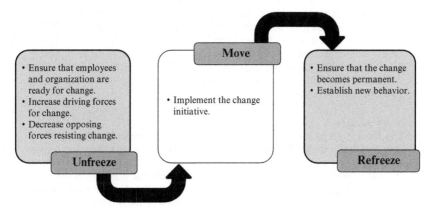

*Figure 12.2   Lewin's change model*

the clarification or diagnosis of the client systems problem; (5) the examination of alternative routes and goals, establishing goals and intentions of action; (6) transformation of intentions into actual change efforts; and (7) the generalization and stabilization of change and achieving a terminal relationship. Cummings and Worley (2009) refer to Lippitt et al.'s seven steps as: scouting, entry, diagnosis, planning, action, stabilization and evaluation, and terminating. Over the years, there have been some differences as to the terminology used to describe the Lippitt et al. model but the relationship to Lewin's planned change process remains clear (see Table 12.1).

BOX 12.2   APPLICATION OF LEWIN'S PLANNED CHANGE
PROCESS FOR IMPLEMENTATION OF BAR-
CODED MEDICATION ADMINISTRATION (BCMA)

**Unfreezing Stage**
The first step of Lewin's planned change process involves identifying the change focus; specifically, implementing a bar-code scanning system of medication delivery at a large psychiatric facility. Key components of this step are communicating with all stakeholders including frontline nurses, managers and administration. The inclusion of front line staff in planning groups and key decision-making processes promotes a feeling of empowerment that helps to overcome their resistance to the change and enables them to understand the importance of the project and how it will beneficially affect client care.

During the unfreezing stage, round table discussions with the purpose of teasing out the driving and restraining forces will help identify barriers that may need to be overcome. In this facility some restraining forces might be staff resistance to using computerized devices, the possibility of workarounds, lack of computer experience, lack of trust in the organization, and aversion to using a new system. Driving forces would be the forces that will help move the project to completion such as adequate financial investment, support from upper level management, potential for ease of use and better time management. The important point here is that this exercise actively engages all parties to work towards accentuating the positive driving forces and diminishing the restraining forces so that BCMA is successfully adopted without the use of dangerous workarounds with full nursing investment in the outcome.

**Moving Stage**
The moving stage represents the period of actual change including the planning and implementation stages of the project. Implementing bar coding across the facility will require sustained effort from various teams, some of which include information technology (IT), pharmacy, clinical information services (CIS), nursing, program managers, clinical nurse educators and administrators. A project of this magnitude will affect all of these departments in different ways, so planning an effective roll out with the assistance and inclusion of all stakeholders is imperative. It is recommended to actively involve nursing staff, to create a feeling of ownership of the success of the project. Some areas to consider at this facility are implementation timelines, reliability of the equipment, educational training needs, and effects on workflow, organizational culture and leadership. It is also important to have a project leader to oversee and monitor a project of this magnitude through all phases. Challenges in this stage may include discovering the use of workarounds that can be resolved through further education.

**Refreezing Stage**
In this final stage of Lewin's planned change theory, the process of freezing or refreezing the changed practice occurs and leads to a time of "stability and evaluation." Ongoing support of the nurses on the frontline and technology support to all stakeholders should continue until the change is deemed complete and

all users are comfortable with the technology. Once completed and fully operational, an evaluation and summary of problems encountered, successes realized,
and challenges encountered throughout the project should be done, for future
reference.

*Source:*   Sutherland (2013). Reprinted with permission.

*Table 12.1   Comparison of planned change processes*

| Lewin | Lippitt et al. |
|---|---|
| Unfreezing | Phase 1: Diagnose the problem |
|  | Phase 2: Assess motivation and capacity for change |
|  | Phase 3: Assess change agent's motivation and resources |
| Moving | Phase 4: Select progressive change objective |
|  | Phase 5: Choose appropriate role of the change agent |
|  | Phase 6: Maintain change |
| Refreezing | Phase 7: Terminate the helping relationship |

*Source:*   Mitchell (2013).

In addition to Lippitt et al. (1958), Kotter (1995, 1996) expanded upon
Lewin's change model, identifying eight steps for managers to follow
for successful organizational change. As related by Borkowski (2011),
Kotter's first four steps change the status quo (unfreezing), steps five
through seven introduce new policies (change), and step eight institution-
alizes the changes (refreezing). The eight steps are as follows (Borkowski,
2011, p. 379):

1.   Establish a sense of urgency. Management often fails to establish a
     sense of urgency about the need for change. The first step should be
     to "unfreeze" the organization by examining market and competitive
     realities and discussing crises, potential crises, or major opportunities.
2.   Create a powerful guiding coalition. Management needs to create a
     powerful guiding coalition, a group that spans both the functions and
     levels of the organization (that is, include members who are not part
     of senior management).
3.   Develop a vision. Management must create a vision to direct the
     change effort and develop strategies for achieving that vision.
4.   Communicate the vision. Management must use every vehicle possible
     to communicate the new vision and strategies, including teaching new
     behaviors by the example of the guiding coalition.

5.  Empower others to act on the vision. Management must eliminate barriers to change, and they must encourage risk-taking and creative problem-solving. They must change systems or structures that undermine the vision.
6.  Plan for and create short-term wins. Management must plan for visible performance improvements. In addition, employees who are involved in the improvements must be recognized and rewarded.
7.  Consolidate improvements and produce more change. Management should use the credibility achieved by short-term wins to create more change. This may include hiring, promoting, and developing employees who can implement the vision and reinvigorate the process with new projects, themes, and change agents.
8.  Institutionalize new approaches. Management must reinforce changes by highlighting connections between new behaviors and organizational success. Managers must also develop the means to ensure leadership development and succession.

**The Burke–Litwin Model of Organizational Performance and Change**

One of the main contributions of the Burke–Litwin (1992) change model is that it separates the transformational (that is, radical) and transactional (that is, incremental) factors that drive organizational change. As reflected in Figure 12.3, the transformational factors (external environment, leadership, mission and strategy, and culture) are placed in the top half of the model with the transactional factors in the lower half. The external environment represents the input, the individual and organizational performance denotes the output, and the feedback loops go in both directions. The remaining items represent the throughput aspect of general systems theory and the arrows in both directions convey the open systems principle that change in one factor will eventually have an impact on the others (Burke, 1994). Palmer et al. (2009) point out that although planned change should flow from the top of the model (environment) to the bottom (performance), it is possible that internal organizational factors may impact the environment and not just be on the receiving end of a one-way environmental determinism, hence the need for the feedback loops to be reflected as going in both directions.

As noted by Osatuke et al. (2014), changes in the transformational factors result in major and significant shifting of the organization. Interventions aimed at these factors cause permanent change in the organization's culture and, ultimately, in individual and organizational performances. Whereas with changes in the transactional factors, some features

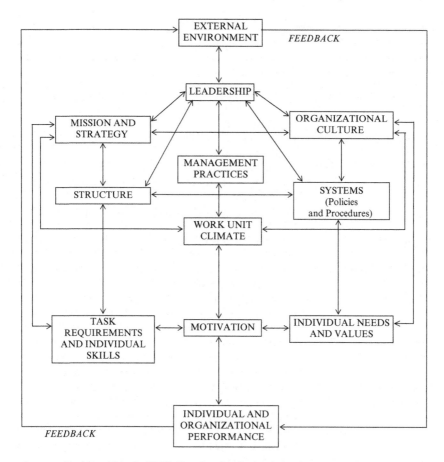

*Source:* Burke and Litwin (1992). Reprinted with permission.

*Figure 12.3   Burke–Litwin model of organizational performance and change*

of the organization may change but the overall nature of the organization remains the same.

In the Burke–Litwin change model, macro-environmental factors (that is, economic, political and regulatory, socio-demographics, technology) are considered to be the most important drivers for change. These external factors impact change in the other transformational elements, similar to a domino effect. As such, managers need to consistently scan their external environment for anticipated changes within these forces so they can identify the implications for organizational change. To better understand

*Table 12.2    The 12 variables of the Burke–Litwin model of organizational performance and change*

| Variable | Sample question |
| --- | --- |
| External environment | Regarding the pace of change (from static to very rapid), what would you say the organization as a whole is experiencing? |
| Mission and strategy | How widely accepted are the organization's goals among employees? |
| Leadership | To what extent do senior managers make an effort to keep in personal touch with employees at your level in the organization? |
| Culture | To what extent are the standard ways of operating in the organization difficult to change? |
| Structure | To what extent is the organization's structure clear to everyone? |
| Management practices | To what extent does your manager communicate in an open and direct manner? |
| Systems | To what extent are the following communication mechanisms in the organization effective? (e.g., grapevine, company newsletter, staff meetings, Intranet/bulletin boards, etc.) |
| Climate | Where you work in the organization, to what extent is there trust and mutual respect among employees? |
| Skills-job match | How challenged do you feel in your present job? |
| Motivation | To what extent do you feel encouraged to reach higher levels and standards of performance in your work? |
| Needs and Values | I have a job that matters. (Indicate extent to which this statement is true for you, from "disagree strongly" to "agree strongly.") |
| Performance | To what extent is the organization currently achieving the highest level of employee performance of which it is capable? |

*Source:*    Burke (1994). Reprinted with permission.

the Burke–Litwin (1992) change model, the 12 variables are described in Table 12.2.

Using the Burke–Litwin framework, the change agent, or organizational development specialist, would conduct interviews along with administering a survey (see Table 12.3) for determining whether significant organizational change is needed (transformational), or whether the organization requires more of an incremental (transactional) change (Burke, 1994).

*Table 12.3   Sample questions for a survey based on the Burke–Litwin model*

| Variable | Description |
| --- | --- |
| External Environment | Any outside condition or situation that influences the performance of the organization, including such things as marketplaces, work, financial conditions, and political / governmental circumstances. |
| Mission and strategy | What employees believe is the central purpose of the organization and the means by which the organization intends to achieve that purpose over an extended time. |
| Leadership | Executive behavior that provides direction and encourages others to take needed action (for purposes of data gathering, this variable includes perceptions of executive practices and values). |
| Culture | The collection of overt and covert rules, values, and principles that guide organizational behavior and that have been strongly influenced by history, custom, and practice ("The way we do things around here"). |
| Structure | The arrangement of functions and people into specific areas and levels of responsibility, decision-making authority, and relationships; an arrangement that assures effective implementation of the organization's mission and strategy. |
| Management practices | What managers do in the normal course of events with the human and material resources at their disposal to carry out the organization's strategy. |
| Systems | Standardized policies and mechanisms that are designed to facilitate work and that primarily manifest themselves in the organization's reward systems and in control systems, such as the organization's management information system, goal and budget development, and human resource allocation. |
| Climate | The collective current impressions, expectations, and feelings of the members of local work units, all of which in turn affect members' relations with supervisors, with one another, and with other units. |
| Task requirements and individual skills/ abilities | The behavior required for task effectiveness, including specific skills and knowledge required for people to accomplish the work assigned and for which they feel directly responsible (this variable concerns what is often referred to as job–person match). |
| Individual needs and values | The specific psychological factors that provide desire and worth for individual actions or thoughts. |
| Motivation | Aroused behavioral tendencies to move towards goals, take needed action, and persist until satisfaction is attained, that is, the resultant net energy generated by the combined desires for achievement, power, affection, discovery, and other important human values. |
| Individual and organizational performance | The outcomes or results, with indicators of effort and achievement including productivity, customer or staff satisfaction, profit, and service quality. |

*Source:*   Burke (1994). Reprinted with permission.

**Positive Model**

The positive model for planned change is a departure from the two previously discussed models as its focus is "what the organization is doing right." This frame of reference is an extension of the social science movement referred to as positive organizational change (Cummings and Worley, 2009). Where the Lewin and Burke–Litwin models are deficit-based (that is, focused on fixing an organization's problems), the positive model "helps members understand their organization when it is working at its best and builds off those capabilities to achieve even better results" (Cummings and Worley, 2009, p. 28). The model is based on the theory that positive expectations give rise to positive outcomes.

The positive model of change is achieved through the use of appreciative inquiry. Appreciative inquiry (AI) is a form of action research that attempts to create new theories, ideas, and images that aid in the developmental change of a system (Cooperrider and Srivastva, 1987). Watkins and Mohr (2005) relate that AI was developed by David Cooperrider in collaboration with Suresh Srivastva while assisting the Cleveland Clinic in the US to diagnosis the problem as to why the organization's employees were experiencing negative anticipation and hopelessness. Using inquiry, Cooperrider focused his analysis on those characteristics that contributed to the clinic's success, ignoring the negative factors (that is, life-centric analysis). Employee participants were asked to focus only on the factors contributing to the highly effective functioning of the clinic when it was at its best. The approach was so powerful and positive that the clinic's Board of Governors asked for ways to use this method with the whole group practice.

The AI model involves five phases: define, discover, dream, design, and destiny. As shown in Figure 12.4 the appreciative inquiry "5-D" model is commonly presented in a circle to reflect the concept that management should keep repeating the process for continuous learning of what works well within the organization (Hammond, 2013).

The focus of each of the five phases of the 5-D cycle is presented in Table 12.4 as well as the decisions that the organization needs to make within each phase (Lee, 2010, p. 64):

# OVERCOMING BARRIERS TO CHANGE

**Resistance**

Change initiatives rarely achieve the substantial success that is intended (Lockett et al., 2014). In fact, estimates of unsuccessful organizational

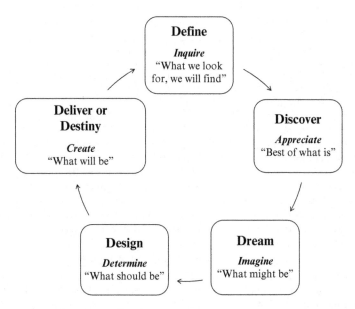

*Figure 12.4 The 5-D cycle of appreciative inquiry*

change may be as high as 70 percent (Miller, 2004). These statements should not come as a surprise. Change requires both organizations and individuals to move from the status quo to an uncertain future. It can (and most times does) cause disruption in the workplace and individual distress by forcing employees out of their comfort zones. As such, resistance to change is a normal process. As Freedman (1997, p. 54) points out, "resistance is a natural and inevitable response to virtually anything that is new or different." Resistance to change should not be ignored if managers wish to avoid risking a failure of their change initiative. By understanding and appreciating the organizational and individual resisting forces, leaders can create a supportive environment that drives change.

At the organizational level, resistance to change typically comes from one of three sources (Cummings and Worley, 2009, p. 167):

- Technical resistance comes from the habit of following common procedures and the consideration of sunk costs invested in the status quo.
- Political resistance can arise when organizational change threatens powerful stakeholders due to various reasons, such as reallocation of power, capital, budgets, and so on.
- Cultural resistance takes the form of systems and procedures that

*Table 12.4    Appreciative inquiry's five phases in the 5-D cycle model*

| Focus of the 5-D Cycle | Decisions to be Made |
| --- | --- |
| *Definition*. Involves introducing decision-makers to Appreciative Inquiry as a process for change, establishing a supporting infrastructure, and engaging participants in the process. AND<br>*Affirmative Topic Choice.* Involves selecting the topics that establish the organization's course for learning and transformation. | – Is appreciative inquiry appropriate for us?<br>– What is our Change Agenda?<br>– Who will serve on our Advisory Team/SC?<br>– What training does our Advisory Team/SC need?<br>– What Form of Engagement will we use?<br>– What will our Inquiry Strategy be?<br>– How and when will we introduce the process throughout the organization?<br>– Who will select the topics?<br>– Which topics will we study?<br>– Who will craft the questions? The Interview Guide<br>– What question will we ask? |
| *Discovery*. Involves conducting interviews, and making meaning of what's been learned. | – Who will we interview?<br>– Who will conduct the interviews? How many each?<br>– What training will our interviewers need?<br>– Who will make meaning of the data? How?<br>– How will we communicate stories and best practices? |
| *Dream*. Involves individual and collective visioning, group dialogues, and enactments of positive images of the organization's future. | – Whom should we involve?<br>– What experiential activity will we use to reveal our images of the future?<br>– What will be the outcome of our dream? |
| *Design*. Involves collaborative identification of the organization's social architecture and crafting Provocative Propositions – descriptions of the ideal organization. | – What are we designing?<br>– Who needs to be involved?<br>– How do we describe our ideal organization? |
| *Destiny*. Involves unleashing self-organized innovation, through which the future will be made real. | – How will we gather stories about what we have achieved?<br>– How will we celebrate?<br>– What are parameters for self-organized action?<br>– How shall we self-organize?<br>– How will we support ongoing support? |

*Source:*    Lee (2010). Reprinted with permission.

reinforce the status quo, promoting conformity to existing values, norms, and assumptions about how things should operate.

At the individual level, resistance to change may involve affective, cognitive and behavioral components (Palmer et al., 2009). The affective component relates to how an employee may feel about the change; the cognitive component is how the employee thinks about the change; and the behavioral component is what the employee does when confronted with the need to change (Palmer et al., 2009).

Hultman (1995) relates that individuals' negative behaviors towards change can fall into two categories: active resistance or passive resistance. Active resistance behaviors include being critical, blaming or accusing, ridiculing, using fear tactics, manipulating facts, and on the extreme side, sabotaging. Passive resistance behaviors include agreeing verbally but not following through (that is, malicious compliance), procrastinating, feigning ignorance, and withholding information and/or support. Understanding why individuals may resist change is critical to achieving success. Hultman (1995, pp. 15–16) outlines the six most common causes of individuals' resistance to change:

1. The individual is comfortable with the status quo because they feel their current needs are being met.
2. The individual sees the change as a threat because it will make it more difficult to meet their current needs.
3. The individual perceives that the change effort outweighs the benefit that the individual believes they will receive.
4. The individual feels that the change is unnecessary to avoid or escape a harmful situation.
5. The individual thinks that the organization is mishandling the change process.
6. The individual believes the change initiative will fail.

**Barriers**

Not all employees will resist change, especially when its outcome benefits them personally, such as an organizational restructuring with the outcome being that the individual is promoted to a more senior position. Even with employee support of an organizational change, the initiative may still fail to meet expectations due to management's failure to create an environment conducive for the initiative to be successfully implemented. For example, in a recent applied research study, focus groups were conducted with frontline healthcare leaders from 11 different functional areas at four community hospitals, to explore why hospital change efforts fail. The researchers, Longnecker et al. (2014, p. 150), identified ten primary barriers to successful hospital change:

1.  Poor implementation planning and overly aggressive timeline.
2.  Failing to create buy-in/ownership of the initiative.
3.  Ineffective leadership and lack of trust in upper management.
4.  Failing to create a realistic plan or improvement process.
5.  Ineffective and top-down communications.
6.  A weak case for change, unclear focus, and unclear desired outcomes.
7.  Little or no teamwork or corporation.
8.  Failing to provide ongoing measurement, feedback, and accountability.
9.  Unclear roles, goals, and performance expectations.
10. Lack of time, resources, and upper-management support.

The above barriers relate, in part, to the organization's lack of capacity to support the change initiative. Capacity for change is defined as the degree of availability of an organization's "financial, material, human, and informational resources necessary to support the introduction, routinization, and sustainability of a new practice" (Alexander and Hearld, 2012, p. 6). Therefore, managers need to assess the organization's capacity to support the change not only during its implementation phase, but also during the post-implementation stage, to ensure that the new practice becomes internalized by the members of the organization. For example, Shea et al. (2014) assessed the organizational capacity (people, processes, and technology resources) for outpatient clinics within an integrated healthcare delivery system for achieving meaningful use of electronic health records. The researchers, using an iterative process involving multiple clinic representatives, developed a structured interview tool that was able to assist in identifying problem areas particularly within the process domain prior to implementation for early interventions that allowed for optimizing existing resources and predicting future resource needs within the institution.

Although change capabilities have become a primary focus as health services organizations attempt to reorganize to meet market and regulatory demands (Kash et al., 2014), the question remains, "What does an organization need to have in place to create a supportive environment for successful change implementation?" To help answer this question, Kash et al. (2014, p. 74) identified ten success factor themes related to implementation of change initiatives from interviews with 61 senior leaders at two large health systems in the USA. The ranked success factors are as follows:

1. Culture and values.
2. Business processes.
3. People and engagement.
4. Service quality and client satisfaction.
5. Coherent planning.
6. Financial resources and accountability.
7. Leadership.
8. Market forces and external demands.
9. Access to information.
10. Communication.

Many factors contribute to the effectiveness of organizational change implementation. For example, the Kash et al. study reflected the "importance of human resource functions, alignment of culture and values with change, and business processes that facilitate effective communication and access to information to achieve change initiatives" (Kash et al., 2014, p. 65). Another crucial factor is referred to as "readiness" which may act to prevent or minimize the likelihood of resistance to change, thereby increasing the potential for change implementation efforts to be more effective (Armenakis et al., 1993).

## READINESS FOR CHANGE

As Weiner (2009, p. 1) notes, "organizational readiness for change is a multi-level, multi-faceted construct." It refers to organizational members' motivation and capability to implement change (Weiner et al., 2008). Although readiness is different from resistance to change, it is most often discussed in conjunction with strategies for reducing resistance (Armenakis et al., 1993). Readiness for change "is comprised of both psychological and structural factors reflecting the level to which the organization and its members are motivated to accept and implement an intentional change to alter the status quo" (see Figure 12.5) (Holt et al., 2009, p. S51).

Weiner (2009, pp. 3–4) explains the diagram's key elements of valance, efficacy, and change-related effort (that is, outcomes) as follows:

> *Change Valence* – Do organizational members value the specific impending change enough to commit to its implementation? Do they think it is needed, important and beneficial?
> *Change Efficacy* – This is a function of organizational members' cognitive appraisal of three determinants of implementation capability: task demands, resource availability, and situational factors. Employees acquire, share, assimilate, and integrate information focused on the questions: Do we know what

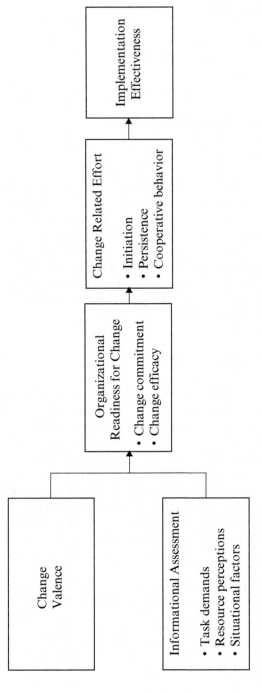

*Source:* Adapted from Weiner (2009).

*Figure 12.5   Determinants and outcomes of organizational readiness for change*

it will take to implement this change effectively; do we have the resources to implement this change effectively; and can we implement this change effectively given the situation we currently face?

*Change-related Effort* – If organizational readiness for change is high, members are more likely to initiate change (e.g., institute new policies, procedures, or practices), exert greater effort in support of change, and exhibit greater persistence in the face of obstacles or setbacks during implementation.

Weiner relates that even though there may be a high degree of organizational readiness, this factor alone will not guarantee a successful implementation, especially if the planned change is poorly designed or the organizational members overestimated their efficacy.

How does a manager create, influence, and manage readiness for change? Armenakis et al. (1993) offer five key elements or strategies for developing organizational readiness: discrepancy, efficacy, appropriateness, principal support, and personal valence. The first element, and the main thrust for creating readiness among employees, is the message for change. This is similar to Lewin's (1947) unfreezing stage or Kotter's (1995) recommendation for creating a sense of urgency. The message must clearly communicate the legitimacy for the needed change. In other words, the message must communicate the difference between the organization's current performance and the desired outcome; for example, a hospital's need to redesign its clinical and administrative procedures to eliminate occurrences of "never-events" and 30-day readmissions due to significant financial losses sustained by non-payment by Medicare and Medicaid and other payors.

The second element is appropriateness. This requires managers to effectively communicate that the planned change (that is, adoption and use of electronic medical records) is the right change to make given the future state the organization needs to achieve (that is, clinically and financially responsible for the health of predetermined patient populations). Employee self-efficacy is the third element. Managers need to provide the resources to assure that employees have the opportunities to develop the right knowledge, skills and abilities to implement the planned change. In addition, the organization needs to have the required infrastructure (technology, policies, procedures, managerial talent) to support the planned change. The fourth element needed is the key leaders' (both formal and informal leaders) visible support of the planned change. These individuals need to clearly demonstrate to employees that they fully support the change initiative. The fifth and final element is for employees to understand what are the intended outcome(s) of the planned change, how the outcome is regarded or valued by the individual, and if the expected outcome will benefit (or not benefit) the employee and to what degree. In other words, this element should answer the question, "What's in it for me?" for the employee.

Similar to the Shea et al. (2014) study which assessed organizational capacity before the implementation of a planned change, managers need to also determine readiness levels of both the organization and employees before planned changes are implemented. This can be accomplishment using assessment tools "to identify gaps that may exist between [leaders'] expectations about the change initiative and those of other members" (Holt et al., 2007, p. 233). For example, using an organizational readiness assessment tool prior to implementing an organization-wide patient safety improvement (PSI) program, Burnett et al. (2010) found two significant issues. First, physicians' support for the PSI was problematic due to low medical engagement; medical engagement was essential for the PSI program to be a success. Second, it was identified that more time and resources were needed to establish the necessary infrastructure to collect and report on a range of process measures that would guide the improvement efforts. "If significant gaps are observed and no action is taken to close those gaps, resistance would be expected, and the change implementation could be threatened" (Holt et al., 2007, p. 233).

## FUTURE RESEARCH

The successful implementation of planned change will continue to remain a challenge for healthcare managers. We need to develop a better understanding and the methods to measure individuals' and organizations' readiness to change. As noted by Alexander and Hearld (2012, p. 6), "without knowledge of successful strategies to increase readiness, change implementation is likely to be hit or miss at best." In addition, the researchers point out that "capacity for change is not well developed both as a construct and as a measure." As such, developing assessment tools to measure organizational readiness and capacity will require the continuing attention of researchers. This continuing focus will assist managers in understanding "why current organizational change and improvement efforts often fail to deliver the desired outcomes" (Longenecker et al., 2014, p. 148).

## CONCLUSION

Today and in the coming years, US healthcare managers will be challenged to successfully implement planned changes as the industry evolves from a fee-for-service fragmented environment into a value-based, patient-centered service. Understanding the complexity of change at both the organizational and individual levels is critical for health service organizations' future success. With declining reimbursements and profit margins, resources are becoming scarcer. This will impact the organization's capacity levels to implement the required changes needed to realign processes and structures to deliver coordinated, integrated care to defined patient populations. As a result, managers need to assure the success of the organization's change initiatives with the efficient use of resources. This is no easy task, given the history of high rates of planned change initiatives failures. However, if the initiative is well designed, the organization's capacity for the implementation and sustained support of the change has been assessed, and employees' readiness for change has been addressed, there is high certainty that the planned change will be successful.

## NOTE

1. Bennis (1966) distinguished between theories of change and theories of changing. Theories of change attempt to answer the question of how and why change occurs. Theories of changing attempt to answer the question of how to generate change and guide it to a successful conclusion (Austin and Bartunek, 2004, p. 311).

## REFERENCES

Alexander, J. and L. Hearld (2012). "Methods and metrics challenges of delivery-system research," *Implementation Science*, 7 (15), DOI:10.1186/1748-5908-7-15, available at http://www.implementationscience.com/content/7/1/15 (accessed 15 September 2014).

Armenakis, A.A., S.G. Harris, and K.W. Mossholder (1993). "Creating readiness for organizational change," *Human Relations*, 46 (6): 681–704.

Austin, John R. and Jean M. Bartunek (2004). "Theories and practices of organizational development," in Walter C. Borman, Daniel R. Ilgen, Richard J. Klimoski, and Irving B. Weiner (eds), *Handbook of Psychology, Industrial and Organizational Psychology* (Volume 12). New York: John Wiley & Sons.

Bate, S. Paul (1995). *Strategies for Cultural Change*. Oxford: Butterworth-Heinemann.

Bennis, Warren G. (1966). *Changing Organizations*. New York: McGraw-Hill.

Borkowski, Nancy (2011). *Organizational Behavior in Health Care*. Burlington, MA: Jones and Bartlett Learning.

Borkowski, Nancy and Barbara Perez Deppman (2014). "Collaborative leadership," in Louis Rubino, Salvador Esparza, and Yolanda Reid Chassiakos (eds), *New Leadership for Today's Health Care Professional: Concepts and Cases*. Burlington, MA: Jones and Bartlett Learning, pp. 193–208.

Burke, W. Warner (1994). "Diagnostic models for organization development," in Ann Howard & Associates (ed.), *Diagnosis for Organizational Change: Methods and Models*. New York: Guilford Press, pp. 53–84.

Burke, W. Warner and George Litwin (1992). "A causal model of organizational performance and change," *Journal of Management*, 18 (3): 523–545.

Burnett, S, J. Benn, A. Pinto, A. Parand, S. Iskander, and C. Vincent (2010). "Organisational readiness: exploring the preconditions for success in organisation-wide patient safety improvement programmes," *BMJ Quality and Safety in Health Care*, 19 (4): 313–317.

Cooperrider, David L. and Suresh Srivastva (1987). "Appreciative inquiry in organizational life," in Richard W. Woodman and William A. Pasmore (eds), *Research in Organizational Change and Development*, Vol. 1. Stamford, CT: JAI Press, pp. 129–169.

Cummings, Thomas G. and Christopher G. Worley (2009). *Organization Development and Change* (9th edn). Mason, OH: South-Western Cengage Learning.

Fischer, E., D. Berwick and K. Davis (2009). "Achieving health care reform: how physicians can help," *New England Journal of Medicine*, 360 (24): 2495–2497.

Freedman, A.M. (1997). "The undiscussable sides of implementing transformational change," *Consulting Psychology Journal: Practice and Research*, 49 (1): 51–76.

Ghoshal, Sumantra and Christopher A. Bartlett (2000). "Rebuilding behavioral context: a blueprint for corporate renewal," in Michael Beer and Nitin Nohria (eds), *Breaking Code of Change*. Boston, MA: Harvard Business School Press, pp. 195–222.

Goldman, E.F. and M.J. Dubow (2007). "Developing and leading successful growth strategies," *Healthcare Executive*, 22 (3): 8–13.

Hammond, Sue Annis (2013). *The Thin Book of Appreciative Inquiry* (3rd edn). Bend, OR: Thin Book Publishing.

Hanson, Heather, Mark J. Moir, and Jason A. Wolf (2011). "Organization development in health care: the dialogue continues," in Jason A. Wolf, Heather Hanson, and Mark J. Moir (eds), *Organization Development in Health Care: High Impact Practices for a Complex and Changing Environment*. Charlotte, NC: Information Age Publishing, pp. 273–279.

Holt, D.T., A.A. Armenakis, H.S. Feild, and S.G. Harris (2007). "Readiness for organizational change: the systematic development of a scale," *Journal of Applied Behavioral Science*, 43 (2): 232–255.

Holt, D.T., C.D. Helfrich, C.G. Hall, and B.J. Weiner (2009). "Are you ready? How health professionals can comprehensively conceptualize readiness for change," *Journal of General Internal Medicine*, 1 Suppl., S50–S55.

Hultman, K.E. (1995). "Scaling the wall of resistance," *Training and Development*, 49 (10): 15–18.

Kash, B.A., A. Spaulding, C.E. Johnson, and L. Gamm (2014). "Success factors for strategic change initiatives; a qualitative study of health care administrators' perspectives," *Journal of Health care Management*, 59 (1): 65–82.

Kotter, J.P. (1995). "Leading change: Why transformation efforts fail," *Harvard Business Review*, 73 (2): 59–67.

Kotter, J.P. (1996). *Leading Change*. Boston, MA: Harvard Business School Press.

Kutscher, B. (2012). "Cancer-care ACO to launch in Florida," *Modern Health Care*, available at http://www.modernhealth care.com/article/20120504/NEWS/305049977# (accessed 15 September 2014).

Lee, Sallie (2010). "Appreciative inquiry foundations and practice," available at http://www.unc.edu/faculty/faccoun/reports/2010-11/specrepts/2010UNCAIWorkbookSallieLee.pdf (accessed 19 September 2014).

Lewin, K. (1947). "Frontiers in group dynamics," *Human Relations*, 1 (1): 5–41.

Lewin, Kurt (1951). *Field Theory in Social Science*. New York: Harper & Row.

Lippitt, Ronald, Jeanne Watson, and Bruce Westley (1958). *The Dynamics of Planned Change: Comparative Study of Principles and Techniques*. New York: Harcourt, Brace & World.

Lockett, A., G. Currie, R. Finn, G. Martin, and J. Waring (2014). "The influence of social position on sensemaking about organizational change," *Academy of Management Journal*, 57 (4): 1102–1129.

Longenecker, C.O., P.D. Longenecker, and J. Gering (2014). "Why hospital improvement efforts fail: a view from the front line," *Journal of Health Care Management*, 59 (2): 147–159.

Meyer, Alan D., Geoffrey R. Brooks, and James B. Goes (1990). "Environmental jolts and industry revolutions: organizational responses to discontinuous change," *Strategic Management Journal*, 11 (5): 93–110.

Meyer, Alan D., James B. Goes, and Geoffrey R. Brooks (1993). "Organizations reacting to hyperturbulence," in George P. Huber and William H Glick (eds), *Organizational Change and Redesign: Ideas and Insights for Improving Performance*. New York: Oxford University Press.

Miller, D. (2004). "Building sustainable change capability," *Industrial and Commercial Training*, 36 (1): 9–12.

Mitchell, G. (2013). "Selecting the best theory to implement planned change," *Nursing Management*, 20 (1): 32–37.

Newman, K.L. (2000). "Organizational transformation during institutional upheaval," *Academy of Management Review*, 25 (3): 602–619.

Osatuke, Katerine, Nancy Yanchus, Steven White, and Dee Ramsel (2014). "Change in the Veterans Health Administration: theory and applications," *Journal of Organizational Psychology*, 14 (1): 77–95.

Palmer, Ian, Richard Dunford and Gib Akin (2009). *Managing Organizational Change: A Multiple Perspective Approach*. New York: McGraw-Hill Irwin.

PricewaterhouseCoopers (PWC) (2013). "PWC's top health industry issues of 2014," available at: http://www.pwc.com/us/en/health-industries/top-health-industry-issues/index.jhtml (accessed 15 September 2014).

Shea, C.M., R. Malone, M. Weinberger, K.L. Reiter, J. Thornhill, J. Lord, N.G. Nguyen, and B.J. Weiner (2014). "Assessing organizational capacity for achieving meaningful use of electronic health records," *Health Care Management Review*, 39 (2): 124–133.

Stempniak, M. (2014). "Physicians pilot population health effort in Michigan," *Hospitals and Health Networks*, available at http://www.hhnmag.com/display/HHN-news-article. dhtml?dcrPath=/templatedata/HF_Common/NewsArticle/data/HHN/Magazine/2014/Jun /IB-population-health-hospital-partnerships (accessed 20 September, 2014).

Sutherland, K. (2013). "Applying Lewin's Change Management Theory to the implementation of bar-coded medication administration," *Canadian Journal of Nursing Informatics*, 8 (1–2), available at http://cjni.net/journal/?p=2888.

Tushman, Michael L. and Elaine Romanelli (1985). "Organizational evolution: a metamorphosis model of convergence and reorientation," in Larry L. Cummings and Barry M. Staw (eds), *Research in Organizational Behavior*, Greenwich, CT: JAI Press, pp. 171–222.

Watkins, Jane and Bernard Morh (2005). "AI history and timeline," Appreciative Inquiry: Change at the Speed of Imagination, available at http://appreciativeinquiry.cwru.edu/intro/timeline.cfm (accessed 21 September 2014).

Weiner, B.J. (2009). "A theory of organizational readiness for change," *Implementation Science*, 4 (67), DOI:10.1186/1748-5908-4-67, available at http://www.implementation-science.com/content/4/1/67 (accessed 15 September 2014).

Weiner, B.J., H. Amick, and S.D. Lee (2008). "Conceptualization and measurement of organizational readiness for change: a review of the literature in health services research and other fields," *Medical Care Research and Review*, 65 (4): 379–436.

# 13. Innovations in healthcare delivery
## Donna Malvey, Alicia Beardsley, Hannah Nguyen and Myron D. Fottler

## INNOVATION THEORY AND APPLICATION

In the United States, innovation is one of top industry issues facing healthcare executives, and healthcare organizations (HCOs) will need to accelerate the pace of innovation to meet the shifting expectations for value, convenience, and patient engagement. Innovation represents both promise and trepidation. It is how providers, payers, and patients expect to become more efficient. Innovation is also perceived as essential to achieving increased access and enhanced quality at lower costs. Because consumers are increasingly using innovative technologies to communicate with their providers, from e-mails to mobile health applications, they also anticipate further development of healthcare innovations.

But according to an extensive study by PWC Health Research Institute (2014), few healthcare companies in the US are managing innovation for maximum efficiency and breakthrough results. This finding is troublesome, given the fact that public sector dollars are becoming increasingly scarce and there is increased competition from those outside the industry.

Innovation requires different skill sets than those of managing the organization's routine day-to-day activities. Peter Drucker, often referred to as the "Father of Modern Management Science," early on recognized that one of the greatest challenges for any organization is to manage the consequences and implications of a future which has already occurred. According to Drucker, "Knowledge constantly makes itself obsolete; with the result that today's advanced knowledge is tomorrow's ignorance" (Drucker et al., 1997, p. 22). But how do managers anticipate the future?

Some do it by assigning responsibility to a research and development (R&D) staff while others go about creating a culture of innovation that involves everyone in the organization. The Cleveland Clinic in the US fosters an innovative employee culture for all of its employees with the creation of the Cleveland Clinic Innovations (CCI). CCI is the commercialization arm of the Cleveland Clinic. CCI turns the breakthrough inventions of Cleveland Clinic employees into patient-benefiting medical products (Cleveland Clinic, 2014). The Kaiser Permanente Garfield Innovation

Center in California uses mock-up versions of patient rooms, operating suites, and nursing stations so that employees may experiment with and simulate ideas prior to the health system committing a major investment (PWC Health Research Institute, 2014).

Thomas Kuhn theorized about paradigm shifts in the 1960s and 1970s as he explored the phenomena and structure of scientific revolutions. A paradigm shift represents a significant change in the rules and regulations that establish or define organizational boundaries, change suggesting that new behaviors will be required within the redefined boundaries. These shifts occur as the result of an industry coming to terms with a crisis or environmental threats such as new regulations. Industries will accept, albeit temporarily, new viewpoints, approaches, and methods to effectively respond to changes that threaten the status quo. The successful new approach becomes the new paradigm through a paradigm shift and ultimately creates change in the industry (Kuhn, 1970).

Healthcare well reflects what Kuhn described. Healthcare is by its very nature a conservative industry. In general, innovation comes from outside with changes in reimbursement and regulation that motivate health providers and payers to do things differently. For example, in the 1980s in the US, changes in reimbursement from cost-based to resource-based diagnosis related groupings (DRGs) resulted in hospitals and physicians increasingly performing work outside the walls of the hospital in ambulatory settings. From surgery to diagnostics, procedures shifted from in-patient to outpatient and took advantage of clinical innovations that permitted such shifts. More recently, the Affordable Care Act (ACA), which has replaced volume-based with value and experience-based reimbursement incentives in the US, has been driving providers and payers alike toward innovations that reflect these new incentives.

Consequently, today hospitals are working with vendors and government partners to test innovations. Furthermore, hospital executives often are called upon to inform the business community about their innovations because healthcare innovations have come to represent a business case. For example, a Florida Hospital executive named Ashley Simpson was interviewed on *Bloomberg West*, a business cable television show, about how wearable technology can improve hospital efficiency by tracking resources throughout the hospital (Simmons, 2014). In addition, hundreds of innovators across the US are participating in models being tested by the US Center for Medicare & Medicaid Innovation to improve patient care quality and reduce costs (Buell, 2014). Thus the private and public sectors simultaneously have become invested in innovation due to implementation of the ACA.

Clayton Christensen, a professor of business administration at Harvard

Business School and reputedly one of the world's top experts on innovation and growth, has written extensively about innovation, specifically disruptive innovation. Christensen's seminal theory of disruptive innovation was explored in his first book, *The Innovator's Dilemma*. Such innovations may disrupt whole industries because they enable less-skilled employees to perform functions previously performed by more skilled and more expensive specialist employees. The newer disruptive innovations are also performed in settings which are more convenient and less costly. In the *Innovator's Dilemma* (Christensen, 1997), which included the results of a multi-industry study, Christensen explained how successful companies could lose market share to new and unexpected competitors because they missed the new waves of innovation.

Clayton Christensen has also argued that companies place too much emphasis on customers' current or existing needs; instead they should concentrate on adopting new technology or business models to meet customers' future needs, needs that have yet to be articulated (ibid.). Christensen et al. (2008) focused on disruptive innovations in healthcare. *The Innovator's Prescription: A Disruptive Solution for Health Care* examines a number of disruptive innovations, including the emergence of retail medicine and medical clinics that will be discussed later in this chapter.

Innovation must also be viewed from the potential of its ability to spread. Diffusion of innovations is a theory which attempts to explain how, why, and at what rate new ideas and technology are disseminated. The theory was developed in 1962 by Everett M. Rogers, a professor of communication studies, and publicized through his book, *Diffusion of Innovations* (Rogers, 1982). Rogers's theory argues that diffusion is a process by which an innovation is communicated through certain channels over time among the participants in a social system. The innovation must be widely adopted in order to achieve sustainability.

To spread an innovation, Rogers suggested a typology of adopters, which included five adopter categories. Different strategies would then be used to appeal to the different adopter categories when promoting an innovation.

1. Innovators. Those who want to be the first to try an innovation. This group is adventurous, open-minded, and willing to take risks. Consequently, they require little encouragement to try something new and different.
2. Early adopters. This group represents opinion leaders who occupy leadership roles. This group welcomes change and the opportunities presented by change. They do not need convincing to change, but look for information on how to effect and implement the change.

3. Early majority. This group usually does not occupy leadership roles, but they are more comfortable adopting new and different ideas before the average person. This group must have evidence of the innovation's effectiveness before they are willing to adopt it.
4. Late majority. This group is skeptical and uncomfortable with change. They will adopt an innovation only after it has been tried by the majority. This group requires information detailing the numbers of people who have tried the innovation and have adopted it successfully.
5. Laggards. This group is traditional and conservative. They are very skeptical of change and will not be easily convinced to change. They will require statistics on successful adoption, and pressure from other adopter groups that will generate fear among them of being left behind (Rogers, 1982).

## STRATEGIC MEDICAL ENTREPRENEURISM

Increased government regulation and market expectations are calling on US healthcare leaders to transform their organizations. The existing model is being upended after decades of focusing on acute care and encouraging volume. The new model reflects value, reductions in utilization, managing population health, convenience, and consumer engagement. It is anticipated that most HCOs will probably fail to successfully make the transition to new models, because historically most transition efforts have reportedly seen little improvement and some have even resulted in worsened outcomes (Wagner, 2013).

Joel Barker, a well-known futurist, has written extensively on paradigm shifts, including observing the role of industry outsiders in promoting these shifts. Barker has suggested that because those outside the industry are not constrained by entrenched legacy systems and bureaucratic structures that often hamper creativity, they are better able to exploit opportunities (Barker, 1993). This would indicate that HCOs should look to non-traditional players for assistance in creating new models.

In response to obstacles and challenges that precipitate paradigm shifts, large US retailers, such as Walmart, Target, CVS, and Walgreens, have identified an opportunity and engaged in what has been termed "strategic entrepreneurship." Strategic entrepreneurship typically involves a large corporation which devotes part of its resources to exploiting new market opportunities not addressed by current participants in the market (Fottler and Malvey, 2007). These strategic entrepreneurs then develop what has been termed a "disruptive innovation" to address the unmet need and enhance their own financial returns. In the case of these retailers, the disruptive innovation was retail medicine and clinics.

What may be needed to survive in the rapidly changing environment is "strategic medical entrepreneurship," which combines the concepts of strategic management and entrepreneurship for the purpose of exploiting resulting opportunities in healthcare. Entrepreneurship, "the identification and exploitation of previously unexploited opportunities" (Hitt et al., 2001), often "involves bundling resources and deploying them to create new organizational and industry configurations" (Schoonhoven and Romanelli, 2001). Doing so may help to develop sustainable competitive advantage.

HCOs exist in an ever-changing environment in which they must evolve and adapt to meet advancements in the field. Whether innovation is created through disruptions or new ways to approach firmly entrenched legacy systems, the development of new ideas is expected to fuel initiative and risk-taking, both of which have been unfamiliar concepts in a traditionally conservative healthcare industry. In addition, HCOs must adapt an entrepreneurial mindset in order to compete with outsiders who see healthcare as an opportunity for employing mobile and other technologies that are transforming other sectors such as retail and shopping.

## FIVE HEALTHCARE SERVICE DELIVERY MODELS TO WATCH

US hospitals, payers, physicians, and entrepreneurs are responding to the rising demand for healthcare, due in large part to greater access to insurance coverage. They are doing so with innovative service delivery models. While innovation in the healthcare delivery system may be viewed as necessary across the board, its impact on delivering health services has received little systematic scrutiny or study.

Below are five healthcare service delivery models that we believe best reflect the impact of innovation, especially disruptive innovation. Particularly noteworthy are the resulting shifting boundaries of service delivery and practice, the presence of non-traditional players, the emergence of consumer-centric care, the anticipated outcomes of reduced costs coupled with enhanced quality and access to care, and the emergence of digital technology in a key role.

### Model One: mHealth

mHealth, which stands for mobile health, is defined as the use of mobile technologies to capture, store, and communicate health information.

mHealth is also recognized as having the potential to transform healthcare. The industry segments expected to benefit most are primary and chronic care, which have significant potential for patients to be more engaged in their own care (Malvey and Slovensky, 2014).

In 2011, then US Secretary of Health and Human Services Kathleen Sebelius referred to mHealth as "the biggest technology breakthrough of our time" (Sebelius, 2011). mHealth has been characterized as a disruptive innovation, displacing prior ways of doing things at much lower costs. There have been and continue to be high expectations for ways in which mHealth can transform healthcare, but few have yet proved functional and sustainable. As it happens, the technology is the easy part of mHealth, and the technology is only as good as the system it is connected to (Rosenberg, 2013).

Mobile technology generally, and the smartphone particularly, has led to the development of an "app culture" among large segments of the world's population, many of whom are eager to use this familiar tool to manage and improve their health. Unfortunately, however, there is insufficient actionable information to inform strategic development, deployment, and use of mHealth in a sustainable productive life cycle. Moreover, the drivers for both using and expanding the use of mHealth as a viable mode of healthcare delivery are yet to be fully recognized. The barriers and limitations that exist in a fragmented, highly competitive healthcare marketplace remain obstacles to successful implementation.

There are some widely recognized healthcare apps with large markets such Blue Button, used by the Veterans Health Administration (VHA) in the US. Blue Button is believed to be driving a patient-centered revolution in VHA healthcare because it offers the consumer the ability to download their personal health data and take control of their own health and healthcare decisions (Downs, 2011). With more than 6 million downloads, iTriage, a product offered by Aetna, one of the US largest health insurers, is one of the most consistently popular health apps in Apple's iPhone App Store. iTriage allows the consumer to do research on a variety of health conditions, find local practitioners, and learn more about their medications (Hempel, 2013). But there are also niche market and social media apps such as PatientsLikeMe where patients, caregivers, and others can join a community of people to both gain and share information about particular diseases (Bradley, 2013).

Smartphones are moving towards clinical applications, and research labs worldwide are focusing on turning smartphones into point-of-care devices. Some patents indicate that smartphones will increasingly be used as diagnostic tools. Apple has reportedly applied for patents to integrate a sensor with the iPhone that detects a user's cardiac activity and a hover, rather than the touch screen, to enable reading electrocardiograms (EKGs) (Schwartz, 2014).

Some suggest that innovation is the primary mechanism for reducing costs, but the power of innovation goes well beyond achieving operational efficiencies. mHealth has the potential to revise the boundaries of health-care in terms of time, space, and who is providing care. As a result, visits to physician offices may become a thing of the past, and care traditionally provided in a hospital may take place outside of the bricks-and-mortar building. What emerges is healthcare that is continuous and asynchro-nous; delivered anywhere and at any time. Healthcare is no longer viewed as "local;" instead, boundaries are disappearing as providers and patients are no longer required to be in the same physical space. Mobile technolo-gies promise opportunities to better understand patients' real-world needs (Shaywitz, 2013). Entrepreneurs and innovators are looking for opportu-nities to help contribute to and create a digital healthcare continuum.

While mHealth is recognized as a disruptive innovation, one that prom-ises to provide needed healthcare access at lower cost than face-to-face encounters, many expected benefits have yet to be realized. Among the remaining challenges to achieving more of the potential for improved access and lower cost in healthcare are information privacy and security concerns, inability to vet applications and assure efficacy, uncertainty in product regulation, adequate business models for product development, and third-party payment for provider services delivered using mHealth (Malvey and Slovenksy, 2014).

**Model Two: Telemedicine**

The American Telemedicine Association (ATA) defines telemedicine as "the use of medical information exchanged from one site to another via electronic communications to improve a patient's clinical health status. Telemedicine includes a growing variety of applications and services using two-way video, email, smartphones, wireless tools and other forms of telecommunications technology" (ATA, n.d.).

At its inception 40 years ago, telemedicine principally focused on provid-ing diagnostic and health monitoring services to patients living in remote or rural areas. Early telemedicine programs were predominantly hospital-based, and telemedicine effectively expanded the market area served and increased referrals to the sponsoring hospital. The most widely used data transmission technology at that time was hard-wired telephone lines, with some opportunities for video interfaces. For patients, the greatest benefits of early telemedicine programs were reduced travel time and costs, and access to specialist consultation services not available locally. Technology innovations supporting high-speed communications and more robust computer processing coupled with reform initiatives have enabled the migration of telemedicine over the past decade to a mainstream healthcare delivery mode supporting a broader array of healthcare services and benefits for both providers and individuals (Galewitz, 2012; Brown, 2013).

The healthcare industry in the past operated very much in a medical model of "sick care," a concept used to describe information transmitted for diagnosis or treatment of specific conditions. As our medical model has grown more inclusive of managing health as well as managing disease treatment, the term "telehealth" has emerged and the terms are used interchangeably, just as we use "medicine" and "health" in our daily language. The distinction is not precise; both refer in general to using telecommunication devices to transmit information related to healthcare.

According to the ATA, growth in telemedicine has occurred because of four main drivers: access to needed services, cost savings, improved quality, and patient interest. A forthcoming driver, changes in reimbursement practices associated with the Affordable Care Act (ACA), may impel the implementation of applications to a level more closely aligned with what can and should be done via remote healthcare, than what HCOs have been financially motivated to do in past years.

From the beginning, telemedicine has promoted the ability to bring healthcare services to patients in distant locations. Not only does telemedicine improve access for patients, but it also allows physicians and health facilities to expand their reach, beyond their own offices. Given the provider shortages throughout the world – in both rural and urban areas – telemedicine has a unique capacity to increase access to millions of new patients.

More recently, telemedicine is also especially critical in reducing readmissions, to both hospitals and emergency departments. Dramatic decreases in hospital readmissions (75 percent) have been seen in a two-year pilot program in the US conducted with Indianapolis-based St Vincent Health, using remote video-conferencing between nurses and discharged patients. Johns Hopkins is using remote patient training and education, including on-demand videos, streamed to patients' hand-held devices that answer patients' questions about post-operative care (Slabodkin, 2012).

Impediments to implementation include Health Insurance Portability and Accountability Act (HIPAA) security issues, reimbursement, and physician liability for telehealth-enabled care (Manhattan Research, 2011). Some of the barriers to telemedicine have absolutely nothing to do with technology. The single biggest impediment to the development of telemedicine is reimbursement. Prior to healthcare reform, there was little financial incentive for US providers to develop telemedicine beyond its basic remote monitoring programs unless it served a specific organization strategic goal. Newly implemented readmission penalties for US providers serving Medicare and Medicaid patients are expected to drive hospitals to develop telehealth programs that monitor and manage post-discharge treatment to prevent unplanned readmissions. And, as healthcare delivery is distributed more fully along the continuum of providers and facilities, these applications will diffuse more broadly as well (Malvey and Slovensky, 2014).

The aging of the population accompanied by chronic illness is increasing. Caring for these patients will be costly unless technology enables new channels for delivering telehealth services. The Internet, computer tablets, smartphones, remote monitoring, wireless applications and devices, including wearable devices such as a wristwatch or a small bandage that can help monitor patients continuously (Brown, 2013), all contribute to the phenomenal technological capability in the telehealth infrastructure.

The growth curve for telemedicine services has accelerated rapidly in the past few years due in large part to technological advances, more applications, and the emergence of wireless connectivity. In particular, consumer familiarity and acceptance of technology is an important part of telemedicine's accelerated progress. Reportedly, 6 billion people on the planet have access to cellphones (Brown, 2013), which creates a world marketplace beyond our imaginings.

Is telemedicine sustainable? Thus far the biggest use of telemedicine in the US has been by the military and the Veterans Administration (VA). A key reason for this fact is that the VA is a single payer system with the infrastructure to facilitate technology diffusion. Although the number of people who would use telehealth if it were it offered to them is unknown, currently not enough people are using it for primary care (Baum, 2012). While HCOs now are capable of delivering telehealth services anywhere, they are not doing so in large volume because they have not figured out how to pay for it through insurance, and they have not produced new business models to support development (Brown, 2013).

Most healthcare experts agree on telemedicine's potential for improving patient access and reducing labor costs, especially in rural and remote areas where there are physician shortages, particularly specialists (Cannon, 2012). The preponderance of research has shown telemedicine programs to be both cost-effective and of good quality. And patient acceptance of programs has been consistently good, due in large part to the convenience factor and the improved access to specialty services in remote or rural areas. Whether telemedicine programs that are deemed successful locally can translate effectively and profitably to a larger national or even international scale has yet to be proven (Malvey and Slovensky, 2014).

**Model Three: Retail Medicine and Clinics**

In 2006, Malvey and Fottler (2006) suggested that a retail revolution was occurring in healthcare. That is, healthcare services were being conceptualized as retail products, sold directly to the consumer. In addition, they observed that in the US large retail chains such as Walmart and Target, also known as "big box retailers," along with large pharmacy chains such as Walgreens and CVS, were moving into the business of healthcare by offering a variety of less expensive, simple, acute care services as well as some preventive services in their stores. These services were typically provided by nurse practitioners and included immunizations, check-ups, and diagnostics and treatment for simple ailments such as colds, bronchitis, and earaches. Furthermore, Malvey and Fottler (2006) speculated about who would be the winners and losers with respect to this new business model, with the winners being those who looked for ways to make use of the new delivery model rather than opposing or ignoring it.

Christensen et al. (2008) later further discussed the emergence of this retail model as a disruptive innovation. Retail medical clinics located inside big box retailers emerged in 2000 with MinuteClinics appearing in Target stores. They also appeared in large grocery chain stores across the US. During the past 15 years, retail medical clinics have adopted a variety of models. Walmart employed contract or lease arrangements and later partnered with health systems to help substantiate the brand. Walgreen and CVS created internal ventures that developed their unique brand of in-store offerings (Fottler and Malvey, 2010).

While retailers experimented with business models, researchers reported on the growth and use of retail clinics. Rand researchers have discussed the popularity of retail clinics in the US; they have grown substantially over the last decade. By 2010 they numbered close to 1200. While visits to retail clinics comprise a small percentage of overall outpatient visits, they quadrupled from 2007 to 2009. Americans made almost 6 million visits to retail clinics in 2009 alone. This rapid growth reflects that these clinics are meeting patient needs for convenience, affordability, and price transparency as most clinics post their charges on a menu-type board. More than 44 percent of retail clinic visits take place when physician offices are closed. Although young adults (18–44) were found to comprise 43 percent of clinic visits, use by seniors is growing, from 7.5 percent in 2000–2006 to 14.7 in 2007–2009 (Rand Health, 2012).

In anticipation of physician shortages and access requirements of the newly insured, due in large part to passage of the ACA, US retailers are in growth mode, expanding not only the number of clinics, but also the types of services offered, such as the trend toward offering chronic and preventive care. CVS, one of the largest pharmacy retailers, has a total of 800 MinuteClinics clinics nationwide and expected to add 150 more in 2014, reaching 1500 clinics by 2017; or almost as many as the more than 1600 retail clinics currently in operation throughout the US. CVS's fast expansion of its clinics reflects an overall growth trend in the industry (Hamilton, 2014).

Meanwhile, Walgreens disclosed that its expansion of chronic and preventive services in 2013 is helping to drive more return visits from patients. The results of its research study demonstrated that its patients are relying more on nurse practitioners at retail clinics to provide chronic and preventive health services. The study also revealed marked increases in the number of patients who are making return visits to clinics. Furthermore, the Walgreens study found the percentage of visits to healthcare clinic locations for preventive services, screening, and chronic visit utilization (combined) increased from 4 percent in 2007 to 17 percent in 2013. The study also found the annual percentage of return patient visits to healthcare clinic climbed from 15 percent in 2007, to more than 50 percent in both 2012 and 2013 (Walgreens Newsroom, 2014).

Walmart, with over 100 retail clinics across its stores, signaled its move into the delivery of primary care services by opening six primary clinics across South Carolina and Texas, with plans to launch six additional clinics before January 2015. The clinics will be staffed by nurse practitioners, in a partnership with QuadMed. What is new about these clinics is that unlike the retail clinics that Walmart hosts through leases with local health systems and hospitals, which have achieved mixed success, the new clinics are fully owned by Walmart and branded explicitly as one-stop shops for primary care. In addition the clinics will have extended hours, open longer and later than competitors: 12 hours per day during the week and eight hours per day on the weekend. Walk-in visits are expected to cost about $40 for the public, with Walmart employees and their dependents receiving discounts: their visits will cost $4 (Diamond, 2014).

ACA may have solved the access to healthcare challenge by giving everyone an insurance card, but an insurance card does not guarantee that a patient will be able to see a doctor. This is especially true in rural areas where the shortage of primary care doctors is particularly severe. Because Walmart has a vast rural network of stores, the introduction of these new primary care clinics may help those who are struggling to get the healthcare they need (Lorenzetti, 2014)

Mobile applications and virtual or online "e-visits" are also trending for retailers that seek to merge technology with convenience and create a new access point for care. CVS is looking to increase access via such technology as telehealth, in addition to expanding its geographic footprint and non-acute services. MinuteClinics is testing telehealth at 28 sites in Los Angeles, San Diego, and Orange County, California where nurse practitioners are providing patient care remotely through sophisticated video technology and audio equipment, with licensed vocational nurses assisting patients (Alexander, 2014).

Kiosks that allow for virtual healthcare check-ups are also being tested. HealthSpot, a Dublin, Ohio-based technology firm, has created HealthSpot Station kiosks that come equipped with a touchscreen monitor, audio system, and high-definition television screens that allow patients to conduct a virtual visit with a physician. Among those testing the kiosks are Cleveland Clinic in its Express Care urgent care clinics (DesJardins, 2013). Walmart is offering self-service kiosk check-ups, too, using SoloHealth, an interactive kiosk that can check blood pressure and weight, and track eating habits (Hutchings, 2013).

**Model Four: Concierge Medicine**

Concierge medicine is an innovation in service delivery for primary care. Also known as "boutique," "personalized," or "private physician" practices, concierge care includes a multitude of structural forms and ranges from in-office visits to telehealth services. Concierge medicine has become increasingly attractive to patients who are tired of long waiting times for appointments and the brevity of office visits. Recent reforms in healthcare and expected shortages of physicians are likely precipitating the growth of concierge medicine in the US. There has been a steady but fairly rapid growth rate of concierge medical practices. Approximately 4400 private physicians participated in 2012, a 25 percent increase over the previous year; and over 1.5 million Americans have become participants, averaging about 350 patients per concierge physician. Concierge medicine has traditionally been regarded as highly personalized services reserved for patients that are willing to pay above the normal price of regular care (Fottler and Malvey, 2010; O'Brien, 2013).

What distinguishes concierge care from other forms of healthcare delivery is its guaranteed 24/7 access to a physician, same-day appointment, and longer face-time with physicians, in exchange for an up-front premium. O'Brien (2013) reports that these premiums average annual fees of $1800. Although the price may seem high, consumers are willing to pay additional costs for the improved service that concierge medicine offers.

While patients appreciate the 24/7 access to care, providers enjoy being able to set their own prices and to determine which services are included in those prices. This allows the provider to focus on quality of care rather than volume. Providers are also able to bypass the application process of becoming "in-network" with an insurance company, which could take upwards of 3–6 months; therefore reimbursement is prompt and consistent. Eliminating insurance billing cuts 40 percent of the practices' overhead expenses, enabling them to keep fees low (Wieczner, 2013). With the stress of billing and worry of "when (and will) I get reimbursed" from insurance out of the picture, providers are able to provide a more positive environment and service to their patients (Leonard, 2012).

Another revolutionary aspect of concierge medicine is the more recent integration of telehealth. Previously, concierge medicine meant that patients had 24/7 access to their primary care physicians. However, through the use of telehealth, patients do not even have to wait for the doctor to be physically present. Instead, the connection is created through a live interactive video service, to consult and diagnose routine medical ailments (PR Newswire, 2014).

With the emergence of partnerships of telehealth and concierge medicine, there is the potential for significant diffusion of the innovation. For example, a smartphone app for doctors, Ringadoc Phone Concierge, a virtual consultation service, provides patients with a quick and easy way to connect with their existing physicians, in exchange for a convenience fee, outside of their insurance coverage (CMTDPC Journal, 2014). The way this app works asks nothing extra of the consumer in the way of activities. Instead, consumers call their primary care physician's office, as normal. The voicemail is immediately transferred to the physician's mobile app and allows the physician to create a direct connection to the patient. This on-demand consultation also allows patients the ability to monitor their symptoms, renew prescriptions, and get referrals to specialists (CMTDPC Journal, 2014). Within a year, this innovative app has reached over 1000 healthcare providers and 1.5 million patients in the US. As concierge medicine and telehealth continue to merge, it is very likely that consumers will see an increase of mobile apps such as Ringadoc.

Concierge medicine may also be a win–win for both the patient and the provider. Patients who decide to use concierge medicine may experience a more personal healthcare experience and easier access to care, as providers offer a closed practice allowing for a limited patient pool.

**Model Five: Innovations in the Emergency Department (ED)**

Are medical entrepreneurs re-inventing the emergency room experience in the US? Some would say yes, and point to the fact that they are putting emergency rooms outside of the hospital, in some cases locating them in a strip mall. Overcrowded EDs have long been a focus of concern due to their influence on rising healthcare expenditures. Even though the ACA emphasizes primary care and offers insurance to the uninsured so that they may establish a routine source of care other than the ED, recent evidence shows and predicts that consumers, especially the formerly uninsured, will continue to use the ED as a source of routine care.

For example, a study led by University of Colorado researchers found that healthcare reform in the United States will lead to an increase in newly insured adults. The study predicted an associated surge in visits to already crowded EDs (Matich, 2012). A 2014 study published in the journal *Science* found that increases in Medicaid coverage led to increases in emergency department use overall. The study looked at Oregon, and this was for a broad range of types of visits and conditions, including those that could be appropriately treated in primary care settings (Rovner, 2014). Consequently, consumers seeking emergency care are exploring alternatives such as free-standing EDs.

Free-standing EDs, also known as free-standing emergency rooms or centers, are walk-in medical facilities that are structurally separate and distinct from the hospital ED that furnishes emergency care to the public at large. Free-standing EDs, as with hospital EDs, are open 24 hours a day, 365 days per year, and are fully equipped to diagnose and stabilize cardiac arrest, breathing difficulties, trauma, and stroke. Free-standing EDs tend to have lower patient acuity. The length of stay ranges from 60–90 minutes in the free-standing ED compared with three hours and longer in hospital EDs. And patients needing higher-acuity care will be transferred to appropriate facilities. Free-standing EDs can be found in about 16 US states, and are typically operated by hospitals, physicians, and non-physician entrepreneurs (Ayers, 2012).

Free-standing EDs are mostly for-profit and thus are primarily chasing profits, even if they also are offering excellent care. Furthermore, the facilities tend to be located in high-income communities with well-insured patients who want convenience. They are not located in the poorer communities or rural areas, or in places with higher populations of uninsured. In addition, some payers have complained that they are more expensive, and include additional facility fees (Feibel, 2013). A backlash has emerged over free-standing EDs charging, or attempting to charge, a facility fee as a hospital ED would. Facility fees are charges that hospitals collect from insurers for operating EDs, and cover the cost of running the departments. Some insurers have sued free-standing emergency departments over their use of the facility fee, which can run to about $1500 per patient (Ter Mat, 2013).

With regard to legal implications, specifically US federal and state laws, the Emergency Medical Treatment and Active Labor Act (EMTALA) requires hospitals participating in government health programs such as

Medicaid and Medicare to provide emergency medical treatment to any patient, regardless of ability to pay. A free-standing ED that is affiliated with a hospital and accepts Medicare and/or Medicaid is generally subject to EMTALA. Meanwhile, an independently owned ED may not be. In addition, many state laws restrict or prohibit free-standing EDs, or require licensure that contains provisions requiring evaluation of all patients for an emergency condition even if the facility chooses not to bill Medicare or Medicaid (Ayers, 2012).

## ASSESSMENT

Table 13.1 summarizes the six innovations we have chosen to describe in this chapter. Of the six, the two most promising in terms of short- and intermediate-term sustainability and growth are telemedicine and retail health. Both are cost-reducing innovations which also provide good or excellent patient access and quality of care. Mobile health faces many challenges or barriers to clear. Lack of a sustainable business model, privacy concerns, and regulatory uncertainty may be addressed over time. However, until they are addressed, mobile health will be utilized primarily as an enhancement to both retail health and telemedicine.

Concierge medicine has potential to expand beyond the small number of patients enrolled in such plans. For higher-income populations, it offers a high-quality, accessible, sustainable model due to high levels of consumer acceptance. However, the higher out-of-pocket costs associated with such plans limit their future growth potential. Free-standing EDs are similarly limited to locations close to high-income populations, and due to an uncertain regulatory environment do not seem to offer a high level of sustainability or growth at this time.

## CONCLUSIONS, FUTURE EXPECTATIONS, AND MANAGERIAL IMPLICATIONS

Technology alone cannot transform the healthcare delivery system nor can it be expected to effectively change health behaviors on its own. But technological innovations can shake up the industry and change the way consumers, providers, and payers interact; from requesting appointments, to receiving diagnoses, to reducing costs and enhancing quality.

With much of healthcare innovation being driven by the consumer, healthcare is focusing its advancements on not only products and services that will provide cost-effective treatment, but convenience. Healthcare has

Table 13.1   Expected impact of mobile health, telemedicine, concierge medicine, retail healthcare, and free-standing emergency department innovations on various evaluation criteria

| Evaluation criteria | Mobile health | Telemedicine | Concierge medicine | Retail healthcare | Free-standing ED |
|---|---|---|---|---|---|
| Quality of care | Uncertain | Good | Excellent | Good | Good |
| Access to services | Excellent | Excellent | Excellent | Excellent | Excellent where utilized |
| Cost vs alternatives | Lower | Lower | Higher | Lower | Higher |
| Consumer affordability | Higher | Higher | Lower | Higher | Higher |
| Value to consumer | Excellent | Good | Varies | Good | Lower |
| Third-party reimbursement | Varies | Varies | Low | Varies | Good |
| Sustainability, greater potential | High | High | High in small numbers | High | Uncertain |
| Challenges, barriers | Privacy concerns, regulations concerning lack of business models | Data security, reimbursement, MD liability | Cost and reimbursement | Some restrictive state regulations, variable reimbursement | State laws, higher cost, limited liability |
| Consumer acceptance | High | Good | Excellent | Good and growing | Uncertain |

become a retail industry in the US, and it is no longer only about what the consumer wants but more about where they can get it. With the patient's expectation of an "anywhere, anytime" healthcare system we are noticing a rise in development of urgent care clinics, retail clinics, and free-standing EDs, and in the near future US patients will be seeing more of these types of convenient healthcare sites (Ayers, 2012).

The future of a cost-effective, patient-centered healthcare delivery system is becoming a reality rather than just discussion as current medical knowledge is being integrated with digital innovations. Healthcare innovation is increasingly becoming about discovering the opportunities of joint projects or new partnerships with technology companies, and these companies and start-ups are more than prepared for the healthcare industry. With a new cloud-based infrastructure, providers are finding the adoption of virtual health technologies less challenging. Having a simple, user-friendly infrastructure, organizations are in a better position to sustain their innovation processes (Banerjee et al., 2014).

Market factors such as the availability of inexpensive technology, partnership opportunities across industry segments, and the growing interest of investors in digital health technologies create a supportive environment for advancement of mHealth products. Ultimately, the success of mHealth will depend on sustainability, which can be defined in terms of acceptance and use by the consumer and also in terms of reducing healthcare costs and achieving improved health outcomes (Malvey and Slovensky, 2014).

Technology appears at the core of much of the disruptive innovation that is fundamentally changing the healthcare industry (Plesk, 2014). Even more disruptive to healthcare is the introduction of robotics in the delivery system. A growing number of hospitals are using robots that automate simple operational tasks or provide new ways for physicians to interact with patients beyond the bedside. Robots are considered as machinery with varying types and degrees of robotic automation. Providers report that the robots can help reduce costs, make operations more efficient, and serve as a marketing tool to position hospitals as early adopters of cutting-edge technology. GE Global Research is working with the Veterans Affairs Department in the US to develop an intelligent system that will sort, sterilize and track surgical tools. The system is expected to be tested at a VA hospital in 2015 (Lee, 2013).

Innovations such as robotics along with telemedicine are addressing healthcare costs, patient expectations, and the physician shortage. Having telemedicine integrated into a practice or organization allows a physician or practitioner to be accessible to their patients regardless of their geographical location. Challenges facing telemedicine largely lie in lack of reimbursement from third-party payers, but concierge medicine is showing that patients may be willing to pay more out of pocket if it is more convenient and accessible, and virtual healthcare provides patients with both.

MedAvail, a company based out of Canada that was formed in 2012, is an innovation company working with US retail pharmacies to deliver Pharmacy Kiosks to patients; a full 24/7 kiosk for patients to have immediate access to their prescriptions, even if their pharmacy is closed (www. MedAvaill.com). Although pharmacy kiosks such as those produced by MedAvail are still in their infancy and the company is working to perfect the system and overcome challenges, it is just another innovation that patients can expect from healthcare in the near future.

The greatest challenge emerging for healthcare in many instances is "big data" and the ability to store, process, and analyze the data being received. But innovation is not just limited to the computer or "cloud" and big data; it is also taking on the challenge of preventative medicine in hopes to build a healthier population. One company taking on this challenge is First Warning Systems which has developed a bra that detects breast cancer, using sensors that detect unusual heat patterns in breast tissue to identify abnormalities before they become a problem (Compton, 2012). Looking forward, healthcare is headed towards a preventative delivery system where patients, healthy or not, will be utilizing wearable technology such as the First Warning Systems cancer detection bra.

Sustainability in the innovation process has proven challenging in the healthcare industry. Still young in its discipline and its quality improvement initiatives, the healthcare industry can ensure success in sustaining its innovation process by building sustainability into the implementation process rather than addressing sustainability after implementation (Minnier, 2014).

## THE FUTURE

Nanotechnology is anticipated to be the next big thing in healthcare innovation as biomedical engineers are looking at nanomedicine for the diagnosis, treatment, and prevention of diseases and traumatic injuries (Patil et al., 2008). Researchers and scientists are using nanotechnology to improve the knowledge of the human body, and in 2001 the US Food and Drug Administration (FDA) approved the PillCam. Created by Given Imaging, the PillCam is a capsule no bigger than a large pill that contains a small light and camera and is used primarily with patients suspected of or already diagnosed with Crohn's Disease in order to look at their small intestine (Globe Newswire, 2013). And in 2014, Given Imaging had its second nanodevice approved by the FDA; this mini camera is intended for colonoscopies and colon cancer patients (Seppala, 2014).

Aside from diagnostics, nanotechnology offers the ability to deliver drug and therapeutic treatments to patients on a more efficient and effective level. For example, researchers are interested in the ability of nanotechnology to deliver treatment to cancer patients. The use of nanotechnology would allow treatment to be delivered specifically to cancer cells without the destruction of the surrounding healthy tissue (FutureMedica, 2010).

In order for innovation of new technologies to be accepted into practice, they have to be proven to contribute to the bottom line, and therefore must be measured. Once reserved only for large organizations, data analysis is finding a place in healthcare and all of its various counterparts, including insurance companies and pharmaceuticals, due to the focus on quality of care. And despite the positive intentions and implementations of new advancements thus far, the high influx of information being recorded with no clear, established way to collect, analyze, and report has made data analysis challenging, and therefore the innovation counterproductive.

Data analytics is also heralded as a pivotal skill set for managers. The goal of data analytics is ultimately to measure the efficiency and effectiveness of practices and new technologies, and reduce readmissions. Providers now have access to information being transmitted from a patient to the doctor or hospital, thereby allowing access to their health status almost immediately. This information is expected to lead to preventative and proactive health strategies. However, the difficulty surrounding data analysis is the resources. Providers are not quite sure what to do with the information they are receiving, and even if they did know, the cost is prohibitive enough to deter them from adopting these care models (McNeill and Davenport, 2014). However, as healthcare innovation continues to evolve, healthcare managers will need to do the same. Future leaders will need to be leaders, to think independently and understand the market, and have the desire and ability to be customer-centered. They must also be prepared to act as the change agent and lead their organization forward.

However, what is missing from the discussion is how the US healthcare system can be reformed through innovation and its ability to provide a structure of healthcare delivery to patients, and the crucial role of value-based competition in driving improvements in clinical quality, service quality, safety, and cost-containment. Competition based on documented results and outcomes widely disseminated through the industry will improve diagnosis, treatment, prevention, and management of specific medical conditions (Porter and Tiesberg, 2006).

Future reform efforts will need to focus on providing all stakeholders with the right information and the right incentives. The Patient Protection and Affordable Care Act represents one small and very flawed step towards universal healthcare in the US. It provides very little more than health insurance expansion, with almost no true health reform. The next step will be more difficult because it will require the major stakeholders to negotiate rules and regulations which will enhance quality, cost containment, and innovation.

# REFERENCES

Alexander, A. (2014). "CVS Caremark's MinuteClinic testing telehealth at 28 sites," available at http://www.drugstorenews.com/article/cvs-caremarks-minuteclinic-testing-telehealth-28-sites (accessed 19 February 2014).

American Telemedicine Association (ATA) (n.d.). Website, available at http://www.amer icantelemed.org/learn (accessed 6 July 2013).

Ayers, A. (2012). "Emerging business models: Freestanding Emergency Rooms," available at http://www.alanayersurgentcare.com/Linked_Files/UCAOA_Freestanding_ER_2011_12_20.pdf (accessed 1 March 2012).

Banerjee, S., Chanmugam, R., and Samtani, M. (2014). "An app a day: Enabling the digital doctor," *Accenture*, 1 (1): 2–6.

Barker, Joel. (1993). *Paradigms: The Business of Discovering the Future*. New York: Harper Business/Harper Collins Publishers.

Baum, S. (2012). "Why a cardiologist started a telemedicine business at Walmart," available at http://medcitynews.com/2012/06/why-a-cardiologist-started-a-telemedicine-business-at-walmart/ (accessed 2 March 2014).

Bradley, R. (2013). "Social media comes to healthcare," *Fortune Magazine*, 6: 52, 54.

Brown, E.M. (2013). "The year ahead for the ATA and telemedicine," *mHealthNews*, available at http://www.mhealthnews.com/blog/year-ahead-ata-and-telemedicine (accessed 4 March 2014).

Buell, J.M. (2014). "Innovation in healthcare: It is possible, and it is happening," *Healthcare Executive*, 29 (3): 32–40.

Cannon, A. (2012). "Another fork in the road for Walmart," *ConvUrgentCare Report*, 5 (8): 1–5.

Christensen, Clayton (1997). *The Innovator's Dilemma*. Cambridge, MA: Harvard Business Review Press.

Christensen, Clayton, Grossman, Jerome H., and Hwang, Jason (2008). *The Innovator's Prescription: A Disruptive Solution for Health Care*. New York: McGraw-Hill.

Cleveland Clinic (2014). "Innovations," available at http://innovations.clevelandclinic.org/About-Us/Innovations-Team.aspx (accessed 17 August 2014).

CMTDPC Journal (2014). "Ringadoc, a $69 medical answering service software for doctor physician," *Concierge Medicine News*, 27 February, 1–2.

Compton, A. (2012). "Bra detects breast cancer: First Warning Systems Bra uses sensors to detect tumors," available at http://www.huffingtonpost.com/2012/10/16/bra-detects-breast-cancer-lifeline_n_1970096.html (accessed 7 November 2013).

Desjardins, D. (2013). "Telemedicine is retail health clinics' newest tool," available at http://www.healthleadersmedia.com/page-2/COM-291947/Telemedicine-is-Retail-Health-Clinics-Newest-Tool## (accessed 19 February 2014).

Diamond, D. (2014). "Healthcare for $4: Are you ready for Walmart to be your doctor?" available at http://www.forbes.com/sites/dandiamond/2014/08/08/health-care-for-4-walmart-unveils-new-primary-care-clinics/ (accessed 11 August 2014).

Downs, S.J. (2011). "Blue button: driving a patient-centered revolution in health care," *Huffington Post*, available at http://www.huffintongpost.com/stephen-j-downs/blue-buttondriving-a-pat_b_958789.html (accessed 7 March 2014).

Drucker, P.F., Dyson, E., Handy, C., Saffo, P., and Senge, P.M. (1997). "Looking ahead: Implications of the present," *Harvard Business Review*, 75 (5): 18–32.

Feibel, C. (2013). "Patients can pay a high price for ER convenience," available at http://

www.npr.org/blogs/health/2013/08/15/211411828/patients-can-pay-a-high-price-for-er-con venience (accessed 5 September 2013).

Fottler, M.D. and Malvey, D. (2007). "Strategic entrepreneurship in the health care industry: The case of Wal-Mart," in J.D. Blair and M.D. Fottler (eds), *Strategic Thinking and Entrepreneurial Action in Health Care.* Amsterdam: Elsevier/JAI Press: pp. 257–278.

Fottler, Myron D. and Malvey, D. (2010). *The Retail Revolution in Healthcare.* Santa Barbara, CA: Praeger.

FutureMedica (2010). Blog: "25 ways nanotechnology is revolutionizing medicine," 19 January, available at http://mritechnicianschools.net/2010/25-ways-nanotechnology-is-revolutionalizing-medicine/ (accessed 28 April 2015).

Galewitz, P. (2012). "Virtual doctors' visits catch on with insurers, employers," USAToday. com, available at http://www.usatoday.com/money/industries/health/sorty/2012-04-427/ virtual (accessed 8 March 2014).

Hamilton, M. (2014). "Why walk-in healthcare is a fast-growing profit center for retail chains," available at http://www.washingtonpost.com/business/why-walk-in-health-care-is-a-fast-growing-profit-center-for-retail-chains/2014/04/04/a05f7cf4-b9c2-11e3-96ae-f2c36d2b1245_story.html (accessed 17 July 2014).

Hempel, J. (2013). "Social media comes to healthcare," *Fortune,* 6: 52, 54.

Hitt, M.A., Ireland, R.D., Camp, S.M., and Sexton, D.L. (2001). "Strategic entrepreneurship: Entrepreneurship strategies for wealth creation," *Strategic Management Journal,* 22: 479–491.

Hutchings, E. (2013). "Walmart offers self-service health check-up kiosks," available at http://www.psfk.com/2013/02/walmart-doctor-check-ups.html#!bKHcZX (accessed 26 August 2014).

Kuhn, Thomas S. (1970). *The Structure of Scientific Revolutions,* 2nd edn. Chicago, IL: University of Chicago Press.

Lee, J. (2013). "Robots get to work," available at http://www.modernhealthcare.com/ article/20130525/MAGAZINE/305259957 (accessed 7 January 2013).

Leonard, D. (2012). "Is concierge medicine the future of health care?," Businessweek.com, available at http://www.businessweek.com/articles/2012-11-29/is-concierge-medicine-the-future-of-health-care (accessed 1 April 2014).

Lorenzetti, L. (2014). "Can Walmart solve the US healthcare-access crisis?," available at http:// fortune.com/2014/08/08/can-walmart-solve-the-u-s-healthcare-access-crisis/ (accessed 11 August 2014).

Malvey, D. and Fottler, M.D. (2006). "The retail revolution in healthcare: Who will win and who will lose?" *Health Care Management Review,* 31 (3): 168–178.

Malvey, Donna and Slovensky, Donna J. (2014). *mHealth: Transforming Healthcare.* New York, Heidelberg, Dordrecht, and London, Springer.

Manhattan Research (2011). "Taking the Pulse – Press Release," available at http:// www. fiercemobilehealthcare.com/press-releases/seven-percent-us-physicians-use-video-chat-co mmunicate-patients-1 (accessed 5 May 2014).

Matich, E. (2012). "Changes in health insurance status linked to greater emergency department use," available at http://www.ucdenver.edu/about/newsroom/newsreleases/Pages/ insurance-changes-emergency-room-use.aspx (accessed 18 August 2014).

McNeill, D. and Davenport, T. (2014). *Analytics in Healthcare and the Life Sciences: Strategies, Implementation Methods, and Best Practices.* Upper Saddle River, NJ: Pearson.

Minnier, T. (2014). *How To Build Sustainability Into the Innovation Process | AHRQ Innovations Exchange.* Innovations.ahrq.gov, available at http://www.innovations.ahrq. gov/content.aspx?id=4157 (accessed 1 March 2014).

O'Brien, E. (2013). "Why concierge medicine will get bigger," Market Watch, 17 January, available at http://www.marketwatch.com/story/why-concierge-medicine-will-get-bigger-2013-01-17 (accessed 28 April 2015).

Patil, M., Mehta, D.S., and Guvva, S. (2008). "Future impact of nanotechnology on medicine and dentistry," 12 (2): 34–40, available at http://www.ncbi.nlm.nih.gov/pmc/articles/ PMC2813556/. DOI: 10.4103/0972-124X.44088.

Plesk, P. (2014). "Harnessing disruptive innovation in health care," *AHRQ Innovations Exchange*, available at http://www.innovations.ahrq.gov/content.aspx?id=4153 (accessed 12 March 2014).

Porter, M. and Teisberg, E.O. (2006). *Redefining Healthcare: Creating Value-Based Competition and Results*. Boston, MA: Harvard Business School Press.

PR Newswire (2014). "What are telehealth services? Let a concierge medicine expert tell you," Los Angeles.

PWC Health Research Institute (2014). "Top health industry issues of 2014," available at http://www.pwc.com/us/en/health-industries/top-health-industry-issues/index.jhtml (Accessed 23 January 2014).

Rand Health (2012). "Special feature: Retail clinics play growing role in healthcare," available at http://www.rand.org/health/feature/retail-clinics.html (accessed 5 September 2012).

Rogers, Everett M. (1982). *Diffusion of Innovations*. New York: Free Press.

Rosenberg, T. (2013). "The benefits of mobile health, on hold," NYTimes.com, available at http://opinionator.blogs.nytimes.com/2013/03/13/the-benefits-of-mobile-health-on-hold/?_php=true&_type=blogs&_r=0 (accessed 30 June 2013).

Rovner, J. (2014). "Medicaid expansion boosted emergency room use in Oregon," available at http://www.npr.org/blogs/health/2014/01/02/259128081/medicaid-expansion-boosted-emergency-room-visits-in-oregon (accessed 7 March 2014).

Schoonhoven, C.B. and Romanelli, E. (2001). "Emergent themes and the next wave of entrepreneurial research," in C.B. Schoonhoven and E. Romanelli (eds), *The Entrepreneurship Dynamic: Origins of Entrepreneurship and the Evaluation of Industries*. Stanford, CA: Stanford University Press, pp. 383–408.

Schwartz, E. (2014). "Can smartphones really cut it as diagnostic tools?" *Mhealthnews.com*, available at http://www.mhealthnews.com (accessed 23 July 2014).

Sebelius, K. (2011). "mHealth Summit Keynote Address," *NCI Cancer Bulletin*, available at http://www.cancer.gov/ncicancerbulletin/121311/page4 (accessed 5 May 2013).

Seppala, T.J. (2014). "FDA approves swallowable 'PillCam' after almost a decade" (video), 4 February, available at http://www.engadget.com/2014/02/04/fda-approves-pillcam-colon-colonoscopy/.

Shaywitz, D. (2013). "Healthcare innovation is not just about cutting costs," *Healthcare Blog*, available at http://thehealthcareblog.com/blog/2013/12/20/healthcare-innovation-is-not-just-about-cutting-costs/ (accessed 2 May 2014).

Simmons, Ashley (2014). "Interview: How wearable tech can improve hospital efficiency," available at http://www.celebrationhealth.com/news/ashley-simmons-featured-bloomberg-tv (accessed 23 July 2014).

Slabodkin, G. (2012). "mHealth Summit 2012: Remote monitoring invaluable for reducing admissions," available at http://www.fiercemobilehealthcare.com/story/mhealth-summit-2012-remote-monitoring-invaluable-reducing-readmissions/2012-12-05 (accessed 23 March 2014).

Ter Mat, S. (2013). "Freestanding emergency department growth creates backlash," available at http://www.amednews.com/article/20130429/business/130429966/4/ (accessed 29 September 2013).

Wagner, M. (2013). "Bringing outside innovations into health care," available at http://blogs.hbr.org/2013/10/bringing-outside-innovations-into-health-care/ (accessed 30 October 2013).

Walgreens Newsroom (2014). "More patients turning to retail clinics for chronic care and preventive services, new Walgreens study shows," available at http://news.walgreens.com/article_display.cfm?article_id=5882 (accessed 27 August 2014).

Wieczner, J. (2014). "Pros and cons of concierge medicine," *Wall Street Journal*. Available at: http://online.wsj.com/news/articles/SB10001424052702303471004579165470633112630 (accessed 1 June 2014).

# 14. Reducing medical errors
## *Joseph G. Van Matre and Donna J. Slovensky*

## INTRODUCTION

Medical errors in the United States engender national economic and policy concerns as well as affecting individuals and organizations. The financial and human costs associated with medical errors in the US have recently been estimated at $17.1 billion (Van Den Bos et al., 2011) and between 210000 and 400000 patient deaths (James, 2013) each year. Medical error and its flip side, patient safety, have been of concern among healthcare providers for many years, but did not emerge as national policy issues until the late twentieth century. Occasional articles appeared in the research literature and trade press, but they rarely engendered sufficient attention or controversy to get the populace involved in advocating for system-wide improvements.

Public records concerning medical data date back at least 500 years when weekly lists of deaths from the plague were enumerated in England. The oldest Bill of Mortality extant, thought to be from 1512, records the deaths of 66 unnamed persons, 34 of whom died from the plague; the cause of death for the other 32 was not specified (Schulz, 2014). From such beginnings as these simple lists, the legal death certificate and the electronic medical record (EMR) have evolved. Data concerning deaths from medical error, whether avoidable (for example, administering penicillin to an individual known to be allergic) or unavoidable (for example, an unforeseen adverse drug event) began to appear in the late twentieth century. The term "iatrogenic" applies to events caused by a physician or his treatment; such events would include those preventable or not, and those involving error or not.

Among the early pioneers of patient safety was Ignaz Semmelweis, a physician in the maternity service of a Viennese hospital. He was the first healthcare professional to establish that hand-washing could prevent infections and he is known today as the father of infection control (Best and Neuhauser, 2004). Although Semmelweis's seminal discoveries were accomplished more than 150 years ago, during the years 1847–1849, hand-washing compliance among clinical providers continues to be a struggle for many hospitals (Marra and Edmond, 2014). A common organizational response to this problem has been to install an antiseptic gel dispenser in a prominent position at the entry to all patient rooms and treatment areas, and to post policy notices about hand-washing. Some organizations engage patients in the compliance effort through patient surveys that ask specifically if all providers followed hand-washing protocols during their encounter.

Florence Nightingale was also achieving fame as a change agent for improving medical care at about the same time as Semmelweis; her success in a military hospital in 1855 during the Crimean War has been called "the most remarkable hospital quality improvement project ever carried out" (Neuhauser, 2003, p. 317). Her actions, primarily addressing sanitary conditions, cut the mortality rate from 42.7 percent of admissions to 2.2 percent in less than six months. Deaths at the hospital, which was located across the Black Sea from the front lines, were largely due to infectious disease and not to wounds inflicted during battle.

Moving to more recent developments, E.M. Schimmel, a Yale physician, was the first to document the extent of hospital-based iatrogenic injury for the scientific literature when he reported that of 20 percent of patients admitted to the Yale–New Haven Hospital medical wards experienced "one or more untoward episodes" (Schimmel, 1964). His study excluded events that arose from inadvertent errors by physicians or nurses as well as postoperative complications, a criterion that surely reduced the total number of untoward events reported.

Seventeen years later Steel et al. published an article in the *New England Journal of Medicine* that sought "to re-evaluate the risks of care in one setting: a medical service in a tertiary hospital." They found that approximately one-third of the patients included in the study had an iatrogenic illness, and for 9 percent of these, "the incident threatened life or produced considerable disability" (Steel et al., 1981, p. 638). Adverse events involving drugs were the leading cause related to iatrogenic complications, with heparin or warfarin involvement in 54 percent of the major drug complications. Events involving provider error were not discussed, although the authors did advocate monitoring of untoward events and "attention . . . to educational efforts to reduce the risks of iatrogenic injury."

A seminal study in the medical error literature, the Harvard Medical Practice Study (HMPS), reviewed 30 121 randomly selected patient records in 51 New York state hospitals. The results of the study were published in two high-profile medical articles (Brennan et al., 1991; Leape et al., 1991). The HMPS was partially inspired by a 20 000-patient study for the California Medical Association (Mills, 1978), that "never had any policy impact" despite its size, being largely ignored because of the unfavorable malpractice implications of its 5 percent iatrogenic event rate (Wachter, 2005). The primary goal of the HPMS was to "develop more current [than the 1978 Mills study] and more reliable estimates of the evidence of adverse events and negligence in hospitalized patients" (Brennan et al., 1991 p.370). The HMPS data provided the first population estimates of adverse medical events and their relation to error, negligence, and disability. Unfortunately, much like the previous studies, the HMPS attracted little attention outside the community of medical scholars (Herman, 2000; Millensen, 1997; Kenney, 2008).

For the HMPS study, an adverse event was defined as "an unintended injury that was caused by medical management and that resulted in measurable disability" (Leape et al., 1991, p.377). Such events occurred in 3.7 percent of patients, and errors in management were identified in 58 percent of these adverse events. Subsequently, the latter measure was revised upward to 69 percent (Leape, 1994, p.1851) after the extent of medical error exposed in these early studies led Leape toward more intensive study of human error. His 1994 *JAMA* article, "Error in Medicine," is considered a seminal work among scholars and researchers in this area.

Leape's article drew from a variety of resources, particularly cognitive psychology, as well as human factors research and the aviation industry. Leape (1994, p.1853) noted: "we have reasonably coherent theories of why humans err, and a great deal has been learned about how to design work environments to minimize the occurrence of errors and limit their consequences." Unlike previous studies, Leape's 1994 report, with its estimate that "180000 people die each year partly as a result of iatrogenic injury" (p. 1351), did gain traction, in part because of the media attention it garnered from an inadvertent association. Two months after the publication of Leape's "error" article, *Boston Globe* health reporter Betsy Lehman died because of a medically prescribed drug overdose (Knox, 1995). The loss of a colleague, coupled with the sad irony of the popular health reporter's demise because of a medical error, stimulated reporters' interest in the topic, resulting in the event being reported "intensively, with 28 front-page headlines over the next three years" (Conway and Weingart, 2005). In pursuing their stories, reporters also found Leape's article and the 1991 HMPS articles. Subsequently, the continuing interest of the media and the public in medical stories, particularly those describing avoidable adverse events, has been pivotal to the impetus of the patient safety movement (Herman, 2000; Rosenthal and Sutcliffe, 2002).

Other research findings published in the 1990s further documented the extent of the healthcare quality problem, such as learning that 6.5 percent of non-obstetrical admissions suffered an adverse drug effect, 28 percent of which were deemed preventable (Bates et al., 1995). The 1990s also saw the beginning of the RAND studies (Schuster et al., 1998), as

Dr. Elizabeth McGlynn and her colleagues attempted to document the extent to which patients receive recommended care, culminating in the disappointing finding that only 55 percent of such care was being provided in 12 metropolitan areas in the USA (McGlynn et al., 2003). However, the major medical error publication event of the decade likely was the September 1999 release of the US Institute of Medicine's report, *To Err is Human* (IOM, 2000), which outlined a strategy for reducing preventable medical errors nationally, using a combination of regulation and market incentives.

The Institute of Medicine (IOM) established the Quality of Health Care in America Committee in 1998 and charged the committee to develop a strategy that would bring about a threshold improvement in quality in the following decade. Early on, the committee determined to focus its first report on issues related to errors and patient safety. Aware that earlier studies had failed to attract sufficient attention to effect systematic industry change despite significant findings, the committee scheduled a day-long meeting with key health journalists to better understand "how the media worked and how the committee could attract coverage for its cause . . . members met with PBS, NBC, the *Washington Post*, the *New York Times*, the *Wall Street Journal*" and other influential individuals (Kenney, 2008, pp. 83–84). The conclusion resulting from the committee's information-gathering and deliberations was that: "The committee's strategy for improving patient safety is for the external environment to create sufficient pressure to make errors so costly in terms of ability to conduct business in the marketplace, market share, and reputation that the organization *must* take action" (IOM, 2000, p. 21).

In 2014 Dr. Robert Wachter, lead editor of two major academic series on medical errors, reflected "on the forces that have promoted safety efforts over the past decade . . . It required the IOM report – particularly its made-for-TV analogy that the deaths from medical mistakes in the US were the equivalent of a jumbo jet crashing every day – to ultimately spark a safety movement" (Wachter, 2009). One should note that the public reporting of healthcare data, begun in 1989 in New York state with risk-adjusted mortality rates for Coronary Artery Bypass Graft (CABG) surgery reported by hospital and surgeon, continues to evolve in coverage and detail, for example hospital infection rates and readmission rates. Such publicly available data, specific to a healthcare organization or a physician, also provides fertile ground for reporters and promotes improvement efforts by providers.

# THE ROLE OF HUMAN ERROR IN MEDICAL ERROR

The first psychologist to attempt to classify error and to seek explanatory principles was James Sully in his 1881 book, *Illusions*. Though this treatise is more esoteric with its focus on dreams, introspection, and beliefs than our current behavioral studies, it is an important reminder that the foundations and causes of human error have long been of scientific interest. Despite other scientific advances after Sully, more than 100 years elapsed before the medical community gave serious attention to errors. As James Reason, a noted expert on system failure, stated, it took "the first Human Error Conference in Maine in 1980 . . . together with Three Mile Island to set the error ball rolling" (Reason, 1990, p. xiv). Building on the work of Jens Rasmussen and Donald Norman regarding the cognitive and motor aspects of error in the fields of safety science and system design, James Reason published *Human Error* in 1990. Though not initially directed at healthcare, Reason's work on human error and system failures was "discovered" by Lucien Leape and cited extensively in his 1994 "Error in Medicine" article, and also in the IOM's *To Err is Human* report. Subsequently, Reason began to apply his work to medical error and published in a variety of medical journals, including some works cited in this chapter.

Human error is a very large subject with application to many fields including airline safety, nuclear reactor safety, and patient injury. Nevertheless, human error takes on a "surprisingly limited number of forms . . . errors appear in a very similar guises across a wide range of mental activities. Thus, it is possible to identify comparable error forms in action, speech, perception, recall, recognition, judgment, problem solving, decision making, concept formulation, and the like" (Reason, 1990, p. 2). Reason's book addresses both the practical and theoretical aspects of human error, and offers a productive way of thinking about error and possible countermeasures. As W. Edwards Deming frequently said in his lectures, "There is nothing as useful as a good theory," and Reason's theoretical approach has been vital to advancing improvements in patient safety. Wachter (2012) describes Reason as "the intellectual father of the patient safety field. I remember reading his book *Managing the Risks of Organizational Accidents* [1997] in 1999 and having the same feeling that I had when I first owned eyeglasses: I saw my world anew, in sharper focus" (Wachter, 2012).

Reason's error classification is best understood when one is familiar with the two forms of thinking described by Daniel Kahneman (2011) in *Thinking Fast and Slow*, aptly titled although the text itself uses the terms

"System 1" and "System 2," respectively. This nomenclature appears frequently in the literature, but some scholars prefer the more descriptive terms of "automatic" or "intuitive" versus "controlled" or "analytical" modes. The automatic mode draws on learned behaviors and rules that are developed primarily through repetitive experiences and are stored in memory and executed without conscious thought. You can brush your teeth, a senior nurse can take blood pressure, or an experienced surgeon can perform an appendectomy, by retrieving a stored routine and executing it automatically. Further, one can tie shoes and hum a favorite song simultaneously because both are stored routines and require no mental effort. However, whether driving a car or cleansing a wound, the actor must perform attentional checks to confirm that all is proceeding normally, and as expected. In the automatic mode, errors occur because of the absence of attentional checks, perhaps due to a distraction. The analytical mode is, however, "limited, sequential, slow, effortful, and difficult to sustain for more than brief periods" (Reason, 1990, p. 50), that is, slow thinking. The effort involved is one reason we prefer to operate in the automatic mode. As Reason asserts, "when confronted with a problem, human beings are strongly biased to search for and find a prepackaged solution [largely based on stored "if–then" rules] before resorting to the far more effortful" analytical mode (Reason, 1990, p. 65). Some cognitive psychologists estimate that we spend about 95 percent of our time in the automatic mode (Croskerry et al., 2013) and thus error is more likely to originate here.

Reason defines error "as a generic term to encompass all those occasions in which a planned sequence of mental or physical activities fails to achieve its intended outcome, and when these failures cannot be attributed to . . . chance" (Reason, 1990). Thus, there are two opportunities for error: (1) in the execution of a plan; and (2) in the selection of a plan; the former is termed slips, and the latter, mistakes. The execution of a plan is performed in the automatic mode, and error results from a slip which includes lapse (memory failure) and fumble (physical failure). However, Reason divides mistakes into two categories: rule-based (RB) mistakes, "if–then" rules that are automatically retrieved; and knowledge-based (KB) mistakes that result despite slow, attentional thinking and could involve limited problem knowledge or selecting the wrong features of the problem space for focus. A defining condition for both RB and KB mistakes is awareness that a problem exists; that is, the actor is engaged in problem-solving decision-making in order to formulate a revised plan that will correct some inadequacy of the current plan, perhaps to deal with a slip. Reason notes that "RB attempts at problem solution will always be tried first . . . then the switch from the RB to the KB level occurs when

*Table 14.1   Forms of human error*

| Error | Thinking | Focus |
|-------|----------|-------|
| Slip | Intuitive (fast) | Execution of a plan |
| RB mistake | Intuitive | Decision-making |
| KB mistake | Attentional (slow) | Decision-making |

the problem solver realizes that none of his or her repertoire of rule-based solutions is adequate to cope with the problem" (Reason, 1990, p. 66). In other words, if the actor encounters a novel situation for which experience and training have not prepared them, then the actor is forced to pursue hard, effortful, slow thinking to create a new plan. Note that the actor may rapidly switch back and forth between the automatic and attentional modes in an attempt to reach a solution. A summary of the forms of human error is shown in Table 14.1.

As an example, consider a patient who presents to the emergency department (ED) with a minor laceration and a possible fracture suffered from a fall. The physician's immediate focus is on the observed injuries and, after cleaning and bandaging the laceration and reviewing an X-ray that ruled out a fracture, the ED physician discharged the patient. The patient was not questioned in the ED about why he fell. Some weeks later, the patient is diagnosed by his family physician as having anemia found to be secondary to colon cancer. If the patient had been questioned about the circumstances surrounding the fall, and reported feeling faint, further investigation might have led to the cancer diagnosis sooner. This error is a slip if the physician intended to question the patient about the circumstances of his fall, but being distracted by other pressing issues in the ED this aspect of the injury was not pursued. Distractions and interruptions are often associated with slips, and they are more likely to occur when the actor is fatigued or preoccupied and the environment is hectic.

Rule-based mistakes occur in decision-making when the actor is automatically seeking a stored "if–then" rule appropriate to the problem at hand out of several choices that may be available. The selection of a rule depends on how completely it matches the situation, and the strength of the rule – how many times it has been applied successfully in the past. Mistakes occur when a "strong but wrong" rule is applied. A rule may come to mind not because of its past success, but because of a recent, vivid experience. For example, an oncologist at the University of Virginia states that:

> despite trials showing the drug Topotecan to be effective against ovarian cancer, he rarely chooses it because he has never had good luck with it himself.

[He] think[s], "The last time, that lady got *so* sick." Bias is very hard. It's easier when you're dealing with test tubes and experimental animals, but when it's real people looking you in the eye, you get wrapped up in their hopes and your hopes from their hopes, and it's *hard*! (Russo, 1999, p. 36)

In other words, a recent vivid experience may trump published clinical trial results.

Research by cognitive psychologists over the last 40 years has identified systematic biases that sometimes impair our judgments. These biases arise from built-in heuristics, or rules of thumb, used by all humans. These useful rules enable us to function quickly and easily, and are appropriate for the vast majority of the time. The availability heuristic assumes that the "if–then" rule that automatically comes to mind does so because its strength is derived from its past success. However, when the rule becomes available for other reasons, such as recency of use alone, mistakes may follow. As the old saw states, "We are always fighting the last war."

The knowledge-based (KB) mistakes arise when the individual is forced to the attentional mode of thinking. Forced, because the problem at hand is novel and the repertoire of stored "if–then" rules has not provided a solution. Interestingly, Reason says the true expert never operates in KB mode; the stored routines and "if–then" rules are sufficient for any difficulty. "At the KB level, mistakes result from changes in the world that have neither been prepared for nor anticipated. By definition . . . no contingency plans or preprogrammed solutions" (Reason, 1997, p. 61). Here too, mistakes can result from a systematic bias. Confirmation bias is the tendency to focus on information and data that support the current hypothesis or diagnosis, and to minimize any data that contradict it. For example, if a diagnosis has been made and if a treatment plan is being followed, and the patient's condition remains unimproved, alternatives must be considered. However, the physician will tend to emphasize new data that is consistent with the existing diagnosis.

## PATIENT SAFETY INITIATIVES

The theories of human error have informed many patient safety initiatives that attempt to prevent medical errors through system design and operational practices, and checklists in particular illustrate the point. The use of checklists has demonstrated great success in, among other error-prone situations, reducing central line infections (Wachter, 2014; Kenney, 2008), surgical site infections (Gawande, 2009), and ventilator-associated pneumonia (IHI, 2012).

A checklist is a tool to enhance the probability that all necessary steps in a procedure are accomplished in the correct order. Thus, it helps ensure that attentional checks are performed and lapses are reduced even in a stressful environment filled with distractions. However, "the successful use of interdisciplinary checklists [e.g., the catheter insertion checklist to minimize central line infections] . . . often requires efforts to improve the culture of safety" (Winters et al., 2009).

Other examples of system solutions to prevent medical errors include both technological approaches and human exchanges. A key factor in the success of these solutions is intervention at the most error-prone steps in a process, or where an error has the probability of causing the greatest harm. A rather large body of literature is available that describes programmed checks in computer information systems that support patient care. For example, most computerized provider order entry (CPOE) systems include robust formularies that are scanned for known drug interactions with current drugs each time a physician enters a new drug order. These formularies are also checked for drug dosage amount and timing of administration; a non-standard order would need to be specifically authenticated as a deliberate decision in response to the individual patient's needs and condition. From the human perspective, most operating room staffs, including the surgeons and anesthesiologists, routinely conduct "time out" checks, visually and verbally verifying patient identification, planned procedures, drug allergies, and other common error possibilities. These preventive efforts have become part of the organizational culture of safety and attention to potential errors.

For many organizations, the National Patient Safety Goals established by the Joint Commission in the USA are important drivers of their safety initiatives. The goals, established in 2002, are developed and revised by the Patient Safety Advisory Group, a national panel (Joint Commission, 2014a). Healthcare organizations (HCOs) tailor the directives of the goals to achieve the greatest return in their known problem areas, as identified through analysis of their internal quality data. For example, Goal 2, "Improve the effectiveness of communication among caregivers," has been approached by some organizations specifically to improve the "hand-off" process, the transfer of care responsibility from one provider to another, either at shift change or when a change in the physical facility location of the patient occurs, such as transfer from a post-anesthesia care unit (PACU) to a regular inpatient care unit. The exchange of accurate and complete information about a patient's clinical status and special care needs at transfer is often critical to the quality of care the receiving provider delivers.

Of note, early attempts to reduce medical error were focused on "the sharp end," where the provider and patient interact. Today, we observe a more balanced view that includes "the blunt end," where staff selection and hiring decisions are made, training standards are set and verified, staffing policies are established, and where the reporting of errors and near misses is encouraged so the system can be improved rather than an individual "blamed and trained." In short, the leaders of the healthcare organization play a most important role in redesigning healthcare systems to improve patient safety.

## LEADERSHIP'S ROLE IN ASSURING QUALITY AND SAFETY

The importance of the organizational leadership in assuring the quality of patient care and service delivery is not a new concept by any means. Arguably, the Joint Commission (www.jointcommission.org) has been the dominant player in establishing the role of leadership in accountability for the quality and effectiveness of patient care provided in US healthcare organizations through its accreditation programs. From its founding in 1951 until today, the Joint Commission has sought to "continuously improve health care for the public" (Joint Commission, 2014b), and has consistently incorporated leadership and governing board requirements in its accreditation standards, delineating their accountability for the organization's clinical quality and organizational effectiveness. More recently, the Sarbanes–Oxley Act of 2002, which established board accountability for corporate governance and financial auditing, has been promoted as logically including hospital boards' accountability for quality of care (Bader, 2010).

And, the US Affordable Care Act (ACA) of 2010, with its national strategy of clinical integration, may further extend the board's responsibility for oversight beyond individual organizations or units. The ACA quality mandates require a focus on the effectiveness of a healthcare system to coordinate patient care "across all conditions, diseases, providers, and care settings, and over time" (Belmont et al., 2011, p. 1282). As payers and healthcare regulatory agencies become ever more diligent about ensuring safe, high quality, and affordable care, the concept of "quality fraud" has emerged. When the board had knowledge about an HCO's quality issues, or in the fulfillment of their board roles they should have known, and the HCO continues to request payment from Medicare and other payers for services provided, the board is committing quality fraud (Gosfield and Reinertsen, 2008), and payers deem charges for poor care as false claims. Under the False Claims Act, HCOs must pay a statutory penalty, often in excess of $10 000 per claim, plus triple the amount charged (Krause, 2002). Thus, with the evolution of the healthcare system toward transparency and accountable care, the board's fiduciary responsibility has encompassed quality more prominently.

Despite this long history of Joint Commission standards, increasing legislation and regulation, and positive influence by other key industry change agents such as the Institute for Healthcare Improvement over the last half-century, research into such issues as board member engagement in HCO quality and safety matters has produced little actionable data to foster widespread expansion of board involvement in HCO quality policy. In fact, some studies found that "quality of care is often not a top priority for hospital boards" (Jha and Epstein, 2010, p. 182), that only 26 percent of 413 boards in a sample of eight US states spent more than 25 percent of their time discussing quality issues (Vaughn et al., 2006), and only 61 percent of boards (n = 562) had a quality committee (Jiang, 2006).

These findings are perhaps intuitive if one considers that US hospital boards were largely composed of honorary appointments until changes in payment structures forced a greater emphasis on effective business practices to ensure the financial viability of the organization. Even when individual board members were recruited for the expertise and experience they could bring to the board table, very often financial management, executive leadership, or other business-based backgrounds were the desirable skill sets. In more recent years following the national call to action via the IOM reports, individuals with quality expertise have been recruited to aid boards in meeting their quality oversight responsibility, including both medical or health professionals and those from service and other industries (Bader and O'Malley, 2006; HRET, 2007). To date, however, representation by health professionals on HCO boards has been primarily physicians (Mason et al., 2007). While physicians certainly bring a wealth of knowledge about clinical practices and other quality and safety concerns, nurses and other health professionals can bring important viewpoints to board discussions as well (HRET, 2007). Over time, this subtle shift in board composition may effect changes in a board's approach to quality oversight, moving the members from supportive but primarily passive information recipients, to engaged participants in crafting a quality improvement strategy.

## EDUCATING BOARDS ABOUT QUALITY AND SAFETY

However desirable a shift toward inclusion of quality and safety oversight in HCO board culture may be, it cannot happen without focused education to provide the board members with the knowledge and analytic skills they need to render the information they receive actionable. These skill sets can be developed using both formal and informal approaches, such as requiring board members to attend conferences and workshops, making site visits to peer or benchmark organizations for observations and discussions with their leaders, and including board briefings by members of the leadership or quality management teams on meeting agendas. Whatever approaches are used, boards need to be knowledgeable about the industry environment as well as facts specific to the organization. Individuals with quality expertise can take the lead in board discussions concerning quality issues, guiding other members toward a better understanding of the organization's performance data and how quality and safety issues may impact the HCO's operations and strategy.

The importance of board education has been underscored by the Institute for Healthcare Improvement's (IHI) "Boards on Board" component of its 5 Million Lives Campaign, which cited learning as one of the "six things all boards should do" (5 Million Lives, 2008, p. 4). The IHI's directive to learn included four broad domains of knowledge:

- Board responsibility and accountability for quality and safety.
- Current state of healthcare quality and safety nationally, locally, and in the organization.
- How board members can affect quality improvement in the organization.
- Strategies to drive continuous improvement.

Some professional organizations and state agencies responded to this call to action by developing board training curriculums that have been made widely available in the USA.

## SETTING THE BOARD AGENDA

Dr. James Reinertsen, a nationally recognized expert in the USA and thought leader regarding board and leadership responsibilities for healthcare quality and patient safety, provides consulting and development services to HCOs seeking to increase leadership engagement in setting their organization's strategic quality initiatives. In Dr. Reinertsen's opinion, "Boards play a key role in quality and safety . . . they generate and maintain the organizational WILL to make changes needed to become safer, better, more reliable . . . [they] *own the problem*" (Reinertsen, 2010). He suggests that the "best" boards:

- Set performance aims for the organization that are both ambitious and specific.
- Hold specific individuals or units accountable for achieving the aims.
- Oversee the development and implementation of plans to achieve the aims.
- "Generate the will" for change management that will get desired results.
- Continuously improve the board's capability to move the organization toward high reliability in quality and safety.

Reinertsen extends the IHI description of leadership's role in improvement of organizational performance to establishing "will to improve, good ideas for improvement, and effective execution of those ideas," to include "constancy of purpose" (Reinertsen, 2007), which was Dr. W. Edwards Deming's Point #1 (Deming Institute, n.d.). This final point is extremely important because achieving organizational transformation is not an easy or speedy process; it is, indeed, a journey.

The tactics that Reinertsen recommends for engaging boards to impose their will include those shown in Table 14.2, namely, putting a face on the data, illustrating the gap between current and desired performance, and being publicly transparent. Intuitively, telling patient stories about individuals who have been harmed, or who experienced near misses, engenders more concern over the issue than reviewing impersonal data reports, and creates a greater sense of organizational responsibility for the event. However, hospital leaders must be selective about the stories shared, choosing them for their potential to initiate meaningful discussion that will motivate change in important areas.

## SCORECARDS AND DASHBOARDS

An additional approach to engaging governing boards and promoting their accountability for the HCO's quality of care and patient safety has been to provide summarized outcomes data to aid in their deliberations and assessment, and to provide a basis for their substantive engagement in

*Table 14.2  Reinertsen's tactics for engaging boards in quality and safety*

| Tactic | Explanation |
| --- | --- |
| Put a face on the problem or data | Tell "stories" about real patients, or let the patients tell their story. Avoid placing individual blame; focus instead on the facts of the event and the harm caused from the patient's perspective. Use recent events in your facility, drawn from current aggregated reports. |
| Illustrate the "gap" between your performance and the "best" performance. | For graphic data reports, include the data points from the "best" or your benchmark organization for a clear visual of the resulting gap. |
| Be transparent about your performance | Share your quality performance data publicly. There is no evidence that public reports drive patients away or cause increased regulatory oversight, but transparency can drive improvement. |

*Source:*  Based on Reinertsen (2007).

directing the HCO leaders' strategies and operational practices. However, clinical outcomes measurement science is still immature and evidence is lacking about which measures provide meaningful data to guide board oversight and policy formulation (Goeschel et al., 2011). Boards may lack training in assessing the data provided or they may fail to give appropriate priority to considering the implications of the data made available to them. Nevertheless, the duty of the board to provide oversight exists, and the accountability burden likely will increase with ongoing healthcare reform legislation.

Because an incredible amount of good, useful data is readily available in any healthcare organization, it can be quite challenging to design a reduced dataset to meet the information and decision-making needs of a specific group such as the board. Despite the need to "put a face on the data," boards most often need reports on whole-system measures rather than detailed clinical improvement measures. These focused reports, often referred to as "dashboards" or "scorecards," aim to provide a quick assessment of performance across key indicators, such as financial ratios, quality outcomes (mortality, infections, and so on), patient satisfaction, and comparison to selected industry benchmarks.

A survey of 109 US hospitals across nine states that prepared dashboards for internal communication included collecting the actual dashboard documents to determine how they were created and used, and how the dashboards affected hospital performance (Kroch et al., 2006). A key finding from this analysis was that, overall, dashboards were used more for "general awareness and focus than used for operational and performance management" (p. 10). However, dashboards that were focused, with content influenced by the board, had stronger associations with quality measures. This finding was supported by other research that led to the conclusion that "a dashboard can't be good unless the leaders design it, so they can use it" (Denham, 2006, p. 51), and is based on three key dashboard design principles: focus, trending capability, and benchmark capability.

Pugh and Reinertsen (2007) recommend the following four categories of dashboards for routine distribution to boards:

- Quality control: ongoing compliance, regulatory, and accreditation measures.
- Patient safety: adverse events, such as falls, surgical complications, infection rates, and other "never" events.
- Improvement projects: current active projects and core measures.
- System-level measures: financial indicators, patient satisfaction, and organizational effectiveness.

Scorecards of this type "create a focal point for critical board discussion[s]" (Pugh and Reinertsen, 2007, p. 65) needed to formulate plans for initiating organizational changes that will foster system-wide improvement, and for allocating the resources needed to effect those changes. Well-designed and well-executed scorecards can provide quick responses to the two priority questions that boards should ask about the quality and safety of patient care in the organization:

- How good is our care compared to the "best" of similar organizations?
- Is our care getting better over time?

While the format and design of the scorecards should be determined in large part by the information to be communicated, some general design features are shown in Box 14.1.

## SUMMARY AND CONCLUSIONS

Since the scope and magnitude of US healthcare quality and safety issues became prominent on the public agenda around the turn of the century,

---

**BOX 14.1  JGV'S DOZEN RULES FOR EFFECTIVE DASHBOARD GRAPHICS**

1. Try to fit all data on a single screen or page. If more than one is required, continue vertically, not horizontally.
2. Include appropriate stretch aims/benchmarks for comparison purposes. You are not striving for the average.
3. Use percentiles to provide context about "where we are compared to others."
4. Provide longitudinal data to answer the "getting better/worse" question.
5. Graph time series data as connected dots, not bars.
6. Use counts, not percentages, for rare or harm (sentinel) events.
7. If symbols are used, make them intuitive; a legend usually should not be required.
8. When applicable, order data by importance.
9. Be conservative in the number of measures reported.
10. Use annotation with restraint; do not "junk up" the visual appearance.
11. Use color, font size, boldface, underlining, and other formatting judiciously to draw attention to key points.
12. Graphic designers may help create an aesthetically pleasing appearance, but they should not be responsible for deciding how to communicate the information.

---

many resource-intensive efforts have been mobilized to effect transformational changes in healthcare delivery at the organization level. Initially, the majority of these interventions occurred at the point of care delivery: the interactions between the patients and clinical providers. Combinations of programmed technology solutions and human attentional checks have prevented many errors. Most healthcare organizations are working diligently to instill a quality and safety culture among their clinical and professional staffs.

An important component of building such a culture is engagement of the governing board in setting the HCO's quality agenda, overseeing the implementation of organizational changes, and monitoring performance outcomes to direct responsive actions. To be effective in discharging their fiduciary responsibility for the quality of care provided in an HCO, boards must be knowledgeable about the political, regulatory, and competitive environments in which healthcare enterprises operate, and they must be well informed about quality and safety concerns within the organization. Effective boards are comprised of individuals with diverse backgrounds and skills, including individuals with clinical expertise and experience in dealing with quality issues.

HCO leaders must be committed to ensuring the ongoing education of the board members to address emerging issues and maintain the personal competence of individual board members. A combination of approaches, such as attending professional conferences, formal information exchanges with other HCOs, and briefings by HCO staff is desirable. Boards may also need to be led toward a culture of dissent and debate to become adept at constructive discussions to build consensus to effect organizational change.

Perhaps the most important role the board plays in improving the quality and safety of care and services provided by the HCO is engendering the organization's "will" to do so. The transformational change required to make healthcare consistently safe, of high quality, and everything the patient needs, cannot be achieved quickly or inexpensively. The board must accept the quality and safety mandate as an important strategic priority as well as their fiduciary responsibility, one that requires diligent attention and dependable resourcing to achieve the desired aims.

# REFERENCES

5 Million Lives Campaign (2008), *Getting Started Kit: Governance Leadership "Boards on Board" How-to Guide*, Cambridge, MA: Institute for Healthcare Improvement.

Bader, B.S. (2010), "Applying Sarbanes–Oxley to Healthcare Quality," *Great Boards*, 10 (1), 2–8, available at http://www.greatboards.org/newsletter/2010/Great-Boards-reprint Sarbanes-Oxley-and-quality-Spring-2010.pdf (accessed 2 September 2014).

Bader, B.S. and O'Malley, S. (2006), "Boardroom Briefing: 7 Things Your Board Can Do to Improve Quality and Patient Safety," *Great Boards*, 6 (1), 1–5.

Bates, D.W., Cullen, D.J., Laird, N., Peterson, L.A., Small, S.D., et al. (1995), "Incidence of Adverse Drug Events and Potential Adverse Drug Events," *JAMA*, 275 (1), 29–34.

Belmont, E., Haltom, C.C., Hastings, D.A., Homchick, R.G., Morris, L., Taitsman, J., Peters, B.M., Nagele, R.L., Schermer, B., and Peisert, K.C. (2011), "A New Quality Compass: Hospital Boards' Increased Role Under the Affordable Care Act," *Health Affairs*, 30 (7), 1281–1289.

Best, M. and Neuhauser, D. (2004), "Ignaz Semmelweis and the Birth of Infection Control," *Quality and Safety in Health Care*, 13 (3), 233–234.

Brennan, T.A., Leape, L.L., Laird, N.M., Hebert, L., et al. (1991), "Incidence and Adverse Events and Negligence in Hospitalized Patients: Results from the Harvard Medical Practice Study I," *New England Journal of Medicine*, 234 (6), 370–376.

Conway, J.B. and Weingart, S.N. (2005), "Organizational Change in the Face of Highly Public Errors: I, The Dana-Farber Cancer Institute Experience," *Perspectives on Safety*, available at www.webmm.ahrq.gov (accessed June 2014).

Croskerry, P., Singhal, G., and Mamede, S. (2013), "Cognitive Debiasing 1: Origins of Bias and Theory of Debiasing," *BMJ Quality and Safety*, 12 (22), ii58–ii64.

Deming Institute. (n.d.), "The Fourteen Points for the Transformation of Management," available at https://www.deming.org/theman/theories/fourteenpoints (accessed 8 September 2014).

Denham, C.R. (2006), "Leaders Need Dashboards, Dashboards Need Leaders," *Journal on Patient Safety*, 2 (1), 45–53.

Gawande, Atul (2009), *The Checklist Manifesto: How to Get Things Right*, New York: Metropolitan Books.

Goeschel, C.A., Berenholtz, S.M., Culbertson, R.A., Jin, L., and Pvonovost, P.J. (2011),

"Board Quality Scorecards: Measuring Improvement," *American Journal of Medical Quality*, 20 (10), 1–7.

Gosfield, A.G. and Reinertsen, J.L. (2008), "Avoiding Quality Fraud," *Trustee*, 61 (8): 12–15.

Health Research and Educational Trust (HRET) (2007), "Building an Exceptional Board: Effective Practices for Health Care Governance," Report of the Blue Ribbon Panel on Health Care Governance. Chicago, IL: Center for Healthcare Governance, available at http://www.americangovernance.com/resources/reports/brp/2007/index.shtml (accessed 11 September 2014).

Herman, R. (2000), "The Human Factor," *Howard Public Health Review*, Fall, 1–5.

Institute for Healthcare Improvement (IHI) (2012), "How-to Guide: Prevent Ventilation-Associated Pneumonia," Cambridge MA: Institute for Healthcare Improvement, available at www.ihi.org.

Institute of Medicine (IOM) (2000), *To Err Is Human: Building a Safer Health System*, Washington, DC: National Academies Press.

Institute of Medicine (IOM) (2001), *Crossing the Quality Chasm: A New Health System for the 21st Century*, Washington, DC: National Academies Press.

James, J.T. (2013), "A New, Evidence-Based Estimate of Patient Harms Associated with Hospital Care," *Journal of Patient Safety*, 9 (3), 22–128.

Jha, A. and Epstein, A. (2010), "Hospital Governance and the Quality of Care," *Health Affairs*, 29 (1), 182–187, DOI: 10.1377hlthaff.2009.0297.

Jiang, H.J. (2006), "Board Engagement in Quality: Findings of a Survey of Hospital and System Leaders," *Journal of Healthcare Management*, 53 (2), 121–133.

Joint Commission (2014a), "2014 National Patient Safety Goals Slide Presentation," January, available at http://www.jointcommission.org/2014_national_patient_safety_goals_slide_presentation/ (accessed 8 September 2014).

Joint Commission (2014b), "History of the Joint Commission," available at http://www.jointcommission.org/about_us/history.aspx (accessed 2 September 2014).

Kahneman, D. (2011), *Thinking Fast and Slow*, New York: Farrar, Straus & Giroux.

Kenney, C. (2008), *The Best Practice. How the New Quality Movement is Transforming Medicine*. New York: Public Affairs.

Knox, R.A. (1995), "Doctor's Orders Kill Cancer Patient, Dana-Farber Admits Drug Overdose Caused Death of Globe Columnist," *Boston Globe*, 23 March.

Krause, J.H. (2002), "Promises to Keep: Health Care Providers and the Civil False Claims Act," *Cardozo Law Review*, 23: 1363; University of Houston Law Center #2007-A-19, available at SSRN: http://ssrn.com/abstract=319101 (accessed 5 September 2014).

Kroch, E., Vaughn, T., Koepke, M., Roman, S., Foser, D., Sinha, S., and Levey, S. (2006), "Hospital Boards and Quality Dashboards," *Journal on Patient Safety*, 2 (1), 10–19.

Leape, L.L. (1994), "Error in Medicine," *JAMA*, 272 (23), 1851–1857.

Leape, L.L., Brennan, T.A., Laird, N., Lawthers, A.G., et al. (1991), "The Nature of Adverse Events in Hospitalized Patients: Results from the Harvard Medical Practice Study II," *New England Journal of Medicine*, 234 (6), 377–374.

Marra, A. and Edmond, M.B. (2014), "Innovations in Promoting Hand Hygiene Compliance," available at http://www.webmm.ahrq.gov (accessed 1 July 2014).

Mason, D.J., Keepnews, D., Holmberg, J., and Murray, E. (2007), "The Representation of Health Professionals on Governing Boards of Health Care Organizations in New York City," *Journal of Urban Health: Bulletin of the New York Academy of Medicine*, 12 November, DOI: 10.1007/s11524-012-9772-9 (accessed 11 September 2014).

McGlynn, E.A., Asch, S.M., Adams, J., et al. (2003), "The Quality of Health Care Delivered to Adults in the United States," *New England Journal of Medicine*, 348 (26), 2635–2645.

Millenson, M.L. (1997), *Demanding Medical Excellence*, Chicago, IL: University of Chicago Press.

Mills, D.H. (1978), "Medical Insurance Feasibility Study: A Technical Summary," *Western Journal of Medicine*, 128 (4), 360–365.

Neuhauser, D. (2003), "Florence Nightingale Gets no Respect: As a Statistician That Is," *Quality and Safety in Health Care*, 12, 317.

Pugh, M. and Reinertsen, J.L. (2007), "Reducing Harm to Patients: Using Patient Safety Dashboard at the Board Level," *Healthcare Executive*, November/December, 62–65.

Reason, J. (1990), *Human Error*, Cambridge: Cambridge University Press.

Reason, J. (1997), *Managing the Risks of Organizational Accidents*, Burlington, VT: Ashgate Publishing.

Reinertsen, J.L. (2007), "Hospital Boards and Clinical Quality: A Practical Guide," Ontario Hospital Association, available at http://www.reinertsengroup.com/pub lications/documents/Boards%20and%20Clinical%0Quality%20Ontario%20Hospital%20 Association%202007.pdf (accessed 8 September 2014).

Reinertsen, J.L. (2010), "The Role of the Board in Clinical Quality and Safety," Presentation to the UAB Health System, Birmingham, Alabama, 6 October.

Rosenthal, M.M. and Sutcliffe, K.M. (2002), *Medical Error: What Do we Know? What Do We Do?* San Francisco, CA: Jossey-Bass.

Russo, F. (1999), "The Clinical Trials Bottleneck," *Atlantic Monthly*, 283 (5), 30–36.

Schimmel, E.M. (1964), "The Hazards of Hospitalization," *Annals of Internal Medicine*, 60, 100–110. DOI:10.7326/0003-4819-60-1-100

Schulz, K. (2014), "Final Forms," 7 April, *New Yorker*, 32–37.

Schuster, M.A., McGlynn, E.A., and Brook, R.A. (1998), "How Good is the Quality of Health Care in the United States?" *Milbank Quarterly*, 76 (4), 517–563.

Steel, K., Gertman, P.M., Crescenzi, C., and Anderson, J. (1981), "Iatrogenic Illness on a General Medical Service at a University Hospital," *New England Journal of Medicine*, 304 (11), 638–642, DOI: 10.1056/NEJM198103123041104.

Sully, J. (1881), *Illusions: A Psychological Study*, New York: Appleton, available at https:// archive.org/details/illusionsapsych02sullgoog (accessed 25 August 2014).

Van Den Bos, J., Rustagi, K., Gray, T., Halford, M., Ziemkiewicz, E., and Shreve, J. (2011), "The $17.1 Billion Problem: The Annual Cost of Measurable Medical Errors," *Health Affairs*, 30 (4), 596–603.

Vaughn, T., Koepke, M., Kroch, E., Lehrman, W., Sinha, S., and Levey, S., (2006), "Engagement of Leadership in Quality Improvement Initiatives: Executive Quality Improvement Results," *Journal on Patient Safety*, 2 (1), 2–9.

Wachter, J. (2012), "James Reason and the Foundation of Patient Safety," available at http://www.kevin md.com (accessed 23 June 2014).

Wachter, R.M. (2005, December), "In Conversation with Troyen A. Brennan, MD, JD, MPH," available at http://webmm.ahrq.gov (accessed 1 July 2014).

Wachter, R.M. (2009), "The Media: An Essential, If Sometimes Arbitrary, Promoter of Patient Safety," available at http://webmm.ahrq.gov (accessed 17 June 2014).

Wachter, R.M. (2014, May), "In Conversation with Peter J. Pronovost, MD, PhD," available at http://webmm.ahrg.gov (accessed 1 July 2014).

Winters, B.D., Gurses, A.P., Lehman, H., Sexton, J.B., Rampersad, C.J., and Pronovost, P.J. (2009), "Clinical Review: Checklists-Translating Evidence into practice," *Critical Care*, 13 (6), 210–219, DOI: 10.1186/cc7792.

# 15. HIT to enhance patient care and organizational performance
*Nir Menachemi, Saurabh Rahurkar and Willi L. Tarver*

## DEFINITIONS

Health information technology (HIT) is defined as "the application of information processing involving both computer hardware and software that deals with the storage, retrieval, sharing, and use of health care information, data, and knowledge for communication and decision making" (Thompson and Brailer, 2004, p. 38). It is a term closely related to and overlapping with the term "health informatics." In its initial definition, health informatics was concerned with the application of methods and technologies from the information sciences to assure the highest quality of healthcare by aiding in problem-solving and decision-making based on archived health information (Graham, 1994). More recently, it has evolved to include "the design, development, adoption, and application of information technology based innovations in healthcare services delivery, management and planning" (Health Services Research Information Central, 2009).

Health informatics has a broad scope due to its interdisciplinary nature with specializations covering basic and applied areas of biomedical sciences (Graham, 1994). The ubiquity of the Internet contributed to the convergence of biomedical, information, and computer sciences in the form of new opportunities and challenges to the healthcare industry. Concerted efforts by healthcare and information technology leaders led to the creation of the term "e-health." It is defined as "an emerging field in the intersection of medical informatics, public health and business, referring to health services and information delivered or enhanced through the Internet and related technologies" (Eysenbach, 2001, p. e20).

In addition to technical development, e-health emphasizes a need for a paradigm shift in healthcare towards a networked, global perspective to improve healthcare by the strategic utilization of HIT applications (Eysenbach, 2001). HIT applications represent a wide range of software and hardware packages that have the potential to influence various aspects of patient care and organizational performance in healthcare. Some key

HIT applications include, but are not limited to, computerized physician order entry (CPOE) systems, clinical decision support (CDS) systems, and electronic medical records (EMRs) or electronic health records (EHRs).

CPOE systems (also commonly referred to as computer-based provider order entry and care provider order entry) are computer-based systems used primarily in the inpatient setting to enter clinician orders for medications, diagnostic studies such as laboratory and/or radiology tests, or other patient services (for example, physical therapy or social service consultation). By computerizing the ordering process, CPOE improves communication and transfer of patient data in the healthcare setting (Sittig and Stead, 1994). In addition, CPOE plays a role in preventing errors that result from difficult-to-read handwritten orders that could cause harm to patients if misinterpreted. Similar to CPOE, electronic prescribing (e-prescribing) is also an HIT application that enables physicians and other providers to enter orders into an electronic system for processing by other health professionals. E-prescribing is similar to inpatient-based CPOE systems except that the term "e-prescribing" typically refers to medication orders used in outpatient settings that directly communicate with community-based pharmacies.

CDS systems "provide clinicians, staff, patients, or other individuals with knowledge and person-specific information, intelligently filtered or presented at appropriate times, to enhance health and health care" (Osheroff et al., 2007, p.141). In other words, CDS systems utilize computer technology and databases to assist healthcare stakeholders in making optimal decisions pertaining to patient care. More importantly, these systems are designed to aid decision-making at the point in time that the decisions are being made (Berner, 2007). A simple CDS system may remind physicians to give an influenza shot to a patient with no contraindications for receiving the vaccine. More sophisticated CDS systems may identify drug–drug interactions that can harm patients; or include a set of algorithms that can help physicians tailor a treatment plan for a complex patient given their laboratory test values, health history, and unique personal circumstances. CDS systems can be stand-alone or used in conjunction with CPOE or EMR/EHR systems.

EMRs/EHRs are digital versions of the patient record used by physicians and other care providers to document patient medical histories, diagnoses, care plans, and treatments. While the term "EMR" is frequently used interchangeably with "EHR," there are subtle differences. Specifically, whereas EMRs include computerized medical data specific to one clinical setting (for example, a medical practice, the emergency department, or a hospital), EHRs are more comprehensive systems defined as "a longitudinal electronic record of patient health information generated by one or more encounters in any care delivery setting" (HIMSS, 2013, para. 1), applicable to a given patient. EHRs build on the functionality of EMRs by allowing for the sharing of health information with other providers involved in the care of the patient. Advantages that EHRs have over a paper-based record include allowing providers to: (1) track data over time; (2) identify patients who are due for preventive screenings or check-ups; (3) check how their population of patients are doing on certain parameters, such as blood pressure readings or vaccinations; (4) monitor and improve overall quality of care; and (5) engage in population health management (Garrett and Seidman, 2011).

The HIT applications mentioned above facilitate the collection of considerable amounts of health information. In order to maximize the benefits of such information, it must flow freely, privately, and securely to places where it is needed; that is, the applications need to be capable of exchanging health data with other applications and organizations electronically (Blumenthal, 2010). In the United States, this electronic movement of health-related information among organizations according to nationally recognized standards is referred to as Health Information Exchange (HIE) (National Alliance for Health Information Technology, 2008). Health information organizations (HIOs) govern this exchange of information among healthcare facilities according to nationally recognized standards (National Alliance for Health Information Technology, 2008). HIOs can comprise local healthcare stakeholders within a defined geographic area which together set policies, make legal agreements, and govern HIE within the catchment area.

## RESEARCH AND POLICY MILESTONES IN HIT

Before reviewing some of the research and policy milestones, it is important to introduce a series of reports published by the Institute of Medicine (IOM). The two reports described here are by no means the beginning of the "safety" and "quality" movement in the USA; however, they are among the most important developments in how and why health information technology (IT) and patient safety have become intertwined.

The first IOM report was released in late 1999 and was titled *To Err is Human* (Kohn et al., 2000). The report generated significant media attention because it shockingly suggested that up to 98 000 people die every year in the USA due to medical errors. Such errors included medication errors, surgical errors, or other errors such as failing to correctly diagnose a patient's condition.

More importantly, the IOM report laid out a compelling argument that most errors in medicine are the result of the poorly designed systems that well-intentioned clinicians are forced to work in. Some characteristics of the error-prone system in which doctors and nurses work included excessively long hours, sleep-deprived training programs, a culture in medicine that does not support open communication, an over-reliance on memory, and the lack of use of information systems that can reduce errors by eliminating the reliance on faulty handwriting, and making information more readily available for medical decision making.

Ironically, the report – even with its shocking statistics – did not present any new data. Instead, it compiled the results of previous studies stemming from the work of researchers including those working on a project known as the Harvard Medical Practice Study. When the report was released, some critics argued that the statistics were inflated. Since then, however, the general consensus among experts is that the statistics were accurate or even possibly underestimated.

Two years after *To Err is Human*, the IOM released a second report entitled *Crossing the Quality Chasm* (Institute of Medicine, 2001). This report made several important contributions to the national quality movement in the USA. First, it defined quality of care as including six main components. The first, patient safety, was defined as freedom from unnecessary injury such as that associated with medical errors. The second and third components of quality were effectiveness and efficiency. Effectiveness refers to care that is evidence-based, while efficiency refers to care processes that are not wasteful of resources.

The fourth component of quality was timeliness; if care is to be high quality, it must be provided in a timely fashion. Next was patient-centeredness; traditionally, healthcare has been provided in such a way that the preferences for convenience of physicians were more prominently emphasized than for that of patients. The IOM report strongly suggested that high-quality care must take into consideration the needs of the patient. These needs can include religious, spiritual, emotional, cultural, physical, and other needs. Lastly, the final component of quality of care is equitable access; if the US healthcare system is to become high quality, everyone must be treated equitably. Clearly, there are many racial, gender, geographic, and other disparities that must be addressed before achieving the "21st century health system" outlined in the report.

Secondly, the report makes the titular suggestion that where we are right now compared to where we should be, is not a gap but a chasm. Lastly, and importantly, the report outlined health IT as playing an important role in addressing quality concerns across all six components of quality.

**Research Milestones in HIT**

In an effort to illustrate the evolving nature of scientific evidence on the impact of HIT, we present a timeline of select published peer-reviewed systematic reviews concerning HIT in the United States (see Figure 15.1). Systematic reviews are research studies that identify, appraise, and synthesize all published studies that meet certain inclusion criteria. As such, reviewing a set of related systematic reviews that span more than a decade is a useful way to rapidly develop an understanding of how scientific evidence on a topic has evolved. The included systematic reviews investigate different elements of HIT, examine HIT's impact on different outcomes, and study HIT in different settings. Ultimately, we selected 11 systematic reviews in our timeline (see Table 15.1), some that focus on CPOE (Kaushal et al., 2003; van Rosse et al., 2009), or CDS (Bright et al., 2012; Garg et al., 2005; Kaushal et al., 2003), EHRs (Buntin et al., 2011; Chaudhry et al., 2006; Poissant et al., 2005; Shachak and Reis, 2009), or HIEs (Fontaine et al., 2010). Moreover, one of the select systematic reviews focuses on the negative impacts of EHRs (Harrington et al., 2011). Overall, these 11 systematic reviews represent hundreds of individual scientific studies.

We begin with a systematic review published in 2003 by Kaushal et al. The authors sought to identify and review studies that evaluate the effects of both CPOE and CDS systems on medication safety. Their review included 12 studies that were either randomized controlled trials or observational studies. Of the 12 included articles in their systematic review, five studies assessed CPOE and seven assessed clinical decision support systems (CDSs). Importantly, half of the studies took place at either the Veteran's Administration Hospital system or the Brigham Women's Hospital in Boston. They found that the use of CPOE and CDS systems in primary care can substantially reduce medication error rates. More specifically, of the five studies that assessed CPOE, two studies showed a decrease in serious medication error rates; one study showed an improvement in corollary orders; one study showed an improvement in five prescribing behaviors in types, doses, and frequencies of drug use; and one study showed an improvement in the drug dose and frequency of use for drugs that are known to cause damage to kidneys. Of the seven CDS studies, three studies found significant improvements in antibiotic-associated medication errors or drug events; and one study showed an improvement in theophylline-associated medication errors. However, three studies showed no significant results (Kaushal et al., 2003).

Another study published in 2005 by Garg et al. systematically reviewed the effects of CDS systems, compared to the standard care without the use

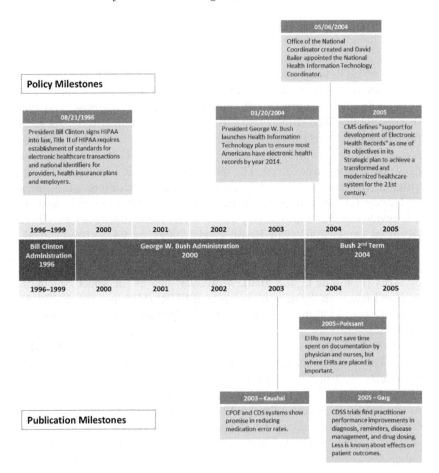

Note:   DSS = Defense Security Service; HIPAA = Health Insurance Portability and
Accountability Act; ARRA = American Recovery and Reinvestment Act; ACO =
Accountable Care Organization; ONC = Office of the National Coordinator (for Health
Information Technology); HITECH = Health Information Technology for Economic and
Clinical Health; PPACA = Patient Protection and Affordable Care Act; PCMH = Patient-
Centered Medical Home.

*Figure 15.1   Policy milestones and findings from systematic reviews in the
HIT field in the United States*

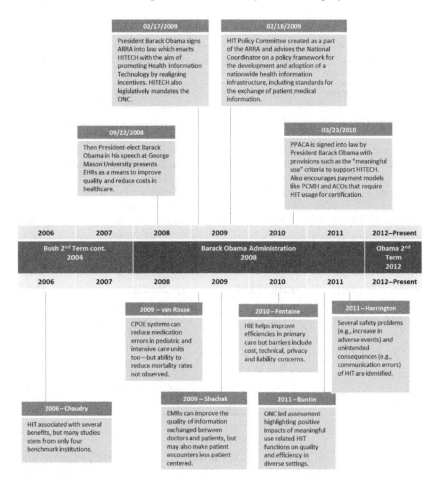

*Figure 15.1* (continued)

of CDSs, on practitioner performance and patient outcomes. This review included randomized and nonrandomized controlled trials and found 100 studies that met the inclusion criteria. Garg et al. found that the use of CDSs led to improvements in practitioner performance in 62 of 97 studies (64 percent). Improvements in outcomes were found in studies using CDS diagnosis systems (4 of 10; 40 percent), reminder systems for prevention (16 of 21; 76 percent) and disease management (23 of 37; 62 percent), and drug dosing and prescription (19 of 29; 66 percent). Findings were not as positive when it came to patient outcomes where improvements were only found in seven of 52 (13 percent) of studies (Garg et al., 2005).

*Table 15.1    A chronology of select research reviews on HIT*

| Research study | HIT application(s) | Outcome(s) of interest | Studies included |
|---|---|---|---|
| Kaushal et al. (2003) | CPOE / CDS | Medication safety / error rates | 12 |
| Garg et al. (2005) | CDS | Practitioner performance/ patient outcomes | 100 |
| Poissant et al. (2005) | EHR | Time efficiency | 23 |
| Chaudhry et al. (2006) | EHR / CDS | Quality / efficiency / costs of medical care | 257 |
| van Rosse et al. (2009) | CPOE | Medication errors / clinical outcomes | 12 |
| Shachak and Reis (2009) | EMR | Patient–doctor communication | 14 |
| Fontaine et al. (2010) | HIE | Motivation to participate | 61 |
| Harrington et al. (2011) | EMR / CDS / CPOE | Safety issues (unintended consequences) | 24 |
| Buntin et al. (2011) | EHR / CDS | Quality / efficiency / costs of medical care | 154 |
| Bright et al. (2012) | CDS | Clinical outcomes, healthcare processes, workload and efficiency, patient satisfaction, cost, provider use and implementation | 148 |
| Weinfeld et al. (2012) | EHR | Quality outcomes | 17 |

Another element of HIT studied is the impact of EHRs on physician and nurse time efficiency. Poissant et al. (2005) published a systematic review that examined the effect of EHR on the documentation time of physicians and nurses and identified factors that may contribute to differences in efficiency. The authors identified 23 studies that met their inclusion criteria, which included five randomized controlled trials, six post-test control studies, and 12 of single-group pre-test and post-test design. Of the 11 studies examining EHRs' impact on the time efficiency of nurses, the study found that six studies showed a reduction in documentation time when nurses used a computer, while the use of bedside terminals increased documentation time in two studies. One study found that documentation time varied based on the information being entered. For example, the documentation of admission information was time-efficient for nurses, while the documentation of registration information required more time using a computer as opposed to paper. Of the ten studies examining EHR impact on the time efficiency of physicians, three studies specifically studied CPOE systems (as a component of EHRs) and seven studies examined other clinical information systems (with or without CPOE functionality). Four of the seven latter studies reported an increase in documentation time (57 percent). It was also found that the location of the EHR may play a vital role in time efficiency. The selection of bedside or central station desktop EHR influenced the documentation time for both physicians and nurses, with nurses being more likely to gain time efficiencies, while the documentation time of physicians increased (Poissant et al., 2005).

In 2006, Chaudhry et al. reviewed the literature to assess the impact of HIT on quality, efficiency, and healthcare costs. Their study included 257 articles that met their inclusion criteria. They found that HIT improves the quality of medical care by increasing adherence to clinical guidelines, enhancing disease surveillance, and decreasing medication errors. Much of this evidence relates to either primary or secondary preventive care, with the major benefit to efficiency being the decreased utilization of care. Another main finding of their review was that a large percentage (24 percent) of studies examining the impact of HIT originated in four benchmark institutions in the USA, namely: (1) the Regenstrief Institute; (2) Brigham and Women's Hospital/Partners Health Care; (3) the Department of Veterans Affairs; and (4) LDS Hospital/Intermountain Health Care. Thus, even though many studies demonstrated the efficacy of HIT in improving quality and efficiency, the fact that so many studies were from four benchmark institutions made generalizing to other organizations challenging. Specifically, at that time, they concluded: "whether and how other institutions can achieve similar benefits, and at what costs, are unclear" (Chaudhry et al., 2006).

In 2009, van Rosse et al. sought to identify and review the CPOE literature with a specific focus on pediatrics and intensive care patients. While the systematic review described above by Kaushal et al. (2003) focused on primary care, this study targeted children, and critical pediatric patients who are more vulnerable and at an increased risk to experience medication errors. The van Rosse study evaluated CPOE exclusively and its effect on medication prescription errors, adverse drug events, and mortality. Twelve observational studies were identified that met their inclusion criteria. The results of their synthesis and analysis showed a significant decrease in medication errors, but no significant difference was observed when it comes to adverse drug events and mortality rates. The authors note that these negative outcomes may have been related to the implementation process of the individual practices (van Rosse et al., 2009).

Shachak and Reis sought to examine the impact of EMRs on patient–doctor communication during consultation. Fourteen articles met the inclusion criteria for their study. The authors found that the use of EMR had both positive and negative impacts on physician–patient communication. The positive impact revolves around information exchange; specifically, EMRs were found to have a positive impact on information-related tasks, especially as they pertain to medications. However, negative impacts were found which deal with the interaction between the physician and patient. Namely, the use of EMR was adversely related to "psychological and emotional talk," establishing a rapport with patients, and patient-centeredness (Shachak and Reis, 2009).

In 2010, Fontaine et al. published a systematic review of HIE in primary care with a specific interest in stakeholder participation in HIE, as well as the benefits, barriers, and overall value of HIE to primary care practices. Sixty-one articles were included in this review. Benefits of participation in HIE identified by the authors included improved access to test results and other data from outside the practice; and improvements in, and decreased staff time for handling, referrals and claims processing. Both of these benefits are related to improved efficiencies. Barriers to HIE as identified in the Fontaine et al. study included implementation and start-up costs, privacy and liability concerns (for example, the unauthorized sharing of confidential information), organizational characteristics (for example, a lack of a strategic plan, a lack of personnel with informatics training, and the ability to counter resistance to HIT), and some technical barriers (for example, the lack of interoperability between different EHR systems). In addition, the authors found that open systems face more barriers as a result of issues across different HIT vendors and organizations, as well as unclear incentives to participate in the sharing of data. The authors also highlighted organizational characteristics that were associated with successful HIE implementation, which included a compelling vision, clear and reasonable expectations, as well as the ability to demonstrate the benefit of HIE to providers (Fontaine et al., 2010).

Despite the many individual studies that identified a link between HIT and various organizational and clinical benefits, Harrington et al. synthesized the literature that examined negative impacts and unintended consequences related to EMR use. Their study reviewed adverse safety issues pertaining to CPOE and CDS systems. The 24 articles in this review included one randomized controlled trial (RCT), one intervention study, one mixed methods (quantitative and qualitative) study, and three case studies. The Harrington et al. study found that safety issues pertaining to CPOE include communication and other unintended consequences. For example, a negative impact of communication includes the use of computers as a substitute for interpersonal communication. CPOE also has the potential to increase the amount of effort it takes for clinicians to coordinate the care of their patients. When it comes to CDS systems, alert fatigue – which occurs when physicians receive too many alerts, causing them to ignore them – was found to lead to medication administration errors due to incorrect physician override of some alerts (Harrington et al., 2011).

In 2011, researchers from the Office of the National Coordinator for HIT (the US federal government's lead agency on HIT issues) published a systematic review that built upon the aforementioned review by Chaudhry et al. (2006), which found a sizeable number of studies on the benefits of HIT stem from four benchmark institutions. In the updated study, Buntin et al. reviewed the literature published between 2007 and 2010, corresponding to the period after the publication of the Chaudhry et al. study. A total of 154 articles met their inclusion criteria. Buntin et al. found that the literature now included more robust evidence about the generalizability of HIT, with studies representing many more institutions other than the benchmark facilities from the previous review. Specifically, they found that 62 percent of studies reported positive outcomes and 92 percent reported either positive or mixed-positive results. Some positive findings include decreases in patient mortality, nurse staffing levels, and the reduction of costs. Some negative findings highlighted e-prescribing as taking marginally longer to enter into the system for processing than creating handwritten prescriptions (Buntin et al., 2011).

A more recent study published in 2012 by Bright et al. evaluated the effect of CDS systems on clinical outcomes, healthcare processes, workload and efficiency, patient satisfaction, cost, and provider use and implementation. Their study, limited to randomized controlled trials, included 148 published articles, highlighting the increased amount of research attention given to this topic over the years. Bright et al.'s findings showed improved healthcare process measures related to performing preventive services, ordering clinical tests, and prescribing therapies. When it comes to clinical outcomes, CDSs only led to improvements in morbidity outcomes. No significant effect was found when it comes to mortality and adverse events, as the strength of the evidence for these two outcomes was low. Although increased attention has been given to the topic of CDS systems' impact on clinical outcomes, Bright et al. concluded that the literature is still sparse when it comes to economic outcomes, workload outcomes, and efficiency outcomes (Bright et al., 2012).

In the spirit of further examining whether the benefits of HIT can be generalized to vulnerable populations, Weinfeld and colleagues examined the potential for EHRs to improve the quality of care in inner-city, rural, and safety-net medical settings. Their systematic review included 17 articles which met their study criteria. They found support for EHRs' potential to improve documentation, process measures, and guideline adherence, as well as outcome measures in underserved settings. More specifically,

EHRs improved documentation of health-promoting information provided to children and their families, risk assessment, and developmental screening of children by primary care providers. However, documentation was not improved for immunizations or lead testing. Documentation was also improved for asthma in an urban federally qualified health center in the US. Another study included in the review found that EHR implementation led to improved process and quality measures, while another found process of care and outcomes in diabetes were significantly better in practices with an EHR (Weinfeld et al., 2012).

**Policy Milestones in HIT**

The contemporary policy timeline (see Figure 15.1) of HIT milestones in the USA can be traced back to 1996 when President Bill Clinton signed the Health Insurance Portability and Accountability Act (HIPAA) into law. It was created to protect insurance coverage for workers and their families in the event that the workers changed or lost their jobs, for reducing insurance fraud and abuse, to protect privacy and confidentiality of protected information, and to establish industry-wide standards for electronic healthcare transactions (Health Insurance Portability and Accountability Act, 1996; White House, 2001). The HIPAA consisted of five titles in total that addressed various aspects of health insurance, including simplification of the administrative processes (Health Insurance Portability and Accountability Act, 1996). Of these, Title II assumes particular importance from the HIT perspective as it defines policies, procedures, and guidelines for preserving the privacy and confidentiality of health information that can or could be used to identify any particular individual. The HIPAA defines protected health information (PHI) as any individually identifiable health information, and regulates its use and disclosure by the covered entities[1] that are in possession of said PHI. Guidelines outlining offenses along with the subsequent civil and criminal penalties are also provided under Title II of the HIPAA. In addition to these provisions, Title II requires the US federal government to adopt national standards for electronic healthcare transactions and national identifiers for providers, health plans, and employers.

This effort by the Clinton administration for streamlining the processes involved in the use of HIT along with addressing the privacy and confidentiality concerns was succeeded by the EHR initiative launched by President George W. Bush during his term. In his 2004 State of the Union address, President Bush delineated a plan to ensure that most Americans had electronic patient records by the year 2014, and presented HIT as a means to "avoid dangerous medical mistakes, reduce costs and improve care" (White House, 2004). The EHR initiative aimed to introduce applications such as EMRs, CPOE, and CDS systems as well as facilitating secure exchange of authorized information among hospitals, private practices, and healthcare providers across the country in order to improve quality, reduce medical errors, and prevent deaths. Later that year the Office of the National Coordinator (for Health Information Technology) (ONC) was created, with David Brailer named as the first National Health Information Technology Coordinator (Brailer, 2009). Presently, the ONC is a part of the US Department of Health and Human Services and has as its primary focus the coordination of nationwide efforts to implement and use the most advanced HIT and the electronic exchange of health information.

Consistent with the President's EHR initiative, the Centers for Medicare and Medicaid Services (CMS) supported HIT to improve quality of care in the Medicare and Medicaid programs. In the context of disease surveillance and prevention, the federal government recognized the value of EHRs in providing early warnings of pandemics and bioterrorism activities. This was operationalized by employing EHRs for collecting preventive and other health quality measures electronically. Furthermore, in its strategic plan for achieving a transformed and modernized healthcare system for the twenty-first century, the CMS explicitly outlined providing support for the development of EHRs and secure electronic data exchange and transactions as one of its objectives (CMS, 2006). Additionally, the strategy prioritized the introduction of HIT applications to health systems with antiquated and inefficient infrastructure, starting with the New Orleans Health System to serve as a model (CMS, 2006).

The commitment to improve the US healthcare system was carried forward by President-elect Barack Obama who in his 2009 address echoed the goals of the EHR initiative outlined by President Bush. This was an important milestone for the HIT community: instead of reversing course on an initiative introduced by his predecessor, Obama, after a politically contentious election, recommitted support thereby demonstrating that HIT was a non-partisan issue. Specifically, Obama expressed his support for meeting the goal of computerizing medical records for all Americans by 2014 (Change.gov, 2009; Obama, 2009). On his election into office, President Obama signed the American Recovery and Reinvestment Act (ARRA) of 2009 (*aka* the Federal Stimulus Package) into law which included the Health Information Technology for Economic and Clinical Health Act (HITECH Act) which provided the resources and means to realize this goal (HealthIT.gov, 2011; White House, 2009).

The HITECH Act focused upon promoting expansion and adoption of HIT by appropriating incentive dollars to reward hospitals and physicians who adopt and/or "meaningfully use" EHRs. "Meaningful use," a term that has now become synonymous with the HITECH Act's incentive program, included specifications regarding how EHRs are to be used in clinical care. Specifically, in order to be a meaningful user, a given provider had to use certified EHRs that included CPOEs or e-prescribing capabilities as well as have certain CDS systems that could facilitate providing care that was safe, efficient, effective, and patient-centered while maintaining privacy and security.

By the first quarter of 2014, the federal government had paid $14.8 billion and $7.7 billion to eligible professionals and hospitals in Medicare and Medicaid, respectively, as a part of the meaningful use incentive program (CMS, 2014a, 2014b, 2014c). In addition, $315 million was paid to Medicare Advantage Organizations for eligible providers (CMS, 2014b).

To facilitate the interoperability of health data across facilities and provider systems, the HITECH Act allocated funds to create a set of standards certifications for EHRs. It also allocated funds for the development and support of local HIEs; these provisions made exchange of health information between systems easier and prevented obsolescence. Regional Extension Centers (RECs) and model communities called Beacons were created to provide technical assistance to providers in HIT adoption and implementation. The resulting increase in EHR activity created by the HITECH Act contributed to the economic stimulus goal of the ARRA, because all the new HIT adoption was creating employment opportunities in sales, manufacturing, implementation support, training, and other HIT-associated services. Ultimately, the aforementioned policy initiatives collectively served to help realize the grand plan of creating a National Health Information Network (NHIN) with the ability to connect local and state HIOs so as to allow health information to be transferred seamlessly from one part of the country to the other.

In late 2012, the NHIN was transitioned to a public–private partnership called the eHealth Exchange which was managed by Healtheway, a non-profit industry coalition (Mullin, 2012). The eHealth Exchange allows for the community of exchange partners to share information under a common trusted framework and standards. As of 2014, it included 34 participants including four federal agencies, 500 hospitals, and 3000 providers (HealthIT.gov, 2014). Governed by a board of directors elected from its membership and federal agencies, the exchange will carry forth the mission of the NHIN by testing and certifying new participants, supporting the exchange's infrastructure including digital certificates, and developing legal agreements and operating policies and procedures for the exchange (iHealthBeat.org, 2012).

## SUMMARY AND LITERATURE GAPS

An IOM report estimated that up to 98 000 people die in the US each year due to medical errors (Kohn et al., 2000). More recent US data suggests that more than 400 000 deaths are attributable to errors in medicine annually (James, 2013). By automating various aspects of care processes, HIT is now believed to be a necessary, but not sufficient, precursor to achieving a high-quality twenty-first-century US healthcare system. The topic of HIT has received considerable attention as a result of the HITECH Act which has subsequently stimulated EHR adoption by hospitals and physicians. Over the past two decades, the research base examining the impact of HIT on patient care and organizational performance has evolved; but several important gaps in the literature remain.

We have learned that achieving the benefits of HIT will be more complex than originally intended. In 2005, researchers estimated that effective deployment of EHR systems could eventually save more than $81 billion annually (Hillestad et al., 2005). These early estimates have been met with criticism because we now know that many of the benefits will likely accrue when health information becomes completely interoperable, which will be facilitated by HIE and the eHealth Exchange (Goodman, 2005; Himmelstein and Woolhandler, 2005). Thus, an important area of future research is the impact of HIE on patient care and organizational outcomes. Specifically, research should further examine HIE's potential to improve quality and patient–provider communication, especially in open systems such as regional health information organizations (RHIOs).

The randomized controlled trial is widely used in HIT research; however, its use tends to be related more to the clinical side of healthcare than to organizational studies. While it is considered to be the gold standard when it comes to research and being able to establish causality, it is not always practical. In the field of health services research, which aims to study ways to reduce healthcare costs, and ways to improve patient treatments and outcomes, researchers use observational analytical methods because randomized trials are frequently not feasible. Observational studies are viewed as less rigorous than randomized controlled trials (Mills, 2012), but advanced analytical methods, stemming from the field of econometrics, are increasingly being used (Heckman, 2008) that can approximate the rigor of randomized trials. The increased adoption of HIT will ultimately create scenarios for health services researchers to more rigorously study the causal impacts of adoption.

In addition, more research should be devoted to address barriers that occur within organizations, which include proper and adequate staff training. Most of the evidence in HIT exists in the area of CDS systems, due in part to the increased attention given to the prevention of medical errors; however, more evidence also needs to focus on HIT's impact on specific disease outcomes. For example, more literature needs to focus on the impact of CDS systems on screening rates for different cancer types, or other specific diseases, as a result of clinical reminders provided to physicians. In addition, HIT applications will also provide physicians with alerts for counseling patients about different preventive measures, including smoking cessation, weight loss counseling, and other evidence-based recommendations. Some of these benefits include the use of these systems to provide more focused, patient-centered care. For example, some HIT systems provide physicians with the preferred language of their patients. This is especially relevant for practices providing care to a diverse population, where such systems can prevent patient–provider language discordance and improve service and care quality.

## MANAGERIAL IMPLICATIONS

The widespread adoption of HIT and the maturation of interoperability have many direct managerial implications. Presently, from an HIT perspective, managerial efforts are primarily directed towards addressing the challenges and needs of HIT implementation and, subsequently, its mean-ingful use by providers. However, this is likely to change as a result of the US federal government's commitment to promoting HIT. We anticipate that the upcoming challenges facing managers will lie in the strategic uti-lization of computerized systems to leverage HIT in order to maximize clinical and organizational performance. Capitalizing on the availabil-ity of data within their organizations created by the new and evolving healthcare landscape, managers will likely address issues such as devising ways to use HIT systems in facilitating population health management, a salient component of the Patient Protection and Affordable Care Act (PPACA). Additionally, the advent of "big data" along with the applica-tion of interdisciplinary methods and technologies (such as machine learn-ing and natural language processing, described below) to this data creates new opportunities to improve quality of care. The following paragraphs discuss these implications in more detail.

The PPACA, enacted in 2010, was created to make healthcare afford-able, to improve the quality of care, and to improve population health (US House of Representatives, 2010). Better health outcomes for the population can be expected by prioritizing proactive management of groups of patients in a practice or groups of practices rather than reactive management of individual patients (Cusack et al., 2010). For example, at the primary care level, individual patient encounters contribute to the population database created by EHRs; this data in turn allows the practices to identify and address the service needs of the populations that need them. HIEs will contribute to the completeness of these databases by adding data from patient encounters with specialists, laboratories, hospitals, radiologists, payers, and even public health agencies, thus creating a comprehensive database of patient health information. In this manner, health data is available at the right place at the right time, allowing for better decision-making regarding the community's health.

Timely availability of information may not only contribute to patient safety by potentially reducing adverse drug events but may also reduce costs by decreasing redundant procedures and diagnostic tests. Furthermore, improved coordination of care can be anticipated due to the availability of up-to-date information at all points of care allowing greater patient-centeredness. Lastly, HIE between individuals and the primary care practices, and the primary care practice and other points of care, may further facilitate management of population health. For example, rapid response and treatment due to early detection of outbreaks of infectious diseases in a community may reduce morbidity and further spread of disease, thus preventing a potential public health crisis. Managers in healthcare organizations that adopt the population health management approach may not only observe improvement in the quality of care and patient outcomes but also fulfill the goals set forth by the PPACA while reducing healthcare costs.

With increasing EHR and HIE adoption, the amount of data collected is expected to increase several-fold. The resulting "big data" – a collection of datasets of an extremely large scale, diversity, and complexity – presents new opportunities from the managerial perspective. Big data has demonstrated utility not only in monitoring seasonal outbreaks but also in predicting their spread (Carneiro and Mylonakis, 2009; Cho et al., 2013; Cook et al., 2011; Hulth et al., 2009). More recently, big data has shown some promise in predicting intention of healthcare utilization and monitoring drug safety (White and Horvitz, 2014; White et al., 2013). Innovations from engineering sciences further add to the value of big data. For example, the application of "machine learning" algorithms allows identification of potential allergies, adverse drug reactions, and disease outbreaks as well as providing intelligent clinical decision support by attributing predictive power to Big Data. Another instance of a borrowed innovation is "natural language processing" (NLP) which is being applied to assist in improving documentation of patient encounters. Ultimately, with the provider's documentation burden lessened, it is believed that more time may be devoted to the patient, allowing for increased patient engagement and an overall better patient experience. Additionally, patient encounters generate vast amounts of textual information requiring manual coding which is both time-consuming and costly; automation brought about by NLP is anticipated not only to reduce costs but also to provide the information in a more timely manner and to improve patient safety by reducing transcription and coding errors (Friedman and Elhadad, 2014). NLP may also help decision-making by reducing patient notes spread across several pages into key points that provide physicians with relevant information at a glance, which may also allow for creation of big data by spanning across patient records and subsequent mining of this data using machine learning algorithms to attribute intelligence to the data (Friedman and Elhadad, 2014). Strategies that focus on early adoption of these technologies based on organizational needs in relation to the market are likely to be the drivers of success.

These are some ways in which the HIT revolution is geared to change the rules about what providers compete around, and are likely to lead to added patient amenities or patient-centered services which may differentiate the choices made by patients as consumers. The interdisciplinary nature of HIT creates a platform conducive to the interaction of ideas and innovations from different sciences. However, the value of these innovations is likely to be determined by organizational needs. The presence of HIT systems in healthcare organizations will facilitate a significantly expanded capacity to conduct more research to better improve care. The accumulation of big data will facilitate longitudinal studies of more rigorous designs which will help healthcare managers and policy-makers learn best practices for improving the care of patients (Kuperman, 2011). A key responsibility for contemporary healthcare managers is to prioritize the monitoring, identification, and utilization of advances in evidence-based HIT applications that best serve the needs of the organization. Skill in fulfilling this responsibility may prove to be pivotal to organizational performance.

## NOTE

1. Any healthcare provider, health plan, public health authority, employer, life insurer, school or university, or healthcare clearinghouse.

## REFERENCES

Berner, E.S. (2007). *Clinical Decision Support Systems: Theory and Practice* (2nd edn), New York: Springer.

Blumenthal, D. (2010). Launching HITECH. *New England Journal of Medicine*, 362 (5): 382–385. DOI:10.1056/NEJMp0912825.

Brailer, D.J. (2009). Presidential leadership and health information technology. *Health Affairs*, 28 (2): w392–398. DOI: 10.1377/hlthaff.28.2.w392.

Bright, T.J., Wong, A., Dhurjati, R., Bristow, E., Bastian, L., Coeytaux, R.R., . . . Lobach, D. (2012). Effect of clinical decision-support systems: A systematic review. *Annals of Internal Medicine*, 157 (1): 29–43. DOI: 10.7326/0003-4819-157-1-201207030-00450.

Buntin, M.B., Burke, M.F., Hoaglin, M.C., and Blumenthal, D. (2011). The benefits of health information technology: A review of the recent literature shows predominantly positive results. *Health Affairs*, 30 (3): 464–471. DOI: 10.1377/hlthaff.2011.0178.

Carneiro, H.A. and Mylonakis, E. (2009). Google trends: A web-based tool for real-time surveillance of disease outbreaks. *Clinical Infectious Diseases*, 49 (10): 1557–1564. DOI: 10.1086/630200.

Centers for Medicare and Medicaid Services (CMS) (2006). *CMS Strategic Action Plan 2006–2009*.

Centers for Medicare and Medicaid Services (CMS) (2014a). Medicaid EHR incentive payments. *Data and Program Reports* (March).

Centers for Medicare and Medicaid Services (CMS) (2014b). Medicare advantage organization payments. *Data and Program Reports* (March).

Centers for Medicare and Medicaid Services (CMS) (2014c). Medicare EHR incentive payments. *Data and Program Reports* (March).

Change.gov. (2009). President-elect speaks on the need for urgent action on an American Recovery and Reinvestment Plan. http://change.gov/newsroom/entry/presidentelect_obama_speaks_on_the_need_for_urgent_action_on_an_american_r/ (accessed 12 May 2014).

Chaudhry, B., Wang, J., Wu, S., Maglione, M., Mojica, W., Roth, E., . . . Shekelle, P.G. (2006). Systematic review: impact of health information technology on quality, efficiency, and costs of medical care. *Annals of Internal Medicine*, 144 (10): 742–752. DOI: 10.7326/0003-4819-144-10200605160-00125.

Cho, S., Sohn, C.H., Jo, M.W., Shin, S.Y., Lee, J.H., Ryoo, S.M., . . . Seo, D.W. (2013). Correlation between national influenza surveillance data and google trends in South Korea. *PLoS ONE*, 8 (12), e81422. DOI: 10.1371/journal.pone.0081422.

Cook, S., Conrad, C., Fowlkes, A.L., and Mohebbi, M.H. (2011). Assessing Google flu trends performance in the United States during the 2009 influenza virus A (H1N1) pandemic. *PLoS ONE*, 6 (8), e23610. DOI: 10.1371/journal.pone.0023610.

Cusack, C.M., Knudson, A.D., Kronstadt, J.L., Singer, M.R.F., and Brown, M.A.L. (2010). Practice-based population health: Information technology to support transformation to proactive primary care. (Prepared for the AHRQ National Resource Center for Health Information Technology under Contract No. 290-04-0016.) Rockville, MD: Agency for Healthcare Research and Quality.

Eysenbach, G. (2001). What is e-health? *Journal of Medical Internet Research*, 3 (2), E20. DOI: 10.2196/jmir.3.2.e20.

Fontaine, P., Ross, S.E., Zink, T., and Schilling, L.M. (2010). Systematic review of health information exchange in primary care practices. *Journal of the American Board of Family Medicine*, 23 (5): 655–670. DOI: 10.3122/jabfm.2010.05.090192.

Friedman, C. and Elhadad, N. (2014). Natural language processing in health care and biomedicine. 255–284. DOI: 10.1007/978-1-4471-4474-8_8.

Garg, A.X., Adhikari, N.K., McDonald, H., Rosas-Arellano, M.P., Devereaux, P.J., Beyene, J. . . . Haynes, R.B. (2005). Effects of computerized clinical decision support systems on practitioner performance and patient outcomes: a systematic review. *JAMA*, 293 (10): 1223–1238. DOI: 10.1001/jama.293.10.1223.

Garrett, P. and Seidman, J. (2011). EMR vs EHR – What is the difference? http://www.healthit.gov/buzz-blog/electronic-health-and-medical-records/emr-vs-ehr-difference/ (accessed 12 May 2014).

Goodman, C. (2005). Savings in electronic medical record systems? Do it for the quality. *Health Affairs*, 24 (5): 1124–1126. DOI: 10.1377/hlthaff.24.5.1124.

Graham, I. (1994). HISA-informatics enhancing health, Melbourne: Health Informatics Society of Australia.

Harrington, L., Kennerly, D., and Johnson, C. (2011). Safety issues related to the electronic medical record (EMR): Synthesis of the literature from the last decade, 2000–2009. *Journal of Healthcare Management*, 56 (1): 31–43; discussion 43-34.

Health Insurance Portability and Accountability Act (1996). HR 3103, House of Representatives, 110 Cong. Rec. (1996).

Health Services Research Information Central. (2009). Health informatics. http://www.nlm.nih.gov/hsrinfo/informatics.html (accessed 12 May 2014).

HealthIT.gov. (2011). HITECH Act – the Health Information Technology Act. http://www.healthit.gov/policy-researchersimplementers/hitech-act (accessed 12 May 2014).

HealthIT.gov. (2014). What is the ehealth exchange? http://www.healthit.gov/providers professionals/faqs/what-ehealth-exchange (accessed 12 May 2014).

Heckman, J.J. (2008). Econometric causality. *International Statistical Review*, 76 (1): 1–27. DOI: 10.1111/j.1751-5823.2007.00024.x.

Hillestad, R., Bigelow, J., Bower, A., Girosi, F., Meili, R., Scoville, R., and Taylor, R. (2005). Can electronic medical record systems transform health care? Potential health benefits, savings, and costs. *Health Affairs*, 24 (5): 1103–1117. DOI: 10.1377/hlthaff.24.5.1103.

Himmelstein, D.U. and Woolhandler, S. (2005). Hope and hype: predicting the impact of electronic medical records. *Health Affairs*, 24 (5): 1121–1123. DOI: 10.1377/hlthaff.24.5.1121.

HIMSS (2013). Electronic health records. http://www.himss.org/library/ehr/?navItem Number=13261 (accessed 12 May 2014).

Hulth, A., Rydevik, G. and Linde, A. (2009). Web queries as a source for syndromic surveillance. *PLoS ONE*, 4 (2), e4378. DOI: 10.1371/journal.pone.0004378.

iHealthBeat.org (2012). NwHIN exchange nearly transitioned to public–private partnership – iHealthBeat. http://www.ihealthbeat.org/articles/2012/10/9/nwhin-exchange-nearly- transitioned to-publicprivate-partnership?view=print (accessed 12 May 2014).

Institute of Medicine (IOM) (2001). *Crossing the quality chasm: A new health system for the 21st century*. Washington, DC: National Academy Press.

James, J.T. (2013). A new, evidence-based estimate of patient harms associated with hospital care. *Journal of Patient Safety*, 9 (3): 122–128. DOI: 10.1097/PTS.0b013e3182948a69.

Kaushal, R., Shojania, K.G., and Bates, D.W. (2003). Effects of computerized physician order entry and clinical decision support systems on medication safety: a systematic review. *Archives of Internal Medicine*, 163 (12): 1409–1416. DOI: 10.1001/archinte.163.12.1409.

Kohn, L.T., Corrigan, J., and Donaldson, M.S. (2000). *To Err is Human: Building a Safer Health System*. Washington, DC: National Academy Press.

Kuperman, G. J. (2011). Health-information exchange: why are we doing it, and what are we doing? *Journal of the American Medical Informatics Association*, 18 (5): 678–682. DOI: 10.1136/amiajnl-2010-000021.

Mills, A. (2012). Health policy and systems research: defining the terrain; identifying the methods. *Health Policy and Planning*, 27 (1): 1–7. DOI: 10.1093/heapol/czr006.

Mullin, R. (2012). NHIN, NwHIN and Healtheway. 11 September. http://www.govhealthit.com/news/nhin-nwhin-and-healtheway (accessed 12 May 2014).

National Alliance for Health Information Technology (2008). Report to the Office of the National Coordinator for Health Information Technology on Defining Key Health Information Technology Terms.

Obama, B. (2009). Text of Obama Speech on the Economy. http://www.cnbc.com/id/28559492/Text_of_Obama_Speech_on_the_Econom (accessed 12 May 2014).

Osheroff, J.A., Teich, J.M., Middleton, B., Steen, E.B., Wright, A., and Detmer, D.E. (2007). A roadmap for national action on clinical decision support. *Journal of the American Medical Informatics Association*, 14 (2): 141–145. DOI: 10.1197/jamia.M2334.

Poissant, L., Pereira, J., Tamblyn, R., and Kawasumi, Y. (2005). The impact of electronic health records on time efficiency of physicians and nurses: A systematic review. *Journal of the American Medical Informatics Association*, 12 (5): 505–516. DOI: 10.1197/jamia.M1700.

Shachak, A. and Reis, S. (2009). The impact of electronic medical records on patient–doctor communication during consultation: A narrative literature review. *Journal of Evaluation in Clinical Practice*, 15 (4): 641–649. DOI: 10.1111/j.1365-2753.2008.01065.x.

Sittig, D.F. and Stead, W.W. (1994). Computer-based physician order entry: The state of the art. *Journal of the American Medical Informatics Association*, 1 (2): 108–123. DOI: 10.1136/jamia.1994.95236142.

Thompson, T.G. and Brailer, D.J. (2004). *The decade of health information technology: Delivering consumer-centric and information-rich health care.* Washington, DC: US Department of Health and Human Services.

US House of Representatives (2010). An Act entitled The Patient Protection and Affordable Care Act, Public Law 111-148.

Van Rosse, F., Maat, B., Rademaker, C.M., van Vught, A.J., Egberts, A.C., and Bollen, C.W. (2009). The effect of computerized physician order entry on medication prescription errors and clinical outcome in pediatric and intensive care: A systematic review. *Pediatrics*, 123 (4): 1184–1190. DOI: 10.1542/peds.2008-1494.

Weinfeld, J.M., Davidson, L.W., and Mohan, V. (2012). Electronic health records improve the quality of care in underserved populations: A literature review. *Journal of Health Care for the Poor and Underserved*, (3 Suppl): 136–153. DOI: 10.1353/hpu.2012.0134.

White, R.W. and Horvitz, E. (2014). From health search to healthcare: Explorations of intention and utilization via query logs and user surveys. *Journal of the American Medical Informatics Association*, 21 (1): 49–55. DOI: 10.1136/amiajnl-2012-001473.

White, R.W., Tatonetti, N.P., Shah, N.H., Altman, R.B., and Horvitz, E. (2013). Web-scale pharmacovigilance: Listening to signals from the crowd. *J Am Med Inform Assoc*, 20 (3): 404–408. DOI: 10.1136/amiajnl-2012-001482.

White House (2001). The Clinton Presidency: Improving the nation's health care. http://clinton5.nara.gov/WH/Accomplishments/eightyears-07.html (accessed 12 May 2014).

White House (2004). A new generation of American innovation. Press release. Available at http://georgewbushwhitehouse.archives.gov/infocus/technology/economic_policy200404/chap3html.

White House (2009). Signed, sealed, delivered: ARRA. Available at http://www.whitehouse.gov/blog/09/02/17/Signed-sealed-delivered-RRA/ (accessed 12 May 2014).

# 16. The many lives of data
## *James H. Willig*

## INTRODUCTION

I begin my consideration of the lives of data with a metaphor: data are raw materials, while statistics are industrial processes that convert these materials into the products of information and insight. The collection and transformation of data into information and insights that aid decision-making, while currently revolutionizing multiple industries, is not entirely novel. Like so many advances, it comes from the approximation of different disciplines; in this case, informatics, statistics, and leadership.

Advances in informatics technology, tools, and methodologies have enhanced our ability to collect, organize, combine, and extract data more efficiently than ever before. The tools of statistical analyses are increasingly used outside the hallways of academia to aid in making decisions as varied as what coupons to send in response to customer purchases, the selection of the correct answer to a jeopardy question, or the evaluation of players in several sports (Davenport and Kim, 2013; Siegel, 2013). I purposefully include leadership as the third discipline, as without institutional vision, direction, and buy-in, an organization will fail to recognize how informatics and statistics can provide the groundwork for improved decision-making and thus fail to drive adoption of these tools to effect meaningful change.

Translational science notes as one of its goals bringing the "bench to the bedside." It seeks to bring laboratory or "bench" research insights to the front lines of designing and delivering patient care as interventions at the "bedside" (Waldman and Terzic, 2010). Data are captured at every step of an individual's contact with the healthcare system and in many cases data capture spills into individuals' home settings in efforts to detect worsening health issues earlier, to enable focused interventions likely to improve clinical outcomes. As data capture grows, the potential to use such data to aid in making decisions at the patient and organizational levels expands accordingly (Davenport and Kim, 2013; Siegel, 2013; Davenport, 2014; Mayer-Schonberger and Cukier, 2013). A well-conceived enterprise data strategy may serve as a broader translational bridge from "bench to bedside to boardroom," as data captured in each of these environments, joined together with informatics tools and subject to statistical analyses, will yield information and insights that can improve decision-making at each of these organizational levels. A well-conceived enterprise data strategy then is critical to the transition that the Institute of Medicine in the United States describes as a "learning healthcare system" (Smith et al., 2013).

In the following sections, I will explore "the many lives of data" and how they impact "the bench, the bedside and the boardroom." I will discuss the need for organizational strategies for the capture, access, sharing, and analysis of data. In healthcare organizations, the establishment of an enterprise data strategy is crucial for long-term success and a foundational step to the transition to a learning healthcare system.

## DATA AS A RESOURCE

Economists describe data as a "non-rivalrous" good, meaning that one person's use does not devalue or negatively impact another person's use of that same good (Davenport and Kim, 2013). In a healthcare organization, data are captured in multiple ways. Some data lend themselves to storage in traditional relational structures, in tables with rows and columns containing detail (for example, medication administration, ordering and purchasing of operating theater materials, hospital laboratory results). Datasets containing such data elements can usually be constructed through extraction of data via querying the underlying relational databases. Such data are often referred to as discrete data. They are collected in tables whose rows and columns often have inclusion and exclusion rules and parameter limits (for example, limits to highest and lowest adult temperatures that can be recorded) that increase the quality of the data collected by limiting data entry errors. Discrete data lend themselves to analyses through a host of options, including descriptive analyses via statistical or visual analytics software (for example, Tableau®, or other options that organize information into visual representations). Such datasets can also be imported and be subjected to more sophisticated analyses (for example, regression analyses, time to event) within more comprehensive statistical software programs and packages (for example, R®, SAS®, SPSS®, STATA®) (Davenport and Kim, 2013).

Other data collected through the process of delivering healthcare services are more difficult to retrieve and analyze, as they do not lend themselves to easy capture and storage in traditional relational database structures. Examples of such data include the free text within caregiver notes (for example, history of present illness, assessment, and plan), as well as images (for example, pathology, radiology) and video data (for example, real-time video surveillance monitoring of patients at risk for falls or seizures). These types of data require either a "transformational step" where the information is reviewed, then reduced and transferred into a relational table structure, or will require altogether different types of analyses. One common "transformational step" used in healthcare for free text data is third-party review or abstraction. For example, a research team member might abstract clinical chart data for those individuals with certain diagnoses, to extract information not available in the relational databases underpinning an electronic medical record, via review of free text notes for a cohort research project. Likewise, a hospital billing or cancer registry employee might review the same free text notes to validate costs associated with an inpatient stay or mandated cancer reporting variables (again, data are a non-rivalrous good). Technological approaches such as natural language processing (NLP) can greatly aid such endeavors, yet the resources to customize NLP to the level to approximate or even surpass a human reviewer are not readily available in most institutions. Likewise, there are technological approaches to aid in either the "transformation" of images and video data or even their direct analyses. These approaches are rapidly changing and form a part of the "big data" movement, where sources of data traditionally not available are increasingly accessible for analysis (Davenport and Kim, 2013; Siegel, 2013; Davenport, 2014; Mayer-Schonberger and Cukier, 2013).

An organization's data represent a key strategic and operational resource. Understanding what data are available provides key insight into the "raw materials" available for analysis and the breadth of questions for which insight can be gained. Access to data is also a key component of an enterprise data strategy. In order to understand more about an organization's data resources, some key questions must be explored:

- Where in the existing business processes are data collected in your organization?
- What types of data are collected (for example, discrete data, free text data)?
- How can you access these data?
- Are there common identifiers that allow you to connect data collected at multiple locations and within multiple software resources throughout the organization?

This last point is particularly important and is a key part of the organization's "innovation space."

## THE INNOVATION SPACE

Healthcare produces a constant flow of data at each layer of the processes that keep an organization running and providing patient care. Historically, a common approach to enhance the efficiency of each layer of processes (for example, billing, bed utilization) has been to provide each process with custom software tools. While some organizations may have built software locally over time, many others purchase existing commercial software solutions, selecting an industry-recognized "best of breed" suite of software tools. Locally developed software or commercial "best of breed" software typically have a focused scope. This focused scope can be both a strength (for example, tools are well adapted to workflow issues because they are built by experts in the subject matter) and a weakness (for example, lack of easy interoperability with other software in the enterprise complicate or, worse, negating data-sharing). For organizations that seek to optimize benefits from the aggregation and analyses of their data, an enterprise populated by individual "best of breed" solutions makes for a fractured collage of data. In such settings, aggregation of data – a necessary step preceding analyses that result in insights – takes tremendous time and resources and often comes to depend on a few experts with copious institutional memory whose bandwidth to process data is easily outstripped by enterprise-wide needs. This is not to say that single, enterprise-wide software solutions are a panacea; rather, the ability to access, aggregate, and analyze data across all layers of the enterprise must be taken into account at the time of purchasing any software solution. This is a key component of an enterprise data strategy and a standard that all parts of an organization must be held accountable to; the data in all individual software must "play well' (interoperate, share data, and so on) with existing data sources, lest the organization lose future analytic flexibility through parochial "best of breed" oversights.

To illustrate the potential of data inherent in an organization, consider its "innovation space." The innovation space, illustrated in Figure 16.1, is defined as the area resulting from the product of the available "data types" and the "methodological expertise" currently present in the organization. This calculation can be illustrated with the following mental exercise: plot a fictional organization's innovation space on a Cartesian plane with the data types on the X-axis, and the methodological expertise on the Y-axis. Now, across the X-axis, imagine that five data types are accessible in this organization (for example, demographic, laboratory, prescription, diagnostic, and hospital readmissions data). At the same time, postulate that four distinct areas of statistical methods expertise are commanded by the available analysts (for example, descriptive,

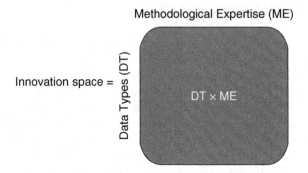

*Figure 16.1   Graphical representation of the innovation space*

time-to-event analyses, logistic regression, and ordinal regression). Once the abilities of an organization have been mapped thus, as shown in Figure 16.2, it is easy to understand the breadth of the questions that may be asked with the available resources by combining the elements mapped in the innovation space.

In the example in Figure 16.2, clinicians in this fictional organization ask, "What factors are associated with hospital readmission within 30 days of discharge for patients with a diagnosis of congestive heart failure?" A cross-reference to the innovation space shows that this analysis would require methodological expertise in "logistic" analyses and would involve the demographic data (to recognize individual patients), diagnostic data (to recognize those with heart failure), and readmissions data (to find out those readmitted at 30 days). Thus, all questions can be mapped to an organization's innovation space, which in turn provides a glimpse of the universe of questions available for analyses.

Another important insight from the innovation space concept is that it presents a blueprint on which to grow an organization's analytics capabilities. Organizations can choose to expand the breadth of their methodological expertise by bringing on new experts or providing training in new statistical techniques to their existing personnel. Furthermore, organizations can choose to expand the available data types by seeking to "data-fy," or record as digital information, an existing or newly created process (Siegel, 2013). It is important to spend time thinking about how data produced by new service layers and corresponding software and data capture added to an organization can be shared and analyzed, and how such endeavors map to an organization's innovation space. It is preferable to discuss interoperability, ease of data extraction, and potential for combination with existing data sources prior to any purchase of information resources.

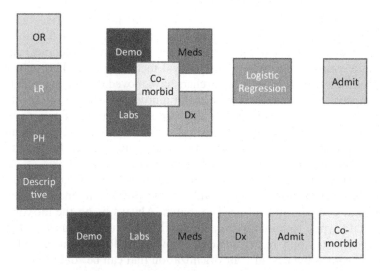

*Note:*  The vertical column shows the statistical methods in which this organization is expert (PH: proportional hazards, LR: logistic regression, OR: ordinal regression); while the horizontal row shows the available data types (demographic, laboratory, medications, diagnoses, admission, co-morbidity). In the center are the data types that will be used as independent or predictive variables (labs, diagnosis, co-morbid conditions, demographics, medications) in a logistic regression analysis of factors associated with the outcome or dependent variable "*30-day readmissions*" that will be derived from the hospital admissions data (admit).

*Figure 16.2   Innovation space in action: prediction of factors associated with hospital readmission within 30 days after a congestive heart failure exacerbation*

The innovation space concept also helps to conceptualize how a small organization can remain relevant against large competitors. For example, the 1917 HIV Clinic at the University of Alabama at Birmingham, USA, despite being relatively small (as of 2014 approximately 3000 clients), represents a thriving clinical and research enterprise. This clinic shares data with various national and international collaborative research groups that have aggregated tens to hundreds of thousands of clinical cases. Imagine a journal editor faced with choosing between two manuscripts of similar scholarship quality, one from a single HIV clinic with a few thousand cases and one from a multi-site research collaborative with tens of thousands of cases. Such an editor would be hard-pressed not to favor the study with the larger sample size, with patients spread across multiple locations, for publication. Thus, a small clinic or a small organization cannot win such a battle (sample sizes, efficiencies of scale, and so on) with a much larger competitor. To continue to thrive from a scholarship perspective, the 1917 HIV Clinic has chosen to add new data types through new technologies for data capture (for example, sensors, patient reported outcomes) and to analyze existing data with new statistical methodologies. Through these approaches, the 1917 Clinic researchers have moved the playing field from a competition on sample sizes to one of innovation, using to their advantage processes that would take a larger competitor months or even years to replicate. This innovation focus has served to differentiate this clinic's work from that of others, making its clinical and research findings more appealing for publication in preferred journals.

Thinking strategically about an organization's innovation space and making its expansion a priority will serve to provide an analytics advantage that competitors will need to match. Always be on the lookout for new data types, technology to facilitate their capture, and new statistical approaches to apply to existing data. Now pause for a moment and cogitate on something new in your organization that can be "data-fied."

# BUILDING AN ENTERPRISE DATA STRATEGY

If one views healthcare delivery in part as an opportunity for continuous data capture on individuals, it is crucial to understand that the aggregation of individual-level data across different parts of an organization can provide population-level insights. This concept lies at the crux of the formulation of an enterprise data strategy. A significant investment in technology and analytic resources as well as a change in organizational culture are important components of such a strategy. While previous sections alluded to some tenets important in an enterprise data strategy, in this section the concepts are discussed in more detail and from a unified perspective.

### Organizational Culture

Data is not the only stone in the foundation of a good decision. There are certainly ways to misinterpret data, and to make mistakes at the data collection, analysis, or interpretation phases that result in suboptimal decisions. However, data may provide a synthesis of past experience and helpful guidance when considered in the context of other variables at the time of making a decision. Viewing data and analytics as tools that can assist decision-making prevents blind over-reliance on individual experience and perception, and recognizes that while no statistical model is a complete reflection of reality, the right model can be quite useful.

A useful analogy is to think of the process of discerning an underlying pattern of illness from a person's disease presentation. One will use history-taking and physical examination skills, laboratory tests, imaging data, and other interventions to analyze a specific presentation and derive a conclusion (diagnosis) prior to deciding on a treatment plan. A sage practitioner knows to consider all sources of insight, to not over-rely by overinflating or undervaluing one source of data. This is analogous to using data and analytics to help provide insight. Analytics represent a remarkably flexible set of tools, a new and powerful set of tools that can greatly aid in making a diagnosis. This does not mean we throw all other tools away, it means we understand that by making these newer tools available, and embracing their utilization, we are contributing to the development of a new and more robust "standard of care" when compared to using only past data to provide insights to decision-making. If experience is indeed the best teacher, why would leaders and clinicians not use the accrued experience of the enterprise to help them make better decisions? Analytics should be an expectation within the organizational culture and an important part of decision-making, to be integrated with other signals to reach the best possible conclusions.

**Informatics Tools, Technology, and Analytics**

"Informatics" is a term that means different things to different academic and professional disciplines: building new software tools to capture data, organizing existing data repositories to communicate with each other, establishing the ability to extract data on demand, are all parts of informatics for data analysis. In addition, having knowledge of how the data are collected and stored, and assisting with the translation of a "question" or its formulation into a statement that can be converted by programmers into lines of code to retrieve the correct data to answer the aforementioned query, is another part of informatics expertise. One must promulgate the idea within the enterprise that different software tools must be able to share data from their corresponding databases. There are many technological means to achieve such interoperability and their discussion is beyond the scope of this chapter, but the key is that leaders must influence the organization to select an effective way to extract data throughout the enterprise, even at the early stages of consideration for purchase of new software tools.

Understanding what data are present in the enterprise, how data are captured, and how much access to data individuals in the organization will need, will provide insight into the type of roles, experts, and investment needed to create a robust informatics and analytics base of operations.

This operation must be ready to interact with all parts of the enterprise and help them gain access to the right data at the right time, and help with high-quality analyses in order to provide timely insights to key enterprise decisions. Many organizations view such investments as unfortunate overheads, when they in fact represent a key investment in business development and an opportunity to improve decision-making throughout the enterprise. A culture that is ready to embrace data-driven insights for decision-making, and an informatics and analytics corps that is ready to collaborate and serve the greater enterprise, are keys to a successful enterprise data strategy.

**Data Quality**

Unfortunately, all too often data quality is an afterthought in healthcare enterprises. Many issues abound, including allowing individuals to customize data collection templates for a limited-scope purpose, knowing that the customization will impede the ability to coalesce different data sources into a complete dataset for future analyses. Though some controls exist in data input fields in many software applications, many times they are insufficient to prevent the entry of incomplete or improper values. The issues with data are legion, yet vigilance and the establishment of systems to review the quality of data and enact changes are often lacking in healthcare.

An internal analysis of data quality at the 1917 HIV Clinic sought to determine how many diagnostic changes (starting or stopping a diagnosis) mentioned in the free text provider notes were made in the corresponding discrete fields of the electronic medical record (EMR) (for example, the Problem List). In the first two-month interval, only 53 percent of diagnostic changes mentioned in provider notes were updated in the Problem List section of the EMR. Furthermore, only 88 percent of medication changes were updated. A logistic regression analysis of factors associated with poor documentation (that is, not updating the EMR) revealed that providers with less than six months' experience using the EMR were 1.6 times more likely to make a documentation error than longer-tenured providers. This led to reconsidering the approach to EMR training, which began to routinely speak to common documentation errors, and carefully monitoring new users during their first six months in the organization, calling and alerting them to documentation issues when they were discovered. In addition, periodic feedback was shared with every provider on where they ranked compared to their peers in regards to the accuracy of their documentation. These tactics resulted in an increase in the documentation of diagnostic data among providers from 53 percent to 78 percent in less than one year.

As one of my statistician colleagues would say, "Every dataset is perfect . . . until analyzed!" The lesson is that important issues with data quality must be aggressively addressed on a continuing basis. Take a moment to ponder potential data quality issues in your enterprise as well as formulating a plan to continuously analyze and improve data quality going forwards. This is an important and often overlooked part of an enterprise data strategy. Better data lead to better insights, and better insights lead to better decisions.

## The Team

The term "data scientist" is growing in popularity and depicts an expert skilled in understanding the informatics resources involved in data collection, and trained in data extraction and the statistical analyses of such data to provide insight to aid in answering questions (Davenport and Kim, 2013). Already dire proclamations exist as to the dearth of such professionals in the workforce juxtaposed with the growing need for their skillsets across multiple industries. While we await the rising tide of newly trained data scientists, what can we do in the short term to provide enterprises with those needed skills? An alternative approach is to create interdisciplinary teams with effective access to data sources throughout the enterprise, and a robust analytics corps. Who should be on such a team and how each could potentially contribute is discussed in the context of my three basic "rules of data," shown in Figure 16.3.

## Team Composition

In the subsequent sections, I will discuss the foundational members and their important contributions to the organization's analytics team. The

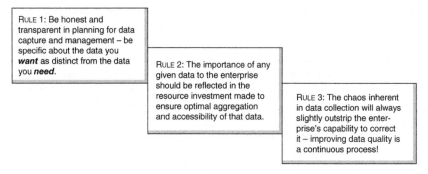

*Figure 16.3   Willig's rules of data*

complexity of the issues addressed by the team may dictate the overall number of members and the mix of skill sets.

**Informatics expertise**

According to the first rule of data, an enterprise must make deliberate, thoughtful decisions about data that are "wanted" (nice to have) versus data that are "needed" (mission-critical). This deliberation requires open and ongoing discussion among multiple individuals and units in the enterprise, and often involves negotiation among the various users of the data. For example, a national reporting mandate (such as cancer case reporting) is a "need" when it comes to data collection for a hospital. Discussion amongst the physician, hospital administrative, and health information management leadership could lead to the development of standardization on how cancer case data are captured by providers, in a way that facilitates or at least minimally disrupts medical care workflow and facilitates the collection of data. This more effective and accurate data collection in turn serves to facilitate national cancer case reporting while providing data to aid the enterprise in attaining insights into the quality and safety of cancer care, and permitting providers and researchers access to a robust set of data to aid in retrospective research and prospective clinical trial enrollment. Recall that data are a non-rivalrous good, so multiple communities can benefit from the same data repeatedly.

To successfully achieve the change in cancer case data collection proposed above would take many concurrent skill sets. First, informatics expertise to understand the whole picture of data collection at the front line of care while envisioning the potential analytic uses of data at the back end is critical to create a navigable compromise that all parties can benefit from. Second, expertise in software development will be needed to either create de novo software tools or modify existing ones to facilitate implementation of the newly proposed cancer case data capture changes. Third, expertise in data extraction is required, including querying databases and/or combining data from multiple existing sources to create an analyzable dataset to provide to the analytics experts. Finally, an organization may also have an existing commercial analytics platform, which must be connected to an enterprise data source to be used to provide real-time visual analytics. The information technology expertise to create and sustain existing enterprise data sources to such a visual analytics platform over the long term will be needed.

There is no one unique informatics skill set that addresses all of these needs. An enterprise must decide its desired architecture to collect and share data, while continuing to remain vigilant to market changes as well as pursuing innovative expansion of new data sources (for example, expanding innovation space) to gain competitive advantages. These enterprise decisions will impact the size and skill sets needed within the informatics team. At this time, consider the second rule of data: in brief, the importance of data's role to the enterprise must be matched by investment in assuring the usability of that data. Be forewarned that this is a critical investment for an enterprise and that, as the saying goes, "You cannot drink champagne on a beer budget." Leaders must make strategic investments for the long-term value that will accrue to the enterprise, not be shortsightedly frugal in consideration of the immediate bottom line. When deciding on investments in informatics and analytics tools and resources, leaders must consider the long-term gains that accrue from enhanced data and analytics capabilities, and their transformational potential for an enterprise.

**Analytics expertise**
Expertise in the various techniques of statistical analysis is critical here. Once an analyst receives a dataset, the first step is to run general descriptive measurements to detect inconsistencies in the data (for example, missing values). A more laborious step of analysis comes next, "cleaning" the dataset, or seeking to validate, understand, and correct inconsistencies that become apparent upon investigation. A key goal of teaming up informatics experts with analytics experts is to spend time on the conceptual construction of the dataset and the subsequent extraction of data elements from existing databases to avoid as many inconsistencies as possible and to minimize subsequent time spent "cleaning the data" as far as possible. This will allow analysts to receive datasets that need very little "cleaning" activity to be ready for analysis or providing insights. In the 1917 Clinic, my colleagues and I at the University of Alabama at Birmingham go to great lengths to protect our analysts' time in order to allow them to focus on analyzing data, not on tasks that other informatics experts can accomplish. This focus increases the individual analysts' efficiency and the potential for the analytics unit's tasks to favorably impact the enterprise, both from a financial perspective and from the research and practice communities' responses to dissemination of clinical and research findings.

Using these approaches, we have achieved increased efficiency of our analysts in three important ways. First, we established a program for continuous data quality monitoring and improvement. Second, we established a necessary step in the process where those who seek to formulate a data-based question must participate in meetings where both the informatics and analytics experts help refine the list of specified data elements requested and the proposed analysis plan (for example, questions being asked). Third, we have formal and frequent communication between those extracting and those analyzing the data.

The need for continuous monitoring and improvement of data quality speaks both to this neglected component of enterprise data strategies as well as to the third rule of data: the chaos inherent in data collection. Data quality is an ongoing effort. We strive to correct inconsistencies in our data consistently, independent of any single analysis. Our goal is to diminish existing quality issues within our existing data, preventing our analysts from having to spend time in the future "cleaning" data or reconciling the same issues within our data in subsequent analyses over time. Meetings in which the individual seeking data-derived information engages with those who will enact the actual data extraction and analysis force the definition of the question, and ensure that the requested data will provide the necessary insight, ultimately saving every team member time and producing more valid and reliable results. Establishing relationships and good communication among those extracting and analyzing the data also help team members to better understand how to more effectively work together and facilitate their collaborative work. For example, an analyst might request the person extracting the data to organize it a certain way that will facilitate importing the dataset into the statistical software package used for data analysis.

By adopting this combination of strategies at the 1917 Clinic, we were able to significantly impact quality reporting across approximately 20 patient outcomes, to decrease the time to process our monthly billing, and to increase our scientific productivity from approximately three published manuscripts per year between 2000 and 2006 to around 16 manuscripts per year between 2007 and 2012 within our established group of collaborators. In addition, we were able to easily interact with collaborators bringing new ideas into the group, as the interdisciplinary meeting quickly shaped vague queries into concise and answerable questions that were expediently converted to constructed datasets that were subsequently analyzed to the benefit of the organization, as evident through improvement in clinical practice and research productivity. A non-trivial by-product of this accumulation of clinical evidence was the contribution to scholarly manuscripts that accrued to our faculty at the University of Alabama at Birmingham, particularly those on track for promotion and tenure review.

**Domain experts**
Individuals who do not fall into one of the prior two categories likely have a different area of expertise within the enterprise. Whether that area is administration or direct patient care, their experience provides valuable insight into processes that have the potential for improvement in

organizational processes and outcomes. These insights, borne from longitudinal experience and careful examination, give rise to insightful questions. It is important for leaders to create venues where these questions are asked in a room with informatics and analytics experts, so that they can be shaped into queries that can be processed through the data extraction and analysis systems present in the enterprise. As described above, we were able to build such a forum in regularly scheduled interdisciplinary meetings in the 1917 HIV Clinic. Analytics teams work together with domain experts to "frame the question," recognized by some as the first step of quantitative analysis, and followed by the stages of "solving the problem," which encompasses data collection and analyses, and "communication and acting on results" (Davenport and Kim, 2013). Domain experts play critical roles in initiating questions, communicating results, and fomenting changes in organizational behavior as the result of analytic findings.

**Who Is the Most Important Team Member?**

While one might ask which is the most important piece of data strategy – the informatics, analytics, or domain experts – I would posit that none of them is the most important. The key to success lies in establishing a spirit of collaboration born from the overarching goal of raising the standards of excellence throughout the enterprise. I would argue that the informatics and analytics experts need to have a "service mentality," understanding that they need the domain experts to trust and communicate with them to bring impactful questions to the forefront. Meanwhile, informatics and analytics experts must trust that domain experts will take their findings, communicate them throughout the organization, and act as a fulcrum to incite change, validating their work.

It is crucial for enterprises to integrate individuals who have good understanding or some knowledge of two expert domains and add them to the data and analytics teams, as these individuals will help bridge the communication gap between those with one strong area of expertise. Let me posit an example where an analysis of the factors associated with readmission to the hospital after a specific surgical procedure is performed through logistic regression analyses. Upon hearing which variables were identified by the statistical model as increasing the risk of hospital readmission, the surgical service administrator ponders significant changes to existing processes for post-surgical care. In such a situation, it is crucial that the analysts in the room are able to explain the ecologic fallacy to the administrator so that they understand that association does not imply causation, and that logistic regression is merely pointing to things that in that dataset were associated with increased odds of the outcome. (Moving directly to process changes on the basis of a statistical finding alone is rarely the correct approach.)

The impact of sample size, or correction for multiple measures from the same patient, and many other subtleties of statistical analyses need to be factored into the interpretation of results, and the administrator in this example must hear in clear and succinct language just how much weight the analyses carry. My fictional example ends with the administrator relenting from enacting sweeping reactionary changes based on the evidence thus far, and working with informatics experts on capturing new data and the analytics experts in devising an analysis strategy that will yield additional insights that will ultimately guide a future decision. This example illustrates the extensive degree of collaboration and communication required for this or any other team to be effective. Thus, perhaps a "most important" team member can be identified after all. I highlight *collaboration* as the "most important" team member. When a service mentality and the goal of favorably impacting enterprises at multiple levels overshadows individual goals and is combined with the integration of individuals who can bridge the communications gap between disciplines, a data and analytics team can transform an institution.

## THE CLINICAL AND ENTERPRISE LIVES OF DATA

The electronic medical record is the virtual location where the collection of clinical data is centralized. Several types of data are captured within the repository, including imaging, discrete, and free text data. Discrete data are stored in relational tables and can be retrieved reliably (Davenport and Kim, 2013). Examples of discrete data include vital signs (body temperature, pulse rate) or the numerical results of a laboratory test, such as a blood cell count. Such information can be readily retrieved using tools to query the underlying database. Imaging and free text data are at present more challenging as such information has a different structure in its storage. To contrast, one may readily request all female hospital patients with a heart rate greater than 100 over a specific week, yet one may not similarly query for all individuals with chest radiographs showing a right third rib fracture during the same time period from the electronic medical records' underlying data structures. Indeed, one of the promises of big data would be to use technology to extract the data in this example, perhaps using image analysis software or natural language processing of chest radiographs and their reports to find those with a right third rib fracture, by organizing such unstructured data into formats that may be queried.

Whether structured or unstructured, the data in the electronic medical record serves to allow communication between all the involved health professionals. Thus, an omission of a patient's medication allergies in a prior encounter can place the patient at risk in the present encounter (Kohn, 2001). Thus, a mistake made by one healthcare provider creates a problem for all future healthcare providers who must now make decisions based on inaccurate data. Patients often suffer the effects of poor documentation as we fail to reconcile their medication regimens at the time of hospital admission or discharge, often leading to adverse events and increased rates of readmission (Provine et al., 2014; Kilcup et al., 2013; Shekelle et al., 2013). Accurate documentation is central to the clinical care, quality and safety, and research missions of a healthcare facility.

It is critical to understand the potential for harm from inaccurate documentation in the clinical life of data. For example, many commercially developed electronic medical record systems are able to detect and alert serious drug–drug interactions when incompatible medications are jointly prescribed. This important software function is undermined and its benefits are lost to patients if a provider writes a handwritten prescription and fails to record that medication in the electronic medical record. Efforts to facilitate quality documentation, to make electronic medical records more user-friendly, and to establish systems to gauge, monitor, and enhance the quality of documentation can improve data quality. An organization with high-quality data will have a stronger base from which to derive insights to create processes to enhance the quality and safety of care, contribute new research to discover new treatment strategies, and use its data to trigger interventions to provide new services to its patients. In regard to the latter, researchers at the 1917 Clinic have used electronically self-reported patient information regarding depression status to detect active suicidality and intervene in high-volume clinical settings (Lawrence et al., 2010). The capture and analysis of high-quality data empowers organizational improvement.

## THE RESEARCH LIFE OF DATA

The University of Alabama at Birmingham counts among its valuable resources an outpatient clinic to care for people living with HIV/AIDS, the 1917 Clinic. The story of this clinic's creation and evolution is told in the book *Positive*, written by the clinic's founder, Dr. Michael S. Saag. The story I would tell of the 1917 Clinic is a more mundane one. It is the story of how a small healthcare facility was able to use its data strategically to contribute greatly to the transformation of HIV/AIDS from a uniformly

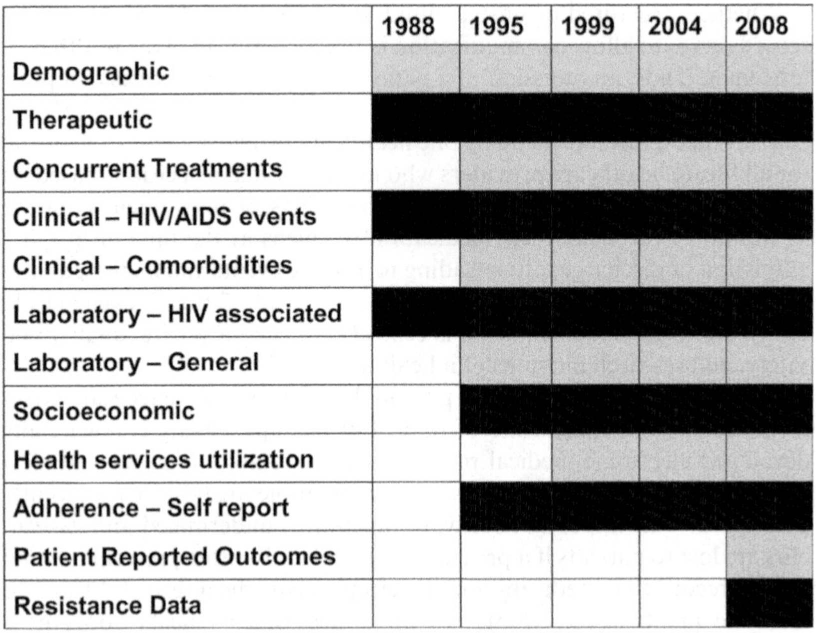

|                              | 1988 | 1995 | 1999 | 2004 | 2008 |
|------------------------------|------|------|------|------|------|
| Demographic                  |      |      |      |      |      |
| Therapeutic                  |      |      |      |      |      |
| Concurrent Treatments        |      |      |      |      |      |
| Clinical – HIV/AIDS events   |      |      |      |      |      |
| Clinical – Comorbidities     |      |      |      |      |      |
| Laboratory – HIV associated  |      |      |      |      |      |
| Laboratory – General         |      |      |      |      |      |
| Socioeconomic                |      |      |      |      |      |
| Health services utilization  |      |      |      |      |      |
| Adherence – Self report      |      |      |      |      |      |
| Patient Reported Outcomes    |      |      |      |      |      |
| Resistance Data              |      |      |      |      |      |

*Figure 16.4   The growth of data capture by year at the 1917 HIV/AIDS Clinic*

lethal diagnosis to a chronically managed illness. Figure 16.4 illustrates the addition of data elements captured over a 20-year time span. Each row represents a data type, while each column denotes the year in which it became available at the 1917 Clinic. The 1917 Clinic data story begins in 1988.

In 1988, a diagnosis of HIV/AIDS was considered fatal. Knowledge of how the disease affected patients was actively being collected. At the 1917 Clinic, the collection of blood samples was being undertaken, and each sample shared an identifier with a small clinical record recorded in a relational database that included only some basic patient demographics (for example, age, gender), clinical HIV/AIDS events as defined by the Centers for Disease Control (CDC) at that time, results of a few basic laboratory tests, and information on therapies that were being used. This modest collection of data allowed clinic providers and associated scientists to use the information to isolate samples for studies on patients with specific criteria (for example, men having suffered a specific opportunistic infection). This ability facilitated local research and allowed collaboration with researchers throughout the US as specific patient types could be readily detected and their samples shared. Over the next few years, the 1917 Clinic was able to participate in seminal studies that uncovered much of how the virus affected patients, how disease activity could be measured, and set the stage to pursue treatment trials. Indeed, many HIV/AIDS medications saw their first use in this small clinic in Alabama.

By 1995, therapy with one and two agents had failed and highly active antiretroviral therapy (a combination of three agents from two drug classes) was beginning to show efficacy. In this remarkable time patients began to live, and the era of effective HIV therapy began. Clinic data capture grew in the setting of these advances. Now a team of health information specialists would abstract paper charts and enter information into an MS ACCESS® database. New data types included concurrent treatments, comorbid diseases, expanded capture of laboratory studies, socioeconomic variables, and self-reported medication adherence. The last two became more and more important as the cost of medications was prohibitive and providers came to learn that despite drug availability, other issues interfered with patients taking medications, and non-adherence to therapy was recognized as a growing threat. The capture of these data allowed the clinic to expand its innovation space and contribute to the burgeoning literature on the efficacy of new agents, the unintended side effects and consequences of these new agents, as well as continued success in basic sciences research, uncovering further insights into how the disease progressed and affected patients.

Only four years later, in 1999, multiple options for effective HIV/AIDS therapy existed. Many individuals had successfully achieved the suppression of viral replication for several years. Our health system began the centralized capture of service utilization data, and this expanded our innovation space. Now, we could look at the hospital utilization of different stages of illness and the associated costs (Chen et al., 2006). The longitudinal data captured on individuals under care for several years began to provide insights into more chronic impacts of these still new antiretroviral medications, and the established basic science research continued to thrive. Data quality was checked regularly as separate medical record personnel duplicated the abstraction of a subset of charts, comparing their findings with those of their colleagues.

By 2004, HIV was recognized as a chronic condition. Life expectancy on long-term therapy is expected to equate to that of people without HIV (Samji et al., 2013). Here, the Clinic transitioned to real-time data capture through a locally developed electronic medical record. Now the clinic had electronic data at a time when such information began to be shared with other national and international HIV collaborations, allowing widespread aggregation of HIV/AIDS data and potentiating research throughout such data-sharing networks. The clinic struggled with data quality, and a system was established whereby a third party read all medication and diagnostic notes, and medication side effects mentioned in the free text notes were confirmed to have been updated in the corresponding discrete fields in the electronic medical record. Through adopting new technology and changing the nature of the data capture, the clinic was able to facilitate external data-sharing and grow all established areas of research. A data and analytics team was established and processes to facilitate and guide collaboration with that team were put in place. The next few years showed an increase from three manuscripts to 16 manuscripts published per year with clinic data. Not only investigators, but clinic leadership began to benefit from data access as clinic billing and internal quality of care and safety analyses were improved collaboratively with the data and analytics team.

In 2008, the time of one pill, once a day HIV/AIDS therapies arrived. HIV/AIDS is truly treated as a chronic illness, and the causes of mortality have shifted from those related to advanced disease to the causes of mortality that afflict the general population (Palella et al., 2006). The study of multi-morbidity or the impact of additional health conditions on the lives of those with HIV/AIDS had grown in importance (Burkholder et al., 2012; Crane et al., 2011; Kalayjian et al., 2012; Kim et al., 2012; Tate et al., 2012; Vance et al., 2011). The clinic's use of hospital utilization data evolved to support a growing research line into linkage and retention in care, which soon became a key component of the US National AIDS Strategy (Kozak et al., 2013; Mugavero et al., 2012; Mugavero et al., 2009). The clinic's innovation space expanded with the integration of HIV/AIDS drug resistance data, which allowed participation in a new facet of collaborative research as this information was combined with that of other treatment sites. In addition, the clinic added electronically captured patient reported outcomes (PRO) data using standardized survey instruments administered to patients during their visits. PRO data allows new insights that impact patient care, and new research data that vastly expand the clinic's innovation space and impact all established research lines and allow new types of behavioral research (Lawrence et al., 2010; Kozak et al., 2012; Schumacher et al., 2013).

The 1917 Clinic continues to thrive. Its aggressive and deliberate expansion of its innovation space through the constant addition of new data types over time has resulted in tens of millions of dollars of research funding that has not only improved care to the local HIV/AIDS population, but has changed and extended the lives of those living with HIV/AIDS throughout the world. Data capture has played a key role in this transformation, and an expanded innovation space has consistently led to better patient care, more effective enterprise operations, and more robust research agendas.

## ONE (INTEGRATED) LIFE FOR DATA

The Institute of Medicine has advanced the vision of a learning healthcare system. In a learning healthcare system, data are continuously collected, shared, analyzed, and used to propel the clinical care, research, and educational missions of an enterprise. In a learning healthcare system, the optimization of patient service, the enhancement of the quality and safety of clinical care, and the development of new advances to further the science that drives improvements in patient outcomes become integrated processes that potentiate and inform each other (Smith et al., 2013; Smith et al., 2012). Both the learning healthcare system and predictive, preventive, personalized, and participatory (P4) medicine rely heavily on the effective collection, analysis, and use of data and the transformation of data to information and insight that strengthen patient care, research, and education (McHattie et al., 2014). The knowledge necessary to control costs, to manage the health of patient populations, to improve in-hospital care through the reduction of errors and variations in clinical practice, is a direct result of an institution's data and analytics infrastructure. Both the learning healthcare system and P4 medicine promote the integration of research and clinical practice in a mutually beneficial cycle of knowledge and understanding.

When it comes to data, healthcare organizations face a challenge in how to expand the understanding and the ability to use data to bring innovative solutions to the strategic and operational objectives of a healthcare system. The elements listed as foundational to an enterprise data strategy include informatics and analytics tools, data quality, and organizational culture. Using the framework of the innovation space, it can be seen that answering questions is the result of the interaction of data types and statistical methodologies, a process which remains the same regardless of whether the question is of a financial, quality and safety, research, or other nature. An effective enterprise data strategy creates one ecosystem to use data effectively, one where disparate healthcare system functions all draw benefit from a common repository of information and tools for data access and analysis, where all the lives of data become integrated into one.

# REFERENCES

Burkholder, G.A., Tamhane, A.R., Salinas, J.L., et al. (2012) "Underutilization of aspirin for primary prevention of cardiovascular disease among HIV-infected patients," *Clinical Infectious Diseases: An Official Publication of the Infectious Diseases Society of America*, 55 (11), 1550–1557.

Chen, R.Y., Accortt, N.A., Westfall, A.O., et al. (2006) "Distribution of health care expenditures for HIV-infected patients," *Clinical Infectious Diseases: An Official Publication of the Infectious Diseases Society of America*, 42 (7), 1003–1010.

Crane, H.M., Grunfeld, C., Willig, J.H., et al. (2011) "Impact of NRTIs on lipid levels among a large HIV infected cohort initiating antiretroviral therapy in clinical care," AIDS, 25 (2), 185–195.

Davenport, Thomas H. (2014) *Big Data at Work: Dispelling the Myths, Uncovering the Opportunities*, Boston, MA: Harvard Business Review Press.

Davenport, Thomas H. and Jin Ho Kim (2013) *Keeping Up with the Quants: Your Guide to Understanding and Using Analytics*, Boston, MA: Harvard Business Review Press.

Kalayjian, R.C., Lau, B., Mechekano, R.N., et al. (2012) "Risk factors for chronic kidney disease in a large cohort of HIV-1 infected individuals initiating antiretroviral therapy in routine care," *AIDS*, 26 (15), 1907–1915.

Kilcup, M., Schultz D., Carlson J., and Wilson B. (2013) "Postdischarge pharmacist medication reconciliation: Impact on readmission rates and financial savings," *Journal of the American Pharmacists Association: JAPhA*, 53 (1), 78–84.

Kim, D.J., Westfall, A.O., Chamot, E., Willig, A.L., Mugavero, M.J., Ritchie, C., Burkholder, G.A., Crane, H.M., Raper, J.L., Saag, M.S., and Willig, J.H. (2012) "Multimorbidity patterns in HIV-infected patients: The role of obesity in chronic disease clustering," *Journal of Acquired Immune Deficiency Syndrome*, 61 (5), 600–605.

Kohn, L.T. (2001) "The Institute of Medicine report on medical error: overview and implications for pharmacy," *American Journal of Health-System Pharmacy: AJHP: official journal of the American Society of Health-System Pharmacists*, 58 (1), 63–66.

Kozak, M.S., Mugavero, M.J., Ye, J., Aban, I., Lawrence, S.T., Nevin, C.R., Raper, J.L., Mccullumsmith, C., Schumacher, J.E., Crane, H.M., Kitahata, M.M., Saag, M.S., and Willig, J.H. (2012) "Patient reported outcomes in routine care: Advancing data capture for HIV cohort research," *Clinical Infectious Disease*, 54 (1), 141–147.

Kozak, M., Zinski, A., Leeper, C., Willig, J.H., Mugavero, M.J. (2013) "Late diagnosis, delayed presentation and late presentation in HIV: Proposed definitions, methodological considerations and health implications," *Antiviral Therapy*, 18 (1), 17–23.

Lawrence, S.T., Willig, J.H., Crane, H.M., et al. (2010) "Routine, self-administered, touch-screen, computer-based suicidal ideation assessment linked to automated response team notification in an HIV primary care setting," *Clinical Infectious Diseases: An Official Publication of the Infectious Diseases Society of America*, 50 (8), 1165–1173.

Mayer-Schonberger, V. and Cukier, Kenneth (2013) *Big Data: A Revolution That Will Transform How We Live, Work and Think*, Boston and New York: Eamon Dolan/Houghton Mifflin Harcourt.

McHattie, L.S., Cumming, G., and French, T. (2014) "Transforming patient experience: health web science meets medicine 2.0," *Medicine* 2.0, 3 (1), e2.

Mugavero, M.J., Amico, K.R., Westfall, A.O., Crane, H.M., Zinski, A., Willig, J.H., Dombrowski, J.C., Norton, W.E., Raper, J.L., Kitahata, M.M., and Saag, M. (2012) "Early retention in HIV care and viral load suppression: Implications for a test and treat approach to HIV prevention," *Journal of Acquired Immune Deficiency Syndrome*, 59 (1), 86–93. doi:10.1097/QAI.0b013e318236f7d2.

Mugavero, M.J., Lin, H.Y., Willig, J.H., Westfall, A.O., Ulett, K.B., Routman, J.S., Abroms, S., Raper, J.L., Saag, M.S., Allison, J.J. (2009) "Missed visits and mortality among patients establishing initial outpatient HIV treatment," *Clinical Infectious Diseases*, 48 (2), 248–256.

Palella, Jr, F.J., Baker, R.K., Moorman, A.C., et al. (2006) "Mortality in the highly active antiretroviral therapy era: changing causes of death and disease in the HIV outpatient study," *Journal of Acquired Immune Deficiency Syndromes*, 43 (1), 27–34.

Provine, A.D., Simmons, E.M., and Bhagat, P.H. (2014) "Establishment and Evaluation of Pharmacist-Managed Admission Medication History and Reconciliation Process for Pediatric Patients", *Journal of Pediatric Pharmacology and Therapeutics: JPPT: Official Journal of PPAG*, 19 (2), 98–102.

Samji, H., Cescon, A., Hogg, R.S., et al. (2013) "Closing the gap: increases in life expectancy among treated HIV-positive individuals in the United States and Canada," *PloS one*, 8 (12), e81355.

Schumacher, J.E., Mccullumsmith, C., Mugavero, M.J., Ingle-Pang, P.E., Raper, J.L., Willig, J.H., You, Z., Batey, D.S., Crane, H., Lawrence, S.T., Wright, C., Treisman, G., and Saag, M.S. (2013) "Routine depression screening in an HIV clinic cohort identifies patients with complex psychiatric co-morbidities who show significant response to treatment," *AIDS Behavior*, 17 (8), 2781–2791.

Shekelle, P.G., Wachter, R.M., Pronovost, P.J., et al. (2013) "Making health care safer II: An updated critical analysis of the evidence for patient safety practices," Evidence Report/Technology Assessment No. 211, Rockville MD: Agency for Healthcare Research and Quality.

Siegel, Eric Hoboken (2013) *Predictive Analytics: The Power to Predict Who Will Click, Buy, Lie or Die*, Hoboken, NJ: John Wiley & Sons.

Smith, M., Halvorson, G., and Kaplan, G. (2012) "What's needed is a health care system that learns: Recommendations from an IOM report," *Journal of the American Medical Association*, 308 (16), 1637–1638. DOI: 10.1001/jama.2012.13664.

Smith, M., Saunders, R., Stuckhardt, L., and McGinnis, J.M. (eds) (2013) *Best Care at Lower Cost: The Path to Continuously Learning Health Care in America*, Washington, DC: National Academic Press.

Tate, T., Willig, A.L., Willig, J.H., Raper, J.L., Moneyham, L., Kempf, M.C., Saag, M.S., and Mugavero, M.J. (2012) "HIV infection and obesity: Where did all the wasting go?" *Antiviral Therapy*, 17 (7), 1281–1289. Epub 2012/09/07.

Vance, D.E., Mugavero, M., Willig, J., Raper, J.L., and Saag, M.S. (2011) "Aging with HIV: A cross-sectional study of comorbidity prevalence and clinical characteristics across decades of life," *Journal of the Association of Nurses in AIDS Care*, 22 (1), 17–25.

Waldman, Scott A. and Terzic, A. (2010) "Clinical and Translational Science: From Bench-Bedside to Global Village," *Clinical and Translational Science*, 3 (5), 254–257.

# 17. Managing clinical professionals

*Timothy R. Huerta, Ann Scheck McAlearney and Eric W. Ford*

## INTRODUCTION

Managing clinical professionals is a daunting task for any healthcare manager in the United States. The management of clinical professionals is a required healthcare administration competency made more complicated by contentious historical relationships, conflicting belief systems, competing values, employment trends, and policy influences. Historically, US physicians made clinical determinations (for example, diagnosis and treatment), commanded the resources to carry out the task (for example, prescribing) and directed how other caregivers' work would be performed (for example, issued orders). This is no longer the case.

Ideological, economic, political, clinical, technical, and organizational change, occurring within a framework that is moving from provider-driven to buyer-driven care environments, all influence the care management. Authority for clinical responsibilities has devolved and extends to a variety of professions in recent years, with more change yet to come. Further, the expectation placed on the entirety of the healthcare system to provide high-quality care has created an implicit interdependency that can both strengthen and weaken the system's ability to provide that care. This chapter will explore these issues to provide insight about the challenges of managing clinical professionals.

The chapter first explains the cultural dynamics associated with medical professions to provide some context for how clinicians view management. Then, we discuss trends in the general environment in the USA (for example, demographic, political and economic forces) that influence managers. Next, prevailing trends in the health sector's task environment (for example, clinical professional supply, public policies targeting the sector) that influence organizational forms and professional norms are described. Expanding clinical autonomy among nurses and other allied health workers creates new interprofessional dynamics and poses significant management challenges. The organizational design section then describes how patient-centered medical homes (PCMHs), accountable care organizations (ACOs), and other new organizational forms are changing workforce dynamics in the US. Lastly, the new leadership para-digms that look beyond treating clinical professionals as either "locals" or "cosmopolitans" (Gouldner, 1957) are discussed, and how to engage them more fully is explored.

## CULTURAL DYNAMICS: WHAT DOES IT MEAN TO BE A CLINICAL PROFESSIONAL?

On the face of it, to be a clinical professional means to be a practitioner of a profession that provides care. A profession refers to a vocation in which the practitioners acquire expertise through extensive training (both educational and vocational) and assume a relationship of responsibility toward clients both individually, through training in an ethical code, and communally, through professional organizations that reinforce that code. In addition, professionals tend to have a highly specialized vocabulary and language that sets them apart from others intellectually and culturally. This definition is important to achieving a greater understanding of the challenges associated with managing such professionals.

There are two main categories of clinical professionals – doctors and nurses – and both have idiosyncratic trajectories for their training. The professional journey of a physician in the United States typically includes four years of baccalaureate-level training, followed by a rigor-ous entrance examination and application process as individuals seek entrance to one of 171 accredited Doctor of Medicine (MD) or Doctor of Osteopathic Medicine (DO) granting institutions. Upon completion, phy-sicians in practice are generally required to complete a residency, a period during which the individual receives vocational training in the profession, including training in the culture of care and the practice of medicine. The shortest residencies add three years of training, while the longest can add six years or more beyond medical school. Successful completion of a resi-dency program is a requirement to practice medicine in many jurisdictions. A residency may also be augmented by a fellowship in one of 22 specialty or sub-specialty areas. While doctors may be working as physicians during their residencies and fellowships, they are doing so under the guidance of mentors and other professionals. After completing all elements of formal training, doctors are later required to complete ongoing training in the form of continuing medical education (CME) to ensure maintenance of their knowledge and skills in their chosen field.

During the formal training period, doctors are being admitted to a com-munity of practice (CoP). A CoP has been defined as a self-organized, voluntary, focused community of people and organizations working toward common understanding on a given issue (Wenger, 1998; Wenger and Snyder, 2000). In Wenger's words, "Communities of practice are groups of people who share a concern or a passion for something they do and learn how to do it better as they interact regularly" (Wenger, 2005). The CoP represents a model for the persistent, sustained social network of individuals who share and develop an overlapping knowledge base, set of beliefs, values, histories, and experiences focused on a common practice and/or mutual experience (Barab et al., 2003). The CoP model is built on an intrinsically collaborative paradigm based on shared knowledge, values, and beliefs with overlapping histories among members who contribute to a level of mutual interdependence, common practice, or mutual enterprise (Barab and Duffy, 2000). CoPs generally meet the collaborative structure requirements articulated by Gray (1989) for relationships that can develop shared perceptions of problems to determine and undertake agreed courses of action.

CoPs have been found to use resources efficiently, help drive strategy, elucidate and transfer best practices, cultivate partnerships, develop professional skills, and promote rapid dissemination of knowledge within teams and groups with a common purpose (Wenger and Snyder, 2000); they are ideally suited to the complex and changing knowledge environment within healthcare (Best et al., 2003; Gao et al., 2003; Knights et al., 1993). CoPs allow for the capture and sharing of knowledge, and in a manner that complements existing organizational structures by galvanizing knowledge-sharing, learning, and change (Smith, 2001). The generation of knowledge in a CoP occurs when people participate in problem-solving and share the knowledge necessary to solve problems (Wenger, 1998).

While formal technique is developed during the training, so too is the development of a professional ethical responsibility toward clients both individually, through training in an ethical code, and communally, through professional organizations that reinforce that code. The Hippocratic Oath, "First, do no harm," is one rule that is interpreted to mean that one must weigh a treatment's costs in light of the potential benefits. Further, training increases professional camaraderie and reliance is reinforced; research indeed shows that the diffusion of innovation is more likely to emerge from professional relationships than dissemination via the literature. One downside to a closed group mentality is that it can lead to combative relationships with other professions for control over "turf." For physicians, these "turf wars" often occur with another profession: nursing.

If we apply the CoP construct to the nursing profession, we find a similar career trajectory to physicians. Nurses receive specialized education and vocational training. Nursing professionals are in short supply in many markets. The nursing profession is also trending toward higher education levels as a means of increasing nurses' clinical autonomy. Taken together, the supply shortage, increasing demand, and elevated professionalization of nurses gives them significant leverage in the workplace, resulting in higher short-term costs, but increasing the ability of healthcare organizations that employ them to deal with more complex care.

The US healthcare sector has faced recurrent short-term nursing shortages (Bovbjerg et al., 2009). Over the next 20 years, aging trends in US society will lead to more people needing healthcare services, further aggravating the nursing shortage. Labor shortages among nurses and the severity of those shortages vary by state and are normal to some extent. For example, the economic downturn triggered by the financial crisis in 2007–2008 led many nurses who had left the profession to return, temporarily alleviating the shortage in many areas. However, the returning nurses highlighted a demographic challenge facing the profession: an aging nursing workforce tending to an increasingly aging society.

The impact of nursing shortages on cost is clear. In the face of a shortage, an organization must pay a premium to secure these clinical professionals and provide an environment conducive to long-term tenure. As the aging population continues to grow, the healthcare system will rely more heavily on nursing homes and long-term care facilitates. Studies have reported the average annual nurse aide turnover rate in US nursing homes as between 74 percent and 100 percent, with California having rates as high as 400 percent (Castel and Engberg, 2006). Nursing staff turnover results in higher financial costs, lower productivity, and lower-quality care and employee morale (Brannon et al., 2002).

### The Advancement of Advanced Practice Nurses

One major difference in the nurses' versus physicians' paths to the terminal degree is work experience (Minnick et al., 2013). Unlike physicians, who typically go from baccalaureate degrees directly to medical school, nurses often have extensive work experience at the bedside prior to entering advanced education. Moreover, many advanced practice programs are designed to allow the nurse to continue to work. Such an educational structure provides both opportunities and challenges to managers.

Originally it was common for hospitals to train their own nursing staff. These "diploma nurses" were provided pragmatic training in the practice of nursing. However, just as specialization brought increased prestige, more interesting engagement, and a trajectory for advanced practice for physicians, nurses are becoming more advanced in their clinical expertise by achieving higher education levels (Tagliareni and Malone, 2013). The supply shift from hospital-prepared "diploma nurses" to colleges of nursing in universities focused on baccalaureate education (Bachelor of Science in Nursing – BSN) as the emerging professional standard has greatly reduced the number of programs producing nurses. Hence, the nursing workforce supply mechanism has decreased significantly, and staffing the educational institutions is now a challenge (Nickitas and Feeg, 2011).

Along with increased education, nurses also now seek to gain greater professional autonomy. Nursing's expanded scope of practice allows health system managers to seek more cost-effective delivery models (Robiner, 2006). In particular, many healthcare managers rely on nurses as less expensive alternatives to physicians. Yet as the last cohorts of diploma nurses leave the workforce, the labor shortage will become more acute in markets where the higher education system did not replace the lost hospital programs and the faculty are not currently available to staff university-based programs. Overall, the labor market challenges endemic to the nursing profession will likely persist into the foreseeable future. Effective recruitment and retention of nurses will remain a major managerial challenge. Moreover, other changes in the nursing profession will alter the way nurses interact with other clinical professions, complicating health system managers' jobs further still.

To that end, the nursing profession has bolstered its educational offerings to include the Nurse Practitioner (NP) focus. NPs have the authority to prescribe medications in 49 US states and the District of Columbia (Duffy et al., 2002) and are considered "complementary" to physicians rather than being "substitutes" because they are under physician supervision. While the extent of physician oversight varies by jurisdiction, the trend is toward greater NP autonomy and changes in legislation to more accurately reflect the reality of many situations where NPs act, for all intents and purposes, with little or no oversight, particularly in underserved areas.

However, the extent of such training, while similarly regulated, occurs in a wider variety of ways. While both professions have continuing education requirements, nurses are far more likely to seek additional academic experiences leading to higher degrees. Nurses progress through different levels of licensure, from Licensed Vocational or Practice Nurse (LVN/LPN), through completion of training to achieve Registered Nurse (RN) status and to Advance Practice (AP) standing, which include nurse practitioners, nurse anesthetists and midwives. What is different in the educational trajectory is that most doctors proceed through training in a continuous fashion, while nurses are not required to do so. The resultant cultural difference that emerges provides support for ongoing formal education among nurses, even as a discontinuous process. Further, nurses speak of being "in the trenches" together, strengthening the CoP as a buffer against managerial encroachment.

Current trends in nursing education and licensure have the doctorate of nursing practice (DNP) as the terminal degree. The Doctorate in Nursing Practice (DNP) was a degree initially offered beginning in 2004 and it was envisioned that it would become the terminal degree for clinical practice. The DNP option was intended to supplant the Master's degree by 2015 (Dracup et al., 2005), and by 2013, over 200 DNP programs had been launched (Dunbar-Jacob et al., 2013). In the future, these programs will produce a significant number of DNPs to staff and manage many clinical settings – although the supply is still unlikely to meet demand.

Having and using the title "doctor" applied to nurses has caused an intra-professional debate over the use of such labels. Physicians would like to reserve the term for themselves in clinical settings to avoid confusion among patients as to who has the apex authority level. Ironically, physicians appropriated the term "doctor" from other learned professions to increase the legitimacy of their authority, along with the famous white coats (Blumhagen, 1979). Given these cultural forces, we can see reasons why physicians and nurses rebuff management's efforts to influence care delivery and experience intra-professional strife. One point that physicians and nurses agree on is that managers are lacking in clinical skills and the training that would align them to the ethical codes supporting the CoP.

**The Broadening of the Clinical Enterprise**

If the domain of clinical professionals were limited to physicians and nurses, management might be more straightforward. However, there has been an increase in professionalization across almost all domains of clinical care. Most notably the emergence of electronic health records (EHRs) has created an opportunity for the development of a new domain of clinical experts. Biomedical informaticists, nurse informaticians, and clinical informatics fellowships for training physicians have created the opening for the development of yet another specialization whose role is to deal with the technological changes occurring in both the general and task environments. Similarly, in the context of allied health professionals seeking this training, allied health professions have identified the management of data as an opportunity to level the expertise landscape.

Further, there has been a shift to increase the expertise available to manage the care of patients beyond the traditional physician–patient dyad. The complexity of patients' needs and the technologies available to meet those demands are so varied and sophisticated that no individual can master them to deliver care optimally. However, the technical and cultural demands that historically put physicians in sole command of the health system have evolved dramatically. Given the costs associated with physician-provided care and the fact that medical care only influences 20 percent of health outcomes, the inclusion of clinical and non-clinical professionals, such as social workers and case managers, in the clinical endeavor is the new normal.

Interestingly, diversification of the clinical team is seen as a strategy by some professions to address supply imbalances and improve access in a community. Consider that current professional programs supplying pharmacists exceed demand (Brown, 2013). Yet including pharmacists as members of multidisciplinary teams of care opens a new opportunity to absorb the excess supply and may generate new demand. The move to the new "team" model of care represents a response to environmental and policy pressures to transform care delivery.

## THE ENVIRONMENTAL CONTEXT FOR MANAGING CLINICAL PROFESSIONALS

If we look back 100 years, we see that care was provided in a much different way in the US. First, a century ago, a doctor typically made house calls without a nurse – he was a team of one (if you don't count the horse he rode in on), likely a man, and often trained as a surgeon. Two dynamics then changed that relationship: the urbanization of the US, where more people were in one place and scale economies could be leveraged; and the invention and dissemination of increasingly technical tools for the purpose of diagnosis, including the X-ray, which required stationary doctors. While hospitals existed before then, doctors took on an increasingly central role in these new facilities. In particular, they took control of directing other professions that had previously acted under their own volition, when facilities were truly used for hospice care and nurses (often nuns) were both the managers and lead professionals.

As medical science advanced and the complexity of managing the treatment of conditions became clearer, physicians used sub-specialization to address care delivery's ever-increasing complexity. The first medical specialty, opthalmology, founded in 1916, identified the need for individuals who specialized in the care of conditions related to the eye who could and should be held to a higher standard of training that specialization affords. Similar to other economic forces, specialization re-enforced the stationary physician with the clients coming to institutions (that is, doctors' offices or hospitals) for the provision of care. However, health sciences' extraordinary technological advancements and medical schools' limited ability to meet the demand for new physicians made the single-profession model untenable if consumers' needs were to be effectively managed. In addition, cultural, economic, organizational, and practical considerations made the model with a single profession dominating health services delivery anachronistic. The result of these pressures is a healthcare environment where disciplinary roles are blurring across professions; care is delivered in experimental organizational forms designed to take advantage of multidisciplinary teams; and managers are faced with challenging human relations paradigms.

**Fast Forward to the Present**

Healthcare's general environment's dynamics are changing the organizational forms and professional norms for service delivery (Bourgeois, 1980). The most rapidly changing environmental feature is the demographic shift toward an aging society as the "baby-boomers" grow older and require more services. The second demographic shift that is remaking the healthcare workforce is related to the increased importance and power of women in US society. With increasing numbers of women participating in the workforce, there have also been advances in their educational attainment and the range of career opportunities open to them, beyond traditional roles such as nursing and elementary education. Lastly, information-empowered consumers are changing the way healthcare organizations are perceived, how they compete, and how they interact with engaged customers rather than passive patients.

**The Aging of America in the Era of Higher Demand for Healthcare Services**

The aging of the US population is among the most important challenges health system managers will face in coming years. In 2010, there were nearly 40 million Americans over 65 years of age (Vincent and Velkoff, 2010). By 2020, there will be nearly 55 million people of 65 years or older. In addition to the rapid growth in the number of elderly in absolute terms, they also represent a larger percentage of the population and they wield that influence in policy circles. The change in age distribution creates both demographic and economic challenges for managers. This rapid growth in the elderly population will strain the supply pipelines for clinical professionals. Chronic disease management has become increasingly important for the elderly, and primary care physicians (PCPs) have taken the responsibility for much of this effort. This creates an increasing pressure to locate and retain PCPs. Unfortunately, PCPs are paid some of the lowest salaries, and therefore medical students often seek to specialize in order to increase their lifetime earnings, because of an interest in a particular area of medicine, or due to professional norms that place higher value on sub-specialties. Family medicine, general internal medicine, and obstetrics and gynecology, all have lower wages than their specialist peers, which inhibits staffing these areas that are experiencing shortages.

The result of a misallocated medical professional is a "double whammy" of fewer professionals trained to support the care needs of larger elderly cohorts, combined with an increase in demand with no increase in pay-ments. In most cases, the cost for a care visit is determined by contractual reimbursement rates, and these rates are not sensitive to financial pres-sures caused by market factors associated with increased competition for clinical professionals. The result is an expectation that more must be extracted from the same resources, or that less expensive clinical expertise (for example, nurse practitioners) should provide care for patients who have traditionally been managed by physicians. In practice this has led to both professional tension between doctors and nurses, as well as conflict between clinical care providers and managers.

## The Changing Roles of the Consumer

Consumers, or patients, used to accept being treated as passive partici-pants in their healthcare experiences. However, one major event and a fun-damental change in society have irrevocably altered that norm. The major event was the publication of *To Err is Human: Building a Safer Health System* (Clancy, 2009; Kohn et al., 1999), which shattered consumers' confidence. No longer were healthcare providers perceived to be infal-lible and wise beyond reproach. It became clear that in many instances care-givers were making catastrophic mistakes on a regular basis. The realization of healthcare's patient safety challenges gave rise to calls for greater transparency, quality monitoring, and consumer engagement (Scanlon et al., 2008). Coupled with the emergence of the Internet as a powerful information collection and dissemination medium, the rise of the empowered healthcare consumer has begun in earnest.

Consumer empowerment in healthcare purchasing, care-giver selec-tion, and clinical decision-making is evolving rapidly. Whether it is implementing an effective personal health record (PHR) system, creating a social media presence to attract customers, or merely avoiding poor ratings from websites such as HealthGrades (www.healthgrades.com) or the Leapfrog Group (www.leapfroggroup.org), meeting the needs of empowered consumers is a major managerial challenge. Collectively, the demographic, educational, and consumer empowerment changes in the larger society have a direct impact on the health sector's task environment.

Notably, the shift from clinical professional driving decision-making to one where patients are central has served to fundamentally alter the basic relationship between these two key stakeholders of the healthcare system. For instance, the advent of the Internet has both undermined the role of the physician as the "knower," and raised the expectations of patients as participants in the management of their disease. These changes have come to transform the American healthcare system. The trend toward greater government involvement in the healthcare sector continues to challenge professional norms and managers' abilities to meet traditional organizational goals.

## THE HEALTHCARE CONTEXT: SHIFTING DEMAND, THE PRACTICE PATTERNS THEY ENGENDER, AND THE CHALLENGES THEY CREATE

In economics, the concept of efficiency is defined as the ability to utilize resources to produce the maximum output level. In the hospital context, there is a distinction between human and capital as resources, and the tensions between these two components are significant. For instance, automation has increased the throughput of many hospital laboratories, resulting in higher capital costs for automated equipment, yet the labor cost is reduced. However, as an economic sector, healthcare remains a human capital-intensive endeavor with a cost structure that grows faster than that of the other industries that are almost completely mechanized.

Economists note that two identical facilities can produce different output levels while having comparable inputs. The differences in organizational efficiency are attributed to the so-called "management effect." The efficiency loss of the management effect is, put another way, the loss attributable to one of four factors: the poor allocation of resources to match the environment, an insufficient demand to support the scope of the enterprise, the enumerated value of the services performed, or the inability to coax from labor or capital their best demonstrated use.

### Allocation–Environment Mismatch

The allocation problem involves an incorrect balance between labor and capital. In practice, this relates to the development of an organization that allocates too many resources to labor at the expense of capital, or vice versa. While organizations are constantly striving for a sufficient care environment to ensure high-quality care, they can also view high-touch environments as resources focused on raising satisfaction of both the staff and the patients. Imagine entering a care environment where it is clear that the employees are overworked and understaffed. One would expect a greater number of errors and higher turnover. In contrast, the opposite would reflect an environment where people felt very comfortable, but there was insufficient investment in rooms, technology and infrastructure such as high-quality electronic health record (EHR) systems. Allocation match is about balancing the needs of the clinical enterprise, and poor allocation undermines efficiency.

For the management of clinical professionals in a hospital setting, this means finding the right mix of specialists, internists, nurses, psychologists, social workers, and technologists that provide the mix of care that is appropriate to the care needs of the patient population, and balanced against the investment in infrastructure these same clinical professionals need to effectively practice their art. There is a debate about whether or not there is a physician shortage in the US (Sloan and Hsieh, 2012). Irrespective of the conclusion that an individual draws about the number of physicians available, one feature that has almost universal agreement is that a labor force misallocation exists between specialists and primary care physicians. In particular, the short supply of PCPs is creating access issues for at-risk populations.

**Demand–Scope Mismatch**

In this context, we look at the environment in which an organization is embedded to determine if it is the right size for the market it operates in. While beyond the scope of this chapter, matching the enterprise size to the community in which it is embedded is a significant issue, and that dynamic has implications for the management of clinical professionals. Most notably this is influenced by trends in the clinical professional workforce. Paradoxically, labor force shortages and increased specialization in both medical and nursing professions have been instrumental in diminishing the scope of physicians' clinical authority and increasing the scope of nursing authority. Trends in the medical and nursing professions are each considered.

Populations in rural and poor inner-city regions are more likely to experience difficulty in accessing primary care. There is also an acute shortage of gerontologists needed to care for the rapidly aging population cohort discussed earlier (Simon et al., 2013). There have been attempts to address this misallocation through the creation of medical schools with missions and curricula focused on primary care and serving rural constituencies (Brooks et al., 2002). A more blunt approach to dealing with the perceived shortage has been simply to create more medical schools and expand the capacity of existing programs. From 2006 to 2013, there was a 30 percent increase in the number of medical school slots available to future doctors (Iglehart, 2013). Despite these efforts, the medical profession's ability to adequately meet patients' needs is expected to grow even worse over the next few decades.

**Professional Productivity**

The two professions that most US managers struggle to coordinate effectively are doctors and nurses. While other allied health disciplines, such as pharmacy, have increased their education rigor significantly and are striving for greater authority, the doctor–nurse working relationship is undergoing the greatest change. The forces driving the changes to professional norms are the way doctors and nurses are educated, and its concomitant impact on the supply and demand for each in the workforce.

As described above, there are a number of forces fueling changes to the clinical professionals' labor force, its education options, forms of licensure, and scope of work. From many health professionals' perspectives, the hope is that having terminal degrees will create parity among the healthcare disciplines. In particular, several professions desire to work with physicians as peers rather than subordinates. From the managerial and policy perspectives, the new professional designations and privileges are both an opportunity and a threat to effective management. On the one hand, the expansion of professional autonomy beyond physicians has given managers increased staffing alternatives to address the complexity of today's healthcare system. On the other hand, a greater range of professional disciplines with the autonomy to direct organizational resources creates additional complexity and new managerial challenges. Chief among these changing professions is nursing, as described earlier.

**Changing Organizational Forms to Accommodate New Clinical Professional Paradigms**

There are two major changes under way in the task environment that are influencing how care is delivered in the US. The first paradigm shift is toward a holistic, integrated care system designed to coordinate various clinicians' efforts for more efficacious outcomes. To that end, both medical groups and hospitals are growing, to gain the scale economies required to achieve the coordinated care aim. Two new organizational forms are the patient-centered medical home (PCMH) (Hahn et al., 2014) and the accountable care organization (ACO) (Fisher and Shortell, 2010). The second trend is to make primary care more readily available in smaller, more convenient settings or through virtual means. Small, primary health clinics situated in high-traffic locations or within other businesses are becoming more commonplace as outlets for routine services (for example, immunizations, wellness check-ups, and minor illnesses). Alternatively, virtual clinical encounters are gaining in popularity as web-based communication technologies become ubiquitous.

**Patient-centered medical homes**
The team-based care model employed by the new PCMH models of care will change primary care physicians' work (Peikes et al., 2014). Under the PCMH model, physician's assistants (PAs), nurse practitioners (NPs), pharmacists and allied professionals each deliver care traditionally considered to be the physician's domain in order to increase efficiency and effectiveness beyond the levels achieved by doctors alone. Such "team-based care" is designed in part to help overcome PCP shortages by shifting some tasks to other professions (Altschuler et al., 2012). Managers who can leverage the PCMH model to create effective intra-team communication and problem-solving may realize a competitive advantage through continuous quality improvement (Taylor et al., 2013).

Although the PCMH's team-based approach has potential benefits, it may cause communication and management challenges. In particular, the difficulty in delineating responsibilities among multiple team members may lead to service delivery fragmentation instead of the desired continuity of care. The managerial challenge arises because the care process disaggregates the work of one person into the work of many people and the relational continuity; and while this model is associated with better quality and lower costs, gains may be disrupted as more staff are actually seeing each patient (Saultz and Lochner, 2005).

How to achieve the appropriate or optimal staffing composition for PCMH is an area of health services research that is only beginning to provide managers with actionable insights. Research shows that most small and medium-sized practices – where the vast majority of primary care is delivered – do not use team-based approaches (Rittenhouse et al., 2011). One explanation may be inadequate or inefficient staffing with other allied health professionals, as physician-managers struggle with ceding clinical authority.

**Accountable care organizations**

Another new organizational form is the accountable care organization (ACO). Recognizing that healthcare in the US is both costly and poorly coordinated, ACOs are being developed by providers as a type of delivery and payment system reform (Berwick, 2011, 2012a, 2012b; Baxley et al., 2011). The "ACO" term, coined by Fisher et al. in 2009, has been defined as "groups of providers who are willing and able to take responsibility for improving the overall health status, care efficiency, and health care experience for a defined population" (DeVore and Champion, 2011). ACOs are emerging across the country as coordinated networks of providers who share responsibility to provide patient care that is both high quality and low cost.

Early adopters of the ACO model were part of the Centers for Medicare and Medicaid Services (CMS) Shared Savings Program (MSSP), or the Pioneer ACO Program (Ginsburg, 2011; Fisher et al., 2012). More recently, commercial payers have entered the mix (Higgins et al., 2011; Baldwin, 2011), and these private market ACOs enjoy more flexibility in the market because they are able to develop multiple contracts with multiple payers rather than being restricted by the MSSP and Pioneer model constraints.

ACOs have their own governance and management structures (Longworth, 2011), and the management structure has both clinical and administrative sides (Correia, 2011; Smith, 2012). Clinician leadership is critical, and highly valued (Abramson et al., 2012; Grauman et al., 2012). For governance, the governing body must be at least 75 percent controlled by providers, including hospitals, physicians, and community organizations (Correia, 2011; Longworth, 2011), with the aim of participants having "appropriate proportionate control" of the board (Correia, 2011).

For the ACO model to survive, the organization must engage clinicians and clinical professionals so that they focus on clinical quality as well as cost. The importance of clinical coordination and integration is consistently emphasized, providing important roles for clinical professionals to lead development and implementation of ACOs and model innovations. Additionally, accurate and timely data on care processes and coordination of care are critical to ensure operational success, and managers who can work with clinical professionals to understand and interpret these data will be well positioned in these new organizations.

## LEADERSHIP PARADIGMS AND HOW TO ENGAGE CLINICAL PROFESSIONALS

The leadership paradigm for healthcare organizations is changing, and with these changes come challenges in how to maintain engagement of clinical professionals. Clinical professionals are shifting into non-clinical roles, and new job titles are being created. For instance, the chief information officer (CIO) position is typically held by an information technology (IT) specialist, but the new title of chief medical information officer (CMIO) has emerged to accommodate a clinical professional with both medical and IT expertise. There is also a blurring of inter-professional boundaries as clinicians obtain advanced education and technical expertise and choose take on leadership roles, whether or not they continue with clinical practice. Rather than have a single chief operating officer (COO), many healthcare organizations have expanded their "C-suite" to include individuals with hybrid clinical–administrative professionals such as the chief medical officer (CMO) and the chief nursing officer (CNO). Key leadership positions such as chief executive officer (CEO) and chief quality officer (CQO) may be held by clinicians who play the role of administrators, or by trained administrators who have accumulated training and experience to ensure understanding of clinical concerns.

Engagement of clinical professionals is key to successful healthcare management. The challenge of managing the healthcare enterprise is characterized by the need to do the right things for the right people at the right time, and non-clinical managers must rely upon the judgment of clinical professionals to ensure that occurs. Whether in collaboration with clinicians or coordination of their work, managers must keep in mind the expertise of these professionals and strive to maintain a balance between task management and organizational leadership.

# REFERENCES

Abramson, R., Berger, P., and Brant-Zawadzki, M. (2012). Accountable care organizations and radiology: threat or opportunity? *Journal of the American College Of Radiology: JACR*, 9 (12), 900–906. doi:10.1016/j.jacr.2012.09.013.

Altschuler, J., Margolius, D., Bodenheimer, T., and Grumbach, K. (2012). Estimating a reasonable patient panel size for primary care physicians with team-based task delegation. *Annals of Family Medicine*, 10 (5): 396–400. doi: 10.1370/afm.1400.

Baldwin, G. (2011). ACO Barriers. *Health Data Management*, 19 (10): 24. Available from MEDLINE with Full Text, Ipswich, MA (accessed 13 July 2012).

Barab, S.A. and Duffy, T. (2000). From practice fields to communitites of practice. In D. Jonassen and S.M. Land (eds), *Theoretical foundations of Learning Environments*. Mahwah, NJ: Lawrence Erlbaum Associates, pp. 22–25.

Barab, S.A., MaKinster, J.G., and Scheckler, R. (2003). Designing system dualities: Characterizing a Web-supported professional development community. *Information Society*, 19 (3): 237–257.

Baxley, L., Borkan, J., Campbell, T., Davis, A., Kuzel, T., and Wender, R. (2011). In pursuit of a transformed health care system: from patient centered medical homes to accountable care organizations and beyond. *Annals of Family Medicine*, 9 (5): 466–467. doi:10.1370/afm.1305.

Berwick, D. (2011). Launching accountable care organizations – the proposed rule for the Medicare Shared Savings Program. *New England Journal Of Medicine*, 364 (16):e32.

Berwick, D. (2012a). ACOs – promise, not panacea. *JAMA: Journal of the American Medical Association*, 308 (10):1038–1039.

Berwick, D. (2012b). Making good on ACOs' promise – the final rule for the Medicare shared savings program. *New England Journal of Medicine*, 365 (19): 1753–1756.

Best, A., Moor, G., Holmes, B., Clark, P.I., Bruce, T., Leischow, S., . . . Krajnak, J. (2003). Health promotion dissemination and systems thinking: towards an integrative model. *American Journal of Health Behavior*, 27 (Supplement 3): S206–S216.

Blumhagen, D.W. (1979). The doctor's white coat: The image of the physician in modern America. *Annals of Internal Medicine*, 91: 111–116. doi:10.7326/0003-4819-91-1-111.

Bourgeois, L.J. (1980). Strategy and environment: A conceptual integration. *Academy of Management Review*, 5 (1): 25–39.

Bovbjerg, R.R., Ormond, B.A., and Pindus, N. (2009). The nursing workforce challenge. 31 August, Jonas Center for Nursing Excellence, http://www.urban.org/research/publication/nursing-workforce-challenge/view/full_report.

Brannon, D., Zinn, J.S., Mor, V., and Davis, J. (2002). An exploration of job, organizational, and environmental factors associated with high and low nursing assistant turnover. *Gerontologist*, 42: 159–168.

Brooks, R.G., Walsh, M., Mardon, R.E., Lewis, M., and Clawson, A. (2002). The roles of nature and nurture in the recruitment and retention of primary care physicians in rural areas: a review of the literature. *Academic Medicine*, 77 (8): 790–798.

Brown, D.L. (2013). A looming joblessness crisis for new pharmacy graduates and the implications it holds for the academy. *American Journal of Pharmaceutical Education*, 77 (5), 90.

Castel, N.C. and Engberg, J. (2006). Organizational characteristics associated with staff turnover in nursing homes. *Gerontologist*, 46 (1): 62–73.

Clancy, C.M. (2009). Ten years after "To Err is Human." *American Journal of Medical Quality*, 24 (6), 525–528. doi: 1062860609349728 [pii] 10.1177/1062860609349728.

Correia, E. (2011). Accountable care organizations: The proposed regulations and the prospects for success. *American Journal of Managed Care*, 17 (8): 560–568.

DeVore, S. and Champion, R. (2011). Driving population health through accountable care organizations. *Health Affairs*, 30 (1): 41–50. doi:10.1377/hlthaff.2010.0935.

Dracup, K., Cronenwett, L., Meleis, A.I., and Benner, P.E. (2005). Reflections on the doctorate of nursing practice. *Nursing Outlook*, 53 (4): 177–182. doi: http://dx.doi.org/10.1016/j.outlook.2005.06.003.

Duffy, F.F., West, J.C., Wilk, J., Narrow, W., Hales, D., Thompson, J., and Manderscheid, R. (2002). Mental health practitioners and trainees. *Mental Health, United States*, 3938: 327–368.

Dunbar-Jacob, J., Nativio, D.G., and Khalil, H. (2013). Impact of doctor of nursing practice education in shaping health care systems for the future. *Journal of Nursing Education*, 52 (8): 423–427.

Fisher, E., McClellan M., and Safran, D. (2012). Building the path to accountable care. *New England Journal of Medicine*, 365 (26): 2445–2447.

Fisher, E., McClellan M., Bertko, J., Liberman, S., Lee, J.J., and Skinner, J. (2009). Fostering accountable health care: Moving forward in Medicare. *Health Affairs*, 28 (2): w219–w231.

Fisher, E.S. and Shortell, S.M. (2010). Accountable care organizations: Accountable for what, to whom, and how. *JAMA*, 304 (15): 1715–1716.

Gao, F., Li, J.M., and Nakamori, Y. (2003). Critical systems thinking as a way to manage knowledge. *Systems Research and Behavioral Science*, 20 (1): 3–19.

Ginsburg, P. (2011). Spending to save – ACOs and the Medicare Shared Savings Program. *New England Journal of Medicine*, 364 (22): 2085–2086.

Gouldner, A.W. (1957). Cosmopolitans and locals: toward an analysis of latent social roles: I. *Administrative Science Quarterly*, 2 (3): 281–306.

Grauman, D., Graham, C., and Johnson, M. (2012). 5 pillars of clinical integration.

*Healthcare Financial Management: Journal of the Healthcare Financial Management Association*, 66 (8): 70–77.

Gray, B. (1989). *Collaborating: Finding Common Ground for Multiparty Problems.* San Francisco, CA: Jossey Bass.

Hahn, K.A., Gonzalez, M.M., Etz, R.S., and Crabtree, B.F. (2014). National Committee for Quality Assurance (NCQA) patient-centered medical home (PCMH) recognition is suboptimal even among innovative primary care practices. *Journal of the American Board of Family Medicine*, 27 (3): 312–313.

Higgins, A., Stewart, K., Dawson, K., and Bocchino, C. (2011). Early lessons from accountable care models in the private sector: partnerships between health plans and providers. *Health Affairs*, 30 (9): 1718–1727.

Iglehart, J.K. (2013). The residency mismatch. *New England Journal of Medicine*, 369 (4), 297–299. doi:10.1056/NEJMp1306445.

Knights, D., Murray, F., and Willmott, H. (1993). Networking as knowledge work – a study of strategic interorganizational development in the financial services industry. *Journal of Management Studies*, 30 (6): 975–995.

Kohn, L.T., Corrigan, J.M., and Donaldson, M.S. (eds) (1999). *To Err is Human: Building a Safer Health System.* Washington, DC: National Academy Press.

Longworth, D. (2011). Accountable care organizations, the patient-centered medical home, and health care reform: what does it all mean? *Cleveland Clinic Journal Of Medicine*, 78 (9): 571–582. doi:10.3949/ccjm.78gr.11003.

Minnick, A.F., Norman, L.D., and Donaghey, B. (2013). Defining and describing capacity issues in US Doctor of Nursing Practice programs. *Nursing Outlook*, 61 (2): 93–101. doi: http://dx.doi.org/10.1016/j.outlook.2012.07.011.

Nickitas, D.M. and Feeg, V. (2011). Doubling the number of nurses with a doctorate by 2020: Predicting the right number or getting it right?. *Nursing Economics*, 29 (3): 109–110, 125.

Peikes, D.N., Reid, R.J., Day, T.J., Cornwell, D.D.F., Dale, S.B., Baron, R.J., ... Shapiro, R.J. (2014). Staffing patterns of primary care practices in the Comprehensive Primary Care Initiative. *Annals of Family Medicine*, 12 (2): 142–149. doi: 10.1370/afm.1626.

Rittenhouse, D.R., Casalino, L.P., Shortell, S.M., McClellan, S.R., Gillies, R.R., Alexander, J.A., and Drum, M.L. (2011). Small and medium-size physician practices use few patient-centered medical home processes. *Health Affairs*, 30 (8): 1575–1584. doi: 10.1377/hlthaff.2010.1210.

Robiner, W.N. (2006). The mental health professions: Workforce supply and demand, issues, and challenges. *Clinical Psychology Review*, 26 (5): 600–625. doi: http://dx.doi.org/10.1016/j.cpr.2006.05.002.

Saultz, J.W. and Lochner, J. (2005). Interpersonal continuity of care and care outcomes: A critical review. *Annals of Family Medicine*, 3 (2): 159–166. doi: 10.1370/afm.285.

Scanlon, D.P., Christianson, J.B., and Ford, E.W. (2008). Hospital responses to the Leapfrog Group in local markets. *Medical Care Research and Review*, 65 (2): 207–231. doi: 1077558707312499 [pii] 10.1177/1077558707312499.

Simon, M.A., Gunia, B., Martin, E.J., Foucar, C.E., Kundu, T., Ragas, D.M., and Emanuel, L.L. (2013). Path toward economic resilience for family caregivers: Mitigating household deprivation and the health care talent shortage at the same time. *Gerontologist*, 53 (5): 861–873.

Sloan, F.A. and Hsieh, C.-R. (2012). *Health Economics*, Cambridge, MA: MIT Press.

Smith, C. (2012). How to build an ACO: Medicare's shared savings program includes specific structural and governance requirements. *Journal for Hospital Governing Boards*, 65 (2): 1341–1342.

Smith, E.A. (2001). The role of tacit and explicit knowledge in the workplace. *Journal of Knowledge Management*, 5 (4): 311–321.

Tagliareni, E. and Malone, B.L. (2013). Nursing education policy: The unending debate over entry into practice and the new debate over doctoral degrees. In D.J. Mason, J.K. Leavitt and M.W. Chaffee (eds), *Policy and Politics in Nursing and Healthcare*, St Louis, MO: Elsevier Saunders, pp. 383–392.

Taylor, E.F., Peikes, D., Genevro, J., and Meyers, D. (2013). Creating capacity for improvement in primary care: The case for developing a quality improvement infrastructure, Washington, DC: Mathematica Policy Research.

Vincent, G.K. and Velkoff, V.A. (2010). The next four decades: The older population in the United States: 2010 to 2050. US Department of Commerce, Economics and Statistics Administration, Washington, DC: US Census Bureau.

Wenger, E. (1998). *Communities of Practice: Learning, Meaning and Identity*. Cambridge: Cambridge University Press.

Wenger, E. (2005). Communities of practice. 21 November. Retrieved from http://www.ewenger.com/theory/ (accessed 1 April 2014).

Wenger, E.C. and Snyder, W.M. (2000). Communities of practice: The organizational frontier. *Harvard Business Review*, 78 (1): 139–145.

# 18. Healthcare insurance and finance
*Dean G. Smith*

## INTRODUCTION

Research on the theory and practice of healthcare insurance and finance has the potential to guide organizations towards more accurate reporting, improved financial decision-making and higher levels of performance. If healthcare organizations in the United States are to apply evidence-based management practices in the area of healthcare insurance and finance, creation and utilization of a research base is profoundly important (Finkler et al., 2003). Textbooks and the professional literature provide adequate guidance to management for many aspects of routine reporting and analysis (Gapenski and Pink, 2013; Smith, 2014). It is less clear that managers have adequate evidence for decision-making for non-routine analyses. Unlike evidence-based medicine, there is not a large cohort of scientists looking to publish results on the management of healthcare insurance and finance. This chapter provides an outline of selected healthcare insurance and financial management topics, with an indication of recent research and directions for future research that will provide managers with the needed evidence base for their work.

The lack of research and the gap between research and the needs of practice are not unique to healthcare insurance and finance. In the closely related field of public sector accounting there is a notable gap between research and practice (van Helden and Northcott, 2010). Some three-quarters of research in public sector accounting is aimed at understanding motivations behind the adoption and use of management accounting techniques. Only one-tenth of the research is aimed at developing the evidence base for practice through evaluating the effectiveness of existing techniques, or identifying the conditions for the successful implementation of techniques. At close to 20 percent of gross domestic product, the healthcare field deserves an evidence base to guide financial management.

Healthcare insurance and finance, broadly defined, cover the range of financial activities related to the management of healthcare organizations. Insurance is the primary source of revenues for healthcare provider organizations in the USA. Management of contracts, coding and billing, reporting, and responding to incentives are among the financial activities related to insurance. Clearly much has changed in the United States in recent years with regards to the insurance marketplace. Managing the finances of a provider organization is challenged by the ebb and flow of managed care, the growth of pay-for-performance and other contacting schemes, and, of course, the Affordable Care Act, which includes the introduction of insurance exchanges and the expansion of Medicaid coverage in many states. Consideration of changes in healthcare management related to changes in the insurance marketplace would require more than one full book. Changes in financial management related to changes in the insurance marketplace are more limited and are discussed in the next section of this chapter.

Finance, in the context of healthcare management, consists of the fields of financial accounting, managerial accounting, and corporate finance. Financial accounting is the practice of keeping track of resources. It involves recording and compiling business and financial transactions, assuring the accuracy of transactions, and preparing reports of the results. Requirements for reporting of financial results are continuously changing. Significant reporting changes and management responses are considered later in this chapter.

In many ways, managerial accounting has the opposite focus and process to financial accounting. Financial accounting produces financial statements that strictly follow externally imposed rules to provide persons outside the organization with a clear overview of its current financial position. Managerial accounting produces reports that follow internal conventions to provide information for decision-making on the future of the organization. Among the most important managerial accounting reports are those that concern the cost of providing services. Despite repeated calls over more than a couple of decades for more advanced cost accounting in US healthcare, progress in this regard has been slow, as noted below.

Corporate finance, as a distinct field of study and practice from accounting, is concerned with planning, analysis, acquisition, and management of resources. What is different between accounting and finance, since the terms used to describe them look so similar? Without splitting too many hairs, the focus of accounting tends to be on the details of operations and reporting in real time (financial accounting) and for the near term (managerial accounting). The focus of finance tends to be on planning and acquisition of funds for the long term. Corporate finance is concerned with analysis of investments, the cost of capital, long-term risk, and the level of debt taken on by an organization. Research in healthcare corporate finance is considered in the final section of this chapter.

# INSURANCE: NEW MODELS MEAN NEW MANAGEMENT

For all organizations, management of the revenue stream is critical to long-run viability. Among the unique aspects of healthcare financial management in the USA is the predominant role of insurance companies as a third party in the patient–provider relationship. Management of provider organizations in the US changed profoundly in the early 1960s with the introduction of Medicare and Medicaid. Government financing came with fundamental changes in how healthcare organizations are paid. Initially, hospitals were paid according to a cost-based reimbursement process that led to rapid escalation in healthcare costs.

In an effort to control costs, payment changed from reimbursement of expenses to a set of fixed prices for operating expenses starting in 1983, and to a set of fixed prices for capital expenses starting in 1991. To distinguish the new payment method, fixed prices were termed "prospective payment." US hospitals became responsible for their bottom line and therefore had incentives for efficient financial management, including collections of receivables, debt management, and investment of financial assets. It may be hard to imagine now, but until 1991, some hospitals kept all of their financial assets in checking accounts, as reimbursement of net interest expense meant that interest expenses were reimbursed net of any interest earnings or investment income. Since 1991, hospital cash balances (actually investments) have increased substantially and management of investments has become critical to financial success for many organizations, though not to the point where financial investments can completely overcome operating losses (Gentry, 2002; Rivenson et al., 2011; Singh and Song, 2013).

Prospective payment means that organizations are now subject to variability in their own costs and fluctuations in the macroeconomy. Following the introduction of prospective payment, some reduction in hospital expenses was noted. However, much of the change was associated with hospital accounting practices, allocating costs away from prospectively paid inpatient services and towards cost-based payment for outpatient services (Eldenburg and Kallapur, 2000). To facilitate changes in accounting practices and to understand costs, expenditures on general accounting (ledgers, budgets) and patient accounting (billing) increased for hospitals after the introduction of prospective payment, especially for hospitals confronting price competition (Krishnan, 2005). Further, the risk induced by fixed payments was associated with a shift of expenses from fixed expenses (plant, equipment, and salaried employees) to variable expenses (Kallapur and Eldenburg, 2005). This behavior is consistent with a real options financial analysis, even if it is highly unlikely that any hospitals were using real options as an analytical tool.

Immediately following prospective payment for capital expenses, which uses a formula that attempts to pay each hospital the average capital cost for all hospitals, there was a regression to the mean of capital expenditures among hospitals (Barniv et al., 2000). Hospitals changed their expense patterns to match revenues, although the managerial process by which this happened is unknown. It would be very interesting to know if the change in fixed expenses that was observed around the implementation of operating prospective payment by Kallapur and Eldenburg (2005) was also observed around the implementation of capital prospective payment.

With respect to changes in the macroeconomy, fluctuations in the financial markets can lead to high investment earnings during good times and losses during bad times (Song et al., 2008). Analysis surrounding the 2008 recession revealed that profits of private US hospitals declined during the recession and returned to pre-recession levels in three years (Bazzoli et al., 2014). For neither investments nor operations have researchers assessed the contributions of financial management practices that might provide an evidence base for managerial decisions related to changes in the macroeconomy.

It appears that over the past three decades since the implementation of prospective payment, organizations have become much more financially sophisticated and able to manage alternative payment arrangements. Early patterns of inappropriate underpayments due to complicated managed care contracts have largely been eliminated, with greater attention to reporting and monitoring of payments (Smith and Betley, 2000). Higher levels of financial sophistication would likely be more so the case were it not for the constant changes in policies and procedures as the US federal and state governments and private insurers attempt to rein in the growth in healthcare spending. Policies and procedures have been aimed at curtailing utilization and prices, with limited success (Wu et al., 2014). Similarly, the evidence on the early years' effects of pay-for-performance has indicated no significant change in revenues, expenses, or profits (Kruse et al., 2012). As with changes in the macroeconomy, no pattern of financial management tools to manage payment arrangements has been identified in published research.

To no one's surprise, research has found that having more patients who do not pay is associated with lower revenues for healthcare organizations (Leleu et al., 2012). If the only effect of the Affordable Care Act is to provide Medicaid-level insurance coverage to a portion of currently uncompensated care patients, research suggests that there may be as much as a 4 percent increase in emergency department margins (Wilson and Cutler, 2014). Perhaps somewhat surprising is the observation that having more patients whose care is paid for by government programs may influence revenues from private sector payers, through a process termed "cost-shifting." Textbook models of full cost pricing imply that cost shifting would be a justifiable practice for hospital pricing. It was once thought that financial managers established charges for private sector payers based upon costs and known government prices, evidence that hospitals were not seeking to maximize profits even in markets where they had the capacity for price discrimination (Clement, 1997; Reinhardt, 2006). More recent evidence suggests that the magnitude of cost-shifting may not have been very large (Frakt, 2011) and that the capacity to cost-shift may have been exhausted (White, 2013; White and Wu, 2014). Research on pricing and cost-shifting has focused on summary outcomes, perhaps appropriately, rather than the financial management practices that yield observed prices.

Managing the finances of a provider organization with revenues coming from both government and private sector sources is challenged by the ebb and flow of managed care, the growth of pay-for-performance, and other contracting schemes. Managed care consists of practices aimed at curtailing utilization and curtailing prices. There are few tools in the financial management toolkit to address direct utilization management. Risk-sharing or risk-shifting through capitation may induce indirect utilization management. Capitation had a challenging start in the 1990s, a halting in the 2000s and perhaps a revival in the 2010s (Frakt and Mayes, 2012). Whether provider organizations can form coalitions to manage capitation at a large scale has yet to be demonstrated. The failures of current managed care utilization and payment systems to curtail total medial expenditures will undoubtedly lead to further experimentation. The push towards value-based payment by Medicare and other payers will require more attention to quality measures and integration of clinical information with financial information, though the efficacy of such work is uncertain (Ryan and Damberg, 2013).

Addressing lower prices requires either practices to change coding to realize higher prices from the same fee schedule or changing production costs. Recent research has found that hospitals have not used (or may not be able to use) electronic health records as a means to change coding and realize higher payments (Adler-Milstein and Jha, 2014). Analysis of production costs is addressed below under the heading of managerial accounting.

# FINANCIAL ACCOUNTING: REPORTING REQUIREMENTS AND EARNINGS MANAGEMENT

There once was a concern that US hospitals did not follow a uniform system of accounting and were therefore difficult to understand and manage (Banfield, 1902). Following the implementation of recommendations by the Advisory Committee on Accounting of the American Hospital Association, standardized financial statements have been in place for quite some time (Rorem and Carroll, 1936). Even with what appears to be a uniform system of accounting, the adequacy of reporting and disclosures may be insufficient for the public interest (Sherman, 1986; Watkins and Brenner, 2003). In 1990, reporting of charity care was moved to a footnote and away from revenue with an offsetting deduction (Eldenburg and Vines, 2004). In 2011, reporting of charity care at cost was clarified and bad debt was moved to a deduction from revenue and away from an expense (Reinstein and Churyk, 2013).

A comparison of the income statements for one hospital in 2013 from its Medicare cost report, using older accounting standards, and audited financial statements, using new accounting standards, is presented in Table 18.1. Medicare cost reports list revenues as charges and present contractual allowances for the differences between charges and payments. Audited financial statements now start with expected payments and ignore charges. Audited statements also include bad debt as a deduction from revenues rather than as an expense. For a simple organization that has only a hospital entity, net patient revenues and operating revenues are very similar. The presentation of expenses is similar for many items (for example, salaries and depreciation expenses), yet sufficiently different to result in a negative operating margin of −2.0 percent with a cost report, and +1.7 percent with audited statements. Net income is nearly identical. Observing differing results based upon the accounting standards used among sources of data requires a careful assessment of the source in the interpretation of analyses (Ozmeral et al., 2012).

In addition to variation in reported operating margins among sources, there may also be variation in the possible values reported within a source, based upon managers' motivations for providing information. Making strategic choices among alternative decisions in the financial accounting process is termed "earnings management." An example of earnings management is the selective estimation of accruals to achieve earnings targets (Leone and Van Horn, 2005). Similarly, hospitals with pressures to show efficiency may shift costs from administrative categories toward program service categories (Krishnan and Yetman, 2011). An alternative form of earnings management is to actually reduce (increase) expenditures

*Table 18.1   Medicare cost report income statement and audited statement of revenues and expenses for one hospital, 2013*

| Medicare cost report | | Audited statement | |
|---|---:|---|---:|
| **Operating Revenue** | | **Operating Revenue** | |
| Inpatient Revenue | 38 725 280 | Patient Service Revenue | 95 905 971 |
| Outpatient Revenue | 80 409 256 | Provision for Bad Debts | (4 148 471) |
| Total Patient Revenue | 119 134 536 | Net Patient Service Revenue | 91 757 500 |
| Contractual Allowances | (23 228 556) | Other Operating Revenue | 3 576 298 |
| Net Patient Revenues | 95 905 980 | Total Operating Revenue | 95 333 798 |
| **Operating Expenses** | | **Operating Expenses** | |
| Salary Expense | 41 114 856 | Salaries | 41 114 862 |
| Fringe Benefits | 5 335 714 | Employee Benefits | 9 197 571 |
| Contract Labor | 219 507 | Professional Fees | 11 940 869 |
| Depreciation | 5 007 908 | Depreciation | 5 677 134 |
| Interest expense | 243 075 | Interest expense | 873 955 |
| Supplies | 19 308 738 | Supplies | 18 858 647 |
| Operations of the Plant | 4 148 111 | Utilities, Maintenance | 4 568 893 |
| Other Operating Expenses | 22 479 203 | Insurance | 1 476 687 |
| Total Operating Expense | 97 857 112 | Total Operating Expenses | 93 708 618 |
| **Operating Income** | **(1 951 132)** | **Operating Income** | **1 625 180** |
| Income from Investments | 272 314 | Investment Income | 389 113 |
| Other Income (Contrib.) | 9814 | Net Realized Gains (losses) | 227 731 |
| Misc. Non-Patient Revenue | 4 951 879 | Other Non-Operating Income | 1 040 866 |
| Total Non-Patient Revenue | 5 234 007 | Total Non-Operating Income | 1 657 710 |
| **Net Income or (Loss)** | **3 282 875** | **Revenues over Expenses** | **3 282 890** |

*Source:*   Medicare Cost Report data, slightly modified to disguise the institution, was obtained through American Hospital Directory® (www. ahd.com). Audited financial statement data, slightly modified to disguise the institution, was obtained through Digital Assurance Certification, LLC, DAC Bond® (www.dacbond.com).

in non-operating areas for short periods of time when confronting below- (above-) target earnings, so-called "real earnings management" (Eldenburg et al., 2011). A review of the literature revealed a number of examples of earnings management in hospitals and managed care organizations (Hofmann and McSwain, 2013). Observations of earnings management call into question the reliability of financial statements as a source of information on short-run organizational performance.

Despite questions of reliability, use of financial statements to characterize the position of healthcare organizations has been the subject of research for many years. In 1951, US hospitals with total profit margins in excess of 5 percent were associated with revenues at the unsustainable level of $21.53 per patient day (Pennell et al., 1954). More recent research has utilized a standard set of ratios and attempted to gain the greatest amount of information with the fewest variables (Cleverley, 1981; Sherman, 1986; Counte et al., 1988; Zeller et al., 1996). Pooling ratios using the commonly used DuPont method has been found to reveal little additional information for healthcare organizations (Chang et al., 2014). Interestingly, there is rarely a caveat in studies using financial ratios concerning the reliability of the data and possible earnings management. Quite the opposite: there are calls for broader use of financial ratios to assess performance for healthcare organizations that have not done so in the past (Suarez et al., 2011).

The final step in the financial accounting process is the end-of-year audit. In the USA the Sarbanes–Oxley Act of 2002 set new standards and expectations both of organizations and their external auditors. Not-for-profit healthcare organizations are not required to follow all of the provisions of Sarbanes–Oxley, though many have voluntarily agreed to provisions that improve internal controls (Loubeau and Griffith, 2012). There is some evidence that the selection of a particular type of auditor affects the reporting of deficiencies in internal controls. Two studies of hospitals found that audits performed by Big Four firms were less likely to report internal control deficiencies than audits conducted by other firms (Rich et al., 2013; McGowan et al., 2014). One study found the opposite association (Pridgen and Wang, 2012). Whether the results of audits affect the financial management practices of healthcare organizations is not known and is worthy of investigation.

## MANAGERIAL ACCOUNTING: MOVING TOWARDS ACTIVITY-BASED COSTING

Among the most important aspects of managerial accounting is the determination of the costs of service lines and specific services. Keeping track of revenues and expenses at the level of the service line or specific service requires more sophisticated accounting systems and/or the application of managerial accounting techniques. Healthcare organizations have been slow to adopt sophisticated accounting systems, perhaps due to the very complicated service mix of many institutions. At the end of the 1980s, by which time having detailed accounting information was clearly important, fewer than two in five US hospitals had cost accounting systems (Hill, 2000). Explaining the reasons behind development of cost accounting systems likely requires further understanding of hospital stakeholders and decision-making processes (Cardinaels and Soderstrom, 2013).

Absent formal cost accounting systems, management accounting has developed techniques for the approximation of costs. For the analysis of costs at the service line (that is, department) level, standard financial accounting systems are often capable of tracing salaries and many other expenses directly to the department. Limitations of accounting systems will leave many expenses unassigned to departments. Further, general administrative expenses and others may truly be joint costs among departments that cannot be directly assigned. For the allocation of expenses that are indirect costs to departments, direct allocation, step-down and other managerial accounting methods are commonly employed. The requirement to prepare departmental cost estimates in Medicare cost reports based upon the step-down method has led to its widespread use in the United States. Internationally, the UK, the Netherlands and Sweden require use of the direct allocation method, and France and Germany require use of the step-down method (Tan et al., 2014). Analysis of hospitals in Washington state found that inefficiencies are similar among departments within a hospital, though it is not clear whether these results are attributable to direct cost similarities as opposed to indirect cost allocations (Murphy et al., 2011).

For the analysis of costs at the service (that is, patient) level, costs at the department level may be further allocated using the ratio of costs to charges (RCC), relative value units (RVU) or assigned to services using an activity-based costing (ABC) process. Costs estimated by RCCs, though quite simple, have been found to be a close approximation to costs estimated by RVUs (Shwartz et al., 1995). Nevertheless, a more sophisticated approach using ABC methods would likely yield more accurate estimates of costs, along with directions for managing costs. Kaplan and Porter (2011) have suggested that ABC methods are essential to effective control of healthcare costs.

Organizations that have adopted ABC methods have reported clear advantages in useful cost determination (Brandt et al., 1998; Cinquini et al., 2009; Demeere et al., 2009). As one example, costs of abdominal surgery patients at a French hospital were found to average €2331 using an RVU method and €2186 using an ABC method (correlation = 0.73). Though many managers may find these values to be similar enough for some purposes, the ABC method reveals the components of costs that may direct managerial action. For-profit healthcare providers have used ABC methods to enhance profitability, and not-for-profit providers have used ABC methods to improve revenue management, if not cost control or profitability (McGowan et al., 2006).

An early survey revealed that RCC was commonly used in practice in the USA (55 percent of respondents) and that RVUs were not commonly used (9 percent) (Orloff et al., 1990). A more recent poll of conference attendees found that RCC is still commonly used in practice (69 percent of attendees), with many using the RCC values obtained from the Medicare cost report (47 percent) (HFMA, 2012). Despite the acknowledged limitations of the Medicare cost report, its availability is associated with widespread use (Magnus and Smith, 2000). A larger portion of hospitals now employ RVUs (35 percent), or values derived from a specialized cost accounting system for which the underlying methods are not known (39 percent), and many hospitals use ABC for some portion of their cost analyses (30 percent) (HFMA, 2012). This last result would be impressive if the conference attendees were at all representative of hospitals nationally in the USA. In 2005, a survey found that fewer than 5 percent of chief financial officers had implemented ABC in their hospitals (Emmett and Forget, 2005).

Service line or service costs may be of value in their own right, as well as in how these costs can be further used in analyses. As one example, conducting breakeven analysis requires the ability to distinguish between fixed and variable costs (Laskaris and Regan, 2013). The ability to distinguish between fixed and variable costs is not universal among healthcare organizations. A survey found a mean of 5 among hospitals, on a scale of 5 = "not at all" to 7 = "completely," on the ability to distinguish between fixed and variable costs (Pizzini, 2006). In part, the lack of ability may be attributable to changes in the composition of fixed and variable costs associated with changing payment systems (Holzhacker et al., 2014). Having cost information available on a timely basis was associated with improved financial performance in a sample of US hospitals (Pizzini, 2006). For a sample of Italian hospitals, the use of cost information, not merely its availability, was weakly associated with profitability (Macinati and Pessina, 2014).

# FINANCE: CAPITAL BUDGETING AND ANALYSIS OF RISK

Among the more dramatic changes in financial management after the introduction of prospective payment was the increase in sophistication of corporate finance practices, particularly capital budgeting. Surveys of hospitals have found widespread use of modern capital budgeting practices, including the use of formal assessment processes, discounting cash flows, and formal assessment of risks, particularly among hospitals within multi-hospital systems (Reiter et al., 1999; Smith and Wynne, 2006; Kocher, 2007). A further increase in the sophistication of capital budgeting may be required to guide organizations in the upcoming decade of US healthcare reform (Reiter and Song, 2013). Specifically, organizations will need to consider a broader range of priorities in capital budgeting for accountable care organizations, focus more on strategic investments that include information technology and primary care initiatives, and carefully consider the cash flows and risks associated with new paradigms of care management.

In a world of perfect capital markets, healthcare organizations would make their capital budgeting decisions based solely on the available market opportunities. Generally speaking, real opportunities for provision of medical services are the largest drivers of capital spending (McCue, 2011). In the imperfect real world, hospitals also consider available cash, financial market performance, and debt capacity when making spending decisions. Given not-for-profit organizations' limits on access to equity capital, stock market performance – though interestingly not bond market performance – was found to be positively correlated to capital spending (Reiter and Song, 2011). The recent financial crisis left many organizations with substantial net asset losses, at least on paper, which were associated with reduced capital spending on health information technology (Dranove et al., 2013). Debt capacity, as measured by target levels of debt, owing to the peculiar arbitrage opportunity available to not-for-profit organizations in the USA that can issue tax-exempt debt, appears to influence borrowing and perhaps even capital spending (Wedig et al., 1996).

In a deeper examination of specific financing vehicles employed, Stewart and Smith (2011) found that healthcare systems relied on operating cash flows, public issues of insured variable rate debt, and accumulated investments to meet their capital financing needs. Their analysis further found that during the recent financial crisis, the use of interest rate derivatives created significant risk exposures, just as was the case for corporations generally (Stewart and Smith, 2011). Subject to availability, US healthcare organizations prefer to issue bonds issued by state-wide authorities to realize lower costs, to the extent that yields offset higher issuance costs (Carpenter and Bernet, 2013).

Just as financial markets may influence investments, so a firm's position in financial markets may also influence real operations. Provision of uncompensated care and other community benefits may be a source of future philanthropy, but not a level that makes it an effective financing strategy (Smith et al., 1995). Hospitals that had higher debt levels were found to provide more uncompensated care and have lower levels of operational efficiency in the 1990s (Magnus et al., 2004a; Magnus et al., 2004b).

A cornerstone of corporate financial analysis is the measurement of risk and the application of risk measures in decision-making processes. Healthcare organizations using modern financial analysis tools generally seek to integrate risk as a component of their cost of capital. Despite the importance of risk, there is surprisingly little research on the cost of capital in healthcare. Wedig et al. (1989) calculated US hospitals' costs of capital from 1974 to 1982, including many idiosyncrasies associated with payment systems at that time. A more general method of calculating capital costs is using the weighted average cost of capital and the capital asset pricing model, along with payment considerations as proposed by Wheeler and Smith (1988).

Current estimates of risk measures (denoted as beta, $\beta$) for large healthcare companies are presented in Table 18.2. Interestingly, after the implementation of the Affordable Care Act in the United States, risk measures for healthcare providers are all less than one, and risk measures for health

*Table 18.2  Capital asset pricing model, $\beta$*

| Company | $\beta$ |
|---|---|
| WellPoint | 0.57 |
| UnitedHealth Group | 0.63 |
| Cigna | 0.77 |
| Aetna | 0.84 |
| DaVita HealthCare Partners | 1.22 |
| Tenet Healthcare | 1.63 |
| Universal Health Services | 1.82 |
| Community Health Systems | 1.82 |

*Source:* Yahoo! Finance. https://finance.yahoo.com/, accessed August 1, 2014 for each company listed. Beta is calculated using monthly price changes relative to the Standard & Poor's 500 over three years (https://help.yahoo.com/kb/finance/SLN2347. html?impressions=true).

insurers are all greater than one. The absence of substantive research on risk measures and cost of capital for more than two decades suggests a clear void in the literature that might guide evidence-based financial management.

A concluding observation on research on the theory and practice of healthcare insurance and finance is that evidence-based financial management might not be all that important. To be sure, understanding the financial implications of insurance practices is critical to the management of a healthcare provider. Also, it is certainly important that proper financial accounting occurs, that audits are performed using good standards, and that organizations have a reasonable understanding of the costs of providing services. Whether it is critical that organizations conduct corporate financial analyses correctly is another matter. Cleverley and Felkner (1984), like researchers before them and after them, found no association between financial management techniques, other than having a plan, and financial performance. The causation of this finding is certainly debatable. Do organizations only seek to apply sophisticated finance techniques in the face of poor performance, or do the techniques just not provide enough information and control to enable better performance? As with many of the aspects of healthcare financial management considered in this chapter, further research is required.

## REFERENCES

Adler-Milstein, J. and Jha, A.K. (2014). No Evidence Found That Hospitals Are Using New Electronic Health Records To Increase Medicare Reimbursements. *Health Affairs*, 33 (7): 1271–1277.

Banfield, M. (1902). Some Unsettled Questions in Hospital Administration in the United States. *Annals of the American Academy of Political and Social Science*, 20: 24–51.

Barniv, R., Danvers, K., and Healy, J. (2000). The Impact of Medicare Capital Prospective Payment Regulation on Hospital Capital Expenditures. *Journal of Accounting and Public Policy*, 19 (1): 9–40.

Bazzoli, G.J., Fareed, N., and Waters, T.M. (2014). Hospital Financial Performance in the Recent Recession and Implications for Institutions that Remain Financially Weak. *Health Affairs*, 33 (5): 739–745.

Brandt, M.T., Levine, S.P., Smith, D.G., and Ettinger, H.J. (1998). Activity-Based Cost Management Part I: Applied to Occupational and Environmental Health Organizations. *American Industrial Hygiene Association*, 59 (5): 328–334.

Cardinaels, E. and Soderstrom, N. (2013). Managing in a Complex World: Accounting and Governance Choices in Hospitals. *European Accounting Review*, 22 (4): 647–684.

Carpenter, C.E. and Bernet, P.M. (2013). How the Choice of Issuing Authority Affects Hospital Debt Financing Costs. *Healthcare Financial Management*, 67 (5): 80–84.

Chang, K.J., Chichernea, D.C., and HassabElnaby, H.R. (2014). On the DuPont Analysis in the Health Care Industry. *Journal of Accounting and Public Policy*, 33 (1): 83–103.

Cinquini, L., Vitali, P. M., Pitzalis, A., and Campanale, C. (2009). Process View and Cost Management of a New Surgery Technique in Hospital. *Business Process Management Journal*, 15 (6): 895–919.

Clement, J.P. (1997). Dynamic Cost Shifting in Hospitals: Evidence from the 1980s and 1990s. *Inquiry*, 34: 340–350.

Cleverley, W.O. (1981). Financial Ratios: Summary Indicators for Management Decision-Making. *Hospital and Health Services Administration*, 26 (1): 26–47.

Cleverley, W.O. and Felkner, J.G. (1984). The Association of Capital Budgeting Techniques with Hospital Financial Performance. *Health Care Management Review*, 9 (3): 45–58.

Counte, M.A., Glandon, G.L., Holloman, K., and Kowalczyk, J. (1988). Using Ratios to Measure Hospital Financial Performance: Can the Process be Simplified? *Health Services Management Research*, 1: 173–180.

Demeere, N., Stouthuysen, K., and Roodhooft, F. (2009). Time-Driven Activity-Based Costing in an Outpatient Clinic Environment: Development, Relevance and Managerial Impact. *Health Policy*, 92 (2): 296–304.

Dranove, D., Garthwaite, C., and Ody, C. (2013). How Do Hospitals Respond to Negative Financial Shocks? The Impact of the 2008 Stock Market Crash. NBER Working Paper w18853.

Eldenburg, L. and Kallapur, S. (2000). The Effects of Changes in Cost allocations on the Assessment of Cost Containment Regulation in Hospitals. *Journal of Accounting and Public Policy*, 19 (1): 97–112.

Eldenburg, L. and Vines, C. (2004). Non-Profit Classification Decisions in Response to Change in Accounting Rules. *Journal of Accounting and Public Policy*, 23 (1): 1–22.

Eldenburg, L.G., Gunny, K.A., Hee, K.W., and Soderstrom, N. (2011). Earnings Management Using Real Activities: Evidence from Nonprofit Hospitals. *Accounting Review*, 86 (5): 1605–1630.

Emmett, D. and Forget, R. (2005). The Utilization of Activity-Based Cost Accounting in Hospitals. *Journal of Hospital Marketing and Public Relations*, 15 (2): 79–89.

Finkler, S.A., Henley, R.J., and Ward, D.M. (2003). Evidence-Based Financial Management. *Healthcare Financial Management*, 57 (10): 64–68.

Frakt, A.B. (2011). How Much do Hospitals Cost Shift? A Review of the Evidence. *Milbank Quarterly*, 89 (1): 90–130.

Frakt, A.B. and Mayes, R. (2012). Beyond Capitation: How New Payment Experiments Seek to Find the "Sweet Spot" in Amount of Risk Providers and Payers Bear. *Health Affairs*, 31 (9): 1951–1958.

Gapenski, L.C. and Pink, G.H. (2014). *Cases in Healthcare Finance*, 5th edn. Chicago, IL: AUPHA Press/Health Administration Press.

Gentry, W.M. (2002). Debt, Investment and Endowment Accumulation: The Case of Not-for-Profit Hospitals. *Journal of Health Economics*, 21 (5): 845–872.

Healthcare Financial Management Association (HFMA) (2012). *Building Value-Driving Capabilities: Business Intelligence*. Westchester, IL: HFMA.

Hill, N.T. (2000). Adoption of Costing Systems in US Hospitals: An Event History Analysis 1980–1990. *Journal of Accounting and Public Policy*, 19 (1): 41–71.

Hofmann, M.A. and McSwain, D. (2013). Financial Disclosure Management in the Nonprofit Sector: A Framework for Past and Future Research. *Journal of Accounting Literature*, 32 (1): 61–87.

Holzhacker, M., Krishnan, R., and Mahlendorf, M. D. (2014). The Impact of Changes in Regulation on Cost Behavior. *Contemporary Accounting Research*, accepted manuscript online: DOI: 10.1111/1911-3846.12082.

Kallapur, S. and Eldenburg, L. (2005). Uncertainty, Real options, and Cost Behavior: Evidence from Washington State Hospitals. *Journal of Accounting Research*, 43 (5): 735–752.

Kaplan, R.S. and Porter, M.E. (2011). How to Solve the Cost Crisis in Health Care. *Harvard Business Review*, 89 (9): 46–52.

Kocher, C. (2007). Hospital Capital Budgeting Practices and Their Relation to Key Hospital Characteristics: A Survey of US Manager Practices. *Journal of Global Business Issues*, 1 (2): 21–30.

Krishnan, R. (2005). The Effect of Changes in Regulation and Competition on Firms' Demand for Accounting Information. *Accounting Review*, 80 (1): 269–287.

Krishnan, R. and Yetman, M.H. (2011). Institutional Drivers of Reporting Decisions in Nonprofit Hospitals. *Journal of Accounting Research*, 49 (4): 1001–1039.

Kruse, G.B., Polsky, D., Stuart, E.A., and Werner, R.M. (2012). The Impact of Hospital Pay-for-Performance on Hospital and Medicare Costs. *HSR: Health Services Research*, 47 (6): 2118–2136.

Laskaris, J. and Regan, K. (2013). The New Break-Even Analysis. *Healthcare Financial Management*, 67 (12): 88–95.

Leleu, H., Moises, J., and Valdmanis, V. (2012). How Does Payer Mix and Technical Inefficiency Affect Hospital Net Revenue? IESEG School of Management Working Paper No. 2012-ECO-01.

Leone, A.J. and Van Horn, R.L. (2005). How Do Nonprofit Hospitals Manage Earnings?. *Journal of Health Economics*, 24 (4): 815–837.

Loubeau, P.R. and Griffith, A.S. (2012). Some Empirical Evidence of Sarbanes–Oxley Implementation in the Hospital Sector. *Coastal Business Journal*, 11 (1): 39–47.

Macinati, M.S. and Pessina, E.A. (2014). Management Accounting Use and Financial Performance in Public Health-Care Organisations. Evidence from the Italian National Health Service. *Health Policy*, 117 (1): 98–111.

Magnus, S.A. and Smith, D.G. (2000). Better Medicare Cost Report Data are Needed to Help Hospitals Benchmark Costs and Performance. *Health Care Management Review*, 25 (4): 65–76.

Magnus, S.A., Smith, D.G., and Wheeler, J.R. (2004a). The Association of Debt Financing with Not-for-Profit Hospitals' Provision of Uncompensated Care. *Journal of Health Care Finance*, 30 (4): 46–58.

Magnus, S.A., Wheeler, J.R., and Smith, D.G. (2004b). The Association of Debt Financing with Not-for-Profit Hospitals' Operational and Capital-Investment Efficiency. *Journal of Health Care Finance*, 30 (4): 33–45.

McCue, M.J. (2011). Association of Market, Organizational and Financial Factors with the Number, and Types of Capital Expenditures. *Health Care Management Review*, 36 (1): 67–77.

McGowan, A.S., Holmes, S.A., and Martin, M. (2006). The Association Between Activity Based Costing System Adoption and Hospital Performance. AAA 2007 Management Accounting Section (MAS) Meeting. Available at http://dx.doi.org/10.2139/ssrn.921471.

McGowan, M.M., Yurova, Y.V., and Chan, S.H. (2014). Audit Firm Size and Audit Quality in Nonprofit Hospitals: Evidence from Circular A-133 Audits. *Academy of Accounting and Financial Studies*, 19 (1): 19–24.

Murphy, S.M., Rosenman, R., McPherson, M.Q., and Friesner, D.L. (2011). Measuring Shared Inefficiency Between Hospital Cost Centers. *Medical Care Research and Review*, 68 (1): 55S–74S.

Orloff, T.M., Littell, C.L., Clune, C., Klingman, D., and Preston, B. (1990). Hospital Cost Accounting: Who's Doing What and Why. *Health Care Management Review*, 15 (4): 73–78.

Ozmeral, A.B., Reiter, K.L., Holmes, G.M., and Pink, G.H. (2012). A Comparative Study of Financial Data Sources for Critical Access Hospitals: Audited Financial Statements, the Medicare Cost Report, and the Internal Revenue Service Form 990. *Journal of Rural Health*, 28 (4): 416–424.

Pennell, M.Y., Altenderfer, M.E., Sigmond, R.M., and Altman, I. (1954). Hospital Income and Expense Ratios, 1951. *Public Health Reports*, 69 (10): 947–952.

Pizzini, M.J. (2006). The Relation between Cost-System Design, Managers' Evaluations of the Relevance and Usefulness of Cost Data, and Financial Performance: An Empirical Study of US Hospitals. *Accounting, Organizations and Society*, 31 (2): 179–210.

Pridgen, A. and Wang, K.J. (2012). Audit Committees and Internal Control Quality: Evidence from Nonprofit Hospitals Subject to the Single Audit Act. *International Journal of Auditing*, 16 (2): 165–183.

Reinhardt, U.E. (2006). The Pricing of US Hospital Services: Chaos Behind a Veil of Secrecy. *Health Affairs*, 25 (1): 57–69.

Reinstein, A. and Churyk, N.T. (2013). New Financial Statement Reporting Requirements for Healthcare Entities and Insurers. *Journal of Hospital Administration*, 2 (3): 21–27.

Reiter, K.L., Smith, D.G., Wheeler, J.R., and Rivenson, H.L. (1999). Capital Investment Strategies in Health Care Systems. *Journal of Health Care Finance*, 26 (4): 31–41.

Reiter, K.L. and Song, P.H. (2011). The Role of Financial Market Performance in Hospital Capital Investment. *Journal of Health Care Finance*, 37 (3): 38–50.

Reiter, K.L. and Song, P.H. (2013). Hospital Capital Budgeting in an Era of Transformation. *Journal of Health Care Finance*, 39 (3): 14–22.

Rich, K.T., Lopez, D.M., and Smith, P.C. (2013). Auditor Size and Internal Control Reporting Differences in Nonprofit Healthcare Organizations. *Journal of Public Budgeting, Accounting, and Financial Management*, 25 (1): 41–68.

Rivenson, H.L., Reiter, K.L., Wheeler, J.R., and Smith, D.G. (2011). Cash Holdings of Not-for-Profit Hospitals. *Journal of Health Care Finance*, 38 (2): 24–37.

Rorem, C.R. and Carroll, M. (1936). Uniform Hospital Accounting. *Accounting Review*, 11 (2): 157–164.

Ryan, A.M. and Damberg, C.L. (2013). What Can the Past of Pay-for-Performance Tell Us About the Future of Value-Based Purchasing in Medicare? *Healthcare: The Journal of Delivery Science and Innovation*, 1 (1): 42–49.

Sherman, H.D. (1986). Interpreting Hospital Performance with Financial Statement Analysis. *Accounting Review*, 61 (3): 526–550.

Shwartz, M., Young, D.W., and Siegrist, R. (1995). The Ratio of Costs to Charges: How Good a Basis for Estimating Costs? *Inquiry*, 32 (4): 476–481.

Singh, S.R. and Song, P.H. (2013). Nonoperating Revenue and Hospital Financial Performance: Do Hospitals Rely on Income from Nonpatient Care Activities to Offset Losses on Patient Care? *Health Care Management Review*, 38 (3): 201–210.

Smith, D.G. (2014). *Introduction to Healthcare Financial Management*, San Diego, CA: Bridgepoint Education.

Smith, D.G. and Betley, C.L. (2000). Cost Management Activities of PPOs. *Journal of Risk and Insurance*, 67 (2): 219–233.

Smith, D.G., Clement, J.P., and Wheeler, J.R. (1995). Philanthropy and Hospital Financing. *HSR: Health Services Research*, 30 (5): 615–635.

Smith, D.G. and Wynne, J. (2006). Capital Budgeting Practices in Hospitals. *International Journal of Healthcare Technology and Management*, 7 (1): 117–128.

Song, P.H., Smith, D.G., and Wheeler, J.R. (2008). It Was the Best of Times, It Was the Worst of Times: A Tale of Two Years in Not-for-Profit Hospital Financial Investments. *Health Care Management Review*, 33 (3): 234–242.

Stewart, L.J. and Smith, P.C. (2011). An Examination of Contemporary Financing Practices and the Global Financial Crisis on Nonprofit Multi-Hospital Health Systems. *Journal of Health Care Finance*, 37 (3): 1–24.

Suarez, V., Lesneski, C., and Denison, D. (2011). Making the Case for Using Financial Indicators in Local Public Health Agencies. *American Journal of Public Health*, 101 (3): 419–425.

Tan, S.S., Geissler, A., Serdén, L., Heurgren, M., van Ineveld, B.M., Redekop, W.K., and Hakkaart-van Roijen, L. (2014). DRG Systems in Europe: Variations in Cost Accounting Systems Among 12 Countries. *European Journal of Public Health*, 24: 1–6.

Van Helden, G.J. and Northcott, D. (2010). Examining the Practice Relevance of Public Sector Management Research. *Financial Accountability and Management*, 26 (2): 0267–4424.

Watkins, A.L. and Brenner, V.C. (2003). Regulating External Reporting in the Municipal Bond Market: the Relevance of Nonfinancial Information in Evaluating Hospital Financial Performance. *Accounting and the Public Interest*, 3 (1): 21–35.

Wedig, G.J., Hassan, M., and Morrisey, M.A. (1996). Tax-Exempt Debt and the Capital Structure of Nonprofit Organizations: An Application to Hospitals. *Journal of Finance*, 51 (4): 1247–1283.

Wedig, G.J., Hassan, M., and Sloan, F.A. (1989). Hospital Investment Decisions and the Cost of Capital. *Journal of Business*, 62 (4): 517–537.

Wheeler, J.R. and Smith, D.G. (1988). The Discount Rate for Capital Expenditure Analysis in Health Care. *Health Care Management Review*, 13 (2): 43–51.

White, C. (2013). Contrary to Cost-Shift Theory, Lower Medicare Hospital Payment Rates for Inpatient Care Lead to Lower Private Payment Rates. *Health Affairs*, 32 (5): 935–943.

White, C. and Wu, V.Y. (2014). How Do Hospitals Cope with Sustained Slow Growth in Medicare Prices? *Health Services Research*, 49 (1): 11–31.

Wilson, M. and Cutler, D. (2014). Emergency Department Profits Are Likely To Continue As The Affordable Care Act Expands Coverage. *Health Affairs*, 33 (5): 792–799.

Wu, V.Y., Shen, Y.C., and Melnick, G. (2014). Decomposition of the Drivers of the U.S. Hospital Spending Growth, 2001–2009. *BMC Health Services Research*, 14: 230–247.

Zeller, T.L., Stanko, B.B., and Cleverley, W.O. (1996). A Revised Classification Pattern of Hospital Financial Ratios. *Journal of Accounting and Public Policy*, 15: 161–182.

# 19. Long-term care
## Carol Molinari and Ting Zhang

## INTRODUCTION

The US population is aging. The growing proportion of elders (aged 65 years and older) in the US is projected to account for one in every five Americans by 2030 (Vincent and Velkoff, 2010). Even during the recent weak economic recovery and recession phase in the US, there has been stable growth in healthcare spending that reflects the non-cyclical and steady demand for healthcare. In 2011, older Americans spent 12.2 percent of their total expenditures on health, almost twice the proportion spent by all Americans (6.7 percent) (AoA, 2014).

Long-term care reflects a broad array of home, community-based, and residential services to maximize a person's ability to function and enjoy a quality of life. The continuum of long-term care covers various settings that range from home-based to institutional services. Long-term care personnel typically include direct care workers and aides, registered nurses, licensed practical and vocational nurses, licensed social workers, physical therapists, occupational therapists, physician medical directors, and administrators (Stone and Harahan, 2010).

Today's elders demand more medical and health support personnel, particularly for long-term care to help them in their later and final years, and are likely to spend more time with the long-term care system as compared to the acute medical delivery system (Yee-Melichar et al., 2014). Increased demand for long-term care across the continuum is enhancing the likelihood of shortages among long-term care workers, such as nursing assistants, home health and home care aides, and other workers. The Bureau of Labor Statistics projects that job growth in the long-term care sector will exceed that in many other sectors of the US economy (US Bureau of Labor Statistics, 2008–2009). Together these forces are driving demand for long-term care now and into the future (Zhang, 2008).

Healthcare managers and leaders increasingly need to understand the key types and forms of long-term care to assist clients and communities to rethink ways to meet social and health needs of aging individuals within the constraints of workforce shortages. The focus of this chapter is to provide an overview of the delivery and management of long-term care and to discuss emerging workforce challenges associated with care coordination across the continuum to promote the safety and health of seniors. An emphasis is placed on home- and community-based care due to seniors' strong preferences to age safely and healthfully in place.

This chapter is organized into two main sections. Section I defines and discusses the broad continuum of long-term care. Information related to the main types of care and services, payment structures, and pertinent regulations provides an understanding of factors related to the growing demand for diverse long-term care options available to seniors and their families especially those related to home- and community-based services being encouraged by the Affordable Care Act (ACA), 2010.

Section II focuses on key supply-side factors related to the long-term care workforce. An analysis of projected shortages among direct care workers and aides helps to identify some of the pressing managerial challenges for healthcare managers and leaders to consider in light of new long-term care delivery models supported by the ACA (2010).

# I  CONTINUUM OF LONG-TERM CARE

Section I discusses key programs and services across the continuum of care from home, community, and institution that are designed to help older adults lead quality lives in their respective communities. As shown in Figure 19.1, six common options across the continuum of care will be discussed in terms of services, payment, and related regulations.

### Home-based care
Home care for seniors typically involves assistance with activities of daily living (ADLs) that reflect self-care, for example, eating, dressing, toileting, and mobility; and instrumental activities of daily living (IADLs) associated with more complex tasks of living independently, for example, shopping, preparing meals, housekeeping, paying bills, and taking medications (Goldman et al., 2014). These activities require a combination of informal and formal care-giving in the home and are not considered medical services.

### Informal home care
Family care-giving is the most common form of informal care provided to seniors in the home. However, care-giving extends beyond family to include friends, neighbors, and community members, although the majority of informal care-giving is done by spouses (Cohen et al., 2000). It is estimated that about 9 million elders are receiving home long-term care (National Center for Assisted Living, 2011). A key point to note is the

*Figure 19.1    Main types of service options in long-term care*

growing amount of home care-giving for elders needing daily assistance with ADLs from informal care-givers, and how these demands can create significant physical and psychological stress on the family or informal care-giver (Schultz and Sherwood, 2008).

*Payment*    Family and informal care-givers are mainly unpaid and make care-giving affordable and accessible to many seniors living at home. Non-medical home care agencies that provide unskilled custodial care in the US are not covered under Medicare. This type of home care is the fastest-growing, with fees varying by region and types of services provided.

*Regulation*    For informal home care, an important issue that is getting more attention relates to family members' responsibility for care-giving. Many states have filial responsibility laws that require adult children to care for elderly parents in need (Scharlach, 2008). However, many questions about the needs of children versus those of elderly parents have not yet been addressed by state regulation (Scharlach, 2008).

### Formal home care

Formal home care is referred to as home healthcare and typically involves skilled medical services or custodial, non-medical care (Goldman et al., 2014). Home healthcare broadly covers health and social services to help meet needs of the individual. Home healthcare helps individuals recover from acute illness or injury as well as helping individuals with chronic conditions, disabilities, and terminal illness. Providing non-medical home healthcare (providing help with ADLs and IADLs) is the fastest-growing type of home care (Kelly et al., 2011).

An estimated 12 million individuals receive home care (National Association for Home Care and Hospice, NAHC). A key benefit of home healthcare is that seniors with moderate needs can remain in their homes and communities even without informal home care support. Home health agencies often provide skilled care. There are numerous providers of home care, that include home care agencies, visiting nurses associations, government agencies, health and hospital organizations, and rehabilitation services. There are also non-medical home care agencies that provide unskilled custodial care, and these home health workers comprise the fastest-growing workforce sector in the long-term care industry (Kelly et al., 2011). States license home health agencies that provide skilled nursing and home care aide services.

*Payment*   Varying levels of home healthcare are provided by certified home health agencies and covered by Medicare and Medicaid government programs. Medicaid funds can be used in states with Medicaid waivers to pay for custodial and non-medical home care. Home health agencies that are licensed by the state and are Medicare certified can offer skilled care that is covered under Medicare programs.

Medicare finances long-term care (LTC) only tangentially through its limited skilled nursing facility and home health benefits, and then only after the patient first meets the requirement of a minimum three-day hospitalization. For homebound persons needing part-time skilled nursing care or physical or other therapy services, Medicare may pay for home healthcare, including personal services provided by home health aides (US Department of Labor, 2000).

Private resources include unpaid or donated care from family members or friends, out-of-pocket spending, commercial insurance payments (although these payments are typically limited), and private LTC insurance (Spinelli and McSweeney-Feld, 2011). Private long-term care insurance is in the form of individual rather than group policies, leading to high administrative costs. A specialized private insurance policy that pays for home-based care usually specifies a maximum daily benefit level of reimbursement and thus may not cover all of the costs (Spinelli and McSweeney-Feld, 2011). A growing challenge is the effort and time required to coordinate and monitor home care, especially insurance and payment, in addition to selecting care-givers, and altering home services as individuals' needs change.

*Regulation*   Home care agencies that provide medical services must be licensed as home health agencies, and if they serve Medicare beneficiaries they also need to be Medicare certified (Goldman et al., 2014). To become a Medicare or Medicaid certified home health aide requires less than two weeks of training together with passing a competency test (Stone and Bryant, 2012). Many states have Medicaid programs that cover personal care and home- and community-based services waiver programs. These programs have requirements for training and monitoring that vary by state. Thus, knowing the state regulations for Medicaid waiver is critical for clients, families, and providers.

State regulation for custodial and non-medical home care also varies. In some states, there is no licensure and monitoring for home care agencies providing non-skilled home care. Currently, 29 states require a license for non-medical home care providers; some also require home care worker training (Kelly et al., 2011).

Regulation of direct care aides working in assisted living and personal care and home care settings depends on the state (Stone and Bryant, 2012). Usually workers in these settings receive little or no training (Seavey, 2007), and there are few competencies specific to long-term care.

**Community-Based Services**

Community-based services and programs help clients live independently in their homes. Common community-based services for seniors are senior centers, adult day centers and adult day health centers, and care management.

**Senior centers**

Senior centers are places for seniors to socialize and receive information about the various needs of aging. Senior centers offer seniors opportunities for recreation and education in a group or a congregate setting. They do not provide direct personal care or healthcare. Participants have a high level of independence in terms of getting to the senior center, as transportation is typically not provided. Some of the usual programs or services offered include nutrition and meals, health and fitness programs, public benefits counseling, social and recreational activities, and volunteer opportunities. Interestingly, about 1 million adults are served in senior centers daily in the United States (NISC, 2011), making senior centers the most-used community-based services by older adults (Gelfand, 2006). Women comprise the majority (70 percent) of participants, most of whom live alone. About 75 percent are low-income individuals.

Senior center participants demonstrate better outcomes, which include higher satisfaction levels (NISC, 2011) and lower levels of loneliness (Malone-Beach and Langeland, 2011). Senior center participants also report improved overall health and well-being. Given the growing numbers of aging baby boomers (born between 1946 and 1964), there is growing interest to develop senior centers with activities and services preferred by these seniors.

*Payment*   In 1973, the Older Americans Act provided US federal funds to develop and operate senior centers. About 11 000 senior centers serve 1 million adults daily (NISC, 2011). Senior centers vary in their funding: some are public, others are not-for profit; their ownership status determines the extent to which participants pay for services at the center. Often those centers that charge do so on a sliding scale.

*Regulation*   The 1999 Olmstead decision in Georgia shows that states have made progress in terms of providing community-based alternatives to institutional long-term care (Hood, 2011). Although licensure is not required to operate a senior center, there is a National Senior Center Accreditation Program (Beisgen and Kraitchman, 2003) that centers can apply to for accreditation that attests to the quality of programming offered. Over 200 centers in the US are accredited (NISC, 2011).

### Adult day centers and adult day health centers

Adult day centers (ADCs) started as a social program in the 1970s (Pratt, 2010). However, they have expanded to include rehabilitative and transitional care, as well as short-term rehabilitation following hospitalization (NADSA, 2014). The purpose of ADCs is to help older clients and their families with daily challenges from chronic health conditions and disability. ADC programming supports participants while providing breaks and respite for care-givers. Since much of care-giving is provided by spouse or family members, this community-based alternative helps clients to remain in the home by supporting the main care-giver. It also helps to reduce unnecessary and costly use of long-term care facilities that include assisted living or nursing homes.

ADCs include some social programming and monitoring in a group setting. These community-based services can provide group care, supervision, and assistance with daily activities at an on-site center (Werdegar et al., 2014). Most of these centers operate at regular business hours to support day attendance by participants. There are over 4600 day programs in the US (NADSA, 2014), and the number of these is rapidly increasing in response to older clients' health and medical needs.

There are two types of day programs, adult day centers (ADCs) and adult day health centers (ADHCs). The purpose of the ADC is to provide a safe and structured environment to those who may have functional limitations and thus need some help (Werdegar et al., 2014). ADCs are based on social care models and do not provide nursing or other health services. In contrast, ADHCs offer a medical model that includes health, social, and recreational services (Pratt, 2010).

Typically, adult day centers provide transportation to and from the center. Both participants and care-givers are served in ADCs, and transportation is usually provided. They can also provide meals and snacks, social services and activities, recreational activities, as well as help with everyday activities of self-care (personal care) as well as more complex instrumental activities related to independent life (shopping, managing money, taking medications, and so on).

The ADC model of care is designed for those who need some personal care help but have limited healthcare needs (Werdegar et al., 2014). This is appropriate for clients who can benefit from assistance due to dementia or cognitive problems. It also provides respite for care-givers. The ADC program offers socialization and recreational activities to clients. The clients can have functional limitation and cognitive impairments without significant health needs.

There are about 11 000 senior centers that serve 1 million adults daily, reflecting that these senior centers are used more than any other community-based program (Gelfand, 2006). There are more than 3500 adult day health programs in the US that provide care to over 150 000 older adults (NADSA, 2014). ADHCs have emerged as demands for assistance increase among seniors with medical needs who desire to age in place. Because of this demand ADHCs have grown as the need for health services has increased among the elderly. Typically, ADHCs provide rehabilitative care that includes short-term rehabilitation after hospitalization (NADSA, 2014).

Clients served by ADHCs suffer from multiple chronic problems and functional impairments; these clients are typically frail with multiple care needs associated with physical and emotional health problems that affect daily activities (Werdegar et al., 2014). ADHCs are part of the community-based continuum of care that serves as an alternative to LTC institutional care. Over half (52 percent) of ADHC participants have some level of dementia (NADSA, 2014).

Care management refers to the coordination of services within a community-based delivery of services. It involves coordinating various services and care systems to support quality of life and independence for older adults (Cress, 2012). Care management involves assessment, planning, coordination, and facilitation of options and services to meet an individual's health and human service needs (CMSA, 2008). Case managers manage care, not the client, as they help advocate for available resources to provide quality and cost-effective care and outcomes. Care management includes a variety of areas: healthcare, acute care, hospice, rehabilitative, mental health, home care, disabilities, and so on.

In the 1970s federal and state governments helped develop community-based health and supportive services. Waivers of Medicaid requirements allowed state governments to create demonstration projects designed to assist the frail and disabled. (Werdegar et al., 2014). The Program of All-Inclusive Care for the Elderly (PACE) program was created to provide community-based care options to populations of older adults. The PACE program has been a successful model delivering LTC to a vulnerable population of frail elderly, and has documented effectiveness compared to institutional care (CMS, 2011).

The On Lok program is an example of the PACE program. The On Lok Senior health services created a new model of delivering a continuum of long-term care services. It provided a community-based system of care delivered to frail elderly in their home and day center as an alternative to nursing home care. In 1980s this On Lok model was tested in other Centers for Medicare and Medicaid Services (CMS) demonstration projects across the US (CMS, 2011). The success of these projects in offering comprehensive and cost-effective healthcare and support services to a vulnerable population led to the designation of PACE as a Medicare program.

*Payment*   Federal support to develop senior centers began in the 1970s (Niles-Yokum and Wagner, 2011). Funds to develop and operate these centers were allocated as part of the Older Americans Act (OAA). The OAA requires Area Agencies on Aging (AAAs) as centers for comprehensive and coordinated services to seniors (Beisgen and Kraitchman, 2003). In fact the majority of senior centers are designated to provide these services to seniors in the community (NISC, 2011).

The financing of community-based programs and services comes from a variety of sources, including Medicare, Medicaid, private insurance, and private pay. Medicare is the primary payer source for acute care costs, but typically does not cover social programs such as adult day care (Werdegar et al., 2014).

*Regulation*   Adult day centers and adult day health centers are licensed by states. ADHCs can offer specialized programming for some groups, such as dementia care. The vast majority of these facilities are operated as public or non-profit enterprises (NASDA, 2011). There is no specific license to operate a senior center. However, the National Institute of Senior Centers (NISC) offers and administers an accreditation program (Beisgan and Kratchmen, 2003). Accreditation specifies standards of operation that promote quality of services.

Care management is critical to delivery of healthcare across the continuum of care, yet it is not a licensed or regulated profession. Providers can be licensed in their profession (for example, registered nurses, social workers). Accreditation and certification in care management can be obtained. For example the National Association of Professional Geriatric Care Managers (NAPGCM) monitors the certification process for managing geriatric care.

Frail elderly have been the main participants and users of care management (Cress, 2012) to help these older adults manage complex health and social problems. There is a growing need and demand for geriatric care managers as the US population ages.

Care management is a guiding principle in the Patient Protection and Affordable Care Act, 2010. This is evident in its provisions to promote modest and voluntary changes in the delivery of healthcare; for example, the creation of accountable care organizations for the purpose of providing and coordinating a broad array of health services for consumers, which would increase the quality and efficiency of care while lowering costs (McDonough, 2014).

**Naturally occurring retirement communities**
As seniors become a larger proportion of the US population, communities with high concentrations of older residents are becoming more common across the society. The growing popularity of the naturally occurring retirement community (NORC) model reflects older Americans' preference to age in place. There are a range of different types of residences in NORCs. Some include residential buildings, single family homes, multilevel apartments, or neighborhoods of housing where 40 percent or more of households are seniors. The key characteristic is having a critical mass of seniors to create efficiencies of scale to facilitate the cost-effective provision of health and social services (O'Shaughnessy and Napili, 2006).

There is some variation in the definition of NORCs, making it hard for researchers to provide an accurate number of NORCs operating in the US. It is estimated that about 5000 NORCs exist in American cities that represent about 10 million people (Masotti et al., 2006). The number of seniors living in NORCs is growing. These communities are important for consumers because they reflect the growing interest of seniors to age in place; and for managers to identify and target needs to enable seniors to live safely in these communities.

It is important to note that the needs of members in NORCs vary. A common type of naturally occurring retirement community is one with a support service program (NORC-SSP). These are affiliations and/or partnerships that bring together housing, residents, and health and social services providers to allow residents to live independently and healthfully (Kain et al., 2014).

The Village is another type of NORC-SSP where residents identify a need in their community and then pursue resources, contrasted with the NORC-SSP model in which providers assess residents' needs (ibid.). A familiar example is the Beacon Hill Village in Boston, Massachusetts. The Village model is member-based and member-directed. The Village model is set up to serve all older residents, not just the frail, disabled, or wealthy. The purpose of the Village is to promote healthy aging based on help from volunteers and neighbors for minor activities, that is, help with carrying groceries and so on. Seniors report that they prefer to ask volunteers rather than friends or family, so as not to burden them (Accius, 2010).

### Payment
Between 2005 and 2006, the US government provided funds to support NORC-SSP through the formation of the community innovation for aging in place initiative (Jewish Federation of North America, 2012). This government support spurred the creation of 40 NORC-SSPs that serve 20 000 older residents (Kain et al., 2014).

In contrast, Villages are set up as non-profit organizations that are funded by membership dues, donations, and other fund-raising activities (McWhinney-Morse, 2009). Villages give members the opportunity to actively participate in the community with regard to their needs and wants (McWhinney-Morse, 2009). Membership fees vary from $100 to $2000 year depending on location and services provided.

### Regulation
Given the voluntary nature of NORC-SSPs, there are no additional regulations for providers who participate in NORCs. Professional providers who partner with NORC-SSPs may have discipline-specific professional

licensure requirements. These villages set up their own policies and members identify needs and volunteers.

**Assisted Living Communities**

There has been dramatic growth in assisted living in the US. It is estimated that 1 million older adults resided in assisted living arrangements in 2005 (Mollica et al., 2007). There are several key reasons for this growth that relate to consumer preferences for a less expensive and restrictive alternative to nursing home care. Generally, assisted living is considered as providing personalized care and supervision outside of an institutionalized environment, which encourages physical and psychological independence (Flores et al., 2014).

Assisted living communities include residential services and arrangements. The term "assisted living" refers to the physical features of a facility as well as a philosophy of care (Flores et al., 2014). The Assisted Living Federation of America defines assisted living as follows: assisted living is designed for individuals who require assistance with everyday activities such as meals, medication management or assistance, bathing, dressing, and transportation. Some residents may have memory disorders including Alzheimer's or they may need help with mobility, incontinence, or other challenges (ALFA, 2011). For practical purposes, "assisted living" will be used here to refer to all types of supportive housing.

A recent report based on 2009 data from five national associations (Flores et al., 2014) found the following:

- The average age of assisted living resident was 86 years.
- Almost three-quarters (74 percent) were women.
- The average resident is mobile but needs help with about two activities of daily living.
- More than 900 000 residents live in assisted living communities.

**Payment**

The majority (two-thirds) of assisted living residents pay for this type of living arrangement (Flores et al., 2014). Options for private payment include personal assets, family assistance, and LTC insurance benefits. Low- to moderate-income residents typically use income from the sale of their homes plus other savings and investments to pay for assisted living. Families paid between 11 percent and 24 percent of the total costs for assisted living of residents (ibid.). Private LTC insurance remains a source of payment for a very limited number of elderly, due to its high costs and premiums.

Public payment for assisted living comes from Supplemental Security Income (SSI), Medicaid benefits based on income eligibility, and veterans' programs. SSI monthly payment is the most common payment source for assisted living (Flores et al., 2014). In most states, Medicaid programs will pay for some type of assisted living. Recent national estimates indicate that only one in five residents is a Medicaid recipient (Park-Lee et al., 2011). Veterans Administration (VA) benefits cover a small number of assisted living residents; in 2009, 7 percent of assisted living residents received VA benefits payments (American Association of Homes and Services for the Aging et al., 2009).

**Regulation**
It is important to understand that there are differing views regarding the types of services provided in assisted living. One perspective is that assisted living should provide social services not medical care. Others argue that assisted living should be able to provide some medical services to reduce the need to transfer older residents to a nursing home. There is considerable variation regarding services provided in licensed assisted living housing. States regulate allowable services and levels of care (Mollica et al., 2007) and thus states can stipulate allowable services.

The vast majority (43 out of 50) states have a licensing category or statute for assisted living (Flores et al., 2014). Forty-two states allow Medicaid to fund services in assisted living facilities (Mollica et al., 2007). States vary in how they define assisted living. Some states require that assisted living be in a licensed facility. Others define assisted living as a service that can be delivered in non-licensed settings.

States vary in whether and how they apply state health regulation. States employ a consumer-focused philosophy that adapts the delivery of care to the needs of the consumer. For some states, consumer privacy is emphasized so that assisted living arrangements must be private. Other states allow shared residences (Flores et al., 2014). The importance of how the state defines assisted living relates to the ways in which states regulate home- and community-based services and costs; admission criteria, which include the health and condition of the resident; rights of residents, that includes, personal rights, disclosure; staff requirements and training for the facilities; and administrator requirements and qualifications for assisted living facilities.

**Continuing care retirement communities**
The purpose of continuing care retirement communities (CCRCs) is to provide a broad range of services in one residential setting to allow elders to age in place without relocating when care needs change (Milford et al.,

2014). There are many different types of CCRCs; however they typically span the continuum of services that include independent apartments and homes, assisted living services, and a skilled nursing facility. The intent is to provide varying levels of services to residents as they move along the continuum of care, so that residents can remain in the CCRC as they age and their care needs change.

There are about 1900 CCRCs in operation in 48 states in the US (US Government Accountability Office, 2010). Many states have statutes to protect elders in CCRCs, yet 12 states do not any have specific CCRC regulations (Milford et al., 2014). There is no federal regulation of CCRCs.

It is important to note that a CCRC offers the resident an agreement that guarantees a specified monthly fee unrelated to care needs and levels of service. Many elders sell off their assets to pay CCRC entrance and monthly fees. Their sense of security depends on the long-term viability of the CCRC.

Most CCRCs are not-for-profit agencies that benefit the communities served. The financial model for CCRCs depends on residents' entrance and monthly fees. The high entrance fee helps to build the CCRC's reserves, while monthly fees are used to pay for operational costs for all residents. Monthly fees from independent residents living in apartments help to subsidize costs of services provided to residents in assisted living or nursing homes. To ensure that not-for-profit CCRCs meet the needs of residents and clients, excess revenue is needed to reinvest in the operations. Consequently, pricing of fees in CCRCs is important, to cover costs of resident services and to have the reserves needed for unexpected expenses.

**Payment**
Typically, residents pay for continuing care retirement communities from their personal assets. The resident contracts for services provided in the CCRC specifies benefits and payment. For example, the contract identifies the entrance fee and monthly fee paid by the resident. There are three main types of CCRC contracts: extensive, modified, and fee-for-service (Milford et al., 2014). These contract types stipulate the extent to which the resident will receive any or all needed health services in addition to housing. An extensive contract, also called a "life care agreement," usually includes housing, residential services, amenities, and unlimited health-related service with little or no increase in monthly payments (Milford et al., 2014). In contrast, fee-for-service contracts can include housing, residential services, and amenities; however, healthcare services are not included.

**Regulation**

Once a CCRC is operational, it is subject to financial review and site visits by state licensing regulators. Typically, independent and assisted living apartments are monitored by state Community Care Licensing regulators, and skilled nursing homes are evaluated by state regulators. CCRC developers usually based in the state Department of Social Services or Department of Insurance provide consumers with a process of credentialing. Once operational, CCRCs are subject to balance sheet review by state licensing agencies to monitor their financial viability and sustainability (Milford et al., 2014).

**Skilled Nursing Facility**

A skilled nursing facility (SNF), also referred to as a nursing home, is designed to meet the physical, social, and mental needs of residents. Nursing homes provide institutional care on a 24/7 basis. Nursing homes have been in operation in the US since the nineteenth century. Recent reports indicate that there are almost 16 000 licensed nursing homes in the US (Briesacher et al., 2009). These facilities house about 1.6 million residents (Breisacher et al., 2009). However, fewer seniors have sought placement in nursing homes over the past decade than in the past (Breisacher et al., 2009), because of the growing availability of home- and community-based services and assisted living options that allow more elders to age in place.

Over half of nursing home residents cannot perform three or more ADLs e.g., eating, bathing, dressing, walking, etc. (Breisacher et al., 2009). The most common diagnoses among nursing home residents are circulatory diseases and cognitive disorders (Jones et al., 2009). An important point to underscore is that half of nursing homes admissions are for short-term rehabilitative stays (Jones et al., 2009).

The average age of a nursing home resident is 79. Most are white (86 percent) and 71 percent are women (Jones et al., 2009). Between 1999 and 2008, white residents declined nationally and Hispanic residents increased by 55 percent, Asian residents increased by 54 percent, and African American residents by 11 percent. These rates exceed the population growth among these ethnic and racial groups. The drop among white residents may also indicate access to other options such as assisted living and home-based services.

**Payment**

Medicaid and Medicare are the public programs primarily responsible for financing nursing home care. Additionally, the Department of Veterans

Affairs and the Social Services Block Grant program also fund some of the costs. In contrast, most European countries finance LTC expenses through public benefit or insurance programs, unpaid care from family members and friends, and out-of-pocket resources.

Medicaid is a state-administrated, means-tested federal insurance program that pays for medical care and other supportive services for low-income individuals, the disabled, and poor elderly persons. Within broad federal guidelines, the states establish eligibility standards; determine the type, amount, duration, and scope of services; set the rate of payment; and administer their own programs. To receive a Medicaid waiver for alternative community services, the patient must first be evaluated for 90 days in a nursing home. To qualify for Medicaid a person must spend-down their liquid assets to $2000. Medicare is the federal health insurance program for individuals over age 65, those on Social Security disability benefits for more than two years, and those with end-stage renal disease. It has four parts and covers care provided in SNFs for up to 100 days as well as home care. As Day (n.d.) specifies, Medicare will pay for 20 days of a skilled nursing care facility at full cost, and the difference between $114 per day and the actual cost for another 80 days. Private Medicare supplement insurance usually pays the 80-day deductible of $114 per day, if a person carries this insurance and the right policy form. However, Medicare often stops paying before reaching the full 100 days. There is a misconception that Medicare automatically covers up to 100 days of all nursing home stays. In reality, 100 full days of Medicare coverage is not that likely.

Medicare covers nursing care for up to 120 days. According to a US Department of Labor (2000) report, it is estimated that the value of LTC services provided by family members exceeds the cost of nursing home care by about 170 percent; family members and close friends continue to be the primary care-givers for LTC services and will likely continue to be an important source of care-giving in the future.

### Regulation

Practically all of US nursing homes are certified so that they can receive payment from Medicare and Medicaid (Breisacher et al., 2009). The Federal Nursing Home Reform Act, often referred to as OBRA (the Omnibus Budget Reconciliation Act), regulates the operations of all nursing homes. OBRA monitors the key areas of quality of care and quality of life in nursing homes. Quality of care requires nursing homes to establish individual care plans based on a minimum dataset (MDS) assessment for each resident at defined time intervals. This MDS information allows state and federal regulators to examine and oversee nursing home quality of care on a regular and continuous basis (Cabigao and Cherney, 2014).

State laws and regulations related to nursing homes were included in 1965 Medicare and Medicaid legislation and reflect federal regulations related to quality of care. States vary in terms of level of nursing home regulation. For example, California requires specified staff levels for direct care nurses. An important point to note is that state boards license nursing home administrators. Similar to the federal government, states have the authority to issue fines and penalties for nursing home violations.

States work with the federal government to ensure quality nursing home care, as reflected in their respective roles. States license skilled nursing facilities (SNFs) and the federal government certifies SNFs to participate in Medicare and/or Medicaid programs. Certification is carried out by the state; state agencies contract with the federal government to certify or recertify SNFs (Cabigao and Cherney, 2014).

## II MANAGING LONG-TERM CARE HUMAN RESOURCES

This second section of the chapter focuses on the long-term care human resources that provide the continuum of services. Specifically, this section discusses the main types of long-term care workers, as well as analyzing the supply and demand forces that include the expansion of home- and community-based long-term care associated with the Patient Protection and Affordable Care Act (2010). Additionally, emerging staffing needs based on this federal legislation will be included in comments and conclusions related to the management and delivery of long-term care.

### Long-Term Care Human Resources

There are a variety of healthcare providers and professionals in the delivery of long-term care. They can be classified as (1) long-term care aides; (2) administrative professionals; (3) clinicians; (4) ancillary personnel; and (5) social support workers (Singh, 2010). The types of human resources vary according to the level of LTC services delivered in a given setting. For example, independent living and retirement centers may employ one or two administrative professionals and a small staff of ancillary staff. A nursing home tends to be more structured and typically has all five categories of LTC professionals.

#### Direct care workers: long-term care aides
Long-term care services heavily rely on non-medical care-givers who give most of the hands-on supportive and personal care and assist patients

with all activities of daily living (ADLs). They also change bed linen and serve meals to patients. These include home health aides, therapy aides, and personal care attendants. They constitute the largest group of healthcare workers in the LTC industry (Singh, 2010). Aides provide clients help with ADLs in settings across the continuum of care ranging from home care to skilled nursing facilities. These positions are close to the bottom of the organizational hierarchy as reflected in low wages and heavy workloads. A key point to note is the low-level training requirements that includes less than two weeks of training plus passing a test to become a Medicare or Medicaid certified long-term care aide. However, aides do not need to be certified to practice.

In most LTC organizations, these aides work under the direction and supervision of skilled workers that include nurses, therapists (physical, occupational, and speech), and social workers. In community-based adult day centers, aides provide help with ADLs, transportation, and social and recreational activities. They also provide support for home and family care-givers.

### Administrative professionals

Long-term care administrators are needed to manage resources, coordinate each function in an organization, oversee compliance with regulations, and ensure that services are delivered in accordance with established professional standards and policies. Administrators need to have a good understanding of not only financing, budgeting, and marketing, but also legal and ethical constraints, as well as having the necessary interpersonal communication and leadership skills.

According to Medicare Conditions of Participation for home health agencies, the administrator must either be a licensed physician, a registered nurse, or someone who has training and experience in health services administration and at least one year of supervisory or administrative experience in home healthcare or related health programs (CMS, 2005a, 2005b). Agencies often employ a registered nurse or someone with a business degree as administrator (Singh, 2010).

Many states now require administrators of assisted living facilities to be licensed, but education and experience requirements vary from state to state. On the other hand, the National Association of Long Term Care Administrator Boards (NAB) has established requirements for licensure as a residential care/assisted living (RC/AL) administrator. To be licensed, individuals must complete a 40-hour state-approved course covering the domains of practice and pass the NAB's licensure examination. A state may also require working experience with a trained preceptor. A preceptor is a nursing home or assisted living administrator who meets prescribed qualifications and has been certified to mentor interns in an administrator-in-training (AIT) program (Singh, 2010).

A nursing home administrator (NHA) must be licensed by the state. Qualifications required for licensure vary widely from one state to another. NHAs not only typically have a broad range of managerial responsibilities as most administrators in general do, but also are closely involved in day-to-day operational details.

### Clinicians

*Nurses*   The two main categories of nurses in LTC settings are registered nurses (RNs) and licensed practical (or vocational) nurses (LPNs or LVNs). All nurses must be licensed by the state in which they practice. The two main educational programs today for RNs are the associate's degree (ADN) programs offered by community colleges, and Bachelor of Science degree (BSN) programs offered by four-year colleges and universities. Regulations require the delivery of skilled nursing services to be under the supervision of RNs.

In LTC settings, RNs compose only a small percentage of the workforce. They mostly hold administrative and supervisory positions such as director of nursing or head nurse. An adequate number of RNs in nursing homes is critical to the care quality (Singh, 2010). The majority of nurses in LTC settings are LPNs/LVNs who are graduates of one-year practical nursing programs offered at community colleges or vocational technical schools. LPNs/LVNs render treatments and administer medications. LPNs also function as charge nurses and team leaders and supervise the work of direct care aides.

*Non-physician practitioners*   Non-physician practitioners (NPPs) are clinical professionals who practice in many of the areas in which physicians practice, but who do not have an MD (Doctor of Medicine) or DO (Doctor of Osteopathy) degree. The two main types of NPPs who practice in LTC settings are nurse practitioners and physician assistants.

Nurse practitioners (NPs) are advanced practice nurses who provide healthcare services similar to those of primary care physicians. They can diagnose and treat a wide range of health problems. Some physicians employ NPs to follow up on the medical care of their patients. Studies of NPs in nursing homes suggest that they enhance the medical services available to residents, and prevent unnecessary hospital admissions (IFAS, 2005). NPs receive advanced graduate-level education and clinical training beyond what is required for RN preparation. Most have Master's degrees; some specialize in geriatrics (American Academy of Nurse Practitioners, 2007).

Physician assistants (PAs) are increasingly employed to provide LTC services under the direction of a physician. Both NPs and PAs are sometimes referred to as "physician extenders" because they enable physicians to see more patients. Admission to a PA training program requires roughly two years of science-based college coursework. After enrolling in a PA program, students study the basic medical sciences and physical examination techniques, followed by clinical training that includes classroom instruction and clinical rotations in primary care and several medical and surgical specialties. Overall, the PA student completes more than 2000 hours of supervised clinical practice prior to graduation. Their scope of practice includes performing physical examinations, diagnosing and treating illnesses, ordering and interpreting laboratory tests, and making rounds at LTC facilities (American Academy of Physician Assistants, 2007).

Both NPs and PAs can prescribe drugs when authorized to do so under state law. As Singh (2010) comments, their generalist training and emphasis on patient relationships make them particularly valuable in LTC care-giving.

**Care managers**
While case management by public health nurses and social workers dates back to the early 1900s, the coordination of services has become more complex and critical, especially for seniors and their families. Being able to navigate and access community-based services to support seniors remaining at home in their communities has been and continues to be the rationale for care management. In the 1970s, Medicaid and Medicare demonstration projects hired social and human service workers to coordinate medical and social services within the community for low-income frail elderly. The intent was to maintain this vulnerable population in the community by supporting community-based services, thereby preventing unneeded and costly institutionalization and hospitalizations (CMSA, 2008).

Care management is carried out by several disciplines, mostly in nursing and social services. Care managers provide service across various specialties (acute, palliative, mental health, long-term care, HIV, and so on) and in home, community, and institutional settings (Werdegar et al., 2014). "Care management" refers to social service coordination within a community-based delivery of services. The case manager is an advocate who assesses needs and coordinates referrals to support direct services and assistance (Werdegar et al., 2014). Typically, case management is not a licensed or regulated profession; however, licensed healthcare professionals – that is, nurses and clinical social workers – can practice case management. Geriatric care management is an emerging profession to manage the needs of the growing numbers of elders and to minimize costly fragmentation of care associated with the growth in the senior population (Cress, 2012).

### Social support professionals

Social support professionals include social workers and activity professionals. In LTC settings, social workers engage in the diagnostic assessment of patients' cognitive, behavioral, and emotional status; counseling; and conflict resolution. They help people cope with various types of issues in their everyday lives. They also have community resource expertise that is often called upon to obtain professional services available in the community.

A bachelor's degree in social work (BSW) is the minimum requirement for social work positions in nursing homes and assisted living facilities (Singh, 2010). Activity professionals are long-term workers who provide a variety of recreational programs for groups and individuals to improve and maintain the patients' physical, mental, and emotional well-being. Programs include arts and crafts, games, music, movies, dance and movement, social celebrations, and community outings. Passive activities such as reading and working with puzzles are prescribed for those who prefer solitude. No specific degrees are specified for activity professionals.

### Demand and Supply Analysis of the Long-Term Care Workforce

According to the National Center for Health Statistics (NCHS)'s 2012 National Study of Long-Term Care Providers, nearly 1.5 million full-time equivalents (FTEs) were nursing-related staff working in home-, community-, and institution-based long-term care settings. Clearly aides comprised the vast majority of FTEs. For adult day services centers and residential care (assisted living) communities, aides are certified nursing assistants. For home health agencies, aides are home care aides, personal care aides, personal care assistants, technicians, or medication aides. For home health agencies and hospices, aides are home health and personal care aides. For nursing homes, aides are certified nurse aides and medication aides (NCHS, 2012).

The relative distributions (as percentages) for the nursing employees within each type of long-term care provider are exhibited in Figure 19.2. The distribution of nursing employees reflects the level of medical care needed. According to the 2012 National Study of Long-Term Care Providers, most of the nursing employee FTEs in residential care communities (82 percent), adult day services centers (70 percent), and nursing homes

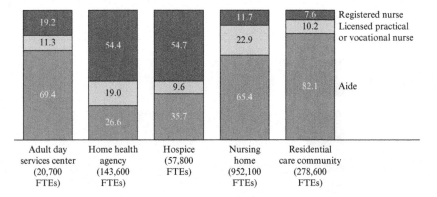

*Note:* Percentages may not add to 100 because of rounding.

*Source:* Harris-Kojetin et al. (2013).

*Figure 19.2 Share of nursing employee FTE types within each long-term care service provider, United States, 2012*

(65 percent) were aides. However, slightly over half of nursing employee FTEs in hospices (55 percent) and home health agencies (54 percent) were RNs. Please note that contract staff who work for these providers were excluded because comparable information was not available.

According to the 2012 National Study of Long-Term Care Providers, for every measure of nursing staff type examined (that is, all nursing staff, all licensed nursing staff, RN only, LPN and LVN only, and aides only), the average staff hours per resident or participant day were higher in nursing homes than in residential care communities and adult day services centers (Harris-Kojetin et al., 2013). Figure 19.3 exhibits the details. This study calculated the staff hours in the following manner:

- For adult day services centers, average hours per participant per day were computed by multiplying the number of full-time equivalent (FTE) employees for the staff type by 35 hours, divided by average daily attendance of participants, and by five days.
- For nursing homes and residential care communities, average hours per resident per day were computed by multiplying the number of FTE employees for the staff type by 35 hours, divided by the number of current residents, and by seven days.

The average total hours for the nursing employees that this study covered (RNs, LPNs and LVNs, and aides) for each resident or participant

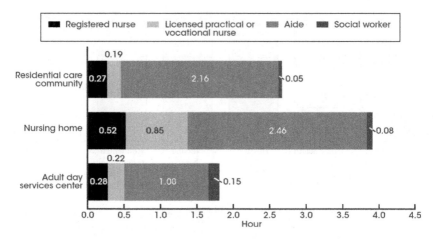

*Note:*    Percentages may not add to 100 because of rounding.

*Source:*    Harris-Kojetin et al. (2013).

*Figure 19.3    Average staffing hours per resident or participant per day for each provider by staff type, United States, 2012*

per day were: 3.8 for nursing home residents; 2.6 for residential care residents; and 1.6 for adult day participants.

Aides accounted for: 85 percent of staff hours in residential or assisted living; 68 percent of staff hours in adult day centers; and 66 percent of staff hours in nursing homes. In contrast, the average licensed social worker hours per resident or participant per day for adult day services centers were nine minutes, for nursing homes five minutes, and for residential care communities only three minutes. From an administrator's perspective, these data reflect an important challenge: growing consumer demand for direct care workers with minimal training and skills.

**Workforce Challenges Related to Direct Care Aides in Long-Term Care**

Direct care workers, especially aides, represent the largest component of the long-term care workforce. It is widely believed that the development and sustainability of a quality direct care work force is a major challenge in the twenty-first century (Institute of Medicine, 2008). Although demand for such workers is increasing, it is difficult to recruit staff due to non-competitive wages and benefits, negative industry image, and inadequate training (Stone and Harahan, 2010).

Turnover rates among aides are high. Estimates for turnover among home health aides range between 40 and 60 percent (National Direct Service Workforce Resource Center, 2008), while turnover for nursing assistants in assisted living facilities was 29 percent (National Center for Assisted Living, 2011). Low, non-competitive wages and benefits are major contributing factors to these high turnover rates. Forty-four percent of direct care workers lived below 200 percent of the poverty level (PHI, 2010). Over a quarter of direct care workers (28 percent) were uninsured (PHI, 2010). Understandably, nursing, home health, and home care aides do not feel their jobs are respected and valued (Bishop et al., 2008).

This low-prestige image of long-term care occupations is exacerbated by media reports that feature poor-quality care by providers; in addition, rules and regulatory policies on long-term care focus primarily on protecting consumers, rather than on responding to workers' concerns (Stone and Wiener, 2001). Long-term care occupations are also reported as having limited career opportunities, and inadequate training and preparation for evolving roles and responsibilities (Stone and Harahan, 2010).

As more chronically ill seniors opt to stay in their homes and communities, helping seniors to manage complex physical and mental health needs requires direct care workers to have more skills in areas such as medication management, palliative care, and dementia (Stone and Bryant, 2012). Empowerment of direct care workers and effective supervision are needed to prepare direct care staff. The minimal training and preparation for direct care positions are increasingly incongruent with the demand for long-term care and its practice (Stone and Bryant, 2012). For example, the minimal two weeks training required to become a Medicare or Medicaid certified home health aide may need to be increased commensurate with the scope of practice for aides. So that nurses can delegate more tasks to empowered aides and likely reduce costs (Reinhard, 2012).

Additionally, there is a major shortage of personnel to educate and prepare direct care workers for long-term care careers, making it more difficult to prepare direct care workers with the skills and knowledge to help manage chronically ill or disabled elders. Direct care workers need more training and education to enable them to implement new service delivery models that are consumer-centered and utilize information technology to help coordinate care for seniors.

**Turnover cost**

A major workforce concern related to long-term care is the high turnover rate of the long-term care workforce, such as for nursing homes and home health programs personnel. This human resources turnover issue was reflected in a major targeted performance goal in 2011, for the Advancing Excellence in America's Nursing Homes Campaign: "The average annual turnover rates for participating nursing homes will be at or below 65 percent for registered nurses, 35 percent for licensed practice nurses, and 65 percent for certified nursing assistants" (American Health Care Association and the Alliance for Quality Nursing Home Care, 2011, p. 40.)

It is increasingly evident that, costly turnover among certified nursing assistants and licensed practice nurses poses major challenges for long-term care administrators and leaders in terms of staffing levels, and quality of care for residents. An important point to consider is the extent that nursing home staff will choose to leave for long-term care opportunities in home and community-based settings.

**Healthcare Reform: Effects on the Long-Term Care Workforce**

The Patient Protection and Affordable Care Act (ACA) is the first federal legislation to identify the workforce shortages among those caring for older Americans over the next two decades (Stone and Bryant, 2012). A brief overview of the key related provisions will be presented here, to provide an understanding of the pressing workforce challenges facing healthcare administrators and leaders striving to keep seniors living safely and healthfully in their communities.

The provisions of the ACA that address service delivery reform are focused on consumers with chronic conditions and disabilities, and thus often use and rely upon healthcare and long-term care systems for older adults. Recent studies and research confirm that older Americans prefer to remain in their homes and communities as they age (AARP, 2010). The Affordable Care Act of 2010 provides a solid foundation for widespread reform of the continuum of care. The ACA legislation uses financial incentives for providers to redesign and reorganize ways to coordinate care and services (Molinari, 2014). The ACA includes several delivery reforms designed to encourage a coordinated and integrated continuum of care that is participant- or person-centered, provides the person with control and choice over home- and community-based services, and improves quality.

Dual eligible (Medicare and Medicaid) beneficiaries have been the target for reform under the ACA 2010. An estimated 10.2 million low-income Americans are eligible for both Medicare and Medicaid (CMS, 2013). These individuals represent some of the most chronically ill and costly individuals served by Medicare and Medicaid programs. Many have multiple and serious chronic problems and long-term care needs. The majority (two-thirds) are also older than 65 years, so dual eligibles are a critical group to target for policy and regulatory reform.

While the majority of older Americans prefer to remain in their homes and communities, the public Medicaid program that finances long-term care for eligible seniors is strongly institution-based; that is, nursing homes. A key provision of the ACA legislation allows states to enroll Medicaid beneficiaries into home- and community-based services with incomes up to 300 percent of SSI level (Shugarman and Whitenhall, 2011). This legislation offers financial incentives to states to move Medicaid beneficiaries from nursing homes into home- and community-based environments. In addition, participating states are required to have case management services to help beneficiaries navigate the continuum of care.

**New service delivery: medical homes**
Several components of the legislation are dedicated to transform the delivery of long-term care through expanding home- and community-based options (Justice, 2010). ACA established a "medical home" program for Medicare beneficiaries with chronic conditions, and offers states the opportunity to enroll Medicaid beneficiaries in "health homes" (Rousseau, 2010). This legislation encourages and supports care coordination by providing incentives to establish accountable care organizations (ACOs), which are responsible for managing health needs for a minimum of 5000 Medicare beneficiaries over three years at the least (McClellan et al., 2010).

Several provisions of the ACA give states some options for financing home- and community-based services and supports (HCBS). These provisions are time-limited, incentive grant programs that seek to shift the balance of state Medicaid fund for long-term services and supports (LTSS) to the community (Justice, 2011). These programs offer Medicaid matching payment for HCBS to those states adopting initiatives to increase the level of long-term services and support delivered in non-institutional settings.

The ACA legislation also includes a grants program for state and local partnerships that develop the healthcare workforce. One key provision focuses on developing a quality and stable direct care workforce that is capable of providing coordinated care in return for reasonable pay and benefits (Stone and Bryant, 2012).

Specifically, the legislation provides start-up funding for new training for direct care workers in home-, community- and institution-based long-term care. The ACA provides $67.5 million in grants and incentives for training, recruitment, and retention of direct care workers, and to improve management of direct care staff working in community-based organizations or organizations delivering long-term care (Stone and Bryant, 2012).

Additionally, a demonstration program has been set up within the grant programs to develop core competencies in care coordination and team skills, to enhance direct care workers' job skills and job satisfaction, and satisfaction with services for the clients and families served. This provision is limited to six states for three years, so serves as a preliminary step towards addressing widespread staffing challenges in the industry (ibid.).

## CONCLUSION

The Affordable Care Act provides far-reaching federal legislation that underscores the workforce shortages to care for seniors. Consequently, it helps to focus attention on the key management challenges related to the growing demand for long-term care that likely will exceed the supply of long-term care workers over the next two decades. An inadequate number of direct care aides, and other long-term care workers with minimal preparation and training, are likely targets for improvement and innovation in the US long-term care delivery system.

New service models described in provisions of the ACA – that is, medical homes, accountable care organizations, and contracted home- and community-based services – require that workers in these service settings have the necessary skills and competencies to coordinate and integrate care for an individual client as well as for the organization. These skills include working with interdisciplinary teams to deliver care, develop and use information in a timely manner, anticipate and address client issues when clients move from one setting to another, and keep the client and family at the center of care decisions (Counsell et al., 2007).

The ACA's emphasis on a shift from institutional to home- and community-based care is likely to increase demand for direct care workers in home health, home care, and personal care (Stone and Bryant, 2012). To ensure that innovative service models achieve the goals of high quality and lower costs, this requires that health workers, especially direct care staff, receive training in assessing and responding to clients'/consumers' changing needs and preferences. Workers caring for Medicare beneficiaries pose significant workforce challenges due to lack of training on how to care for a person as a whole, rather than the disease itself. Today's workforce needs to pay attention to individuals' functional needs and to emphasize improvement and wellness. Workers also need to recognize the full continuum of care that may be needed to address individual needs over time, and to work with interdisciplinary teams to deliver coordinated care (Boult et al., 2008).

Therefore, the recruitment and retention challenges for direct care workers will continue to be major concerns for healthcare administrators. Training for these workers to deliver quality care across the continuum of long-term care has not been funded through the ACA. However, state-based demonstration grants (for feasibility studies) administered through Health Resources and Services Administration are examining how worker training for home care and personal care aides can be integrated into the delivery of home- and community-based service systems. This is the first national initiative to recognize the needs for competency-based training for direct care long-term workers (Stone and Bryant, 2012).

Realistically, there are very limited public funds to support the recruitment and retention of direct care long-term care workers. Thus the challenge for new and established home- and community-based services will be to develop a learning culture that supports training and change, while providing workers with opportunities that empower them to develop and grow in ways that enhance the quality and efficiency of care and coordination. Workforce training and learning will likely become competitive forces used by innovative home- and community-based services to attract competent care workers over the next few decades.

# REFERENCES

AARP (2010). Home and community preferences of the 45 + population. http://assets.aarp.org/rgcenter/general/home-community-services-10.pdf (accessed 1 April 2014).

Accius, J.C. (2010). The village: A growing option for aging in place. AARP Public Policy Institute Fact Sheet 177. March. Retrieved from www.aarp.org/ppi (accessed 29 April 2014).

Administration on Aging (AoA) (2014). Administration on aging: A profile of older Americans: 2013. Available at http://www.aoa.gov/Aging_Statistics/Profile/2013/docs/2013_Profile.pdf (accessed 1 April 2014).

American Academy of Nurse Practitioners (2007). Frequently Asked Questions: Why choose a nurse practitioner as your healthcare provider. Available at http://www.npfinder.com/faq.pdf (accessed 1 April 2014).

American Academy of Physician Assistants (2007). Physician assistant practice in long-term care facilities. Available at http://www.aapa.org/gandp/issuebrief/ longtermcare.htm (accessed 11 April 2014).

American Association of Homes and Services for the Aging, American Seniors Housing Association, Assisted Living Federation of America, National Center for Assisted Living and National Investment Center (2009). *Overview of assisted living*. Washington, DC: Stratton Publishing and Marketing.

American Health Care Association and the Alliance for Quality Nursing Home Care (2011). 2011 Annual Quality Report: A comprehensive report on the quality of care in America's nursing and rehabilitation facilities. Available at http://www.ahcancal.org/quality_improvement/Documents/2011QualityReport.pdf (accessed 2 April 2014).

Assisted Living Federation of America (ALFA) (2011). ALFA's care provider philosophy. Available at http://www.alfa.org/alfa/Care_Provider_Philosophy.asp (accessed 2 April 2014).

Beisgen, B. and Kraitchman, M. (2003). *Senior Centers: Opportunities for Successful Aging*. New York: Springer Publishing Company.

Boult, C., Christmas, C., Durso, S., Leff, B., and Fried, L. (2008). Perspective: Transforming chronic care for older persons. *Academic Medicine*, 83 (7): 627–631.

Briesacher, B.A., Field, T.S, Baril, J., and Gurwitz, J.H. (2009). Pay-for-Performance in Nursing Homes. *Health Care Financing Review*, 30 (3). Available at https://www.cms.gov/Research-Statistics-Data-and-Systems/Research/HealthCareFinancingReview/downloads/09Springpg1.pdf.

Cabigao, E. and Cherney, C. (2014). The skilled nursing facility. In Yee-Melichar, D., Flores, C., and Cabigao, E. (eds), *Long-Term Care Administration and Management*. New York: Springer. Available at http://www.asaging.org/blog/addressing-health-disparities-among-older-asian-americans-data-and-diversity.

Case Management Society of America (CMSA) (2008). *Core Curriculum for Case Management* (2nd edn). Philadelphia, PA: Lippincott, Williams & Wilkins.

Centers for Medicare & Medicaid Services (CMS) (2005a). CMS's Health Care Information System (HCIS), 1998–2004. Available at http://www.cms.hhs.gov/FilesForOrderGenInfo/ (accessed 2 August 2005).

Centers for Medicare & Medicaid Services (CMS) (2005b). *State Operations Manual*. Chapter 2 – The certification process. Available at http://www.cms.gov/Regulations-and-Guidance/Guidance/Manuals/downloads/som107c02.pdf.

Centers for Medicare & Medicaid Services (CMS) (2011). Program for all inclusive care for the Elderly (PACE) – Overview. Baltimore, MD: CMS. Available at http:/www.cms.gov/pace (accessed 1 April 2014).

Centers for Medicare & Medicaid Services (CMS) (2013). Commission on Long-Term Care; Report to Congress. Available at http://www.medicareadvocacy.org/wp-conte nt/uploads/2014/01/Commission-on-Long-Term-Care-Final-Report-9-18-13-00042470.pdf.

Cohen, M., Weinrobe, M., and Miller, J. (2000). Informal caregivers of disabled elders with long-term care insurance. Available at http://aspe.hhs.gov/daltcp/reports/icdeltci.pdf (accessed 12 May 2014).

Counsell, S., Callahan, C., Clark, D., Tu, W., Buttar, A., Stump, T., and Ricketts, G. (2007). Geriatric care management for low income seniors. *Journal of the American Medical Association*, 298 (22): 2623–633.

Cress, C. (2012). *Handbook of Geriatric Care Management* (3rd edn). Sudbury, MA: Jones Bartlett Learning.

Day, T. (n.d.). About nursing homes. National Care Planning Council. Available at http://www.longtermcarelink.net/eldercare/nursing_home.htm (accessed 2 June 2014).

Flores, C., Newcomer, R., and Hernandez, M. (2014). Assisted living communities. In Yee- Melichar, D., Flores, C., and Cabigao, E. (eds), *Long-Term Care Administration and Management*. New York: Springer, pp. 69–90.

Gelfand, D. (2006). *The Aging Network: Programs and Services* (6th edn). New York: Springer.

Goldman, D.D., Khurin, R., Tingley, D.W., and Yee-Melichar, D. (2014). Long-term care at home. In Yee-Melichar, D., Flores, C., and Cabigao, E. (eds), *Long-Term Care Administration and Management*. New York: Springer, pp. 3–26.

Harris-Kojetin, L., Sengupta, M., Park-Lee, E., and Valverde, R. (2013). *Long-Term Care Services in the United States: 2013 Overview*. Hyattsville, MD: National Center for Health Statistics.

Hood, A. (2011). The Affordable Care Act and older Americans. *Journal of American Society on Aging*, 35 (1): 4–5.

IFAS (2005). *The Long-Term Care Workforce: Can the Crises be Fixed?* Washington, DC: Institute for the Future of Aging Services.

Institute of Medicine (2008). *Retooling for an aging America: building the health care workforce*. Washington (DC): National Academies Press.

Jewish Federation of North America (2012). Jewish Federation of North America's Washington office. Retrieved from http//www.jewishfederations.org/Washington-office,aspz.

Jones, A.L., Dwyer, L.L., Bercovitz, A.R., and Strahan, G.W. (2009). The National Nursing Home Survey: 2004 overview. National Center for Health Statistics. *Vital Health Statistics*, 13 (167): 1–155.

Justice, D. (2010). Long-term services and supports and chronic care coordination: Policy advances enacted by the Patient Protection and Affordable Care Act. National Academy for State Health Policy. Available at http://www.nashp.org/node/1903 (accessed 1 April 2014).

Justice, D. (2011). States, stakeholders, and climate change: The Affordable Care Act offers a new environment for long-term care advocacy. *Generations: Journal on the American Society of Aging*, 35 (1): 32–37.

Kain, N., Donovan, C., and Yee-Melichar, D. (2014). Naturally occurring retirement communities. In Yee-Melichar, D., Flores, C., and Cabigao, E. (eds), *Long-Term Care Administration and Management*. New York: Springer, pp. 53–68.

Kelly, C.M., Morgan, J.C., and Jason, K.J. (2011). Home care workers: Interstate differences in training requirement and their implications for quality. *Journal of Applied Gerontology*, 20 (10): 1–29.

Malone-Beach, E. and Langeland, K. (2011). Boomers' prospective needs for senior centers and related services: A survey of persons 50–59. *Journal of Gerontological Social Work*, 54 (1): 116–130.

Masotti, P., Fick, R., Johnson-Masotti, A., and MacLeod, S. (2006). Healthy naturally occurring retirement communities: A low-cost approach to facilitating health aging. *American Journal of Public Health*, 96 (7): 1164–1170.

McClellan, M., McKethan, A.N., Lewis, J.L., Roski, J., and Fisher, E.S. (2010). A national strategy to put accountable care into practice. *Health Affairs*, 34 (4): 982–990.

McDonough, J.E. (2014). Health systems reform in the United States. *International Journal of Health Policy and Management*, 2 (10): 1–4.

McWhinney-Morse, S. (2009). Beacon Hill Village: A civic-minded group of older adults forms its own supportive community and becomes an international model. *Journal of the American Society on Aging*, 33 (2): 85–86.

Milford, J., Griffeath, D., and Yee-Melichar, D. (2014). Continuing care communities. In Yee- Melichar, D., Flores, C., and Cabigao, E. (eds), *Long-Term Care Administration and Management*. New York: Springer, pp. 91–104.

Mollica, R., Sims-Kastelein, K., and O'Keeffe, J. (2007). Residential care and assisted living compendium, 2007. Washington, DC: US Department of Health and Human Services, Office of the Assistant Secretary for Planning and Evaluation, Office of Disability, Aging and Long Term Care Policy and Research Triangle Institute. Available at http://aspe.hhs.gov/daltcp/reports/2007/07alcom.htm (accessed 1 April 2014).

Molinari, C. (2014). Does the Accountable Care Act aim to promote quality, health, and control costs or has it missed the mark? Comment on "Health system reform in the United States." *International Journal of Health Policy Management*, 2: 97–99. DOI: org/10.15171/ijhpm.2014.23.

National Adult Day Services Association (NADSA) (2014). Overview and facts. Fuquay Varina, NC: NADSA. Available at http://nadsa.org/consumers/overview-and-facts/ (accessed 12 April 2014).

National Center for Assisted Living (2011). Findings for the NCAL 2010 assisted living staff vacancy, retention, and turnover survey. Available at http://www.ahcancal.org/ncal/resources/Documents/2010%20VRT%20Report-Final.pdf (accessed 12 April 2014).

National Direct Service Workforce Resource Center (2008). A synthesis of direct service workforce demographics and challenges across intellectual/developmental disabilities, aging, physical disabilities, and behavioral health. Available at http://rtc.umn.edu/docs/CrossDisabilitySynthesisWhitePaperFinal.pdf (accessed 12 April 2014).

National Institute of Senior Centers (NISC) (2011). Senior centers: fact sheet. Washington, DC: National Council on Aging. Available at http://www.ncoa.org/assets/files/pdf/FactSheet_SeniorCenters.pdf.

NCHS (2012). National study of long-term care providers. US Centers for Disease Control and Prevention's National Center for Health Statistics. Available at http://www.cdc.gov/nchs/data/nsltcp/NSLTCP_FS.pdf (accessed 12 April 2014).

Niles-Yokum, K. and Wagner, D. (2011). *The Gaining Networks: A Guide to Programs and Services* (7th edn). New York: Springer.

O'Shaughnessy, C. and Napili, A. (2006). CRS Report for Congress (P.L. 109-365) The Older Americans Act: Programs, Funding, and 2006 Reauthorization. Available at http://www.nasuad.org/documentation/policy_priorities/OAAReauth2006_OShaughnessyCRS.pdf.

Park-Lee, E., Caffrey, C., Sengupta, M., Moss, A., Rosenoff, E., and Harris-Kojetin, L. (2011). Residential care facilities: a key sector in the spectrum of long-term care providers in the United States. NCHS Data Brief, No. 78. Washington, DC: US Department of Health and Human Services, Centers for Disease Control and Prevention, National Center for Health.

PHI (2010). Who are the direct care workers: 2009 data update. Facts 4. Issue Brief supported by a grant from the SCAN foundation.

Pratt, J. (2010). *Long-Term Care: Managing across the Continuum* (3rd edn). Sudbury, MA: Jones & Bartlett.

Reinhard, S.C. (2012). Money follows the person: un-burning bridges and facilitating a return to the community. *Generations: Journal on the American Society of Aging*, 36 (1): 52–58.

Rousseau, D. (2010). Dual eligibles' Medicaid enrollment and spending for Medicare beneficiaries in 2007. Report from Kaiser Commission on Medicaid and Uninsured, Washington, DC.

Scharlach, A. (2008). Historical overview. *American Journal of Nursing*, 108 (9 Suppl.): 16–22.

Schulz, R. and Sherwood, P. (2008). Physical and mental health effects of family caregiving. *American Journal of Nursing*, 108 (9 Suppl.): 23–27.

Seavey, D. (2007). Written statement of Dorie Seavey, PhD. Testimony before the House Committee on Education and Labor, Subcommittee on Workforce Protections, Washington, DC. 25 October.

Shugarman, L.R. and Whitenhill, K. (2011). The affordable care act proposes new provisions to build stronger continuum of care. *Generations: Journal on the American Society of Aging*, 35 (1): 11–18.

Singh, D.A. (2010). *Effective Management of Long Term Care Facilities*. Sudbury, MA: Jones & Bartlett.

Spinelli, R. and McSweeney-Feld, M.H. (2011). Financing long-term care services. In McSweeney-Feld, M.H. and Oetjen, R. (eds), *Dimensions of Long-Term Care Management: An Introduction*. Washington, DC: Health Administration Press.

Stone, R. and Bryant, N. (2012). The impact of health care reform on the workforce caring for older adults. *Journal of Aging and Social Policy*, 24: 188–205.

Stone, R.I. and Harahan, M.F. (2010). Improving the long-term care workforce serving older adults. *Health Affairs*, 29 (1): 109–115.

Stone, R.I. and Wiener, J.M. (2001). Who will care for us? Addressing the long-term care workforce crisis. US Department of Health and Human Services. Available at http://aspe.hhs.gov/daltcp/reports/ltcwfes.htm (accessed 12 May 2014).

US Bureau of Labor Statistics (2008–2009). *Occupational Outlook Handbook (OOH), 2008–09 ed.* Washington, DC: DOL. Available at http://www.bls.gov/oco/.

US Department of Labor (2000). Report of the Working Group on Long-Term Care. Employee Benefits Security Administration. Available at http://www.dol.gov/ebsa/publications/report2.htm (accessed 10 June 2014).

United States Government Accountability Office (2010). Report to the Chairman, Special Committee on Aging, US Senate. Older Americans: Continuing Care Retirement Communities Can Provide Benefits, but Not Without Some Risk. Available at http://www.gao.gov/new.items/d10611.pdf.

Vincent, Grayson K. and Velkoff, Victoria A. (2010). The next four decades, the older population in the United States: 2010 to 2050. Current Population Reports, p25-1138. Washington, DC: US Census Bureau.

Werdegar D., Flores, C.M., and Caldwell, A. (2014). Community-based programs and services. In Yee-Melichar, D., Flores, C., and Cabigao, E. (eds), *Long-Term Care Administration and Management*. New York: Springer, pp.27–52.

Yee-Melichar, D., Flores, C., and Cabigao, E. (2014). *Long-Term Care Administration and Management*. New York: Springer.

Zhang, T. (2008). *Elderly Entrepreneurship in an Aging US Economy: It's Never Too Late*. London, UK; Singapore; Hackensack, NJ, USA: World Scientific.

# 20. Ethical challenges in healthcare
## Kurt Darr and Carla J. Sampson

## PERSONAL ETHIC AND PROFESSIONAL CODES

### Ethics and Law

Ethics and law are not necessarily synchronous. Laws that result from a democratic process generally reflect the majority's views of justice and fairness. Some may consider a law unjust or immoral and risk or invite punishment by breaking it. Classic contemporary examples are the widespread recreational use of marijuana in the United States, and engaging in civil disobedience to protest government or private actions considered morally wrong by the protesters.

Law is the minimum performance expected in society. Professions ask their affiliates to obey the law, but simultaneously ask more of them. Thus, a profession's code of ethics requires members to act in ways different from other members of society.

### Personal Ethic

The guidelines that direct our behavior as human beings arise from family, religious training, professional affiliations and allegiances, and an often ill-defined personal code of moral conduct which is in itself an amalgam of intellect, reasoning, experience, education, and relationships. A personal ethic is a moral framework for decision-making that allows persons to refine guidelines, judgments, and actions. Membership in a professional association with a code of ethics, and employment in a health service organization (HSO) with an organizational philosophy reflected in values, mission, and vision statements, are not substitutes for a coherent, consistent, and comprehensive personal ethic. Each person is a moral agent whose actions, inactions, and misactions have moral consequences for which they must bear responsibility. Morally, conduct cannot be excused by claims such as "I was only following orders," or "That's not my area of direct responsibility." Demands from lawfully constituted public authorities pose special problems. Moral agents who judge such orders to be unjust disregard them at their peril and must bear any sanctions. Ethical (moral) implications of an act must be considered independently of the act.

## Ethical Theory

Ethical theories and derivative principles guide the development of rules that produce specific judgments and actions. Four principles to guide health services managers are respect for persons, beneficence, nonmaleficence, and justice. These principles are derived from moral philosophies including rule utilitarianism, Kantian deontology, the Natural Law, and virtue ethics.

### Respect for persons

The principle of respect for persons has four elements. First, autonomy requires that persons act toward others in a way that enables them to be self-governing. To choose and pursue a course of action, persons must be rational and uncoerced (unconstrained). Physical or mental conditions may cause persons to become nonautonomous. Nonetheless, they are owed respect, even though special means are needed to allow them to be autonomous. Autonomy underlies consent for treatment, as well as how HSOs view and interact with patients and staff. Autonomy is in dynamic tension with paternalism. The Hippocratic Oath is antecedent to paternalism in the patient–physician relationship and directs that physicians act in the patient's best interests – as the physician judges those interests. The modern view of autonomy limits paternalism to specific circumstances.

The second element of respect for persons is truth-telling, which requires managers to be honest in all they do. At its absolute, truth-telling eliminates "white lies," even if knowing the truth causes harm to the person learning it.

Confidentiality, the third element, requires managers and clinicians to keep secret what they learn about patients and others in the course of their work. Legal requirements necessitate morally justified exceptions to confidentiality.

The fourth element is fidelity, defined as doing one's duty or keeping one's word. Sometimes called promise-keeping, fidelity, like the other three elements of respect for persons, requires managers to be respectful of persons, whether they are patients, staff, or others.

### Beneficence

A second principle important to a personal ethic is rooted in the Hippocratic tradition. Beneficence is defined as acting with charity and kindness. Current applications of beneficence are broader, including a positive duty. Beneficence anchors one end of a continuum, the opposite of the principle of nonmaleficence, defined as refraining from actions that aggravate a problem or cause other negative results.

Beneficence comprises conferring benefits and balancing benefits and harms. The former is well established in medicine; failing to provide benefits when it is possible violates an ethical obligation of clinicians. Appropriately modified, beneficence applies to managers too. Beneficence requires HSOs to do all that they can for patients. There is a lesser duty toward potential rather than actual patients. This distinction varies with the HSO's values, mission, and vision, and with the population served.

The second part of beneficence is balancing an action's benefits and harms, which is a utilitarian basis for cost–benefit and risk–benefit analyses. Utility is but one of several considerations in health services decision-making. Utility cannot morally justify overriding patients' interests and sacrificing those interests to a greater good.

### Nonmaleficence

The third principle relevant to a personal ethic is nonmaleficence. It, too, has deep historical roots in medicine. Nonmaleficence is *primum non nocere*: first, do no harm. This dictum to guide physicians applies also to health services managers.

Nonmaleficence gives rise to specific moral rules, but neither the principle nor derivative rule is absolute since it may be appropriate (with the patient's consent) to inflict harm (for example, administer cancer chemotherapy) to avoid worse harm (for example, a surgical procedure, or death), and it may be appropriate to compromise truth-telling if telling the truth will result in significant mental or physical harm. In addition to relationships with patients, nonmaleficence means that managers have duties to staff, so that putting staff at unnecessary or extraordinary risk to their health and safety violates a manager's duty to them, even if the result meets the principle of beneficence to patients.

### Justice

The fourth principle, justice, is important in managerial decision-making such as the allocation of resources or the development and application of human resources policies. Some definitions of justice require that all persons get their just deserts: what they are due. Rawls defined justice as fairness. How are just deserts and fairness defined? Aristotle defined justice as equals being treated equally, and unequals treated unequally; a concept common to public policy analysis. Equal treatment of equals is reflected in liberty rights such as freedom of speech for all. Aristotle's concept of justice as unequals being treated unequally is expressed by more health services being provided to those who are more ill and with greater medical needs. At a minimum, clinicians and managers act justly if they consistently apply clear and prospectively determined criteria in decision-making.

# HEALTH SERVICES CODES OF ETHICS

## Managers

The American College of Healthcare Executives (ACHE) adopted its first code of ethics in 1939, six years after being founded. In its several iterations, the code has gained specificity. In 2014, the code had five sections that detailed the healthcare executive's responsibilities to the profession, to patients or others served, to the organization, to employees, and to the community and society. The final section charges affiliates with a positive duty to communicate the facts to the committee on ethics when they have reasonable grounds to believe that another affiliate has violated the code (ACHE, 2011). Biomedical ethical issues receive little attention. The ACHE publishes ethical policy statements to guide affiliates on issues such as medical records confidentiality, decisions at the end of life, and professional impairment. The committee on ethics investigates allegations and makes recommendations regarding breaches of the code. Expulsion is the maximum disciplinary action.

The American College of Health Care Administrators (ACHCA) code of ethics guides managers of long-term care facilities, usually called nursing facilities. The four "expectations" for managers are summarized as: (1) the welfare of those receiving care is paramount; (2) maintain professional competence; (3) maintain professional posture, holding paramount the interests of facility and residents; and (4) meet responsibilities to public, profession, and colleagues. Specific areas include quality of services; confidentiality of patient information; continuing education; conflicts of interest; and fostering increased knowledge, supporting research, and sharing expertise. Affiliates are expected to provide information to the standards and ethics committee of actual or potential code violations. No enforcement or appeals process is described (American College of Health Care Administrators, 2014).

## Clinicians

### Physicians
The American Medical Association (AMA) is pre-eminent among professional associations for allopathic physicians in the USA. The AMA's first Principles of Medical Ethics, adopted at its founding in 1847, were based

on the code of medical ethics developed by the English physician and philosopher Sir Thomas Percival (1740–1804) in 1803 (AMA, 1982). After several iterations, the 2001 principles emphasize providing competent medical care, honesty in all professional interactions, and safeguarding patient confidences. Members "shall ... strive to report physicians deficient in character or competence, or engaging in fraud or deception, to appropriate entities" (AMA, 2001). Opinions of the AMA's Council on Ethical and Judicial Affairs interpret the principles. The 2001 principles continue the trend of recognizing responsibilities and rights that began in 1980. The 1980 iteration was "the opening to an ethics based on notions of rights and responsibilities rather than benefits and harms. It is the first document in the history of professional medical ethics in which a group of physicians is willing to use the language of responsibilities and rights" (Veatch, 1980).

### Nurses

The Code of Ethics for Nurses was first adopted by the American Nurses Association (ANA) in 1950. The Code of Ethics for Nurses has nine provisions including various expectations: principles to guide practice, primary commitment to patients' interests, advocating for patients, individual accountability, duties to self and others, improving healthcare, advancing the profession, collaboration, and obligations to the profession. An interpretive statement follows each. Like the ACHE, ACHCA, and AMA, the ANA code obliges nurses to counter or expose problematic practice: "The nurse promotes, advocates for, and strives to protect the health, safety, and rights of the patient" (American Nurses Association, 2015).

### Trade Associations

The American Hospital Association (AHA) is the leading US trade association for hospitals. Its Patient Care Partnership includes high-quality hospital care, a clear and safe environment, involvement in the patient's care, protection of the patient's privacy, help when the patient is leaving the hospital, and help with billing claims (American Hospital Association, 2003).

The American Health Care Association (AHCA) includes for-profit and not-for-profit long-term facilities. Its code of ethics guides the organization and is a model for state affiliates and their members. Provisions include moral responsibility, good business practice, making difficult choices, acting responsibly, providing quality services, dealing with conflicting values, use of information, responsible advocacy, conflicts of interest, respect for others, and fair competition (Langmead, 2013).

The statement of commitment of America's Health Insurance Plans (AHIP) guides member health plans. The three sections are commitments to improve quality; to give all Americans access through public and private coverage and through support for the public health infrastructure; and to improve affordability (America's Health Insurance Plans, 2004).

# ETHICS ISSUES AFFECTING GOVERNANCE AND MANAGEMENT

## Fiduciary Duty

A fiduciary is someone in a position of superior knowledge and authority and in whom trust is reposed. Fiduciaries have specific obligations and duties. Ethically (and legally), fiduciary duties arise in many relationships, including physician–patient, priest–penitent, attorney–client, and professor–student. Fidelity (an element of respect for persons), beneficence, and nonmaleficence underpin the ethical aspects of fiduciary duty as well.

Governing body members of for-profit and not-for-profit corporations are fiduciaries and have special obligations (Bryant, 2005). Fiduciaries have primary duties of loyalty to the organization above all self-interest, and responsibility to exercise reasonable care and diligence in performing their work as trustees. Most "trustees" are not true trustees because they are not responsible for assets held in trust. More appropriately, they should use the title "director" or "corporate director."

## Conflicts of Interest

### Background
The potential for a conflict of interest to arise is described as a duality of interest (Carson, 1994). Dual interests are present in almost all managerial and clinical relationships. Only when a conflicting action is taken, however, does the potential (duality) become an actual conflict of interests. A conflict of interest occurs when someone has more than one duty or obligation that demands loyalty, and decisions based on these loyalties are different or in conflict; for example, meeting one duty makes it impossible to meet the other(s). The element of fidelity (promise-keeping) assists in ethical analysis of conflicts of interest. The principles of beneficence and nonmaleficence also provide an ethical framework to analyze conflicts of interest.

The ACHE code of ethics states only that the healthcare executive shall "avoid financial and other conflicts of interest," an admonition that provides scant guidance. The matter of degree is useful to help determine when a duality of interests has devolved into a presumptive conflict of interest. A conflict of interest is unlikely to arise if a vendor buys a cafeteria lunch for a manager. An expenses-paid, two-week vacation presumes development of loyalties that create a duality of interest that will lead to conflicts of interests. Large gifts are presumed to encourage or reward certain behavior. Many dualities of interests that arise are more subtle.

Is it ethical for a manager to use a position of influence or power to gain personal aggrandizement of titles and position? Is it ethical for a manager to be lax in implementing an effective patient consent process? Is it ethical for managers to keep negative information about their performance from the governing body? Is it ethical for a manager to ignore evidence of quality-of-care problems in a clinical department? Is it ethical for managers concerned about their personal ability to meet the demands of their job to remain in it? Conflicts suggested by questions such as these are identified and understood only with continued questioning and self-analysis.

### Managing healthcare outcomes

The conceptualization of healthcare delivery known as "managing care" originated in the 1920s when it was known as "prepaid group practice." Organized medicine strongly opposed prepaid group practice because it inserted a third party – a payer – between patient and provider, thus diminishing the ideal of a direct, personal relationship. Prepaid practice grew slowly in the USA until World War II when Kaiser-Permanente began providing healthcare to California shipyard workers. Growth of what became known as "managed care" was stimulated by the US federal Health Maintenance Act of 1973. Despite its many names, the basics of managing care are similar: physicians are employed by or under contract to an HSO that provides a benefit package to a defined population for a fixed fee. The latest iteration is the "accountable care organization" (ACO) that focuses on Medicare enrollees. ACOs are authorized by the federal Patient Protection and Affordable Care Act (2010). Nuances among the various types of delivery organizations vary, but the conflicts of interest issues that arise are generic to the basic elements of that type of delivery system.

The duality of interests in managing care predisposes it to conflicts of interest. The goals, purposes, and objectives – the interests – of delivery organizations managing care, as expressed by governance, management, and physicians, often differ from those of their members. Both want a financially strong, well-functioning organization that meets member needs in a timely and effective manner. Beyond this, however, lies significant divergence.

## Marketing and operations
Divergence of interests between the organization and its members (and potential members) begins at the initial stage of marketing when benefits packages and market segments are identified. Is it ethical to market primarily to healthy, low-risk persons? Perhaps, but only if the organization ignores high-risk groups because it has a greater moral duty to current than to potential members. Members want to maximize access to services to meet actual or perceived needs. The goals of organization and members are congruent if members remain healthy with minimal cost and use services appropriately. It is rarely that simple, however. Members of an organization that is straining against adverse selection may experience diminished quality, restricted benefits, and increased premiums.

## Utilization
Using services has the greatest potential for conflicts of interest. In this regard, members may be divided into appropriate users and overusers, whether purposefully so or not. The organization's interests and those of appropriate users are congruent. To be competitive, however, overusers must be controlled, and this can be done through physicians and organization policies. Even appropriate users are a potential financial threat in a competitive environment. To trim costs, the organization may seek to make members underusers. This sharpened duality of interests may result in a conflict of interest.

## MD incentives and disincentives
Members will be concerned about subtle and potentially serious constraints that affect the physicians who are affiliated with the organization that is managing care. There are numerous dual interests among the organization and its members and physicians. Though the Hippocratic tradition clearly directs physicians to act only in their patients' best interests, the organization facilitates or inhibits physician treatment decisions. Employment is an example of self-selection bias: physicians unwilling to accept an organization's rules will work elsewhere. Independent physicians affiliated with an organization that is managing care, whether in a network or an independent practice association, are controlled less directly but they experience similar constraints. Independent physicians may choose to avoid inhospitable organizations by practicing fee-for-service or concierge medicine.

Physicians affiliated with an organization that is managing care face numerous behavior-modifying guidelines: limits on referrals (especially out of the organization) and hospitalization, financial disincentives (and incentives), quotas on numbers of patients seen (used in staff-model health maintenance organizations, HMOs, for example), and peer review. Physician practice patterns that are undesirable result in various actions by the organization. In order of increasing severity, they are: data-based peer pressure, letters of warning or admonition, economic incentives or disincentives, contract non-renewal, and dismissal. Constraints are positive when they encourage judicious but appropriate use of medical resources. This partly explains why organizations managing care, especially HMOs, generally use fewer ancillary services and hospital days.

### Services

Organizations managing care may forgo purchases of high-technology diagnostic and treatment equipment and services, or they may contract with physicians or hospitals without such technology. Both strategies reduce costs. Lower costs that enhance financial integrity and support availability of low-technology services make organizational and member interests congruent. This strategy has no advantage for those who might benefit from an unavailable technology; to them it suggests that a duality of interests has become a conflict of interest. When are constraints excessive and members deprived of needed services? How should wanted services be paid for? When do constraints violate the principles of beneficence and nonmaleficence? Such questions lack simple answers. Constraints are a function of an organization's willingness, prompted by the manager acting as moral agent, to institute safeguards that balance competitiveness and financial viability with members' needs and wants.

### Minimizing Conflicts of Interest while Managing Care

How are conflicts of interest prevented or minimized? An indispensable first step is acknowledging the many dual interests present in the relationships among the organization managing care, and its members and affiliated physicians. Awareness permits avoiding or minimizing them. In addition, verification is needed. An ombudsman or consumer relations specialist can assist members to receive services. Procedures to review members' concerns should be readily accessible. Audits of utilization data and comparisons with similar organizations allow management to determine whether utilization was appropriate. Awareness of how and in what circumstances conflicts of interest arise will help to prevent them or minimize their effect.

### Confidential Information

HSOs and health services are rife with confidential information about patients, staff, and the organization. Managers are ethically and legally bound to use this information properly. Conflicts of interest occur if confidential information is used to benefit a manager or others with whom the manager is associated or related, or to harass or injure.

Misuse of confidential information includes disclosing governing body decisions so that advantageous sales or purchases can be made by the insider's associates; selling or giving patient medical information to the media or attorneys; and disclosing the HSO's marketing strategies to competitors.

### Ethics and Marketing

HSOs are social enterprises with economic dimensions, not economic enterprises with social dimensions. Nevertheless, they all market, and did so long before "marketing" became acceptable. A competitive environment makes marketing necessary. Marketing occurs in the physicians' hospital lounge and dining room, at health fairs and new employee orientations, and in press releases. In addition, the proliferation and relative ease of social media outlets makes marketing even more pervasive.

Marketing and advertising raise questions of how the HSO can meet its ethical obligations toward those potentially in need of its services, while avoiding creating unnecessary demand. Guidance from the Society for Healthcare Strategy and Market Development (SHSMD) of the AHA instructs its professionals that marketing in all channels should be "readily comprehensible [and that] all marketing communications generated by hospitals are factually supportable and are presented with truthfulness and accuracy" (SHSMD, 2010).

Responsible marketing is an important if elusive concept. HSOs whose focus is return on investment will view marketing and competition differently from those with more eleemosynary goals. Being responsible tempers customers' desires and potential demand for a service with objective information as to value and usefulness. Decision-makers must determine whether some expenditures and goals are more worthy than others, a task consistent with mission statements and their expertise as providers. This approach has a significant element of paternalism.

## BIOMEDICAL ETHICAL ISSUES

### Resource Allocation

At both the macro and micro levels, resource allocation embodies the principle of justice. It necessitates making decisions: who has access to what, when, and how. Value-laden criteria such as worth, usefulness, merit, and need are commonly used. Government involvement often brings political motives. Like governments, HSOs use macroallocation criteria to determine what equipment to buy and whether to offer new programs or services. Microallocation includes a physician's willingness to refer, a patient's geographic access to services and technologies, and economic considerations. Often, micro-level decisions are guided (in a sense, predetermined) by policies and procedures of governments or HSOs. Often, the "greatest good" (utility) principle of utilitarianism is used for macroallocation. It is at best a partial answer. Using principles of utility diminishes or ignores issues of need, fairness, and justice.

Allocation theories are varied. At one end of the continuum is egalitarianism: persons are entitled to equal health services. Hyperegalitarianism holds that treatments not available to all should be available to none. Opposite on the continuum is a theory that health services are not a right guaranteed by society; rather, they are a privilege to be earned through merit. This hyperindividualistic position holds that providers have no obligation to render services, but are free to choose whom they will serve. Between the extremes is a view that society is obliged to encourage, develop, and perhaps even provide health services in some situations. The macroallocation theory espoused by Charles Fried (1976) suggests that a "decent minimum" (routine services) should be available to all. Conversely, high-technology services are limited in several ways and should be available on a different basis (Harron et al., 1983). Microallocation (allocation to persons) theories of exotic lifesaving services have been developed by James Childress and Nicholas Rescher. They consider the problem of how (by what criteria) decisions are to be made about whom gets what. Both start by applying medical criteria to determine need and appropriateness for treatment. Then they diverge (Childress, 1970). Rarely do HSOs address the ethical issues of resource allocation in an organized, prospective manner. Knowledge of the criteria used in decision-making allows the public to know that the system of allocation is fair.

### Consent

#### Background
Ethics and law treat "consent" similarly. The former is more demanding. In the USA, consent began at law as freedom from non-consensual touching. Ethicists expanded the legal concept of consent, named it "autonomy," included it in the principle of respect for persons (and self-determination), and found it reflected in the special relationship of trust and confidence (fiduciary relationship) between physician and patient.

Consent reflects the Kantian view that human beings are equal. Ethically and legally, consent must be voluntary, competent, and informed.

**Legal aspects of consent**
The US law recognizes that not obtaining consent can lead to a legal action for the tort of battery. In addition, the tort of negligence occurs if physicians breach a duty to communicate information that the patient needs to make a decision (Hiatt, 1989).[1] Questions of consent arise when patients seek treatment. Consent is implied because the patient has sought treatment. Consent is also implied in life-threatening emergencies. Elective, routine treatment requires only general consent, as compared with the special consent needed for invasive, surgical, or experimental or unusual types of procedures. The law requires consent to be voluntary, competent, and informed.

"Voluntary" means that consent is given without duress that substantially influences the decision. Prisoners are a group whose incarceration greatly diminishes their independence; ethically, it is not possible for them to give voluntary consent to be research subjects, for example. Voluntariness is diminished if inducements to participate are such that one becomes greedy, imprudent, or incautious. Similarly, there are circumstances when even small inducements reduce voluntariness; for example, starving persons may agree to take part in a risky medical experiment if they are offered food. Beyond such obvious problems, the concept of voluntariness is elusive. Patients may be under duress to accept a physician's recommendations because they fear being marked as difficult and lose the physician's good-will and cooperation. Patients are influenced by family and friends and may be persuaded (even coerced) by them to accept (or reject) treatment. Perhaps one's freedom to accept or reject medical care is reduced to only that of the right to refuse procedures or treatment (Katz, 1977).

"Competent" means that the patient knows the nature and conse-quences of the decision. For example, children and those with a mental illness or a developmental disability are presumed incompetent.

Historically, the legal standard for informed consent required disclosure of the condition for which treatment was proposed, all significant facts about it, and an explanation of alternatives and likely consequences and difficulties related to the proposed treatment. This standard was based on the amount of information that a reasonable physician would provide. By comparison, ethical criteria suggest more active patient participation. Criteria developed by the President's Commission for the Study of Ethical Problems in Medicine and Biomedical and Behavioral Research state that patient sovereignty with complete participation in the process is preferred (President's Commission, 1982).

## End-of-Life Decisions

The historical definition of death as the cessation of blood circulation and of circulation-dependent animal and vital functions such as respiration and pulsation (heartbeat) proved inadequate as technology advanced. Since the mid-1990s, all US states have recognized alternate criteria to determine death: irreversible cessation of circulatory and respiratory functions, or irreversible cessation of all functions of the entire brain, including the brain stem (brain death). Most states have enacted the Uniform Determination of Death Act, which incorporates these two sets of criteria for determining death (Capron, 2001).

### Life-sustaining treatment

Decisions about life-sustaining treatment are a point of convergence for ethics and law. Hospitals and nursing facilities often face ethical issues regarding withholding or withdrawing life-sustaining treatment. Historically, risk of legal liability caused a reluctance to withdraw life support, absent court approval. The first case receiving national attention in the United States, *In re Quinlan*, was decided in 1976 (*In re Quinlan*, 1976). In 1990, the US Supreme Court first ruled on a case involving life-sustaining treatment, *Cruzan v. Director, Missouri Department of Health*. The court distinguished the rights of competent persons, who are assumed to have a constitutionally protected right to refuse life-sustaining hydration and nutrition, from the rights of incompetent persons such as Nancy Cruzan. The court ruled that the US Constitution does not prevent Missouri from requiring "clear and convincing evidence" that an incompetent person in a persistent vegetative state (PVS) would not wish to be kept alive artificially. Cruzan's parents succeeded in withdrawing life-sustaining treatment.

### Advance Medical Directives

Patient participation in and control of healthcare decisions in the US were enhanced with passage of the federal Patient Self-Determination Act (PSDA) in 1989. The PSDA requires HSOs participating in Medicare and Medicaid to give all patients written information about their rights under state law to accept or refuse treatment and to formulate advance medical directives (AMDs). Medical records must document whether a patient has an AMD, and the HSO must educate staff and the community about AMDs. All US states recognize AMDs (ABA, 2004). State AMD forms are available online (http://www.caringinfo.org/i4a/pages/index.cfm?pageid=3289).

Only 15 percent–25 percent of patients complete AMDs; the majority will do so only after a significant hospital event (Wissow et al., 2004). Only 12 percent of patients with AMDs are asked by their physicians or nurses about their preferences for end-of-life care. About 70 percent of physicians were unaware their patients had AMDs (AHRQ, n.d.).

### Living wills

Living wills have been used since the 1960s to allow persons to communicate their wishes regarding medical treatment if they are not able to do so. In theory, living wills allow patients to control treatment. Absent state law, however, living wills have no legal status in the US; patients must rely on the willingness of care-givers to follow their directives.

### Natural death Act statutes

Interest in living wills and public reaction to situations in which seemingly excessive treatment was provided led to state laws that codify the right of a competent adult to control treatment. This is a clear instance in which ethics (autonomy) and law merge. Common titles for natural death Act statutes are living wills laws, natural death Acts, or death with dignity laws.

### Substituted judgment

Surrogates make decisions for persons incompetent to make them because they are too young or have physical, intellectual, or mental disabilities. Before AMDs, surrogates were appointed on petition to a court. Statutes in almost all US states have eased this cumbersome and expensive process. By 2011, 42 states and the District of Columbia had authorized surrogate decision-making for persons without AMDs (ABA, 2014).

### Powers of attorney

Powers of attorney (PoAs) are another type of decision-making by a surrogate. They may be general or limited and are prepared prospectively. PoAs are "durable" if authority continues beyond the grantor's incompetence. Titles vary, but all have the effect of granting the healthcare agent and surrogate a durable PoA for healthcare decisions. These limited PoAs enable the surrogate to make legally binding decisions for the grantor. By 2004, all states and the District of Columbia allowed appointment of healthcare agents with durable powers of attorney (ABA, 2004).

### Do-not-resuscitate orders

Do-not-resuscitate orders (DNRs) are a type of AMD common to delivery of services. Patients without a DNR order are presumed to want a "full code," or maximum cardiopulmonary resuscitation (CPR). Despite best efforts, CPR is very unlikely to be successful. The violence of CPR may cause collateral damage such as broken ribs and internal injuries, especially in the frail elderly (Shmerling, 2012). Since few patients have AMDs, HSOs should develop policies covering resuscitation of terminally ill patients and those for whom life-continuation decisions must be made, such as patients in PVS. A DNR policy should affirm the legal right of patient or surrogate to direct care, and identify specific chemical and mechanical technologies and their use. Key to use of DNR orders is that patient wishes about CPR mesh with physicians' perceptions of patients' wants (Teno et al., 1995).

Pre-hospital DNR orders are a recent development that allows persons to refuse CPR in medical emergencies. They may be known as emergency medical services (EMS) DNR orders, EMS-DNRs, or durable DNRs. They make patients' decisions about treatment legally binding in non-hospital settings. By 2012, 43 US states and the District of Columbia had authorized pre-hospital DNR orders.

### Euthanasia

The Hippocratic tradition prohibited physicians from giving a deadly drug, and euthanasia (Greek for "good death" – *eu* and *thanatos*) described care that made an inevitable death pain-free. In contemporary use, however, euthanasia often describes mercy killing: active steps to cause death. It is important to make the ethical distinction between actively hastening death and providing palliative care that allows a pain-free, dignified death as a natural course of the disease. The latter is known as allowing natural death (AND).

Euthanasia has four permutations: voluntary active, voluntary passive, involuntary active, and involuntary passive. Voluntary means the person has consented freely. Involuntary means the person either has not consented freely or cannot consent freely, but is presumed to want to die. Active means steps are taken to cause death, or killing. Passive means death is not hastened; it is natural death. Passive euthanasia includes palliative care.

### Physician-assisted suicide

Physician-assisted suicide (PAS) is not euthanasia. It has aspects of voluntary, active euthanasia, but has an important difference. PAS occurs when a physician provides the means, medical advice, and (sometimes) assurance that death will result, but the person, not the physician, performs the act that causes death. Broadly defined, PAS is *eu thanatos* because it tends to relieve suffering and is likely pain-free. The first widely publicized PAS occurred in 1990 when Dr Jack Kevorkian, a retired Michigan pathologist, provided PAS by using a device that enabled persons wishing to commit suicide to self-administer chemicals, after initial help from a physician (Gibbs, 1990). The case focused public attention on active, voluntary euthanasia and aid in dying.

### Legal aspects of PAS

Oregon became the first US state to legalize PAS in 1997. By 2014, four states had legalized PAS: New Hampshire, Oregon, and Washington State by statute; Montana by decision of its Supreme Court (CBC News, 2013). Oregon's law is paradigmatic. It permits physicians to prescribe, but not administer, fatal doses of oral drugs to competent, terminally ill adults with fewer than six months to live. The physician's minimal role of assisting in suicide distinguishes Oregon's law from Kevorkian's PAS. In Oregon, the physician's prescription allows access to medications necessary for self-administered *eu thanatos*, without the guarantee of death that a physician's presence would provide. Absent this modest physician assistance and the legality conferred by the statute, such self-inflicted death would simply be a suicide. The first suicide under the Oregon law was reported in March 1998 (Booth, 1987). The Blue Cross and Blue Shield plans of Oregon began covering PAS in early 1998 (AHA, 1998). In late 1998, the Oregon Health Plan (which covers Medicaid patients) added PAS to end-of-life palliative care and hospice care (AHA, 1998). Between 1998 and the end of 2013, a total of 752 Oregonians had been assisted in suicide. This was about 0.2 percent of persons who died in Oregon during that period (Oregon Public Health Division, 2014).

A national survey found that 7 percent of physicians responding who regularly care for the dying had either given lethal injections or written prescriptions so that patients could kill themselves. This occurred at a time when physician assistance in suicide was illegal. The survey also found that roughly 50 percent of doctors would write prescriptions for deadly doses at the patient's request, and that one-fourth would give lethal injections, if they were legal. Opiates such as morphine were the drugs given most often by physicians to help patients die (Boyd, 2014).

## ORDINARY VERSUS EXTRAORDINARY CARE

"Ordinary" and "extraordinary" do not mean "usual" and "unusual," respectively. Instead, the measure is hope of benefit compared with excessiveness of expense, pain, or other inconvenience. Absent hope of benefit, any medicine, treatment, or operation is extraordinary. If there is hope of benefit, using the same medicine, treatment, or operation is not excessive and is ordinary treatment (Gerald, 1951). Normally provided hydration and nutrition are ordinary; those artificially provided are extraordinary, if they offer no hope of benefit.

Comparing benefits and burdens is another way to judge treatment. Proportionality – proportionate and disproportionate – may be more descriptive than ordinary and extraordinary. Proportionate care and disproportionate care are measured much as are ordinary and extraordinary care. The type of treatment and its complexity or risk, cost, and appropriateness are studied and compared with the results to be expected, taking into account the state of an individual's health and physical and moral resources (Vatican, 1980). Using this calculus, treatment is ethical if the benefit justifies the burden. These comparisons of treatment are qualitative.

**Futile Treatment**

In many ways, futility theory is old wine in new bottles. Its origins lie in the differences between ordinary and extraordinary care which, as noted, are distinguished by hope of benefit, and excessive expense, pain, or other inconvenience. These distinctions make it ethical to withhold any medicine, treatment, or operation that offers no reasonable hope of benefit or that cannot be obtained or used without excessive expense, pain, or inconvenience. Medically futile treatment is defined as any treatment that, within a reasonable degree of medical probability, has little likelihood of having a positive physiological effect on the patient's condition; reversing the patient's imminent decline; or restoring the patient's cognitive, affective, and interactive functions (Trinity Health, 2007).

Futility theory has quantitative and qualitative aspects. The quantitative is concerned with the probability of success if a treatment were continued or attempted. Probability of success means the likelihood that the treatment can be successfully performed and achieve its intended purpose. For example, tube-feeding will maintain the life of a patient in PVS, but will not restore cognition. "Qualitative" assumes a successful treatment that achieves its intended purpose, but asks if the result is such that the treatment ought to be undertaken. The quantitative determination is made by clinical experts. The qualitative determination (judgment) can be made only by the patient or, as necessary, the patient's surrogate. Futility theory limits the qualitative decision.

**Futile-treatment guidelines**
The use of futile-treatment guidelines has been stimulated by perceptions that patients and/or surrogates demand treatment that clinicians

deem to have little or no likelihood of benefiting the patient. Consent and autonomy drive the initial phases of decision-making for patients able to participate. Patients should receive information so as to make an informed choice about treatment or no-treatment options. Patients bear the brunt of continuing treatment that is futile, a fact that likely makes them more willing than surrogate decision-makers to limit what will be done. If patients' decisions (or demands) will not result in efficacious medical treatment or will only prolong suffering and the dying process, clinicians have a moral obligation to withhold or withdraw treatment. Guidelines for withholding or withdrawing life-sustaining treatment usually require agreement of attending and consulting physicians that treatment is futile.

Futile-treatment guidelines or policies should emphasize that physicians have no moral obligation to provide treatment that they judge inappropriate. Physicians' professional integrity is compromised and they fail to meet their duty to their patients if they provide treatment that has neither benefit nor hope of benefit. Physicians fail, too, in their ethical obligation to use resources parsimoniously if ill patients consume them.

All but 12 states give physicians and hospitals latitude in refusing to provide end-of-life treatment that is futile (NRLC, 2012). In Virginia, families have 14 days to find a facility that will accept the patient. Texas allows families ten days to find another facility before withdrawing treatment (Moreno, 2007). Despite such laws, however, it seems doubtful that either physicians or hospitals will refuse to provide treatment that they deem futile, except after considerable continued treatment and when the prognosis is beyond reasonable challenge. The potential for accusations from the public and media that passive, involuntary euthanasia is occurring, or patients are being treated cruelly or killed, is too great. Reactions to highly publicized futile treatment cases show significant ignorance among the public. In such a milieu, strictly enforcing futile-treatment guidelines will cause a public relations nightmare. HSOs must have guidelines or a policy on futile treatment, nonetheless. It is their ethical obligation.

Guidelines will encourage physicians to address the futility of a patient's treatment. Thus encouraged, their frank discussions with patients or surrogates may allow futile treatment to be withheld or withdrawn. By informing patients or surrogates of their moral objection to continuing medically inappropriate (and harmful) treatment, physicians may gain assent without invoking the HSO's guidelines. The "transfer out" option is unlikely to be viable, but is useful to convince patients or surrogates how seriously physicians view the problem. In practical terms, patients may be too ill to transfer; more likely, no facility will accept them. The concept of futile treatment is not without its critics (Valko, 2003).

**Implications**

Futility theory goes well beyond the contemporary concept of patient autonomy, which is a negative right. Autonomy, expressed as the need to consent, is the right to be free from unwanted treatment; the right to say "No, thank you." Futility theory limits the exercise of what is asserted to be a positive right: the "right" to demand treatment after a determination that neither medical benefit nor hope of benefit will accrue from receiving it. No such positive right exists at law or in ethics.

The most compelling ethical issue when considering futile treatment is that the right to die may become a duty to die. Do futile treatment policies put HSOs and healthcare providers on a slippery slope? Will the policies become broader and more focused on the quality of life that clinicians decide would be (or should be) acceptable to the patient? These questions can be answered only in retrospect, in itself not a cheery prospect.

# ORGANIZATIONAL RESPONSES TO ETHICS PROBLEMS

As noted, *In re Quinlan* (1976) first focused national attention in the United States on a clinical ethics issue. It stimulated the development of institutional ethics committees. That interest became quasi-regulatory in 1992 when the Joint Commission mandated that accredited hospitals have a means by which to address ethics issues arising from patient care (Caulfield, 2007). Institutional ethics committees (IECs) help determine the policies that guide the ethical problem-solving outlined in the previous sections, and are typically responsible for case review and guiding institutional decision-making that has ethical dimensions. However, there is little guidance as to selecting, training, and constituting this important group.

HSOs receiving federal reimbursement and providing care to handicapped infants are encouraged by the government to establish an infant care review committee (ICRC). This committee develops policies and procedures concerning treatment decisions for infants with certain clinical conditions. Guidance is given for the expertise that should be sought for the ICRC. The suggested model includes a representative from the HSO's medical staff who serves as chair; a pediatric specialist; a nurse; an attorney; a public member; and a representative from a disability organization (Title 45, n.d.-a, n.d.-b).

Institutional review boards (IRBs) are required by the federal government for the protection of human subjects in federally funded research. There are minimal review requirements for research that can be defined

*Table 20.1  Administrative and/or clinical ethics research topics*

| Topic | | Administrative and/or clinical ethics issue |
|---|---|---|
| Institutional Ethics Committees | IEC composition, function, effectiveness, and role | Both |
| | Role and use of IECs beyond clinical aspects of healthcare delivery | Both |
| Consent | Patient consent process and role of the HSO and its staff | Both |
| Resource allocation | Process and criteria used for capital expenditure decisions | Both |
| | Understanding effects of futile care policy on resource use at end of life | |
| End-of-life decisions | Effects of futility theory policies, and advance medical directives on end-of-life decisions | Both |
| | Effects of decision-making when family members act as surrogates | Both |
| | Attitudes of physicians regarding physician-assisted suicide and the role of the HSO | Both |
| | Effects on clinical practice of greater availability and use of living wills | Clinical |
| Staffing | Implications of increasing numbers of licensed independent practitioners employed by hospitals | Both |
| | Effects of using hospitalists employed by the hospital | Administrative |
| | Conflicts of interest, self-dealing, and nepotism in HSOs | Administrative |
| Effects of profit motive | Role and activities of for-profit HSOs compared with not-for-profit HSOs | Administrative |
| | Comparing for-profit and not-for-profit HSOs' focus on values and mission and economic performance | Administrative |
| | Comparing for-profit and not-for-profit HSOs' focus on values and mission and customer satisfaction | Administrative |
| Integrating delivery of healthcare | Linking care in various parts of an integrated healthcare system | Both |

as exempt or expedited. IRB protection extends to personally identifiable information of the research subject, as well as data collected about the subject during the research or derived from the research intervention. The IRB assures that research subjects are treated ethically and that researchers observe established research protocols, especially regarding consent (Bozeman et al., 2009). Required IRB membership includes a public member and reflects a diversity of expertise including the sciences and a gender balance, although gender cannot form the basis for selection (Title 45, n.d.-a, n.d.-b).

## TOPICS FOR FUTURE RESEARCH

Several decision-making areas with clinical or administrative ethical implications will benefit from further healthcare management research. Table 20.1 identifies several of them.

## NOTE

1.  Contrast this view with a case in Japan, in which a physician told a patient that she had gallstones rather than frighten her by telling her that she actually had gall bladder cancer. She delayed surgery (Hiatt, 1989). The cancer spread and she died. Her family sued. The court said that the patient herself was to blame because she had not followed the physician's advice to have the surgery, and that the physician had no obligation to inform her of the true condition.

## REFERENCES

American Bar Association (ABA) (2004). "Health Care Power of Attorney and Combined Advance Directive Legislation." Chicago, IL: American Bar Association, Commission on Legal Problems of the Elderly (Mimeo).

American Bar Association (ABA) (2014). "Default Surrogate Consent Statutes." http://www.americanbar.org/content/dam/aba/migrated/aging/PublicDocuments/famcon_2009.authcheckdam.pdf (28 June 2014).

American College of Health Care Administrators (2014). "Code of Ethics." http://www.achca.org/content/pdf/Code%20of%20Ethics_ACHCA%20Non-Member_140430.pdf (accessed 28 June 2014).

American College of Healthcare Executives (ACHE) (2011). "ACHE Code of Ethics." Amended by the Board of Governors on 4 November. http://www.ache.org/abt_ache/code.cfm (accessed 28 June 2014).

American Hospital Association (AHA) (1998). "Assisted-Suicide Coverage Could Be Expanded." *AHA News*, 34 (43): 6.

American Hospital Association (AHA) (2003). "The Patient Care Partnership: Understanding Expectations, Rights, and Responsibilities." http://www.aha.org/aha/content/2003/pdf/pcp_english_030730.pdf (accessed 28 June 2014).

American Medical Association (AMA) (1982). "Current Opinions of the Judicial Council," vii. Chicago, IL: American Medical Association.

American Medical Association (AMA) (2001). Principles of Medical Ethics. http://www.ama-assn.org/ama/pub/physician-resources/medical-ethics/code-medical-ethics/principles-medical-ethics.page? (accessed 28 June 2014).

American Nurses Association (2015). "Code of Ethics for Nurses." Washington, DC: American Nurses Association.

America's Health Insurance Plans (AHIP) (2004). "A Commitment to Improve Health Care Quality, Access, and Affordability." Board of Directors Statement, Washington, DC.

Booth, William (1987). "Woman Commits Doctor-Assisted Suicide." *Washington Post*, A7.

Boyd, Andrew (2014). University of Texas Southern at Dallas. "Physician-Assisted Suicide: For and Against." *American Medical Student Association.* http://www.amsa.org/AMSA/ Libraries/Committee_Docs/PhysicianAssistedSuicide.sflb.ashx, (accessed 28 June 2014).

Bozeman, B., Slade, C., and Hirsch, P. (2009). "Understanding Bureaucracy In Health Science Ethics: Toward A Better Institutional Review Board." *American Journal of Public Health*, 99 (9): 1549–1556.

Bryant, L. Edward, Jr (2005). "Ethical and Legal Duties for Healthcare Boards." *Healthcare Executive*, 20 (4): 46, 48.

Capron, Alexander Morgan (2001). "Brain Death – Well Settled Yet Still Unresolved." Editorial. *New England Journal of Medicine*, 344 (16): 1244.

Carson, T.L. (1994). "Conflicts of Interest." *Journal of Business Ethics*, 13: 387–404.

Caulfield, Sharon E. (2007). "Health Care Facility Ethics Committees: New Issues in the Age of Transparency." *Human Rights Magazine*, 34 (4).

CBC News (2013). "Dying with Dignity Legislation to Be Tabled at National Assembly." http://www.cbc.ca/news/canada/montreal/dying-with-dignity-legislation-to-be-tabled-at-national-assembly-1.1361088 (accessed 28 June 2014).

Childress, James F. (1970). "Who Shall Live When Not All Can Live?" *Soundings, An Interdisciplinary*, 57: 339–355.

Fried, Charles (1976). "Equality and Rights in Medical Care." *Hastings Center Report*, 6: 29–34.

Gerald, Kelly (1951). "The Duty to Preserve Life." *Theological Studies*, 12: 550.

Gibbs, Nancy (1990). "Dr Death's Suicide Machine." *Time*, 18 June: 69–70.

Harron, Frank, Burnside, John, and Beauchamp, Tom (1983). *Health and Human Values: A Guide to Making Your Own Decisions.* New Haven, CT: Yale University Press.

Hiatt, Fred (1989). "Japan Court Ruling Backs Doctors." *Washington Post*, 30 May, A9.

Katz, Jay (1977). "Informed Consent – A Fairy Tale." *University of Pittsburgh Law Review*, 39: 137–174.

Langmead, S. (2013). Personal communication, 12 July.

Moreno, Sylvia (2007). "Case Puts Texas Futile-Treatment Law Under a Microscope." *Washington Post.* http://www.washingtonpost.com/wp-dyn/content/article/2007/04/10/ AR2007041001620.html (accessed 13 July 2013).

National Right to Life Committee (NRLC) (2012). "Will Your Advance Directive Be Followed?" Robert Powell Center for Medical Ethics. http://www.nrlc.org/uploads/med ethics/WillYourAdvanceDirectiveBeFollowed.pdf (accessed 28 June 2014).

Oregon Public Health Division (2014). *Death with Dignity Act Annual Report 2013.* http://public.health.oregon.gov/ProviderPartnerResources/EvaluationResearch/ DeathwithDignityAct/Documents/year16.pdf (accessed 15 July 2014).

President's Commission (1982). President's Commission for the Study of Ethical Problems in Medicine and Biomedical and Behavioral Research. "Making Health Care Decisions," 1.

Shmerling, Robert H. (2012). "CPR: Less Effective than You Might Think." InteliHealth. Updated and revised 23 October. http://www.intelihealth.com/article/cpr-less-effective-than-you-might-think (accessed 28 June 2014).

Society for Healthcare Strategy and Market Development (SHSMD) (2010). "SHSMD Advisory: Principles and Practices for Marketing Communications in Hospitals and Health Systems."

Teno, Joan M., Hakim, Rosemarie B., Knaus, William A., Wenger, Neil S., Phillips, Russell S., Wu, Albert W., Layde, Peter, Connors, Alfred F., Dawson, Neal V., and Lynn, Joanne (1995). "Preferences for Cardiopulmonary Resuscitation: Physician–Patient Agreement and Hospital Resource Use." *Journal of General Internal Medicine*, 10: 179–186.

Title 45 (n.d.-a). "Title 45: Public Welfare Part 84 – Nondiscrimination On The Basis Of Handicap In Programs Or Activities Receiving Federal Financial Assistance §84.55 a,f."

Title 45 (n.d.-b). "Title 45: Public Welfare Part 46 – Protection of Human Subjects §46.107–46.110."

Trinity Health (2007). "Trinity Health Guidelines on Medically Futile Treatment." Novi, MI: Trinity Health.

Valko, Nancy (2003). "Futility Policies and the Duty to Die." *Voices*. www.wf-f.org/03-1-Futility.html (accessed 13 November 2013).

Vatican Congregation for the Doctrine of the Faith (1980)."Declaration on Euthanasia." 26 June. Rome.

Veatch, Robert M. (1980). "Professional Ethics: New Principles for Physicians?" *Hastings Center Report*, (June): 17.

Wissow, Lawrence S., Belote, Amy, Kramer, Wade, Compton-Phillips, Amy, Kritzler, Robert, and Weiner, Jonathan P. (2004). "Promoting Advance Directives among Elderly Primary Care Patients." *Journal of General Internal Medicine*, 19 (9): 944–951.

# 21. The future of healthcare: the editors weigh in
*Myron D. Fottler, Donna Malvey and Donna J. Slovensky*

## INTRODUCTION

The present chapter provides the opportunity for the co-editors of this book to speculate on how the healthcare industry and management of that industry must or may change to accommodate future challenges. In the future, we will experience both evolutionary and revolutionary changes in all countries as we struggle to balance the necessity for enhanced patient access and quality with the need to contain costs. Such pressures will be particularly acute in developing countries in managing these goals with an aging population and workforce.

The nature of the chapter necessitates judgments regarding which societal and healthcare trends will accelerate, decelerate, or discontinue as new challenges arise. Our judgments may turn out to be prescient, partly validated, and/or significantly off the mark. We approach this task with a great deal of humility since none of us can claim 100 percent accuracy on our previous prognostications.

The topics we will cover on future trends and management challenges are divided into four sections:

1. The future of health reform.
2. Managing continuous change through effective stakeholder management.
3. Managing the future.
4. Big data and enterprise information governance.

## FUTURE OF HEALTHCARE REFORM

### The Patient Protection and Affordable Care Act

Since the passage of Medicare in 1965, the United States federal and state agencies have required more and more data from healthcare providers to receive reimbursement for covered services. Private insurers followed suit, thus creating an increasingly complex bureaucracy to regulate and control the healthcare industry. The problem was that the promises that had been made by politicians and corporations regarding services they would pay for turned out to be unsustainable.

In 2010, the US took an additional giant step towards a bureaucratized healthcare system, with even more power and control centralized at the federal level, with the passage of the Patient Protection and Affordable Care Act (ACA). This legislation is the only major social legislation (that is, social security, civil rights, and welfare reform) passed with a totally partisan vote. Seemingly, those who voted to pass the bill did not read it; and those who read it voted against it. Additionally, there were minimal congressional hearings on the bill and no pilot projects to test the key features of the law.

The American public has been continuously negative regarding the 2700-page law before, during, and after its passage. Moreover, thousands of pages of regulations to provide specific guidance for provider implementation were still being written as this book went to press in 2015. One major reason for the negative response of the American public is because the ACA was 90 percent health insurance expansion and only 10 percent healthcare system reform. A more appropriate and transparent title for the legislation would have been "The Health Insurance Expansion and Income Redistribution Act."

Most of the politicians who pushed through the legislation (Obama, Pelosi, Reid, and Baucus) did not have any background or experience in the healthcare industry. Moreover, they refused to listen to those in Congress or those from outside who did have relevant experience. They also bought off wavering Democratic senators in swing states to vote in favor of the legislation, which was later dubbed the "Corn Husker Kickback" and the "Louisiana Purchase." Even more important than the political process has been the substance of the legislation. The effects of the most significant provisions are outlined in Box 21.1.

### Evaluation

The assumption of the legislation that "one size fits all," despite the diversity and cultural differences in different geographical regions of the United States, was unrealistic. The entire thrust of this bill is to standardize benefits and how they will be paid and provided, regardless of individual choices or ethical convictions. Insurance should be a contract by which an insurance company pays for large, unanticipated expenses, in return for premium. It is a bad idea for small, regular, predictable expenses to

---

BOX 21.1 EFFECTS OF MAJOR COMPONENTS OF THE PATIENT PROTECTION AND AFFORDABLE CARE ACT

- The bill will add $1 trillion to the US deficit and national debt, since no money was saved or put aside to pay for it. In the longer run this means higher taxes and more inflation as well as the direct cost of the bill.
- It imposes an unprecedented governmental mandate for everyone to buy health insurance or pay a $750 fine.
- All individuals must purchase health insurance, which is defined as "minimal, essential coverage." Failure to do so on the part of the individuals or corporations leads to mandatory penalties. Congress justifies such penalties under the "Commerce Cause" which was passed to prevent states from erecting state trade barriers.
- Cuts Medicare by $500 billion and increases taxes by $500 billion.
- It expands the federal workforce by funding the hiring of 16 500 Internal Revenue Service (IRS) agents to enforce its tax provisions.
- It provides a "play or pay" plan where employers of more than 50 employees are encouraged to cover their employees with penalties associated with non-coverage. However, many workers have been pushed off their health insurance and forced to buy a government-subsidized plan.
- It nationalizes the regulations of health insurance premiums recently made by state governments and reduces the normal market forces that would otherwise encourage innovations and efficiencies.
- It ignores the real cost drivers in healthcare, such as third-party payment systems which promote overconsumption, and payment mechanisms that encourage doctors to provide more services but not necessarily require better outcomes.
- It creates disincentives for providers and patients to make cost-effective, quality choices.
- It empowers a "comparative effectiveness board" that will influence providers' decisions on which treatments are best for which patients.
- It reduces previous appropriations for Medicare.
- It creates a new Medicare Independent Advisory Board of unelected bureaucrats who choose where to cut future Medicare benefits.
- Physicians were slated to absorb a 30% cut in their reimbursement, which is very unlikely to be implemented.
- Since it applies to full-time workers (defined as those working 30+ hours a week), it has expanded the ranks of involuntary part-time workers.

---

be covered, and it is even a worse idea for consumers to have all their expenses covered (that is, no co-pays, whereby the insured pays a specified amount towards costs). Full coverage results in overutilization and lack of concern for cost on the consumer side.

The dollar numbers presented to the public were ludicrous in that the Congressional committees gave the Congressional Budget Office (CBO) assumptions that made no sense. As a result, the CBO concluded that 32 million more people could be added to the health insurance rolls (mostly Medicaid) without adding to the US deficit or national debt based upon the timing for implementation for various provisions. They actually claimed that the legislation would save money. Medicare's top actuary was quoted as follows, prior to passage of the bill: "The Financial Projections do not represent reasonable expectations for actual program operations in either the short range or long range."

Moreover, if the 30 percent cut in physician reimbursement was implemented, seniors and the poor would have an insurance card with no doctors to provide the services covered. Consequently, the proposed cuts in Medicare and Medicaid have not and will not be implemented.

Some pieces of the legislation have already been repealed or are in the process of being repealed even by Democrats (coverage of long-term care) or by presidential executive orders (mandates for unionized workers). Moreover, some provisions of the legislation such as the Accountable Care Organizations (ACOs) are not and will not be sustainable in the future.

Relative effectiveness panels (that is, Death Panels) were built into the legislation through the establishment of the Independent Payment Advisory Board (IPAB) in order to address the expected rising costs resulting from increased insurance enrollment, and diminishing incentives to contain such costs. Basic economics suggest that when something is subsidized more of it will be utilized, and when something (that is, full-time employment) is penalized, less of it will be utilized. The law gives the board sweeping authority to contain Medicare costs with virtually no constraint. The effectiveness panel is the attempt to minimize the expected cost increases. It can control cost by lowering physician reimbursements (reducing physician incentives to treat Medicare patients) and by reducing the services eligible for reimbursement. Finally, this board cannot be checked by the executive, legislative, or judicial branches of government.

One goal is to force young, healthy individuals, and those disinclined to purchase health insurance, to overpay for such insurance in order to pay for heavy users. The $750 penalty per person will not be sufficient to induce helping young people to purchase health insurance to offset high utilization rates of middle-aged enrollees. Annual premiums for young people which exceed the penalty will create an enrollment disincentive for the young.

However, the legislation is unsustainable and will not be sustained in its present form. The percent of gross domestic product (GPD) accounted for by federal government spending has averaged 20 percent over the last quarter of a century. The three-and-a-half-year Obama Administration average was 24 percent prior to implementation of Obama Care. The most recent Congressional Budget Office report estimates that the cost of Obama Care is not the $900 billion over the next ten years in the original estimate. Rather, it is now $2.2 trillion. The ultimate outcome is a debt crisis similar to that currently being experienced by countries in the European Union.

## Market-Based Healthcare Reform

As an alternative to the Affordable Care Act, many well-informed analysts have advocated a market-based healthcare reform that would address the issue of consumer and provider incentives to provide high clinical and service quality, expand access, and contain costs for health-care services. Components of such an alternative are outlined in Box 21.2. While space limitations preclude a detailed discussion of each component, interested readers may consult a variety of other sources to access such detail (Abrams, 2012; Flower, 2012; Melhado, 2014; Shore, 2012).

One analyst believes that there is now a clear path to repeal and replace the ACA in 2015 (Barnett, 2014). In Fall 2014, the Supreme Court agreed to hear *King v. Burwell*, which challenges the legality of the IRS rule allowing ACA subsidies in states that have not built their own insurance exchanges. Rather than asking the court to establish some grand constitutional principal, the justices are merely being asked to hold the IRS to the actual wording of the law. Unfortunately, the Supreme Court affirmed the ACA in June 2015.

Now there appear to be fewer incentives for major stakeholders to invest in designing a replacement for the ACA (Barnett, 2014). The Supreme Court justices were reluctant to invalidate a law upon which many citizens rely. It would have been easier for the justices to enforce the law's existing language if they knew there was a viable alternative enacted by both the houses and signed by the President. Obviously, the components of such a bill would have consumer choice including catastrophic-only insurance, medical savings accounts, tort reform, allowing insurance to be sold across state lines, and broadening employer-based tax benefits to all health insurance products. In sum, a favorable ruling in *King* would have been more likely if Congress had crafted bipartisan market-based replacement. Consequently, we are unlikely to construct a consumer-oriented, market-based health insurance system in the future.

---

BOX 21.2    COMPONENTS OF MARKET-BASED HEALTH
REFORM

- Enact medical malpractice reform (tort reform).
- Make a real investment in minimizing medical fraud and abuse.
- Increase federal funding for training programs to enhance the supply of primary care physicians, nurse practitioners, and physician assistants.
- Repeal all state laws prohibiting health insurance from being sold across state lines.
- Support high-deductible health insurance options coupled with medical savings accounts to cover routine services.
- Repeal all government mandates specifying what services insurance companies must cover.
- Allow markets to work by enhancing price transparency to allow consumers to make informed choices (i.e., public websites with price information for all services).
- Reimburse based on patient outcomes (clinical and service).
- Incentivize employers to offer catastrophic insurance for major expenses supplemented by health savings accounts for small expenses, as they do in Singapore. Every individual needs to have "skin in the game."
- Put decision-making in the hands of the consumer by removing legal obstacles, legal mandates, and government bureaucratic rules.
- Incorporate patient cost-sharing in all health products and services.
- Equalize tax laws to treat employer and individual health insurance the same from a tax perspective.
- Convert Medicaid to a block grant program for states.
- Provide Medicare beneficiaries with an option to choose either the current Medicare entitlement program or a premium support program for purchasing private insurance.
- Encourage defined contribution insurance where employers would give their employees a fixed dollar payment to allow them to choose from a menu of coverage options based on their own situations and pay the marginal cost of higher-priced plans.

---

**The Future of Healthcare Reform**

There are four possible scenarios for the future of health reform:

1.  Maintain the ACA more or less as is.
2.  Amend the ACA with as many aspects of market-based reform as possible.
3.  Repeal the ACA and adopt a single-payer (that is, the US government) system.
4.  Repeal the ACA and adopt a market-based reform model.

The four scenarios listed above are outlined in Table 21.1 along with their implications for a variety of healthcare outcomes. We will now discuss the scenarios of each of the four possible outcomes, together with their implications and probability of adoption over the next 6–10 years (2016–2024).

Continuation of the ACA as it is currently constituted, with minor tweaks, may be attempted but will fall short. Such attempts to "improve" the increasingly bureaucratic system will ultimately result in soaring costs, restriction in access to expensive services, and higher taxes for middle- and upper-income citizens. Access to services will be higher for lower-income citizens and stable for everyone else. Clinical quality of care and service quality will erode as providers respond more to governmental rules than to consumer preferences.

The second scenario is to amend the ACA by incorporating more market-based scenarios to mitigate the above-stated negative outcomes. As noted in Table 21.1, the positives of amending the ACA include slowing the growth of healthcare costs, reducing financial deficits, and reducing the higher taxes for middle- and upper-income groups. It would also enhance service quality, consumer choice, growth of non-regulated services, and long-term sustainability. However, as noted in Table 21.1, there is only a 20 percent chance that this will happen. This scenario will not occur unless or until the American people elect a President and Congress which will allow market-based healthcare reform consistent with the US Constitution. The most likely outcome is a continuing increase in bureaucratic rules and regulations in an attempt to solve these problems. But Americans will become increasingly frustrated and become amenable to scenario 3: a single-payer system.

The third scenario is the repeal of the ACA and the adoption of a single-payer system for the US. This has the highest probability of occurrence in the long run. The reason is that the US is unlikely to adopt market-based reforms of the ACA, and the first scenario will result in increased bureaucratic decisions and increased costs. Therefore, Americans will exert pressure for adopting a single-payer system, like that of most developed countries, over the next 6–10 years. The result of a single-payer system, as noted in Table 21.1, will be higher levels of consumer access to standardized services but not unapproved non-standardized services, rapid growth in healthcare costs, taxes, and the federal deficits. Quality of care will be lower overall, as well as consumer choice. Major growth will be seen in non-regulated services such as concierge services as many more affluent Americans will try to escape the single-payer system.

The fourth and final option is to repeal the ACA and adopt a

Table 21.1  Four scenarios for future healthcare reform in the United States, and the implications of each

| Implications | Scenario 1: Maintain the ACA as is (20% probability) | Scenario 2: Amend the ACA, incorporating many market-based reforms (20% probability) | Scenario 3: Repeal the ACA and adopt single-payer model (50% probability) | Scenario 4: Repeal the ACA and adopt a market-based model (10% probability) |
|---|---|---|---|---|
| Consumer access | Higher for lower income; lower for others | Higher | Higher | Higher |
| Cost trajectory | Rapid growth | Slower growth | Rapid growth | Slower growth |
| Deficit trajectory | Rapid growth | Slower growth | Rapid growth | Slower growth |
| Non-regulated service trajectory | Stable | Moderate growth | Significant growth | Significant growth |
| Tax changes | Higher for middle and upper incomes | Slightly higher for middle and upper incomes | Higher for middle and upper incomes | None needed |
| Quality of care | Slightly lower | No change overall | Lower | Higher |
| Service quality | Lower | Higher | Lower | Higher |
| Consumer choice | Lower | Higher | Lower | Higher |
| Long-term sustainability | Not sustainable | Sustainable | Not sustainable without major access restrictions | Sustainable |

market-based model. As noted in Table 21.1, it is the least likely to occur, with a 10 percent probability, and would require major support by both houses of Congress and the President. Unfortunately, the fourth scenario is also the scenario with the most positive outcomes, including increased consumer access, slower growth of costs, reduced deficits, no tax increases, higher clinical and service quality, greater consumer choice, and higher levels of long-term sustainability.

## Managerial Implications for the Scenarios

Managerial implications for scenario 1 will require healthcare providers to identify and standardize services for which government reimbursement is approved, and continue to modify such services in response to government regulation. Also, providers will need to focus on generating revenues from non-regulated services such as retail clinics and medical tourism to help relieve some of the negative aspects of the ACA.

Partnerships with those providing health services in non-regulated markets may also be helpful in maintaining revenue streams. Since the ACA provides some small reimbursement benefits for providing high levels of clinical and service excellence, providing and documenting such high levels would also be in order. A continuing challenge for health-care providers of all types is how to provide necessary treatments for patients requiring unusual or non-standardized services for which federal authorities will be restricting access.

The second scenario, amending the ACA with market-based reform, provides a more positive outcome for healthcare executives. There should be no problem maintaining clinical quality, and service quality will be undoubtedly higher as market-based solutions are expected to focus on consumer preferences. However, non-regulated health services are likely to grow much faster than under scenario 1 since there are more options available to physicians, patients, and healthcare organizations. Lower levels of government standards and regulations will result in more options and greater competition which will mitigate and help to contain costs. A continuing focus on non-regulated health services is likely to result in faster growth in these areas.

Scenario 3 occurs where a single-payer model is adopted due to rapid increases in costs and high federal deficits. This will cause the federal regulators to reduce access for certain services that are deemed high-cost, have undocumented need, or are unnecessary. Healthcare executives will need to avoid such services and become highly responsive to changes in federal rules, regulations, and reimbursement changes. Since consumer choice will be lower, the role of healthcare marketing will decline and the role of political connections will increase. The country is likely to experience a significant growth in non-regulated health services, with non-affluent consumers having more out-of-pocket costs.

Finally, the fourth scenario, where the ACA is repealed and a market-based reform is adopted, provides the most positive outcomes with highest levels of managerial choices as well as consumer choices. In other words, this option "would allow one thousand flowers to bloom." This would result in greater competition, but also stimulate much higher levels of managerial and clinical innovation to the benefit of consumers and the country as whole. Strategic management and marketing will be major managerial functions fostering the success of the organization. Higher levels of innovation would also tend to mitigate higher costs of health services. A major growth in non-regulated services would also expand under this scenario.

Despite the optimistic position of Barnett (2014) the most likely long-term scenario is scenario 3, where the system becomes increasingly bureaucratized and the negative outcomes noted above become obvious. While this conclusion may seem pessimistic, the most negative aspects could be mitigated by increased innovation in less regulated or unregulated sub-markets of healthcare. Innovations will expand in these areas and may mitigate the overall aspects of the system. Examples of areas that may expand are concierge medicine, retail medicine, inbound medical tourism, and other private sector innovations that are able to avoid the worst aspects of government regulation.

## MANAGING CONTINUOUS CHANGE THROUGH EFFECTIVE STAKEHOLDER MANAGEMENT

The only constant in life and in managing healthcare organizations is change. No healthcare executive or student of the field should expect that they or their organization will prove to be an exception to the above rule in the twenty-first century. In today's highly competitive healthcare environments, competition is broadening and becoming global, while innovation is continuous. Healthcare reform efforts such as the Affordable Care Act in the US are just one aspect of a wide range of environmental changes which will impact healthcare in the future. Being able to adapt is the key to capturing opportunities, overcoming obstacles, and organizational survival itself.

The nature of organization change and specific strategies to address it have been previously discussed in Chapter 13 in this volume. A common denominator in all such strategies is that they require healthcare organizations to engage in a continuous change management process. Such a process is a systematic way of bringing about and managing changes at both the individual and the organizational levels.

While most staff members understand the concept of continuous change, they tend to resist it because it requires them to modify or adapt familiar and successful current ways of working. Individuals, groups, and organizations tend to resist change because they are accustomed to the usual way of doing things and/or they perceive the change to be threatening to their status and influence (Austin, 2009). Healthcare executives need to envision the future, communicate that vision to all stakeholders, set clear expectations for future performance, and invest in the human and other resources to achieve the new vision. More specifically they need to (Bolman and Deal, 1999; Stern, 2005):

- Link the expected changes to achieving the goals and objectives to the strategic plan.
- Show how the change creates benefits which will positively impact all key stakeholders.
- Engage key stakeholders in the change process so the plan changes will contain benefits that are widely shared.
- Invest human and financial resources in the change and sustaining process.

To overcome such resistance to change, managers and executives need to address two questions pertaining to change: what to change and how to change it. The issue of what to change requires the identification of the challenge or problem, then deciding what combination of strategic, structural, cultural, technological, and/or workforce attitudes and skills that will best address this challenge. Strategic, structural, and technological change will fail without the support of key stakeholders. Thus, any successful organizational change will invariably require change in employee's attitudes, skills, and behaviors. Establishing how to change the organization requires executives and managers to (Kotter, 1996; Abrahamson, 2000; Herald et al., 2007):

- Establish a sense of urgency.
- Mobilize commitment from key stakeholders.
- Develop and communicate a shared vision.
- Help employees make the change.
- Use short-term accomplishments to produce more change.
- Reinforce new processes to organization systems and procedures.
- Monitor and assess progress.

Since implementation is usually the weakest part of the change implementation process, managing the above steps is easier said than done. The reason is obvious: resistance to change among one or more of the key stakeholders involved. Knowing how to plan for and address actual stakeholder resistance is key to successful change efforts.

**Effective Stakeholder Management**

Few healthcare organizations have developed, articulated, and integrated key stakeholders as a key to successful change management. Healthcare leaders require a detailed approach as well as specific tools and techniques to effectively manage their key stakeholders (Blair and Fottler, 1990, 1996, 1997). A summary of this approach involves the following major steps:

- Identify all external, interface, and internal stakeholders relevant to the particular change process.
- Diagnose each stakeholder by their potential for threat or cooperation.
- Ensure that the diagnosis for each stakeholder is relevant for the specific change issue facing the organization.
- Classify such stakeholders as supportive, mixed-blessing, or non-supportive based upon their potential for threat or cooperation.
- Formulate generic stakeholder management strategies: involve the supportive stakeholder, collaborate with the mixed-blessing stakeholder, defend against the non-supportive stakeholder; and monitor the marginal (non-key) stakeholders.
- Implement these generic strategies by developing specific implementations, tactics, and programs for each stakeholder.
- Determine which specific internal stakeholders should be assigned responsibility for managing the implementation process for each stakeholder.
- Continuously evaluate the success of the stakeholder management process for each stakeholder and make adjustments as necessary.

The latter two steps might involve either the human resources department and/or specific managers explaining the need for change, asking employees to help design the change, providing incentives and sanctions to guide employee behavior, and giving inspirational speeches (Furst and Cable, 2008). Such managers need to continuously monitor stakeholder behavior which either detracts or contributes to the change efforts.

As changes to management occur, the commitment of new managers may not be equal to that of the manager who initiated the change process.

Throughout any change process, success is dependent on "champions" who will lead the way and inspire others to follow. Simply assuming that the new managers will reflect the values and attitudes of those whom they replace may prove problematic. The necessity for continuous communication regarding the change effort is an ongoing process.

## MANAGING THE FUTURE

Can healthcare executives manage the future, and can they manage the future to achieve success and assure survival? Management is about getting things done through and with people, but how can executives be expected to meet the challenges of what is unknown, uncertain, and often beyond their control? As the discussion of the future of healthcare reform demonstrates, there are a variety of scenarios that healthcare executives can use to determine what their strategies and courses of action will be in the coming years. In their leadership role, healthcare executives are called upon to lead their workers to the future. In this respect, healthcare executives have relied on their vision of the future, their ability to communicate that vision, and finally, their ability to assist and support their employees in moving past whatever obstacles they encounter to realize that vision. These executives have also assured that the vision was tied to realistic goals with necessary resources to fund their achievement.

Can healthcare executives be expected to continue to lead their followers to the future? What challenges await them? What can healthcare executives do to overcome these challenges? What follows are seven challenges to managing the future. Executives must respond to these challenges to assure the success and survival of their healthcare organization (HCO) in the coming years.

### Challenge #1: Find the Future

The first challenge is finding the future. Finding the future is complicated by the fact that the future is neither a stable nor a known place. Healthcare executives may believe that they are future-oriented, but in reality not recognize that chaos in the environment is obscuring what is going on. Consequently, executives may not always know what is being missed; that is, regardless of how adept a manager is at planning for and predicting the future, they potentially will always be missing something. And that something can be very significant for the HCO's future. The problem in today's hyper-change environment is that overlooking major developments such as the shift to mobile technology can have disastrous impacts on the future. Facebook almost missed the mobile revolution, which would have limited its future and opened up opportunities for Facebook's competitors. In healthcare, executives cannot afford to miss important revolutions either.

Yet it is easy to "miss" an important "disruptive" event that will revise the way things are done in an industry and across industries. In 2008, *Businessweek* highlighted what it did not see coming. Turns out it missed YouTube, Twitter, Wikipedia, Facebook, and iTunes (Baker and Green, 2008). If *Businessweek* overlooked the emergence and impact of these significant sites and services, how can healthcare executives work to avoid misjudging the future?

Executives will make errors about the future and how it will play out, but they will likely commit fewer transgressions if they are attuned to emerging phenomena such as mobile technology and also health policy developments. In addition, they will probably be more responsive to change if they are open to admitting a loss of control about the future as it plays out. While management involves controlling (planning, organizing, monitoring), the leadership aspect of management calls for letting go of traditional ways, being willing to take risks, and embracing change with a view toward the future.

### Challenge #2: Devise Mechanisms to See the Future Coming

This challenge derives from recent thinking about innovation: big bang disruption, which suggests that there are new kinds of innovators that can wipe out incumbents in an instant. And these disruptions can come from anywhere, including outside the industry. Conventional navigation product makers such as Garmin and Magellan found themselves overtaken by free navigation apps that are preloaded on smartphones. Furthermore, these apps are constantly improving because of robust platforms of iOS (iPhone, iPod Touch, iPad) and Android operating systems. While managers have been alerted to disruptive technologies and new entrants or upstarts that can offer less expensive substitutes and capture markets, there has been little attention given to big bang disruptors that cause rapid product or service adoption and pull consumers away in every segment almost simultaneously. This kind of innovation is previously unknown and therefore game-changing (Downes and Nunes, 2013).

Big bang disruptors can come out of nowhere and almost immediately wipe out mature products and lead to shorter product life cycles. Consequently, consumers are becoming accustomed to an accelerated lifecycle in which they anticipate that every product, service, or device will decline in price and improve in quality over a relatively brief time span. To survive them, HCOs need to develop new tools to detect radical change and develop strategies to slow down the disruptors. For example, hospitals have been reluctant to embrace telemedicine, which offers the ability to provide quality, affordable healthcare regardless of location. Thus, there remains an opportunity for big bang disruptors to take advantage of large-scale inefficiencies (Downes and Nunes, 2013). Again, executives must look for ways to put big bang disruptors on their radar if their HCOs are to survive them.

**Challenge #3: Defy Gravity**

The third challenge involves defying gravity; that is, ignoring the gravitational pull of hyper-change and institutional pressure to copy what everyone else is doing, especially when it comes to technology. You cannot transform healthcare delivery and behaviors by technology alone. Furthermore, you cannot rely on technology for problem-solving or decision-making – other than as assistive in the process. The healthcare executive must use technology as a tool to solve problems, but technology on its own does not solve problems, people do. Ultimately executives are both responsible and accountable, as these commitments are inherent in being a manager.

It is difficult to avoid following the leader in an industry and copying what they do. In graduate school, managers are taught that one size does not fit all, which means that every HCO has unique attributes, challenges, and environments and adopting a model successfully used by another HCO will not necessarily guarantee similar success across organizations. Unfortunately, too often executives follow what others are doing in their industry regardless of the differences among organizations. For example, small hospital systems might adopt models that work well in larger systems, only to find out that small systems lack advantages of scale that underwrite successful implementation.

In the past, HCOs have consolidated because of regulatory, reimbursement, or other threats in the environment. For example, in the 1990s, hospitals moved to integrate vertically in order to offer a continuum of health services. This move was in response to the impact of changes associated with the prospective payment system (PPS) and diagnosis-related groupings (DRGs). However, in the following decade, many of these same hospitals opted out of vertical organizational structures because they could not support the service continuum. We see similar movement today with US hospitals acquiring physician practices and consolidating in response to the ACA that incentivizes a shift from volume to value.

In addition, executives should also examine how organizations outside of healthcare are adapting to changes in their environments. Often there will be clues to how to revise operations for success. Recognizing the unique context of HCOs, managers may be able to take away ideas for revising operations based on what is occurring outside healthcare. For example, many HCOs today practice lean systems, a method that was adapted from Toyota, an automobile industry giant.

**Challenge #4: Do Not Give Away Your Power to Others**

This challenge involves resisting becoming overwhelmed by what you do not know or understand and believing that others know more than you do about the future. In healthcare, it is easy to feel out of the loop given the preponderance of clinical, legal, and technical jargon. With the rapid rise of technology, including mHealth services and devices, executives are facing a future in which knowing what to do involves relying on others such as technicians who represent information systems and data management knowledge and expertise. Executives should recognize that these technicians are support for decision-making, not decision-makers. Some would advise executives to take courses or upgrade their skills in the emerging technical areas. If only it were that easy. What executives require is someone in the organization who can interface with the new technical workforce and translate what is actually going on so that executives can make critical decisions based on understanding.

Among the more interesting unintended consequences of the mHealth explosion are the emerging executive positions needed to better integrate and manage technology in delivering healthcare services. Many health facilities are adding new positions to the "C-suite" to meet specific challenges created in large part by rapid advances in technologies. Suggested new positions include a chief innovation officer who would identify leading-edge processes and technology to help the organization adapt to future needs. Also recommended is a chief integration officer or transformation executive. This position would lead the digital side of the clinical and medical operations infrastructure. These executives could be called upon to figure out how to best merge the wireless needs and devices of patients, staff, physicians, and community to maximize the healthcare delivery system (Honaman, 2013).

**Challenge #5: Communication Must Remain Personal**

Managing the future requires communicating with workers on a variety of levels, ranging from the most educated, such as physicians, to the least educated, usually those workers who perform manual tasks such as maintenance. We have been repeatedly told and shown evidence demonstrating the importance of interpersonal skills, but with the emergence of the Internet and mobile technologies, communication is often more frequent but also less personal. In fact, the workforce is routinely inundated with e-mails and other messages that have little meaning or relevance, nor do they contribute to maintaining and sustaining a relationship, especially with upper management. Given the trend toward flatter organizations, there is less opportunity for upper management to effectively connect with workers below them.

The elimination of middle management positions has created an environment where there is no go-between for those who make the decisions and those who carry them out, especially the front-line workers. Some believe that flatter organizations are more cost-effective and efficient because middle management represented an unnecessary layer of supervision. In fact, that middle layer serves a critical function as it translates the decisions and strategies into implementable actions, including figuring out the resource allocation and coordination of work processes. Furthermore, middle management traditionally was viewed as the mechanism by which what was occurring on the front lines could be communicated upwards in the HCO. For example, if there were implementation problems, front-line workers would tell their supervisors, who in turn would let upper management know about them and possibly recommend how to revise the work processes to accommodate the reality of application. However, communication technologies, including socially focused apps like Facebook and Twitter, may ultimately assist in making flatter organizations more productive.

It is also incumbent upon executives to attempt to communicate on a personal level with the workforce, and to do so in a meaningful way. Because communication technology creates opportunities to create workplace communities, executives can work to join those communities and promote relationships that are continuous and open, rather than hit-or-miss and one-way. The traditional suggestion box can be replaced with an online tool such as a website where employees post their ideas for improvement. Similarly, executives can share ongoing developments in real time so that employees are truly involved in the day-to-day goings-on of the HCO. For example, if employees discovered that their organization was going to engage in lay-offs by way of the local news program, they would be very upset and could unleash a Twitter backlash that could damage the HCO's reputation in the community. Executives do not have to reveal all of their strategies and tactics, but should realize that it is difficult to keep much news private these days and employees should not be excluded, especially if there is a potential for a backlash by attempting to keep them in the dark.

### Challenge #6: Discover the Benefits of Mindfulness

This challenge is about mindfulness; that is, managers really paying attention to what is going on around them instead of behaving as if on autopilot. Mindfulness is a process of actively noticing new things (Beard, 2014, p. 60). The benefits of mindfulness have been documented, and include enhanced performance as well as improved ability to pay attention, creativity, and the ability to take advantage of new opportunities. Instead of clinging to what is familiar and known, what may have done in the past, mindfulness opens executives up to change and instability. They become more accepting and less controlling when it is beneficial to do so. Thus, instead of attempting to solve today's problems with yesterday's solutions, executives are able to exist in a state that is future-oriented, not looking backwards to the past for answers (Beard, 2014).

However, the past should not be totally ignored. The past has many lessons to teach us, but even though we are often reminded that the past is prelude to the future, what occurred in the past will not be repeated identically. For example, in the 1990s, US hospitals purchased physician practices in response to incentives of PPS and DRGs. They soon discovered that physician productivity plummeted as a result of making physicians salaried employees. Consequently, most HCOs dispensed with physician employment arrangements. However, with the ACA and creation of ACOs, hospitals are once again purchasing physician practices, but this time the employment arrangement includes productivity measures and other mechanisms to assure performance levels of physician employees.

### Challenge #7: Grow a Culture of Authenticity

It is incumbent upon executives to continuously search for the future; that is, to monitor the environment, engage others in the organization in doing the same, and also to look outside the industry and see how others view the world. There must be an open environment, which encourages the honest exploration of possible futures. Executives must assure that their employees are encouraged to engage in authentic conversations. An HCO in which top management is in total agreement about the future is an organization that is delusional. It might make everyone feel comfortable to agree, but the outcome may not. History is replete with examples where consensus leads to near-disaster or actual disaster, such as the Space Shuttle Challenger disaster in 1986, when the shuttle broke apart within minutes after launch. In the aftermath of this disaster, group-think was identified as contributing to the outcome. Engineers and other technical staff felt compelled to go along with the group's decision to launch even though they had severe reservations based on evidence of the launch's potential jeopardy (Hughes and White, 2010).

Top management as well as front-line employees must feel able to express their views without expecting censure. Executives should create a culture where people are allowed to question: Why? Why are we doing this? Where will this lead us? What are the advantages of doing it this way versus doing it other ways? Have we considered all alternatives? Executives must learn to recognize warning signals, such as when employees are reluctant to come forward and share concerns. Executives should also gain input from externals, those outside the organization and also outside the industry. Customers, front-line employees, industry analysts, and others may inform executives about the radical change that is coming (Downes and Nunes, 2013).

**Playing it Forward**

Prior to passage of the ACA, only two examples of revolutionary or discontinuous change in US healthcare had been documented. The first occurred in 1965 with the federal government's intervention into healthcare as a major purchaser of health services by way of the Medicare and Medicaid Acts. The second took place in 1982–1983 with the federal government's establishment of a prospective payment system (PPS) that included diagnosis-related groupings (DRGs) that initiated a transition from cost-based reimbursement to incentives based on efficient resource usage. In both instances, these interventions radically affected the delivery of health services in the US through reimbursement and structural incentives (Scott et al., 2000). Ultimately these revolutionary changes were unsuccessful in fixing the healthcare system, and instead contributed to outcomes of ongoing problems and rising healthcare costs.

In addition, as we suggested in 2006 and later described in more detail in 2010, there may also be occurring another type of revolutionary change in healthcare: that is, the entrance of new retail players including large "big box" retailers such as Walmart and Target, and large pharmacy chain retailers such as CVS and Walgreens (Malvey and Fottler, 2006; Fottler and Malvey, 2010).

The French have a saying, "The more things change, the more they stay the same" (Karr, 1849). It would appear in healthcare, however, that the more things change, the worse things get, or at least the problems remain unfixed and the costs are not contained. Could this also be the fate of the ACA; that is, failing to fix existing problems and contributing to escalating costs?

Healthcare managers recognize that passage of the ACA represents the third example of radical or revolutionary change, change that would upend existing systems of access, quality, and cost. In fact, managers understand better than anyone that they are at ground zero. Furthermore, they expect to see more disruptive innovation and big bang innovators in the aftermath of the legislation. Whatever comes their way, managers will be prepared if they attempt to manage their future instead of letting events and circumstances dictate what they should do.

## BIG DATA AND ENTERPRISE INFORMATION GOVERNANCE

Healthcare is inarguably a data- and information-intensive industry. Despite the historical reputation of health care organizations (HCOs) being laggards in the adoption of integrated information technology, once engaged, most HCOs aggressively embraced health information technology (HIT), quickly evolving to the current philosophy of "no data left uncaptured." And for many HCOs, once captured, no data is ever truly purged or deleted, particularly in this digital age when the clouds seem to have no limits with regard to available storage capacity. However, information, considered by many as the most important strategic asset in an organization, also has much to offer from a liability perspective. One only has to consider the cost of data security breaches – suggested by some research to average $3.5 million dollars per incident (Ponemon Institute, 2014) – to bring this fact to the forefront.

Whereas clinical data and information have always been essential tools for diagnosing and treating patients, these same data are now pivotal to decisions about payment for providing those services. The needs and uses for accurate, complete, and timely data are pervasive throughout HCOs, and other needs continue to emerge. The challenges inherent in balancing information accessibility needs with privacy and security risks have been and continue to be of paramount importance to HCOs. In fact, most HCOs have robust, comprehensive information security practices in place that are designed in compliance with regulatory requirements and incorporate industry best practices. And, despite the best efforts of highly skilled and committed employees, security breaches continue to occur and essential data are not always available to meet the organization's needs. A particularly vulnerable category of data with regard to both security and access is described as "dark data," or data stored or transmitted outside their officially designated location (Butler, 2014). Examples include files e-mailed between employees, a file copy saved on a desktop for convenient future access, data stored on employees' personal mobile devices, or even paper documents retained in a file drawer after being scanned into an electronic system. These data sources may have utility for their users, but they typically are not protected by the facility's established processes, and may create data integrity issues if they re-enter the official systems along with alternate versions.

Despite the data challenges that exist at the organization level, the industry is moving toward an "open information" orientation, as decades of stored data from many sources (that is, clinical, research, claims and cost, and patient behaviors), are aggregated into "big data" that can be mined to create new knowledge (Groves et al., 2013). Such an information environment was inconceivable until recent years, when technological capabilities, industry standards, and delivery and reimbursement models aligned sufficiently to impel change of this magnitude. The knowledge that can be gleaned from big data is expected to lead to improvements in clinical quality, reduced costs of providing healthcare, better business models for providers and suppliers, and ultimately a healthier population.

Although the sheer magnitude of big data can compensate for some degree of data quality issues, volume alone will not suffice to overcome factors such as differing database structures and data characteristics compiled from diverse sources. And data-sharing on such a scale has comparably scaled security risks. As big data initiatives evolve, leaders in HCOs will be dually challenged: first, to protect and optimize their local information assets as feeders to big data; and second, to derive strategic advantage for their organizations from big data's capability to produce business intelligence. A robust enterprise information governance program will be an important foundation to address these challenges.

**Information Management vs. Information Governance**

The American Health Information Management Association (AHIMA), a national professional association established in 1928 that currently boasts more than 71 000 members, is described on its website (ahima. org) as the "leading source of 'HIM knowledge'." The AHIMA is recognized across the United States healthcare industry as an authoritative source regarding standards, guidelines, and best practices with regard to the information resources in HCOs. Information governance has been a key strategic initiative for the AHIMA in 2014 (Gordon, 2014) and some important resources to guide HCOs in establishing an information governance program are available on their website and from other AHIMA publications.

The AHIMA defines information governance (IG) as "an organization-wide framework for managing information throughout its lifecycle and for supporting the organization's strategy, operations, regulatory, legal, risk, and environmental requirements" (AHIMA, 2014, p. 2). The strategic nature of IG, with its "top-down" driven focus, is an important distinguishing characteristic when contrasted with information management, which is operational and "bottom-up" in orientation (Empel, 2014). Certainly, both strategic objectives and operational tactics are essential to organizational success, but information resources have received less top-down attention due to their emergence from operational units.

While information management remains an essential function, the governance of information is increasing in importance as a leadership responsibility, fueled by such issues as the aforementioned security breaches, "meaningful use" requirements from the Health Information Technology for Economic and Clinical Health Act (HITECH Act), payment models based on demonstrated clinical quality, and a national focus on improving patient safety. Although the business case for information governance is solid, whether viewed from a proactive or a reactive stance, a survey of more than 1000 clinical and non-clinical executives and managers reported that only 35 percent of HCOs in the study have a comprehensive IG strategy (Dimick, 2014).

**Principles of Information Governance**

The AHIMA (2014) recommends eight principles that should underlie an HCO's IG structure. These principles are intended to be reflective of characteristics associated with health information, such as trust and integrity, and the obligation of HCOs to maintain privacy, confidentiality, and security of health information. The principles are:

- Accountability, defined as senior leadership.
- Transparency, demonstrated by published policies and procedures.
- Integrity, maintaining information that is authentic, timely, accurate, and complete.
- Protection, securing data against breach, corruption, or loss.
- Compliance, adherence to applicable laws, regulations, standards, and policies.
- Availability, ensuring timely, accurate, and efficient retrieval.
- Retention, maintaining information for an appropriate time period.
- Disposition, either destruction or transfer of permanent custodianship.

**Protecting HCO Information Resources**

In rating the maturity of existing IG components, Dimick (2014) reported privacy and security policies as most mature, and deletion and destruction policies as the least mature. However, all IG maturity ratings were below desirable levels for the types of information maintained by an HCO.

Information security is a constant concern for HCOs, although categories of risk and management of those risks have evolved along with the mechanisms for capturing data and the media for storing data. As the industry moved from relatively secure paper-based storage where one could always physically lock a storage area; to removable media such as microfilm, tapes, and disks; to the current digital environment, security has become more of a challenge and protection approaches have become more sophisticated. The current shift to mobile technologies brings a new set of challenges, because their inherent beauty of mobility is also their weak spot (Malvey and Slovensky, 2014). Of 538 publicly reported health information security breaches in the USA involving more than 21.4 million patient records, 38 percent were attributed to mobile devices such as unencrypted laptops (Redspin, Inc. 2013). Specific policies for mobile devices, and rigorous auditing for compliance, are essential.

HCOs have not been early adopters of cloud computing – a distributed network configuration based on wireless connection via the Internet – due in large part to perceived security risks (Glandon et al., 2013). However, big data is by definition distributed, and HCOs likely will need to explore cloud options. From a global data perspective, a large information service provider has suggested that by 2020, more than one-third of all data will live in or pass through the cloud (CSC, n.d.). Among the most important decisions to be made will be selection of the cloud service provider (CSP), and the cloud type: private, public, or hybrid. CSP attributes to explore from an IG perspective include the following (QuinStreet, 2013):

- Transparency about controls, technology, and location.
- Risk mitigation strategy.
- Demonstrated proof of capabilities.
- Customization and integration options.
- Breadth of experience across industries.

Electronic health information exchange (HIE), transferring patient medical information among providers and patients, is a fact of the current US system, and one that is federally supported and incentivized (HealthIT. gov, n.d.). Driven in part by meaningful-use requirements and demands by payment plans, HCOs must incorporate HIE into their strategies for care coordination to improve efficiency of services provided and clinical out-comes. Among the governance issues that must be considered are interop-erability of systems and trust among strategic partners.

In summary, the obligation of the HCO to protect the privacy and security of its information is not new. The complexity of the systems for data capture, storage, and transfer and the diversity of stakeholders for the HCO's information use and protection are growing and will continue to grow. An information governance program, and designated account-ability for its oversight to experienced, skilled information professionals, are critical success factors for the HCO.

## Exploiting Big Data

Selby and Sherer (2013) suggest that the risks and benefits associated with big data have been an important driver in accelerating IG, with its demands for "good organization of records, taxonomy, retrieval, and defensible destruction policies." They also neatly describe big data's fundamental challenge to leaders as striking "the right balance between the need to mine data assets for valuable information . . . and the cost of storing ever-increasing amounts of data; maintaining its security, and complying with relevant laws, regulations, and litigation holds."

In the opinion of one of the co-authors (Slovensky), this statement of challenge is the crux of the leader's role with regard to the information assets of an organization. As noted previously, HCOs can and do capture and maintain an enormous volume of information, much of which has no utility for making clinical, financial, or administrative decisions. Much of this data is flawed, inaccessible, or redundant. Through information governance, HCOs can make thoughtful, informed decisions about how (and why) their data and information are captured and maintained for accessibility by those who have a legitimate need for it: patients, provid-ers, payors, strategic partners, researchers, policy-makers, and others both internal and external to the organization.

The healthcare industry is in the early stages of establishing standards for HIE and meaningful use of technology to enhance the quality and safety of healthcare delivered by providers. HCO leaders must monitor current and pending legislation related to HIT and engage with stra-tegic partners to enhance relationships based on information-sharing. Additionally, HCOs must migrate their technology architecture, not only to comply with emerging industry standards but also to be able to exploit big data in its many forms, including unstructured media.

# REFERENCES

Abrahamson, E. (2000). Change Without Pain. *Harvard Business Review*, 78(4): 75–79.

Abrams, M.N. (2012). Market-Based Care. *Trustee*, 65(8): 40–41.

American Health Information Management Association (AHIMA) (2014). Information Governance Principles for Healthcare (IGPHC). Available at http://www.ahima.rog/topics/infogoveranance (accessed 3 October 2014).

Austin, J. (2009). Mapping Out a Game Plan for Change. *HR Magazine*, 54(4): 39–42.

Baker, S. and Green, H. (2008). Beyond blogs. *Businessweek*, 5 June: 45–50.

Barnett, R.F. (2014). Obamacare Can Be Repealed. *USA Today*, 5 December: 8A.

Beard, A. (2014). Mindfulness in the Age of Complexity, An Interview with Ellen Langer. *Harvard Business Review*, 92(3): 68–73.

Blair, J.D. and Fottler, M.D. (1990). *Challenges in Healthcare Management: Strategic Perspectives for Managing Key Stakeholders*. San Francisco, CA: Jossey-Bass.

Blair, J.D. and Fottler, M.D. (1996). *Strategic Leadership for Medical Groups: Navigating Your Strategic Web*. San Francisco, CA: Jossey-Bass.

Blair, J.D. and Fottler, M.D. (1997). Effective Stakeholder Management: Opportunities and Strategies. In Duncan, W.J., Kinter, P.M., and Swain, N.E. (eds), *Handbook of Healthcare Management*. Malden, MA.: Blackwell Publishers, pp. 19–54.

Bolman, L.G. and Deal, T.E. (1999). Four Steps to Keeping Change Efforts Heading in the Right Direction. *Journal of Quality and Participation*, 22(3): 6–11.

Butler, M. (2014). Digging Out from Data Hoarding. *Journal of AHIMA*, 85(10): 24–28.

CSC. (n.d.). Big Data Universe Beginning to Explode. Available at http://www.csc.com/insights/flxwd/78931-big_data_universe_beginning_to_explode (accessed 5 October 2014).

Dimick, C. (2014). Slow to the Information Governance Starting Line. *Journal of AHIMA*, 85(10): 44–48.

Downes, L. and Nunes, P.F. (2013). Big Bang Disruption. *Harvard Business Review*, 91(3): 46–52, 54, 56.

Empel, S. (2014). The Way Forward. *Journal of AHIMA*, 85(10): 30–32.

Flower, J. (2012). *Healthcare Beyond Reform: Doing it Right for Half the Cost*. Boca Raton, FL: CRC Press.

Fottler, M.D. and Malvey D. (2010). *The Retail Revolution in Health Care*. Santa Barbara, CA: Praeger Publishers/Greenwood Publishing Group.

Furst, S. and Cable, D. (2008). Employee Resistance to Organizational Change: Managerial Influence Tactics and Leader–Member Exchange. *Journal of Applied Psychology*, 93(2): 453–462.

Glandon, G.L., Smaltz, D.H., and Slovensky, D.J. (2013). *Information Systems for Healthcare Management*, 7th edn. Chicago, IL: Health Administration Press.

Gordon, L.T. (2014). The Time for Information Governance is Now. *Journal of AHIMA*, 85(10): 23.

Groves, P., Kayyali, B., Knott, D., and Van Kuiken, S. (2013). *The 'Big Data' Revolution in Healthcare: Accelerating Value and Innovation*. McKinsey & Company Center for US Health System Reform, January.

HealthIT.gov. (n.d.). Nationwide HIE Strategy. Available at http://www.healthit.gov/providers-professionals/health-information-exchange/nationwide-hie-strategy (accessed 5 October 2014).

Herald, D., Fedor, D.B., and Caldwell, S.D. (2007). Beyond Change Management: A Multi-Level Investigation of Contextual and Personal Influences on Employee Commitment to Change. *Journal of Applied Psychology*, 92(4): 942–951.

Honaman, J.D. (2013). The Jobs of Tomorrow. *Healthcare Executive*, 28(3): 76.

Hughes, P. and White, E. (2010). The Space Shuttle Challenger Disaster: A Classic Example of Groupthink. *Ethics and Critical Thinking Journal*, September. Available at http://connection.ebscohost.com/c/case-studies/57804160/space-shuttle-challenger-disaster-classic-example-groupthink (accessed 27 September 2014).

Karr, Jean-Baptiste Alphonse (1849). Quote from *Les Guêpes* (January). Available at http://en.wikipedia.org/wiki/Jean-Baptiste_Alphonse_Karr (accessed 28 September 2014).

Kotter, J.P. (1996). *Leading Change*. Boston, MA: Harvard Business School Press.

Malvey, D. and Fottler, M.D. (2006). The Retail Revolution in Healthcare: Who Will Win and Who Will Lose?. *Health Care Management Review*, 31(3): 168–178.

Malvey, D.M. and Slovensky, D.J. (2014). *mHealth: Transforming Healthcare*. New York: Springer.

Melhado, E.M. (2014). Health Insurance in Historical Perspective II: The Rise of Market-Oriented Health Policy and Healthcare. *Encyclopedia of Health Economics*, Waltham, MA: Elsevier, pp. 380–387.

Ponemon Institute (2014). Ponemon Institute Releases 2014 Cost of Data breach: Global Analysis. 5 May. Available at http://www.ponemon.org/blog/ponemon-institute-releases-2014-cost-of-data-breach-global-analysis (accessed 4 October 2014).

QuinStreet (2013). QuinStreet Executive Brief: 5 Things to Look for in a Cloud Provider When it Comes to Security. *Oracle*. Available at http://www.oracle.com/us/solutions/cloud/oracle-cloud-security-final-1964475.pdf (accessed 17 November 2013).

Redspin, Inc. (2013). Breach Report 2012 Protected Health Information Breach Analysis. February. Available at http://www.redspin.com/docs/Redspin_Breach_Report_2012.pdf (accessed 18 September 2013).

Scott, W.R., Ruef, M., Mendel, P.J., and Caronna, C.A. (2000). *Institutional Change and Healthcare Organizations*. Chicago, IL: University of Chicago Press.

Selby, J. and Sherer, J. (2013). A Year-end Review of Information Governance. InsideCounsel.com, 10 December. Available at http://www.insidecounsel.com/2013/12/20/a-year-end-review-of-information-governance (accessed 4 October 2014).

Shore, D.A. (ed.) (2012). *Forces of Change: New Strategies for the Evolving Health Care Marketplace*, San Francisco, CA: Jossey-Bass.

Stern, J. (2005). Forever Changing. *Management Today*. Available at http://www.managementtoday.co.uk/news/461019/.

# Index